The ... ...tion

The Law of Assisted Reproduction

By

Seamus Burns, LLB (Hons)(QUB),

MA Biotechnological Law and Ethics (Sheff. U.),
PG Dip F&H Ed (Sheff. Hallam U.), CPLS (QUB)

Solicitor, Senior Lecturer in Law at Sheffield Hallam University,
President of the South Yorkshire Medico-Legal Society (2012–13)

Bloomsbury Professional

Bloomsbury Professional Limited, Maxwelton House, 41–43 Boltro Road, Haywards Heath, West Sussex, RH16 1BJ

© Bloomsbury Professional Ltd 2012

Bloomsbury Professional is an imprint of Bloomsbury Publishing plc

A CIP Catalogue record for this book is available from the British Library.

ISBN: 978 1 84766 695 6

Typeset by Phoenix Photosetting Ltd, Chatham, Kent
Printed and bound in the UK by www.printondemand-worldwide.com

Contents

Contents

Contents

Preface

The purpose of this book is to highlight the key major features of the Human Fertilisation and Embryology Act 2008 (effective on 1 October 2009). The 2008 Act preserved unaltered the vast bulk of the original pioneering Human Fertilisation and Embryology Act 1990, but made a number of significant and highly controversial amendments to some provisions of the earlier trail-blazing legislation, which had established the legislative architecture and ethical foundations regulating much of the assisted reproductive treatment and medicine landscape and human embryonic research.

The book will focus on a number of the more important and pivotal areas of change in the 2008 Act, including permitting the creation of saviour siblings, deleting the 'need for a father' clause in s 13(5) of the 1990 Act and replacing it with the need for supportive parenting clause, permitting the creation of the new type of embryo (the human admixed embryo) for research purposes, the ban on sex selection for social reasons and the legal recognition of new family structures and families in the context of children born following certain assisted reproductive treatments. In addition the book will consider specific and discrete areas, including the changes to birth certification, major problems still existing with the unavailability of IVF in approximately 75 per cent of cases and the availability of the remaining 25 per cent on a postcode lottery basis, the potential impact of human rights in the assisted reproductive sphere, the role and imminent demise of the independent, statutory quango the Human Fertilisation and Embryology Authority, consideration of the changes to the Abortion Act 1967 (as amended) that were suggested but ultimately not included in the 2008 Act, an assessment of attempts at regulating stem cell research in the United States and by the EU, and an evaluation of the role and the critical importance of our 'ethical compass' in the field of embryonic research and assisted reproductive medicine, namely Parliament, as witnessed in Parliamentary debates and proceedings.

I have attempted to state the law as at 17 November 2011. However, given the controversial nature of the law and the seemingly intractable gulf between many Parliamentarians on the meaning of certain provisions and language deployed in the 2008 Act, never mind what subliminal or neon signals or messages they send out to society at large, as is clear in Parliamentary debates, that may remain a moot point for some on occasion.

I would like to thank Sarah Thomas and Andy Hill (at Tottel Publishing initially, and since October 2010 at Bloomsbury Professional), in particular for putting their confidence and faith in me to write the book. Furthermore I would like to thank Bloomsbury Professional for all their help with the myriad tasks in converting an idea for a book into an actual book. Also I would like to thank Kiran Goss for her encouragement and support over the last year in general and her Herculanean efforts over the last few weeks in particular in reading and editing the draft manuscript. Also, I would like to thank the anonymous reviewer who read a specimen chapter and provided me with such constructive and incredibly helpful comments. I would like to thank the second anonymous reviewer for their comments too. Furthermore, I would like to put on record my great appreciation to Paul Crick for the tremendous amount of care, time, attention to detail and professionalism he has shown in editing my book.

I would like to dedicate the book to my wife, two daughters and my parents. Finally I would like to thank my wife Finola for her tremendous support, infinite encouragement and love and care throughout the past two years. Finola kept my feet, spirit and brain firmly fixed to terra firma (an incredibly difficult task!) and had to endure my long absences from our family, when I was in the office and in our study at home glued to computers typing – or should I say word-processing! – and magnificently kept our family and home ticking round, as she always does, as well as doing her own very demanding job as a university lecturer. This book is dedicated to Finola primarily. I would also like to thank my two daughters, Isabel (Issie) and Eleanor, for their love in helping to sustain me over the last two years writing the book. To paraphrase Arnold Schwarzenegger, 'Daddy will be back' now, at long last! Love you both lots! Finally I would like to thank my parents, John and Kathleen Burns, (Daddy and Mammy), for all their love and support over many years.

Seamus Burns

November 2011

Table of statutes

Table of statutory instruments

Table of cases

R

S

V

W

Y

List of abbreviations

AID	Artificial insemination by donor
ALB	Arm's length body
ART	Assisted reproductive technology
CNR	Cell nuclear replacement
CoP	Code of Practice
DI	Donor insemination
ECHR	European Convention on Human Rights
ECtHR	European Court of Human Rights
ESCs	Embryonic stem cells
GIFT	Gamete intrafallopian transfer
hESCs	Human embryonic stem cells
HFE Bill	Human Fertilisation and Embryology Bill
HFEA	Human Fertilisation and Embryology Authority
HLA	human leukocyte antigen (tissue typing)
HTA	Human Tissue Authority
ICSI	Intra-cytoplasmic sperm injection
IPS	Induced pluripotent stem cells
IVF	in vitro fertilisation
OHSS	ovarian hyper stimulation syndrome
PCT	Primary Care Trust
PGD	pre-implantation genetic diagnosis
SET	Single embryo transfer
SHA	Strategic Health Authority
The 1990 Act	Human Fertilisation and Embryology Act 1990
The 2008 Act	Human Fertilisation and Embryology Act 2008

Chapter 1

Introduction

WHY LEGISLATE?

1.1 Following the birth in 1978 of Louise Brown, the first test-tube/IVF baby, and the publication of the seminal Warnock Report in 1984, the original Human Fertilisation and Embryology Act 1990 (the 1990 Act) signalled the clear intent of Parliament to regulate the relatively new science of assisted reproduction. Parliament was keen to permit the new science to develop, but in a strictly regulated fashion under the aegis of the 1990 Act and the Human Fertilisation and Embryology Authority (HFEA), the independent, specialist regulatory and licensing body/authority created under the 1990 Act. Parliament thus rejected both leaving the field of assisted reproduction treatment and research unregulated (as it was prior to 1990), or alternatively, as some wished, prohibiting these activities. By passing the 1990 Act, Parliament incontrovertibly legitimised assisted reproduction, or, depending on one's view, at least built clear steps to prevent going down any alleged ethical slippery slope.

1.2 Not only did the 1990 Act regulate the field of assisted reproduction (eg providing IVF treatment, storing embryos and doing research on embryos), but it also substantially reformed the law on abortion, as contained in the Abortion Act 1967, by HFEA 1990, ss 37 and 38. Both a legislative precedent and an ethical foundation and moral framework had therefore been set in 1990, which subsequent Parliaments could build on to take account of technological developments in the sphere of assisted reproduction and simultaneously to reflect changes in social attitudes to those developments and to their possible uses. Parliament built on the solid legal, ethical and moral foundations enshrined in the 1990 Act with the Human Fertilisation and Embryology Act 2008 (the 2008 Act), which became effective on 1 October 2009. Much of the legal parameters and ethical/moral framework contained in the 1990 Act remained intact and was preserved in the 2008 Act, but there were a number of considerable (and controversial) changes and additions made to the original regulatory regime.

1.3 The potential scope and impact of Parliament's latest attempt, as contained in the 2008 Act, to map out the regulatory scope and ambit of the assisted reproduction treatment research etc landscape has been commented on by this author. The introduction and enactment of the 2008 Act was both timely and apposite, given:

> 'the development of new, yet ethically controversial scientific procedures – unimagined when the HFEA 1990 was passed … its enactment signals a shift in public opinion regarding the scope and possible applicability of new technologies to a range of innovative areas … [T]herefore the HFEA 2008 [the 2008 Act] can be viewed as Government and Parliament's considered

attempt at legislative "catch-up", ie the "old law" (HFEA 1990 [the 1990 Act]), hence, being re-crafted and updated, not scrapped, and repealed (indeed, much of the essence and content of the HFEA 1990 is specifically retained), to address the challenges posed by 18 years of scientific research and development, to deal with the "new" medicine, so that the juggernaut of the "new" medicine is properly regulated, scrutinised and fully accountable, and more likely to be "fit for purpose".'[1]

1.4   Elsewhere, in assessing the enormous potential scope and ethically controversial and seismic impact of the provisions and general amendments made by the 2008 Act, the author has said that:

'it heralds potentially significant changes to:
- the sphere of assisted reproduction regulation (which, arguably, will have major ramifications for society's notion of what constitutes a family);
- the permissible uses of certain types of embryo;
- the ethical value attached to embryos in the light of recent scientific developments in the fields of assisted fertilisation and embryology; and
- thorny, controversial and sometimes intractable arguments over legal parentage, the welfare of the child and consent.'[2]

GENERAL STRUCTURE OF THE 2008 ACT

1.5   The 2008 Act is split into three Parts. Part 1 (comprising ss 1–32), deals with amendments to the 1990 Act. Sections 1 and 2 cover the principal terms used in the 1990 Act. Then ss 3 and 4 deal with activities governed in the 1990 Act. Sections 5–10 deal with the HFEA itself. Section 11 considers the scope of licences, ss 12–14 deal with licence conditions and ss 16–21 cover the grant, revocation and suspension of licences. Then, ss 22 and 23 deal with Directions and the Code of Practice (CoP; the latest version of the CoP is the 8th edition, effective from 1 October 2009). Sections 24 and 25 cover information, s 26 covers mitochondrial donation, and ss 27–32 deal with a variety of miscellaneous matters.

1.6   Part 2 of the 2008 Act (ss 33–58), comprises a number of provisions covering parenthood in cases involving assisted reproduction. These include s 33 concerning the meaning of the term 'mother'. Section 34 deals with the application of ss 35–47, then ss 35–41 cover the important issue of the meaning of the term 'father' under the Act. Perhaps more controversially for some, ss 42–47 cover cases in which a woman will be the other parent. Section 48 deals with the effect of ss 33–47. Sections 49–50 cover references to parties to marriage or civil partnership. Sections 51 and 52 concern further provision about registration made by virtue of ss 39, 40 or 46. Section 53 deals with the interpretation of references to father, etc where a woman is the other parent. Next, ss 54 and 55 cover parental orders. Section 56 addresses amendments of enactments and finally ss 57 and 58 deal with general issues.

1   *Current Law Statutes Annotated,* 'Human Fertilisation and Embryology Act 2008, Chapter 22' (Sweet & Maxwell 2009), pp 1–210, at p. 4.
2   S Burns, 'Fit for Purpose?' (2008) Fam LJ 73(Feb)16–18.

1.7 The final Part of the 2008 Act is Part 3, covering miscellaneous matters (ss 59 and 60) and general matters (ss 61–69).

INFERTILITY/CHILDLESSNESS – A DISEASE OR SOCIAL CONDITION?

1.8 Quite apart from difficult questions about how one defines the term infertility or childlessness, critical questions also arise regarding whether infertility/childlessness is a disease or medical condition necessitating medical intervention financed by the public purse (ie the NHS), or whether it is merely a social condition or state that infertile couples/individuals have to accept or alternatively try to fix themselves with their own money. People want a bigger house, better car, or a nicer holiday in a better destination, but that does not mean the state has to satisfy this want or social condition/desire. Critics of the use of limited taxpayers' money in a recession with a huge public deficit of £162 billion in 2010 might express misgivings about the wisdom of the State spending millions of pounds on trying to assist the infertile to have children by assisted reproductive treatments (eg in vitro fertilisation (IVF) treatment). Quite apart from concerns about a world that is already very overpopulated and putting a huge strain on land availability and access to food/water/housing/ amenities etc, and given the huge numbers of abortions that occur globally,[3] some opponents of both the greater availability of IVF/infertility treatments and research in this area would ask profound questions about whether infertility is even a disease at all, warranting the assistance of public funding, or whether it is just a social condition. Lord Winston rhetorically asked:

> 'People may say, why should infertile people get their medical treatment for free? Nobody dies from infertility. For that matter, nobody suffers physical pain through it either. After all, infertility isn't a disease, it is repeatedly said.'[4]

1.9 However he counters that this fallacious perception of what childlessness is shows 'a widespread lack of understanding about what it means to be infertile'. Rather, he submits, 'Infertility actually causes most of its victims extraordinary pain' and a pain 'moreover which is private and difficult to express (and therefore to resolve) because it is so personal.' This pain can, inter alia, lead to, or manifests itself in couples or individuals as, 'anxiety', 'inadequacy', 'loss of self-esteem', 'feelings of worthlessness', 'guilt', 'recrimination between partners', strain on relationships, 'anger' and social 'isolation'. He adds that:

> '[two] consequences follow the failure to recognise that infertility is not caused by a disease process. Firstly, it means that health care resources need not be provided in so many cases. Secondly it results in infertility being treated without a diagnosis being made.'[5]

IVF is, therefore, offered inappropriately in some cases.

---

3   In the UK alone in 2010 there were over 196,000 abortions.
4   Prof R Winston, *Making Babies* (BBC Books, 1996) pp 20–21.
5   *Ibid*, p.25.

1.10   Some critics would contend that infertility and assisting the infertile to have healthy children in a loving family have become increasingly 'medicalised' since the late 1970s. Infertility and trying to treat it, whether immediately, by offering various assisted reproductive treatments, or in the long-term, by undertaking different types of research using embryos, now including human admixed embryos (and of course doing research not just to alleviate or cure infertility, but for a growing variety of other purposes), firmly moors in many – doctors, patients and the public – the belief that infertility is a genuine disease that needs tackling, rather than a mere social condition.

STATISTICS OF ASSISTED REPRODUCTION

1.11   Since 1978 and the birth of Louise Brown, the first IVF 'test-tube' baby, according to the HFEA[6] up to and including 2005 at least 286,588 patients have received IVF in the UK. In the same period (1978–2005), at least 527,000 IVF treatment cycles have occurred and at least 89,280 births have occurred, resulting in at least 119,583 babies being born. This explosion in the therapeutic assisted reproduction revolution has not been confined to the UK but is very much a worldwide phenomenon extending to many other countries. Indeed the HFEA notes that:

> 'A study by the International Committee for Monitoring Assisted Reproductive Technology estimated that over three million IVF babies were born around the world between 1978 and 2006.'[7]

1.12   The Human Fertilisation and Embryology Authority in its publication *Fertility Facts and Figures 2008*, published on 8 December 2010 (the HFF&F Report), furnished statistical data concerning around 50,000 treatments performed each year in the UK fertility sector, which was provided by licensed clinics and covers treatments between 1 January and 31 December 2008.[8] The report noted initially[9] that: 'Infertility is defined as "failing to get pregnant after two years of regular unprotected sex" by the National Institute for Health and Clinical Excellence (NICE).' It also noted that: '[A]fter pregnancy, infertility is the most common reason for women aged 20–45 to see their GP', and very worryingly revealed the prevalence of infertility, noting that '[F]ertility problems affect one in seven couples in the UK – approximately 3.5 million people.' Thus infertility is arguably a significant, if not huge social and medical problem. The HFF&F Report noted also that: 'Most couples (about 84 out of every 100) who have regular sexual intercourse (that is, every 2–3 days) and who do not use contraception will get pregnant within a year,' and furthermore: '[A]bout 92 out of 100 couples who are trying to get pregnant do so within 2 years.'

1.13   Some salient headline statistics from the HFF&F Report include, inter alia, that the number of IVF treatment cycles performed and the number of patients treated has continued to rise.[10] There were 50,687 IVF treatment cycles in licensed clinics in 2008, compared to 44,275 in 2006, 39,879 patients

---

6   www.hfea.gov.uk/1317.html
7   www.hfea.gov.uk/1320.html
8   See p 2, 'a snap shot of data'. These are the latest figures available.
9   Page 3.
10   Page 4.

treated in 2008, compared to 34,885 in 2006, 12,211 successful births giving rise to 15,082 babies in 2008 compared to 10,242 successful births giving rise to 12,596 babies in 2006. Also, the live birth rate per cycle started rose from 23.1 per cent in 2006 to 24.1 per cent in 2008 – an improvement of 1 per cent. The downside was that the multiple birth rate following IVF also rose 0.5 per cent in that two-year period – rising from 22.7 per cent in 2006 to 23.2 per cent in 2008.

1.14   The HFF&F Report noted too that: 'Intra-cytoplasmic sperm injection (ICSI – a technique used to overcome some problems caused by the quality of sperm) represented 46 per cent of all IVF treatment in 2008 … The remainder was conventional IVF.'[11]

1.15   Concerning donor insemination (DI), the HFF&F Report found that there was a decrease in the number of DI treatment cycles from 4,225 in 2006 to 3,938 in 2008, and that there was also a decline in the number of patients from 2,106 in 2006 to 1,916 in 2008. The number of successful births (455) giving rise to 489 babies in 2006 declined to 451 successful births giving rise to 487 babies in 2008. The DI live birth rate per cycle started rose from 10.8 per cent in 2006 to 11.5 per cent in 2008, but unfortunately – and not surprisingly – the multiple birth rate also rose from 6.8 per cent in 2006 to 7.8 per cent in 2008.

1.16   The HFF&F Report noted:

'The likelihood of getting pregnant following IVF or DI treatment is strongly linked to the age of the woman being treated. On average, a woman aged under 35 is substantially more likely to conceive than a woman who is older.'[12]

The IVF live birth rate in 2008 is shown below:

Age range	Percentage
Under 35	33.1%
35–37	27.2%
38–39	19.3%
40–42	12.5%
43–44	4.9%
Over 44	2.5%

The DI live birth rate as shown in the table below was even lower.

Age range	Percentage
Under 35	15.3%
35–39	11%
40–42	4.8%
43–44	1.1%
Over 44	0%

11   Page 4.
12   Page 5.

These figures are particularly significant given the clear evidence of women delaying having children until later on in their reproductive lives because of careers; sadly their biological clocks do not take cognisance of this career choice occurring at a woman's most fertile time of life.

1.17   Regarding the frequency of fresh compared to frozen IVF cycles and their respective success rates, in 2008 the HFF&F Report noted, that 'Just over 80 per cent of IVF cycles were fresh cycles [39, 334], the remainder used frozen embryos [8,959].'[13] Not surprisingly therefore the number of births in fresh IVF cycles, 10,010, and the number of babies born, 12,480, was considerably higher than those using frozen embryos, respectively 1,618 and 1,855. However, the benefit and value of fresh embryos in maximising the likelihood of, for example, the couple getting a baby, was clear when one considers live birth rates by age. Using fresh embryos in IVF resulted in a live birth rate for women under 35 of 33.1 per cent compared to 22.2 per cent using frozen embryos – a significantly lower success rate. For age 35–37 it was 27.2 per cent for fresh embryos compared to 17.8 per cent for frozen embryos, and for 38–39 year olds the difference was not as marked – 19.3 per cent compared to 15.8 per cent. However, for women who were 40 and over, using frozen embryos was paradoxically more successful, with a live birth rate of 11.9 per cent, compared to 10.7 per cent using fresh embryos.

1.18   In addition it was reported that 63 clinics offered IVF treatment using donated eggs in 2008. That translates into 1,700 IVF treatment cycles, resulting in 485 births and 630 babies being produced, with a live birth rate of 28.5 per cent. The women using donated eggs may well be mainly older women, some post-menopausal, yet the live birth rate is comparatively high, because the donated eggs come from women donors under 35 in accordance with the HFEA's Code of Practice, so the eggs are going to be 'better' for maximising the chance of a live birth than using, for example, an older recipient woman's eggs.

1.19   The HFF&F Report also revealed that in 2008 10 licensed clinics offered Pre-Implantation Genetic Diagnosis (PGD), and that there were 214 IVF treatment cycles using PGD, resulting in a live birth rate of 25.2 per cent, with 54 successful births producing 66 babies compared to those using IVF or ICSI on its own – a small number.

TREATING INFERTILITY – A RISKY BUSINESS?

1.20   The British Fertility Society (BFS), in their factsheet entitled 'Risks and complications of assisted conception'[14] pertinently and correctly observed: 'No medical treatment is entirely free from risk and infertility is no exception.' However that is why, inter alia, s 13(6) was inserted into the 1990 Act and Parliament insisted on the requirement of informed consent and various information being given to a patient prior to, for example, receiving IVF treatment – forewarned theoretically meant forearmed! However, the BFS also

---

13   Page 6.
14   Published August 2005; see p 1.

noted that while it was important for the patient to have information about risks concerning, for example, IVF, nevertheless it was 'also important to appreciate that most women go through IVF and other assisted conception treatments without serious problems.' Infertility treatments, and particularly IVF, are not fraught with danger or risk for the patient. The BFS categorised the risks of infertility treatment, including IVF, into four distinct categories or areas. These were:

'1. The risks associated with the drugs used to stimulate egg production
2. The surgical risks associated with egg removal during IVF, ICSI and egg donation
3. The risks associated with pregnancy resulting from any treatment
4. The risks of producing an abnormal baby following IVF, ICSI or egg donation.'

1.21 Taking each of these in turn, the BFS noted two main risks associated with drugs used to stimulate egg production.[15] These were firstly the risk that a woman whose ovaries were stimulated by drugs would produce more eggs than she naturally would each month, developing ovarian hyperstimulation syndrome (OHSS), and secondly therefore the risk of her developing ovarian cancer. Regarding the risk of excess stimulation of the ovaries causing OHSS, the BFS noted: 'The majority of cases are a mild to moderate form, occurring in up to 5% of all patients undergoing IVF … Less commonly a more severe case occurs … This happens in 0.5–1% of all IVF cycles.' The risk of the woman possibly developing ovarian cancer is much more tentative. The BFS referred to two studies from North America, which suggested that the risk of ovarian cancer developing increased in women using the drug clomifene, but added that subsequent studies had not confirmed this risk.

1.22 Regarding the surgical risks associated with egg removal during IVF and related procedures, the BFS flagged up three risks, namely:

1. The risks associated with patients receiving general anaesthetics and intravenous sedation. The risk of serious harm is very low (1 in 10,000) and is similar to that of other elective surgery.
2. Egg collection and the risk of damage to other structures (eg the woman's bowel or bladder or a major blood vessel could be accidentally punctured in the egg collection procedure using the laparoscopy – indeed a couple of women have in fact died because of this). The BFS assessed that the risk of a significant haemorrhage from an internal blood vessel is approximately 1 in 2,500.
3. The risk of pelvic infection, where the risk of serious pelvic infection is likely to be less than 1 in 500.

1.23 Next, the BFS pointed out the risks associated with pregnancy resulting from any treatment (ie not just IVF treatment). These were:

● multiple pregnancy;
● ectopic pregnancy;
● heterotopic pregnancy; and
● miscarriage.

15 Page 2.

As the BFS correctly and fairly commented: 'Multiple pregnancy can result from any treatment involving the use of drugs to stimulate egg production or when more than one embryo is replaced during IVF/ICSI or egg donation treatment.' Hence most people associate multiple births with IVF, but in fact multiple births can result following the use of fertility drugs to stimulate the woman's ovaries without having IVF. Merely giving women fertility drugs is not regulated by either the 1990 Act or the 2008 Act, nor by the HFEA. The Mandy Allwood case is a good illustration of the use and problems associated with fertility drug use, where she became pregnant with seven embryos following her being provided with fertility drugs, but sadly lost (miscarried) all of the septuplet embryos. The BFS noted also that IVF and related treatments increase the risk of an ectopic pregnancy to 1–3 per cent, about twice the normal rate.

1.24   The BFS also noted, regarding the risk of an abnormal baby following IVF/ICSI and related technologies, that as of August 2005, there have been over a million babies born following IVF and ICSI treatment worldwide and that in the UK between 1 and 2 per cent of all babies are conceived following IVF and its related technology. It goes on to say:

'Many studies have reported the incidence of abnormal babies but most have been too small or of insufficient quality to provide a reliable answer ... At this time [the BFS] cannot conclusively say whether or not there is a cause and effect relationship between IVF/ICSI and specific abnormalities, however, it is clear that, if such a risk exists, it is small and that further monitoring of children resulting from such treatment is necessary to answer this question.'

1.25   Finally the BFS refer to the psychological and emotional risks of infertility treatment, stating it can be:

'stressful because of the emotional "roller-coaster" of expectation, disappointment and success and the marked hormonal changes that occur during the cycle of treatment.'

Dr Jim Monach, formerly at the University of Sheffield, stated that:

'There is no longer any disagreement that infertility is a distressing experience ... Indeed some studies have suggested that it is one of the most distressing medical conditions treated in the health service, especially where infertility lasts for a long period and is never resolved ... Prior to and during treatment this commonly takes the form of:
● Depression
● Anxiety
● Sexual anxiety/difficulty
● Relationship problems with partner, family and friends, and
● Increased sense of self-blame and guilt (especially in the subfertile partner).'[16]

1.26   He adds that following unsuccessful treatment (70–75 per cent approximately of treatment is after all unsuccessful):

---

16   BFS Factsheet (February 2005).

'all of the above feelings are still very commonly reported and also [regrettably]:

- Poor coping skills
- Sense of helplessness
- Increased marital/partner tensions
- Heightened anger and
- Sense of loss or bereavement.'

Worryingly too he notes that 'there is evidence that high levels of psychological distress, of whatever kind, will make conception less likely,' which creates a real and vicious infertility circle.

MULTIPLE BIRTHS – THE BIGGEST RISK

1.27   The HFF&F Report also flagged up one of the major medical, and arguably ethical, disadvantages of IVF, namely the risks of multiple births. Indeed, it states that multiple births where twins or triplets are born were the single biggest health risk associated with fertility treatment. It went on to outline the risks that multiple births carry to the health of both the mother and the babies:

- Mothers have a higher risk of miscarriage and other complications in pregnancy.
- The babies are more likely to be premature and to have a low birth weight.
- The risk of death within the first week of life is more than four times greater for twins than for a single baby.
- The risk of cerebral palsy is five times higher for twins and 18 times higher for triplets than for a single baby.

1.28   Not surprisingly, given these risks, the HFEA Code of Practice in an attempt to protect women from these very real dangers and tangible harm imposed limits on the numbers of embryos transferred into women. But the Report concedes:

'However, whilst this has effectively reduced triplet births, the proportion of twin births remains high. The only way to reduce the risk of multiple births is to transfer just one embryo (single embryo transfer) in the patients who are most likely to get pregnant and therefore also most at risk of having twins.'[17]

1.29   The HFF&F Report noted that the HFEA took proactive steps to promote the transfer of single embryos in January 2009 by introducing a policy to promote single embryo transfer and minimise the risk of multiple births from IVF treatment. The HFEA sets a maximum multiple birth rate that clinics should not exceed and this is lowered each year with an ultimate aim of 10 per cent multiple births. The Year 1 (2009) target was 24 per cent multiple births and the Year 2 (2010) target was 20 per cent. On 9 February 2012, the HFEA announced that licensed IVF clinics' current target that no more than 15 per cent of births should be twins or triplets, would be cut from October 2012 to no more than 10 per cent of births being twins or triplets. This incremental policy (introduced in January 2009) of the HFEA to encourage clinics to promote

17   Page 7.

single embryo transfer (SET) is a very telling and tangible manifestation of the statutory regulator acting to safeguard the interests of the patient and thus avoid potential harm, in the guise of reducing the frequency of multiple pregnancies with all their associated significant risks to both the mother and child. Indeed Alan Doran, Chief Executive of the HFEA, observed on 9 February 2012:

> 'Since the introduction of the policy in January 2009, the proportion of single embryo transfers has increased, the multiple pregnancy rate has decreased and the overall pregnancy rate has remained steady.'

Despite these undoubtedly reassuring words, some paying patients (paying patients make up 75 per cent of patients), desperate for a child, may nevertheless disregard them and demand or expect that paid clinicians ought to transfer two or three embryos to maximise their chance of having a child. Is the customer always right? All centres had their own strategy setting out how they would not exceed the maximum multiple birth rate.

1.30 The Report highlights that:

> 'The data presented in this report is for treatments started in 2008, before the HFEA single embryo transfer policy was introduced. However the most recent pregnancy data shows that the multiple pregnancy rate has decreased as centres carry out more single embryo transfers in patients most at risk of conceiving a multiple pregnancy.'

1.31 The multiple birth figures for all types of IVF in 2008 revealed that multiple births are generally more common in younger women: 'The high rate of multiples in women aged over 44 is thought to occur because they are more likely to be treated with donated eggs which will have come from younger women.'[18] The figures for multiple births for all types of IVF are set out in the table below:

Age range	Singleton births	Multiple births	Proportion of live births which are multiple
Under 35	4,555	1,694	27.1%
35–37	2,509	681	21.3%
38–39	1,259	255	16.8%
40–42	813	136	14.3%
43–44	143	31	17.8%
Over 44s	97	38	28.1%

Donor Insemination

1.32 The multiple birth figures for donor insemination (DI) are considerably lower and better than for IVF as seen in the table below.

---

18   Page 8.

Age range	Singleton births	Multiple births	Proportion of live births which are multiple
Under 35	232	25	9.7%
35–37	111	6	5.1%
38–39	47	3	6.0%
40–42	24	1	4.0%
43–44	2	0	0%
Over 44s	0	0	0%

AVERAGE AGE OF WOMAN TREATED

1.33 The HFF&F Report noted that the average age of women treated in 2008 was 35.2 years for IVF and 35.1 years for DI, and that this has not changed since 2007. However, since the creation of the HFEA in 1991, the average age of women treated has increased by 1.6 years from 33.6 for IVF, and 3.2 years from 31.9 for DI. Again this is clear evidence that women are increasingly delaying having children until later on in their reproductive life. Hence the need and demand for IVF. The detailed breakdown of the age of women starting treatment in 2008 was as follows:

- 40.3 per cent of those seeking treatment were under 35;
- 24.6 per cent were 35–37;
- 15.6 per cent were 38–39;
- 13.9 per cent were 40–42;
- 3.8 per cent were 43–44; and
- 1.7 per cent were over 44.

Therefore, almost three out of every five women seeking treatment were aged 35 or over.

REASONS FOR PATIENTS UNDERGOING FERTILITY TREATMENT

1.34 The Report disclosed that: 'Approximately equal numbers of patients sought treatment for male (29.7 per cent) or female (28.5 per cent in total) factors. A further one in ten patients received treatment because of both male and female factors.'[19] Very significantly it noted that: 'Nearly a quarter of patients treated had unexplained infertility.' The fact that 23.9 per cent of infertility is unexplained arguably provides sufficient justification for scientists and doctors to use human embryos or human admixed embryos for research purposes. Indeed, under Sch 2, para 3(2)(a) of the 1990 Act, one of the original five permitted research purposes for using human embryos, and still one today, was if the use of the embryo was 'necessary or desirable for the purpose of [...] promoting advances in the treatment of infertility.'

19 Page 10.

1.35 The detailed breakdown of the reasons patients sought fertility treatment in 2008 was:

- male factor – 29.7 per cent
- ovarian failure – 1 per cent
- tubal disorders – 12.4 per cent
- endometriosis – 3.5 per cent
- ovulatory disorders – 7 per cent
- uterine factors –0.4 per cent
- multiple female factors – 4 per cent
- menopausal – 0.2 per cent
- male and female factors –10.3 per cent
- other factors – 4.7 per cent
- avoid genetic disorder – 0.5 per cent
- no male partner – 1.4 per cent
- unexplained infertility – 23.9 per cent.

EGG, SPERM AND EMBRYO DONATION

1.36 One of the many problems with assisted reproduction is that you need a supply of eggs/sperm/embryos. Generally these will come from the couple, but if one of them cannot produce gametes then gamete/embryo donation becomes imperative. However, there are not enough gamete and embryo donors and demand from would-be parents exceeds the supply from existing donors. The HFEA noted in 1992 (it had been created in August 1991) that there were 346 new sperm donors and 449 new egg donors. The number of new sperm donors peaked in 1994 and 1996 with 417 new sperm donors registering at an HFEA licensed clinic, and the number of new egg donors peaked in 2001 with 1,289. The most recent figures in 2008 reveal that 396 new sperm and 1,150 new egg donors respectively were registered.

UK v overseas donors?

1.37 There appears to be good statistical evidence that the pool of UK sperm donors is declining (although donation remains the main source of sperm), and that UK licensed clinics are having to rely increasingly on overseas sperm donation to address the needs of infertile couples. Thus the HFEA noted that in 2005, out of a total of 257 sperm donors, 226 (88 per cent) were from the UK compared to 31 from overseas (12 per cent). However, in 2008, of the total of 442 sperm donors, 347 (79 per cent) were from the UK compared to 95 (21 per cent) from overseas sperm donors.[20]

1.38 Regarding egg donors the picture is totally different. In 2005 there was a total of 944 egg donors and of those 904 (96 per cent) were UK egg donors compared to 40 (4 per cent) who were overseas egg donors. In 2008, of 1,184 egg donors in total, 1,155 (98 per cent) were from the UK, as against just 29 (2 per cent) from overseas. Thus, the percentage of UK egg donors, very high in 2005, is even higher in 2008.[21]

---

20 See hfea.gov.uk/3413.html
21 *Ibid.*

1.39   However, the bottom line is that there are not enough gamete donors or gametes available for donation.

Donor conception births

1.40   HFEA statistics found that in 1992 there were 1,790 children born following sperm donor treatment, 122 using eggs and 19 using embryos, making a total of 1,931 children (42 per cent) born following all donation out of 4,569 babies born as a result of all IVF/DI donor treatment whether using own or donated gametes. However there has been a decline in the number of children born following donor treatment and a much steeper drop in the percentage of children born from donation compared to the overall number of children born from IVF/DI. So in 2008 there were 1,600 children (11 per cent) born following donor treatment, comprised of 977 children born following sperm donor treatment, 541 using eggs and 82 using donated embryos. But there were 331 fewer children born from all donations and there were 15, 237 babies born from all IVF/DI, whether using donated or own gametes; so the percentage of children born from all donations plummeted from 42 per cent to a mere 11 per cent in the 16-year period from 1992 to 2008.[22]

Egg share v non-patient egg donors

1.41   The HFEA states that egg donors can either 'donate all their eggs in a treatment cycle (non-patient egg donors) or share their eggs with up to two recipients in each cycle (egg share donors).'[23] In 2000 (the year they first registered as a donor), out of a total of 1,245 egg donors, 376 (30 per cent) were egg share donors and 869 (70 per cent) were non-patient egg donors. In 2007 the total number of all egg donors had declined to 986, of whom 477 (48 per cent) were egg share donors and 509 (52 per cent) were non-patient egg donors. So in 2007 nearly half of all egg donors were egg share donors, in other words giving up some of their eggs in return for cheaper IVF. In 2008 the total number of all egg donors increased to 1,164, comprised of 400 egg share donors (34 per cent) and 764 non-patient egg donors (66 per cent). This percentage still represents quite a significant proportion of all egg donors.

RESEARCH

1.42   On the HFEA website[24] there are 21 licensed clinics undertaking research involving human embryos. Some of these research projects include:

- The Centre at LIFE, Newcastle-upon-Tyne, with two research projects – 'Pluripotency, reprogramming and mitochondrial biology during early human development (R0152)' and 'Mitochondrial DNA Disorders preventing transmission (R0153)'.
- The Centre for Stem Cell Biology, University of Sheffield, 'Development of human embryonic stem cell lines to Good Manufacturing Practice for treatment of degenerative diseases and conditions (R0104)'.

22 See www.hfea.gov.uk/donor-conception-births.html
23 See www.hfea.gov.uk/3412.html
24 www.hfea.gov.uk/166.html

- Guy's Hospital, London had two research projects licensed, one of which was entitled 'Improving methods for biopsy & preimplantation diagnosis of inherited genetic disease of human embryos (R0075)'.
- London Fertility Centre, 'Analysis of chromosomes in human preimplantation embryos using FISH and CGH (R0169)'.
- Scottish Biomedical, 'Derivation of a human embryonic stem cell line for the development of drugs for human disease (R0182)'.
- The University of Newcastle-Upon-Tyne, Centre for Stem Cell Biology & Developmental Genetics, Institute of Human Genetics, 'Derivation of Embryonic Stem cell Lines from Interspecies Embryos produced by Somatic Cell Nuclear Transfer (R0179)'. This research licence and research project arguably signals an important new direction of future research using human admixed embryos.
- The Welcome Trust Centre for Stem Cell Research, University College Cambridge, 'Derivation of pluripotent human embryo cell lines (R0178) (Previously R0132–Institute of Stem Cell Research, Edinburgh)'.

Interestingly at least 14 of the research projects involve stem cell research or use of embryos to develop treatments for diseases, etc and thus have little or nothing to do 'with promoting advances in the treatment of infertility', arguably one of the main original permitted research purposes under the 1990 Act. For some this is further evidence of the ethical slippery slope, but for others (the majority) it is evidence of the further good uses (ie research) that can be made of human embryos, and, since the 2008 Act, the use of the new human admixed embryos, hopefully for the benefit of mankind in the least harmful way.

PARLIAMENT – THE UK'S ETHICAL AND LEGAL COMPASS?

1.43 The debates in Parliament, (in both the House of Commons and House of Lords), that preceded the enactment of the Human Fertilisation and Embryology Act 2008, which eventually received the Royal Assent on 13 November 2008, characterised the fiercely controversial and divisive nature of several key features of the Act, and the seemingly unbridgeable chasm that exists between a sizeable proportion of Parliamentarians on a raft of legal, ethical and medical/scientific issues. Whilst those debates incontrovertibly, and not surprisingly, generated considerable and passionate heat, they nevertheless shed much light on extremely complex areas of cutting-edge medicine and scientific development. Parliament met the challenge and criticism of marrying 'old laws to new medicine' (per Professor Sheila McLean), and demonstrated that Parliament was in Bagehot's terms an 'efficient', ie a fully functioning, effective, working body, attempting to successfully regulate a fast-moving area of science/medicine/research, rather than being merely a 'dignified', ie ineffective, rubber-stamping mechanism, blindly and obsequiously in thrall to the latest whims and diktats of science.

IVF, ETC – CONVENTIONAL MEDICAL TREATMENT AT LAST?

1.44 The fact that the creator and pioneer of in vitro fertilisation (IVF), Professor Robert Edwards (who along with Patrick Steptoe created the first 'test-tube' baby in 1978, Louise Brown), received the Nobel Prize for

Physiology or Medicine on 4 October 2010, 32 years after the birth of Louise Brown is welcome, if somewhat belated recognition of the massive contribution the science of IVF and its application, IVF treatment, have made to mankind.[25] It is a timely award too, given how much IVF is taken for granted by most people nowadays as a routine medical procedure and treatment, albeit generally only available to those who can pay for it privately. As *The Times* editorial of 5 October 2010 correctly notes, since Louise Brown's birth in 1978, which demonstrated that IVF could be safe and effective:

> 'IVF treatment, has since become commonplace, given some 12,000 IVF babies are born in the UK each year. Worldwide, almost four million babies have been born after IVF treatment … It will appear trite to describe those births as miraculous; it is also untrue, for they are the outcome of methods devised by science. Yet to couples who want children and are unable to conceive, IVF has given them something precious and incomparable: a realistic chance [on average 25–30 per cent] of creating and guiding a human personality through its earliest years.'

1.45 The editorial recognised that IVF can involve the destruction of embryos – maybe 12–15 eggs are fertilised in the IVF process, and only two are generally implanted in the woman, the rest being frozen or even discarded then or subsequently, but it countered that:

> '… there is nothing anti-life in IVF: the embryos are created to produce babies and allow the chance of parenthood to couples who want a child of their own … Nature itself creates and fertilises many more eggs than become babies.'

Nature is more profligate and wasteful of life than science. Why should we demand more exacting standards from science than those that occur naturally, one might ask?

1.46 Equally, the editorial in *The Times* was fulsome in its praise of the promise of embryo stem cell research in helping mankind. It noted:

> 'The embryonic cell can also be taken apart, at an early stage, to yield stem cells … Research using stem cells offers the promise of finding a cure for debilitating conditions such as Parkinson's disease … those same forces who object to IVF treatment, also object to embryonic stem cell research, but that, the objections are similarly misguided … The successes of IVF in creating new life may yet indirectly improve the lives of adults.'

BARREN BRITAIN?

1.47 On 19 May 2011 the *Daily Mail* cited a study by the Organisation for Economic Co-Operation and Development (OECD) which considered women in 24 countries (ie industrialised nations) who were born in 1965 and all of whom are now around 46, so most will have finished their reproductive careers

---

25 Paradoxically the Medical Research Council rejected an application from him in the 1970s when he sought to establish the first clinic to treat infertility by IVF, citing 'safety concerns, including a claim that IVF rats "were born with small eyes", and the belief that "infertility should not be treated because the world was overpopulated"' (Hannah Devlin in *The Times* on 5 October 2010).

and some will be entering the menopause. The survey found that, at this stage of life, rates of childlessness in the UK – 18.9 per cent to be exact – are beaten only by 24 per cent in Italy and 20 per cent in Germany and Finland. The article added: 'Experts believe the Barren Britain phenomenon could have arisen because until recently women here were far more likely to pursue careers than those in the rest of Europe, meaning many put off having children until too late.'

AN EXPLOSION OF DEVELOPMENTS

1.48 The frequency and pace of scientific developments in the sphere of assisted reproduction being reported in the media highlights the importance placed on helping to alleviate the pain and suffering of people afflicted with a range of diverse diseases and debilitating conditions, as well as the faith many people place in science and medicine in helping to find possible cures and treatments for those diseases and conditions. However the emphasis, if not the total direction, of the assisted reproduction industry appears to have moved away from merely helping the infertile to have children they otherwise would not have, to harnessing and manipulating the new technologies and techniques of the assisted reproduction industry for a wider range of other purposes. Some recent examples of this burgeoning utilisation of the research and therapeutic tools of assisted reproduction science are outlined here.

Genetic screening using PGD

1.49 In 2010, it was reported[26] that Dr Richard Scott had developed a genetic screening test to pick the best embryos for couples having fertility treatment, which can improve the chances of a successful pregnancy. This screening test, said the article, 'is likely to be of particular value to women over 35, who have a higher chance of producing embryos with chromosomal abnormalities as the quality of their eggs declines.' Using pre-implantation genetic diagnosis (PGD) following IVF, this test is used to filter out the implantation of embryos with chromosomal abnormalities, in order that the chances of implanting 'healthy' embryos in the woman, to maximise the likelihood of a successful pregnancy, can occur. Dr Scott conceded that screening embryos could add 'between £1,000 and £2,000 to the cost of IVF', but 'provided the best chance of success when implanting a single embryo in the womb'. This genetic screening test using PGD is not cheap, but might mean only one good quality embryo being implanted in the woman, and thus less likelihood of multiple births and a greater chance of a successful pregnancy. This would appear to be a commendable ethical pathway to follow and of course it ties in with the HFEA policy of promoting single embryo transfers in clinics.

Woman gives birth to own grandson

1.50 On 26 February 2011, the *Daily Mail* reported that Pamela Butler, aged 57, had given birth to her grandson, Josef, by Caesarian section in August 2010 because her daughter Nichola, aged 35, was medically unable to have a child and, in the process became the oldest surrogate mother in Britain. Moreover,

---

26 *The Times,* 27 October 2010.

'[I]t took four heartrending attempts at IVF treatment – in which eggs were harvested from Mrs Pagett and fertilised with her husband's sperm before being implanted into Mrs Butler's womb – for Josef to be born.'

First baby from flash frozen egg

1.51 On 4 April 2011, the *Daily Mail* reported that Olivia Bates was:

'the UK's first baby to born from an egg that was flash frozen – frozen in less than 60 seconds. Months later the egg was thawed, fertilised and placed in her mother Karen Bateman's womb [...] With normal freezing techniques, which takes about two hours, 65 per cent of eggs survive the thawing process. With vitrification this rises to 95 per cent.'

1.52 Dr Gillian Lockwood of Midland Fertility Services, who carried out the treatment, noted that: 'Because it is frozen so quickly, the egg undergoes less structural damage which means it has a better chance of surviving the thawing process.' She also added the new technique and the happy outcome of a healthy baby (Olivia):

'gives hope to the many young women who want to preserve their fertility before they have life-saving cancer treatment – and also to those women who know that they want to be mothers one day, but can't try for a baby now.'

She added that the further benefit was:

'Because so many more eggs survive this thawing process, it means that women can have just one cycle of treatment and get enough eggs to freeze, instead of having to have several treatment cycles.'

1.53 A therapeutic assisted reproduction lifeline has, therefore, been thrown to a number of women by the creation of this technique. However, whilst there would be enormous sympathy and support for a woman using this technique before she receives, for example, life-saving chemotherapy, many would be unhappy with its use by women or couples delaying having children at, for example, 30 for social, career or other non-health related reasons, until later in life, for example 45 or 50.

Eggs developed from girls' ovaries

1.54 In the *Sunday Times* on 22 May 2011 it was announced that a team of researchers from Edinburgh University are developing eggs '[from] removed tiny strips of tissues from the ovaries of girls as young as eight using keyhole surgery. At this age, the ovaries contain undeveloped eggs inside follicles.'

These young girls have been left infertile by cancer treatment and the hope is to develop these eggs and ultimately fertilise them and replace them in the girls when they grow up and want to start a family, in order to give them at least the opportunity of becoming a parent if they wish. The *Sunday Times* noted that if the researchers' plan is successful:

'the embryos would be the first developed from eggs grown outside the body [...] In adult patients, eggs can be removed and kept in the laboratory for possible IVF treatment if the woman is left infertile. Until now, however, this has been of no use for children, whose eggs are too undeveloped to turn into embryos.'

1.55   Professor Anderson stated: 'If you take a piece of ovarian tissue and start from that then you could potentially have hundreds of eggs or more.' There is, therefore, an ethical argument that this avenue of research and hopeful therapy promises a better supply of developed eggs for fertilisation and subsequent use by the girl when she grows up. The potential demand and use of this research and ultimately therapy is clear, given that the *Sunday Times* noted that about 1,500 children under 15 are diagnosed with cancer each year in Britain.

Mitochondrial genetic disease

1.56   On 28 May 2011, it was reported at the European Society of Human Genetics annual conference that Dutch researchers had developed a test which predicts which mothers at risk of passing on mitochondrial genetic disease to their children are likely to have a healthy baby. It was also reported that PGD can give women at risk of passing on a mitochondrial DNA disorder to their offspring a good chance of being able to give birth to an unaffected child. The prevalence of mtDNA disorders is 1 in 5,000, which means that the families of about 146,000 patients in Europe would now have the option of having a healthy child, a choice they do not currently have. This development emphasises the ethical principle of autonomy.

MoD asked to pay for freezing of sperm from soldiers on combat duty

1.57   On the 9 June 2011, it was reported by BBC News that Sgt Rick Clement from Blackpool, who lost both of his legs in a roadside bomb in Afghanistan and cannot because of his terrible injuries conceive a baby with his wife Leanne,[27] has called on the Ministry of Defence to pay for soldiers to freeze their sperm before combat duty.' However, the BBC reported that an MoD statement said that it did not fund 'pre-deployment fertility preservation'.

Lowering risk of twins

1.58   Furthermore, on 5 July 2011 BBC News reported that:

> 'At a meeting of the European Society for Human Reproduction and Embryology (ESHRE), in Stockholm experts heard, 'how running through a simple checklist of questions about the patient could bring down the risk of causing twins to virtually "normal".'[28]

The research was led by Dr Jan Holte of the Uppsala Science Park, who, with his colleagues over a four-year period between 1999 and 2002 analysed over 3,000 of the IVF cycles performed at their clinic, taking note of different factors that played a role in the treatment's success. They found that:

---

27   www.bbc.co.uk/news/uk-england-lancashire-13709751
28   www.bbc.co.uk/news/health-14012498

'four factors – age of the woman, how many eggs she produced, quality of the resultant embryo and past success or failure with IVF – could predict the chances of pregnancy.'

Keeping up the IVF live birth rate or even increasing it, whilst at the same time cutting the multiple birthrate is arguably one of the many holy grails of IVF treatment/research.

Breeding out genetic disorders

1.59 In a BBC news report on 5 July 2011, it was revealed that a South Shields teacher Daniel Stanley, following the death of his 28 year old sister, Natasha, from breast cancer, (who had discovered that the cancer had a genetic basis on one of two breast cancer genes, BRCA1 and BRCA2), had undergone a test and discovered that he had the same gene. This result had 'placed him on the horns of a very difficult dilemma because he wanted children, but did not want to pass on the gene.' Following genetic counselling he was offered PGD to screen IVF-created embryos for this genetic disorder. It was noted that:

'PGD has been offered by the NHS for more than a decade for serious diseases that come early in childhood, like cystic fibrosis or Tays Sachs, a neurological disease [...] for a treatable adult disease the ethics are debatable, and so the first child free of the breast cancer gene by PGD was born only in 2009.'

Some critics would demonise this as tantamount to doctors playing God, and acquiescing in creating designer children, and furthermore cite this as further evidence of a descent down the ethical slippery slope. Even some eminent researchers cautioned whether 'weeding out' embryos with mutant genes was necessarily a therapeutic panacea. Professor Michael Baum, a leading researcher in breast cancer raised the phenomena in genetics and cellular development called co-expression in which two genes can be stuck together and noted: 'If you have the mutant gene, that might be co-expressed with favourable components of the human genome.' He cautioned that 'if you breed out the BRAC1 and BRCA2 mutation you may inadvertently breed out something of value.' For example, if one were able to 'select out' embryos with thalassaemia in IVF, preventing that terrible disease might be a very good thing, but arguably some embryos have these genes to protect against malaria, so if a country was 'hit' by a malaria epidemic, more people would be affected by that disease because the thalassaemia had been 'screened' out by not implanting those embryos with the thalassaemia genes. As Professor Baum argues, we may be inadvertently be selecting out 'something else that has an evolutionary advantage.' However Daniel Stanley believed that going through PGD was 'almost a kind of duty,' and added: 'If science has given me that power to do something about it then really I should use that power.'

Non-invasive and cheaper screening of IVF embryos

1.60 On 6 July 2011, BBC News also reported that fertility doctors said they had found a non-invasive and cheaper way to screen IVF embryos for genetic abnormalities, which means PGD, which experts fear may be harmful, does not need to occur.[29] The lead researcher, Dr Elpida Fragouli, from Oxford University, explained that in the ovary the eggs are surrounded by a cloud of tiny cells, known as cumulus cells. Cumulus cells are routinely stripped off eggs during IVF treatments and are usually discarded, so it should be straightforward to obtain them for analysis. The research involved Dr Fragoulli's team examining cumulus cells from 26 women undergoing genetic screening prior to IVF treatment. They found abnormalities in the cumulus cells that appeared to tally with genetic errors in the eggs they had surrounded. Dr Fragouli said: 'We are still in the process of establishing the usefulness of these genes as non-invasive markers of egg chromosome status and quality.' As well as being much cheaper and much less invasive than PGD, Stuart Lavery said that the new procedure could permit doctors to pick the best embryo from the best egg, which will hopefully mean a move towards single embryo transfer in line with existing HFEA policy.

Stem cell register

1.61 On the same day, BBC News reported that a survey carried out by the Antony Nolan charity which questioned 2,049 members of the public found that most people (54 per cent) would consider joining the stem cell register.[30]

Adult stem cell growing made easier

1.62 On 17 July, 2011 BBC News reported that a new plastic surface, that is 'nano-patterned', which overcomes the difficulties associated with growing adult stem cells, has been developed by researchers at Glasgow and Southampton universities.

Fixed sum payment for egg donors

1.63 On 19 October 2011, it was announced that the HFEA had agreed to approve a fixed sum payment of £750 per treatment cycle for egg donors in an attempt to increase the number of donors, and in response to the growth of fertility tourism (people seeking egg donors abroad), or egg donation through unregulated websites. The main reason for this is the acute shortage of human eggs, but for some egg donation should be based on altruism, not commerce. Also, will poorer women be exploited by richer women? What price human life?

NEGATIVE CONSEQUENCES OF ASSISTED REPRODUCTION?

1.64 Clearly not all coverage of the spin-offs of the IVF business has been rose-coloured eulogies. Some have seemingly highlighted risks and downsides of IVF, and sounded a cautionary note about the 'promise' and benefits of the technology.

---

29 www.bbc.co.uk/news/health-14029983
30 www.bbc.co.uk/news/health-14030891

Malformation of babies

1.65 The *Sunday Times* reported on 13 June 2010 that research led by Dr Geraldine Viot, clinical geneticist at the Maternite Port-Royal hospital, Paris, into the health of 15,162 babies born after assisted conceptions found that 4.24 per cent had serious malformations, roughly double the rate for all children. The study, carried out in France, is the largest of its kind.

PCTs create additional criteria

1.66 On 4 October 2010, the *Daily Mail* flagged up how some PCTs were creating their own additional criteria to effectively both preclude certain individuals from accessing IVF, and at the same time reducing their expenditure on healthcare treatment. Thus:

'Up to one in five of … PCTs … in England say that they would refuse treatment to couples if either of them drink more than the Department of Health's recommended weekly limit of 14 units for women and 21 for men.'

Mother freezes eggs for sterile daughter

1.67 On 11 January 2011, the *Daily Mail* reported that 'Penny Jarvis', aged 25, and a mother of four children, wanted to freeze her own eggs so that Mackenzie, her two-year-old daughter, who was born with Turner syndrome, a potentially devastating chromosomal abnormality which inter alia causes sterility, and who was born without ovaries, can use them to have babies by IVF.

Removing current compensation limit to discourage fertility tourists

1.68 On 17 January 2011, the *Daily Mail* reported that the HFEA had unveiled a consultation policy about removing the current limit of £250 compensation for donating eggs under a plan to help more infertile women conceive. Quite simply, there are not enough egg donors or eggs for donation; hence the necessity of trying to encourage more egg donors to come forward with the inducement or carrot of an increase in compensation for the egg donors, which is being mooted by the independent statutory regulator, the HFEA. The plans would also aim to prevent hundreds of 'fertility tourists' being driven abroad every year because of the drastic shortage of eggs in this country. The implication is that some of these 'fertility tourists' seeking eggs for donation would be exposing themselves to potential harm by obtaining these eggs in countries not enjoying the rigorous control of donation of eggs as in the UK.

Down's Syndrome risk

1.69 On 4 July 2011 BBC News reported that UK researchers at the European Society of Human Reproduction and Embryology's annual conference in Sweden who looked at 34 couples think drugs used to kick-start ovaries for IVF in older women disturb the genetic material of the eggs and may increase their risk of having a baby with Down's syndrome. Apparently all of the women in the research sample were over 31 and had been given drugs to make their ovaries release eggs for subsequent IVF treatment. When the researchers studied these now fertilised eggs they found some had genetic errors, which could either cause the pregnancy to fail or mean the baby would be born with a genetic disease. The report went on to say that a closer look at 100 of the faulty eggs revealed that many of the errors resulted in an extra copy of chromosome 21, which causes Down's syndrome. But unlike 'classic' Down's syndrome which is often seen in the babies of older women who conceive naturally, the pattern of genetic errors leading to Down's in the IVF eggs was different and more complex. This led the researchers to believe that it was the fertility treatment that was to blame. The lead researcher on the project, Professor Alan Handyside, the Director of the London Bridge Fertility Gynaecology and Genetics Centre (and the creator of PGD) stated:

> 'This could mean that the stimulation of the ovaries is causing some of these errors. We already know that these fertility drugs can have a similar effect in laboratory studies. But we need more work [ie research] to confirm our findings.'

1.70 Clearly, if this further research were to confirm these findings, questions would arise as to whether it was wise, safe and ethically acceptable to expose women to the greater risk of possibly having a handicapped child by using certain drugs on women's ovaries to produce eggs. Also, this research could also help identify which women might be better off using donor eggs for IVF instead, which of course avoids the need to stimulate the infertile woman's ovaries. This research could be challenging conventional wisdom that chromosomal abnormalities like Down's syndrome are attributable to the age of the egg. Stuart Lavery noted:

> 'What this work shows is that a lot of the chromosomal abnormalities are not those that are conventionally age-related. It raises the concern that some of the abnormalities might be treatment-related.'

Pro-life advocates might again point to an ethical slippery slope here and state that IVF treatment and research involves mass experimentation that no-one has consented to, least of all the innocent, silent, defenceless embryo.

STRUCTURE OF THIS BOOK

1.71 This work is set out as follows:

- Part One examines the legalisation governing the creation of human admixed embryos for research purposes and consider the arguments raised in both Houses of Parliament supporting and opposing this highly significant new legal development.
- Part Two considers the legalisation governing the creation of so-called 'saviour siblings' for, inter alia, saving the life of or helping therapeutically an existing sick child, and the ethical dimensions and repercussions of this new dispensation, as well as looking at Parliament's views on this development.
- Part Three considers the highly significant and symbolic change made to the 'welfare of the child' provision (s 13(5) of the 1990 Act), the deletion of the need for a father clause and its replacement by the need for supportive parent clause, and the huge ethical, moral and social fissures this created in both chambers of Parliament.

- Part Four examines some of the changes to the existing abortion legislation (the Abortion Act 1967, as amended) proposed by legislators, mainly in House of Commons, and considers some of the ethical arguments underpinning these.
- Part Five considers, inter alia, the key changes wrought by the 2008 Act to the parenthood provisions in the earlier 1990 Act and to the creation of a new order of legal parenthood in the UK, arguably more in tune with 2011 and beyond.
- Part Six focuses on the impact of human rights and various ECHR rights in the context of the provision of fertility treatments.
- Part Seven examines the role and impact of the Warnock Report in setting out a moral and ethical compass to assist in navigating the frequently choppy waters of infertility provision and regulation. It also covers the creation, role and functions of the HFEA, and considers the changes to the HFEA made by the 2008 Act.
- Part Eight considers two highly controversial aspects of fertility treatment, namely the lottery of accessing IVF treatment, and the vexed question of sex selection.
- Part Nine examines the great potential and promise of stem cell research and the real fears about where it will lead, and considers the seemingly different stances taken to it by some in the US and in the EU.
- Part Ten considers the role of our democratically elected and representative Parliament, our main ethical compass, in setting the legal parameters and ethical boundaries for infertility research and treatment in the UK, and examines whether it remains a fit-for-purpose forum to continue to do so.
- The concluding chapter assesses the potential overall impact of the 2008 Act and tentatively looks to the future.

Part 1

Human Admixed Embryos: New Eden or Manufactured Humanity?

Chapter 2

Frankenstein Humanity – Promethean Hubris?

BACKGROUND

2.1   Sadly there is an acute lack of human eggs being donated for the treatment of infertile women and couples and for undertaking research into, for example, infertility, so there is a certain logic, if not a scientific imperative and ethical compulsion to explore alternative possible sources for eggs or even to create new types of embryos for both treatment purposes and for research. Put bluntly, there are not enough eggs available to grow embryos for research, and getting these eggs is difficult and not without some (small) risk and discomfort to the woman, so if scientists could use enucleated animal eggs with, for example, human DNA or a human nucleus inserted, they could develop these embryos and harvest stem cells from them for therapeutic drugs testing or research on diseases etc. Unsurprisingly, permitting the creation of such human admixed embryos generated huge controversy and implacable opposition in many. However, as Gregory Pence observed, 'knee-jerk condemnations stem from fear and ignorance; they should not be mistaken for moral wisdom.'[1] He conceded that:

> '[whilst] ethics is partly based on emotion, it is also more than that ... reasonable creatures, humans want reasons why a certain act is judged to be wrong' [ie creating human admixed embryos] ... If the balance of reasons favors one side over another, we know that the right side is the one with the better reasons.'[2]

He argues that decisions should be anchored in reasons, arguments and evidence, and not on the basis of 'a conditioned "yuck factor"'. However, who decides which are the better reasons and how? Are decisions to permit or ban an activity always necessarily based exclusively on the quality of the reasons advanced? The debates in Parliament on permitting the creation of human admixed embryos highlighted graphically the use of reason, evidence and argument versus the use of emotion, intuition, gut feeling, and 'yuck factors' on both sides of the debate. Pence also challenged those who were opposed to scientific development such as IVF because of the risks associated with it, contending that: 'no reasonable approach to life avoids all risks. Without some risk, there is no progress, no advance.' That logic could be extended to human admixed embryo research.

NEW DAWN OF CREATION

2.2   On 23 July 2011 it was reported in the *Daily Mail* that 155 'admixed' embryos containing both human and animal genetic material, have been

---

1   *Who's Afraid of Human Cloning*' (Rowman & Littlefield,1998), p 2.
2   Ibid, pp 5 and 6.

created since the introduction of the 2008 Act. Allegedly, the hybrids had been produced secretively over the previous three years by researchers looking into possible cures for a wide range of diseases. This figure of 155 human admixed embryos being created was revealed to cross-bench peer Lord Alton following a Parliamentary question. Lord Alton was forthright in condemning this development, stating that he had earlier:

'argued in Parliament against the creation of human-animal hybrids as a matter of principle … None of the scientists who appeared before us could give us any justification in terms of treatment.'

He also contended that, '[E]thically it can never be justified – it discredits us as a country … It is dabbling in the grotesque.' He continued his vituperative denunciation of the creation of human admixed embryos for research thus:

'At every stage the justification from scientists has been: if only you allow us to do this, we will find cures for every illness known to mankind …This is emotional blackmail.'

Further, he claimed that all the 80 treatments and cures which have come about from stem cells have come from adult stem cells and not embryonic ones. This claim suggests that the promise of cures/treatments from embryonic stem cell research been over-sold and over-hyped. He concluded: 'On moral and ethical grounds this falls; and on scientific and medical ones.'

2.3 Another leading critic of embryonic stem cell research, Josephine Quintavalle, of the pro-life pressure group Comment on Reproductive Ethics, (CORE), stated that she was, 'aghast that this is going on and we didn't know anything about it.' She added, 'Why have they kept this a secret? If they are proud of what they are doing, why do we need to ask Parliamentary questions for this to come to light?' and she claimed that: 'The problem with many scientists is that they want to do things because they want to experiment. That is not a good rationale.' However, clearly one of the aims of these Parliamentary questions is to hold the government to account, to get information from them on controversial matters and issues that might be occurring largely unknown to the general public.

2.4 The *Daily Mail* noted that: 'Earlier this week, a group of leading scientists warned about "Planet of the Apes" experiments' and called for new rules to prevent lab animals being given human attributes, for example by injecting human stem cells into the brains of primates. They stated that lead author Professor Robin Lovell-Badge, from the Medical Research Council's National Institute for Medical Research, said the scientists were not concerned about human-animal hybrid embryos because by law these all have to be destroyed within 14 days. This is similar to human embryos which cannot be developed or kept beyond 14 days. In justifying that he added that:

'The reason for doing these experiments is to understand more about early human development and come up with ways of curing serious diseases, and as a scientist I feel there is a moral imperative to pursue this research … As long as we have sufficient controls – as we do in this country – we should be proud of the research.'

The *Daily Mail* noted, however, that he called for stricter controls on another type of embryo research, in which animal embryos are implanted with a small amount of human genetic material.

THE NUMBERS GAME

2.5   Critics of embryonic research cite the extraordinarily high numbers of embryos that have been used for research purposes and indeed the even greater number of embryos that have been discarded and destroyed in the provision of IVF treatment. Lord Howe, the Health Minister, revealed the huge extent of the sacrifice of human embryos in a written answer in the House of Lords to Lord Alton. The *Daily Mail* reported on 23 July 2011 that the figures show that 3,144,386 embryos have been created in UK laboratories since the passage of the 1990 Act and that a total of 1,455,832 embryos were discarded in the course of treatment, 101,605 were given for research in destructive experiments, and 764,311 were frozen for later use. The rest were implanted, resulting in 94,090 births, meaning that in the region of 32 embryos are created for every live birth. The *Daily Mail* commented that: 'Hundreds of thousands have been simply thrown away or destroyed in the name of scientific research over the past 20 years.' Lord Alton, commented on these high numbers thus, describing them as 'staggering' and adding:

'We are creating and destroying human embryos on an industrial scale ... the figures reveal the folly of spending huge amounts of money on treatments which usually fail at a time when there are 600 abortions a day and only 70 babies put up for adoption each year.'

Lord Alton said that whilst we could 'celebrate with joy' the IVF birth of a baby to a family, nevertheless 'we shouldn't remove from the debate how many other human embryos are discarded without any thought in order to achieve that object.' Human embryos should not be used as a means toward an end and consequently become fundamentally devalued morally and ethically. Human embryos are not commodities.

2.6   Commenting on whether there was an ethical alternative to this – presumably adult stem cell research and use of cord blood – Lord Alton said:

'I think the real work that should be going on in fertility treatment is to fund the development of implantation techniques which don't require the destruction of human embryos.'

Josephine Quintavalle, of CORE, endorsed Lord Alton's concerns, stating that: 'Human life begins at the point of conception. It should not be created as a surplus in such a careless way.' Thus, embryos should not be manufactured and manipulated without consent in mass experimentation, and then be either discarded or destroyed. That may be considered both morally and ethically unacceptable.

THE NEW LAW: EDEN REVISITED?

2.7   The new law enshrined in the 2008 Act is in many ways playing legislative 'catch-up' with the rapid developments in scientific research that have taken place since the original 1990 Act was enacted, and is arguably a necessary attempt to make the new law fit for purpose to match and regulate this emerging and developing science. Concerning the creation of interspecies embryos (human admixed embryos), this author observed that:

'In 1990 it simply was not technologically possible to create an inter-species embryo. Thus, the 1990 Act does not refer to this novel type of embryo. However, this type of embryo can now be physically created by scientists/doctors (whether they ought ethically to do so, is a different question).'[3]

The author also noted that:

'The recent decision by the Human Fertilisation and Embryology Authority (HFEA) to approve in principle the creation of interspecies embryos – or cytoplasmic hybrids to give them their correct scientific designation – to be used for research purposes by scientists to create cell models for diseases with a genetic basis, has not been greeted with unanimous approval.'[4]

However he added:

'Nightmarish visions of mad scientists secretively creating half-human/half-animals in some grotesque Frankenstinian experiment and unleashing these ghoulish creatures into the world to cause mayhem, are gross hyberbole and a total distortion of the reality of the proposed science and the proposed use to which it is intended to be put.'[5]

2.8 Harris raises these concerns too, stating that:

'The spectre of Dr Frankenstein, the representative "mad scientist", is standardly invoked as a dire warning of what to expect when researchers tamper with the ultimate constituents of what matters.'[6]

He adds that:

'[the] storm of … protest that this work has attracted and continues to attract [is] not on account of what is being done but for fear of what the work demonstrates can or might be done.'

Thus the fear of science pushing society down new research and technologic/therapeutic pathways and avenues in the future alarms some and engenders caution in many that we may be descending down the ethical slippery slope. Harris counters these fears of ethical slippery slopes, arguing:

'We would be both irrational and immoral if we cut ourselves off from options we clearly perceive to be the beneficial products of the procedures now being developed because we fear that we will be insufficiently resolute to resist the dangers.'[7]

He cites that effective contraception, for example, is not outlawed because we fear that to practise population control is effectively stepping on the ethical slippery slope that, 'leads inexorably to the extinction of the human race.' That said, the author adds:

'However, HFEA admits there is ignorance among the general public about the scope, limitations and possibilities of the new cytoplasmic hybrid research: "There is a clear demand from people to know more about what researchers are doing and their plans for future work, highlighting a need

---

3   'S Burns, Fit for purpose?' (2008) 73(Feb) Fam L J 16–18, at p 17.
4   S Burns, 'It's a cow!' (2007) 157 NLJ 1521.
5   Ibid.
6   J Harris, *The Value of Life: An Introduction to Medical Ethics* (Routledge, 1985), p 111.
7   Ibid, p 127.

for better communication about science and research from both the scientific community and ourselves as regulators".'[8]

2.9 Ignorance of the new science and its possible uses by a large swath of the general public must be confronted and addressed by the scientists, regulators and by government and cannot be simply glibly dismissed as mere ignorant prejudice. As the author states, the new type of embryos:

'... are going to be used as research and investigative tools/models by scientists, and most definitely are not being manufactured with a view to being placed in a woman using in vitro fertilisation (IVF) procedures, in order that the world's first cytoplasmic hybrid human embryo is born.'[9]

The new law

2.10 Section 1 of the 2008 Act (one of the key definition provisions in the new legislation) provides that:

'(1) Section 1 of the 1990 Act (meaning of "embryo", "gamete" and associated expressions) is amended as follows.

(2) For subsection (1) substitute—

"(1) In this Act (except in section 4A or in the term "human admixed embryo")—
(a) embryo means a live human embryo and does not include a human admixed embryo (as defined by section 4A(6)), and
(b) references to an embryo include an egg that is in the process of fertilisation or is undergoing any other process capable resulting in an embryo."'

The term 'human admixed embryo' is the one used in the 2008 Act, rather than 'interspecies embryo', the term used in the earlier parliamentary debates in the House of Lords.

2.11 The 2008 Act fundamentally, inter alia, distinguishes between two types of embryo, namely a 'live human embryo' (referred to as an 'embryo') and 'a human admixed embryo' (as defined in the new s 4A(6), discussed later). It may be argued that in this clear legal distinction is an implicit moral and ethical distinction between the two types of embryo. The new science creates new ethical/moral issues and concerns constantly.

2.12 The new s 4A of the 1990 Act, referred to in s 1(2) above, inter alia, outlines prohibitions in connection with genetic material not of human origin, (and will be discussed elsewhere).

2.13 Thus, crucially, the new s1(1)(a) of the 1990 Act clearly defines an embryo as being specifically a live human embryo and that therefore it excludes equally clearly a human admixed embryo, which variety of embryo is defined in new s 4A(6).

8 Ibid, p 1521.
9 S Burns, 'It's a cow!' (2007) 157 NLJ 1521.

2.14 Newly inserted s1(2)(b) is obviously aimed at addressing the apparent lacuna in the law caused by s1(1)(a) and (b) of the 1990 Act, which defined an embryo as meaning 'a live human embryo where fertilisation is complete', and also included 'an egg in the process of fertilisation', thus seemingly not therefore covering an embryo created by cell nuclear replacement (CNR), the technique used to create Dolly the sheep in 1996 whereby an adult nucleus is inserted into an enucleated egg to create an embryo by this method rather than by fertilisation. This was eventually clarified in the *Quintavalle* case,[10] when the Court of Appeal, inter alia, held that an embryo created by CNR was covered by the 1990 Act, even though the embryo had not been created by fertilisation. The 1990 Act was primarily aimed, inter alia, at the strict regulation of the creation and use of embryos outside the body. An embryo created by CNR, although patently not created following fertilisation, was nonetheless an embryo and as such fell under the regulatory aegis of the 1990 Act.

2.15 This change is also contained and reflected in s1(1)(3) of the 2008 Act, which substitutes a s 1(2)(a) which provides:

'references to embryos the creation of which was brought about *in vitro* (in their application to those where fertilisation or any other process by which an embryo is created is complete) are to those where fertilisation or any other process by which the embryo was created began outside the human body whether or not it was completed there.'

2.16 Furthermore another highly significant change is made by s 4 of the 2008 Act, which is headed 'Prohibitions in connection with genetic material not of human origin'. This crucially includes human admixed embryos. Section 4 makes the following amendments to s 4 of the 1990 Act:

'(1) In section 4 of the 1990 Act (prohibitions in connection with gametes)—
   (a) in subsection (1), omit—
       (i)   paragraph (c), and
       (ii) the word 'or' immediately before it, and
   (b) in subsection (5), after "section" insert "or 4A".'

2.17 Section 4(1)(c) of the 1990 Act had basically provided that no person could mix gametes with the live gametes of any animal unless they were licensed to do so by the HFEA. The only exception to this major and clear prohibition was contained in Sch 2, para 1(1)(f) of the 1990 Act which permitted human sperm to be mixed with hamster eggs to test the motility/mobility of the human sperm. Clearly the justification for this testing was the scarcity of human eggs for this type of testing and the absence of any ethical concerns with the practice. Schedule 2, para 1(1)(f) provided that a licence under this paragraph may authorise a number of procedures in the course of providing treatment services including:

'(f) mixing sperm with the egg of a hamster, or other animal specified in directions, for the purpose of testing the fertility or normality of the sperm, but only where anything which forms is destroyed when the test is complete and, in any event, not later than the two cell stage'.

10   *R (on the application of Quintavalle) v Human Fertilisation and Embryology Authority* [2003] EWCA Civ 667.

Thus, even under the original 1990 Act mixing of human and animal gametes was permitted, albeit for a specific and very limited purpose (ie testing human sperm fertility/normality), and subject to the very important safeguard that following the testing anything which formed was destroyed, and, failing that, that anything that formed when the testing was completed was destroyed no later than at the two cell stage, (ie when the thing that had formed had started dividing). This again was a clear ethical bright line in the 1990 Act.

2.18   Also, s 4(2) of the 2008 Act amends s 4(5) of the 1990 Act, so that it now reads:

> '(5)   Activities regulated by this section or section 3 or 4A of this Act are referred to in this Act as "activities governed by this Act".'

Section 4(2) provides that new s 4A is inserted after s 4 of the 1990 Act, concerning prohibitions in connection with genetic material not of human origin. This provides, inter alia, that:

> '(1)   No person shall place in a woman—
>> (a)   a human admixed embryo,
>> (b)   any other embryo that is not a human embryo, or
>> (c)   any gametes other than human gametes.'

Quite simply it is a very serious criminal offence for anyone, including a maverick doctor or scientist, to put a human admixed embryo in a woman. The penalty if a person is caught doing this and is subsequently prosecuted and convicted is 10 years' imprisonment (maximum), which is a draconian penalty but emphasises the seriousness with which Parliament takes the creation and use of human admixed embryos and that they should be created and used only strictly in accordance with how Parliament, by legislation, stipulates that they be created and used. Human admixed embryos are being permitted to be created and used only for specific research purposes and most definitely are not being permitted for reproductive purposes, ie creating the first ever human admixed person! That would be completely beyond the ethical and moral pale and would signal a steep descent down the slippery slope. The author has further commented on these provisions elsewhere, stating that:

> '[they continue] to prohibit the placing of non-human embryos in a woman, which is intuitively morally repugnant and offensive to most observers, and is a glaring example of an activity beyond the ethical pale (as well as exemplifying the so-called "yuck factor").This prohibition preventing non-human embryos being placed in women extends also to non-human gametes. Furthermore, no person can place an inter-species embryo in a woman, so that a mad or fame-seeking doctor cannot lawfully place an inter-species embryo in a woman, in order to create the first ever inter-species child born to a woman.'[11]

2.19   Section 4A(1)(b), which provides that no person can place any other non-human embryo (eg a gorilla or orang-utan embryo) in a woman, replicates its predecessor (s 3(2)(a) of the 1990 Act). Again, violation of this provision incurs a very serious penalty if a person is convicted under it (ie 10 years' imprisonment maximum). Equally, s 4A(1)(c) provided by the 2008 Act is

---

11   'S Burns, Fit for purpose?' (2008) Family Law Journal, February 2008, No 73, pp 16–18, at 18.

virtually identical to the prohibition in s 3(2)(b) of the 1990 Act, and prohibits a person placing any live non-human gametes in a woman. This too would be ethically repugnant.

2.20   Of fundamental importance to the legislation is new s 4A(2) of the 1990 Act (provided by s 4(2) of the 2008 Act), which provides that:

> '(2) No person shall—
> - (a)   mix human gametes with animal gametes,
> - (b)   bring about the creation of a human admixed embryo, or
> - (c)   keep or use a human admixed embryo,
> except in pursuance of a licence.'

Thus, creating, keeping or using a human admixed embryo necessitates a licence. The HFEA is the only body that can grant such licences. If a scientist, doctor, businessman or indeed anyone else does not possess a licence and proceeds to create, keep or use such a human admixed embryo, they are committing a serious criminal offence. If they are caught, prosecuted and convicted, the maximum penalty is two years' imprisonment – again quite a severe punishment, but arguably a warranted one, given the controversial and sensitive nature of Parliament actually permitting the creation of human admixed embryos for research purposes. The fact that Parliament set up a statutory licensing system and insisted that doing research by creating and using human admixed embryos must be licensed by an independent statutory licensing regulator/body (the HFEA) signals to society and those engaged in the assisted reproduction industry, both consumers and providers (given that three quarters of eg IVF treatments are only available privately) that Parliament will not allow the business to be undertaken lightly, and that moreover it must be conducted to rigorous and robust legal, ethical and medical standards.

2.21   New s 4A(3) provided by the 2008 Act again replicates and basically re-grafts s 3(3)(a) and s 3(4) of the 1990 Act into the new law contained in the 2008 Act to cover the new type of embryo that can be used for research purposes, namely the human admixed embryo.

2.22   Section 3(3)(a) had clearly provided that a licence could not authorise keeping or using an embryo after the appearance of the primitive streak, and s 3(4) had defined the primitive streak thus;

> '(4) For the purposes of subsection (3)(a) above, the primitive streak is to be taken to have appeared in an embryo not later than the end of the period of 14 days beginning with the day when the gametes are mixed, not counting any time during which the embryo is stored.'

2.23   Thus human embryos could not be developed beyond 14 days after fertilisation, nor experimented on or researched on beyond 14 days, a significant ethical bright line and one enforced by the criminal law. Persons violating s 3(3) who were then prosecuted and convicted under s 41(1) are 'liable on conviction on indictment to imprisonment for a term not exceeding ten years or a fine or both.'

2.24   The new s 4A(3) therefore extends this prohibition to human admixed embryos and hence provides:

'(3) A licence cannot authorise keeping or using a human admixed embryo after the earliest of the following—
  (a) the appearance of the primitive streak, or
  (b) the end of the period of 14 days beginning with the day on which the process of creating the human admixed embryo began, but not counting any time during which the human admixed embryo is stored.'

Section 4A(3) is virtually identical to the terms of s 3(3) and s 3(4); the only difference is that the word 'embryo' is replaced with 'human admixed embryo'. The bottom line is that the strict net of regulation created by the 1990 Act, and extended by the 2008 Act, is applicable equally to human embryo and human admixed embryo alike. The author comments on this:

'Hence the human admixed embryo is treated in an identical manner to the human embryo in that it cannot be kept/used or developed (albeit it can of course be stored – presumably frozen in liquid nitrogen) beyond 14 days or the development of the primitive streak, whichever is "the earliest". Human admixed embryos are thus not a morally/ethically second- class or inferior status embryo – surely compelling evidence challenging arguments about their commodification.'[12]

2.25   Next, s 4A provides that:

'(4) A licence cannot authorise placing a human admixed embryo in an animal.'

Again for most people this is merely explicitly outlawing a potentially ethically repellent and intuitively repugnant practice from taking place. The thought of an animal being some sort of surrogate mother or incubator for a human admixed embryo would be totally objectionable and nauseating.

2.26   Arguably very sensibly, s 4A(5) makes provision for future Parliaments to possibly limit the keeping or using of human admixed embryos by being able to pass secondary legislation regulating both their keeping and use. It provides:

'(5) A licence cannot authorise keeping or using a human admixed embryo in any circumstances in which regulations prohibit its keeping or use.'

DEFINITION OF 'HUMAN ADMIXED EMBRYO'

2.27   Section 4A(6) provides quite a lengthy and compendious, but arguably not very felicitous definition of what constitutes a 'human admixed embryo'. It provides:

'(6) For the purposes of this Act a human admixed embryo is—
  (a) an embryo created by replacing the nucleus of an animal egg or of an animal cell, or two animal pronuclei, with—
      (i) two human pronuclei,

---

12 *Current Law Statutes Annotated,* 'Human Fertilisation and Embryology Act 2008, Chapter 22', (Sweet & Maxwell 2009), pp 1–210, at p 74.

       (ii) one nucleus of a human gamete or of any other human cell, or

       (iii) one human gamete or other human cell,

   (b) any other embryo created by using—

       (i) human gametes and animal gametes, or

       (ii) one human pronucleus and one animal pronucleus,

   (c) a human embryo that has been altered by the introduction of any sequence of nuclear or mitochondrial DNA of an animal into one or more cells of the embryo,

   (d) a human embryo that has been altered by the introduction of one or more animal cells, or

   (e) any embryo not falling within paragraphs (a) to (d) which contains both nuclear or mitochondrial DNA of a human and nuclear or mitochondrial DNA of an animal ("animal DNA") but in which the animal DNA is not predominant.'

2.28 The author, commenting on the potentially seismic nature of this new s 4A, observed that:

'This new s4A is hugely controversial and pioneering in that it permits the creation of human admixed embryos, and these embryos, which contain both human and animal DNA, are subject to regulation under the 1990 Act, like 'conventionally' created embryos.' and that, 'This new section builds on the ethical foundations and prohibitions set out in the earlier Act, whilst adding new prohibited activities in light of significant scientific developments made in the 18 years since the passage of the 1990 Act.'[13]

However he notes that:

'Critics of this considerable extension of the existing grounds for using and manipulating embryos would regard this new and additional liberalisation as evidence of legislators being in thrall to the whims of over-zealous scientists pushing for the availability of ever increasing raw materials (here human embryos) to further their research, as well as cheapening and devaluing human life (albeit at a very early stage of development), by commodifying it, and using it only as a means towards achieving some allegedly greater end.'[14]

But the author balances that criticism by stating that:

'Those in favour of permitting the range of human embryos that can be used and researched on would counter that this does not signal a further descent down the hypothetical ethical "slippery slope", but is a considered, rational and sensible incremental extension and refinement of the existing statutory regime, which will hopefully in time lead to ultimately major therapeutic benefits for a range of patients with terrible diseases.'[15]

Thus under the new s 4A as provided in the 2008 Act, human admixed embryos can be created in five different ways.

---

13 *Current Law Statutes Annotated,* 'Human Fertilisation and Embryology Act 2008, Chapter 22', (Sweet & Maxwell 2009), pp 1–210, at p 74.

14 Ibid.

15 Ibid.

Section 4A(6)(a)

2.29   Here the human admixed embryo is created by replacing the nucleus of an animal egg or of an animal cell, or two animal pronuclei with:

(i)   two human pronuclei; or
(ii)   one nucleus of a human gamete or of any other human cell; or
(iii) one human gamete or other human cell.

The author comments:

'This type of admixed human embryo would be created essentially using the cloning technique used to create Dolly the sheep in 1996. The embryo thus created would be virtually, almost entirely human, except for the presence of animal mitochondria contained originally in the animal enucleated egg.'(or animal cell) and 'These admixed human embryos are technically called cytoplasmic hybrids or cybrids, because of the animal DNA left and contained in the mitochondria in the cytoplasm of the animal egg.'[16]

Section 4A(6)(b)

2.30   The second variety of human admixed embryo (seemingly the new generic or umbrella term for such entities) is defined as any other embryo created by using human gametes and animal gametes or one human pronucleus and one animal pronucleus. Commenting on this variety, the author observes:

'Human admixed embryos of this variety (human-animal hybrid embryos) would be created by mixing either a human sperm and an animal egg or alternatively an animal sperm with a human egg. Also a human-animal hybrid embryo could be created by combining the pronucleus of a human with the pro-nucleus of an animal.'[17]

Section 4A(6)(c)

2.31   The third type of human admixed embryo contained in the 2008 Act is a human embryo that has been altered by the introduction of any sequence of nuclear or mitochondrial DNA of an animal into one or more cells of the embryo. The author notes that:

'These human admixed embryos are called human transgenic embryos – literally transgenic by virtue of the fact that animal DNA has been introduced into a cell or cells of the embryo.'[18]

Section 4A(6)(d)

2.32   The next variety is defined as a human embryo that has been altered by the introduction of one or more animal cells. The author comments here that:

16   Ibid.
17   Ibid.
18   Ibid.

'These human admixed embryos are referred to as human-animal chimeras, that is human embryos that have been altered by the introduction of one or more cells from an animal.'[19]

Section 4A(6)(e)

2.33   The fifth and final definition and type of human admixed embryo is arguably a 'catch-all' type, but a catch-all type with a very ethically controversial sting in the tail, which generated much angst and debate in Parliament. This fifth type is any embryo not falling within paragraphs (a) to (d) which contains both nuclear or mitochondrial DNA of a human and nuclear or mitochondrial DNA of an animal, but in which the animal DNA is not predominant. The author observes:

'Worryingly for those opposed to the creation of human admixed embryos and who fear we are spiralling down the slippery slope to the ethical/morality abyss, s4A(6)(e) defines a possible fifth type of human admixed embryo'.[20]

The author is concerned and queries what exactly is meant by the rather vague and woolly expression 'predominate'. Thus he asks:

'What does Parliament mean by predominate? Does that mean an admixed human embryo could be 49 per cent animal and only be 51 per cent human? Seemingly yes?'

FURTHER PROVISIONS

2.34   New s 4A(7) then defines two further terms, namely animal cells and human cells, referred to in the key s 4A(6) thus:

'(7) In subsection (6)—
    (a)   references to animal cells are to cells of an animal or of an animal embryo, and
    (b)   references to human cells are to cells of a human or of a human embryo.'

Under the Act, animal cells can originate from two sources, namely either a cell from an animal or a cell from an animal embryo, and human cells can similarly emanate from two sources, ie cells of humans or cells from a human embryo.

2.35   Furthermore new s 4A(8) states and clarifies that:

'(8) For the purposes of this section an "animal" is an animal other than man.'

One could argue that man is basically a type of animal. Certainly, if one accepts Darwin's theory on evolution, as opposed to eg creationism, man is descended from apes (an animal) so from an evolutionary perspective humans are basically animals, sharing 99.7 per cent of our DNA with our simian relatives. However the 2008 Act clearly distinguishes and demarcates the two legally, and, it might be argued, ethically and morally. The author comments:

---

19   Ibid.
20   Ibid.

'Just in case there is any doubt, s 4A(8) states explicitly that when the legislation refers to animal gametes or animal cells, the term "animal" refers to an animal other than man, eg an elephant, chimpanzee or dolphin. Man, of course, is a type of animal – that much is implicit from subs (8), albeit one in a very privileged position and status.'[21]

2.36 Again, an additional clarifying provision is included in s 4A(9), which arguably provides a definitive and totally clear definition of what constitutes an embryo. It provides:

'(9) In this section "embryo" means a live embryo, including an egg that is in the process of fertilisation or is undergoing any other process capable of resulting in an embryo.'

2.37 Commenting on s 4A(9) the author states:

'The latter part of the subsection, namely, "or is in the process of resulting in an embryo", is again designed to plug the apparent hole in the 1990 Act, which referred in s1(1)(a) and (b) respectively and thus, "(a) embryo means a live human embryo where fertilisation is complete, and (b) references to an embryo include an egg in the process of fertilisation, and for this purpose, fertilisation is not complete until the appearance of the two- cell zygote", which arguably did not cover an embryo created in the manner that Dolly the sheep was created (ie cell nuclear transfer), which was not a form of fertilisation.'[22]

This was clarified in the *Quintavalle* litigation,[23] where it was held, inter alia, that a human embryo created by CNR was indeed covered by the 1990 Act.

2.38 Section 4A(10) defines and elaborates on what is meant by the terms 'eggs' and 'gametes' respectively. It provides:

'(10) In this section—
 (a) references to eggs are to live eggs, including cells of the female germ line at any stage of maturity, but (except in subsection (9)) not including eggs that are in the process of fertilisation or are undergoing any other process capable of resulting in an embryo, and
 (b) references to gametes are to eggs (as so defined) or to live sperm, including cells of the male germ line at any stage of maturity.'

Commenting on s 4A(10), the author notes that:

'Eggs and sperm therefore, includes immature and not fully developed eggs (oocytes) in the woman's ovaries and sperm developing in the man's testicles. Thus, if the woman has difficulty producing eggs or the man sperm, they can be retrieved at an earlier stage, but both types of gametes are included in the definition of eggs and gametes under the 2008 Act.'[24]

---

21 Ibid.
22 Ibid.
23 *R (on the application of Quintavalle) v Human Fertilisation and Embryology Authority* [2003] EWCA Civ 667.
24 Ibid.

2.39   The newly inserted s 4A(11) provides:

> '(11) If it appears to the Secretary of State necessary or desirable to do
> so in the light of developments in science or medicine, regulations
> may—
> (a)   amend (but not repeal) paragraphs (a) to (e) of subsection (6);
> (b)   provide that in this section "embryo", "eggs" or "gametes"
>   includes things specified in the regulations which would not
>   otherwise fall within the definition.'

2.40   Finally, s 4A(12) adds that:

> '(12) Regulations made by virtue of subsection 11(a) may make any
> amendment of subsection (7) that appears to the Secretary of State to
> be appropriate in consequence of any amendment of subsection (6).'

The author notes here:

> 'Again, Parliament sensibly confers another additional regulation-making
> power on the Secretary of State, if it appears to him, "necessary or desirable
> to do so in the light of developments in science or medicine", to pass
> regulations amending, but not repealing, paras (a) to (e) of subs (6), ie the
> definition of what constitutes a human admixed embryo, and to add, "include
> things" in those regulations which are not included in the definitions in subs
> (6). Any proposed future regulations either amending subs 6, or adding
> things to those definitions, are subject to the affirmative resolution procedure
> in Parliament, thus ensuring some degree of notional parliamentary
> accountability and scrutiny.'

Chapter 3

House of Lords Debates

INTRODUCTION

3.1 The debates in the Upper House underlined the fundamentally different perspectives peers held concerning legalisation of human admixed embryos for research purposes under the aegis of the 2008 Act and the regulatory oversight of HFEA. However, both the technical expertise (on the scientific, moral, medical and legal issues), and the forensic scrutiny displayed by peers on all sides served to illustrate the importance and pivotal nature of the second chamber in revising and improving government legislation.

DEBATES

3.2 Lord Darzi, in introducing the HFE Bill,[1] emphasised that one of the 'key aims' of the Bill was to clarify the regulation of 'inter species' embryos for research and also to 'increase the scope of legitimate embryo research activities, subject to controls.'[2] Hence the government, and ultimately Parliament, with the introduction of the 2008 Act, deliberately and in a calculated manner extended the permitted use of embryos in research by permitting the creation of the new type of embryo – the human admixed embryo – for research purposes in the future, albeit after much effort in trying to carefully define these new embryos and ensure they were captured in the controlling, existing legislative and regulatory net of the 1990 Act and the HFEA. The term 'inter species embryos', was used initially in Parliament, but due to its provocative and arguably misleading connotations, it was changed, in what became ultimately the 2008 Act, to the less obviously controversial, and for some less ethically repugnant, definition of human admixed embryos. Presciently, Lord Darzi said that Parliament was likely to devote considerable time, attention and energy to this vexed issue of legalising the creation of these human admixed embryos. As he stated:

> 'Two matters are … likely to occupy us particularly. The first is the whole issue of embryos containing both human and animal material and the ethical considerations surrounding that idea. The second is the extent to which the regulator should be given discretion in judging which entities may be created for research under licence.'[3]

3.3 The Lord Bishop of Leicester outlined the Church of England approach to the creation of human admixed embryos, emphasising that great caution and care must be taken, within a tightly controlled regulatory regime,

---

1   *Hansard*, 8 November 2007, col 141.
2   Ibid, p 142.
3   Ibid, col 148.

before permitting the creation of both cloned embryos and human admixed embryos, and that actual therapeutic benefits must be the only basis for such groundbreaking and ethically controversial research, stating that:

> '[w]e remain deeply cautious about the creation of cell nuclear replacement embryos [again another definition to further muddy and obfuscate!], that is, cloned embryos – and especially about the creation of human/animal hybrids. We will continue to press for very tight controls on embryo experiments and for constant review of the licensing of research into hybrids to ensure that the claimed therapeutic benefits are the only rationale for continuing research programmes.'[4]

3.4   Lord Harries of Pentregarth, (a former interim Chairman of the HFE Authority), referred to the creation of what he described as 'cytoplasmic hybrids', (again another different description or definition of human admixed embryos), as being a 'fundamental' issue, which really ought to be decided by Parliament, and not by the HFEA. As he said: 'It is right that major issues of principle, about which the public are hesitant if not hostile, should be decided by Parliament.' Lord Harries then outlined what he considered to be the role of the regulator, stating:

> 'A regulatory body regulates only on the basis of what Parliament has decided, making general decisions about good practice, while properly leaving other decisions to professional bodies and clinicians.'

3.5   Lord Harries then made the important observation that 'The legal advice to the HFEA was that cytoplasmic hybrids were embryos within the meaning of the 1990 Act and were in principle within our remit to regulate'[5] (on the basis of the *Quintavalle* decision[6]). However, Lord Harries was of the opinion that:

> '[nevertheless] this is a development of such significance that it is absolutely right that it should be considered by Parliament.'

He adds, concerning the correct parameters that the regulator (the HFEA) operates in, and regarding its relationship with the legislature, that, regarding permission for the creation and the subsequent use of human admixed embryos:

> '... it is right that Parliament should consider it. A good number of highly significant decisions have to be made by regulatory bodies – they cannot look to Parliament all the time – but fundamental issues arise which should be referred.'

HFE BILL: SECOND READING

3.6   Lord Darzi, in laying the foundations for Parliament's acceptance of creating and using human admixed embryos, points to the position of the UK at the forefront of technological advance in the sphere of assisted reproductive technologies, and of the huge benefits reaped by patients as a result of this assisted reproductive revolution. He said that:

---

4   Ibid, col 156.
5   Ibid, col 197.
6   *R (on the application of Quintavalle) v Human Fertilisation and Embryology Authority* [2003] EWCA Civ 667.

'This country has a proud record of pioneering new techniques for the alleviation of infertility and for exploring new avenues of scientific research ... Key developments in new research techniques, such as the creation of Dolly the sheep happened in British laboratories ... These and other developments have brought hope to countless thousands of people who might otherwise have been unable to have children, and offer enormous potential for the future treatment of serious disease.'[7]

This is a constant theme of the advocates of the creation and use of human admixed embryos, namely either giving children to the infertile or alternatively the promise of harvesting a bumper crop of potential treatments for serious diseases that afflict humanity.

3.7 Commenting on the existing statutory regime contained in the 1990 Act, Lord Darzi stated that '[I]n 1990, Parliament set out the legal boundaries and parameters of a scheme of regulation,'[8] and that moreover '[the] 1990 Act represented a will to find common ground in a framework broadly acceptable to society.' Hence the 1990 Act was in many ways a compromise piece of legislation, ie creation, use and research of embryos would be permitted, but it would be strictly regulated by a robust licensing scheme. Lord Darzi added that the Government 'recognised that the 1990 Act had worked well, but like any cutting-edge legislation, needed to be reviewed from time to time.' The Act was passed in 1990, but in late 2007 developments in assisted reproductive technologies and techniques had outpaced the 1990 Act. Thus, he stated: 'Our aim in undertaking the review was to ensure that the law remained effective and fit for purpose in the 21st century.'[9]

3.8 Lord Darzi then elaborated on the scope of the HFE Bill, which 'will update the regulation of assisted reproduction, ensuring that it is effective and reflective of modern society',[10] ie not only must the Bill be instrumental and actually work, it must be supported by and reflect what society feels ought to be permitted. Lord Darzi said: '[It] is needed to ensure that legitimate medical and scientific uses of human reproductive technology can continue to flourish.' He added that:

'The Bill will help maintain the UK's position as a world leader in ground-breaking research for the treatment of serious diseases, including through embryonic stem cell research. Its provisions are an overhaul of the existing law and will promote public confidence together with best regulatory practice.'

Lofty ambitions indeed.

3.9 That said, Lord Darzi emphasised that the HFE Bill did not signal the jettisoning of the original 1990 Act:

'We have not, however, proposed to abandon the basic foundations on which the existing law is based. We have not tried to fix what is not broken, nor have we thrown the baby out with the bathwater.'[11]

---

7   *Hansard*, 19 November 2007, col 663.
8   Ibid, col 663.
9   Ibid, cols 663, 664.
10 Ibid, col 665.
11 Ibid.

Much of the the 1990 Act is indeed retained, both the legal framework and the ethical principles that moor the Act, but as Lord Darzi said:

'Nevertheless, technology has moved on and so have attitudes ... These developments demand a rigorous examination in Parliament of the regulatory framework, and a resetting of the controls and boundaries for the future.'

3.10   Lord Darzi was clear on the scope and remit of HFE Bill, stating:

'[its] main provisions will ensure that all human embryos outside the body, whatever the process used in their creation, are subject to regulation. The existing law refers to the process of fertilisation, which has cast doubt on whether embryos produced by more novel processes are within the regulator's remit.' [12]

As stated earlier, this specifically addresses the situation encountered in the *Quintavalle* case,[13] where an embryo was created by cell nuclear transfer (CNR), rather than by fertilisation. The important point decided there by the courts was ultimately that the product, namely a human embryo, however it was created, was the important thing or mischief that the 1990 Act was aimed at, rather than the process, ie how that human embryo was created. All human embryos, however created, fell within the net of regulation under the 1990 Act. Lord Darzi said:

'It is important for the future of embryo research that there should be clarity about what is regulated, and moreover to ensure that human embryos cannot be created and used lightly.'

3.11   In addition regarding the creation and use of human admixed embryos, or 'interspecies embryos', as he calls them, Lord Darzi said:

'The Bill will clarify the regulation of interspecies embryos for research. The original legislation was concerned almost entirely with human embryos.' [14]

Clearly in 1990 creating human admixed embryos would have been generally ethically repugnant and unacceptable. As he notes, the 1990 Act 'banned the mixing of human and animal gametes, other than for the limited purpose of testing the fertility of human sperm.' This was the so-called hamster testing, whereby the mobility/motility of human sperm was tested by mixing it with hamster eggs. Anything created had to be destroyed at no later than the two-cell stage.[15]

3.12   However what is sought in the HFE Bill is a further extension of this solitary ground for mixing human and animal gametes. (Some would cite this as evidence of the slippery slope, ie permitting an arguably dubious action for a noble or good reason, and then permitting something else for a more dubious reason). As Lord Darzi said:

'Technology has moved on and promising avenues of research have expanded. For example, scientists now wish to use animal eggs in place of

---

12 Ibid.
13 *R (on the application of Quintavalle) v Human Fertilisation and Embryology Authority* [2003] EWCA Civ 667.
14 *Hansard*, 19 November 2007, col 666.
15 See para 1(1)(f) of Sch 2 of the 1990 Act.

human eggs for the purpose of creating embryos for stem cell research, in part to overcome the shortage of human eggs available for research.'[16]

The reality is that there are not enough human eggs available for treatment purposes, never mind for research purposes, and therefore sheer necessity compels other sources and types of eggs to be used, or, as here, literally created. Lord Darzi stated: '[T]he aims of such research would be, for example, to explore the potential for treatment of degenerative conditions such as Parkinson's disease.' This is the promise of using such human admixed embryos.

3.13 Clearly if the Government, through Parliament, and by means of primary legislation, were permitting the creation and use of this new type of embryo for research purposes, ie the human admixed embryo, then safeguards needed to be built into that legislation to reassure the public against possible abuse and misuse of that new, innovative statutory provision. Thus, Lord Darzi reassured Parliament that:

'Again, it is essential that the law and regulations are clear about what falls within the Human Fertilisation and Embryology Authority's remit. We are proposing that interspecies embryos can be created for research, subject to the HFEA's decisions to license individual research projects as being necessary or desirable.'[17]

Lord Darzi is thus effectively saying that a major safeguard is that Parliament must clearly define what is meant by an interspecies embryo, and that further safeguards, applicable equally when human embryos are being used for research, are that for a research project to use interspecies embryos for research, they must be licensed by the HFEA, and that furthermore a research project will only be licensed if the use of interspecies embryos is both necessary and desirable. As Lord Darzi says: 'These are exactly the same controls as apply for embryo research projects using human embryos, and subject to the same safeguards.' Further safeguards are that '[T]he embryos cannot be kept beyond 14 days' development, nor can they be placed in a woman or an animal.'

3.14 Lord Mackay of Clashfern, a former Lord Chancellor, and one of the key legal brains behind the 1990 Act, referred to the *Quintavalle* decision,[18] where the court decided that the wording of the 1990 Act was sufficiently broad to capture an embryo however it was created, thus echoing Lord Darzi.[19] He also urged the government to consider having 'a working definition of interspecies embryos as a whole – one that was not only a list of particular cases but a description of what is meant by the phrase in the Bill'.

3.15 Baroness Tonge, an enthusiastic backer of creating and using human admixed embryos for research, again extolled the virtues of the UK regulatory regime which permits scientists to operate at the vanguard of the assisted reproduction revolution, and for the UK to assume the mantle almost of worldwide leadership in the development of new technologies.[20]

---

16 *Hansard*, 19 November 2007, col 666.
17 Ibid, col 666.
18 Above, fn 13.
19 *Hansard*, 19 November 2007, col 668.
20 Ibid, cols 670–671.

3.16   Human eggs are patently very scarce and very difficult to retrieve from women so an alternative less costly, physically, emotionally and ethically for the egg donor, is prima facie to be commended.

3.17   Baroness Tonge acknowledged the powerful concerns of critics of the Bill regarding the creation of hybrids but stressed that a number of safeguards were built into the Bill specifically to prevent abuses and to reassure the public.[21]

3.18   The hyperbole and scaremongering surrounding creating a latter day *Island of Dr Moreau* scenario, ie creating a new breed of half-men/half animals of different types and mixtures enters the realms of science fiction, and departs from the realm of science fact, and indeed what is scientifically and ethically desirable. The safeguards include the prohibition on keeping embryos and experimenting on them beyond 14 days, (see s 3(3)(a) of the 1990 Act, and s 3(4), which defines the primitive streak), and that, 'no interspecies embryo – human embryo or interspecies embryo … must be implanted in a woman's uterus.'

3.19   Baroness Tonge advocated keeping all options (including inter species) for beneficial research open, and not cutting off possible promising research avenues or routes,[22] but said that whilst encouraging this route, it was important that there is regulation. She said that, 'we need all avenues of research if we are going to conquer the diseases that persecute the human race.' Thus, permitting this new research will be strictly regulated (by Parliament, the HFEA, and clinicians' sense of professionalism), and is therefore not tantamount to acquiescing in a scientific research free-for-all.

3.20   Baroness Tonge then addressed several other objections and concerns to interspecies embryo research First: 'The objectors will say human life is sacred, full stop'.[23] However: '[T]he difficulty is to define exactly what is a human being?' Can a human admixed embryo be regarded as a person/human life/a human being warranting the same full legal protection afforded to, eg an adult/child/new-born human baby? Is there a person from the moment of conception, or at birth, or when the entity acquires/possesses certain attributes (eg consciousness, self awareness, communication, ability to remember/plan, etc), or is it at some other stage of development? There is no conclusive or definitive answer to this philosophical and ethical conundrum.

3.21   Baroness Tonge said there is no doubt that: '[T]he sufferers of the diseases I mentioned are certainly human, and their lives could be transformed if this work is successful. Do we want to deny them that?' Might this be seen as emotional blackmail by the advocates of permitting the new science, given its infancy?

3.22   Baroness Tonge then made the fair and accurate scientific point that women lose thousands of eggs naturally throughout their reproductive life. They have their full complement of eggs whilst a foetus in their mother's womb and start losing the eggs from then until menopause. Again, after conception,

21   Ibid, col 671.
22   Ibid, col 671.
23   Ibid.

women lose up to 30 per cent of fertilised embryos naturally in the first three months of pregnancy (ie through natural miscarriages).[24]

3.23   Concerning research for mitochondrial disorders, she said:

'People worry about the transmission of infection via mitochondria but, if that is a possibility, the only way we can develop ways to combat it is to allow the research to go ahead to find out what happens.'

3.24   She then addressed the spectre and shibboleth of mad scientists/doctors (latter day Frankensteins), creating monsters in their laboratories and unleashing them on the public, or alternatively the monsters escaping from captivity and wreaking havoc on the population at large. The potential for some bad apples in the barrel (rogue scientists trying to create monsters), must not, she said, stop or spoil all the good apples, the vast majority of doctors/scientists who wish to use the science to try and improve the lives of many very ill patients.

3.25   The Lord Bishop of St Albans, another Anglican peer, posed the question whether human admixed embryo research (for example) needed regulation.[25] 'Why not let scientific and therapeutic market forces rip?' he said and highlighted a number of dangers of permitting such a *laissez-faire* approach. One could challenge all these as being manifestations of illusionary slippery slopes and of course the bottom line is that interspecies research, far from being unregulated, would in fact be tightly regulated under the HFE Bill.

3.26   Baroness Jay of Paddington reiterates the compelling scientific and pragmatic arguments in favour of creating and using interspecies embryos for research, namely the acute shortage of human eggs and embryos.[26]

3.27   Lord Alton of Liverpool vehemently opposed the creation and use of interspecies embryos for research purposes. He, and many of the opponents of stem cell research, repeatedly pointed out how few therapies have been developed as a result of this allegedly over-hyped science, and feared that the alleged exaggerated claims and promises of new cures/therapies using stem cell research would be replicated with interspecies embryonic research. That is in marked contrast to using adult stem cells for research, which poses none of the ethical problems and objections as those posed by using embryonic stem cells, less specifically created interspecies embryos. He referred to an editorial in *Nature Biotechnology* in 2005 which stated: 'One estimate is that there are currently over 80 therapies and around 300 clinical trials underway' using adult cells. This, he said, and not embryonic stem cell research, much less interspecies embryonic research, is the ethical and right direction that Parliament and the scientific community should be embarking on.

3.28   Lord Alton reminded peers that the hype and promise of permitting embryonic cloning of stem cells in 2001 had not translated into tangible, effective therapies and emphasised that there was an ethically uncontroversial alternative to embryonic (and interspecies embryonic) research available,

---

24   Ibid.
25   *Hansard*, 19 November 2007, col 675.
26   Ibid, col 678.

namely adult stem cell research, "where the future lies', which he strongly supported.

3.29 Finally Lord Alton endorsed the adoption of what he describes as the 'Hunt test', concerning the use of human embryos for research purposes. Explaining what the 'Hunt test' means, he referred to the words of Lord Hunt in a House of Lords debate in 2001, who said:

'the 1990 Act already provides the answer to the question of what happens if and when research into adult cells overtakes research using embryos: embryonic research would have to stop because the use of embryos would no longer be necessary for that research.'[27]

Under Sch 2, para 3(2) of the 1990 Act a research licence, 'cannot authorise any activity unless it appears to the Authority to be necessary or desirable' for one of the specified research purposes in the 1990 Act, or additional specified research purposes include in subsequent regulations, or future primary legislation, like the 2008 Act. Hence, under the Hunt test the use of human embryos must be either necessary or desirable for the research, before the HFEA will grant a research licence. Lord Alton was basically arguing that if there is an effective, ethically uncontroversial alternative to using human embryos (or interspecies embryos) for a research project, ie by using adult stem cells, then axiomatically it is neither necessary nor desirable to use either embryonic stem cells or interspecies embryos for research.[28]

3.30 Lord Jenkin of Roding also highlighted the safeguards built into the legislation, including 'the 14-day rule', the promising potential of the research in curing 'debilitating' diseases, but 'subject to proper ethical and regulatory control.'[29]

3.31 Baroness Williams of Crosby, one of the leading peers opposed to embryonic stem cell research and interspecies embryonic research stressed the success of adult stem cell research.[30] Fundamentally adult stem cells have two enormous advantages over using embryonic and interspecies embryos: first, they come from an ethically uncontroversial source and secondly the problem of sick patients' immune systems rejecting transplanted foreign cells from an embryo or interspecies embryo are overcome.

3.32 Lord Walton of Detchant, inter alia the life president of the Muscular Dystrophy Campaign, agreed with the general safeguard enshrined in the 1990 Act, which prevents experimentation on human embryos after 14 days, (a safeguard and prohibition applicable also to human admixed embryos).[31] He welcomed the fact that it was now technically possible and feasible to use PGD to test for the presence of muscular dystrophy in embryos and to prevent the birth of children suffering from that 'dreadful disease.'

3.33 Moreover he challenged pro-life supporters who objected to the huge waste and disposal of human embryos involved in embryonic treatment,

---

27 *Official Report*, 22 January 2001, col.120.
28 *Hansard*, 19 November 2007, col 683.
29 Ibid, cols 684–5.
30 Ibid, cols 685–686.
31 Ibid, col 708.

testing and research, and reminded Parliament that innumerable ova were lost naturally.[32] What he is really saying is given this waste of millions of human embryos, what logically and sensibly could be the objection to creating human embryos and especially human admixed embryos for research purposes that will hopefully yield significant future therapeutic benefits for very ill patients?

3.34 Lord Walton referred then to the Human Fertilisation and Embryology (Research Purposes) Regulations 2001, which extended the original five permitted research purposes outlined in Sch 2, para 3(2)(a)(e), 'to allow embryos and stem cells derived from them to be available for the treatment of human disease, legalising therapeutic but not reproductive cloning.' He flagged up a major problem with adult stem cells, immunological rejection, a problem overcome, by contrast, if one creates and uses interspecies embryos.[33] The massive downside is that, 'it is not easy to obtain ova from even the most public-spirited of women.' He concluded that the HFE Bill, 'is a crucial Bill. It carries enormous potential benefits for human health ... It is our duty to generations in the future to see this Bill enter into law.'

3.35 Lord Winston, an eminent obstetrician and gynaecologist, scientist and Chancellor of Sheffield Hallam University was strongly of the opinion that assisted reproduction is generally over-regulated, and too strictly regulated.[34] Quite a few medical procedures, by contrast, are unregulated; for example obstetric practice, paediatric care for neonates, intensive care, tubal surgery, administration of drugs and other treatments 'that are routinely given are not subject in any way to this kind of regulation.' Why therefore is, eg, IVF treatment being singled out for regulation? Of course other treatments are subject to regulation, eg abortions by the Abortion Act 1967, as amended, organ transplantation, by the Human Tissue Act 2004, and consent partially by the Mental Capacity Act 2005.

3.36 Baroness O'Cathain was totally opposed to the creation of human admixed embryos for research purposes and was concerned that there was 'also built into the Bill a level of flexibility which would permit the extension of many of the quasi-prohibitive aspects of the Bill, without the need for full parliamentary approval.'[35] She worried: 'Is this not opening the door to creating legislation without true limits?' In other words a Minister by secondary legislation, without proper and full Parliamentary scrutiny and debate in the open can amend or relax the quasi-prohibitive safeguards currently in the Bill. That is completely unacceptable. The HFEA would be a law unto itself, deciding what it can and cannot license.

3.37 Interestingly Baroness O'Cathain drew support for her opposition to the clauses in HFE Bill by reference to the book of Genesis in the Bible. As she states:

> 'God created man in His own image and likeness, and, as is written in Genesis 1:28. He ordained that man should have, "dominion over the fish of

---

32 Ibid.
33 Ibid, cols 708–9.
34 Ibid, col 710.
35 Ibid, col 713.

the sea, and over the fowl of the air, and over every living thing that moveth upon the earth".'[36]

Thus, on the basis of the book of Genesis, she argues that '[T]here is a clear definition between the species, which is how it must remain.'

3.38 Baroness Emerton observed that there was insufficient public engagement and consultation on the radical proposals in the Bill permitting the creation/use of interspecies embryos which 'touches the very roots of human dignity.'[37]

3.39 Baroness Neuberger, (a former member of HFEA, a rabbi and the president of Liberal Judaism in the UK) observed that analogies between permitting hybrid embryos and the excesses of Nazi Germany were 'particularly odious'.[38] She was referring to the alleged slippery slope of eugenics/Nazism occasionally lurking behind debates about embryonic research, abortion, euthanasia/assisted suicide and here creating and using interspecies embryos. Interestingly, unlike some advocates of creating or using interspecies embryos, she did not dismiss out of hand the need to confront and challenge logically and rationally the belief of those opposed to such a significant development. The arguments of opponents should not be dismissed out of hand or ignored, but rather should be challenged on the basis of evidence, arguments and reasons. Sticking one's head defensively in the sand, ostrich fashion, is not a very wise response. Unlike Lord Winston, she believed, 'that regulation is needed and I support it.'

3.40 Concerning the ethical and moral status of the human embryo (never mind the arguably much more complex status of the human admixed embryo), she correctly noted that:

> 'there is clearly an irreconcilable difference between those who believe that ensoulment happens at the time of conception and those who believe in a more gradual acquisition of human status over the development of the foetus ... Those two positions can never be brought closely together because they come from totally different standpoints ... Whatever we do in this area is a compromise.'

Rather than accept either stance or position, or do nothing, Parliament had opted for the compromise option (obviously where the compromise is pitched exactly generates equally fierce debate too). Baroness Neuberger said:

> 'The compromise to which we have come, rightly in my view, is to set an absolute limit of 14 days or the appearance of the primitive streak, whichever is earlier, and to forbid implantation of cloned embryos – no reproductive cloning. And that seems about right.'

3.41 Baroness Neuberger wisely said that legislators, difficult though it may be under the deluge of paper and documents and evidence (lots of it contradictory), must be able to see the wood from the trees, concerning what is the heart of the matter regarding the creation and use of interspecies embryos and to try and consider and wrestle with the ethical, legal and moral

36 Ibid.
37 Ibid, col 715.
38 Ibid, col 716.

implications of the science fact (wood), as opposed to the science fiction,(trees), which is an enormously difficult task in itself.[39] She added that she could understand the concerns if 'we were likely to see an army of half-sheep/half-men walking across Westminster Bridge'. Her use of hyberbole indicated that this dreadful spectre will not happen. The reality is diametrically opposed to this nightmarish, speculative image. The scientific reality/science fact is that: 'Researchers are working on developing a way to replace with healthy cells the dopamine-producing nerve cells that have died in Parkinson's disease.'[40]

3.42 Baroness Neuberger readily acknowledged the ongoing research using cells from cord blood and also the research on adult stem cells, but argued that:

'[that] does not mean that we do not have still to use these interspecies embryos where we can for research until new techniques are established that make that unnecessary.'[41]

Some would say this is sensibly keeping all avenues of potentially beneficial research open, others would argue it is an unethical stop-gap which is giving scientists carte blanche to engage in immoral research. She said:

'If we want to continue with research that is very promising ... we need to do it in this way for the alleviation of present human suffering. That is the point.'

Furthermore she emphasises the important ethical bright-line in the sand:

'No one is suggesting implanting these eggs into any woman. No one wants to create hybrid creatures, half-man/half-cow ... [The slippery slope/science fiction nightmare] ... This technique of interspecies embryos is to be used to protect women from having their ovaries over-stimulated, of which there is a minor but not insignificant risk in fertility treatment, to get more eggs.'[42]

3.43 Another massive advantage of using interspecies embryos for research is that it avoids having to use human embryos for research. So if one is objecting to research using precious and scarce human embryos, which some regard as persons with the same ethical status as adults/children/babies, surely using an alternative non-human embryo, ie an interspecies embryo for research, is to be preferred, or is at least the lesser of two evils? No human eggs are involved in this new research and furthermore the manufactured creation/product of the mixing of human sperm and animal egg 'is in no sense a person.'

3.44 Addressing the myriad objections of those opposed to the creation and use of interspecies embryos for research, including that the technique allegedly blurs the boundaries between humans and animals, undermines human dignity, offends the image of God, transgresses the Biblical prohibitions on mixing kinds and fundamentally alters the very essence of humanity, Baroness Neuberger said:

'I beg to differ. The use of such eggs for research and not for cloning in no way blurs the difference between animals and humans but merely provides

39 Eg ibid, col 717.
40 Ibid, cols 717, 718.
41 Ibid, col 718.
42 Ibid. The risk is of ovarian hyperstimulation syndrome (OHSS), a risk of roughly 1–2 per cent.

material on which to conduct research; material which is not fully human and therefore, according to this line of argument, less deserving of respect.'[43]

3.45 Baroness Warnock, was the Chairman of the Warnock Committee, whose Report formed the basis of the 1990 Act. She 'greatly' welcomed the HFE Bill, saying, 'It is timely and necessary to update the 1990 Act.' She agreed with Lord Winston that the regulation should not be heavy-handed, but that nevertheless it was 'futile to suggest that we now go back and have no regulation, nor would I advocate that.'[44] Not surprisingly Baroness Warnock advocates regulation rather than either prohibition or alternatively permissiveness (ie research to be left unregulated). She states that:

'the possible future uses of the new embryology in the wider context of genetic disease [have] so vastly increased that they constitute a positive moral imperative upon government to allow research to continue, to be properly funded and to be regulated with not too heavy a touch.'

3.46 Not surprisingly, given her background as an eminent philosopher, Baroness Warnock underlines that the broad underlying philosophy underpinning The 1990 Act was utilitarianism. She stated:

'At the centre of the moral thinking behind the 1990 Act was a broad utilitarianism ... As legislators, parliamentarians have to be utilitarian in the broadest possible sense. They have to consider the consequences of any legislation they propose and carry through and, in considering the consequences, they have to weigh the harms that may be done to society as a whole against the benefits to society as a whole. It is a morality that gives thought to the common good in so far as it can be ascertained. That is an important principle.'[45]

Furthermore she said that the Warnock Committee, 'thought that utilitarianism in this broad sense was the philosophy that must lie behind any legislation – weighing up harms against benefits'.

3.47 Baroness Masham of Ilton attacked the creation of interspecies embryos on the basis that it is contrary to nature, stating: 'Mixing animal and human life is disturbing as it is so against nature. Both human and animal life should be respected.'[46]

3.48 Lord Brennan urged that, concerning the prospects of future embryonic testing: '[H]umility before hubris in science is a wise approach', and cautioned against 'gross overselling' about the prospects of genetic science – first, as to the range of cures, and, secondly, as to when they might occur.[47]

3.49 Baroness Paisley of St George's, a DUP peer, who, inter alia, was stridently opposed to the creation of interspecies embryos for research, warned the House to: 'reject the proposals in this iniquitous and immoral Bill',

---

43 Ibid, col 719.
44 Ibid, col 720.
45 Ibid, col 721.
46 Ibid, col 725.
47 Ibid, col 727.

contending that their creation was undermining 'human dignity' and altering 'the very nature of humanity', a very disturbing and damning indictment against the new science, if correct, and invoked the Biblical prohibitions against:

> '… mixing species as laid down in Holy Scripture, [which] would be an offence to the Creator Himself who made man in His own image. These proposals would also unleash an untameable monster on an already morally diminished people, the end result of which is too fearsome to contemplate.'[48]

3.50   Clearly, no one can doubt the passionate, principled and powerful objections here to the creation of interspecies embryos for research, but in a UK society which is increasingly secular, agnostic, atheistic or at least apathetic to religion generally, and given the development of a multicultural, diverse, less homogenous society, arguments based on a particular reading of scripture are unpersuasive and unconvincing for many. Again, Baroness Paisley was clearly using the slippery slope argument to good effect to bolster her argument that giving the green light to creating interspecies embryos for research is a bad idea, with potentially apocalyptic consequences.

3.51   The Lord Bishop of Newcastle, an Anglican peer, noted that one of the main themes of the HFE Bill, to ensure Britain remains at the forefront of medical research, albeit 'laudable', could not be 'at any price'.[49] Thus, the government's aim that embryonic and interspecies embryonic research in the UK should be at the forefront of developments in this exciting new science (arguably an economic imperative) should not be at the expense of sacrificing ethical concerns and moral objections to certain aspects of that technology. He added that Parliament must regulate the fast-moving science to retain 'public confidence and trust'.[50] He had fundamental concerns with the term 'interspecies embryo', and urged that respect was shown for the embryo. The embryo may not be a person, or full human being, nor be a potential person, nor even possess any rights, but unquestionably it must be accorded respect.

3.52   Lord Elton was also unhappy with the blunderbuss term 'interspecies embryo'.[51] He referred to Lord Mackay's revelation that:

> 'even the experts brought in by the Joint Committee that scrutinised the Bill were unable to understand the definition proposed of the interspecies embryos'.[52]

3.53   Lord Ahmed stated that: 'As a Muslim, I believe deeply that all life is sacred'.[53] As well as deploring the six million abortions that have taken place since 1967, he was 'disturbed to be a member of a society that … [has] … condoned the manufacture and destruction of around 2 million human embryos'. This is of course the conclusion of all research on animals, human embryos and interspecies embryos, namely the eventual destruction of that entity. He also highlighted the distinction between what is scientifically possible and what is scientifically ethical, moral and desirable.

---

48   Ibid, col 730.
49   *Hansard*, 21 November 2007, col 839–40.
50   Ibid.
51   Ibid, cols 841–42.
52   Ibid.
53   Ibid, col 844.

3.54 Lord Patel strongly supported the use of interspecies embryos for research by scientists because, 'this avoids the problem of graft rejection'.[54] Furthermore, he contended:

> 'A perfect solution would be the availability of adult stem cells – every stem cell research worker in the world is chasing this Holy Grail right now – but these cells are not available ... Growing adult stem cells is not easy. There are many cell types that adult stem cells are unlikely to be able to give rise to.'

These are two major drawbacks or at least limiting factors concerning using adult stem cells. They are not a silver bullet on their own. By contrast: 'Embryonic stem cells, on the other hand, have the potential to give rise to any stem cell.'

3.55 Lord Patel explained that there are currently only two ways of obtaining patient specific embryonic stem cells: first, by somatic cell nuclear transfer and cytoplasmic hybrid embryos, ie creating interspecies embryos, and secondly: 'obtaining pluripotent patient specific ES cells ... by the direct reprogramming of adult somatic cells into ES-like cells.'[55] Scientists want to do the former now because pragmatically, 'there is not a ready supply of human oocytes and large numbers of oocytes will be required.' Lord Patel highlighted how technically difficult it was to secure embryonic stem cell lines.

3.56 Regarding the second method for obtaining pluripotent patient-specific ES cells, by the direct reprogramming of adult somatic cells into ES-like cells, Lord Patel referred to the work of Professor Yamanaka in Japan and to a second research team's work in Wisconsin with this second method, 'using mouse skin fibroblasts and adding four factors, four genes.'[56] Explaining the science, he added that one of those genes was an oncogene – a gene that causes cancer, which induces pluripotency in the skin fibroblast. However sadly there are huge downsides to adult stem cell research. Lord Patel flagged up that the mouse that developed in the Yamanaka research was full of cancer tumours. Thus the major practical and ethical problem with adult stem cell research is: how could you use it and implant cells in a sick person that might help their underlying serious illness, but simultaneously expose them to the risk of getting cancer? The point being you could not ethically do such testing in humans if this is the possible or probable consequence when experimenting on mice. As Lord Patel stated: 'We cannot conduct such chimeric experiments in humans.' He argued basically that we need to learn to walk (that is to understand embryonic stem cells) before we learn to run (understand adult stem cells). Thus he says:

> 'We need to understand how embryonic stem cells behave to be able then to understand how to manipulate cells that we have derived from human skin to behave like pluripotent embryonic stem cells ... Embryonic stem cells are the gold standard against which other pluripotent cells derived from human skin will be tested. That is the Holy Grail that every scientist chases, and it is why we must not stop research at this stage on any aspect of any stem cell

---

54 Ibid, cols 854–855.
55 Ibid, col 855.
56 Ibid.

research-adult, embryonic, umbilical, cold-blood, on the cord itself or any other adult cells.'[57]

3.57　Baroness Barker noted that:

'The principle of the developing moral status of the embryo has not been accepted universally [but] ... that it forms the cornerstone of good governance, appropriate legislation and ethical practice in this most difficult of areas.'[58]

She also noted two clear ethical, bright lines: interspecies embryos cannot be implanted in women, nor can they be experimented on beyond 14 days, (like human embryos) She noted the necessity of having 'absolute clarity with regard to terminology' and 'the utmost importance that all lines of research continue.'[59]

3.58　Earl Howe referred to the Warnock Report with approval for having given 'much of the ethical and practical underpinning for our present regulatory regime,' and for striking the correct balance between conflicting considerations.[60] He referred to the 'concept of the special ethical status of the human embryo', with regard to when they can be used,[61] enshrined in ss 3 and 4 of the 1990 Act and ,eg Sch 2, para 3(2)(a)–(e). However, he noted his concern that there was no ethical Warnock foundation to the 2008 Act. Parliament was thus legislating in the absence of an ethical compass that had been carefully thought out and also in the absence of a proper evidence base, which was worrying for the legitimacy of the resulting legislation passed.

3.59　Earl Howe referred to the sharply polarised views of advocates and opponents of research using 'cytoplasmic hybrid embryos' but contended that there was an onus on opponents to articulate 'the alleged harms to society'.[62] He referred to the Animals (Scientific Procedures) Act 1986 which already sanctioned the mixing of human and animal genetic material, the point being that the mixing of human and animal genetic material already occurs, and has done so for some time. Moreover, he did not agree 'that the recent emergence of techniques which may one day make embryonic stem cell research unnecessary is reason enough for Parliament to make embryonic stem cell research illegal.' If that was true then using, eg, human embryos or interspecies embryos was still both necessary and desirable. In addition he strongly urged that all three possible routes to the applied use of stem cells remained open under the aegis of the HFEA licensing and regulatory regime.[63]

3.60　In winding up the debate Lord Darzi said: 'There remains a general desire for a scheme of regulation with clear boundaries, but with a light touch.'[64] He agreed that all avenues of research should be explored, ie adult and umbilical cord, but including interspecies embryonic research and human

---

57　Ibid, col 856.
58　Ibid, col 859.
59　Ibid, col 860.
60　Ibid, cols 862–3.
61　Ibid.
62　Ibid, col 864.
63　Ibid.
64　Ibid, col 866.

embryonic research. This was a clear statement of intent from the government that all research options and potential opportunities be kept open.

3.61 Regarding funding of respectively adult and embryonic stem cell research, Lord Darzi stated:

'From 2004–05 to 2005–06 the Medical Research Council provided funding of £14.7 million for adult stem cell research and £16.5 million for embryonic stem cell research.'[65]

3.62 Lord Darzi noted that the Bill:

'brings some interspecies embryos within the scope of the regulator where licences may permit their creation subject to the requirement that the project is necessary or desirable for the purposes described in legislation.'

In addition, there is in the Bill:

'a regulation-making power to extend the definition of interspecies embryos [that] will provide future flexibility to ensure that the law keeps pace with technological developments.'

Lord Darzi also said that:

'The definitions in the Bill are intended to ensure that embryos at the human end of the spectrum of research involving the mixture of animal and human material are clearly within the HFEA regulatory remit'[66].

3.63 Finally, by way of emphasising the effective safeguards contained in the Bill he said that the clauses in the Bill 'make it clear that no animal embryo can be implanted in a woman and that only certain types of human embryos can be implanted.'[67]

HFE BILL: COMMITTEE STAGE

3.64 At the Committee stage, Lord Alton expressed concerns about light touch regulation or no regulation which might have the practical effect of society effectively entering 'a brave new world'. The need for strict regulation in this controversial ethical minefield was imperative to reassure the public. Strict regulation does not equate with being anti-science, but is recognition that society and scientists need to proceed cautiously and always ethically. Lord Alton believed Parliament needed to emphasise that 'good science and good ethics march hand in hand.' Moreover Parliament needed to provide a strong lead in setting out the legal and ethical parameters that science operates within and must not appear to be in thrall to the dictates of science, unethical or undesirable as they may appear.[68]

3.65 Furthermore Lord Alton warned against legislators being 'seduced and subverted by the dazzle of these various proposals' (eg permitting the creation, keeping and use of human admixed embryos for research purposes), and that:

---

65 Ibid, col 867. There was, therefore, roughly parity between the two distinct types of research.
66 Ibid.
67 Ibid, col 868.
68 *Hansard*, 3 December 2007, col 1501.

'To sleep walk into provisions that might have irreversible effects, and to do so in the absence of a legislative, ethical and regulatory framework, would be a dereliction of our duty.'[69]

He referred to the science fiction writings of CS Lewis, who warned of 'technological brutalism', and of TS Huxley, who in *Brave New World* 'foresaw a world populated from vast hatcheries and peopled with entities and intelligences ranging from alpha to epsilon', and also to HG Wells' *The Island of Dr Moreau*, where Dr Moreau 'specialised in creating animal-human hybrids'. He also noted concerns that eugenics and designing babies lurked behind some of the new science. He commented that 'futuristic, speculative writing ... is fast becoming reality because of the extremely permissive flexibility of provisions' in the 2008 Act.

3.66   Lord Alton referred to the House of Lords Science and Technology Committee, who following the BSE crisis, and after the 'saga of genetic crops', noted that '[S]cience's relationship with United Kingdom society is under strain', and questioned:

'Do we seriously believe that the creation of animal-human hybrid embryos about which there is deep unease, will heal that fractured relationship?'[70]

3.67   He also referred again to the viable and successful alternative to embryonic stem cell research and using human admixed embryos, namely adult stem cell research, and particularly to the research of Professor Yamanaka in Japan and Professor James Thomson in America, and noted in particular the research of Yamanaka.[71] Moreover he argued there was not 'overwhelming, compelling evidence that true hybrids are urgently required for medical use.'[72] In addition he drew support for his contention that there was no demand or necessity for permitting creating human admixed embryos from evidence given by Sir Liam Donaldson, the Chief Medical Officer, to the Joint Committee on the draft Bill on 6 June 2007, that:

'... there was no clear scientific argument as to why you would want to do it, and, secondly, a feeling that this would be a step too far as far as the public are concerned.'

Lord Alton had no doubt that those who voted for embryonic cloning in 2001 and those who would vote for animal-human hybrid creation, 'did so out of a genuine humanitarian desire to help those who suffer from disabling diseases,' but the new research was not a panacea.

3.68   Lord Alton concluded by stating that experimentation using human embryos following the 1990 Act had resulted in no significant cures or advances in treatment, and that in 2001, when three additional research purposes were added to the original five contained in Sch 2, para 3(2)(a)–(e):

'when close to 1 million human embryos had been destroyed ... No one could point to a single cure, yet we then authorised the cloning of human embryos. Seven years later we are now being asked to permit the creation of

69   Ibid, col 1502.
70   Ibid, cols 1518, 1519.
71   Published in *Nature Biotechnology* on 30 November 2007.
72   *Hansard*, 3 December 2007, col 1520.

interspecies embryos. Although some 2 million human embryos have now been destroyed or experimented upon, the answer to the question remains the same. Cures – around 80 are now documented – are coming through adult stem cells, not through interspecies manipulation.'[73]

3.69 Lord Harries of Pentregarth adopted a less sanguine and more optimistic approach to, inter alia, the new science of creating, keeping and using inter species embryos, and repudiated the fallacious and bogus argument that the new research was 'unnatural' and 'artificial', claiming, 'it is natural for us to use our minds in order to enhance human welfare and well-being.'[74] He added that it was clear:

'... there is a great shortage of human eggs. If it were possible to do this research using animal eggs, there would be a virtually unlimited supply.'[75]

Moreover, he argues that what is being talked about is 'research that is essential for the future.'

3.70 Thirdly, he admitted that the Yamanaka research was very exciting and promising. However, he added correctly that the HFEA would only permit embryo use if necessary. Under Sch 2, para 3(2), a research licence cannot authorise any activity, unless it appears to the HFEA to be necessary or desirable for one of the permitted research purposes.

3.71 Lord Patel acknowledged fully the potential significance of the new research concerning adult stem cells referred to by Lord Alton and published in *Nature Biotechnology*:

'It heralds tremendous promise for achieving every stem cell scientist's holy grail ... of being able to reprogramme an adult cell to a pluripotent cell and differentiate it in the cell types that they need to treat the diseases. That is what every scientist is chasing.'[76]

However, he emphasised that all research avenues should be kept open.

3.72 Lord Patel extolled the promise and benefits of stem cell research and noted somatic cell nuclear transfer (SCNT) had three specific aims, namely:

'to create disease-specific stem cell lines that can be used to model disease processes and open up new opportunities for developing therapies;

to generate stem cell lines with particular genetic backgrounds to be used in drug development assays; and

to create patient-specific stem lines for therapeutic use, which would avoid rejection by the recipient immune system, either because they are created using a patient's donor cell nucleus or selected to be immunocompatible.'[77]

3.73 Lord Patel noted the recent promise of SCNT techniques, which 'have proved effective in numerous animal species,' but flagged up the problem that

73 Ibid, col 1522.
74 Ibid.
75 Ibid, col 1523.
76 Ibid.
77 Ibid.

many eggs are needed to develop SCNT techniques to derive stem cells. Scarce human eggs are desperately needed for treatment purposes as a priority before one can consider them being used for research purposes, and sadly harvesting human eggs comes at a price (potentially physically harmful, emotionally difficult etc) for the woman they are being harvested from. That being the reality, he contended:

'It may therefore be more acceptable to use animal rather than human eggs, since they could be used to generate cytoplasmic hybrid embryos for the derivation of embryonic stem cell lines of essentially human nature.'

He claimed that when harvested from the blastocysts, 'most of the genetic material' is '99.9 per cent human … or more'. The other major advantage is that animal eggs are readily available from abattoirs – in other words there is a ready, easy and ethically uncontroversial supply line to meet the demands of the burgeoning research community.

3.74   In addition Lord Patel argued that, as scientists became more technically skilled and proficient in manipulating and working with a virtually unlimited stream of animal eggs using SCNT technology, a huge positive ethical spin-off would be that fewer human eggs would need to be used for this purpose. A further positive consequence of embracing and permitting the new SCNT technology using animal eggs was that: 'The information and technique would also be relevant in research looking at deriving stem cells by programming adult somatic stem cells.'[78]

3.75   Lord Patel reiterated that the Thompson and Yamanaka adult stem cell research 'are exciting and welcome,' but nonetheless raised a number of concerns, including the telomere, or the aging process:

'If these cells are used for therapy there will always be a problem because of the loss of telomeres when inserted for treatment. They may produce cancers in the patients treated because of the limited senescence of these cells.'

This problem arguably occurred with Dolly the sheep who showed signs of premature aging with arthritis and dying earlier than normal for a sheep. Was this due to the unsafe nature of SCNT? Of course, 277 eggs had to be used before Dolly was created too.

3.76   Lord Patel concludes that stem cell research should not sensibly be shoe-horned in one direction, and moreover highlighted the criminal offences which are clear ethical prohibitions (safeguards) created in HFE Bill concerning the use of interspecies embryos.

3.77   Baroness Neuberger welcomed the use of animal eggs too because it will lessen the risk posed to women from overstimulation of their ovaries (one such risk being OHSS).[79] Lord Winston echoed this concern saying:

'one could argue that the stimulation of the ovary under any circumstances may produce abnormal eggs. There is growing evidence that the lesser the

---

78   Ibid, col 1525.
79   See above.

stimulation, the better the quality of the egg and the better the chance of the embryo implanting and being viable.'[80]

Statistically using the current methods, Lord Winston contended;

'If during stimulation you get 10 follicles, on average you will get nine or 10 eggs. From these, on average about six will fertilise, of which, on average, two or three will produce an embryo. Even then, those embryos will not necessarily be viable.'

Hence, 'an alternative method' – using animal eggs – 'would be extremely useful.'

3.78   Baroness O'Cathain flagged up that the UK is virtually out on a limb in Europe by permitting the creation of human embryos for research, and stated 'all avenues of research should not be open; only ethical avenues should be pursued.' Although those in favour of using animal eggs for research would argue strongly that it is a very ethical avenue to pursue. She specifically alluded to the 'initial reaction' to such research as the 'yuck factor' and was concerned about its removal of any respect for human dignity and crossing 'the human-animal species barrier.'

Lord Walton of Detchant conceded that no cure for a human disease has been yet achieved by the use of embryonic stem cells, but that:

'a great deal of research has been done in using stem cells to treat animal models of disease, with as yet some significant and quite encouraging results … This type of research is measured in years, not months and days.'

3.79   Research by its very nature does not produce instant results (eg cures or therapies). He argued that permitting research on cybrids in the HFE Bill 'is crucial for the future management and treatment of human disease.'

Finally he refers to Professor Ian Wilmut, creator of Dolly the sheep, who argued that we should continue work on cybrids and embryonic stem cells as well as adult stem cell research.[81] He added 'That work must go on in parallel with this new work on adult skin cells.'

3.80   Earl Howe was concerned that regarding interspecies embryos, 'we currently lack an ethical or moral compass for decision-making in relation to this type of entity', a compass which Baroness Warnock had provided for the 1990 Act. He argued that:

'Some fundamental ethical questions present themselves. Is the ethical status of an entity which is 99 per cent human on an equal footing with the status of something that is 50 per cent human?'

Where, and at what point or percentage is the humanity, and axiomatically, presumably, the consequent legal and ethical status and protection conferred on such an entity? Is there going to be a system of apartheid effectively in operation regarding different types of interspecies embryo?

---

80   Ibid, col 1526.
81   *British Medical Journal* of 3 December 2007.

3.81   He also noted that interspecies embryos are not surplus to, eg, IVF treatment, but have been deliberately created, manufactured solely and expressly for research purposes.

3.82   Lord Darzi said the House of Commons Science and Technology Committee and the Joint Committee as well as the scientific community favoured the extension (research on human admixed embryos), to enable research involving such embryos, subject to strict regulation. He added that 'interspecies embryos', defined arguably quite broadly, are, 'those embryos created using human and animal components where the resulting embryo is towards the human end of the spectrum.' He stated the reason for the need to permit such research was abundantly self-evident, and emphasised the safeguards (ethical and legal 'boundaries') in both the 1990 Act and the HFE Bill to guard against potential abuse, eg the requirement to possess a research licence from HFEA, no placing of an interspecies embryo in a woman, no keeping or use of an interspecies embryo after 14 days, etc. He hoped that:

'Research using interspecies embryos may one day provide more clues to the mechanics of human cells and lead to a better understanding of the nature of disease and provide effective treatments.'

3.83   Rebutting the accusations that creating interspecies embryos is intuitively repugnant and unnatural, Lord Darzi, stated that:

'Not only is it very difficult to specify … what "unnatural" means, but it is not clear why unnaturalness should be bad. IVF is an unnatural process; vaccination is an unnatural process; but those scientific advances have created modern medicine as we know it today.'[82]

3.84   Regarding the presence of a regulation-making power in the HFE Bill to add to or amend the definition of what constitutes a human admixed embryo (ie s 4(11)(a) and (b) in the 2008 Act), Lord Darzi argued that:

'[this] regulation-making power would provide the future flexibility we need to ensure that the law keeps pace with any technological developments in the creation of part-human, part-animal embryos … Building in mechanisms of flexibility to legislation in order to respond to new scientific developments and changed circumstances in the future is arguably no bad thing.'

3.85   Lord Darzi was emphatic that interspecies embryos should not be used for research lightly or without necessity and must be shown respect. It is not treated as a person or potential person, nor does it have rights, but it is not a mere product. He confirmed too, that in the HFE Bill:

'[the government] have proposed the same level of regulation and control on the use of interspecies embryos and research throughout the Bill as we have on the regulation and control of human embryos.'[83]

Human embryos and human admixed embryos are therefore treated equally from the point of view of the licensing regime and the criminal prohibitions and safeguards concerning their use in research.

---

82   *Hansard*, 3 December 2007, col 1535.
83   Ibid, cols 1536, 1537.

3.86 Lord Alton referred to another successful use of adult stem cells by Professor Carlos Lima in therapy in spinal cord injury cases and stated that: 'where good science and good ethics march hand in hand, we should all get behind it.'[84] He insisted that what he dubbed 'the Hunt test' be incorporated into the granting of all licences, that either human embryos or human admixed embryos can only be used for research where this is necessary or desirable, ie where there is no alternative. The 'Hunt test' refers to the government minister, Lord Hunt who in 2001 said that:

'the 1990 Act already provides the answer to the question of what happens if and when research into adult cells overtakes research using embryos: embryonic research would have to stop because the use of embryos would no longer be necessary for that research.'[85]

Lord Hunt had previously stated that the Act:

'must satisfy itself that there is no other way of doing the research, avoiding embryo use.'[86]

3.87 Lord Alton refers to *Forbes* magazine which, he says:

'recommends that investors do not do what the British Government have done. It says that only dumb public money is going into embryonic stem cells.'[87]

He also referred to a 2005 editorial in *Nature Biotechnology*, which flagged up the obvious alternative to embryonic stem cell research (and presumably to interspecies embryonic research too):

'Meanwhile forward steps continue to be made in the field of adult stem cell therapy. One estimate is that there are currently over 80 therapies and around 300 clinical trials under way using such cells.'

He queried, 'Can the Government truly say that it was necessary to destroy or experiment on 2 million human embryos?'[88]

3.88 Lord Winston challenged Lord Alton, by pointing out the reality that IVF at present results in large numbers of human embryos being wasted. Implicit in this is the argument that, if that is the case, some of these surplus embryos could be used for research purposes, so that some potential good can come from them.

3.89 Lord Patel noted:

'The whole purpose of interspecies embryo work is to be able to develop disease because many diseases are specific to humans; they do not occur in animals. The point of much of the research is to create disease-specific stem-cell lines that reflect the human specific gene mutations and abnormal functioning involved in the disease.'[89]

---

84 Ibid, col 1539.
85 *Hansard*, 22 January 2001, col 120 (HC).
86 *Hansard*, 19 December 2000, col 214 (HC).
87 *Hansard*, 3 December 2007, col 1541.
88 Ibid, col 1542.
89 Ibid, cols 1543, 1544.

3.90   Lord Harries endorsed Lord Patel, arguing:

'you cannot predict exactly a research outcome. The whole point about research is that you are testing something. You may not get out what you are expecting and hoping to get out. That result might still be useful to future scientific work.'[90]

3.91   Earl Howe revealed that the HFEA had given him on 3 December 2007 figures for the number of embryos donated to research by patients in the course of treatment between 1990 and 2005. The total was 82,955.

3.92   Lord Darzi reiterated the practical reality;

'Not all research is successful. In fact, researchers in almost every field of science undertake significant research to yield only a few positive results. The results however, are significant ... A specialist regulator [ie the HFEA] is in place to assess the necessity of each embryo research project, and legislation has set out which scientific goals are suitable for embryo research ... This system has worked well in the past, and is the best arrangement that we can hope for to permit embryo and interspecies embryo research while ensuring that the special status of the embryo is upheld.'[91]

3.93   Lord Alton disputed the HFEA figures of 82,955, saying that the figures he had been using were of the numbers of embryos that have been destroyed or experimented on. He was also concerned that mere scientific curiosity was driving the debate and that, 'surely we have a duty to say that other factors must be held to account.'

3.94   Lord Winston repeated that IVF process 'destroys a large number of embryos that cannot be used for fertility treatment.'

3.95   Lord Mackay of Clashfern expressed concerns about the type of interspecies embryo that the government are seeking to capture and very sensibly stated that: 'When we are talking about interspecies embryos ... it is essential to know what it is we are talking about.'[92] He added:

'When you want to regulate something ... it is vital that the area to be regulated is clearly defined. It is about as mad to have flexibility in that area as it would be to have flexibility in a fence around an animal enclosure.'[93]

3.96   Lord Winston then helpfully distinguished between the various properties of stem cell, explaining:

'True stem cells, at best, are totipotent; that is, they can develop into any one of numerous cell types – in the case of the human body, it is about 220 different cell types. There are various degrees of potency. Some stem cells are pluripotent, which means that they can develop into many tissues, but not all. Some stem cells – mostly, it seems, from adult sources – have even more limited potential and can grow only into certain tissue. Look at the genes or

---

90   Ibid, col 1544.
91   Ibid, col 1546.
92   Ibid, col 1549.
93   Ibid, col 1551.

look at the tissues which are produced in vitro in the laboratory. One of the best tests – it is almost the prime test, and the one that has been most used in the literature and the most valuable – is to mix stem cells with an animal embryo, usually that of a mouse, to see what happens to the human cells during that animal's development,.'[94]

3.97   Earl Howe insisted, concerning adequate definition of interspecies embryos, that:

'the Government and Parliament need to approve a legal architecture that would straddle all types of interspecies embryo – an architecture that rests on the foundations of ethics and science and which has clear guidelines but which allows for a sensible degree of autonomy by the regulator in taking decisions.'[95]

3.98   Regarding whether and when an organism can be classified as a human, in the context of creating interspecies embryos, Lord Patel, rhetorically asked

'As for how much of a mouse or another organism is human, when we share nearly 30 per cent of our genome with a banana, we could ask: is a banana human?'[96]

Lord Patel, like most of the advocates of permitting the creation of interspecies embryos for research, strongly rejected putting unnecessary hurdles and imposing bureaucratic restrictions on potentially beneficial research. As he said: 'Even if the work were not banned, introducing additional regulations would be a major setback for the speed at which such research could progress.' He added that the use of transgenic animals is fundamental to biomedical research and that testing the pluripotency of stem cells was critical for realising the therapeutic potential of stem cells, not only embryonic stem cells. He noted moreover the importance of transgenic models, used in both basic and applied medical research, inter alia in the modelling of human diseases, drug development and drug testing.[97]

3.99   Lord Winston went further in extolling the virtues of transgenic technology and stated that it was the single most important advance in human medicine in the past two decades.[98]

3.100   Lord Darzi stated that:

'The spectrum of human animal embryo research is broad ... warrants the regulation warranted under the 1990 Act – strict regulation and strict limits placed on the creation and use of such embryos.'[99]

Concerning who would regulate interspecies embryos, (ie add to the number or types of these), he said that: '[T]he regulations in question would be for the House to debate in the form of an affirmative resolution.'[100]

94   Ibid, col 1553.
95   Ibid, col 1557.
96   Ibid, col 1558.
97   Ibid, col 1558.
98   Ibid, col 1560.
99   Ibid, cols 1561–62.
100   Ibid, cols 1561–62.

3.101 Lord Alton noted, interestingly, that:

'Following a freedom of information request by Comment on Reproductive Ethics, it is acknowledged that the HFEA has never turned down a research application to the best of its knowledge.'

He controversially claimed:

'So indifferent is the HFEA to widespread hostility to creating animal-human hybrids that it has totally disregarded its own consultation which demonstrated that of more than 800 submissions, only one in eight supported the creation of hybrids.' [101]

3.102 Lord Patten scathingly poured sceptical caution on the promises of benefits emerging from interspecies embryonic research, stating:

'It sometimes strikes me that we are being taken on a magical mystery tour, where we should automatically canonise what a lot of clever scientists think is a very good thing.'[102]

3.103 The informed and intelligent contributions of a wide array of peers from such a diverse pool of different professional backgrounds and expertise unquestionably fashioned a considerable improvement in the final legislative product on this occasion. Whilst the debates, discussions, and legislative skirmishes in the second chamber were impassioned and powerful on many occasions they nevertheless highlighted the deeply held principles and convictions of the contributors, and served to underline the vitally important role of our parliamentarians, even here our unelected ones, in articulating the views, fears and concerns not just of those peers, but of wider society regarding highly controversial yet potentially critical legislative changes in the sphere of assisted reproductive medicine and research. This is to the enormous credit of our sometimes unfairly maligned, currently unelected, second chamber.

---

101 Ibid, col 1582.
102 Ibid, cols 1584–1585.

Chapter 4

House of Commons Debates

INTRODUCTION

4.1   The House of Commons debates mirrored those in the House of Lords. If the arguments were not advanced with quite the same technical expertise and authority as by certain peers, MPs certainly did not lack passion, conviction or principle in putting their respective cases.

DEBATES

4.2   In introducing the HFE Bill in the House of Commons for its Second Reading, Alan Johnson MP, the Secretary of State for Health, set out the main thrust of the government's policy concerning the Bill:

'Parliament's main objective has always been to support scientific advances that benefit patients and their families, through a clear legal, moral and ethical framework that provides proper controls and safeguards and reflects their concerns that many people have about research involving stem cells and embryology.'[1]

Moreover, he said that the HFE Bill was quite simply 'a flagship Government Bill, in respect of which we are building on a precedent that has gone on for 18 years.'[2] He added that the purpose of the Bill 'is to ensure that the 1990 Act is revised to keep pace with new avenues of scientific research and to reflect wider change in our society.'[3]

4.3   Lembit Opik MP supported the HFE Bill, emphasising its huge potential promise for curing terrible diseases and lessening suffering, stating that:

'Many people face a sentence of death because of incurable diseases such as motor neurone disease, and are depending on the opportunities provided by parts of the Bill to find cures for such dreadful and debilitative wasting diseases.'[4]

4.4   Mark Pritchard MP countered by asking Mr Johnson:

'does he also accept that the scientific breakthroughs.., have to date come only from existing adult stem cell research, not embryo research or stem cells extracted from embryos?'[5]

---

1   *Hansard,* 12 May 2008, col 1063.
2   Ibid, col 1065.
3   Ibid, col 1066.
4   Ibid, col 1067.
5   Ibid.

This is one of the central planks of the argument of those opposed to both interspecies and embryonic stem cell research, namely there is a very good alternative to them, ie adult stem cell research, which is ethically uncontroversial. However Mr Johnson demurred, contending that:

> 'the induced pluripotent stem cell breakthrough that seeks to transform adult stem cells back to the embryonic stage could not have been reached without legislation that allowed embryonic research in the first place.'[6]

In other words the superstructure of adult stem cell research was built on the foundations of embryonic stem cell research, and the former would not have been possible without the latter. Again the Health Secretary reiterated what his colleague Lord Darzi stated in the House of Lords, that all avenues of research should be supported and kept open and that Parliament should be loath to direct research down one path or route alone, stating that every opportunity available should be used.

4.5   Moreover, Mr Johnson claimed that:

> 'The clear and consistent message from the wide consultation … and from the debates we have already had, is that the current Act cannot keep pace with scientific developments that have occurred since its enactment … Over the last 18 years, methods that are not explicitly governed by the 1990 Act, such as cell nuclear replacement … and parthenogenesis, where an egg is stimulated either electrically or chemically to develop into an embryo, has been developed.'[7]

He was equally clear that

> 'Similarly, there is no explicit provision for the regulation of the use of admixed embryos, which combine human and animal genetic material for scientific research … That development is recognised by scientists across the world as an essential building block for establishing cures for many life-threatening diseases, such as multiple sclerosis, Parkinson's and Alzheimer's.'[8]

4.6   The reason for creating and using human admixed embryos for research is entirely pragmatic, ie because of a lack of human eggs. He adds that human admixed embryos are 99.9 per cent human, and that no scientist anywhere in the world wants to implant such an embryo in a woman or animal, and moreover could not do so legally: 'Such actions will remain a criminal offence under international law.'

4.7   Alan Johnson then emphasised that, in addition, the HFE Bill 'will ensure that all human embryos created for research – regardless of how they are created – are subject to the same regulatory framework.' In response to Geraldine Smith MP's observation that full hybrids ie embryos that are 50 per cent animal and 50 per cent human are permitted under HFE Bill, he added that true hybrids had been used in the past, and cited 'the famous hamster test done years ago used true hybrids'. Indeed, he goes further arguing that, '[I]n fact,

---

6   Ibid.
7   Ibid.
8   Ibid, cols 1067, 1068.

cytoplasmic embryos are the most exciting development that most scientists wish to use', whilst not ruling out other important areas of research.

4.8   Phil Willis MP pointed out that a cytoplasmic hybrid embryo will have just 0.1 per cent of animal tissue in it, but that 'in reality, once we mix in any element of animal, the principle of using hybrids for research purposes is established'.[9] Whether a cytoplasmic hybrid embryo is 0.1 per cent, 1 per cent or 10 per cent comprised of animal tissue is academic – the principle of mixing has been conceded and accepted.

4.9   Sally Keeble MP favoured permitting the creation of admixed embryos, because, 'the alternative to using admixed embryos, which is using human eggs, is itself unethical because of the risk that it poses to women, and the pain that it involves'.[10]

4.10   Mr Johnson wanted to put on the record, in agreeing with Jim Devine MP the fact that the Bill was not about creating Frankenstein-type monsters. In the past 18 years, he said, scientists in the UK had pioneered medical advances that could not have been anticipated in 1990. He noted that:

'The "unknown and threatening seas" to which Baroness Warnock referred have been navigated successfully thus far, thanks to the lodestar provided by Parliament, which has allowed scientists to reap the benefits of embryonic stem cell research … Specialist regulation of reproductive technologies and clear legal boundaries have united scientific breakthroughs with public confidence in their development and use … Among other things, that represents a considerable triumph for parliamentary scrutiny and debate.'[11]

He concluded:

'Stem cell research has enormous potential to develop new cures for degenerative and other life-threatening diseases. It brings hope to hundreds of thousands of sufferers and their families. This Government believe that we should continue to support such research in order to exploit advances in medical science, but only provided there are clear safeguards, within the ethical and moral framework that Parliament has established with such skill and sensitivity.'[12]

4.11   Andrew Lansley MP, the shadow Health Secretary agreed that the 1990 Act had been a success and a positive example for policy making worldwide but importantly stressed that:

'research required to be established within an ethical framework so that science is bounded [ie cannot do what it wants without any limitations] … some forms of research are prohibited, and all research on human embryos requires a licence.'[13]

He emphasised too that '[T]he fact that scientists can do something does not mean that they should', and that '[E]thical boundaries do not shift in a

---

9   Ibid, col 1068.
10   Ibid, col 1069.
11   Ibid, cols 1072, 1073.
12   Ibid, col 1073.
13   Ibid.

mechanistic way to reflect the utility of new research techniques.' Mr Lansley however acknowledged that the legislation needed to be updated and referred to the decision of the HFEA in January 2008 concerning two projects involving the use of animal eggs from which the nucleus had been removed. He observed that:

> 'Despite the fact that the 1990 Act prohibits the mixing of animal and human gametes, other than to test the fertility of sperm, the authority regarded the embryo created as human and that, as such, it could licence research.'

On that basis he argued:

> 'The HFEA's decisions and interpretation of the 1990 Act suggest that substantial research using hybrid embryos would continue even if there were no legislation, so the Bill is necessary to provide clarity and to update the law.'

His argument here is that it would be better to set this out clearly in an Act than leave it to a specialist, but ultimately unelected quango, to decide. The other positive spin-off of legislation is that:

> 'scientists feel far more confident about the nature of what they are doing, and of public support for it, when Parliament has provided an ethical and legal framework.'[14]

4.12   Like Lord Darzi, Alan Johnson and a wide range of other MPs and peers, Mr Lansley accepted:

> 'that there is a need to pursue different models by which stem cells can be created or reprogrammed to provide potential therapeutic benefit. Although research on reprogramming adult stem cells is encouraging, it would be foolhardy to block embryonic stem cell research and it is increasingly evident that the availability of human eggs for research purposes will be a serious constraint on the conduct of such experiments.'[15]

He flagged up the crucial safeguard that human admixed embryos should not be created lightly or frivolously, contending that:

> 'Those who promote such projects must demonstrate that they are necessary and desirable. It is clear from the structure of the Bill that, if an alternative route-not using embryos-were available, the HFEA should not licence such a research project.'[16]

Mr Lansley said there was consensus on research, but that:

> 'the consensus rests on the proposition that embryonic stem cell research is one of several models of research, which may deliver substantial therapeutic benefit in future, and on the fact that constraints emerged on the availability of human eggs, which meant that there were significant benefits to be derived from using animal eggs'[17]

---

14   Ibid, col 1074.
15   Ibid, col 1075.
16   Ibid.
17   Ibid, col 1076.

However, he said that there was no consensus on the matter of creating human-animal embryos in which there is a substantial mix of human and animal nuclear DNA. Mr Lansley submitted:

'It would be the job of the authority, when undertaking its licensing, to ensure that embryonic stem cell research was minimised, not that it was excluded. That is the balance that I seek.'[18]

4.13 Concerning funding of the two competing, but complementary types of research, namely embryonic and adult stem cell research, Mr Lansley stated that the split was broadly speaking 60 per cent for embryonic stem cell research and 40 per cent for adult stem cell research. He noted that there were also other options.

4.14 Kevin Barron MP welcomed the HFE Bill, arguing that 'it was not about creating monsters ... and it never was'. He referred to the clear ethical and legal boundaries that the scientists must operate within and rejected the assertion that medical science had become out of control.

4.15 Norman Lamb MP, the Liberal Democrat Health Spokesman, said the Bill was necessary because the history in this area had been of legislation trying to keep pace with scientific endeavour and developments, ie old law trying to keep up with and regulate new science. Thus, because the new science had raised correspondingly new ethical, legal and social issues, 'in order to maintain public confidence legislation must be able to meet new challenges; hence the need for updating.' He argued that it was Parliament's task and duty to regulate the new science and it must ensure, as best it can, that its laws are future-proofed. Thus he argued:

'Ultimately, it has to be Parliament that sets the framework – the boundaries within which scientists and the medical profession can lawfully operate ... In setting the framework here and now, we have to look forward and anticipate new breakthroughs, in order to make sure that the legislation is as durable as possible.'

Mr Lamb emphasised that the Liberal Democrats' policy position was to be pro-science and in favour of research, but within proper limits and with proper safeguards. Having witnessed the horror of degenerative and genetic conditions, he believed that there was a powerful case for research, increasing understanding and ultimately leading to cures. He said:

'If there is a chance of our finding cures or treatments, that is surely a worthy objective ... Any such research would, of course, be subject, under this Bill, to tight control.'[19]

4.16 Mr Lamb was in favour of creating and using human admixed embryos, because there was a genuine problem of a shortage of human eggs hampering research, and there was the safeguard that they can only be developed up to 14 days. He argued:

'Surely it makes sense to save human eggs for IVF treatment, so if we really want research that has the potential to deliver cures of treatments for some

18   Ibid, col 1077.
19   Ibid, col 1086.

of these awful conditions to be done, there must be a compelling logic to making use of admixed embryos.'

He conceded there were concerns regarding creating and using human admixed embryos:

'because we are dealing with a challenging concept and there is a sense that it blurs the distinction between animals and humans, creating unnatural entities.'[20]

4.17   A staunch and leading opponent of the creation and use of human admixed embryos, Geraldine Smith MP, opposed the provisions in HFE Bill that would add to the two million human embryos that since 1990 have been destroyed or experimented upon. Furthermore, she found the aim of the Bill in, inter alia, creating hybrid animal-human embryos, 50 per cent 'animal' and 50 per cent human, 'revolting'. She was scornful of the failures of embryonic stem cell research to deliver any cures for terrible diseases, stating that as well as having serious misgivings about the ethics of this issue, she had real concern about the lack of progress in embryonic stem cell research. She argued that resources ought rather to be targeted at new methods that had been developed to produce stem cells with greater potential than embryonic stem cells. She was in no doubt that many of those who had voted for embryonic cloning in 2001 and who would vote in favour of creating and using human admixed embryos:

will do so out of a genuine humanitarian desire to help those who suffer from disabling diseases ... [but] ... Six years on from the hype of 2001, not only have the hopes of those who were desperate for a cure for their illness been raised and dashed, but no therapies have been developed anywhere in the world using embryonic stem cells.'[21]

Furthermore she detailed the record of success using adult stem cells, an ethical alternative, thus:

'Advances continue to be made in adult stem cell therapy, which involves no moral hazards. Indeed, there are more than 80 therapies and about 300 clinical trials under way using such cells ... Worldwide, children are being treated successfully for leukaemia using stem cells obtained from cord blood. There are also early clinical trials using adult stem cells in the treatment of diabetes, heart disease, multiple sclerosis and spinal injuries ... Surely, the future lies in the development of ethically sound, adult stem cell research techniques.'[22]

4.18   John Bercow MP, an enthusiast for the new research said that he adopted in the debate:

'an empiricist, pragmatic, instrumental view, rather than the view that some abstract principle should inveigh against the possibility that such research should be allowed or extended.'[23]

20   Ibid, col 1087.
21   Ibid, col 1098.
22   Ibid, col 1099.
23   Ibid, col 1100.

He rejected the argument that ethically non-controversial alternatives exist to both embryonic and human admixed embryo research, which ought to make such research unnecessary, and believed that parliamentarians should not 'act as the exclusive arbiters in favour of one source, rather than of either of the other two main sources that are on the table at the moment.'[24] He recognised some MPs 'feel an almost overwhelming revulsion at the idea' of human admixed embryos, but he was motivated by the pursuit of results and believed that the pragmatic arguments were strong, including the shortage of human eggs, the fact that the whole process of egg harvesting is difficult, burdensome and hazardous, and that for a small proportion of women, it is potentially fatal.[25] Later on he passionately argued that regarding someone who is withered and debilitated by the most appalling disease he could not, 'simply turn away, saying that some abstract theory, dogmatic reasoning or religious insistence prevents me from giving the go-ahead to that work.'[26]

4.19 Dr Brian Iddon MP drew attention to the promise of human admixed embryo research finding cures or improvements for terrible diseases that ravage and inflict terrible suffering on individuals. Such cures, he said, do not just simply appear from nowhere but are generally based on lots of prior and painstaking research. He claimed that stem cell research 'is a remarkable field of research, which is advancing more quickly than the legislation to deal with it.'[27] Whilst conceding that adult stem cell research was important, he reminded the House of the dangers associated with it. The solution, he said, is that '[A]ll three lines of research must continue, because faults are inherent in each of them.'

4.20 Gary Streeter MP welcomed scientific progress, but progress not made in an ethical and moral vacuum. We should, he said, always possess a functioning moral and ethical compass, and added that: 'Nor should we discard the wisdom of the ages: the wisdom that places humans as important moral objects, distinct from other animals.' Man is an animal but a unique animal, for some created in the image of God, and arguably at the apex of evolutionary animal development. He said that he was not closing the door on research, but argued that there was a better way of conducting that research. He also wanted to ensure that public money is spent more effectively, reiterating that:

> 'We are constantly told that more than 80 therapies have been developed from adult stem cell research, while so far no therapies at all have been developed as a result of embryonic stem cell research.'[28]

Concerning the therapeutic benefits yielded from embryonic stem cell research, he conceded too that, 'of course, it takes a long time, but we have had 20 years.'

4.21 Dawn Primarolo MP replied that:

> 'the technologies under discussion have existed only in the past few years. He refers to science and developments that have been around for longer.'[29]

---

24 Ibid, col 1101.
25 Ibid, col 1100.
26 Ibid, col 1102.
27 Ibid, col 1104.
28 Ibid, col 1106.
29 Ibid.

Mr Streeter voiced the intuitive opposition of many MPs to creating human admixed embryos, encapsulating perfectly the 'yuck factor', stating he was instinctively against it for moral reasons, that it was 'plain wrong' and moreover was 'a slippery slope to who knows where'.

4.22 He added that:

'The creation of induced pluripotent cells.., or adult cells with embryonic stem cell properties, now, it seems, provides a credible alternative to embryonic stem ... The Bill ... promotes research into gas lamps when electricity has already been invented.'[30]

He concluded by pointing to our European counterparts who do not permit the creation of human admixed embryos for research and stated that we could learn lessons from their example. He thus says 'Most European countries – France, the Netherlands and Germany, to name but a few – have banned the process of somatic cell nuclear transfer, which is used in the creation of human admixed embryos.' So, he said, should the UK.

4.23 Dr Ian Gibson MP, a former Chairman of the Select Committee examining stem cell research, again sensibly cautioned against over-optimism concerning immediate or relatively quick results and beneficial therapies emerging from embryonic and human admixed embryo research, stating:

'As with everything in science, we live in hope that something will happen, but it is never possible to swear to it. I am 99.9 per cent sure that the sun will rise tomorrow morning, but who knows?' [31]

Amusingly Dr Gibson concluded that we should not get too outraged by the thought of creating human admixed embryos, given that:

'There are people in this House ... who have parts of a pig attached to their heart. That keeps them alive. We do not need hypocrisy in this matter. We can have combined pigs and human beings to keep people in this House – and elsewhere – alive.'[32]

4.24 Robert Key MP tellingly commented that Parliament was not only our national bioethics commission, but the best bioethics committee concerning permitting the highly controversial creation of human admixed embryos. He stated there are three crucial moral principles. These are that:

(1) all human tissue is special and uniquely demanding of respect;
(2) embryos can only be used for up to 14 days, the point at which the primitive streak emerges: and
(3) no embryo that has been used for research may ever be implanted in a woman.

He states that these 'are pillars that are fundamental to the morality of this legislation.'[33] He also argued that: 'a human embryo needs protection because it has the potential to develop as a person, or persons, made in the image of God',

---

30 Ibid, col 1108.
31 Ibid, col 1110.
32 Ibid, col 1114.
33 Ibid.

and added that the HFE Bill was both sensible and practical, having 'gone through the mill of the opinion of both Houses of Parliament.' It was 'a great force for good and a step in the right direction, rather than the wrong one' and was, 'a natural evolution of the current position', but, he cautioned scientists, 'just because you can do something, that does not mean you should.'[34]

4.25 Chris McCafferty MP warmly supported the Bill, submitting that it would strengthen regulation in important areas of scientific research, including embryo and stem cell research, which he observed was currently a very grey area. The law ought to be clear. Unclear law is arguably bad law. Scientists, doctors, patients and the public needed to know where they stood. Is an action lawful or unlawful? The legal frontiers and ethical boundaries had been clearly demarcated over the last 18 years, since the 1990 Act was enacted. He contended that the therapeutic benefits of this pioneering research may not necessarily be immediately apparent, or even become so in the short- to-mid term, but this research demanded more long-term thinking. The promise was great.

4.26 Phil Willis MP agreed that a much clearer definition regarding what constituted human admixed embryos was needed, and that the HFE Bill did not change law or scientific practice 'radically, but rather incrementally'. Additionally, he referred to the Science and Technology Select Committee Report, 'Government proposals for the regulation of hybrid and chimera embryos', which:

'found that there was a pressing need to clarify the law in relation to hybrid embryos, and that research allowing the creation of human-animal chimera or hybrid embryos was necessary and desirable.'[35]

However, research into both adult and cord blood stem cells was of equal importance rather than one or the other, and all 3 types of research had to be regulated, not outlawed.

4.27 Responding to the argument that research using embryonic stem cells has not yielded results, Mr Willis countered:

'If the House legislated by saying that we had to know the answer before we could permit the research, we would end up with the most sterile research community ever.'

4.28 Mr Bercow mentioned again the reality that human eggs were scarce and difficult to harvest, but that animal eggs were in bountiful abundance by contrast. He stated:

'In the abattoir this afternoon, hundreds of thousands of oocytes were flushed down the drain. Not only could all of them be used for research purposes but they would also allow human embryos-human oocytes–to be used sparingly and effectively, because techniques to do so would have been developed elsewhere.'[36]

---

34 Ibid, col 1116.
35 Ibid, cols 1120–21.
36 Ibid, col 1122.

Religious objections

4.29 Iris Robinson, DUP MP for Strangford, 'speaking as a born-again Christian' warned the House to approach the Bill, 'through the central fact that we are all created in the image of God' in the book of Genesis in the Bible. For her mankind is 'fundamentally different from the rest of creation, including animals', and so:

> We are not just another animal. We are created special, and that fact must be treated with respect … That tenet is central to human identity.'[37]

She was emphatic that 'The creation of hybrid embryos undermines our dignity and is fundamentally disrespectful of the boundaries of nature.' She then outlined a series of what she regarded as catastrophic consequences if human admixed embryos are permitted, namely:

> 'It would tarnish the "image of God" present in all of us, would breach the biblical prohibition of the mixings of kinds, would confuse lineage, would fundamentally affect all human relationships, especially marriage and the family, and would cross an ethical line by creating something essentially new but unnecessary.'

She drew succour and further support for her detestation of what is, for her, ethically and morally repellent science from the Bible accordingly:

> 'Corinthians 15 provides us with a clear statement of the difference between humans and animals in God's order. Verse 39 reads: "All flesh is not the same: Men have one kind of flesh, animals have another, birds another and fish another." I stand by that.'[38]

4.30 Basically her opposition to the creation and use of human admixed embryos was rooted and moored in the Bible. Some would argue that opposition should be more firmly based on scientific facts and rationality rather than faith and superstition. Others might counter that science has itself become a faith akin to a religion, with the doctors and scientists at the 'cutting-edge' of technological development assuming the mantle and mitres of the priests in a religion.

4.31 More pragmatically she contended:

> 'To date, human embryonic stem cell research has absorbed a huge amount of taxpayers' money but delivered no therapies, whereas adult stem cell research, which involves no ethical hazards, has delivered around 80 therapies for patients, and some 350 clinical trials are currently under way. That is a fact.'[39]

The balance sheet is seemingly very much in credit and in favour of adult stem cell research, regarding successful delivery of therapies that benefit patients, and equally patently in debit and not in favour of the ethically controversial use of embryonic and now human admixed embryos for research.

---

37 Ibid.
38 Ibid, col 1124.
39 Ibid, cols 1124–1125. As opposed to a matter of faith, or a gut reaction!

4.32   Dr Desmond Turner welcomed the enormous boost embryonic stem cell research and research in assisted reproduction generally has provided the UK economy. This progress needed to be harnessed and further developed in other fields, eg human admixed embryo research, and certainly hurdles and obstacles ought not to hinder this seismic, cutting edge science. He argued that none of this would have been possible 'without the confidence-building framework of the 1990 Act.'[40] He argued that UK science in this field is so successful that there had allegedly been a reverse brain drain in stem cell research, with top American scientists coming to work in the United Kingdom:

'because they can work with surety, knowing that they will not be subject to legal challenge for their activities, whereas in many states in America they are actively discouraged and prevented from carrying out that research.'

4.33   Dr Turner interestingly highlights the value of regulation, as opposed to no regulation, as was the case in several other EU countries. He mentioned Italy, which had just passed laws controlling IVF, but:

'Prior to that, the issue had been completely unregulated and all manner of things had been going on. A scientist had been threatening to clone a human being; that would clearly be absolutely impossible in this country under this legislation.'[41]

The problem in the UK, and axiomatically why the law in the UK needs updating, is that the HFEA has been called on to make 'judgments that stretch the framework to its limits. Once that happens, there is judicial review and there are challenges in the courts.' he added that the courts, however, were not the places in which to make ethical or medical decisions – by implication Parliament is.

4.34   Dr Turner crucially noted with admixed embryos that:

'the DNA involved is 99 per cent human, and all the nuclear DNA is human. The 1 per cent that remains is the mitochondrial DNA, which does not determine the character of what might grow.'[42]

He castigated the popular image of human admixed embryos, fanned by some sensationalist tabloid headlines, such as 'Human-Cow Embryos in the UK!', saying that he had 'visions of the bovine equivalents of centaurs trotting down the streets', and that this was 'absolutely absurd, because no such thing is happening or will be allowed to happen.' He concluded that parliamentarians should 'make decisions based on true facts and not misrepresentation or sensationalism.'

4.35   David Burrowes MP, stated that opponents did not want to impede sound research, but rather 'to see Britain leading the way … on a sound ethical basis'. He asserted:

'The Bill is by no means what it says on the tin in being a blueprint for the future in leading scientific research and producing results … It hides within its laudable exterior proposals that strike at the heart of the value of

40   Ibid, col 1127.
41   Ibid.
42   Ibid, col 1128.

human life and commodifies a child's life as an instrument for the benefit of another.'[43]

Additionally, he claimed: 'The major problem with the Bill is that the Government are marching us up to the top of the hill of embryonic research.'[44] Paraphrasing Rev Martin Luther King, he said that the government were claiming that embryonic and human admixed stem cell research would help reach the summit of the mountain and the promised land of cure, therapies and medicines for a series of terrible diseases. However, the reality check was:

'as a country we have been marched up the hill since 1990 … The summit of treatments is still far off, as it was in 1990. The government want us to follow another path to the summit now, using human admixed embryos, as well as pursuing the embryonic stem cell route … Everyone agrees, though, that the prospect of treatment and clinical trials is a long way off.'

4.36   Furthermore, he said:

'It does not give us reassurance when we look at the summit, which many would say is over-hyped and could be false. The real progress has been made with adult stem cell research and umbilical cord blood stem cells.'[45]

He added that whilst the funding imbalance between adult and umbilical and embryonic stem cell research has been 'rebalanced', nevertheless umbilical cord blood remained the poor relation of the stem cell therapy world. He argued that '[W]e should be marching up a different hill to ensure that we have regenerative medicine that produces results, relieves suffering and reduces health care costs', and observed that:

'Cord blood is producing more than 80 treatments in leukaemia and other areas of immune deficiency and moving into degenerative diseases. If the Government took umbilical cord blood collection and banking seriously, controversial parts of the Bill would not be necessary.'

The ethically non-controversial alternative has not been fully explored, he said, and added:

'It frustrates me that the Bill condones the creation of commodity humans and part animal, part human entities, but refuses to make provision for the valuable resource of cord blood, which is simply treated as waste in 98.5 per cent of all cases.'

Concluding, he described the Bill:

'as a Humpty Dumpty type of Bill – it is broken and ethically flawed. The king's horses and all the king's men have sought to put Humpty together again, but it is flawed fundamentally.'[46]

4.37   Mrs Claire Curtis-Thomas MP, one of the leading opponents of the Bill, scathingly said '[M]ost reasonable people would say that to combine an animal and human embryo is, by definition, monstrous.' Far from that view being hype and sensationally exaggerated, she argued:

---

43   Ibid, col 1129.
44   Ibid, col 1131.
45   Ibid, col 1132.
46   Ibid.

'If anyone was guilty of hype it was those who favoured embryonic stem cells, which have not produced any therapies despite 18 years of research, over adult stem cells, which have already produced more than 80 treatments.'[47]

She then proceeded to criticise 'The scientific community, which sees the embryo as nothing more than a clump of cells', and thus 'denies any respect for the sanctity of life or human dignity.' She is certain that 'a human embryo is a potential human being, the personhood of which needs to be respected.' She says she is pro-life, but argued that 'Many of the proposals in the Bill are anti-life because many embryos will be killed to achieve the aims of the research and procedures.'

4.38   She slammed the Bill which permits the creation of animal-human hybrids, which 'is based on a utilitarian mentality that human life can be treated simply as research material if it benefits the common good.' In other words human life is used instrumentally as a means toward an end and not valued intrinsically as an end or good in itself. That is ethically wrong. 'Most crucially', she claimed, 'it violates the dignity of the human person.' She also said:

'The United Kingdom has already breached Article 18 of the European Convention on Human Rights and biomedicine by the creation of human embryos for research purposes … Many European countries would not even consider the creation of animal-human embryos.'

The shortage of eggs is no excuse for this new departure – only ethical avenues of research should be allowed. She also stated that there was little appreciation of how far out of a limb the UK was in relation to the creation of human admixed embryos and cited Australia, Canada and the United States as having prohibited such research.[48] She concluded:

'Launching into ethically dubious areas will not solve the ethical problem – it will compound it. "Progress" in this area is actually a backwards step that takes us further down the slippery slope of moral decline by crossing the species barrier and treating humans no better than animals.'

Finally, she worryingly asserted:

'In fact, legislation in this country gives animals better protection than the human foetus because under the Animals (Scientific Procedures) Act 1986, an animal embryo becomes a protected animal after half its gestation period, which is equivalent to 20 weeks for a human being.'[49]

She was also worried about the health and safety issues surrounding the use of animal eggs, that is, the risk of creating new diseases, and that 'No consideration has been given to safety issues in the Bill, and cow eggs are simply obtained from local abattoirs.'

4.39   Mrs Jacqui Lait MP supported the creation of human admixed embryos for research under the strictest regulatory regime, and challenged the instant

47   Ibid, col 1133.
48   Ibid, col 1134.
49   Ibid.

or quick gratification exponents regarding new therapies from the new technologies:

'There is an unspoken demand for instant results from embryonic stem cell research ... It could well take decades before there are results from embryonic stem cell research, but let us go with it.'[50]

4.40 Dr Evan Harris MP, one of the leading advocates of most of the changes made by the Bill, emphasised from the outset that 'it is important to stress that we are not discussing a matter that pitches science against morality' (simplistically science would permit such developments, whereas morality would oppose it). He added correctly:

'there are morality and ethical codes on both sides ... I do not accept the view that it is only science that is in favour of the measure and that the opposition to the Bill has all the moral and ethical arguments.'[51]

He would rather argue 'that it is ethically wrong to seek to stand in the way of some of that research.'

4.41 He challenged the argument, 'that after 20 years of embryonic stem cell research there were still no therapies.' He countered:

'however, the technology is relatively recent; indeed, it was only possible to pursue it in this country following the passage of the 2001 cloning regulations.'[52]

Dr Harris also explained that:

'Once one accepts that it is legitimate to do destructive medical research on human embryos, there is no ethical reason to give greater protection to things that are not human embryos. It would be an inversion of everyone's ethical compass to say that certain embryo entities require greater protection than a fully human embryo.'[53]

He was adamant that:

'It would be wrong to have a ban in primary legislation, however, because a non-ethically difficult use might come along in a few years' time, and the House might then be required to pass new primary legislation.'

4.42 Dr Richard Taylor MP attempted to reconcile the apparently irreconcilable difference between advocates of the new embryo research and religious opponents, and reiterated the use of blood from the umbilical cord:

'[Cord blood] is a completely wasted resource. The Anthony Nolan Trust estimates that 65,000 litres of cord blood are discarded every year. Cord blood is taken after the baby is born, so there is no risk to the baby. It is wasted, yet it can be an excellent source of stem cells.'[54]

---

50 Ibid, cols 1135–1136.
51 Ibid, col 1137.
52 Ibid, col 1138.
53 Ibid, col 1139.
54 Ibid, col 1142.

4.43   Alastair Burt MP, an avowed Christian, was concerned as to why his opinion 'should carry less weight than those of others because it has a base of faith', concerning his objections to many of the elements contained in the HFE Bill.[55]

4.44   David Amess MP scathingly denounced the pretence of scientific objectivity (reflected in the main proposals of the Bill) pitted against the alleged superstition, subjectivity, prejudice, and gut reaction of the opponents of the Bill. That was a total misrepresentation. He argued that '[N]one of us should hide behind a façade of scientific objectivity. The Bill deserved to be opposed 'because the principles enshrined in it are unjust and contrary to human rights.'[56] He also contended that the Bill:

> 'weakens the prohibition on so-called reproductive cloning and reduces the status of the human embryo by permitting new abuses and extending those already permitted ... Creating human embryos in the laboratory and treating them like commodities abuses them, thus dehumanising all human beings.'

He also argued that creating human admixed embryos, 'would be a radical violation of human dignity.' He concluded by stating he believed that the public 'are being fed the same false hopes' that they were in 1990 (with human embryo research) and in 2001 (with embryonic stem cell research), and that, in 2008:

> Now, we are told that the creation and destructive use of human-animal hybrid embryos will lead to cures for diseases. I fear that that will not be the case ... since 1990 there have been no such cures derived from human embryo research or embryonic stem cell research. I see no reason to believe that we will get any cures from so-called admixed embryos.'[57]

4.45   William Cash MP, an opponent of the Bill and of creating human admixed embryos, stated:

> 'Our choice should be based on deep and instinctive repugnance towards the proposition that a thing, however defined, whose sole purpose or object is that it may be a human life, should be subjected to experiment and destroyed for the acquisition of knowledge. We should maintain that fundamental tenet.'[58]

He argued that religion and science were complementary and not mutually exclusive. The two are inextricably bound up and go hand in hand. He referred to Albert Einstein who stated, 'Science without religion is lame; religion without science is blind.'

4.46   Dr John Pugh MP, very thoughtfully contributed to the debate on legalising human admixed embryo research by highlighting what he described as 'six unquestioned and unquestionable truths.' These are:

> (1) It is uncertain whether important therapies will come from embryonic stem cell research.

---

55   Ibid, col 1144.
56   Ibid, col 1147.
57   Ibid, col 1148.
58   Ibid, col 1149.

(2)   If they come, it is probable that they are a long way off. (However what is meant by a 'long way off'? Is it 5, 10, 15 years or longer?)

(3)   No substantial therapies have so far come from embryonic stem cell research.

(4)   In marked contrast, many therapies have come from adult stem cell research. The figure of 80 such therapies was referred to by several parliamentarians.

(5)   It is ultimately adult stem cell research – this point has not yet been made – that holds the key to mass-producing and industrialising the production of stem cells.

(6)   Adult stem cell research – cord blood use and so on – is morally unproblematic.[59]

4.47   Dr Pugh cited the main substantive objection to extending research to embrace this new human admixed embryo as being a diminution of respect for human life generally:

'the main, fundamental reason is the possible encouragement that the research gives to a casual attitude to, or a lack of respect for, human life.'

The possibilities of therapeutic advances afforded by this new type of research have tended to instrumentalise the human embryo and to cheapen life. He added that:

'every embryo is the blueprint of an individual and the code of a human life no different from ours ... [it is] mere human material ... [but] that is not the view of the existing law ... [It] requires good reasons for experimenting on ... embryos. If that was not the case, we would be comfortable with embryos being used in cosmetics, foodstuffs and so on.'[60]

However, he said, the law of Parliament insists: 'We require good reasons, namely the hope of scientific advance or medical therapy', ie there need to be, potentially at least, good reasons before permitting the research, thus: 'The potential risks and harms are set against the potential goods in a utilitarian fashion.'

4.48   Dr Pugh noted that Baroness Warnock 'made it clear that this is a utilitarian debate', but criticised this saying: 'Utilitarianism seldom works, because people weigh risks and harms differently.'[61] He queried how one decides what type of research ought to be permitted, stating 'If one looks for a clear principle that explains the boundary between the permissible and the impermissible, one does not find it in the Bill', and added:

'The real limit is the imagination and endeavour of the scientific community – the ad hoc, post hoc baptising of what decent scientists do, as opposed to rogue, usually foreign scientists.'

Very worryingly, he added;

'There is no rule that can be provided to differentiate the two categories, other than the claims that the decent scientists have good ethical reasons,

---

59   Ibid, col 1150.
60   Ibid, cols 1150–1151.
61   Ibid, col 1151.

that their work may minimally advance understanding, and may, but not will in all probability, lead to therapy.'

He asked 'What research programme, when one thinks about it, could not meet that standard?' He then proceeded to note that: 'Perhaps that is why the HFEA has refused none hitherto', before scathingly, but arguably pertinently, stating:

'If we have no clear idea what we want to rule out, we can have no clear idea what we want to rule in. We are a society in moral and intellectual confusion, and that is embodied in the debate, drawing ad hoc, post hoc temporary limits, and wrapping legislation round existing practice.'[62]

4.49   Interestingly, and ironically, Dr Pugh condemned those who advocate permitting the creation of and research on human admixed embryos primarily because of their faith in the huge potential benefits it will yield, yet those same advocates of the new science attack vehemently the opponents of the new science because their objections are based on a mixture of faith, religion, superstition, intuition and subjectivity. Science is one of our modern day faiths, but all faiths are not infallible.

4.50   Dr Pugh concluded that more experiments did not necessarily mean better research or more therapies, regardless of the ethical justification for that research. He was highly critical that the case for creating human admixed embryos was 'based not on existing research objectives but on the possibility that someone might have a research objective,' and that the case fails to properly address 'the moral issues and the possible waste of time and money', and excoriated the Bill, saying 'This is blank cheque legislation.'[63]

4.51   Mark Simmonds MP emphasised that 'true hybrids' 'are the only ones that are 50–50 and the only ones to merge the sex cells of animals and humans', and that there was a shortage of human eggs – hence the need to use animal eggs – but that 'it must be understood that the animal eggs that are used only as a vessel to ensure an ample supply of eggs for research.' He also claimed that Professor Yamanaka's team 'does not want embryonic stem cell research to cease.'[64]

4.52   Dawn Primarolo MP, Minister of State at the Department of Health said, 'the Bill seeks a pragmatic fusion between science and the social mores of today … Its overall effect is that of evolution, not revolution.'[65] She referred with approval to the 1990 Act being, 'a considered response to concerns that there should be limits and barriers in law under a scheme of regulatory regulation', and went on to say, 'The Bill is a recasting, in a similar mould, to ensure that the law and regulations can tackle the challenges of today and tomorrow.' She also admitted that:

'the Government's expressed aim is to ensure that the United Kingdom is at the forefront of developments in cutting-edge science and technology, which promises so much for individuals and their families and for society.'

---

62   Ibid.
63   Ibid, cols 1151–1152.
64   Ibid, col 1153.
65   Ibid, col 1157.

This was a constant theme and sales pitch for the legislation. She then really sells the overwhelming merits of the Bill thus:

> 'Advances in technology go hand in hand with those in regulation. They are united through proper accountability and public confidence ... [The HFE Bill] is an attempt to maintain that unity, keeping the established foundations that have proved sound, and updating them when necessary ... Failure to address those matters would lead inevitably to a loss for society ... Doubts about what is regulated or what is allowed would endanger public confidence. Confusion about legal duties and responsibilities would harm public accountability ... The impact would be felt through slower or stopped progress in understanding and treating infertility and serious medical conditions.'[66]

4.53   The Bill is designed and aimed, inter alia, at capturing all embryos, however created, including the new human admixed embryos, within the legal net of regulation. She stated, inter alia, that the matter should not be left open to interpretation, and not surprisingly added that in her opinion the Bill as drafted provided the necessary clarity. She highlighted the various safeguards in the existing 1990 Act, all applicable to human admixed embryos in the 2008 Bill, and added that research will not now be skewed in one direction, She called these 'genuine safeguards'. She finally stated that the HFE Bill 'is about introducing regulation that takes us into the 21st century.'[67] The House then voted 340–78 (a large majority of 262) in favour of the Bill.

HOUSE OF COMMONS COMMITTEE DEBATE

4.54   At the Committee stage Edward Leigh MP, another leading opponent of the controversial changes included in the HFE Bill, raised three fundamental objections to the raft of changes, namely, that it was 'ethically wrong', that it was 'almost certainly medically useless', and 'if it is not useless, that there is no evidence to substantiate it.'[68] He argued strongly that leaving the matter to be regulated was not good enough and that treating and using human admixed embryos for research quite simply ought to be banned outright:

> 'It is said by those who resist the amendment that we can rely on regulation, but we do not believe that regulation is enough. We believe that the move is a step too far and should therefore be banned.'[69]

He furthermore argued that stating that admixed embryos would be allowed to live for only 14 days was no reassuring safeguard for those concerned and that an entirely new ethical boundary was being crossed. In addition, he contended:

> 'there is no overwhelming or large-scale body of scientific evidence that suggests that such research, which crosses the ultimate boundary between animals and humans, will cure anything. That is our point.'[70]

---

66   Ibid.
67   Ibid, col 1161.
68   *Hansard*, 19 May 2008, col 22.
69   Ibid, col 23.
70   Ibid.

Thus research using human admixed embryos is tantamount to speculative research which is likely to yield little of tangible therapeutic benefit to suffering patients. He continued:

> 'The public has been misled – cruelly, in many cases –into thinking that such research could lead to early and useful cures by exaggeration, misinformation and hyberbole.'[71]

4.55   Mr Leigh emphasised that the Bill caught not just cybrids in its legislative net, but also chimeras and true hybrids, which was very alarming, saying:

> 'Contrary to what has been said, the provisions apply not only to cybrids – when the nucleus is removed from an animal egg and replaced with a human nucleus – but to the creation of chimeras, which are a mixture of animal and human cells, and true hybrids, which are created by fertilising an animal egg with human sperm or vice versa … That is truly pushing the boundaries.'

He claimed the Bill 'legalises true hybrids, which are genuinely and absolutely 50 per cent animal and 50 per cent human.' He also argued that it was not entirely true that cybrids are only 0.1 per cent animal and warned the House against being 'blind[ed] … with science' regarding the percentage mixture (human versus animal) concerning these human admixed embryos. He accepted the lack of scientific consensus one way or the other, but for that reason advocating extreme caution when proceeding. Moreover, he contended that 'the human race is special and different from the animal race, and that we should take the issue seriously for that reason.'[72]

4.56   Dr Evan Harris MP retorted that 50 per cent of a cybrid's mitochondrial DNA might come from a human and 50 per cent from an animal, but that was not inconsistent with a very small percentage overall coming from the animal, given that over 95 per cent of the DNA in such a cybrid is nuclear DNA. He said that Mr Leigh was talking only about the split of less than 5 per cent, and probably less than 1 per cent, of the mitochondrial DNA. However Mr Leigh countered that the science editor of *The Daily Telegraph* had stated that mitochondrial DNA was very important and that tiny changes in DNA could cause very serious illnesses in adults, so the point was not minor and should therefore be carefully treated. One cannot have it both ways. If it is virtually a human embryo (ie 99 per cent human), then the human admixed embryo should be accorded the same legal protection and ethical status, as a human embryo. Mr Leigh also cited Sir Liam Donaldson's evidence to the Select Committee, in arguing against the creation of admixed embryos – 'there was no clear scientific argument as to why you would want to do it' – and that there was 'a feeling that this would be a step too far as far as the public was concerned.'[73]

4.57   Addressing the argument that admixed embryos need creating because of the shortage of human eggs or embryos, he stated:

> we know that there is no such shortage because there are many left from IVF treatment … It is said that there is a shortage of eggs, but eggs are needed for

71   Ibid, col 24.
72   Ibid, col 25.
73   Ibid.

cloning only … There is enormous difficulty even in animal-animal cloning – more than 270 attempts were necessary to create Dolly the sheep – and there are enormous difficulties with therapeutic cloning. How much greater will be the difficulty in creating an animal-human clone!'[74]

4.58   Mr Leigh criticised various red herrings being used, such as the hamster test, to bolster the case that the research that is being discussed is already being done, stating:

'but the hamster test was used only to test human sperm … [for motility/ mobility] … [A] human entity was not being created. Today, we are talking about creating a new entity, so we should be very careful about what we do.'[75]

Moreover most other European countries do not engage or indulge in this ethically controversial and pointless research. Why should the United Kingdom be the odd man out? He stated:

'We should ban what 21 other countries have banned. No other country in Europe is going down this route yet. In terms of embryonic research, we will almost be like a rogue state.'

4.59   Dr Brian Iddon MP challenged Mr Leigh's use of the words 'entities, species and beings' to describe the human admixed embryos being used here, saying that the stem cells would be harvested at the blastocyst stage, so there would be 50 to 150 cells at the most. At that stage, there was no sign of development of an entity, being or species. He is really arguing this human admixed embryo is not a person/potential person and possesses therefore no rights. However this stance was not accepted by Mr Leigh who responded: 'an embryo is not a thing. It has been fertilised, and I believe that human life begins at conception.'[76]

4.60   Chris Bryant MP likened the opposition of those to creating human admixed embryos 'to those in the Churches and elsewhere who opposed vaccination.' He said:

'Those people believed that it was uncertain that vaccination would provide the benefits claimed by scientists and that it was wrong to use a vaccination developed in cows, through cowpox, to solve a human medical problem, namely smallpox. They were wrong.'[77]

Mr Bryant stated that Mr Leigh was using basically the same argument as those advanced by the opponents of vaccination over a hundred years ago and was as wrong in 2008 as they had been. However Mr Leigh refuted this comparison as being odious, saying that the creation of an entirely new part-animal, part-human entity, was different from research into smallpox, which clearly does not involve creating a new entity. He added that the very potency of embryonic stem cells meant that they could cause tumours and his concern was that voting for animal-human research was not a vote for hope, but for false hope. He said

---

74   Ibid.
75   Ibid.
76   Ibid, col 26.
77   Ibid, col 27.

'we should not take that risk. It is not good enough to say that such research will be tightly regulated', and he added:

> 'In many ways, our age is one of technology giants and ethical infants – we are like children playing with land mines, because we have no idea of the dangers posed by the technology that we are handling.'

Our scientific advances and the possible technological and therapeutic benefits that may accrue are greatly outstripping the development of a suitable ethical framework to operate in.

4.61   He moreover cautioned against putting 'all our faith' in regulation rather than in principle, and asserted:

> 'We do not have to be Christians to believe that we are all created in God's image. We can surely accept that embryos contain the genetic make-up of a complete human being and that we should not be spliced together with the animal kingdom.'[78]

A further detrimental consequence of permitting the new type of embryo was that it would perpetuate the destruction of human embryos, and he stated that 2.2 million had already been destroyed.

4.62   Finally he likened permitting the creation of human admixed embryos to the creation of Frankenstein's monster, noting that 'a monster does not have to be big and ugly; it could be a monstrous creation.' He concluded:

> 'Science should be our servant, not our master. Science should not tell us what to do on all occasions; it can tell what can be done, but should not necessarily tell us what to do.'

Scientific possibility is not the moral compass that should dictate what is ethically permissible.

4.63   By contrast, Gerald Kaufman MP argued that the provisions in the Bill do 'not have a path; all they have is a possibility', and the language used in the Bill 'admit that it is a remote possibility'. Fundamental questions about our being were raised by permitting the creation of human admixed embryos.

4.64   Mark Simmonds MP agreed that 'all, irrespective of party, want science and research to proceed if it is possible to find solutions', and this needs to take place within an ethical framework. He noted that there had in fact been advances in the new science, given that the HFEA had already granted two licences for cytoplasmic hybrid research, which entailed various hurdles. Mr Simmonds acknowledged there was a dearth of human eggs available for research and highlighted a major snag with adult stem cell research:

> '... there are significant differences between embryonic stem cells and adult stem cells, particularly given the versatility of embryonic stem cells, which can transfer themselves into almost every cell in the body, which adult stem cells currently cannot do.'[79]

---

78   Ibid, col 28.
79   Ibid, cols 30–31.

4.65   Lembit Opik MP, who was also President of the Motor Neurone Disease Association, said the association agreed strongly that stem cells derived from human admixed embryos offered a potential source of motor neurones for research and that using animal eggs 'as empty vessels' to be used to create human embryos overcame the limiting factor of the availability of donated eggs. He contended:

> 'Although there are ethical issues in using animal eggs, surely it would be unethical not to use a methodology that could save 16,000 lives a year in the UK alone.'[80]

4.66   Mr Burrowes MP noted the more than 80 treatments that have already been developed worldwide from umbilical cord blood research and was concerned about the opportunity cost imposed by the Bill. He argued also that:

> 'The cost of focussing our attention today, and resources and funding subsequently, on admixed embryo research is surely that other areas and ethical alternatives will not receive the attention and funding that they deserve.'[81]

4.67   Mr Simmonds disagreed, arguing that all possible avenues within the ethical framework that the House believed in must be permitted and followed, to maximise the opportunities to find a resolution to such awful diseases and illnesses. Keeping research options open rather than going down one route into a research cul de sac, would appear to be a much more prudent course. He noted Professor Yamanaka's research team was keen that he understood that:

> 'embryonic stem-cell research is a key part of pluripotent stem-cell research. It forms a fundamental benchmark and comparison against which they can monitor and measure the progress of induced pluripotent stem-cell research.'[82]

Definitions

4.68   Mr Simmonds MP then helpfully explained the four different types of admixed human embryos, because they are very different, and explained why true hybrids should be prohibited.

(1) The first type of embryo is the cytoplasmic hybrid, which is euphemistically called a cybrid and involves removing the nucleus from an animal egg cell and replacing it with one from a human. It is essentially a vessel to compensate for the shortage of eggs that are needed to produce embryonic stem cells. Mr Simmonds MP noted two licences for that practice had recently been granted by the HFEA. He claimed mitochondria, which are in the area around the cell nucleus, were neither animal nor human, but were autonomous, and that this aspect of the law needed to be clarified because the 1990 Act had not foreseen cybrids coming along. HFEA had granted two licences for such work to be carried out, 'jumping ahead of legislation.'

---

80   Ibid, col 31.
81   Ibid, col 32.
82   Ibid.

(2) The second category of embryo is the human transgenic embryo, for which animal DNA is put into one or more cells of a human embryo. In this type of embryo, both nuclear and mitochondrial DNA are inserted such that there will be a DNA sequence that controls the expression of the DNA already in the human sample. Mr Simmonds MP added that DNA is not intrinsically human or animal. Sections contain proteins that are identical between animals.

(3) The third category of embryo is the chimera, which involves adding animal cells to a human embryo; it has two or more cells from different organisms. A chimera could contain two different mouse cells, such as a mouse stem cell in a mouse embryo. Mr Simmonds further noted chimera are useful research tools for the observation of disease and treatments and in a chimera the human cells significantly outnumber those from animals.

(4) The final category of admixed embryo is known as the true hybrid. It combines human gametes with animal gametes, which are also egg or sperm. As noted already the so-called hamster test, lawful under the 1990 Act, permitted the creation of true hybrids, subject to the caveat and safeguard that such entities be destroyed no later than the two-cell stage. Significantly, under the new law that limit would be extended to 14 days. Mr Simmonds added that the use of ICSI significantly reduced the need for that type of assessment in clinics, which might even become largely irrelevant according to Dr Robin Lovell-Badge.

4.69 Mr Simmonds was emphatic that:

'The HFEA, many scientists and I believe that embryonic stem-cell research is necessary … It is a research requirement that the research could not be achieved by any other means than by embryonic research.'[83]

He furthermore contended that there were significant differences between true hybrids and other hybrids, and that the true hybrid was not always at the human end of the spectrum. He claimed, arguably arbitrarily, that there was an ethical difference between a cell that is 99 per cent human and one that is 50 per cent human. 'Why choose 50 per cent?' might be the obvious retort. He added that there was also a significant difference between the transfer of genes and chromosomes and the mixing of gametes, which are sex cells. This explained why he was opposed to the creation of true hybrids, but not to the creation of the three other types of human admixed embryos that he categorised.

4.70 Dr Ian Gibson MP acknowledged:

'It is … the desire of all stem cell scientists one day to take an adult stem cell and reprogramme it to be just like an embryonic stem cell – one that can, with growth factors, be turned into different types of tissues.'[84]

He referred to this lofty aim as the 'El Dorado' of stem cell research.

4.71 He re-emphasised some of the problems with reprogramming adult stem cells, apart from using retroviruses:

---

83   Ibid, cols 32, 33.
84   Ibid, 32 col 35.

'Only very few of the colony cells that are treated develop any kind of resemblance to an embryonic cell. It is something in the region of 10 out of 50,000 cells that take on some of the properties associated with embryonic cells.'

4.72   Concerning using adult cord cells, he agreed that they were very effective in certain haemopoietic diseases – blood diseases, anaemias and so on – but they were unable to turn into other cell types. He agreed that single patients could be treated with adult stem cells, but a culture of embryonic stem cells could be grown to treat lots of different patients with a particular condition. 'That is the El Dorado; that is the dream. Degenerative disease can be handled in a larger arena than the single individual.'

4.73   Regarding the charge that little progress and no therapies have been developed from embryonic stem cell research, Dr Gibson replied that stem cells were something quite new too. He said their isolation was achieved only in 1998 in Wisconsin, that stem cell research was only legalised here in 2001, and that the first research licences for this type of research were only granted by the HFEA in 2003, just five years along the line, but people were expecting major results – ridiculously optimistic and a wholly unreal expectation in his view. He noted:

'How long does it take any good company in this country or in the USA to develop a drug? It takes 20–40 years. Do we ever hear people being critical of drug companies being slow? They have many, many tests to go through, which we should be glad about.'

Again he adopted the mantra 'keep all options open' regarding the types of stem cell research that should be encouraged and supported, arguing that everything should be tried:

'There is no easy bet that one will be better than the other. We might need all different types for different types of disease.'[85]

4.74   Dr Gibson continued to flag up some of the practical difficulties relating to adult stem cells:

'It is extremely difficult to obtain adult stem cells from the human body … The longer a stem cell stays in the body, the more likely it is that an ageing effect will lead to mutations, while an embryonic cell at the start of a process does not show any of the changes in DNA that we call mutations.'[86]

He said it was untrue to say no embryonic stem cell tests were in progress, citing experiments in the United States using embryonic cells to deal with spinal cord injuries. He also noted that neuronal cells had been placed in people, where they were shown to have repaired spinal damage. Dr Gibson emphasised that any research using human admixed embryos would have to be licensed by the HFEA, and described it as 'a tight, tough regulatory agency.' He added that many new discoveries and technologies would be developed out of human DNA understanding and that, therefore:

85   Ibid, col 37.
86   Ibid, col 38.

'we need to make sure that we can take science on, and that when new science comes through that is useful, the legislation allows for that, ie future-proofing legislation.'[87]

The reason why we need to use animal cells is patently obvious he said, because 'we cannot get human eggs at this stage.'

4.75 Bill Cash MP, an opponent of legalising human admixed embryos, stated that opposition to the controversial research was, 'not just a matter of religious belief, which I certainly hold; it is also a question of practicalities.' He asked: For whom would it be made available? Who would benefit from it? Would the procedures be made universally available? He then drew comparisons with the availability of, eg, assisted reproductive procedures and claimed correctly that about 80 per cent are paid for privately. He therefore submitted that:

'Whatever the objectives of relieving pain and suffering, or improving health, it is almost impossible that the benefits of such research could be made universally available.'

He went on to reflect on the fact that life is not perfect, and said that however much we might seek to do so, we cannot, for example, extend our lives indefinitely. He also stated:

'At the heart of some of the moral questions that we must struggle with is whether we are crossing a Rubicon to try to achieve the unachievable. It is not just a question of science or ethics, but of realities, on which all the best morality is ultimately based.'[88]

4.76 Will this research, if it ever materialises into successful therapies, benefit the masses or only the select paying few? 'We must be extremely cautious', he says, 'The idea that the research would be available primarily for those who could afford it is very worrying.' But then again this accusation could be levelled at IVF, which is available in 75–80 per cent of cases only to those who can afford it. He further added that he did not want to stop all research, but rather felt that the route of embryonic cell research should be avoided while there are alternatives such as adult stem-cell research. He said:

'We need to be conscious that there is a vast amount of commercial investment in this field, and research is not done exclusively for altruistic purposes ... [and] ... If adult stem-cell research becomes viable, it should then be the only kind of research available. It is ultimately about the dignity of man.'[89]

4.77 David Drew MP, in introducing his amendments, stated he was not just opposed to genetic modification of crops and animal species but was also 'against the genetic modification of human beings.'[90] He elaborated:

'To use another cricketing metaphor, it seems that we want to hit the ball every which way, but we are not sure which strokes we are playing, and whether we can be caught out if we play the wrong stroke.'

---

87 Ibid, cols 39, 40.
88 Ibid, col 44.
89 Ibid, col 45.
90 Ibid, cols 46–47.

The argument is that the new law was fundamentally unclear and therefore flawed. Unclear law is thus, bad law.

4.78   Lembit Opik MP, however countered that should Parliament limit such research through proper regulation, there would be no problem with the 'fly-by-night opportunists', ie maverick and rogue scientists.

4.79   Dr Evan Harris MP explained that the Liberal Democrat Party's policy supported the use of cloned embryonic stem cells for research and therapeutic purposes, but that this was a free-vote issue for their MPs. He added that legalising human admixed embryo research 'is an issue of conscience but that does not mean that it is a case of science versus ethics', ie science is not ethics-free and does not and ought not to operate in an ethics- or morality-free universe. The notion too that science, in favour of creating or using the new human admixed embryos, was pitted against ethics and morality, which are opposed in a principled fashion against this new dispensation, was a completely erroneous dichotomy. He correctly observed that both sides have an ethical viewpoint, and of course not every MP, still less every individual, fits neatly into a 'side'.

Strict regulation?

4.80   Dr Harris responded to Mr Drew's assertion that the Bill was 'in a sense, a moveable feast', because the Government kept changing their mind on key issues in it, by replying he was watching the Government 'like a hawk' on these measures, and that the principles of the 1990 Act applied in this Bill. He argued that embryo research would still be heavily regulated in at least five ways:

(1) 'No embryo research could be carried out without a licence – that would be a criminal offence, so the Bill is certainly no walkover in that respect': again the centrality of the prerequisite of a licensing regime underpinning all assisted reproductive activities is emphasised here.

(2) 'No embryo could be kept beyond 14 days': applicable to human embryos and human admixed embryos alike – the principle of indivisibility.

(3) 'no research embryo could be implanted': hence no slippery slopes or *Island of Dr Moreau* monsters to be created.

(4) 'researchers would have to show that it was necessary or desirable for medical research purposes to do the embryo research': again this was a central pillar in the regulatory regime created by the 1990 Act and continued in the 2008 Act, regarding research using human admixed embryos, again signalling an ethical bright line and moral Rubicon that cannot still be crossed, and moreover was enshrined clearly in primary legislation.

(5) 'and, finally and crucially … researchers would have to demonstrate that it was necessary to use embryos and that the same research could not be obtained by techniques that did not use embryos. It is critical to recognise that.'

4.81   Dr Harris contended that the HFE Bill was not a radical departure from the principles of the 1990 Bill. He also noted that the 1990 Act permitted 'that true hybrid entities should be created, albeit only up to the two-cell stage', using the hamster test, but that, '[N]o one, however, can argue that there is a huge ethical distinction between the two-cell, eight-cell and 16-cell stages', which is what the HFE Bill would permit.

4.82   Sarah Teather MP was not convinced that the HFEA licensing system was as rigorous and strictly enforced. She observed that the HFEA has turned down only one application for a licence, and that decision was overruled on appeal. 'It is difficult to say that the process is tightly regulated.'[91] Dr Harris disagreed. He pointed out that in fact;

> 'The way in which science works is that before someone gets to the HFEA stage, they have to get funding. They must get ethical approval and they have a research proposal. That is a huge job. People's jobs depend on being able to get permission, and scientists apply to the HFEA only at an extremely late stage.'[92]

He referred to Lord Winston, and the Newcastle team and others who complained that the process for getting a research licence from the HFEA 'is too burdensome.' He added that 'A walkover it is not.' Mr Burrowes, however, disagreed, contending the 1990 Act 'did not legalise full hybrids, but via the hamster test, it legalised the testing of human sperm.'

4.83   Dr Harris rejected the argument that the UK was out on a limb internationally in supporting permitting the creation and use of human admixed embryos for research. He said: 'I want to stress that we are not the only country that permits such research ... Significant numbers of countries do so.' Furthermore the United States has no regulation in the private sector, ie it is totally unregulated. He said:

> 'The fact that we have tight regulation and, yes, burdensome regulation, means that many scientists recognise that this country has deliberated over the issue and that there is a framework ... The flipside ... of the fact that most scientists are successful is that there have been no prosecutions for research on embryos without a licence and there are plenty of people looking for opportunities to make accusations ... To the extent that no prosecutions indicate success, one can say that the process has been successful.'[93]

Scientists are acting legally and ethically in their research endeavours.

4.84   Dr Harris very powerfully and convincingly asserted:

> 'The 1990 Act, together with the 2001 cloning regulations, voted for under a free vote in the House, permitted cybrid embryo creation and research. The legal advice that the HFEA got and that the Select Committee on Science and Technology got was that the 1990 Act and the regulations permitted it. Whether it was envisaged in 1990 is a separate matter, but the Government are putting the legal advice and the HFEA policy that it is based on into statute.'[94]

Surely the fact that it is enshrined explicitly in an Act of Parliament is a good thing and should not be deprecated? Thus he contended:

---

91   Ibid, col 50.
92   Ibid.
93   Ibid.
94   Ibid, col 51.

'People who are worried about such matters should be grateful to the Government for placing them onto a statutory footing so that there is clarity and we do not rely on the random – or perhaps not so random – views of a judge or judges in the High Court or the Court of Appeal, and do not get bogged down in judicial review.'[95]

A graphic illustration of this would be the *Quintavalle* case and litigation. Parliament – an elected and accountable legislature, the 'great consult' and effectively our Bioethics Commission – really ought to be deciding these hugely important ethical/medical/legal issues, and not the unelected, unrepresentative judges.

4.85 Dr Harris stated that he shared the concern about giving false hope, re using embryonic stem-cell therapy, but submitted that he has never claimed that:

'we are considering the certain prospect of cures and treatments for millions of people with serious diseases …Scientists hope that that will happen, and there is an expectation that we will learn about at least the cause of disease and be able to test treatments in a Petri dish in a cell model, which is difficult to obtain.'[96]

Parkinson's disease cells cannot realistically or ethically be obtained from patients: 'However, if they can be grown from an embryonic stage and drugs can be tested on them, that must offer hope.'

4.86 He claimed that 'authoritative groups of people', eg the Academy of Medical Sciences, the Royal Society, the Medical Research Council, the Wellcome Trust and the medical research charities, 'which jealously guard the money that they raise and do not want to waste it on useless treatments – one finds that they all support the research.' He also crucially noted:

'The UK Parliament is not deciding whether those entities should be created but whether the HFEA should have the ability to approve a licence, if a scientific case is made to show that it is necessary or desirable for medical research, and there is no way in which to do that that does not involve embryos.'[97]

4.87 Dr Harris addressed the charge that embryonic stem cell research has yielded no beneficial therapies when compared to the many successful therapies developed from adult stem cell research by pointing out that '[A]dult stem cells have featured in clinical trials since the 1950s and it would therefore be a shock if we did not have therapies as a result.' He then proceeded to chart the relatively short history of embryonic stem cell research:

'The first human embryonic stem cell lines were derived in the UK by Stephen Minger's group at King's College in 2003. The first ES cells worldwide were created only in 1998. Since it takes 15 years to get a molecule into patients, it is not surprising that it will take some years yet to experience the clinical benefits of the research. Arguing that it has not been done in five years, so it

---

95 Ibid.
96 Ibid, col 52.
97 Ibid.

should therefore be thrown out, is preposterous and the worst argument that I have heard from opponents of the research.'[98]

4.88   He said that proposals for trials were currently being considered. There was a trial for spinal nerve repair on hold and there were also applications for treating macular degeneration using pigmented epithelium cells from an embryonic derivation.

4.89   Concerning the ethical objections, he said:

'There are those who object to the measures ethically, because they believe that life begins at conception and therefore they object to all embryo research. They are arguably absolutists, but are consistent in their ethical objections. However, some people have picked out hybrid embryos as a separate ethical issue, even though they might not oppose embryo research.'[99]

Dr Harris regarded this latter category of opposition as 'peculiar', and asked:

'Are such people arguing that hybrid embryos are too human and therefore ought to have greater protection than human embryos? ... If it is ethically acceptable to use up and destroy fully human embryos, with all the potential that they have, as has been done, how can it be right to provide hybrid embryos, which clearly have less potential, in terms of viability, with greater protection? That does not make sense.'

How can one logically give greater protection/safeguards to a human admixed embryo than to a human embryo?

4.90   Dr Harris provided reassurance that there was no prospect of any hybrid embryo being implanted or injected into anyone or anything: 'That is clear in the law.' He added:

'It is much more likely that hybrids will be used to perfect the technique, so that we do not use up precious human eggs. Only fully human embryos will be the source of stem cells and stem-cell lines that could be used for treatment.'[100]

4.91   Finally Dr Harris claimed that the scientific organisations made it clear that true hybrids are necessary for research. He also cited the Select Committee on Science and Technology and the Joint Committee on the Bill who favoured using true hybrids for research.

4.92   Dawn Primarolo MP, the Minister of State at the Department of Health, summed up why the creation and use of human admixed embryos needed to be permitted in the Bill, stating that the lack of human eggs created a significant barrier to the continuation of embryonic stem-cell research and the 'pragmatic solution' to this was using animal eggs to create human admixed embryos. She re-affirmed that the Bill does clearly define what is meant by a human admixed embryo. The aim was to ensure these new embryos are covered by the regulatory regime of the 1990 Act and the watchful scrutiny of HFEA. The use of human

98   Ibid, col 53.
99   Ibid, col 53.
100 Ibid, col 54.

admixed embryos must be necessary for the research, thus reiterating one of the basic safeguards contained in the1990 Act, before using human embryos.

4.93   Again, she detailed further legal safeguards and ethical bright lines built into the 1990 Act and consolidated and extended to embrace human admixed embryos by virtue of the 2008 Bill:

'No human admixed embryo that has been created may be implanted into a woman or an animal, or be cultured for more than 14 days or after the appearance of the primitive streak. Equally any research done using human embryos must satisfy the HFEA that it is necessary or desirable for one of the statutory purposes.'

She argued the whole point of permitting this research:

'is about giving scientists the ability within clear boundaries – which have been discussed in the House before, particularly in 1990 – within which to advance technologies that could help in the development of treatments for devastating degenerative conditions, in continuing research into male infertility and in learning more about what makes embryonic stem cells so different from any other cell.'[101]

4.94   She added that the use of animal eggs:

'will provide a valuable resource to embryo research scientists, giving them the ability to perfect the techniques that could one day help to develop our understanding of diseases and to speed up the development of their cures.'

Her argument was that it is better to perfect the techniques on human admixed embryos and animal eggs than in the much rarer human eggs and precious and valuable human embryos. Also she agreed that the Government:

'cannot promise that this research will definitely lead to those treatments; it is an aspiration that it could do so, if it is permitted, along with the rest of the research that is being carried out.'[102]

4.95   The procedure for getting human eggs is difficult, costly and not risk-free for the egg donor. Hence Ms Primarolo contended:

'Researchers have been looking for a solution to the shortage and they believe that they have found one in the form of animal eggs, which are widely available and believed to be as useful in the creation of embryos as human eggs. If successful, they could advance embryonic stem-cell research by many years.'[103]

She cited the support of, inter alia, the Academy of Medical Sciences, the Royal Society, the Wellcome Trust and the Medical Research Council, who all said that:

'true hybrids offer significant potential for research to improve our understanding of infertility, sperm function and stem-cell development and must not be prohibited.'[104]

---

101 Ibid, col 57.
102 Ibid.
103 Ibid.
104 Ibid, col 58.

4.96   On behalf of the Government, Ms Primarolo said that the hamster test would remain in the HFE Bill, and also noted that the Bill:

'prohibits the transfer of such embryos to a woman. That is underpinned by an international consensus that prohibits such practice and the Bill also reinforces the point.'[105]

She added that Government amendments Nos. 33–39 amend the definition of human admixed embryos. The Bill uses the term 'human admixed embryo' as an umbrella term for four types of embryo containing human and animal genetic material ranging from those that are – in simple terms – 99 per cent genetically human through to those that are 50 per cent genetically human. This hopefully addressed the need for clarifying definitions. A catch-all category to the definition of human admixed embryos in the Bill was also added, providing further clarity of the scope of the term, and, Ms Primarolo also stated, hopefully ensuring that all new forms of embryos that may be developed that contain both human and animal DNA will, where the animal DNA does not predominate, fall within the regulation.[106]

4.97   Mr Burrowes MP, one of the leading opponents of the creation or use of human admixed embryos, again raised the unsatisfactory nature of the definitions of what constituted human admixed embryos:

'When dealing with legislation that needs to be applied by regulations – no doubt it will be challenged in due course by lawyers and others – it is important that the House at least leave the Bill in a state of clarity and with clear definitions so that we know what we are dealing with, although that is extremely complex … The reality is that this science is a moveable feast – moving towards human and animal.'[107]

4.98   Addressing the government argument that all avenues of research, including embryonic and human admixed embryo, must be kept open, he noted that when one looked through the Bill, one could see that all avenues are not left open. 'The Government would wish us to close off various avenues in various arenas', he said – and one such avenue closed off in the Bill concerned sex selection. He was clear that the House had the duty of building an ethical framework that could properly lead to good science. Moreover it was important that the framework:

'[is] sound, lasts for a considerable time and deals with future developments, but is based solidly on ethics and a firm belief in and respect for human life and the dignity of human life, which the House needs to send out and establish clearly in the Bill … There is perhaps no greater duty on the House than ensuring that we are clear about that. It cannot be left to chance. It cannot be left to whim.'[108]

It was, therefore, incumbent that the HFE Bill 'has not only clarity of definition, but clarity of ethics.'

105 Ibid.
106 Ibid, col 59.
107 Ibid, cols 59–60.
108 Ibid, cols 60–61.

4.99   Again Mr Burrowes, like many of the other opponents of embryonic stem cell and human admixed embryo research, extolled the virtues and advantages of adult and cord blood stem cell research, stating that the latter had led:

> 'and are leading us beyond the normal route of blood immune deficiency to the regeneration of nerves, bone, cartilage, tendon, vessel tissue and beyond. That is an exciting area, but sadly this country is lagging way behind in the league table for collecting cord blood.'[109]

4.100   He then considered the clinical trials throughout the world in the context of stem cell research and noted:

> 'There are 1,987 [trials] in relation to adult stem-cell research and 106 on cord blood. There are none on embryonic stem-cell research. That is a significant context, but it should not necessarily be given undue weight when one is considering the context of the Bill.'[110]

4.101   He argued that the human admixed embryo provisions seek to take us to a new level of the human embryo stem-cell project (a level to which many object), and that the high expectations for embryo stem-cell research should perhaps be dampened down. He observed:

> 'We should take note and be cautious in relation to the fact that embryo stem-cell lines do not work in mature tissues ... Embryo stem-cell lines develop tissues. There are fundamental engineering problems. Once embryo stem-cell lines are differentiated, the concern is that what is involved will stop being a stem cell and lose its "stemness". It has difficulty turning into a tissue type.'

4.102   Mr Burrowes then raised a number of concerns about the cloning processes involved in stem cell research:

> 'The concern, though, is that we do not simply deal with the problems of embryo stem-cell research; the issue is human hybrid embryos and whether there are alternatives ... In the development of embryo stem-cell research, one has to focus on cloned human embryos. Those are particularly difficult to create. They are very inefficient and defective. There is difficulty that leads to abnormality ... When one looks at the research, one sees that there are problems. The problems develop when dealing with the structure of cloned human animal embryos.'[111]

He said:

> 'The concern [in the creation or use of human admixed embryos or animal eggs] goes beyond risk of infection, immune logical reactions and the tumours that develop. The development of cloned human animal embryos represents taking another leap ... That is the focus of the Bill, which will establish that we must move into the area of cytoplasmic hybrids. Taking the scientist's view, one struggles to see how one could get to the point of curing diseases, which is what we all want.'

109 Allegedly 13th.
110 Ibid, col 61.
111 Ibid.

4.103 Mr Burrowes rained on the government parade which highlighted the many future benefits of the new research, saying:

> 'if one goes back a stage to cloned human embryos the reality [rather than the hype] is that they cannot properly be used for therapies for genetic diseases. The genetic flaw would remain in the tissue, as the genes would come from a person with a disease.'[112]

He then turned his fire on human admixed embryos research, saying:

> 'it would be even worse, as they would contain the genetic flaws and the additional genetic and epigenetic flaws because of the way they are created … The human genome would have been reprogrammed with reprogramming factors from the animal egg, and there would be a degree of mismatch between relevant human and animal material. There would also be the risk of the creation of new diseases … there may be the risk of immune rejection, as mitochondria have proteins that can cause an immune reaction. Some animal mitochondrial proteins would be present in the cells, and they might cause an even stronger immune reaction than human mitochondria.'[113]

4.104 He concluded that:

> 'The concern is that, looking back, embryonic stem cells have caused dangerous tumours … it is far too dangerous medically to attempt to use embryo stem-cell lines for therapies. Looking to take that a stage further in terms of human animal cloned embryos, it would be even less safe to use them for therapies.'[114]

He said that the Government claimed and sought to be a world leader but that there had been rapid progress in other areas of alternative stem cell research, not least in the area of induced pluripotent cells, and claimed that Professor Ian Wilmut, the creator of Dolly the sheep, had stated that 'reprogrammed adult cells – induced pluripotent stem cells – showed much more potential' than cybrid research.

4.105 Mr Burrowes urged the House:

> '[to] support the research that has already taken those steps and clearly has great potential, rather than supporting an area of research that is not only very speculative but ethically challenging.'[115]

He said that when exploring all avenues ethical considerations must be respected, and that the new permissive clauses on human admixed embryos, 'transcend people's concerns about proper respect for the dignity of human life. It is not a case of all avenues being equal.' He said that the government was leading everyone into areas that other countries do not even consider and that human admixed embryonic research and using animal eggs is a 'false dawn.'

4.106 Mr Bercow countered by saying this was a 'monopolist' approach, ie 'excluding lines of enquiry that others think it prudent and sensible to pursue.'[116]

---

112 Ibid, cols 61, 62.
113 Ibid, col 62.
114 Ibid.
115 Ibid, col 63.
116 Ibid.

Mr Burrowes responded by stating that as a Conservative who does not favour monopolies, he subscribes to the Conservative principle of payment by results. In this country more than 80 therapeutic treatments had been made possible by adult stem-cell research, and there had been more than 350 clinical trials. He also emphasised again the gravity of the important principle of the dignity of human life, and pointed out that the lack of a water-tight definition of human admixed embryo was 'a fundamental ethical concern that takes us beyond the realms of results.'

4.107 Mr Bercow, like Dr Harris, countered the accusations about the comparative lack of success of embryonic stem cell research compared to adult or cord blood stem cell research saying that this was not comparing like with like:

'[T]his is a case of comparing something that has been possible for only five years with something that has been possible for half a century ... That is an absurd comparison [Critics] ought to give the opportunity for admixed embryo research a decent span before rushing into judgment against it.'

4.108 Mr Burrowes countered that in recent years progress had been made by leaps and bounds in induced pluripotent stem-cell research, and that MPs should be very cautious about adopting a route that was 'ethically problematic':

'[MPs] are charged with the duty of ensuring that there is a proper ethical framework, and we should be extremely cautious about taking this route unless its therapeutic value is clear. Why should we not invest properly in areas that are producing the results that we all want?'

He argued further that there was no real evidence that embryonic stem-cell research, particularly involving admixed embryos, was likely in the foreseeable future to produce treatments. He concluded that, 'We should respect the dignity of human life by prohibiting human admixed embryos.'

4.109 Gordon Marsden MP very wisely said that in this debate, like other scientific debates, 'no one in the scientific and medical communities has the tablets from Sinai any more than does anyone else.' He said that in reaching decisions on the proposals on human admixed embryos, MPs 'have to use our judgment. It is not our job in this House to canonise scientists, any more than it is our job to canonise cardinals.' He added that scientists are not 'different from the rest of us' and 'there are no tablets from Sinai in science.'[117] He said:

'sadly, clinical hybrid animal trials conducted at cell stage do not always produce the results in humans that the trials show – they do not even produce these results in different groups of human beings. Therefore, it is unreasonable to hold the view that hybrid research will automatically open up matters in the way that has been suggested.'

4.110 Sir Patrick Cormack MP overtly and unapologetically adopted an absolutist line saying: 'I think there are cases where one has to face up to the fundamental question of whether the ends[118] justify the means.'[119] He said that, 'we all wish to see cures, [but] we must also accept the mortality of man. We

---

117 Ibid, col 65.
118 Presumably a raft of promised cures for terrible diseases.
119 Presumably creating and using human admixed embryos for research and using animal eggs.

have to accept that there are certain things that man should not seek to do.' He adopted a deontological approach, rather than looking at the consequences of an act to assess its morality. He said, 'The mixture of embryos – the creation of something that is part animal and part human – is a line beyond which I am not prepared to go.'[120]

4.111 Fiona MacTaggart MP said:

'Asking women to go through the process of hyperstimulation of their ovaries to make eggs for other people's research is frankly a step too far, yet we know that it is possible, through embryonic research, to create a model of some of these terrible diseases in a dish. That is what this Bill offers; it does not offer hybrid, would-be people: it offers the possibility of creating cell lines that contain these terrible, debilitating diseases.'

She concluded that MPs 'have an opportunity tonight to make a real difference, perhaps not in the short term, but in the future, on chronic diseases, particularly on these devastating neurological diseases'. This was an opportunity the House must grasp.

4.112 Mr Leigh MP concluded that the clauses in the Bill supporting human admixed embryo research and use of animal eggs must be opposed because 'it crosses an ethical line in mixing animal and human embryos.'

4.113 MP's voted by 336 to 176 in favour of legalising the creation and use of human admixed embryos, a majority of 160. Amendment No 10 (laid down by Mark Simmonds MP) and Amendment No 33 (Mr David Drew MP) were defeated quite narrowly, (286–223) – a majority of 53 only. Finally Mr Drew MP's Amendment No 44 was defeated 314–181. The elected chamber thus give a clear if not ringing endorsement of creating or using human admixed embryos and animal eggs for research purposes.

CONCLUSIONS

4.114 The advent of the creation and use of human admixed embryos for research purposes permitted under the 2008 Act signalled for some a huge incursion over the ethical and moral Rubicon. However given that human sperm could lawfully be mixed with hamster eggs since the enactment of the 1990 Act, albeit only to test the mobility and motility of human sperm and subject to anything created being destroyed no later than the two-cell stage, research using human admixed embryos could arguably be legitimately described as a logical, incremental extension or development of sperm testing. It could be contended that it was a necessary consequence of the acute shortage of human eggs and an imperative step to harness the great potential of embryonic stem cell research generally. Also, the rigorous safeguards built into the 2008 Act would guarantee that there was no ethical or legal free-for-all for would-be maverick scientists to act as latter-day Frankensteins spurred on by Promethean hubris, to the obvious detriment of society.

---

120 Ibid, col 65.

Part 2

Saviour Siblings – Commodifying Life?

CHAPTER 5

Saviour Siblings

DEFINING 'SAVIOUR SIBLINGS'

5.1   There is no specific definition of what a 'saviour sibling' is in the original legislation governing assisted reproduction, the Human Fertilisation and Embryology Act 1990 (the 1990 Act), nor in the later amended legislation, the Human Fertilisation and Embryology Act 2008 (the 2008 Act). The term 'saviour sibling' arguably has religious undertones, as a child sent into the world by God, to save not mankind, as in the case of Christ, but another already existing sick child. Such a child is selected by doctors or scientists and parents because they are a tissue match with an existing sick child, and free from the serious illness afflicting that child; umbilical cord blood, bone marrow or other tissue is used to save or improve the quality of life of that existing sick child.

5.2   Thus, whilst the purpose for creating and sending a saviour sibling into the world may not be quite as far-reaching as that contained in the Bible, nevertheless, for the individual sick child and their devoted and loving parents, the creation and use of a saviour sibling is a lifeline, thrown out to save the sick child and/or spare it from pain. The creation of the saviour sibling is clearly beneficial for that sibling, as it has been given the gift of, hopefully, a long, healthy and happy life. 'Hopefully', as there are no guarantees or certainties in life (apart from death and taxation, as Benjamin Franklin famously once said). However, leading obstetricians, gynaecologists and consultants in human reproductive medicine at the top assisted reproductive clinics in the country never guarantee that they can create a live, perfectly healthy baby. They would be very foolish to do so considering all the factors militating against a successful live, healthy birth, disregarding the pitfalls of then being able to harvest tissue from the saviour sibling to successfully treat the sick child.

THE SCIENCE OF CREATING SAVIOUR SIBLINGS

5.3   Several scientific processes have to be undergone before a saviour sibling can donate stem cells from cord blood, bone marrow or other tissue to be used to save the life of an existing sick sibling or to improve the quality of their life. These include:

- in vitro fertilisation (IVF);
- pre-implantation genetic diagnosis (PGD);
- human leucocyte antigen (HLA) tissue typing; and
- implantation (part of IVF).

Then there is a nine-month pregnancy, hopefully similar to a 'normal' or 'natural' pregnancy, birth, and finally a live, healthy baby born, who subsequently will have stem cells from their umbilical cord, bone marrow or other tissue transplanted successfully into the sick existing child.

In vitro fertilisation

5.4　In vitro fertilisation (IVF) is of course not a new technology. The first IVF, or 'test tube', baby Louise Brown, was born in the United Kingdom in 1978, over 33 years ago. In fact, she was the first IVF baby born in the world. IVF is now arguably a routine and conventionally accepted treatment for tackling infertility. A small minority of individuals and organisations would still oppose it, but the vast majority of the public and medicine and indeed the great bulk of our legislature would support its availability and use in treatment.

5.5　IVF involves a woman being given superovulatory drugs to increase the number of eggs her ovaries produce. Instead of her ovaries producing one egg (the female gamete), they produce many eggs, which are harvested (retrieved) by laparoscopy. There are risks associated with both the woman's ovaries being over-stimulated to produce extra eggs, and with the invasive procedure of laparoscopy. With the former, there is the risk of the condition ovarian hyper stimulation syndrome (OHSS), variously assessed at between 1 per cent and 2 per cent, which can be painful and damage the woman's ovaries in some cases. With the laparoscopy procedure, which necessitates the woman being anaesthetised and a laparoscopy tube being inserted into her ovaries to harvest the eggs, there could be (albeit it mercifully in very rare instances) the risk of death. A number of women have died when the laparoscopy tube or pipette was inserted by mistake into an artery, rather than the ovary.

5.6　The procedure will harvest 12–15 eggs (possibly more), which are then mixed with her husband/partner's sperm (male gametes) in a petri dish. The term 'in vitro' fertilisation literally means fertilisation in glass (the glass petri dish), as opposed to 'normal' or 'conventional' fertilisation occurring 'in vivo' (ie in the womb of the woman). This is the genesis of the popular term 'test-tube babies'.

5.7　Clinics will need to inform the woman of the nature of this procedure, ie what is involved (including the risks associated with the process), under the terms of s 13(6) of the 1990 Act, and the Code of Practice.[1] This is in essence the informed consent requirement enshrined in the legislation. If the woman (and her husband/partner) desperately wants a saviour sibling to save the life or health of a sick existing child, and the woman gives a fully informed consent to the IVF procedure, thus exercising her autonomy, that is her decision and choice.

5.8　When the woman's eggs are mixed with her husband/partner's sperm in the petri dish, hopefully all the eggs will be fertilised with her husband/partner's sperm, although of course some may not be. Once fertilisation occurs successfully an embryo is created (an 'embryo' being the name given to the fertilised egg, or new human entity). The embryo then starts to divide and grow. At the eight-cell stage of the embryo, normally three days after fertilisation, ie when the embryo is made up of 6–8 cells, PGD can take place.

1　8th edition (2009).

Pre-implantation Genetic Diagnosis (PGD)

5.9 Pre-implantation genetic diagnosis (PGD) was developed in 1989 by Professor Robert Winston and Dr Alan Handyside. In explaining what is involved in PGD, Mr Justice Maurice Kay in the *Quintavalle* case stated regarding pre-implantation genetic diagnosis or PGD that;

'This technique involves three stages: (1) an *in vitro* embryo is permitted to develop to the 6–8 cell stage which occurs three days after fertilisation; (2) one or two cells are removed from it by the process of embryo biopsy; (3) genetic material from the extracted cells is then taken and analysed.'[2]

Basically then when the extracted cells are examined by scientists, the examination determines if the genetic material from those extracted cells reveals the presence of certain types of genetic diseases, eg beta thalassaemia or cystic fibrosis, which will be present in that embryo if it is implanted, so thus that diseased embryo is not implanted in the woman and is discarded (allowed to perish). The process of PGD is undertaken on all the created embryos. Of the original, eg, 15–16 embryos created, there may be only 1–2 disease-free ones that are also a tissue match for an existing sick sibling. These will then be implanted in the woman, and hopefully she will then get pregnant, and have a disease-free, tissue compatible (with the sick existing child) baby, born nine months later. That is the hope and theory at any rate.

Human Leucotype Antigen (HLA) typing, ie 'Tissue Typing'

5.10 Human leucotype antigen typing (HLA), commonly or popularly referred to as 'tissue typing' testing, can be carried out at the same time as PGD. The idea is that the HLA tissue typing testing reveals if the embryo is a tissue match to the sick existing child who needs the transplant. As Lord Phillips of Worth Matravers MR stated: 'Because this process involves examination of proteins known as human leucocyte antigens (HLA), this form of PGD is described as HLA typing.'[3] As Maurice Kay J stated in the High Court:

'It [tissue typing] is a technique which enables an embryologist to ascertain whether an embryo will produce a child whose tissue will match that of an existing child'[4]

If the embryo is such a tissue compatible match, and is also disease-free of the condition suffered by the existing child, then the embryo ('saviour sibling' embryo) can be implanted in the woman, and result then in a pregnancy, birth and use of that saviour sibling for the benefit of its sick existing sibling.

'Normal' pregnancy?

5.11 One or two embryos will, as stated above, be implanted in the woman, she will become pregnant and, hopefully, give birth nine months later to a

---

2   *R (on the application of Quintavalle) v Human Fertilisation and Embryology Authority* [2002] EWHC 3000 (Admin) at para 1.
3   *R (on the application of Quintavalle) v Human Fertilisation and Embryology Authority* [2003] EWCA Civ 667 at para 4.
4   *R (on the application of Quintavalle) v Human Fertilisation and Embryology Authority* [2002] EWHC 3000 (Admin) at para 1.

healthy, disease-free baby that is tissue-compatible (compatible, that is, with the existing sick, older, sibling). This follows the pattern of a 'normal' conventional pregnancy (including an IVF created pregnancy), although many would argue that the selection and creation of such a saviour sibling embryo is anything but normal and is highly controversial and ethically wrong.

SUBSEQUENT 'USE' OF THE SAVIOUR SIBLING

5.12 When the saviour sibling is born the doctors will retrieve, keep and extract stem cells from the umbilical cord of the saviour sibling. The umbilical cord is discarded in the vast majority of pregnancies (98 per cent or more), which is a huge waste of a potentially invaluable medical tool kit, so this utilisation of a resource that is just discarded or disposed of in most instances is to be commended. Alternatively the saviour sibling may have bone marrow extracted from them at some point in the near future, again to either save the life of the saviour sibling or lessen their suffering or improve their quality of life. The third potential 'use' of the saviour sibling, probably the most controversial ethically, and the most harmful and invasive of the bodily integrity of the saviour sibling, is the use of 'other tissue', ie the harvesting and use of part organs, regenerative tissue or other tissue, for the benefit of the saviour sibling.

LEGAL BACKGROUND

5.13 Section 5(1) of the Human Fertilisation and Embryology Act 1990 (the 1990 Act) created and established the Human Fertilisation and Embryology Authority (the HFEA). The general functions of the HFEA, which are quite wide and extensive, were set out in s 8 of the 1990 Act:

'(1) The Authority shall—
- (a) keep under review information about embryos and any subsequent development of embryos and about the provision of treatment services and activities governed by this Act, and advise the Secretary of State, if he asks it to do so, about those matters,
- (b) publicise the services provided to the public by the Authority or provided in pursuance of licences,
- (c) provide, to such extent as it considers appropriate, advice and information for persons to whom licences apply or who are receiving treatment services or providing gametes or embryos for use for the purposes of activities governed by this Act, or may wish to do so, and
- (d) perform such other functions as may be specified in regulations.'

5.14 Fundamentally, though, despite the scope of the above functions, the HFEA is tasked essentially with granting licences to clinics. As s 9(1) of the 1990 Act provides:

'The Authority shall maintain one or more committees to discharge the Authority's functions relating to the grant, variation, suspension and revocation of licences, and a committee discharging those functions is referred to in this Act as a 'licence committee'.'

Hence the HFEA is a body whose primary function and role is to grant licences to clinics, to police the licensed clinics and ensure that they comply with the legal and regulatory regime contained in the 1990 Act and in the 2008 Act, and in the Code of Practice.

5.15   The HFEA grants three types of licences to clinics: treatment, storage and research licences, as outlined by s 11 of the 1990 Act. A clinic must possess a licence issued by the HFEA before it can, eg, treat patients using IVF, ICSI or DI, store and freeze embryos or gametes, or undertake research on embryos (or, since 1 October 2009, hybrid embryos). To offer various assisted reproductive treatments, store embryos or experiment on embryos without a licence is a serious criminal offence. Section 3(1) provides that;

'(1) No person shall—
(a)   bring about the creation of an embryo, or
(b)   keep or use an embryo,
except in pursuance of a licence.'

Section 41(2) of the 1990 Act then proceeds to provide that:

'(2) A person who—
(a)   contravenes section 3(1) of this Act …,
[…]
is guilty of an offence.'

Under s 41(4) of the 1990 Act:

'(4) A person guilty of an offence under subsection (2) […] above is liable—
(a)   on conviction on indictment, to imprisonment for a term not exceeding two years or a fine or both, and
(b)   on summary conviction, to imprisonment for a term not exceeding six months or a fine not exceeding the statutory maximum or both.'

5.16   Thus, experimenting on, storing or using embryos without a valid licence from the HFEA is a serious criminal offence, with arguably draconian penalties for violation. The embryo may not be regarded as a person or as potential person, nor possess rights under the regulatory regime, but it can only be kept, used, stored or experimented on if the clinic seeking to do any of these activities has a licence from the statutory regulatory authority and licensing body, namely the HFEA. The seriousness and gravity with which Parliament treats this important safeguard or overarching principle is evident in the involvement of the Director of Public Prosecutions (DPP), under s 42 of the 1990 Act. The DPP must either institute himself, or alternatively give his consent to, any prosecution for any of the criminal offences created by either the 1990 Act or its 2008 equivalent. Thus s 42, inter alia, provides:

'No proceedings for an offence under this Act shall be instituted—
(a)   in England and Wales, except by or with the consent of the Director of Public Prosecutions,
(b)   […].'

5.17   Under s 11(1) of the 1990 Act, the HFEA is empowered to grant treatment, storage and research licences, and may not grant any other licences. Treatment licences under s 11(1)(a) under para 1 of Sch 2 to the Act are licences authorising activities in the course of providing treatment services. One of the central issues in the *Quintavalle* litigation was whether the HFEA had the power or discretion to authorise the creation of saviour siblings using PGD in conjunction with HLA tissue typing.[5]

5.18 'Treatment services' as referred to in s 11(1)(a) of the 1990 Act were defined in s 2(1) as meaning:

'medical, surgical or obstetric services provided to the public or a section of the public for the purpose of assisting women to carry children.'

Paragraph 1 of Sch 2 of the 1990 Act provided in turn, inter alia, that:

'(1) A licence under this paragraph may authorise any of the following in the course of providing treatment services—
- (a) bringing about the creation of embryos *in vitro*
- (b) keeping embryos
- (c) using gametes,
- (d) practices designed to secure that embryos are in a suitable condition to be placed in a woman or to determine whether embryos are suitable for that purpose,[6]
- (e) placing any embryo in a woman,'

5.19 Paragraph 2(2) of Sch 2 also provides that:

'Subject to the provisions of this Act, a licence under this paragraph may be granted subject to such conditions as may be specified in the licence and may authorise the performance of any of the activities referred to in sub-paragraph (1) above in such manner as may be specified.'

This paragraph essentially allows the HFEA licensing committees to impose additional conditions (safeguards) on treatment licences, permitting eg the creation of saviour siblings. Furthermore, under para 2(3) of Sch 2, it is provided that:

'A licence under this paragraph cannot authorise any activity unless it appears to the Authority to be necessary or desirable for the purpose of providing treatment services.'

This sub-paragraph is almost identical to the wording in Sch 3 concerning the use of embryos for one of the permitted research purposes, namely that the activity is necessary or desirable, and not just merely convenient or handy for the doctors, scientists or clinic, etc for the purpose of providing treatment.

5.20 On 13 December 2001, the HFEA issued a press release entitled, 'HFEA to allow tissue typing in conjunction with pre-implantation genetic diagnosis'. This press release described the PGD process and referred to tissue typing as 'an additional step whereby the embryo is simultaneously tested for its tissue compatibility with an affected sibling.' The HFEA press release then proceeded to state:

'Before this technique can be used in treatment, approval will be required from an HFEA Licence Committee which will consider applications on

---

5   See below.
6   Again what exactly was meant by the term the embryo being 'in a suitable condition' prompted much discussion and disagreement in the *Quintavalle* litigation.

a case-by-case basis. If licences are issued, these will be subject to strict conditions.'

This was the background against which the *Quintavalle* litigation emerged and developed.

'CORE' OBJECTIONS: THE *QUINTAVALLE* LITIGATION

5.21   When the HFEA issued their press release of 13 December 2001 (above), the HFEA had an application for a treatment licence from a clinic to perform PGD screening for beta thalassaemia and tissue typing in relation to the Hashmi family. On 22 February 2002 the Licensing Committee of the HFEA granted the clinic a licence to, inter alia, perform PGD pre-implantation genetic screening for aneuploidy, subject to many conditions, including one forbidding the use of information derived from tests on an embryo or any material removed from it to select embryos of a particular sex 'for social reasons'.

5.22   Mrs Josephine Quintavalle then sought an application for judicial review of the decision of the HFEA to grant a treatment licence on 22 February 2002 to the clinic to undertake PGD and HLA tissue typing for the Hashmi family. In the words of Maurice Kay J:

'In a nutshell, the case for CORE is that (1) tissue typing is prohibited by section 3(1)(b) as it involves the use of an embryo but (2) it cannot be licensed under Schedule 2 because it cannot be said to arise in the course of providing "treatment services" or to be necessary or desirable for the purpose of providing "treatment services". This is said to flow from the definition of "treatment services" as services "for the purpose of assisting women to carry children" and the fact that the purpose of tissue typing is not to assist a woman to carry a child but to relieve the suffering of another child.'[7]

In other words Mrs Quintavalle and CORE (Comment on Reproductive Ethics) were arguing that the term 'treatment services' be given a narrow and restricted interpretation and should be read literally. The fact that tissue typing would not literally assist Mrs Hashmi to carry a child, but rather was primarily only being used for the hopeful benefit of an existing child (Zain Hashmi), meant they contended that the procedure (HLA tissue typing) could not therefore be licensed by the statutory regulator and granter of licences, namely the HFEA. However, in marked contrast, Maurice Kay J stated:

'the primary submission on behalf of the HFEA is that tissue typing does not in itself require a licence because it is performed not on an embryo but on cells extracted from an embryo.'[8]

The implicit argument is that the embryo is the remaining six cells, not the 1–2 cells that have been extracted and analysed in biopsy, using PGD and then HLA tissue typing. That said, the HFEA argued that tissue typing could be regulated by the imposition of conditions on a licence permitting PGD. Indeed:

'In Supplementary Grounds of Opposition dated 31 July 2002 it was suggested that suitable conditions to be imposed on a licence might include

---

7   *R (on the application of Quintavalle) v Human Fertilisation and Embryology Authority* [2002] EWHC 3000 (Admin) at para 6.
8   Ibid.

(a) that no material recovered from an embryo may be subjected to a test which supplies genetic information about the embryo that is not listed in an annex to the licence or specifically approved by a licence committee in any particular case; and (b) that no embryo may be transferred to a woman where any material removed from it has been subject to a test which supplies genetic information about the embryo that is not listed in an annex or approved by a licence committee in any particular case.'[9]

In fact, these very conditions were among those imposed in the licence which was granted on 22 February 2002.

QUINTAVALLE: HIGH COURT

Roles

5.23   At first instance interestingly (and, for some, worryingly, and arguably not completely accurately), Maurice Kay J stated that it was 'common ground' that the task of the court in deciding even an ethically and morally controversial case of this nature was 'legal rather than ethical', and furthermore was 'one of statutory interpretation', an exercise that judges feel a lot more comfortable in dealing with than grappling with thorny and intractable ethical decisions. They are trained in law after all, not ethics or moral philosophy. This appears to be an articulation and defence of the traditional and arguably conservative approach of the judges merely declaring what the law is, ie construing Acts of Parliament and sections in them narrowly and literally. Judges are tasked thus with locating, stating and applying laws, and most definitely cannot make laws, nor give sections in Acts strained interpretations to fill in gaps in the law, particularly as here to cover technological advances (tissue typing) that were not possible in the 1990 Act technological world.

5.24   Significantly Maurice Kay J refers to the response of the House of Commons Select Committee on Science and Technology Report[10] in response to the Chairman of the HFEA (Dame Ruth Deech, as she then was), who had stated it was desirable that the HFEA take decisions about permitting tissue typing because 'this protects Members of Parliament from direct involvement in that sort of thing'. The Committee replied that:

'Parliament does not need protecting and democracy is not served by unelected quangos taking decisions on behalf of Parliament.'[11]

Parliament is quite capable and adept at making decisions on these scientific developments that raise huge ethical and moral issues (as the calibre of debate in both Houses amply demonstrated), and moreover it is a responsibility it does not want to shirk.

Interpretation

5.25   In many ways this is a harbinger of Maurice Kay J's ultimate decision in the High Court, namely to give the words in Parliament's statute a restricted,

9   Ibid.
10   Published on 18 July 2002.
11   At para 26 of the Report.

narrow, literal interpretation and confine their meaning within sensible and safe limits, rather than be creative and give a bolder, more purposive and broader construction which would facilitate tissue typing falling within the net or aegis of treatments for which the HFEA has the power to issue treatment licences.

5.26   Maurice Kay J referred specifically to the Court of Appeal decision of *R (Quintavalle) v Secretary of State for Health*[12] for support, saying 'I respectfully agree with it.' and adding that:

'I take the view that, in relation to an area such as this, the purpose of the legislation must play a very important part in its interpretation if that interpretation is open to doubt.'[13]

Again this is in keeping with the traditional approach of judges to statutory intention (ie what do the words of the statute mean and how should they be applied), that the judges need to ascertain the Parliamentary intent behind the words. Thus judges need to tread warily and cautiously before deciding to depart from this safe, traditional approach to construing statutes.

5.27   In *Quintavalle*,[14] the primary issue was whether an organism created by cell nuclear replacement (the technique used to create Dolly the sheep) came within the definition of an embryo in s 1(1) of the 1990 Act.[15] The argument of Bruno Quintavalle and CORE was that cell nuclear replacement, ie where an adult nuclear cell was placed in an enucleated egg and fused, resulting in an embryo, did not involve fertilisation and was therefore outside the regulatory regime of the 1990 Act. However, this argument was ultimately rejected by the Court of Appeal. As Maurice Kay J stated: 'The Court of Appeal, on the basis of a purposive construction, held that it did.' Essentially the court held that the purpose of the legislation (the Parliamentary intent) was, inter alia, aimed at regulating strictly human embryos, created outside the body, and using them for treatment, storage or research. The product, namely the embryo, was the critical consideration, not the process or manner (here created by cell nuclear replacement (CNR)) of its creation. Hence embryos created by CNR (the 'Dolly the sheep method' of creation), whilst they may not have been created by fertilisation, as it was strictly or usually understood, were nevertheless embryos and covered and included by the 1990 Act.

5.28   Lord Phillips of Matravers MR, in the Court of Appeal, described the policy of the 1990 Act thus:

'The Act brings the creation and use of embryos within a regulatory regime which very severely restricts the right to indulge in those activities. The reasons for legislating to impose those restrictions are not in doubt. They are essentially ethical.'[16]

Moreover, it was essential to do so in order to give effect to the intention of Parliament – the purpose of statutory interpretation.

---

12   [2002] EWCA Civ 29.
13   [2002] EWHC 3000 (Admin) at para 9.
14   [2002] EWCA Civ 29.
15   Section 1(1) of the 1990 Act provides that except where otherwise stated, 'embryo means a live human embryo where fertilisation is complete'.
16   [2002] EWCA Civ 29 at para 36.

Key questions

5.29 Maurice Kay J is, therefore, absolutely clear what the central issue in the case is:

'The issue is whether the Human Fertilisation and Embryology (HFEA) has the power to permit tissue-typing in conjunction with pre-implantation genetic diagnosis or PGD.'[17]

He added that while no one doubted that saviour sibling technology was capable of helping existing very sick children, it nevertheless raised serious ethical issues. He then adopted the two headings used by the HFEA in their skeleton argument to pose two questions: first, was tissue-typing governed by the 1990 Act; and secondly, could tissue typing be authorised under the 1990 Act.

(1) Is tissue typing governed by the Act?

5.30 Maurice Kay J stated: 'The first question is whether tissue typing involves the "use" of "an embryo" within the meaning of section 3(1)(b) [of the 1990 Act].'[18] In addressing that question he noted that the HFEA accepted that embryonic biopsy involved the use of an embryo, but that carrying out further tests on them did not. The six cells are the embryo, and the 1–2 cells are merely the extract to be biopsied. However, he rejected this contention, stating:

'First, tissue typing involves the testing of an embryonic cell, a term … consonant with the language of the HFEA press release: … "an additional step whereby the embryo is simultaneously tested for its tissue compatibility with an affected sibling." Secondly, section 3 is headed "Prohibitions in connection with embryos". The words "in connection with" militate against a narrow construction. Thirdly, it is common ground that tissue typing has a potential for misuse.[19] That is why the HFEA would only countenance it—in the words of its Chief Executive—"in very rare circumstances and under strict controls." Although the HFEA is entrusted by the Act with the making of many difficult decisions, it acts within ground rules set by the Act. I find it inconceivable that an Act which goes to great lengths to provide for the statutory control of the persons by whom and the places at which controversial activities are carried out and subject to inspection, was intended by Parliament to leave an activity such as tissue typing outside the direct control of the Act. It cannot have been the intention of Parliament to draw a line between the extraction of embryonic cells, which in itself gives rise to no real ethical problem, and the subsequent genetic testing of them, which has the potential for misuse. The distinction is artificial, unattractive and unnecessary, having regard to the policy of the Act as explained by the Master of the Rolls.'[20]

Finally, Maurice Kay J stated:

'Fourthly, when one considers the structure of the Act as a whole, it is plain to see that, to the extent that it addressed the testing of embryonic material, it

---

17 [2002] EWHC 3000 (Admin) at para 1.
18 Ibid, para 11.
19 True, but hardly a convincing basis or reason for preventing it!.
20 [2002] EWHC 3000 (Admin) at para 12.

did so within the context of the licensing system. Schedule 2, paragraph 1(1) provides that a licence may authorise:

> "any of the following in the course of providing treatment services ...
>
> (d) practices designed to secure that embryos are in a suitable condition to be placed in a woman or to determine whether embryos are suitable for that purpose."

That is a licence in relation to the "use" of an embryo within the meaning of section 3(1)(b). The fact that the licences enabled by Schedule 2, paragraph 1(1), are limited to those there specified or "such other practices as may be specified in, or determined in accordance with, regulations" (paragraph 1(1) (g)) suggests that anything not specified in paragraph 1(1) is unlawful unless its licensing is permitted by some future regulation.'[21]

Thus he concludes at para 14: 'For all these reasons I am satisfied that tissue typing falls within the prohibition of section 3.'

(2)   Can tissue typing be authorised under the Act?

5.31   The second question then arises: can tissue typing be authorised under the 1990 Act? The HFEA submitted that if tissue typing was an activity governed by the 1990 Act, it could lawfully be authorised by the HFEA by a licence. By contrast (not surprisingly), Mrs Quintavalle and CORE argued that tissue typing cannot be authorised by way of a licence, contending, inter alia, firstly that the 1990 Act provides an exhaustive list of activities which may be authorised by a licence. Secondly, a licence under Sch 2, para 1, cannot authorise any activity 'unless it appears to the Authority to be necessary or desirable for the purpose of providing treatment services'.[22] Thirdly, 'treatment services' are services provided 'for the purpose of assisting women to carry children'.[23] Fourthly, and of considerable importance, the purpose of tissue typing is not to assist women to carry children but rather instead to ensure that a child born to the particular woman will have tissue compatibility with an affected sibling.

5.32   Maurice Kay J is clear that there could be no doubt that the Act provided an exhaustive list of activities which may be licensed by the HFEA, and he justified this conclusion by stating, '[t]his is made clear by the language of section 11(1)—'may grant the following *and no other licence*'.[24] In other words this is a definitive, closed and complete, and exhaustive list, which permits of no additional licensed activities, such as tissue typing, as sought by the Hashmi family and supported by the HFEA.

5.33   Maurice Kay J said that the fundamental question in the case was, therefore, whether the purpose of tissue typing was one of 'assisting women to have children'. The Hashmi family and the HFEA contended that it was and pressed for the court to adopt:

---

21   Ibid, para 13.
22   See Sch 2, para 1(3) of the 1990 Act.
23   See s 2(1) of the 1990 Act.
24   [2002] EWHC 3000 (Admin) at para 16.

'a broad construction of the Act in the following stages: (1) the definition of 'treatment services' in section 2(1) is intended to be a wide definition of the forms of treatment falling within the Act and should be construed as being broadly synonymous with 'fertility treatment': (2) paragraph 1(3) of Schedule 2 does no more than to make it clear that the HFEA cannot authorise an activity under a licence unless it considers such an activity to beat least desirable for the overall purpose of providing fertility treatment; and (3) to assist a woman to carry a child with a particular characteristic whether it be freedom from genetic disorder or tissue compatibility with an affected sibling is an activity which is desirable for that permitted purpose.'[25]

However, if that is the construction of the Act that is accepted and the pathway chosen to proceed, then, Maurice Kay J added, 'such a construction might open the door to the use of PGD for what is sometimes called "social selection" for example based on sex.' Again the spectre of slippery slopes is being raised here. If this seemingly innocuous activity is permitted, then the door may be opened to a whole raft of very bad and ethically disastrous activities. However, Maurice Kay J noted that Dinah Rose (counsel for the HFEA) countered that frightening contingency ever arising, reminding the court that she had said:

'it is the job of the HFEA to determine what is acceptable and what is not through the licensing system and the HFEA, as a mixed body of clinicians, religious leaders, ethicists and others, can be trusted to grapple with the difficult issues that arise.'

Clearly at the operational and daily level it is correct that the HFEA has been entrusted to reach decisions in individual cases and has the power to grant or refuse licences, as well as revoking and suspending them. It is also correct that the HFEA is comprised of a diverse range of individuals from a wide professional or business background (albeit all of them are broadly supportive of eg embryonic research, storage of embryos and using embryos in treatment).

5.34　However, Maurice Kay J emphatically concluded that the construction for which Miss Rose (and obviously the HFEA and the Hashmi family) contend was not correct. Moreover, he states that:

'When "treatment services" have been defined with a high degree of specificity by section 2(1), it is not appropriate to rewrite that definition as being "broadly synonymous with fertility treatment". Moreover, section 2(1) expressly defines "treatment services" by reference to a single purpose—that of "assisting women to carry children".'[26]

Applying this principle to the instant case of the Hashmi family, Maurice Kay J, contends:

'it is not suggested that those problems arise from an impaired ability to conceive or to carry a child through pregnancy to full term and birth. The sole purpose of tissue typing is to ensure that any such child would have tissue compatibility with its older sibling.'

In other words the saviour sibling's only purpose for being created was to be used as some form of tissue donor, or organ donor or blood donor for an older, sick sibling, and therefore it had only instrumental value. Thus it was being

25　Ibid.
26　Ibid, para 17.

created and used solely as a means toward an end (saving a sibling), and was not being valued (created or brought into existence) as an end in itself, ie its own inherent value or worth was paradoxically being blithely ignored. This instrumental creation or narrow use of the sibling was unethical.

5.35 Maurice Kay J continued:

'I do not consider that it can be said to be "necessary or desirable" for the purpose of assisting a woman to carry a child. The carrying of such a child after implantation would be wholly unaffected by the tissue typing.'[27]

Maurice Kay J effectively construed the words in the 1990 Act in a very limited and restrictive fashion, and interpreted them to literally mean that PGD and HLA tissue typing as requested by the Hashmi family was not necessary for Mrs Hashmi to successfully carry a child to term. Tissue typing will not assist with the viability of a pregnancy. Whether the embryo implants in the woman has got absolutely nothing to do with whether tissue typing is permitted. Therefore, how can tissue typing be said to be either necessary or desirable in this case?

5.36 Maurice Kay J therefore stated:

'It seems to me that the language of the Act does not bear the strain which would be necessary to read "with particular characteristics" into the carrying of a child. Nor do I find it appropriate to resort to the Warnock Report as an aid to construction. The Report was indeed the catalyst for the Act and the HFEA but it did not anticipate the detailed statutory structure which is highly specific and restrictive, as the Master of the Rolls observed in the other *Quintavalle* case. There is no reason to give the language of the Act anything other than its ordinary meaning in the context of the purpose which was identified in that case.'[28]

He also rejected the submission that:

'as section 3 of the Human Rights Act 1998 requires me to construe the 1990 Act compatibly with Convention rights so far as it is possible to do so, the right of the parents to respect for their private and family life (Article 8) and the right of life of the existing child (Article 2) compel the construction for which [Miss Rose] contends.'[29]

He rejected the submission because 'I find no incompatibility between the proper construction (as I have held it to be) and Convention rights.'

5.37 In addition, Maurice Kay J stated:

'This case is in the form of a challenge to the HFEA on the basis that it has exceeded the powers which Parliament conferred on it. Parliament plainly enjoyed a margin of appreciation in that respect. It seems that the activity which the HFEA seeks to licence is one which is unlawful in most, if not all, Convention countries. In these circumstances it is difficult to see how the present case exhibits breaches of Convention rights.'[30]

---

27 Ibid.
28 Ibid.
29 Ibid, para 18.
30 Ibid.

The judge therefore draws support for his assessment that tissue typing cannot be authorised by the HFEA granting a licence for it, by virtue of the fact that the procedure is unlawful in most if not all other countries who are party to the Convention.

5.38　Maurice Kay J, therefore, concluded that the application for judicial review of the decision of HFEA to licence tissue typing succeeded. He conceded:

> This is a difficult area of medical science and ethics. On any reading of it, the legislation has been tightly drawn so as to ensure that the ground rules within which the HFEA operates restrict the potential for misuse of science and technology. The pace of development in this area in the last decade shows the sense of that.'[31]

The HFEA then appealed the decision of the High Court to the Court of Appeal.

QUINTAVALLE: COURT OF APPEAL

Lord Phillips of Matravers MR

5.39　Lord Phillips of Matravers MR delivered the leading judgment of the Court of Appeal.[32] He gave some interesting statistics concerning the likelihood of a saviour sibling being tissue compatible (and disease-free):

> '[s]tatistically Mrs Hashmi has one chance in four of producing a child with matching tissue, although the odds are somewhat longer of producing such a child who is not affected with beta thalassaemia major.'[33]

Regrettably for Zain Hashmi (the existing older sibling who was suffering from beta thalassaemia major), none of his three elder siblings had tissue that matched his.

5.40　As well as stating that IVF can only be carried out in this country under a treatment licence issued by the HFEA, and moreover that for some years PGD screening against genetic disease had been carried out as part of IVF treatment licensed by the HFEA, nevertheless it needed to be pointed out that tissue typing had never been carried out as part of such treatment.[34] Dr Simon Fishel, the Managing and Scientific Director of Centres for Assisted Reproduction Limited (CARE), the largest single provider of in vitro fertilisation (IVF) services in the United Kingdom, told Mrs Hashmi that tissue typing required express authorisation from HFEA, and, therefore, CARE accordingly applied to the HFEA for a ruling as to whether an IVF clinic could properly apply for a licence to administer treatment including tissue typing.

5.41　As mentioned already the HFEA announced their decision in the press release of 13 December 2001 that they would in principle be prepared to grant a licence for treatment including tissue typing, subject crucially to a number of

---

31　Ibid, para 20.
32　*R (on the application of Quintavalle) v Human Fertilisation and Embryology Authority* [2003] EWCA Civ 667.
33　Ibid, at para 2.
34　Ibid, para 5.

conditions. The HFEA said that tissue typing should only be permitted where PGD was already necessary to avoid the passing on of a serious genetic defect – clearly here beta thalassaemia major was considered such a serious genetic defect. They also said that licences permitting PGD in conjunction with tissue typing should only be granted on a case-by-case basis. Treatment licences involving tissue typing would only therefore be granted subject to the following conditions (which were arguably rigorous and demanding):[35]

'(a) The condition of the affected child should be severe or life threatening, of a sufficient seriousness to justify the use of PGD;

(b) The embryos should themselves be at risk of the condition affecting the child[36]

(c) All other possibilities of treatment and sources of tissue for the affected child should have been explored[37]

(d) The techniques should not be available where the intended recipient is a parent[38]

(e) The intention should be to take only cord blood for the purposes of the treatment

(f) Appropriate counselling should be given to the parents

(g) Families should be encouraged to take part in follow-up studies

(h) Embryos should not be genetically modified to provide a tissue match'.[39]

5.42   As stated previously, HFEA granted a licence to Park Hospital, operated by CARE in Nottingham to carry out IVF treatment including PGD for beta thalassaemia in conjunction with HLA tissue typing for the Hashmi family.

5.43   Lord Phillips, commenting on how difficult it was (and is) to frame legislation covering controversial areas in the assisted reproduction sphere,[40] referred to the words of Lord Bingham of Cornhill in *R (Quintavalle) v Secretary of State for Health* who said:

'There is no doubting the sensitivity of the issues. Nor can one doubt the difficulty of legislating against a background of fast-moving medical and scientific development. It is not often that Parliament has to frame legislation apt to apply to developments at the advanced cutting edge of science.'[41]

He also stated:

'It is, however, plain that while Parliament outlawed certain grotesque possibilities (such as placing a live animal embryo in a woman or a live human embryo in an animal) it otherwise opted for a strict regime of control. No activity within this field was left unregulated. There was to be no free for all.'

---

35   Ibid, para 6.

36   So the PGD is not just being done for the benefit of another, arguably helping to negate the accusation that the saviour sibling is being used solely as a means toward an end.

37   Evidence surely that the HFEA view PGD and HLA tissue typing as an option of last resort, only to be deployed if absolutely necessary.

38   PGD in conjunction with HLA tissue typing ought only to be available to eg save an older sibling, not a different generation, ie a parent.

39   [2003] EWCA Civ 667 at para 6.

40   Ibid, para 12.

41   *R (on the application of Quintavalle) v Secretary of State for Health* [2003] 2 WLR 692, at para 12.

5.44 Lord Phillips refers to Chapter 9 of the Warnock Report (published in 1984, 18 years before *Quintavalle*), which 'contemplates the possibility of avoiding transmission of a gender linked hereditary disease by PGD screening for gender to avoid implantation of embryos with the vulnerable gender.'[42]

5.45 Lord Phillips also referred to the Government's White Paper, which preceded the 1990 Act, which, at para 49, stated that those who support the licensing of research:

'envisage the development of techniques including embryo biopsy which might allow the very early detection of embryos which had single gene or chromosome defects which would result in seriously abnormal babies. In the UK some 7,000 babies a year (about 1 per cent of all babies) are born with an obvious single inherited defect. Pre-implantation diagnosis could ultimately result in some fall in that number.'

Thus, the promise of PGD for improvement of human happiness is being sold here. Use of PGDs can prevent children being born with serious congenital disorders which will prevent that child suffering a life of misery and prevent its family sharing in that suffering. Also it obviates the need for an abortion, if one 'weeds out' the embryo at this 6–8 stage cell period. There is less biological investment and arguably less ethical and moral status in an embryo than in a foetus or unborn child who will be aborted at a much later stage of gestation. As the White Paper added:

'It could, however, give the possibility in some instances of rejecting defective embryos in favour of healthy ones and reducing the number of requests for abortion on grounds of fetal abnormality.'

5.46 Lord Phillips flags up para 30 of the White Paper as being highly significant to the instant case. Paragraph 30 provides:

'It will be a criminal offence to carry out any procedures on a human embryo other than those aimed at preparing the embryo for transfer to the uterus of a woman; or those carried out to ascertain the suitability of that embryo for the intended transfer.'

He comments on this, stating:

'The latter is plainly the origin of the provision that ultimately became s 1(1) (d) of Schedule 2. It is to be noted that suitability is not defined, but that procedures carried out to ascertain suitability for transfer were considered to be appropriate for licensing, whether or not embryo research was prohibited.'

5.47 Lord Phillips pointed out that by the time of the third reading of the HFE Bill in 1990, it was known that Dr Robert Winston had successfully implanted female embryos after genetically screening out male embryos which were, or might have been, affected with gender linked genetic disorders. Theoretical PGD had become reality.

---

42 [2003] EWCA Civ 667 at para 27.

5.48 Again, utilising the rule in *Pepper v Hart*,[43] Lord Phillips relied on the words of the then Health Secretary Kenneth Clarke in the debate on third reading, when he remarked:

'Not all reproductive technologies are aimed at helping infertile couples to have children. Some are designed to help people to have healthy normal children by allowing a range of congenital diseases and handicaps to be detected prenatally by pre-implantation diagnosis. The possibility of preventing genetic disease is one of the reasons most frequently cited in support of embryo research.'[44]

Moreover Ken Clarke, concerning whether a ban on research would lead to a ban on PGD screening for hereditary defects, 'confirmed that that treatment now that it is being developed, could be continued if the amendments were agreed to.'[45]

5.49 Lord Phillips found the arguments of counsel for the HFEA (David Pannick QC) persuasive, namely that:

'paragraph 3(2)(b) of Schedule 2 was significant. This permits the licensing of embryo research activities for the purpose of "developing methods for detecting the presence of gene or chromosome abnormalities in embryos before implantation" ... it would be strange if Parliament approved research to develop a method for achieving an objective which was prohibited elsewhere in the Act. The clear inference of permitting such research was that Parliament approved of PGD to avoid implantation of embryos carrying genetic defects. The phrase "for the purpose of assisting women to carry children" and of "suitable for that purpose" in Schedule 2 paragraph 1(1)(d) had to be read so as to embrace that activity.'[46]

5.50 In a nutshell, Parliament had expressly permitted as a research purpose developing methods to detect gene or chromosomal abnormalities in embryos before implantation. It would be logically absurd if this objective were prohibited under the Act for treatment purposes. Lord Phillips stated:

'Parliament chose to permit the licensing of research. It makes little sense for Parliament, at the same time, to prohibit reaping the benefit of that research, even under licence.'[47]

He then adds:

'The matter is, in my judgment, put beyond doubt by the statement made by the Secretary of State [Ken Clarke] in the course of Parliamentary debate ... The Minister made an express statement to Parliament upon the very issue of construction under consideration and it is clear that the issue in question was of particular concern to Parliament.'[48]

5.51 Lord Phillips then went on to state that the question remained as to whether the two vital phrases 'for the purpose of assisting women to carry

---

43 [1993] AC 593.
44 Quoted at [2003] EWCA Civ 667, at para 35.
45 Ibid, para 36.
46 Ibid, para 36.
47 Ibid, para 40.
48 Ibid, para 41.

children' and 'designed to secure that the embryo is suitable for the purpose of being placed in a woman' were appropriate to describe the object of IVF treatment which is designed not to assist the processes of fertilisation and gestation, but to ensure that the child which is produced by those processes is healthy. In other words should one interpret the words restrictively and narrowly and confine the words to literally mean just helping the women to get pregnant/carry a baby, or should one give them a wider purposive construction to mean so that the woman can carry a healthy baby? In answering that question Lord Phillips conceded that the phrase 'for the purpose of assisting women to carry children' naturally suggested treatment designed to assist the physical processes from fertilisation to the birth of a child. He went on:

> 'But if the impediment to bearing a child is concern that it may be born with a hereditary defect, treatment which enables women to become pregnant and to bear children in the confidence that they will not be suffering from such defects can properly be described as "'for the purpose of assisting women to carry children".'[49]

5.52   Lord Phillips, therefore, believed that it was 'appropriate to give it this meaning in order sensibly to reconcile the provisions of the Act that deal with treatment and those that deal with research', presumably the implication being that Parliament could not have sensibly or deliberately crafted provisions in an Act that were irreconcilable. Secondly, Lord Phillips said that:

> 'It is legitimate when deciding to adopt this construction to have regard to the fact that the more narrow alternative construction would render unlawful a practice which has been carried on for over a decade and which is patently beneficial.'[50]

Surely the implication again is that would be manifestly absurd. One cannot just turn back scientific progress, nor can one put the genie back in the bottle so easily, nor ought one to do so. It is a moot point whether PGD to detect and then prevent the implantation of an embryo with a serious hereditary defect is a beneficial practice—it clearly and demonstrably is. Thirdly, as stated already, Lord Phillips drew support for his construction of the statutory provisions by stating that it was also legitimate to have regard to Mr Clarke's statement to Parliament.

5.53   Concerning whether the actual process of biopsy and PGD are designed to secure that the embryo is suitable for the purpose of being placed in a woman, Lord Phillips stated that:

> 'once satisfied that the treatment as a whole is for the purpose of enabling a woman to carry a child, no further problem arises. The word "suitable" takes its meaning from its context. Where the object of the treatment is to enable a woman to bear a child confident that it will not carry a hereditary defect, an embryo will only be suitable for the purpose of being placed within her if it is free of that defect. PGD is thus designed to secure that the embryo is suitable for this purpose.'[51]

---

49   Ibid, para 43.
50   Ibid.
51   Ibid, para 44.

The treatment, including PGD and HLA tissue typing, should therefore be considered holistically when assessing and ultimately determining if it is for the purpose of enabling a woman to carry a child. Lord Phillips then reiterated that, 'the primary concern about genetic defects was and is not that they imperil the pregnancy but that they lead to the birth of children carrying the defects.'[52]

5.54 Lord Phillips then summarised what he considered is meant by the term 'treatment for the purpose of assisting women to bear children':

'When concern as to the characteristics of any child that she may bear may inhibit a woman from bearing a child, IVF treatment coupled with PGD that will eliminate that concern can properly be said to be 'for the purpose of assisting women to carry children.'[53]

This very obviously gives the words a much wider construction than Maurice Kay J gave them. He continued:

When the Act was passed women who had reason to fear that they would give birth to children with genetic defects were probably the only section of the population for whom it was envisaged that IVF treatment could be justified on this basis.'

However times change and scientific developments advance rapidly, and Lord Phillips stated:

'[N]o evidence suggests that the wish of a woman to bear a child in order to provide a source of stem cells for a sick or dying sibling was anticipated at that time Such a wish is now the reality, and the case of Mr and Mrs Hashmi is not unique.'

5.55 Continuing on from that Lord Phillips noted:

'The activities that the HFEA has licensed in the case of Mr and Mrs Hashmi are the same as those it has regularly licensed for the purpose of assisting women to bear children free of hereditary diseases:

  i   creation of embryos
  ii   biopsies of the embryos
  iii analysis of the cells removed by biopsy by the use of a DNA probe in order to identify those embryos likely to produce children with desired characteristics
  iv   implantation of those embryos'.[54]

Lord Phillips makes the point that the difference in the case of the Hashmi family was as to the desired characteristics. He very tellingly added that that difference may be critical in determining whether or not the HFEA would decide to licence the activities in question, but:

'I cannot see, however, that the difference can be critical in determining whether or not the treatment, including the PGD, is "for the purpose of enabling women to carry children."'

---

52 Ibid, para 45.
53 Ibid, para 46.
54 Ibid, para 46.

5.56 The desired characteristics for the Hashmi family were a disease-free and tissue-compatible embryo to be implanted, not just a disease-free embryo. Lord Phillips therefore concluded:

> 'My conclusion is that whether the PGD has the purpose of producing a child free from genetic defects, or of producing a child with stem cells matching a sick or dying sibling, the IVF treatment that includes PGD constitutes treatment for the purpose of assisting women to bear children.'[55]

5.57 Regarding whether HLA tissue typing allied to PGD was designed to ensure that the embryo is suitable for the purpose of being placed in the woman, Lord Phillips stated:

> 'Just as in the case of PGD screening for genetic defects, the meaning of "suitable" falls to be determined having regard to its context. When the object of the treatment is to enable a woman to bear a child with a tissue type that will enable stem cells to be provided to a sick sibling, an embryo will only be suitable for the purpose of being placed within her if it will lead to the birth of a child with the tissue type in question.'[56]

Context therefore is apparently all. Suitability is context specific. The Hashmi family's context is that only a tissue-compatible (and disease-free) embryo can possibly save their son. Lord Phillips concluded therefore that the HFEA was right to decide that the Act authorised it to licence IVF treatment with PGD for the purpose of tissue typing 'subject to such conditions as it considered appropriate'.

5.58 Lord Phillips concludes by saying that the new technology (HLA tissue typing) allowed couples to make a choice about the characteristics of a child to be born, which in turn raised huge ethical issues about whether and for what purposes such a choice should be permitted. Nonetheless his conclusion was that 'Parliament has placed that choice in the hands of the HFEA'.[57]

Schiemann LJ

5.59 Lord Justice Schiemann made the important observation concerning the use of and experimentation on embryos that common law made no special provision for this new technology and this gave rise to a considerable amount of public anxiety, one of the reasons for the passage of the 1990 Act. He agreed with Lord Phillips that at the root of this case was statutory interpretation – 'The underlying task which faces the Court in the present case is one of construction of this Act [ie the 1990 Act]'[58] – and the construction and interpretation of Sch 2, para 1(3) was 'the crucial provision in this appeal.'[59] He summarised and paraphrased what he considered to be the central question in the case: '*Can the Process in Issue* [ie HLA tissue typing with PGD] *lawfully appear to the Authority as necessary or desirable for the purpose of assisting a woman to carry a child?*' [emphasis in judgment][60] Essentially the question was: is

---

55 Ibid, para 48.
56 Ibid, para 49.
57 Ibid, para 50.
58 Ibid, para 53.
59 Ibid, para 66.
60 Ibid, para 76.

HLA tissue typing with PGD a matter that is prohibited or a matter that can be regulated by the HFEA?

5.60   Schiemann LJ made the accurate observation that in conventional or normal IVF not all the embryos created are used, and that, moreover several perfectly healthy unused embryos can ultimately be allowed to perish, even though they are healthy or disease-free. Patently this was 'not regarded by Parliament as always unacceptable', and nor was using a genetic defect-free embryo, nor the use of embryonic biopsy on an embryo.

5.61   Again, he contended that:

> 'There is in my judgment no indication in the Act that the carrying out of tests on cells extracted from an embryo was regarded by Parliament as unacceptable as such.'[61]

Thus he seems to take the view that, if Parliament has not expressly prohibited the practice or activity, it is not always unacceptable and may take place.

5.62   Schiemann LJ concluded therefore that Parliament was not opposed in principle to permitting the HFEA to allow this practice but 'did not sanction a free for all.' – ie another clearly defined incremental step was permitted, but not the construction of a staircase (the slippery slope). He adds that:

> 'No part of the Process in Issue (with the possible exception of carrying out tests on the extracted cells) can lawfully be done without a licence granted by an Authority specially set up by Parliament to supervise developments in this field.'[62]

The HFEA is the only body permitted by Parliament to issue licences. He then said: 'The phraseology of paragraph 1(3) immediately points to the Authority as the primary decision taker.'

5.63   Schiemann LJ said that one of the tasks of the HFEA was to determine if HLA tissue typing or PGD appeared necessary or desirable for the purposes of assisting a woman to carry a child, and that that involved the HFEA determining whether that process would assist a woman to carry a child and, if so, whether it was necessary or desirable for that purpose:

> 'In my judgment it was lawfully open to the Authority to come to the conclusion that the Process in Issue would assist some women, who would otherwise refrain from conception or abort either spontaneously or deliberately to carry a child'. [63]

It was, therefore, 'lawfully open to the Authority to come to the conclusion that the Process in Issue was necessary or desirable for that purpose.'[64] Thus the HFEA's decision in principle does not infringe para 1(3) of Sch 2. In addition he adds:

> 'Since the Process in Issue does not offend against subparagraph 1 (3) it follows that it will be done for the purpose of assisting a woman to carry a

---

61   Ibid, para 85.
62   Ibid, para 87.
63   Ibid, para 89.
64   Ibid, para 90.

child. If that be so, it will also be done "in the course of providing treatment services" and thus fall within the opening words of paragraph 1(1).'[65]

5.64 In conclusion, Schiemann LJ, in allowing the HFEA's appeal, stated:

'Once one accepts, as I do, that the Process in Issue can in some circumstances lawfully be regarded by the Authority as desirable for the purpose of assisting a woman to carry a child, then this implies in my judgment that the concept of suitability in paragraph 1(1)(d) is wide enough to embrace ensuring that the embryo does not suffer from a genetic defect and tissue incompatibility. I therefore consider that the remaining proposed activities fall comfortably within the phrase 'practices designed to determine whether embryos are suitable' for the purpose of implantation.'[66]

Importantly, Schiemann LJ stated that: 'Parliament did not impose upon the Authority any express obligation to sanction the grant of licences'.[67] The decision of the Court of Appeal was, therefore, not an order or instruction to grant a licence for HLA tissue typing with PGD, but was rather a decision about its lawfulness and about the lawfulness of the HFEA's discretion in granting such a licence. Therefore he adds, 'If the decision of the Authority is upheld in the present case it does not mean that parents have a right to in vitro fertilisation for social selection purposes', ie no slippery slopes.

Mance LJ

5.65 The third judge in the Court of Appeal, Lord Justice Mance, endorsed the basic approach of the other two judges, saying whilst the facts of the Hashmi case excited great sympathy, nevertheless 'the issue is one of law. It involves the construction of the Human Fertilisation and Embryology Act 1990, in the context of scientific developments which go beyond any specifically envisaged at the time of the Act.'

5.66 Concerning the definition of treatment services (as defined by s 2(2) of the 1990 Act – 'medical, surgical or obstetric services provided to the public or a section of the public for the purpose of assisting women to carry children'), LJ Mance made the important point that of course:

'Treatment services extend beyond the activities for which any licence would be required. There are of course many medical, surgical and obstetric services (including advice, medicine and hospital facilities) "for the purpose of enabling women to carry children" which do not involve the creation outside the human body, or the keeping or use, of an embryo.'[68]

So, for example, giving a woman superovulatory drugs to produce eggs would not by itself need a licence from HFEA, nor would surgery to block fallopian tubes, or surgery to retrieve early sperm from a man who was not producing sperm normally.

---

65 Ibid, para 93.
66 Ibid, para 96.
67 Ibid, para 98.
68 Ibid, para 107.

5.67   LJ Mance referred to the words of Lord Bingham in *Quintavalle*,[69] who identified three levels of control imposed by the 1990 Act to the sphere of assisted reproduction, namely those in the Act, the power of the Secretary of State to make regulations, and the powers exercised by HFEA. Commenting on these in turn, Lord Bingham had said that the highest is that contained in the Act itself, ie s 3(1) (no one can create, keep or use an embryo unless they have a licence – penalty for violation two years in jail), or s 3(3) (no one can keep or use an embryo after the appearance of the primitive streak) or (s 3(3)(a)) place an embryo in any animal (the penalty for both of these serious criminal offences is 10 years in jail). Lord Bingham continued:

> 'The next level of control is provided by the Secretary of State, who is empowered to make regulations for certain purposes subject (so far as relevant here) to an effective resolution of both Houses of Parliament (section 45(1), (4)).'[70]

An example of this second level of control would be s 3(3) of the 1990 Act, which empowers the Secretary of State to make regulations prohibiting the keeping or use of an embryo in specified circumstances. Government ministers can add to, amend or flesh out certain parts of the 1990 Act. Finally, Lord Bingham had said that the third level of control was that exercised by the Authority. An example of this would be the granting of licences under s 3(1) of the 1990 Act. The HFEA's arguably main or primary function is to grant licences (and revoke, suspend, renew, vary and effectively police them!) That is a critical role that has been given to them by Parliament. They are the statutory licensing body or authority. There is an overlap here, given that Parliament has stated that persons who create, keep or use embryos without licences commit a serious criminal offence, and this might be considered the highest level of control (making an activity a criminal offence), but nonetheless the HFEA is specifically 'delegated' or charged with issuing and granting those licences (the 'third level of control'). Another example of this third type of control would be the CoP drafted and updated periodically by the HFEA.

5.68   Mance LJ made a very telling observation, really applicable in the context not just of saviour siblings but across the whole of assisted reproductive technologies regulated primarily by Acts of Parliament:

> 'The House of Lords had, as we have, to grapple with at first sight contrasting rules that a statute always bears the meaning that it had when Parliament passed it and that a statute is always speaking, and with the difficulty that arises in deciding whether a modern invention or activity [here PGD with HLA tissue typing] falls within statutory language used at a time when it did not exist.'[71]

Does a judge in 2003 or 2012 interpret the 1990 Act with 1990 spectacles on, or with 2003 or 2012 spectacles? Questions of this profound nature have been vexing members of the US Supreme Court regarding the interpretation of the US written constitution since its writing in 1787. Do we interpret it using 1787 spectacles or spectacles in the year the Supreme Court decision is made? There are, not surprisingly, sharp and fundamental differences of opinion on this issue,

---

69   *R (Quintavalle) v Secretary of State for Health* [2003] UKHL 692; 2 WLR 692.
70   [2003] EWCA Civ 667, at para 108.
71   Ibid, para 109.

depending on whether the commentator, lawyer or academic etc is of a liberal or conservative bent.

5.69 Mance LJ relied on and supports the famous words of Lord Wilberforce, (approved by Lord Bingham and the House of Lords in *Quintavalle*), in *Royal College of Nursing of the United Kingdom v Department of Health and Social Security*[72] on the court's role in this situation:

'In interpreting an Act of Parliament it is proper, and indeed necessary, to have regard to the state of affairs existing, and known by Parliament to be existing, at the time. It is a fair presumption that Parliament's policy or intention is directed to that state of affairs. Leaving aside cases of omission by inadvertence, this being not such a case, when a new state of affairs, or a fresh set of facts bearing on policy, comes into existence, the courts have to consider whether they fall within the Parliamentary intention. They may be held to do so, if they fall within the same genus of facts as those to which the expressed policy has been formulated. They may also be held to do so if there can be detected a clear purpose in the legislation which can only be fulfilled if the extension is made. How liberally these principles may be applied must depend upon the nature of the enactment, and the strictness or otherwise of the words in which it has been expressed. The courts should be less willing to extend expressed meanings if it is clear that the Act in question was designed to be restrictive or circumscribed in its operation rather than liberal or permissive. They will be much less willing to do so where the subject matter is different in kind or dimension from that for which the legislation was passed. In any event there is one course which the courts cannot take, under the law of this country; they cannot fill gaps; they cannot by asking the question "What would Parliament have done in this current case – not being one in contemplation – if the facts had been before it?" attempt themselves to supply the answer, if the answer is not to be found in the terms of the Act itself.'

5.70 Mance LJ disagreed with Maurice Kay J's conclusion that tissue typing itself involved the use of an embryo, arguing that:

'An embryo is distinct from embryonic cell material, which is extracted from an embryo leaving the embryo free to continue to develop.'

He added:

'The creation outside the human body, biopsying and implantation of an embryo all fall within s.3. They can all only take place under a licence, which may impose strict conditions regarding the nature of any testing permissible in respect of any embryonic cell material removed from such an embryo.'[73]

5.71 Continuing, Mance LJ said:

'The central issues are thus whether the activities of bringing about the creation by IVF of an embryo and, particularly, its biopsying are activities capable of being licensed, when the purpose is to test embryonic cells removed from the embryo by PGD, including tissue typing, and only to place

---

72   [1981] AC 800, 822.
73   Ibid, para 111.

the embryo in the relevant if the embryo is both free from genetic disorder and has tissue compatibility with an existing sibling.'[74]

In answering this Mance LJ said that licences could only be granted which authorised activities which satisfied the two initial criteria:

'that they are "in the course of", and appear to the HFEA to be necessary or desirable "for the purpose of" providing treatment services (s.11 and Schedule 2 paras. 1(1) and (3)).'[75]

He criticised the wording of Sch 2, para 1(3), saying that, in providing that any activity must appear to the HFEA necessary or desirable for the purpose of services for that purpose, it is to say the least inelegant, but that the intention had to be that the activity should appear to the HFEA to be necessary or desirable for the simple purpose of assisting women to carry children.

5.72 Mance LJ, in interpreting the words 'practices designed… to determine whether embryos are suitable for that purpose' stated that '[T]hese words go on any view wider than the condition of the embryo, to allow some consideration of its inherent characteristics or qualities.'[76] The words, therefore, are not confined to the condition or viability of the embryo, ie will it implant, but rather permit a wider consideration of the characteristics or qualities of the individual embryo to be implanted, ie is it a tissue match with the sick sibling? He rejected Maurice Kay J's association of the concept of 'assisting women to carry children' with problems arising from 'an impaired ability to conceive or to carry a child through pregnancy to full term and birth', and his observation that the carrying of a child would be wholly unaffected by the tissue typing, stating:

'focusing on the single question whether the woman could conceive and carry a child to full term and birth … eliminated the possibility of any test the main purpose or effect of which could be said to determine whether the child would, after its birth, be healthy or suffer from, or be the carrier of, some abnormality, as well as the possibility of deciding against the implantation of a particular embryo because of any abnormality detected that would affect the viability of the embryo while being carried.'[77]

Indeed, he added: 'It is doubtful whether so limited an interpretation was advanced to the Judge [ie to Maurice Kay J].'[78]

5.73 In addition Mance LJ posed the further question:

'One has also to ask whether Parliament can have intended to limit the assistance given to women to carry children to treatment for infertility, including treatment to determine the viability of an embryo for implantation, carriage to and birth at term; or whether Parliament must be taken to have had a broader concern for the health of the child after birth and future generations.'[79]

---

74 Ibid, para 112.
75 Ibid, para 113.
76 Ibid, para 115.
77 Ibid, para 116.
78 Ibid, para 117.
79 Ibid, para 119.

In answering that question he said that the legislation contained a number of indications telling against any limitation of focus to mere viability. He outlines four such indications in the 1990 Act:

(1) First, Parliament resolved the choice left to it, as a result of the White Paper of 1987, in favour of permitting research under licence on embryos. The 1990 Act permitted research on embryos for five permitted purposes (see Sch 2, para 3(2) (a)–(e)), including 'developing methods for detecting the presence of gene or chromosome abnormalities in embryos before implantation'. The original five were increased to eight permitted research purposes by the Human Fertilisation and Embryology (Research Purpose) Regulations 2001[80] (and in turn by the 2008 Act), examples of the second level of control of assisted reproduction contained in the 1990 Act referred to by Mance LJ earlier. Thus, he added:

> 'While it is theoretically possible that Parliament intended to permit research into methods of detecting abnormalities, or into applications of knowledge acquired about disease, which it would be impermissible to licence for practical use unless the Act was amended, it seems improbable that it was contemplated that research, a particularly contentious matter, should be permissible into methods and applications the use of which in practice Parliament had decided to exclude.'[81]

Research into embryos is clearly more contentious than using embryos for treatment. The benefits of research are not as immediately evident (if they are evident), so it is inconceivable that if research were permitted expressly that the use of that research in practice would be prohibited by implication.

(2) Secondly, according to Mance LJ: 'Under Schedule 2 para. 1(1)(f) licences may be granted authorising the mixing of sperm "for the purpose of testing the fertility or normality of the sperm".'[82] This is the so-called 'hamster' test, whereby human sperm is mixed with hamster eggs to test the motility and mobility of the sperm. The reason why hamster eggs are being used to test the fertility of sperm is the scarcity and difficulty of obtaining human eggs. The important safeguard is that this will be permitted, 'only where anything which forms is destroyed when the test is complete and, in any event, not later than the two cell stage'. There is thus no mention, (or limitation therefore), to testing just for viability.

(3) Thirdly, according to Mance LJ:

> 'there is some support in s.13(5) for a conclusion that Parliament cannot have limited its sights to matters going to the viability of an embryo for the purpose of being implanted, carried to term and born as a child.'

This is a condition applicable in every treatment licence (and clearly therefore applicable to the Hashmi family and their licence). This requirement applies not only before, but continues throughout the administration of treatment

---

80 SI 2001/188.
81 [2003] EWCA Civ 667, at para 120.
82 Ibid, para 121.

services. The HFEA would contend that denying them the power or discretion to use HLA tissue typing with PGD to prevent a child being born with a genetic abnormality which will affect that child, its siblings and parents is denying them 'one most effective way' to promote the welfare of the child who might be born. Thus, he added, 'In short, s 13(5) points towards a wider concern for the future child and siblings, which is better served if the legislation is read as permitting such screening.'[83]

(4) Fourthly, Mance LJ noted that:

> '"treatment services" are defined as "medical, surgical and obstetric services provided to the public or a section of the public". Although their purpose must be to assist women to carry children, they are not services provided exclusively to women. The potential father is someone to whom such services may be provided, and whose natural concerns about future health and welfare would be expected to be relevant.[84] This too tends to point against any conclusion that the legislation focuses solely on the woman's narrow physical ability to become pregnant and give birth.'[85]

5.74 Mance LJ again finds support for his wider interpretation and construction of the words in the legislation by reference to the Warnock Report, which took a positive view towards the wider use of techniques (then in their infancy) as a facility or service available in cases other than infertility (Chapter 9 of the Warnock Report), and even considered that the whole question of the acceptability of sex selection should be kept under review.

> '[The White Paper] contemplated expressly (in paragraphs 29–30) that embryos could under the proposed legislation be screened by PGD, so as to achieve "successful pregnancy leading to a healthy baby", that embryos would only be implanted "if suitable", and that they would be allowed "to perish where they were not to be transferred (eg because an abnormality had been detected)".'[86]

5.75 Thus, he concluded:

> 'I am in those circumstances left in no real doubt that the concept of "medical, surgical or obstetric services … for the purpose of assisting women to carry children" was intended to embrace not merely services to assist women physically to carry to term and give birth, but also services to assist them to give birth to children who would be normal and healthy during their lives and would in turn be able to have normal and healthy children.'[87]

Also, the word 'suitable' in Sch 2 para 1(1)(d) was not just limited to PGD to avoid using an embryo with an abnormality which might just affect that embryo's viability, but also embraced implantation of such an embryo, which might affect any resulting child either during that child's own life or any future generation because the child would be a carrier. A much wider use was captured

---

83 Ibid, para 122.
84 Eg see s 28 of the 1990 Act here too.
85 [2003] EWCA Civ 667, at para 122.
86 Ibid, para 125.
87 Ibid, para 126.

in the net following this more liberal, purposive and wider construction being given. He proceeded to argue:

'[H]ere the statute only identifies the next step or immediate purpose, leaving it to those interpreting it to ascertain from its background and other terms the more distant purposes and wider context that may admissibly be taken into account when judging suitability.'[88]

5.76 Concerning the argument that the suitability of an embryo for implantation is to be assessed objectively without reference to the particular woman in whom it is to be placed, Mance LJ said that that would make no sense – the compatibility of the particular embryo with the particular mother must, at least, be a fundamental consideration. At the end of the day implanting an embryo in a woman is only the first step in a successful pregnancy.

Permissibility of tissue typing

5.77 For the Hashmi family, both the screening out of a genetic defect (they saw the terrible effects of the genetic defect every day in Zain and had to abort a pregnancy of a 'natural' would-be saviour sibling because the foetus was afflicted by the same genetic defect that Zain had) and tissue typing were important purposes of an intended biopsy. Therefore, the biopsy envisaged by the HFEA and the Care Clinic licence had a dual purpose: to authorise both PGD to screen out abnormalities *and* tissue typing.

5.78 Mance LJ stated that:

'the assistance to women to carry children which the Act contemplates is not limited to assistance in the narrow physical operation of becoming pregnant and giving birth.'[89]

Section 13(5) of the 1990 Act was to be used in assessing the individual circumstances of the Hashmi family, and that: 'Whilst that subsection probably had primarily in mind consideration of any adverse effects on the welfare of the future or any existing child, the language does not exclude positive effects.'

5.79 The 'core' of CORE's case is that the services which may be provided do not extend to assisting women to carry children selected for particular characteristics unrelated to any abnormality:

'Screening out genetic abnormalities is one thing. Screening out certain normal characteristics [ie a tissue type] is another. The crucial distinction has been put as being between "screening out abnormalities" and "screening in preferences".'[90]

Addressing this false dichotomy, Mance LJ said:

'That distinction raises a spectre of eugenics and "designer babies". But it is a crude over-simplification to view this case as being about "preferences". The word suggests personal indulgence or predilection and the luxury of a real choice. But there is no element of whim in the circumstances that the

---

88 Ibid.
89 Ibid, para 133.
90 Ibid, para 134.

HFEA had in mind to licence in December 2001, and Mr and Mrs Hashmi are not seeking to indulge themselves. The case is about a family's reaction, understandable in the light of current scientific possibilities, to a cruel fate which one of its members is suffering and will continue to suffer, without a successful transplant.'[91]

The unpredictability of nature has dealt the Hashmi family and Zain a terrible hand. Rather than gambling (ie having babies 'naturally' in the hope that one of them will be a tissue match for Zain), they decided to play a game based more on percentages, assisted by clinicians and cutting-edge science. Who can fault them for this? LJ Mance said:

'Ethical concerns that a child to be born might be used as a vehicle [ie instrumentally or as a commodity] or would not be valued and loved were, for good reason in the circumstances as they appear, not at the forefront of any submissions made to us in the present case.'

5.80   Referring to the Warnock Report,[92] Mance LJ said that the circumstances in the Hashmi case lay conceptually between the two poles of 'good medical reasons' for tests, by which Warnock was referring simply to medical reasons affecting children yet to be born, and testing for 'purely social reasons' which Warnock said would 'obviously affect the individual family and the children involved, and would also have implications for society as a whole'. For Mance LJ the Hashmi family's case lies:

'far closer in spirit … to the former pole than to the latter. There are here good medical reasons for screening any embryo, although they do not relate to any future child's health. The concerns to which the HFEA's decision and the licence for Mr and Mrs Hashmi are directed are anything but "purely social", relating as they do to the health of a sibling and the well-being of the whole family.'[93]

Furthermore Mance LJ contended that:

'[It] is of considerable relevance to this appeal that neither Warnock nor the White Paper recommended any absolute prohibition in relation to embryonic testing or in relation to sex selection for reasons unrelated to the child-to-be-born's medical condition.'[94]

The implication was that the HFEA, licensing Authority, or specially created expert standing statutory body could in the future assess the merits of this development and decide whether to permit it.

5.81   Concerning the ethical status of embryos and the use of them in PGD or HLA tissue typing, Mance LJ commented that embryos enjoyed on any view a higher level of protection. When their use was permissible at all, it was only under the control of the HFEA. However, it was at least clear that there is no absolute bar on sex selection in all circumstances.

5.82   Mance LJ observes that the 1990 Act was framed when using PGD to screen out disabilities was understood as a possibility, and was (as concluded

---

91 Ibid.
92 Chapters 9 and 11.
93 [2003] EWCA Civ 667, at para 135.
94 Ibid, para 139.

in this book) contemplated in certain of its provisions. But, in contrast, tissue typing and other techniques to screen out certain normal characteristics were only speculative possibilities at the time of the Act. However, the concept of 'services for the purpose of assisting women to carry children' seems on its face wide enough to embrace some forms of activity in relation to healthy embryos, eg testing to ensure that the right sperm and egg had been used,[95] although the considerations here differ from those presently under consideration.

On that basis, Mance LJ argued:

'More importantly, once it is recognised that the concept of "services for the purpose of assisting women to carry children" extends beyond purely physical problems affecting the viability of the embryo during pregnancy and birth, and allows the screening of embryos for genetic abnormalities, it becomes clear that such services may have regard to prospective parents and society's concern for others and for the future. The concept is in other words to be read in a general, rather than a restrictive sense.'

5.83   One could couch this approach in terms of justice. Society expects and fairly demands that if techniques are available to select children to benefit families (parents, siblings and sick sibling) and society in general by not having to pay out huge sums for the medical care of a sick existing child, then that is a just and fair treatment and moreover a good use of resources. Furthermore tissue typing may have very good consequences for all these individuals and for society more generally, so if one is wishing to maximise utility and good consequences tissue typing arguably is the way forward. Mance LJ continued:

'The assistance to carry a child provided can be viewed either as assistance to have a child whose addition to the family could, without any invasion of tissue, bring very special benefits for a sibling and for the family as a whole and who would be expected to be valued correspondingly, or more narrowly as assistance to the parents in giving them crucial information to decide whether the potential mother should go ahead to have an embryo placed in her.' [96]

Whether it is the former or latter, it comes within the statutory concept of services designed to assist her to carry children.

5.84   If Parliament had wanted to expressly ban an activity it could have done so. In fact it did ban several activities involving embryos,[97] and the fact is it did not ban even sex selection for social reasons. As Mance LJ noted, it did not include any absolute prohibition in the area of sex selection for 'social purposes'. The inference is that even this was left to be regulated by the licensing authority. HLA tissue typing 'is much less obviously problematic than, and very far removed from, selection for social purposes.'[98] Therefore, he held that:

'it was, in circumstances such as those faced by the Hashmis, open to the HFEA under the Act to conclude that a biopsy for the purpose of selecting an

---

95   See *Leeds Teaching Hospital NHS Trusts v A* [2003] 1 FLR 1091.
96   [2003] EWCA Civ 667, at para 142.
97   See, eg s 3 of the 1990 Act.
98   [2003] EWCA Civ 667, at para 143.

embryo with tissue compatibility with that of a very sick child was an activity necessary or desirable for the purpose of treatment services as defined.'

5.85   Using Lord Wilberforce's terminology, he continued:

'a biopsy for the purpose of tissue typing is, in the wider sense, a form of PGD. Its direct purpose is to establish the embryo's genetic makeup and in that light to decide whether or not it should be implanted. The differences between the testing of embryonic cells for abnormality and for tissue typing lies in the precise aspects of the genetic makeup tested and in the factors taken into account when deciding whether to implant. In the one case, it may be said, the procedures are with a view to ensuring the health of the child to be or of future generations, while in the other they are to promote the health of a sibling and the general welfare of the existing family ... I would regard these as differences falling in Lord Wilberforce's terms within the same genus (even if not the same species) of facts as those to which the expressed statutory policy has been formulated.'[99]

In addition:

'the Warnock Report and the White Paper support the view that Parliament envisaged the possibility or likelihood of future developments (even though it could not know precisely what they would be) and positively intended to bring all such procedures within the sphere of the HFEA, with the exception of those specifically prohibited.'

5.86   Finally Mance LJ rejected the suggestion that Sch 2, para 1(1)(d) is only concerned with characteristics which in objective terms render an embryo unsuitable to be placed in *any* woman. The compatibility of the particular embryo with the woman was, he said, fundamental, and he added tissue typing was aimed at providing assistance matching the felt and perceived needs of the family as a whole and the parents and siblings in particular. Clinics have to bear in mind the interests of siblings and the saviour sibling under s 13(5), and their performance of that role was likely to be assisted by information obtained from tissue typing. He concluded that:

'the suitability of the embryo to be placed in a (particular) woman may be considered in the context of objectively established aims and perceived needs relating to the child-to-be-born's parents and to an affected sibling.'[100]

Mance LJ found in favour of the HFEA, setting aside Maurice Kay J's decision. Mrs Quintavalle and CORE then appealed the decision of the Court of Appeal to the House of Lords.

QUINTAVALLE: HOUSE OF LORDS

Lord Hoffmann

5.87   Lord Hoffmann delivered one of the two key judgments in the House of Lords and initially set out the stark and harrowing circumstances confronting

---

99   Ibid, at para 144.
100 Ibid, at para 145.

the Hashmi family and, in particular, Zain,[101] setting out again the details of his illness, his need for daily drugs and regular blood transfusions to keep him alive and how he could be restored to normal life (and his family) by a transplant of stem cells.

5.88 Lord Hoffmann puts the case for permitting PGD with HLA tissue typing very powerfully: 'There is a way to save the Hashmi family from having to play dice with conception' (namely, create a saviour sibling embryo using PGD/HLA tissue typing). Mrs Hashmi would have been spared the physical and emotional trauma of the abortion if she had had the PGD with HLA tissue typing option. She didn't have it then sadly, but she ought to have it now. The presence of utilitarian reasoning and justifications can be implied here, ie minimising her and Zain's suffering, and maximising their potential happiness and health. Consider, therefore, the many good and beneficial consequences and the overall outcome of permitting the procedure. They greatly outweigh the burdens or risks. Lord Hoffmann said that 'the question in this appeal is whether this can be lawfully done in the United Kingdom', which would spare the Hashmis having to go to, eg, Chicago in the United States to get the procedure done, as the Whitaker family had had to do.[102]

5.89 Lord Hoffmann referred to the 1984 Warnock Report, which had laid the foundations for the later 1990 Act, and noted that:

> 'The centrepiece of the committee's recommendations was the creation of a statutory licensing authority to regulate all research and treatment which involved the use of IVF embryos.'[103]

He added that the source of the authority's power was s 3(1), which makes it a criminal offence to bring about the creation of an embryo or keep or use an embryo except pursuant to a licence from the authority, thus emphasising again the pivotal and most important function of the HFEA.

5.90 Lord Hoffmann said that whether or not the HFEA could grant such a licence to do PGD/HLA tissue typing here depended on the extent of its powers under the 1990 Act. Treatment services are defined in s 2(1) of the 1990 Act. The question, Lord Hoffmann said was whether PGD and HLA typing were activities which the authority could authorise to be done 'in the course' of providing Mrs Hashmi with IVF treatment. To find the answer to that one must consider Sch 2, para 1(3) which provides that the HFEA may licence an activity on the list of activities in that paragraph only if it appears to the HFEA to be 'necessary or desirable for the purpose of providing treatment services'. The activities listed include, '(d) practices designed to secure that embryos are in a suitable condition to be placed in a woman or to determine whether embryos are suitable for that purpose.'[104]

Concerning the meaning of the word 'suitable', Lord Hoffmann said that:

---

101 Now aged six, at 28 April 2005, when the House of Lords delivered their judgment.
102 See paras 5.108–5.110 below.
103 *R (on the application of Quintavalle) v Human Fertilisation and Embryology Authority* [2005] UKHL 28, at para 6.
104 Ibid, at para 11.

'The narrower meaning[105] is particularly difficult to support when paragraph 3(2)(e) lists, among the research projects which may be licensed, "developing methods for the detecting the presence of gene or chromosome abnormalities in embryos before implantation." It would be very odd if Parliament contemplated research to develop techniques which could not lawfully be used.'[106]

Lord Hoffmann makes the point that:

'"Suitable" is one of those adjectives which leaves its content to be determined entirely by context ... a suitable hat for Royal Ascot is very different from a suitable hat for the Banbury cattle market ... The context must be found in the scheme of the 1990 Act and the background against which it was enacted. In particular, one is concerned to discover whether the scheme and background throw light on the question of whether the concept of suitability includes taking into account the particular wishes and needs of the mother.'[107]

5.91 Lord Hoffmann said that if that were the case the HFEA may authorise tests to determine if the embryo is 'in that sense suitable' for implantation in Mrs Hashmi's womb. It was clearly Mrs Hashmi's wish that only a tissue compatible and disease-free embryo be implanted in her. Lord Hoffmann added that the HFEA may authorise tests on that basis, but it is not obliged to do so. It is after all a discretionary power:

'It may consider that allowing the mother to select an embryo on such grounds is undesirable on ethical or other grounds. But the breadth of the concept of suitability is what determines the breadth of the authority's discretion.'

5.92 Warnock had considered cell biopsy and whilst it was not feasible in 1984 made no recommendations that it be banned in subsequent legislation on the matter. The Warnock Report highlighted the advantages of PGD, namely detecting abnormalities before implantation and thus helping parents to avoid traumatic later decisions in pregnancy about aborting the foetus, and the disadvantages, namely the need to use IVF. Lord Hoffmann said:

'For present purposes, the most relevant discussion in the Warnock Report concerned gender identification. The report considered (in para 9.8) the possibility of gender identification of an IVF embryo by single cell biopsy. Such information could be used to select embryos to 'prevent the birth of a child with a sex-linked hereditary disease'. The committee saw no reason why this should not be done: para 9.11. It then went on to consider the use of gender identification to select the sex of a child 'for purely social reasons'. After some discussion of the social issues (population distribution, the role of women in society), the committee said that it was unable to make any positive recommendations. Nevertheless: "the whole question of the acceptability of sex selection should be kept under review (See chapter 13)".'[108]

---

105 Ie that 'suitable' meant only that the embryo would be viable, as held by Maurice Kay J.
106 [2005] UKHL 28, at para 13.
107 Ibid, at para 14.
108 Ibid, at para 16.

The Warnock Report did not therefore recommend expressly or explicitly that sex selection be banned and they did not even make any recommendations on sex selection merely for purely social reasons. Lord Hoffmann concluded:

> 'that the committee contemplated that the authority would decide the circumstances, if any, in which sex selection on social grounds should be authorised. As sex selection on social grounds is the most obvious case of selecting an embryo on grounds other than its health, I would infer that the Warnock Committee did not intend that selection of IVF embryos on grounds which went beyond genetic abnormality should be altogether banned.'[109]

5.93 In considering the relevant context, Lord Hoffmann also referred to the 1987 White Paper which preceded the 1990 Act, and to para 13 in particular:

> '[the government] accepted the "basic principle underlying the Warnock Report recommendations – namely the need 'to regulate and monitor practice in relation to those sensitive areas which raise fundamental ethical questions'" The authority would therefore exercise its functions in areas which included "any [research or] treatment involving human embryos created in vitro."'[110]

The intention was therefore to define the functions of the authority in very broad terms. To ensure that the legislation was flexible enough to deal with as yet unforeseen treatment developments which may raise new ethical issues, the Bill, which ultimately became the 1990 Act, would contain powers to make regulations to add to or subtract from the range of matters coming within the regulatory scope of the Authority. Thus flexibility was built into the 1990 Act from its inception. Of note was that para 37 of the White Paper prohibited certain activities, including designer babies, ie 'the artificial creation of human beings with certain predetermined characteristics through modification of an early embryo's genetic structure.' Cloning by cell nuclear replacement was prohibited. However:

> 'relevantly for present purposes, there was no proposal to include in the "clearly prohibited" list the testing of embryos to enable the mother to choose to carry a child with characteristics of her choice. One infers that while the White Paper intended the fundamental ethical issues which such activities might raise to be determined by the statutory authority, subject to the regulation-making power by which Parliament could impose its own decision.'[111]

The principle that the activity is theoretically or prima facie lawful if it is not expressly prohibited seems to being applied here.

5.94 Lord Hoffmann, said that the 1990 Act created a series of prohibited activities involving the use of embryos (see s 3 of the 1990 Act, which covers a range of criminal offences), but that:

> 'Subject to these prohibitions, the licensing power of the authority is defined in broad terms[112] ... if the concept of suitability in sub-paragraph (d) of 1(1) is broad enough to include suitability for the purpose of the particular

---

109 Ibid, at para 19.
110 Ibid, at para 20. Note that the square brackets and words within them are in the case transcript.
111 Ibid, at para 22.
112 See Sch 2, para 1(1).

mother, it seems to me clear enough that the activity of determining the genetic characteristics of the embryo by way of PGD or HLA tissue typing would be "in the course of" providing the mother with IVF services and that the authority would be entitled to take the view that it was necessary or desirable for the purpose of providing such services.'[113]

5.95　Lord Hoffmann then considered the relationship between Parliament and the HFEA and their respective responsibilities in the regulatory sphere. He stated:

'Let it be accepted that a broad interpretation of the concept of suitability would include activities highly unlikely to be acceptable to majority opinion. It could nevertheless be more sensible for Parliament to confine itself to a few prohibitions which could be clearly defined but otherwise to leave the authority to decide what should be acceptable. The fact that these decisions might raise difficult ethical questions is no objection. The membership of the authority and the proposals of the Warnock Committee and the White Paper make it clear that it was intended to grapple with such issues.'[114]

Parliament therefore sets out the broad sweep and parameters of permissible activities (by prohibiting certain activities), and the HFEA fills in the detail of what is ethically or legally permissible in specific cases. The background and expertise of the HFEA leads one to be confident this is a role they can competently discharge.

5.96　Lord Hoffmann concurred that 'suitable' was not limited to merely producing a viable foetus, since that would effectively outlaw PGD completely, but was also concerned that 'suitable' be interpreted and confined to producing a healthy foetus free of genetic defects. He submitted that this definition itself was not free from difficulty. What actually amounted to a genetic defect? As he said:

'Surely it would be more sensible to concentrate on whether choice on such grounds was ethically acceptable rather than to argue over whether it counted as a genetic defect. The great advantage which Parliament would have seen in using broad concepts to define the remit of the authority is that it would avoid sterile arguments over questions of definition and focus attention upon the ethical issues.'[115]

An excellent illustration of the potential problems encountered if one were to limit PGD to merely detecting genetic defects was the case of *Leeds Teaching Hospital NHS Trusts v A*,[116] where the hospital mixed up sperm (sperm from a black man was mixed up by mistake with a white woman's eggs), and this led to a married white couple giving birth to mixed race twins. Here this was a terrible mistake; there was no genetic defect in the embryos, but if the mistake had been suspected before implantation of the embryo, the narrower construction of suitability canvassed for and pressed by CORE and Mrs Quintavalle would have prevented any tests to check the embryo's DNA. As Lord Hoffmann added:

113 [2005] UKHL 28, at para 24.
114 Ibid, at para 26.
115 Ibid, at para 27.
116 [2003] 1 FLR 1091.

'Likewise, many people might agree with the authority that the tests proposed to be conducted in the present case would be ethically acceptable. It often seemed that an unstated assumption [in the argument of CORE/and Mrs Quintavalle] was that the authority was likely to authorise anything that it was not positively prohibited from authorising or that it could not be trusted to make proper ethical distinctions. But these assumptions are in my opinion illegitimate. The authority was specifically created to make ethical distinctions and, if Parliament should consider it to be failing in that task, it has in reserve its regulatory powers under section 3(3)(c).'[117]

5.97   Lord Hoffmann continued:

'Perhaps the most telling indication that Parliament did not intend to confine the authority's powers to unsuitability on grounds of genetic defects is ... the absence of any reference in the Act to selection on grounds of sex. It could be said that the Act made no reference to HLA typing because neither the Warnock Committee nor Parliament in 1990 foresaw it as a possibility. But there was intense discussion, both in the report and in Parliament, about selection for sex on social grounds. If ever there was a dog which did not bark in the night, this was it. It is hard to imagine that the reason why the Act said nothing on the subject was because Parliament thought it was clearly prohibited by the use of the word "suitable" or because it wanted to leave the question over for later primary legislation. In my opinion the only reasonable inference is that Parliament intended to leave the matter to the authority to decide. And once one says that the concept of suitability can include gender selection on social grounds, it is impossible to say that selection on the grounds of any other characteristics which the mother might desire was positively excluded from the discretion of the authority, however unlikely it might be that the authority would actually allow selection on that ground.'[118]

5.98   Lord Hoffmann referred to the words of Lord Wilberforce in *Royal College of Nursing of the United Kingdom v Department of Health and Social Security*,[119] which were referred to by LJ Mance in the Court of Appeal. However, he observed that like all guides on construction they were more appropriate to some cases than others. He distinguishes this case from the former, because:

'This is not a case in which one starts with the presumption that Parliament's intention was directed to the state of affairs existing at the time of the Act. It obviously intended to regulate research and treatment which were not possible at the time.'[120]

This is the problem with most legislation, but it is a particularly germane consideration when one is dealing with legislation regulating a field of science, and, a fortiori, one that develops so rapidly. Lord Hoffmann also distinguished the first *Quintavalle* case:

'in which the statutory language needs to be extended beyond the "expressed meaning". The word "suitable" is an empty vessel which is filled with meaning by context and background. Nor is it helpful in this case to ask

---

117 Ibid, at para 28.
118 Ibid, at para 29.
119 [1981] AC 800.
120 [2005] UKHL 28, at para 33.

whether some new state of affairs falls within "the same genus" as those to which the expressed policy has been formulated. That would beg the question because the dispute is precisely over what the genus is. If 'suitability' has the meaning for which the authority contends, then plainly PGD and HLA tissue typing fall within it. If not, then not.'[121]

Lord Hoffmann therefore held that both PGD and HLA tissue typing could lawfully be authorised by the authority as activities to determine the suitability of the embryo for implantation within the meaning of para 1(1)(d).

5.99 The fact that the HFEA had from time to time stated its policy on PGD and HLA tissue typing and then relaxed some of the conditions upon which licences are granted, according to Lord Hoffmann, seemed exactly in accordance with the duty of the authority to keep the state of the art under constant review. That should be commended not derided – the HFEA were obviously doing their job properly. A further example of the shifting policy of the HFEA, in the light of changing values, times and science concerns the Hashmi family themselves. The HFEA policy of 2001 (the one under which the Hashmi licence for treatment was granted) had a condition that only cord blood should be taken, but after a review in 2004 HFEA decided to delete this condition, because it was in practice unenforceable as once the embryo had been implanted and the child conceived the case passed out of the jurisdiction of the authority. Lord Hoffmann therefore concludes:

'I have no doubt that medical practitioners take very seriously the law that any operation upon a child for which there is no clinical reason relating to the child itself must be justified as being for other reasons in the child's best interests. If the question appears to be doubtful, a ruling from the court may be obtained.'[122]

Finally he adds that:

'There has never been any suggestion that the authority acted unreasonably in granting a licence. The case has always been that it had no power to do so. In my opinion it did.'[123]

Lord Brown of Eaton-Under-Heywood

5.100 Lord Brown of Eaton-Under-Heywood agreed with Lord Hoffmann that this case was all about the scope of a power, not about its exercise: was the HFEA empowered by the 1990 Act to licence tissue typing? He added that 'the ethical questions raised by such a process are, it need hardly be stated, profound.' They include:

'Is this straying into the field of "designer babies" or, as the celebrated geneticist, Lord Winston, has put it, "treating the offspring to be born as a commodity?"'[124]

Again Lord Brown states that even though the conditions imposed on a treatment licence permitting PGD and HLA tissue typing have been relaxed

---

121 Ibid, at para 34.
122 Ibid, at para 38.
123 Ibid, at para 39.
124 Ibid, at para 43.

since the Hashmis got their treatment licence following the original HFEA policy in December 2001:

> 'Your Lordships are simply not concerned with the conditions under which tissue testing should be licensed, assuming it is licensable at all – nor even, indeed, with *whether* it should be licensed. Your Lordships' sole concern is whether the Act *allows* the authority to licence tissue typing were it in its discretion to think it right to do so.'[125]

Furthermore Lord Brown said it was:

> 'your Lordships' task to decide whether by the 1990 Act, Parliament was conferring power upon the newly created authority to take whatever decisions arose from such unforeseen possibilities as tissue typing, or whether Parliament must rather have been contemplating the need for further primary legislation to deal with whatever ethical questions arose out of such future discoveries.'[126]

Thus the question was: did Parliament leave the decision to its agent, the HFEA, or did it retain that prerogative for itself to permit tissue typing only by future primary legislation authorising it?

5.101 Lord Brown stated:

> 'Whether or not the authority is empowered to licence tissue typing ultimately depends on the true construction of two particular provisions in the 1990 Act, section 2(1) and paragraph 1(1) (d) of Schedule 2.'[127]

Furthermore, he sums up, the critical question, therefore, put compendiously was whether tissue testing is a practice designed to determine whether an embryo is suitable for placing in a woman (para 1(1)(d)) and necessary or desirable for the purpose of providing a medical service which itself is to assist a woman to carry the child (s 2(1)). He says that there are three possible answers to that question:

(1) No – the only type of PGD permitted was that which is necessary to ensure that the woman can carry the child successfully to full term. In other words 'embryonic screening to eliminate just such genetic defects as may affect the viability of the foetus and no other.'(Maurice Kay J's meaning).

(2) No – because while the 1990 Act allowed PGD screening to eliminate gene and chromosome defects such as may affect that child (or be carried by that child to future generations), it does not permit tissue typing (CORE/Mrs Quintavalle's meaning).

(3) Yes – because tissue typing can also be licensed: like PGD screening, it provides information about the characteristics of the embryo which is relevant to the woman's decision whether or not to carry the child (the meaning put forward by the HFEA and the Hashmis).

5.102 Whilst Lord Brown said that he confessed to finding some considerable force in the second argument:

---

125 Ibid, at para 46.
126 Ibid, at para 47.
127 Ibid, at para 48.

'It is one thing to enable a woman to conceive and bear a child which will itself be free of genetic abnormality; quite another to bear a child specifically selected for the purpose of treating someone else.'[128]

However, to read into s 2(1), he said, the notion that the child would be a suitable future donor for the health of another would be to stretch the statutory language too far. Lord Brown rejected the second answer and preferred the construction given to the words in the legislation by the third answer.

5.103 Lord Brown drew support from the Warnock Report, eg Chap 9, para 9.11, which, he said:

'expressly envisaged the future possibility of sex selection "for purely social reasons" and concluded that "the whole question of the acceptability of sex selection should be kept under review"– review which inferentially was to be undertaken by a proposed new statutory licensing authority [ie the HFEA]'.[129]

Hence even sex selection for social reasons was not ruled out by Warnock. Again the White Paper of 1987, para 14, proposed:

'To ensure that the legislation is flexible enough to deal with as yet unforeseen treatment developments which raise new ethical issues, the Bill will contain powers to make regulations (subject to affirmative resolution procedure) to add to or subtract from the range of matters coming within the regulatory scope of [the authority].'[130]

The inclusion of powers in the Bill (the eventual 1990 Act) to make regulations clearly demonstrated that the government were aware that new techniques and treatments might need to come within the regulatory net of the HFEA at some time in the future (like PGD and HLA tissue typing here).

5.104 Lord Brown referred to the specific prohibitions and criminal offences in, eg s 3 of the 1990 Act, and said:

'Consistently with paragraph 14 of the White Paper, there is power to make regulations (subject to affirmative resolution) both to add to the range of matters coming within the authority's regulatory scope – see paragraph 1(1) (g) of Schedule 2 enabling regulations to be made for the licensing of other practices in the course of providing treatment services and to subtract from the licensing powers already conferred on the authority – see section 3(3)(c) which enables regulations to be made prohibiting the keeping or use of an embryo in such circumstances as may be specified.'[131]

Flexibility is thus manifestly evident and patently built into the very DNA of the 1990 Act. Importantly too, Lord Brown stated that:

'The legislative scheme necessarily contemplates that the only fresh practices arising out of unforeseen treatment developments capable of becoming licensable by regulation under paragraph 1(1)(g) will themselves have to be characterisable as being "in the course of," and "necessary or desirable for

---

128 Ibid, at para 51.
129 Ibid, at para 53.
130 Quoted, Ibid.
131 Ibid, at para 55.

the purpose of," providing treatment services, which itself argues for a wide construction to be given to the definition of 'treatment services' in section 2(1). The scheme also, of course, enables section 3(3)(c) regulations to be made restricting the authority's powers if ever it were thought to be dealing inappropriately with the "new ethical issues" arising out of the "as yet unforeseen treatment developments" contemplated by the White Paper.'[132]

Thus 'fresh practices' will themselves have to fit into the strict criteria of the 1990 Act before they will be licensed. The protective umbrella and net of the HFEA regulatory regime is designed to be a wide one, and one that can accommodate expansion and growth to cater with the ever burgeoning technology and treatments being developed in the sphere of assisted reproduction.

5.105 Lord Brown refers to the wise words of Lord Bingham in *R (Quintavalle) v Secretary of State for Health*[133] that:

'[besides] outlaw[ing] certain grotesque possibilities (such as placing a live animal embryo in a woman or a live human embryo in an animal) ... otherwise opted for a strict regime of control. No activity within this field was left unregulated. There was to be no free for all.'[134]

However, Lord Brown emphasises that:

'There is no inconsistency however between that approach and the authority's stance in the present case. There it led to a newly discovered method of creating embryos being held to fall within the scope of regulatory control under the 1990 Act. So too here, the respondent's case is that tissue testing is controlled by the 1990 Act. It is not "left unregulated". There will be "no free for all." Rather the licensing of this new technique is for the discretion of the authority.'[135]

5.106 Commenting on the argument that tissue typing assisted Mrs Hashmi to carry a child because her wish was conditional upon knowing that the birth of that child (the 'saviour sibling') would be capable of curing her son Zain, Lord Brown argued that: 'under this reasoning PGD to ensure that a child had certain characteristics for purely social reasons could also be said to be "for the purpose of assisting women to carry children."' At the end of the day it is ultimately up to the HFEA 'to control PGD so as to ensure that it is not used for such ethically objectionable purposes.' The HFEA is the body entrusted by Parliament to do this. It must discharge its ethical policing role robustly.

5.107 Concerning the central thrust of CORE and Mrs Quintavalle's argument in the House of Lords that PGD and HLA tissue typing could not lawfully be permitted by HFEA under the HFEA 1990, Lord Brown said that:

'Its weakness ... lies in the difficulty ... in establishing a satisfactory and coherent dividing line between embryo selection which is permissible and that which is not – let alone finding support for any such dividing line in the 1990 Act.'

132 Ibid, at para 56.
133 [2003] 2 AC 687 at p 697.
134 [2005] UKHL 28, at para 57.
135 Ibid, at para 58.

Moreover:

'what amounts to a serious genetic defect will itself often be contentious. Still less can one find in the statutory language any basis for saying that the elimination of serious genetic or chromosome defects contributes to the process of "assisting women to carry children" whereas other embryo selection does not.'[136]

Finally Lord Brown stated:

'The fact is that once the concession is made (as necessarily it had to be) that PGD itself is licensable to produce not just a viable foetus but a genetically healthy child, there can be no logical basis for construing the authority's power to end at that point. PGD with a view to producing a healthy child assists a woman to carry a child only in the sense that it helps her decide whether the embryo is "suitable" and whether she will bear the child. Whereas, however, suitability is for the woman, the limits of permissible embryo selection are for the authority.'[137]

He then concludes that:

'In the unlikely event that the authority were to propose licensing genetic selection for purely social reasons, Parliament would surely act at once to remove that possibility, doubtless using for the purpose the regulation making power under section 3(3)(c). Failing that, in an extreme case the court's supervisory jurisdiction could be invoked.'

5.108 Ultimately, if the HFEA were permitting slippery slopes to develop and grow, Parliament could pass secondary legislation, or of course primary legislation reining in any excesses or over-zealous permissiveness in what activities could be permitted. The court's protective and safeguarding role could be invoked too to ensure that there was no ethical free for all in this area. Lord Brown dismissed the appeal too.

CONCLUSIONS ON THE *QUINTAVALLE* LITIGATION

5.109 The author has commented on the House of Lords' decision that:

'[it] is a welcome further example of our higher courts giving a more purposive construction to domestic legislation which prove beneficial to aggrieved claimants in highly controversial ethical areas … Whilst for some, the outcome of the case signals a sharp descent down the ethical slippery slope to the commodification of life and the creation of "designer" babies created purely for social reasons at the whim and behest of parent consumers, it is clear that relaxing those circumstances in which tissue-typing can be used to select embryos for implantation need not result in leaving tissue typing "unregulated'. There will be "no free for all", according to Lord Brown (at paragraph 58). Parliament and its agent in this field, the Human Fertilisation and Embryology Authority, will surely guarantee that.'[138]

---

136 Ibid, at para 61.
137 Ibid, at para 62.
138 S Burns, 'The Law Lords' decision in *Quintavalle*: sensible and sensitive – or a first step down a slippery slope?' (2005) 43(Oct) L Ex 38–39.

5.110 Brownsword argues that such reasoning (ie Parliament leaving the HFEA to take responsibility for the regulation of practice in sensitive areas that raise fundamental ethical questions) passes the ethical parcel to the HFEA.[139] Chico has concerns about the implications of the House of Lords' decision, and indeed the trend of the HFEA, that:

> '[has] relaxed the eligibility criteria, increasing the number of people who can access such treatment. In the face of a rising demand for treatment, it may only be a matter of time before an attempt to create a saviour child goes wrong, generating new grievances that might be articulated as novel legal claims. [eg wrongful birth and psychiatric harm claims]'[140]

She adds that following the House of Lords' decision 'policy decisions regarding access to saviour sibling treatment currently rest solely with the Authority.'

THE *WHITAKER* CASE – A HAPPY ENDING

5.111 Prior to the Hashmi case (ie the *Quintavalle* litigation), the parents of Charlie Whitaker, Jayson and Michelle Whitaker, had sought permission from the HFEA to test and select embryos so that a tissue compatible, disease-free embryo could be implanted in Mrs Whitaker, in order that she might give birth to a disease-free, tissue compatible sibling baby, from whose umbilical cord stem cells would be removed and subsequently implanted in Charlie in order to save his life and hopefully cure him of Diamond Blackfan Anaemia (DBA). The HFEA refused permission. HFEA then permitted HLA tissue typing to test and select embryos to prevent the birth of a baby with a genetic disease, but not to select an embryo to help another child, ie they did not then permit the creation of so-called 'saviour siblings'.

5.112 Because HLA tissue typing was not permitted in the United Kingdom at that time, Dr Taranissi, who was treating the Whitakers, organised for the family to travel to the Reproductive Genetics Institute in Chicago in October 2002, and paid for all their medical treatment both in the United States and the United Kingdom.[141] In Chicago the HLA tissue typing took place on Mrs Whitaker's embryos created using IVF. As Mrs Whitaker stated: 'Six out of 13 [embryos] survived more than six days, three were a tissue match for Charlie, two were implanted and we flew home … One of the embryos took and I had a normal pregnancy.' Interestingly Mrs Whitaker said she felt very emotional when Jamie was born at Sheffield Teaching Hospital because he was so special. The stem cells were removed from the umbilical cord (which is discarded after the pregnancy generally anyway), frozen and stored. The stem cells were then transplanted into Charlie in 2004. Before that he underwent gruelling chemotherapy to kill off his own diseased bone marrow. Charlie then left hospital and very happily, as *The Mail on Sunday* reported, 'Now more than seven years after Jamie's birth, doctors have pronounced his brother cured.'

---

139 R Brownsword, 'Reproductive Opportunities and Regulatory Challenges' (2004) 67(2) MLR 304 at 313.
140 V Chico, 'Saviour siblings: Trauma and Tort Law' (2006) 14(2) Med L Rev 180–218, at 180.
141 As reported in *The Mail on Sunday* on 22 May 2011.

5.113 Jamie, who was three years old when his parents told him he had saved his brother Charlie's life said he was 'happy I did it but I don't really feel like a superhero', and added 'I know I was born to do that instead of being just born for me.' However, 'it makes me feel close to Charlie even though he is nearly a teenager', and 'I also know Mummy and Daddy want and love me and always wanted a big family.' Charlie said that '[the] illness has affected me in several ways. I am a bit of a role model.' Some other children 'really look up to me.' He thinks 'I am more adult than other children my age because of what I have been through', and concluded that 'most children don't come near serious illness. I have and I feel very sorry for people and especially children who are really ill, especially when there isn't a cure.' As Dr Taranissi stated 'I felt very committed to them [the Whitaker family] and wanted it [their treatment] to be successful …You cannot put a value on the feeling I had when I later saw Charlie looking so well.'[142]

142 Ibid.

Chapter 6

Ethical Issues

INTRODUCTION

6.1   The use of PGD with HLA tissue typing to create a saviour sibling, where stem cells from umbilical cord blood, bone marrow or other tissue are collected or transplanted from the saviour sibling into a sick existing older sibling, raises a myriad of ethical issues. Most of these were raised, debated and analysed in the debates in Parliament concerning the progress of the HFE Bill (which was eventually enacted as the Human Fertilisation and Embryology Act 2008 (the 2008 Act) which came into force on 1 October 2009). The issue was clearly highly controversial and generated impassioned and informed contributions from many of the key actors in the Bill's progress and scrutiny in Parliament. Not surprisingly there was a huge and unbridgeable chasm between those strongly in favour of the legislation and those who were strongly opposed to the creation and use of saviour siblings for a range of purposes. However, not all contributors to the ethical discussion and debate were quite so polarised. Legislation, albeit arguably not entirely clear or felicitous, with safeguards (however effective they turned out to be), was passed. Again, the divergence of legal opinion concerning the legality of the practice evident in the courts revealed fissures in the senior judiciary concerning not just interpretation of statutory provisions and terms, but the relevance of ethics to the litigation and particular ethical principles and concerns too.

ARGUMENTS IN FAVOUR OF CREATING AND USING SAVIOUR SIBLINGS

Autonomy

6.2   One of the key arguments in favour of the creation and use of saviour siblings is the reproductive autonomy of the woman (potential mother), and closely associated with this the autonomous choice of the couple, whose gametes will be used to create embryos, hopefully to produce a saviour sibling. It is the choice and decision of the woman (or couple) to create and use the saviour sibling. Autonomy is a word that originates from two Greek words: 'auto' which translates roughly as 'self' and 'nomos' which translates as 'rule'. So autonomy is literally self rule, or self-determination. In other words the woman (obviously with her partner) exercises her choice and control over her body to undergo the process which will hopefully culminate in a live healthy baby being born who will save the life of or improve the quality of life of an existing child. Autonomy is one of the four key ethical principles underpinning medicine and medical treatment, according to Beauchamp and Childress.[1]

1   T Beauchamp and J Childress, *Principles of Biomedical Ethics*, 5th Edn (Oxford University Press, 2001).

6.3   Consent is of course the manifestation of autonomy, so when, for example, a woman or couple consent to IVF, PGD and HLA tissue typing they are exercising their autonomy and choosing to undergo a lengthy, costly, physically, mentally and emotionally challenging procedure with no guarantee of success. However that is the woman and the couple's choice.

6.4   Again, the woman or couple clearly and demonstrably want to save their sick child by the creation and use of the saviour sibling. However, they may also want a second or other child as well. This child will be wanted and loved and valued in its own right. Its value and moral worth does not depend necessarily on how it or a by-product from its birth can be used to save the life of a sick sibling. The child will have intrinsic moral and ethical value and worth, totally independent from any positive spin-offs from its creation and birth for others. Put simply, the autonomous wish of the woman or couple is to have another child (albeit one who is free of the disease afflicting the sick child and who is a tissue match for that child too).

6.5   Autonomy is a fundamental but not an absolute ethical principle of course. Certain types of individual or patient cannot exercise autonomy permanently or temporarily, eg incompetent patients, unconscious patients or minors. The autonomy of the woman to exercise her choice to have a saviour sibling created and used to save the life of a sick child is limited greatly by, eg, financial considerations. Firstly, can she afford IVF, PGD and HLA tissue typing, given that three quarters of IVF is funded privately? Secondly, will the Primary Care Trust (PCT) fund NHS IVF and PGD with HLA for the couple? Thirdly, and crucially, will the HFEA grant a treatment licence to the clinic to use the procedure? The reproductive autonomy of the woman or couple is extremely important ethically, but it is not a trump card.

Informed consent

6.6   Closely associated with autonomy, and arguably an integral part of it, is informed consent. The woman (or couple) needs to be informed before undergoing the medical procedure or treatment (IVF, PGD with HLA tissue typing) about the nature of the procedures involved, the risks, costs (financial and otherwise), chances of success, etc in accordance with s 13(6) of the 1990 Act and the Code of Practice. The woman or couple are thus forewarned and arguably forearmed about the procedures and are provided with an effective safeguard to prevent them being exploited because of their desperation to save the life of their child.

Beneficence

6.7   Another strong, if not compelling argument in favour of creating a saviour sibling is beneficence. The argument is that the creation and use of the saviour sibling is beneficent, ie it is doing good – it is a beneficial act. This is because a new healthy human being has been created, one who would not otherwise have existed and one that because of PGD and HLA tissue typing is guaranteed to be free of the disease which the sick child has. It is also a child loved and wanted by its parents and wider family, and one who will hopefully save the life of its older, sick sibling. The wonders of modern medicine have led to this treatment being developed that promises so much for desperately ill children and their families.

Non-maleficence

6.8 The ethical principle of non-maleficence, sometimes translated as *primum non nocere*, or 'first do no harm' holds that the medical intervention or treatment should not harm the patient. Arguably this is a more important ethical principle than that the treatment should be beneficial for the patient. The question arises: who is the patient in a saviour sibling scenario? Members of the public may superficially and incorrectly believe the patient to be the sick older child; they will not be harmed by the creation of a saviour sibling who possibly saves their life or significantly improves their quality of life. However, the saviour sibling is the relevant party who must primarily not be harmed by the procedure.

6.9 The question is: how has the saviour sibling been harmed? Yes, they have been selected from 14–15 other embryos, primarily because of their tissue type and disease-free status, but if a successful implantation and birth occurs, they will have been given a valuable, disease-free life, which hopefully will be happy and healthy in a loving family, in the knowledge that they have saved or at the very worst been created to try to save an older sick sibling. How many children are 'naturally' created unconditionally, with only that child's interests being considered by their parents? That is a counsel for perfection and simply unrealistic. To paraphrase Immanuel Kant, never a straight thing was made out of the crooked timber of humanity.

6.10 Even in the worst case scenario that the stem cells from the cord blood, or the bone marrow transplantation, or the transplantation from the saviour sibling does not save or cure or improve the sick child and they die, how logically or fairly could anyone blame the saviour sibling for this? How could the alleged psychological harm (guilt or sadness) that they might suffer as a consequence, outweigh the much greater actual (not alleged or possible) benefit they have in being alive and having a healthy life in a loving family?

Sanctity of life

6.11 Perhaps paradoxically, the sanctity of life ethical principle which arguably underpins the practice of medicine and medical treatment could be invoked in favour of creating and using a saviour sibling. The sanctity of life ethical principle recognises that life has an inherent and intrinsic value or worth. Life is sacred and is a good thing in itself, even if that person cannot value their own life. Being alive is the foundation upon which all other rights, interests or wishes are built. Sanctity of life is frequently relied on by people from a religious background arguing against some course of action or in favour of a course of action, but, importantly, it is not confined only to those with a religious faith. To those who do not believe in God or an afterlife, this life is rather important. There is no other life beyond this life, so one's life is extremely precious and valuable. It might be the most important thing in your life.

6.12 Professor Peter Singer[2] argues that the traditional Judaeo-Christian ethical principle of sanctity of life, which underpins the practice of medicine,

---

2 P Singer, *Re-thinking Life and Death-The collapse of our traditional ethics* (St Martin's Press, 1995), p 1.

collapsed following the decision of the UK courts in the *Bland* case.[3] That may be overstating the significance of one precedent. Quite clearly the principle was shaken, but arguably is still a highly significant and relevant ethical principle generally and specifically in the context of the saviour sibling debate. The argument would run that the sanctity of life principle is respected and indeed reinforced by the creation and use of saviour siblings because two lives are either created or saved theoretically, namely the saviour sibling who would not have otherwise existed and the existing, sick older sibling. Both lives have equal moral and ethical value and worth. A much wanted, needed and loved child has been created, and a good consequence of that creation will possibly be the saving of the life of a child who is greatly loved and valued by its parents and family.

Good consequences – utilitarian justifications

6.13 A utilitarian might contend that the creation and use of saviour siblings was ethically and morally justifiable because of the good consequences that would flow from it. These would be most obviously the saving of the sick child's life or improvement in their quality of life, or at the very least giving the sick child a very good chance of being saved or having their quality of life improved. Other good consequences of creating and using a saviour sibling would be the enormous happiness given to the family of the sick child if the treatment was successful, or if it was not at least the satisfaction that they had made every effort to save that child. The benefits to the saviour sibling would be great too. They have been given the gift of healthy life, and will be brought up in a loving family where they are wanted. If their sick older sibling has been saved by, eg, their stem cells from the umbilical cord, then that is another huge benefit. It is very difficult to see what bad consequences there might be.

Justice

6.14 Central to the ethical principle of justice is fairness and entitlement. All equals should be treated equally and fairly. This could apply to the saviour sibling. They are not a drone, or spare part bank, but have equal value and ethical worth to their sick sibling. Once they are born they are a person with equal value to their older sibling. Justice could also be applicable in that if the saviour transplantation is successful, the huge financial costs and resources in keeping the saviour sibling alive can be re-channelled and redirected to other patients in the healthcare system, which unquestionably would be a just outcome.

Welfare of the child

6.15 Section 13(5) of the 1990 Act must be considered before offering a woman or couple IVF, PGD and HLA tissue typing, in the same way as with conventional IVF (ie on its own), intra-cytoplasmic sperm injection (ICSI) or DI. The welfare of the child principle is one of the main legal and ethical pillars underpinning the whole assisted reproduction regulatory regime created by the 1990 Act. That major overarching principle was unquestionably fully considered before eg the Hashmis were offered this treatment.

3   *Airedale NHS Trust v Bland* [1993] AC 789 HL.

1990 Act safeguards

6.16   The very fact that PGD and HLA tissue typing is regulated by the provisions in the 1990 Act is a safeguard itself and hence provides reassurance that the practice will be done in a clinic licensed by the HFEA only if the stringent and robust requirements (legal, ethical and medical) contained in the 1990 Act and the Code of Practice are complied with. The fact that both Parliament and the HFEA have supported this technique's use, and that it was deemed that the HFEA could lawfully at its discretion under the 1990 Act authorise it by the courts, must surely engender trust in the general public that it is prima facie an ethical, if not uncontroversial, or universally accepted medical treatment.

Human rights dimension?

6.17   Arguably, if CORE and Mrs Quintavalle had won their case and the HFEA had not appealed the decision and the Hashmis were prevented from creating and using a saviour sibling, they might have sought to invoke Art 8 of the European Convention on Human Rights (ECHR), in that arguably their right to respect for private and family life had been violated. Their point would be that the decision would be a death warrant for their son Zain, which would shatter their family harmony and family life, and that Zain's own Art 2 right to life had been violated. The clear counter-argument of course would be that neither right (Arts 2 or 8), is absolute, as Arts 2(2) and 8(2) make clear (and indeed quite a number of cases on the scope of these articles respectively).

ARGUMENTS AGAINST CREATING AND USING SAVIOUR SIBLINGS

Commodification

6.18   One of the main and most glaring ethical objections to the creation and use of saviour siblings is the argument that if parents, aided and abetted by embryologists, are permitted to create and use them we are basically commodifying babies and children. Babies and children are not commodities or fashion accessories but persons in their own right. Their value is inherent, intrinsic and not instrumental. They are ends in themselves and not a means towards others' ends, be that saving the life or improving the quality of life of an existing sick, older sibling, or relieving the mental suffering of parents traumatised by witnessing on a daily basis that existing child's suffering. Children cannot be chosen according to whim, taste or preference, but rather are human beings with inherent, intrinsic and fundamental ethical value and moral status, not dependent on whether or not they are particularly useful to others.

6.19   Immanuel Kant, the great German deontological moral philosopher, might be invoked in aid of the opponents of the creation and use of saviour siblings. His philosophical approach (deontology) to the ethics and morality of the actions of individuals was diametrically opposed to that of utilitarians and those who assessed an action by the consequences it produced. Kant favoured by contrast a deontological approach in his moral universe, based on the requirements of his famous categorical imperative. The deontological approach is based on the notions of duties and obligations to do acts (the Greek word 'deon' translates and means an 'obligation' or 'duty') as the basis for assessing the morality and ethical nature of an act rather than focussing on the consequences of that act. The Second Formulation or Second Maxim of Kant's categorical imperative which is highly significant and applicable in the context of the saviour sibling controversy is:

> 'Act in such a way that you treat humanity, whether in your own person or in the person of any other, always at the same time as an end and never merely as a means to an end.'[4]

6.20   Perhaps the classic example to illustrate this is slavery, where the slave is used solely or merely as a means toward an end, eg working on the plantation for the benefit of the slave owner and his land. The intrinsic value of the slave as a person has been obliterated. The slave has become instrumentalised, and is being used only as an instrument to serve the demands of the master. Human trafficking could be another example of instrumentalisation, where the person subject to the human trafficking just becomes very cheap fodder for exploitative work or demanding labour in terrible conditions, or used and sold for prostitution purposes.

6.21   However, if one is reading or translating the German of Kant correctly, he does not say that persons cannot be treated partially or ever as a means toward an end, just that they should 'never' be treated *'merely'* as a means to an end. That distinction is of fundamental importance in the context of saviour siblings. The saviour sibling is not created and used to help a sick sibling and then discarded after it has served that purpose. Mr and Mrs Hashmi tried for a 'naturally' created saviour sibling by the lottery of normal sex, producing their son Haris, who was not tissue-compatible with Zain, but was nevertheless a much loved and wanted child. He was loved equally to Zain and the other siblings.

6.22   As has been stated before, parents have children for a huge variety of reasons, some good and some bad, and indeed have children for no reasons at all or accidentally. Why condemn and vilify and prevent the parents of a would-be saviour sibling from availing of the technology to create such a saviour sibling because the parent may not be able to give an undertaking that they want the saviour sibling for its own sake alone? Why have a different test and apply a different standard to such parents? Professor John Harris correctly notes:

> 'We all [treat people as means] perfectly innocuously much of the time. In medical contexts, anyone who receives a blood transfusion has used the blood donor as a means to their own ends ...'.[5]

Sheldon and Wilkinson add that, 'there is nothing objectionable about creating a baby as a "means to an end" provided that it is also viewed and treated as a human being.'[6] Sheldon and Wilkinson then raise a second more practical

---

4   Immanuel Kant, *Groundwork of the Metaphysic of Morals* (1785).
5   J Harris, *The Value of Life* (London: Routledge, 1985), p 143.
6   S Sheldon and S Wilkinson, 'Should selecting saviour siblings be banned? (2004) 30 J Med Ethics 533, at 534.

objection to the commodification argument advanced by opponents of the creation and use of saviour siblings:

'that it does not adequately distinguish between creating a child as a saviour sibling and creating a child for some other "instrumental" purpose – for example, "completing a family", being a playmate for an existing child, saving a marriage, delighting prospective grandparents, or providing an heir. Perhaps these things are different from creating a saviour sibling but, if they are, the difference isn't that they are less "instrumental" for in all these cases, the child is used as a means.'

Non-maleficence

6.23   Another powerful and commonly raised objection to the creation and use of saviour siblings is that the process will harm them. Generally this harm will allegedly take the form of psychological harm. The saviour sibling will be psychologically scarred and damaged if, eg their stem cells from their umbilical cord, or their bone marrow from a bone marrow transplant shortly after their birth, or more radically their other tissue harvested after their birth, fails to save the life of the sick sibling or improve their quality of life. If the former sadly materialises, the argument runs that they will suffer terrible feelings of guilt, rejection by ungrateful or sad parents and psychological damage and depression. Hard evidence or proof of this psychological damage is very elusive, and tends to be anecdotal. The other point is that even if one accepted the possibility of this in some cases, would it necessarily be true in every saviour sibling case? Would one size fit all saviour siblings? Again, might the benefits of its life not heavily outweigh that alleged psychological harm anyway? Furthermore who would determine if psychological harm had been caused and how?

6.24   One would expect the parents to tell the saviour sibling that it was not only created to save the life of its sick sibling, but was created because its parents and family wanted another child anyway, and that the fact that the sick child has died does not diminish, still less stop their love for it.

Welfare of the child

6.25   Opponents of the creation and use of saviour siblings would also base some of their objections to the technique on the basis that the welfare of that saviour sibling has not been taken account of, or, failing that, has not been taken account of properly or sufficiently. Section 13(5) of the 1990 Act (as amended significantly by the 2008 Act), provides:

'A woman shall not be provided with treatment services unless account has been taken of the welfare of any child who may be born as a result of the treatment (including the need of that child for supportive parenting), and of any other child who may be affected by the birth.'

However, as has been stated already, s 13(5) applies equally to saviour siblings, as much as it does to children born by eg simple or conventional IVF or ICSI. Why will a saviour sibling's welfare necessarily be compromised or affected any more by its process of creation as opposed to an IVF or ICSI child? Where is the evidence of this? Of course no such test of taking account of the welfare of the child is undertaken for the 99 per cent of children born by normal sexual intercourse.

6.26   Arguably the welfare of the child could be compromised or harmed in a number of ways:

- physical harm or damage directly attributable from the process of PGD;
- physical harm from HLA tissue typing; and
- harm of a psychological variety later in life.

6.27   Concerning the first point, a *Lancet* editorial states that:

'embryo biopsy for PGD does not seem to produce adverse physical effects in the short term, but it is too early to exclude the possibility of later effects.'[7]

Looking at this positively, *The Lancet* seems to be contending that there does not appear to be any obvious or apparent evidence that PGD causes the embryo any harm and no real reasons to suspect harm will occur in the mid- or long-term. However, viewed more negatively, or perhaps cautiously, the fact that there does not appear to be any short-term damage is no guarantee there will be no harm mid- or long-term. Again, one could argue the use of PGD is one long ongoing experiment on all children born as a result of the procedure.

6.28   Regarding the second variety of harm, namely harm from HLA tissue typing, the argument would be that if there is no short-term harm apparent from the PGD process, axiomatically there is likely to be no harm either from the HLA tissue typing process, as it is done in conjunction with PGD and testing for the disease-free status of the embryonic cell. Hence no additional harm, if harm has been caused, could have been done to the embryo (with its 6–7 remaining cells).

6.29   One could argue that the potential saviour sibling embryo is being harmed by having 1–2 cells removed from it for biopsy for tissue typing analysis, ie a procedure that will not directly benefit it (but will clearly benefit a sick older sibling), but that argument tends to collapse in the light of the fact that 1–2 cells (the same 1–2 cells) had to be extracted and analysed anyway to establish the disease-free status of the embryo. Also incontrovertibly, establishing that the embryo is disease-free will be of direct benefit to that embryo (and subsequent saviour sibling). Sheldon and Wilkinson argue:

'there is an important difference between using PGD to select a saviour sibling and using it to screen for a serious genetic disorder since only the latter procedure benefits the child created, and so only the latter can be ethically acceptable.'[8]

6.30   Concerning the third type of alleged harm to the saviour sibling – psychological harm – Sheldon and Wilkinson sub-divide this category into two types:

'first, that future child may suffer psychological harm if she finds out that she were wanted not for herself, but as a means to save the life of a sibling, and second, that a child conceived for this reason is likely to enjoy a less close and loving relationship with its parents who are less likely to value and

---

7   'Preimplantation donor selection' *The Lancet*, Vol 358, Issue 9289, p 1195, 13 October 2001 (editorial).
8   Sheldon and Wilkinson, cited above, p 535.

nurture the child given that they wanted it primarily to save the life of the sibling.'[9]

Interestingly, the Hashmis did indeed try 'naturally' to have a child that was a tissue match to Zain. They had a child Haris, who regrettably was not a tissue match with Zain, but the Hashmis love him as much as Zain and their other children. Why logically would a saviour sibling created by PGD and HLA tissue typing, who unfortunately was not a match to Zain, suffer any more psychological harm than Haris, who was a naturally created unsuccessful saviour sibling? Sheldon and Wilkinson state that 'it is far from obvious that considerations of child welfare should count against, rather than for, the practice of saviour sibling selection.'[10]

Beneficence

6.31 Opponents of creating and using saviour siblings would contend that the procedure does not do the saviour sibling any good and is not beneficial to them. Again, however, if one gives the definition of benefit or good a wider construction to include possible benefits to the sick sibling, ie curing them or improving their quality of life, and making their parents happier, less stressed out and worried, and improving the general happiness of the wider family, surely that is a tangible benefit? Also PGD and HLA tissue typing benefits the saviour sibling selected, in that they are then implanted in the woman, because they are a tissue match and disease-free, whereas if they were either not a tissue match or alternatively were suffering from the disease that the saviour sibling was suffering from then they would not have been selected for implantation. The tissue typing process has led to a positive outcome and benefit for them. The tissue typing hasn't cured them of an illness or improved their health, given they were not ill or unhealthy. It is, therefore, not therapeutic treatment but it has nonetheless clearly benefited the saviour sibling.

Justice

6.32 PGD and HLA tissue typing could also be challenged ethically, on the basis that it infringes the justice principle, arguably in several different ways:

- It is an extremely costly process, involving as it does IVF, PGD and HLA tissue typing.
- Also, it is an extremely resource-intensive process. Many embryos have to be created and then discarded because of lack of tissue compatibility. (NB these embryos are, at the end of the day, healthy embryos, and could be donated to other infertile couples, thus potentially increasing their happiness.) Many others have to be allowed to perish because they have the same diseases as the existing sick child. Even if a saviour sibling embryo is selected, implantation of it does not actually guarantee a saviour sibling being born ultimately or the transplantation of the stem cells from the blood, bone marrow transplantation or transplantation of other tissue actually being successful.
- Can all parents who can benefit from the procedure access it equally?

9   Ibid.
10 Ibid, p 536.

Sanctity of life

6.33   Tied in with the previous objection is that many embryos have to be created and discarded, or left in frozen limbo and eventually allowed to perish if they are not donated to other infertile couples, in order to acquire or obtain a tissue matching, disease-free embryo. The wastage is not quite on the scale entailed in creating Dolly the sheep, where 277 eggs were used before Dolly was produced, but given that one is using human embryos, rather than animal eggs or embryos in creating a saviour sibling then the ethical objections multiply exponentially accordingly. The practice of creating and using saviour siblings is immoral and ethically repugnant if one views embryos as human beings, albeit at a very early stage of human life. This is a colossal waste of human life at a very early and vulnerable stage in that human being's life.

Slippery slopes – what next?

6.34   Opponents frequently cite the spectre of the slippery slope against permitting the creation and use of saviour siblings. Sheldon and Wilkinson explain what they understand is meant by the 'slippery slope objection':

> 'if we allow something to happen which, considered in itself, is either acceptable or only slightly bad, it will later cause something else to happen which is very bad or clearly wrong (this being what is at the bottom of the proverbial slope). So applied to saviour siblings, it says that if we allow the creation of saviour siblings (which is only slightly bad) this will lead to something much worse: the creation of fully-fledged designer babies.'[11]

In other words if we permit PGD to prevent the creation of a baby with a serious genetic condition, and maybe if we permit the creation of a disease-free embryo who is also a tissue match for an existing sick child (by using HLA tissue typing), that can exceptionally be justified, but some individuals and doctors will always be driven for dubious and unacceptable reasons to push the ethical boundaries and frontiers even further to select additional characteristics in their embryos. Examples of these characteristics invariably include being blue-eyed, tall, intelligent, more musical or possessing athletic ability. Arguably an embryo chosen for any of these reasons would be chosen for a frivolous reason which is unethical. Clearly selections for these reasons cannot yet be made, and may never be able to be made; even if they could, such selection could be outlawed expressly. This will be the result, the inevitable conclusion or bottom of the ethical slope say some, if tissue typing is permitted. Slipping down the slippery slope is regarded as inevitable. However, critics might counter that steps can be built into slippery slopes to stop sliding, eg the licensing system, a supervisory or policing role for the HFEA, the statutory regulatory scheme and the Code of Practice, imposing conditions on treatment licences. This is what the HFEA in fact did in the Hashmi case with the clinic's treatment licence, etc.

6.35   Those who believe in slippery slopes would point to the example of the permitted purposes for using human embryos for research. In the 1990 Act there were only five permitted purposes for using human embryos for the purpose of a project of research.[12] Those original five purposes were extended to

---

11   Ibid, p 534.
12   See Sched 2, para 3(2)(a)–(e).

eight purposes,[13] and additional research purposes using hybrid embryos have now been included by virtue of the 2008 Act. The slide they would contend is proceeding apace here. What and who is to say that that slide will not be mirrored or repeated with initially permitting saviour siblings, then something else and before one knows it permission to create so-called designer children. Sheldon and Wilkinson comment that the objections to slippery slope arguments fall into three categories:

> 'First, one could reject the premise ... that allowing people to choose embryos with designer characteristics is wrong. Secondly, one could argue that allowing the selection of saviour siblings won't or needn't, cause us to become "permissive" about designer babies. Finally, one could argue that saviour siblings and designer babies are relevantly different and therefore one can oppose the latter and not the former without inconsistency.'[14]

6.36   It is extremely difficult to envisage how creating designer babies, as opposed to saviour siblings, which itself necessitates the creation and discarding, rejection or freezing etc of far more embryos than are usable for that purpose, would be economically or ethically justified, given the potentially huge amount of embryos one would need to create and screen before finally getting the elusive, chosen design or preferred characteristics of the designer baby that the parents wish. At the end of the day can the creation and use of a saviour sibling to save the life of a sick and much loved older sibling in all fairness be equated with or be the precursor to the selection of an embryo by whim or fancy, leading to the creation of a designer baby?

---

13   The additional three being created by the Human Fertilisation and Embryology (Research Purposes) Regulations 2001, SI 2001/188.
14   Sheldon and Wilkinson, cited above, p 534.

Chapter 7

House of Lords Debates

INTRODUCTION

7.1   The Parliamentary debates on legalising the creation of saviour siblings characterised the deeply held convictions, principles and views held by both supporters and opponents of this relatively new and controversial branch of medicine. Once again the legal and ethical status of the human embryo was raised, both directly and indirectly: when and in what circumstances was it permissible to create a human embryo and select it primarily or at least partially for the use and benefit of an existing sibling?

DEBATES

Parliamentary supremacy

7.2   The centrality of legalisation regarding the creation of saviour siblings in certain circumstances, under the umbrella of the statutory provisions contained in the 2008 Act and under the aegis of the HFEA, were evident in the words of Lord Darzi, who said, inter alia, that because technology had moved on, so had attitudes. There was, for example a much-increased capacity to screen embryos for serious genetic diseases. Moreover, he said, one of the key aims of the Bill was to impose a statutory ban on the sex selection of offspring for non-medical reasons.[1] The clear implication was that saviour siblings can be created for medical reasons, eg to prevent future children suffering from sex-related diseases/conditions.

7.3   Lord Darzi contended that the government wanted to convert and enshrine in statute what was presently a matter of HFEA policy, and to give Parliament the opportunity to fully debate the provisions. The Bill would also make explicit the basic parameters for screening and selecting embryos and that should be undertaken only on the grounds of avoiding serious disease. Moreover he submitted that the current situation, which had been the subject of legal challenge, ie the *Quintavalle* litigation, was not sufficiently clear, and Parliament could now provide 'a clear steer for the future'.[2]

7.4   The government wanted to copper-fasten the current existing HFEA policy and enshrine it in a legislative form, thus lending it democratic legitimacy following Parliamentary debate and approval, ultimately manifested in legislation. This is in keeping with the general thrust of regulation in the sphere of assisted reproduction where Parliament sets out the broad sweep of

---

1   *Hansard*, 19 November 2007, col 666.
2   Ibid.

permissible activity and the specifically created expert statutory regulatory body, the HFEA, is given powers to fill in the regulatory detail.

7.5   Baroness Deech[3] welcomed the wider use of PG for creating saviour siblings, but not 'for social reasons.' Furthermore, she stated that the House of Lords should be pleased that the deliberate choice of an embryo that was, for example, likely to be deaf will be prevented by the Bill. For her, and many others, deliberately creating an embryo with a disability, is an ethical, medical and legal bright line that must not be crossed. That would surely be taking reproductive autonomy and choice to highly dubious and ethically unacceptable limits.

Commodification?

7.6   Lord Alton, one of the leading critics, not just of the creation of saviour siblings, but of much of the superstructure and content underpinning the whole edifice of the the 2008 Act, was particularly scathing about the nebulous and vague nature of the language employed in the Bill to describe the type of tissue which may be used from the saviour sibling, and to what extent the saviour sibling would effectively be manipulated and exploited for the benefit not of the saviour sibling but for another individual. He stated that:

> 'deliberately [leaving] it open for children apparently to be created for the sole and explicit purpose of being available to provide any type of tissue at all for an existing sibling is appalling.'[4]

This was 'truly dehumanising society' and was a serious development. Essentially he objected to the commodification of humanity, to a person (like many others, he passionately believes an embryo is a person) being used and treated instrumentally, ie being used as a means toward an end and not valued as an end in itself. However, the counter-argument would run that these so-called saviour siblings are valued as an end in themselves by both the doctors and embryologists who create them and by the parents of the sick child who have requested and want their creation. They will be greatly wanted ,valued and loved by their parents with a love equal to that for the sick child and simply will not be regarded as a spare part bank or drone to be discarded when the, eg, stem cells needed for their sick child have been harvested or mined from the saviour sibling.

Definitions and justification

7.7   Lord Alton was also extremely vexed and concerned about the nature and type of treatments suffered by the existing sick child that could lead to the creation of saviour siblings, stating that:

> 'The Bill [potentially] extends the creation of saviour siblings to the treatment of serious disease rather than just life-threatening disease.'[5]

Therefore saviour siblings could be created to treat a serious disease in an existing child, which lowers the ethical sliding scale considerably further than if one limited treatments to life threatening diseases. Is this a further example

---

3   Chairman of the HFEA (1996–2004).
4   *Hansard*, 19 November 2007, col 681.
5   Ibid.

of an ethical slippery slope? Lord Alton continued that the government used the words 'umbilical cord blood stem cells, bone marrow or other tissue' in the Bill, and that the meaning of "other tissue" is potentially very broad and wide. As he stated: 'The phrase in the Bill does not seem to exclude anything specifically'. In other words there are no limits to what organs or body parts that could theoretically fall within the net of the words 'other tissue'. Essentially he argued that unclear and vague law is potentially bad law and law that can be abused to the detriment of human life.

7.8   In addition Lord Alton drew support for his concerns that badly drafted and uncertain legislation may lead inexorably down the ethical slippery slope when he suggested the term could extend to even autism. Critics might contend that this approach is unduly alarmist and highly unlikely to materialise, given that the causes of autism are so little understood. What therefore would be the purpose of such a saviour sibling?

7.9   Lord Alton was not reassured that the Bill would unequivocally ban the creation of a child to be a kidney donor. Kidneys are of course non-regenerative tissue as defined originally by s 7(2) of the Human Organ Transplants Act 1989, in that if they are transplanted from a donor (saviour sibling) into a recipient (the existing sick child) they will not be replicated or replenished, in contrast to blood or bone marrow, which is regenerative tissue. Kidney transplantation operations involve major surgery with attendant risks to the donor, so arguably the major ethical principle of non-maleficence (sometimes referred to as *primum non nocere*, or 'first do no harm') applies.[6] Incontrovertibly a saviour sibling who was created to provide a matching kidney to a sick existing child and who was subjected to an operation to remove a kidney and give it to their sick sibling would suffer harm. Arguably all living donations involve harm to the donor and hence are prima facie unethical.

Alternatives

7.10   Lord Alton also argued strongly that the creation of a saviour sibling was unnecessary given the availability of less ethically controversial alternatives. He contended:

> Instead of creating saviour siblings … how much better it would be if we were routinely collecting umbilical cord and cord blood. Only four National Health Service facilities do this at present, while 98 per cent is routinely destroyed. That would save lives immediately.'[7]

For Lord Alton this was a scandalous waste on a Biblical scale of a highly valuable potential toolkit and medical resource for sick existing children, which crucially has been obtained in a morally and ethically uncontroversial manner, unlike, he submitted, the manufacturing of a child (saviour sibling) specifically with the aim of harvesting cord blood after birth, or bone marrow in a subsequent bone marrow transplantation procedure, which is a potentially painful and harmful procedure for the saviour sibling, or even subjecting them

---

6   One of the four major ethical principles underpinning the practice of medicine according to Beauchamp and Childress in *Principles of Biomedical Ethics*, 5th Edn (Oxford University Press, 2001).

7   *Hansard*, 19 November 2007, col 681.

to some other invasive procedure to recover tissue for the benefit of another patient.

7.11   The Archbishop of York, Dr John Sentamu, was strident and passionate in his denunciation of feeding voracious consumerism and science's attempt to assuage the wishes and desires of parents desperate to have children, which he believed underlined many of the controversial proposals included in the Bill, eg the right of any prospective parent to have a child by any means necessary, and the creation of saviour siblings.[8] To paraphrase the song that love and marriage go together like a horse and carriage, doctors and scientists are harnessing and yoking the beast of science and technological development and manipulating and bridling it in directions wished for by would-be parents. Just because something is technologically possible to achieve does not axiomatically mean it ought to be done, but the fact that it is possible to do something frequently impels those deciding whether to do it, to do so. Again, just because patients desperately want a saviour sibling to save a very sick existing child, and that scientists can use PGD allied to tissue typing to hopefully create such a child, does not automatically mean it is ethically right to do so, nor that legally it should be permitted. The autonomy and reproductive freedom and choice of parents are clearly of enormous and fundamental ethical significance but they are not absolute. Considerations of the welfare of the child, ie of any child who may be born as a result of the procedure, must be taken account of and act as a brake on the wishes of the prospective parents and on the desire of the scientists and doctors to meet those parental wishes.

Natural wastage?

7.12   Lord Walton of Detchant injected a bit of perspective and context into the debate in the House of Lords regarding the concerns of those opposed to the creation of saviour siblings who argued, inter alia, that it resulted in the discarding of healthy as well as diseased embryos, hence devaluing human life, stating that, in the course of normal human fertilisation, four or five ova are fertilised but only one generally implants. 'All the rest of those fertilised ova are flushed down the toilet. So millions and millions of human embryos are lost every day in life.'[9]

7.13   Hence 'natural' creation of embryos (ie non-IVF assisted creation by sexual intercourse) is incredibly inefficient and wasteful of embryos, resulting in a far greater 'natural' discarding of embryos, yet there is no moral angst or ethical outrage at that. As Lord Winston noted, humans are:

'one of the most infertile of all mammals ... For most couples, regular sexual activity only gives a chance of about 18% each month of a successful pregnancy ... Women, unlike most lower mammals, only produce a single egg, and that at most once a month ... Each healthy man, with a single orgasm, ejaculates enough spermatozoa to produce a pregnancy in all the healthy women of child-bearing age in Western Europe. But most of the sperm are either so abnormal in shape or chemical composition, or move so sluggishly that proper fertilisation is impossible ... Moreover, once an egg is

---

8   Ibid, cols 705–707.
9   Ibid, col 708.

fertilised and a human embryo is formed, there is only about a 20% chance of pregnancy ensuing … Four-fifths of all human embryos are lost in the first few days after conception, before implantation in the mother's womb … Even when implantation has occurred, the trials of the embryo are not over. Human miscarriage is a common event, and it is likely that between 10–15% of early pregnancies will abort spontaneously for reasons which are still largely obscure.'[10]

7.14 As Tennyson famously said, nature is red in tooth and claw. The fact that something is 'natural' is not necessarily good and to be valued or stoically or fatalistically accepted. Conversely, the fact that something is 'unnatural' does not equally mean it is automatically bad or unethical. All medical intervention is arguably unnatural in one sense, although in another it is surely natural to utilise technological, medical or scientific skills to try and improve the human condition generally or help individual patients, rather than stick our heads and intelligence in the sands.

Strict control

7.15 Lord Darzi flagged up a key safeguard against potential abuse:

'the HFEA retains the control of tissue typing via licensing, and the Human Tissue Authority must approve any transplants involving organs from living donors and for children who are too young to consent.'[11]

Ultimately the HFEA must grant a licence for tissue typing. Therefore, there can be no tissue typing done without a licence by doctors or scientists. The HFEA has been created by legislation, charged specifically with making decisions about granting licences to clinics keeping, using, creating or undertaking research on human embryos. Great responsibility, not inconsiderable powers and trust has been delegated to it by Parliament. Parliament set out the overarching principles and parameters in the 1990 and 2008 Acts, and created the HFEA to, inter alia, enforce or police clinics to ensure they comply with the Acts and the Code of Practice.

Prevention v cure?

7.16 Lord Walton[12] flagged up the practical life-saving and enhancing value (as opposed to the abstract or philosophical worth) of PGD in testing embryos for Duchenne muscular dystrophy. The argument here is that prevention is better than cure, and, moreover, preventing an embryo being implanted affected with Duchenne type is much better ethically, given there is no cure for a child with Duchenne muscular dystrophy. PGD is the technique used to ascertain if the embryo has Duchenne type by removing just one cell from the embryonic blastocyst. This removal will not damage or harm the embryo and if the embryo does not contain the Duchenne type it can be implanted in the woman to give her a Duchenne-free child. The argument is that this is in that child's best interests

---

10   Prof R Winston *Making Babies: A Personal View of IVF Treatment* (BBC Books, 1996), p 14.
11   *Hansard*, 21 November 2007, col 869.
12   At *Hansard*, 4 December 2007, col 1641.

and promotes its welfare most effectively, by avoiding a life with considerable suffering. The argument then would be, if you can test the cell of the embryo to check if it is Duchenne-free, you can at the same time test it for tissue type and then implant it in order to create a saviour sibling for a sick existing child. However, is that next step a slide down the ethical slippery slope or a crossing of the ethical Rubicon, or is it by contrast a deliberate and conscious ethical bright line or step?

Terminology

7.17   The difficulty of defining and grappling with terms appropriate to cover the intended target was apparent in Parliament. This is obviously a problem when drafting any legislation, but the problem is particularly exacerbated when dealing with controversial and fast-moving scientific areas.

7.18   Unsurprisingly, Lord Alton took issue with altering the wording in the Bill from 'abnormality' to 'characteristic' and warned the Lords that: 'We have to guard against the mentality that can sometimes lead to wanting designer babies.'[13] Babies should not be selected by consumerist parents on the basis of the their preferences for certain desirable characteristics or traits, eg being tall, blonde, intelligent, athletic, etc – essentially choosing an 'off-the-peg' design or blue-print for a future child. Babies are not products or goods in a free market of choice.

7.19   Baroness O'Cathain fully endorsed the sentiments of Lord Alton, asserting that replacing the word 'abnormality' with 'characteristic' would open Pandora's box, that 'characteristics' could include colour of the eyes, mental ability, physical ability, or whether they are tall, small, white or whatever. She felt that this amendment would create designer babies, and said: 'We are trying to play God once more.'[14] The argument here would be that reproductive choice and autonomy do not equate to reproductive licence or a reproductive 'free-for-all'. The preferred UK method for dealing with the new assisted reproductive technologies is neither prohibition nor laissez-faire, rather it is regulation: whether the regulation is too restrictive of doctors' or scientists' activities or concerning parental wishes to be parents, etc, or whether it is far too permissive, is another matter.

Embryonic testing

7.20   Baroness Royall of Blaisdon, a government minister, then explained what was tantamount to embryo testing under the terms of the Bill, saying it would be permitted in five situations. Arguably this is itself a legal and ethical safeguard, in that doctors or scientists cannot use PGD on human embryos whenever they want to. Society needs to be reassured on this, if respect is to be shown to embryos. She stated:

---

13   *Hansard*, 4 December 2007, col 1645.
14   Ibid.

'Embryo testing involves removing one or two cells of an embryo created in vitro at the eight-cell stage. The Bill introduces five principal purposes for which embryos can be tested.'[15]

7.21 She then set out these five purposes:

(1) 'to determine whether the embryo has a genetic, normally chromosomal, abnormality that would affect its ability to result in a pregnancy'. This purpose appears to accord with the interpretation given by Maurice Kay J in the High Court in the *Quintavalle* case,[16] namely that testing embryos is permissible under the 1990 Act for the viability of an embryo, ie giving the words employed in the Act a narrow, limited construction;

(2) 'to determine whether the embryo has inherited a gene or genes from one or both parents that will mean that any resulting child will have or develop a serious medical condition – this is preimplantation genetic diagnosis, and is what the amendments tabled by the noble Baroness relate to';

(3) 'to determine the sex of the embryo where there is a particular risk that any resulting child will have or develop a gender-related serious medical condition';

(4) 'to determine the tissue type of the embryo where there is an older sibling with a serious medical condition that could be treated with umbilical cord blood, bone marrow or other tissue of the resulting child'; and

(5) 'in the event that there is uncertainty as to whose gametes were used to create the embryo.'

7.22 Commenting on the second purpose, Baroness Royall stated that it allowed embryo testing where there is an inherited condition in one or both parents that could be passed on to any resulting child. She emphasised:

'the criteria that must be met in relation to the risk of the condition for which the embryo is being tested – for example, that it must be a significant risk that a person with the abnormality would have or develop a serious condition, disability or illness.'[17]

7.23 The debate teased out of the Minister the government view that an abnormality as referred to in the Bill means or translates into 'something medically wrong' with the embryo, as opposed to a mere trait or characteristic, ie presumably being intelligent, tall, athletic, etc. Be that as it may, Baroness Royall, stated that the clause was aimed at ensuring:

'that however the trait is described, embryo testing could be carried out only where the trait gives rise to a significant risk of a person having or developing a serious medical condition.'

Embryo testing thus is not carried out lightly or for frivolous reasons. The Minister did not define or explain the difference between a risk as opposed to a significant risk, albeit she provided an example of a 'significant risk':

---

15 Ibid, col 1645.
16 *R (on the application of Quintavalle) v Human Fertilisation and Embryology Authority* [2002] EWHC 3000 (Admin).
17 Ibid, col 1646.

'if the particular abnormality resulted in a serious condition in nine out of 10 people with that condition, this could be considered a significant risk.'[18]

Nor did she nail down precisely what constitutes a 'serious medical condition'. Baroness Royall was adamant and certain that selecting embryos by characteristics or traits including 'sporting ability' was an emphatic no:

'The answer is no – a characteristic would still need to satisfy the criteria leading to a serious medical condition.'[19]

No consent possible

7.24 Lord Alton challenged vociferously the fallacious notion that saviour siblings can be regarded as 'donors'. Organ donation is something that is done altruistically and philanthropically, and certainly in the case of living donations it is imperative that it is done with 'appropriate consent'.[20] Arguably one of the fundamental pillars underpinning medical treatment is the consent of the patient to medical treatment and, more particularly, obtaining the informed consent of the patient to the proposed treatment. Consent is a manifestation of patient autonomy. The autonomy of the saviour sibling is quite simply being ignored in favour of the needs of the existing sick child. Clearly obtaining the informed consent from a saviour sibling is impossible. When did the saviour sibling give consent to the subsequent use of their tissue? Lord Alton argued:

'Let us first dispose of the casuistry that saviour siblings are donors. There is clearly something of a contradiction in using the word "donor", as a donor has to give consent, and that is manifestly impossible in what is proposed. Personal organ donation is often a generous and altruistic act … but it is always an act freely entered into. It is an act of autonomy and personal choice but clearly a baby or a young child does not have any say in this momentous decision.'[21]

Definitions

7.25 In addition Lord Alton was troubled about the dilution of the legislative safeguard, as he saw it, of a saviour sibling being created where the sick sibling is suffering from a 'life threatening condition' to merely suffering from a 'serious condition'. The ethical floodgate barriers have been breached significantly, he believed by this apparently minor, but in reality huge alteration in terminology. As he stated:

'Furthermore, reducing the present hurdle for permitting such an extraordinary presumption from "life threatening" to "serious" conditions – which, as we know in another context [ie abortion] may mean a cleft palate or webbed fingers – should not be allowed to happen without deep and fundamental debate.'[22]

---

18   Ibid, col 1647.
19   Ibid.
20   See the Human Tissue Act 2004.
21   *Hansard*, 4 December 2007, col 1649.
22   Ibid.

Consent

7.26 Lord Alton was particularly vexed and concerned about the creation of saviour siblings as potential organ donors for existing sick siblings and refers to his question to Lord Darzi concerning the meaning of the words 'or other tissue' in the Bill and to Lord Darzi's answer, on 21 November 2007, which, Lord Alton claimed, left the House in no doubt that it included organs, including organs from non-consenting children who are too young to give consent. Lord Alton quoted Lord Darzi:

> "'The Bill does not limit which tissue can be used in the treatment of a sibling... and the Human Tissue Authority must approve any transplants involving organs from living donors and for children who are too young to give consent".– [*Official Report,*21/11/07; col.689]'

Lord Alton concluded that on the basis of Lord Darzi the government Minister's reply:

> 'Therefore, if the embryo is found to be an immune match, it will be implanted deliberately to become a source of spare parts for an existing child – its sibling – even when it is too young to give consent.'[23]

An organ bank?

7.27 Lord Alton raised the spectre of future ethical issues on the moral horizon, contending that even if a child had ostensibly been created only to provide umbilical cord blood, it was nevertheless available to provide any tissue or organ after birth. Thus the saviour sibling, once selected for its tissue compatibility and disease-free status, will be a permanent tissue match and potential source of spare parts for the existing sibling. The temptation will always be there for parents, the sick sibling and doctors to go to the saviour sibling first in the event of the sick sibling needing tissue or organs, etc. The pressure on it to donate later in life might be enormous.

7.28 Lord Alton contended that the words used in the HFE Bill, 'treated by umbilical cord blood' were very much open to interpretation. Treatments come in all shapes and sizes and can be totally curative of a condition, improve a condition, stabilise a condition, prevent deterioration in the condition, prevent some of the associated painful symptoms, make very little or no difference to the condition or maybe even make it worse. The question is how is 'effective' defined and who defines it – the scientist, the doctor, the legislator, the patient? He claimed that the saviour sibling is initially and hopefully being created to harvest beneficial stem cells from the umbilical cord of the tissue compatible saviour sibling, but if that fails other parts of the saviour sibling will be used to benefit the existing sibling.[24]

7.29 Lord Alton, therefore, contended that creation of saviour siblings ought to be a last option. If other routes exist, eg umbilical cord blood from other donors in cord blood banks, then these must be tried and utilised before embarking on creating saviour siblings and using their umbilical cord blood.

---

23 Ibid.
24 Ibid, col 1650.

This is a classic slippery slope argument – something ethically controversial is allowed to be done for an allegedly beneficial reason, but then gradually it is done in a wider range of circumstances which are for bad reasons, or certainly not obviously good reasons.

Loving creation?

7.30 Lord Alton, stated that unlike normal transplantation, saviour siblings are created following 'deliberate intervention'.[25] That may be the case, but of course it denies the fact that the saviour sibling may be loved and valued by its parents for itself, regardless of whether it was initially chosen and created as a saviour sibling. It was created not solely as a means toward an end, but was valued in its own right. It has inherent, intrinsic value. If umbilical cord blood or bone marrow from the saviour sibling proves ineffective in treating the existing child this does not automatically guarantee that its parents will stop loving or valuing it any less. By the same token if the cord blood or bone marrow transplant successfully helps to cure or improve the sick sibling child's condition, this does not mean the parents will love or value the saviour sibling any more, but it does mean the sick child is still alive and may have a better quality of life. As has been argued already children are created for a huge variety of reasons 'naturally'– some for very good reasons, some for very bad, some for very mixed reasons and quite a few for no particular reason at all.

7.31 Lord Alton contended that it was totally understandable for loving parents who are desperate to save the life or prevent the terrible suffering of their child, to try any method to save their child or spare it suffering. However that does not give them, or doctors and scientists, ethical carte blanche to do anything to save that child or prevent or lessen its suffering. Two wrongs do not make a right. As he commented: 'Any parent who has a seriously ill child … will understandably search desperately for cures', adding that a caring society has 'a duty' to continue the search for new and successful cures, but that: 'Medicine, however, cannot function in a moral vacuum and many ethical considerations need to be taken on board'.[26]

7.32 Hard cases make bad law and emotional tuggings at our ethical heartstrings are arguably poor foundations for sound ethical decisions. Lord Alton made the important and telling observation that medicine and scientific development do not operate in a separate sphere of existence which is devoid of ethical and moral considerations. Good medical and scientific development is underpinned by a sound ethical and moral framework.

Gut reactions

7.33 Lord Alton argued that creating saviour siblings is intuitively wrong and that most people would have an intuitive 'gut reaction' against it. However some would argue that gut reactions against things can be misconceived and

25   Ibid, col 1651.
26   Ibid.

be based on prejudice and ignorance and quite simply be wrong. Gut reactions again are not a sound basis for ethics or for framing law. Lord Alton stated:

'Gut feelings are absolutely valid and often represent the greatest wisdom. Our compassion for the welfare of existing children does not legitimise a trade off with our legal responsibilities for the welfare of children, including those created by assisted reproduction.'[27]

An assault?

7.34 Lord Alton raised another objection to the creation of saviour siblings, namely that the removal of, eg, bone marrow from them after birth, or other tissue, and certainly the removal of organs or parts of organs arguably constituted an assault on their person:

'There is no reason why criminal law prohibitions on battery or abusive behaviour towards children should not apply as much to children created by IVF as to everybody else. In the current legal realm, how could any invasive medical intervention performed on a child not for its own benefit, when it could not possibly give consent, not be argued in law to be an assault against the bodily integrity and right to autonomy of that innocent child?'[28]

Balancing ethical principles

7.35 Clearly those in favour of the creation of the saviour sibling would argue that whilst the harvesting of bone marrow from the saviour sibling might be physically painful (ie offend the non-maleficence principle), and not be for the immediate or obvious good (beneficence) of the saviour sibling, and that there is conceivably a violation of the autonomy principle (ie the bodily integrity of the saviour sibling has been compromised), nevertheless, if one gave the best interest test a wider, purposive construction, then saving the life of an existing sick sibling or giving that existing sick sibling the prospect of greatly enhanced quality of life, relieving the tremendous pressure and suffering on loving parents, and promoting holistically the interests and the greater health and happiness of the whole family unit by permitting this notional assault (if that is what it is) would arguably serve justice best. Again, if one were to balance the risks and burdens to the saviour sibling associated with eg harvesting bone marrow from them, arguably tiny and minimal when weighed against the enormous potential benefits to the sick sibling, the parents and other family members, and arguably the benefits to the saviour sibling of knowing they saved their older sibling, then again the scales of justice and ethics favour the treatment being done.

7.36 One could draw further support for this conclusion from a couple of cases on transplantation. The first case, from the United States, involved the transplantation of a kidney from an incompetent adult to his sick sibling, which the Kentucky court held was in the best interests of the incompetent donor even though he clearly lacked the capacity to consent to the procedure.[29] In

---

27 Ibid.
28 Ibid.
29 *Strunk v Strunk*, (1969) 445 SW 2d 145 (Ky,169).

the second case, from the United Kingdom, a bone marrow transplantation involving an incompetent adult woman donor to her sick sister was authorised by the courts on the basis that it was in the best interests of the donor.[30]

Balancing competing principles

7.37   Lord Alton was adamant, however, that:

> 'No child should be created specifically for the benefit of a third party, no matter how pressing the anguish of the parents. That is the absolute principle at stake here, but it must also be added that the therapeutic benefits of creating tissue-matching babies have been inaccurately portrayed to the public as an easy procedure with guaranteed success.'[31]

Again one can hark back to the old chestnut that children are created for an infinite variety of reasons in non-assisted reproduction. Why are double standards being applied and also more exacting standards being required from the parents and doctors who are helping to create a saviour sibling for the parents for the benefit of the existing, sick sibling? Again, Lord Alton would appear to be taking a more deontological approach in his objections to the creation of saviour siblings, in that there is an obligation or duty not to manipulate, exploit, create, utilise a baby or child for the benefit of another – for him an 'absolute principle' not just merely a fundamental one.

A panacea?

7.38   Lord Alton then raised a couple of more pragmatic objections, albeit equally important to his philosophical objections to the creation and use of saviour siblings. First he challenged the misconception of the public that creating saviour siblings and harvesting tissue or bone marrow or even organs, is an 'easy procedure', presumably with little or no risk to the saviour sibling donor. Secondly, he challenged the fallacious notion that creating saviour siblings and utilising tissue or cord blood etc from them inevitably results in a 'guaranteed success', ie keeping the existing sick recipient sibling alive and improving their quality of life. He repudiated the claim that the technology was the only, or ideal, therapeutic route:

> 'In reality, the chances of the matching baby being created successfully are limited. IVF has a low success rate. Pregnancies do not always go to term. There is no guarantee … that there will be sufficient [cord] blood harvested, or that any subsequent transplant will be successful.'[32]

A myriad of imponderables may thwart the successful treatment of the existing sick child using a saviour sibling.

7.39   Furthermore, he believed that using saviour sibling technology may undermine ('be hijacked') and damage best practice in pregnancy, and so cause harm. The interests of the saviour sibling would be further subordinated to those of the sick sibling.

---

30   *Re Y* [1996] Med L Rev 204.
31   Ibid, cols 1651–1652.
32   Ibid, col 1652.

7.40   The technology will result in embryonic waste. For those who regard fertilised eggs or embryos as early human life warranting equal legal protection and having ethical status and moral worth equivalent to any human, and who believe in personhood from the moment of conception, discarding embryos with serious diseases and/or embryos that don't happen to be tissue compatible with the existing sick sibling is tantamount to murder; immoral and ethically unacceptable.

Eugenics

7.41   Lord Alton continued with his critical and scathing scorn of the wisdom and probity of permitting this controversial process:

> 'It is very much a hit or miss technology and it is criticised for some of the eugenics practices associated with embryo selection in the first place.'[33]

Eugenics has connotations with the excesses of Hitler and the Nazis of the Third Reich, but the word 'eugenics' originates from two Greek words, namely 'eu', translated 'good' or 'well', and 'genesis' or 'stock' or 'type', so literally eugenics involves classically sorting by types or stock. In Nazi Germany this sorting by stock or type meant those deemed to be non-Aryans were rounded up, placed in concentration camps, tortured and brutalised and finally exterminated in their millions, as part of the so-called 'final solution'. However recourse to such an argument is for some the wrong vantage point for assessing the ethical acceptability and indeed the legality of a proposed act, such as permitting saviour siblings.

Psychological harm?

7.42   Lord Alton then considered the harm, and specifically the alleged 'psychological burden', placed on a 'tissue-matching child' or 'designed baby' if the process fails and the recipient dies. He argued that burden 'must not be dismissed in a rose-coloured enthusiasm for the benefits that might accrue to a third party.' Again this concern could be met by stating that the alleged harm must be weighed against the enormous benefit and good of creating new life – the benefit accruing clearly to the saviour sibling who has the prospect of a long, happy, disease-free life, and the benefits to their family and to society generally by the potential unique contribution they make to it in the future. There could be psychological burdens, but equally there could be psychological benefits if the use of eg blood or bone marrow is effective.

Alternatives

7.43   Lord Alton pressed the House of Lords to explore and fully develop better alternatives to creating saviour siblings or 'designed' children, stating:

---

33   Ibid.

> 'The lottery of trying to design a saviour sibling is a lengthy and unreliable process at best, making it immensely impractical and never likely to be universally practised.'[34]

He said that instead 'non-controversial' alternatives should be explored, eg cord blood.

7.44   Human embryos can only, under the terms of Sch 2, para 3(2) to the 1990 Act, be used for research purposes under a research licence granted by the HFEA, 'unless it appears to the Authority to be necessary or desirable' for a number of specified reasons (originally there were five in the 1990 Act). Thus, if alternatives to human embryos could be used for the research project (eg animal embryos or computer models, etc) then clearly the use of human embryos was not necessary and would be prevented. Thus Lord Alton argued that the use of saviour siblings is unnecessary given the availability of alternative sources stem cells, ie in umbilical cord banks, which store cord blood and donated cord blood.

7.45   The government, rather than concentrating on legalising a highly dubious and controversial procedure (saviour siblings), which is impractical, lengthy, costly and ultimately a lottery, should rather focus their attention on increasing the availability of cord blood banks. He quoted Colin McGuckin, Professor of Regenerative Medicine at Newcastle University, who stated: 'cord blood stem cells ... already treat 85 clinical diseases.'

7.46   In other words treatments using stem cells from cord blood is not a possible theoretical source of potential treatments for diseases, but is a real, tangible resource in the arsenal of doctors fighting diseases. Crucially these stem cells originate from a universally acceptable and uncontroversial source. He also noted Dr Peter Hollands, who said '98 per cent of cord blood produced in this country is routinely destroyed',[35] and that moreover there were only four NHS facilities in this country at that time that did that collection. This was in marked contrast to, eg, the United States. Rather than direct time, effort and money at the mirage of savour siblings, Lord Alton advised:

> 'If we were to store the cord blood from every baby born in this country, we would have a bank of stem cells of infinite value, and if this was practised internationally on the largest possible scale, the therapeutic potential would be extraordinary.'[36]

Devaluing?

7.47   Earl Howe supported Lord Alton's concerns about the ethical acceptability of creating and using saviour siblings, stating that it devalued that person as an individual. He was concerned the phrase 'or other tissue' implied donating 'an organ', which caused lasting harm to the donor and contended the state had no 'right to raid the body of a child for any part of him that will not naturally regenerate.' The salutary and damaging lessons learned following the

---

34   Ibid.
35   Ibid, at cols1652 – 1653.
36   Ibid, at col 1653.

Alder Hey and Royal Bristol Hospital scandals, when thousands of organs were removed and stored without the specific consent of parents of the dead children come to mind here, the scandals being compounded and exacerbated by the fact that the vast majority of these organs were never actually used for research etc, allegedly the main reason for their retention.

7.48   Earl Howe conceded:[37]

> 'if there is ever a question of a child donating tissue, the Human Tissue Authority is legally charged with taking the decision under the 2006 regulations. Of course, it must do so on the basis of the common law test of "best interests", but "best interests" is a concept capable of being interpreted quite broadly.'[38]

Terminology revisited

7.49   Lord Lloyd of Berwick stated that, given the 'sensitive' nature of human embryology, any legislation should be as precise as is reasonably possible and so he had major reservations on replacing the words "life-threatening disease" with "serious medical disease", which he said was far too vague and wide. It could have covered almost anything, and, furthermore, how could anyone ever be sure that the saviour sibling was donating the kidney truly voluntarily?

7.50   Lord Harries of Pentregarth, the former acting Chairman of the HFEA, said the HFEA gave 'serious ethical consideration' to the legal/ethical issues involved regarding saviour siblings, and encouraged the government to furnish more clarity concerning terms employed like 'serious' and 'other tissue'.

Motives?

7.51   Lord Harries tackled Lord Alton's argument that a saviour sibling was being created and used instrumentally as a means to an end and that that is unethical. Peers would agree, he said, 'with the Kantian principle that we should never treat any other human being simply as a means to an end. That is fundamental to any ethical view.' but, 'However, a woman who is having a baby in this situation probably has a range of motives', ie not just 'purely' to help a sick sibling, but for 'mixed' motives including having the child for 'its own sake.'

7.52   In many ways both Lord Harries and Lord Alton, although approaching the issue of the merits or ethical basis of why the woman or couple are having the saviour sibling from diametrically opposed stances, can only really be making a 'guesstimate' as to the real motives for having such a baby. This area of judging the reasons why parents have saviour siblings is fraught with dangers, in the same way as assessing would-be parents who are seeking IVF, using either the old test in s13 (5) of the 1990 Act (ie including the need of that

37   Ibid, at col 1654.
38   As was evident in both *Strunk v Strunk* (above, fn 29) and in *Re Y* (above, fn 30).

child for a father), or the new test, post 1 October 2009, enshrined in s 13(5) as amended by the 2008 Act (ie including the need of that child for supportive parenting).

7.53   Lord Harries again challenged Lord Alton's contention that there may be a psychologically negative and deleterious effect on the savour sibling for the rest of its life if it felt it had been brought into the world simply for the benefit of another person. He contended 'this is an unknown' if the recipient child died, or it 'could be the opposite' if the transplant was successful. Then the saviour child's 'value' and 'preciousness' would be 'enhance(d)'.

Definitions – moral vacuums

7.54   Lord Patten argued that Parliament should only legislate on a matter if that matter can be clearly and satisfactorily defined, citing the difficulty Lord Darzi and some of the greatest figures in the medical world had in even agreeing a definition of an inter species embryo. He queried the mangling and distortion of the English language in describing a saviour sibling as a 'donor' in the Bill:

'A saviour sibling cannot, by definition, be a donor so as presently drafted the Bill uses highly inexact language.'[39]

Moreover he agreed with Lord Alton that 'medicine cannot and should not proceed in a moral vacuum', or as he dubs it 'a morality-free zone'. Although those in favour of creating and using saviour siblings would unquestionably agree with him on this, they would disagree with him and contend that the 2008 Act and the Code of Practice and the HFEA ensure that doctors, clinics and would be parents are operating in anything but a moral vacuum, but rather are subject to a tightly controlled area of medicine governed by strict and effective regulation in an environment subject to a very clear ethical framework provided both by Parliament and the special expert quango created by Parliament, namely the HFEA. Indeed some[40] would contend the regulatory regime is in certain respects too restrictive.

7.55   The Lord Bishop of Winchester, whilst agreeing that the terminology employed in the Bill is far from clear, eg 'or other tissue' and 'serious medical condition', argued that this is not accidental, but deliberate on the part of the government: 'the phrase is precisely designed not to be clear but to be broadly inclusive.'[41] He agreed about the value of relying on 'gut feelings' (ie intuition) when judging the probity, ethics and acceptability of certain actions, and then seized on one of the main arguments utilised by opponents of creating and using saviour siblings, namely they are being used as a means towards an end, ie being created primarily not for their own benefit but for the benefit of another, which is unethical. He stated:

'Enabling the collusion of parents … in making this individual an instrument, making legal the engagement of the medical profession in such a creation of instrumentality and the lack of choice in being a donor and

---

39   Ibid, col 1656.
40   Eg Lord Winston.
41   Ibid, col 1657.

being an instrument, is a fundamentally serious thing to be doing, and in my judgment, a wrong thing to be doing.'[42]

Human life has more value than mere instrumentality. Humans are not slaves, mere objects or drones. That would be *Brave New World* translated into 2011.

7.56   The Lord Bishop noted that adult donors are free to donate tissue to others, consensually and altruistically, but clearly saviour siblings cannot do so.[43]

Who decides?

7.57   Baroness Deech, the former Chairman of the HFEA referred to the Hashmi and Whitaker cases and the judgments in the former, and made the telling observation that the blame, or responsibility, for giving permission to harvest organs or human tissue from child 'donors' rests with the Human Tissue Authority (HTA), the sister quango of the HFEA, which is responsible for, inter alia, regulating and granting permission for organs and human tissue to be transplanted from certain categories of living unrelated donors and children. The Baroness said:

'Until very recently there would have been no question of a donation from a child who did not have the capacity to consent unless that child was made a ward of court. The judges would consider the case and most likely not give their permission. The fault lies, if there is one, in this new law that the HTA should be giving permission in these cases.' [44]

Baroness Deech flagged up the very low chance of creating a disease-free, tissue- compatible saviour sibling: 'There is only a one in 16 chance of finding an embryo that is free of the disease and is capable of developing into a saviour sibling.' Hence a quango, the HTA, and not the courts now ultimately make the decision about transplantation from children.

Instrumentalisation?

7.58   Baroness Deech was not convinced by the argument that it is unethical that saviour siblings are being created as a means toward an end, and agreed that:

'no one should be used as a means to an end, but until the dawn of the age of contraception very recently there could be no question as to whether there was a good or a bad reason to have a child. People had babies because they came along, maybe to till the land, to inherit a title indeed, or for whatever reason, and there is no question but that parents are likely to love that saviour sibling very much indeed because they have gone to enormous lengths to have it.'[45]

42   Ibid, cols 1657–1658.
43   Ibid, col 1658.
44   Ibid, col 1659.
45   Ibid.

Best interests

7.59   Lord Alton expressed concern at what constitutes the 'best interests' of a child as construed by the HTA, and asked whether they extended beyond the medical questions to psychological, social and emotional issues,[46] noting that if they were incorporated into these tests that would obviously be a wide area indeed on which to make these judgments.

7.60   Baroness Deech, in responding to Lord Alton's question as to what was meant by a child's best interests in relation to the vexed issue of what tissue can be removed from them said that, 'looking back at decisions made in the past, it is very unlikely that a court would give permission for a major organ to be removed from a small child.'[47] Regarding a person being born as a means to an end or treating anyone as a means to an end, Baroness Deech cited the Diane Blood case as an example, saying 'the most egregious example of that was the Diane Blood case where sperm was taken from a dying and then a dead man.'

7.61   However, Baroness Tonge did share the concerns about the meaning of 'other tissue' a phrase which was she said, 'very worrying'.

7.62   Lord Walton of Detchant described the issue of creating saviour siblings as 'a very difficult issue, which bristles with scientific, medical, ethical and social problems.'[48]

7.63   Lord Elton had a number of major ethical objections to the production of saviour siblings: first the 'repulsive idea' of creating a saviour sibling for harvesting organs or tissue; and secondly that 'if the child was not compatible, the embryo would be destroyed.' The ratio of embryos needed to produce one disease-free tissue compatible-match is, therefore, unacceptably high. For every potential saviour sibling created, there will be many (15 according to Baroness Deech) deemed unfit for implantation. Such a huge waste of embryos is unethical, given their scarcity, regardless of their special moral status for some.

Fertility tourism

7.64   Lord Winston, made the telling comment that:

'so far, in practice, most of these diagnostic procedures [tissue typing] which are very rare – they have been done only a very few times – have usually been done in collaboration with other countries, for example in the United States where tissue-typing or a gene-specific diagnosis has been made by a pre-implantation diagnosis overseas.'[49]

The reality is that even if a technique or procedure is unavailable in the United Kingdom for whatever reason, the nature of our increasingly global economy and global healthcare means that a minority of patients can 'shop' around and

---

46   Eg see *Re Y* (above, fn 30).
47   *Hansard*, 4 December 2007, col 1660.
48   Ibid, col 1660.
49   Ibid, col 1662.

travel to other countries to access the therapy or treatment. The Blood case,[50] the phenomenon of transplant tourists, ie people who travel to poor developing world countries and buy organs,[51] and the phenomenon of Irish women travelling to England to access lawful abortions, are obvious examples of this.

7.65 Baroness Deech agreed the reality is that: 'we live in a world of freedom of mobility. There is nothing to stop anyone going abroad to have a procedure that is limited or prohibited here.' That is in fact what the Whitakers did do. They travelled to Chicago and had their embryos tissue-typed. As Baroness Deech noted:

'We have no control in that sense, but we live in a world of globalisation so far as IVF and embryology go ... All we can do is to set standards in this country'.[52]

Terminology

7.66 Lord Winston reiterated that he favoured the term 'life-threatening' because it covered genetic diseases, rather than 'serious', stating that the latter was open to all sorts of interpretations and much looser and gave the following example:

'One genetic disease that could be classed as serious but is certainly not life threatening is colour blindness ... it would be rather unjustified under the purposes of the Bill to screen an embryo for colour blindness, but it might be a serious condition under this vague definition. It is certainly not life-threatening.'[53]

7.67 Lord Mackay of Clashfern, a former Lord Chancellor, stated that he felt that 'life-threatening' had in it the idea of a condition that would certainly shorten the life of the child in question. This was not quite broad enough to cover a situation in which a disease might accompany a person throughout their life, having a very detrimental effect on it and restricting it without shortening it. Regarding the meaning of 'or other tissue' in the Bill, Lord Mackay ventured that it 'means more than umbilical cord blood stem cells and bone marrow and is an additional phrase'.[54]

Safeguards

7.68 Baroness Royall of Blaisdon responded to the concerns of quite a number of the peers and from the outset acknowledged that:

'The screening and selection of embryos for the purpose of providing stem cells to treat a seriously ill child – so-called saviour siblings – is one of the most emotive issues in this controversial field ... the HFEA currently [as at the date of the debate] licenses on a case-by-case basis the screening of

50 *R v Human Fertilisation and Embryology Authority ex p Blood* [1999] Fam 151; [1997] 2 WLR 806.
51 S. Burns, 'Transplant Tourism' (2007) 157 NLJ 20.
52 *Hansard*, 4 December 2007, col 1663.
53 Ibid, col 1664.
54 Ibid, col 1665.

embryos where the intention is that the resulting baby's umbilical cord stem cells or bone marrow stem cells will be used to treat an existing sibling who has a life-threatening or serious illness. The Bill clarified the scope of the HFEA to make such decisions.'[55]

Again this is in keeping with the respective roles of Parliament and the specialist regulator (the HFEA) in the sphere of assisted reproduction: Parliament strategically sets out the broad framework (legal and ethical) within which the assisted reproduction process and industry occurs, and the HFEA fills in the detail (ie performs the important operational role). Baroness Royall was adamant that the debates, discussions and deliberations on the Bill in Parliament, especially in the House of Lords, were not made in a moral vacuum.

Burdens v benefits

7.69   Baroness Royall then assessed the alleged respective burdens and harms of creating saviour siblings, compared to the possible benefits and gains of the process. Concerning the burdens and harmful consequences she submitted that PGD followed by tissue-typing is a safe procedure, in the generally accepted meaning of the term 'safe' – clearly there is no such thing as 100 per cent safety. She observed:

'Although children born as a result of embryo testing are not yet adults, from the thousands of children born following embryo testing there is no such evidence of harm.'[56]

Whether any of these children will develop illnesses or suffer problems long-term (ie in adulthood) over and above 'normally' created children, remains to be seen. Some critics would, on the basis of this, argue that all children born by IVF or ICSI or DI are being subjected to a massive non-consensual experiment, which is totally unethical.

7.70   On the plus side of the ethical, medical and legal scales, Baroness Royall observed:

'In contrast the benefits offered by tissue typing are considerable. The Bill allows potentially life-saving treatments to be offered for children who are affected by serious medical conditions. In practice, tissue typing is only ever considered when all other options are exhausted – in other words, when there are no match donors on the register or within the family.'[57]

Tissue typing is, therefore, not the first treatment option. Furthermore the HFEA has not been issuing licences for tissue-typing like confetti, licensing it for three conditions.

7.71   Baroness Royall agreed wholeheartedly that the government should be doing considerably more to ensure that more cord blood is stored: 'Clearly there is much more that we should do to store cord blood, and we welcome the new cord blood bank.'[58]

---

55   Ibid.
56   Ibid, col 1666.
57   Ibid.
58   Ibid, col 1667.

She noted that the HTA oversees transplants of bone marrow for children, and that the HTA and an independent assessor (IA) would have to be satisfied that the child's best interests had been properly considered and that the HTA's Codes of Practice had been correctly followed. Therefore, she said:

'The Government decided on balance that the creation of embryos where the intention was to collect bone marrow for the treatment of a sick sibling was appropriate, subject to those safeguards.'[59]

Scope

7.72   Significantly, and arguably very worryingly, Baroness Royall then stated, inter alia, that although 'strictly speaking' it could be possible under the provision to test an embryo as a future kidney donor, it was not in any way the intention behind including the words 'or other tissue'. This ministerial reassurance is far from convincing. If 'strictly speaking' it is possible to test an embryo for subsequent organ donation then that loophole ought to be plugged. It is academic that it is not in any way the *intention* behind including the words 'or other tissue' to include organs.

Safeguards emphasised

7.73   Baroness Royall attempted to further allay the concerns of the critics of the Bill, by stating that:

'The role of the HFEA in regulating tissue typing is limited to the creation and testing of an embryo. However, there are further regulatory controls imposed by the Human Tissue Authority, which must approve such transplants. The HTA's code of practice advises that before the removal of a solid organ from a child it is good practice for court approval to be obtained'.[60]

This is similar to decisions about withholding or withdrawing treatment from patients in a persistent vegetative state (PVS), as was decided in the famous case involving Tony Bland.[61] Baroness Royall stated, moreover, that, in practice, since the HTA took on responsibility for approving organ donations from children in September 2006 it had yet to approve a single case.

7.74   A further safeguard made by the government was that saviour siblings will not be permitted to be created to provide parents with treatment for a life-threatening condition. Is this a case of it being unethical to use child donors to benefit adult or older recipients?

7.75   Baroness Royall confirmed that the Bill would have no impact on the Human Tissue Act or the powers of the Human Tissue Authority. It addresses the grounds on which embryos can be selected, not the subsequent controls on interventions on the child that result. Regarding concerns from peers that saviour siblings ought only to be created as a last resort, Baroness Royall stated that people would not choose to do this if there was another option and conceded

---

59   Ibid.
60   Ibid.
61   *Airedale NHS Trust v Bland* [1993] AC 789.

that there are a lot of hurdles to surmount before parents or doctors get a saviour sibling child to help their sick existing sibling: 'Assuming an embryo has the correct tissue type ... the chance of pregnancy is still only likely to be around the 30 per cent mark.'[62] She also noted that the HFEA had produced a Code of Practice with guidance in it for clinics and would-be parents and that for tissue typing 'it includes a list of factors to consider, including the availability of alternative sources of tissue or therapy, now and in the future.'[63]

7.76 Baroness Royall dealt with the issue of assessing the alleged possible psychological impact of being a tissue-type child by stating that the HFEA code of practice required consideration of the long-term emotional and psychological implications for any child who might be born.

Signals

7.77 Lord Alton explained to the House why he objected so strongly to the proposed change and 'signal' being sent in the Bill by the words 'life threatening' being replaced by 'serious', by referring to a 'good parallel here', namely the case of the Reverend Joanna Jepson, who on reading the statistics for late abortions discovered that cleft palate, club foot, hare lip, webbed fingers and webbed feet were being included in the 'serious' category for abortion of a child.[64] Clearly none of those by itself is a life-threatening disease, and thus 'It goes to the heart of how we interpret things'.[65]

Reality

7.78 Baroness O'Cathain sought to burst the bubble of optimism and the promise of guaranteed cures offered by saviour siblings, stating the reality is slightly different from the visionary ideal:

> 'the overarching ethical issue of the legitimacy ... of deliberately creating a human being so that his or her body tissue can be harvested for the benefit of another ... is impossible to justify in any circumstances ... We have a duty to explore the reality rather than the hype of creating tissue matching babies. It is not a simple procedure and it gives no guarantee of a cure.'[66]

The process involves IVF, and there is no guarantee that viable embryos will go to full term. There is the risk of ovarian hyper stimulation syndrome (OHSS), variously assessed as being of the order 1–2 per cent, and moreover:

> 'is it right for a fertile woman to be subjected to infertility treatment carrying risks, bearing in mind her responsibility to her family, including at least one existing child?'[67]

The obvious retort is that it is the woman's autonomous choice if she wants to undergo this very difficult process, with no guarantee of success, and, if she

---

62 Ibid, at col 1668.
63 Ibid.
64 See s 1(1)(d) of the Abortion Act 1967, as amended.
65 *Hansard*, 4 December 2007, at col 1668.
66 *Hansard*, 15 January 2008, at col 1268.
67 Ibid.

gives fully informed consent and is fully aware of what is involved, including risks and possible or probable failure the question as to whether this is right is answered. Also she has a responsibility to a dying child to try and do everything reasonable to save him, and to her husband and family, who will be devastated if the sick sibling dies. Again, why necessarily will she love or consider less the interests of the saviour sibling?

Negatives

7.79   Other negatives and risks of the process are identified and flagged up for major concern by the Baroness, including multiple IVF cycles, which increase the health risks to the mother, to get a matching sibling. Non-tissue matching and/or 'disease- carrying' embryos are destroyed. PGD is an invasive procedure which may negatively affect the survival rate of the embryo. Finally, there are unknown, longer term consequences of PGD, the argument being that this is an unethical form of mass experimentation without consent.

7.80   The Baroness emphasised and reiterated that there was no guarantee of success regarding a tissue-matching sibling, but then there is no guarantee of any treatment or diagnosis made by doctors always being successful. Indeed the tests of standard established by the *Bolam*[68] and *Bolitho*[69] cases involves the doctor only having to act in accordance with a responsible body of opinion (ie body of practitioners in their speciality or field), not that the treatment will necessarily cure the patient, nor that they have to act in accordance with the highest standard of the leading practitioner in their field. So long as they act in accordance with an ordinarily skilled practitioner in the field they discharge their standard of care.

Other countries

7.81   Baroness O'Cathain contended that the United Kingdom is out of kilter with other countries in the world in that no other national Parliament in the world has legislated to allow saviour siblings. That may well be true, but then again, no other 'test-tube' baby had been created in the world till Louise Brown was created in 1978 in the United Kingdom, so that is perhaps not a necessarily convincing argument against legalisation of creation of saviour siblings. Again, in 1990 the United Kingdom was the first country in the world to pass legislation regulating assisted reproduction and embryo research in the world.

Balancing interests

7.82   Baroness O'Cathain sympathised greatly with desperate parents but nonetheless argued:

---

68   *Bolam v Friern Hospital Management Committee* [1957] 1 WLR 582, QB.
69   *Bolitho (Deceased) v City and Hackney HA* [1998] AC 232, HL.

'The interests of the absolute welfare of the child who would be created must encourage us to resist the emotional force of the argument about the sick sibling.'[70]

Principle needs to prevail over emotions otherwise hard cases make bad law and bad ethical decisions. In addition the Baroness noted pragmatic, as well as ethical and philosophical objections to the practice of saviour sibling creation. More universally available streamlined and cost-effective solutions should be sought, such as cord blood stem cells, which are available naturally and are particularly versatile. Clearly the Baroness is arguing that creating saviour siblings violates the justice principle, as it is unfair that only a very few families or sick siblings will benefit from the process, whilst a whole swath of families and sick siblings, whose needs are equally important, are effectively prevented from accessing it.

Ethical objections

7.83 Baroness O'Cathain then outlined a number of 'considerable' ethical objections to the practice of saviour sibling creation and use:

'the ethical objections are considerable and they constitute a fundamental obstacle. First, there is the question of potential harms to the parties involved, most obviously the harm inflicted by the destruction of unsuitable embryos. Secondly, at the very centre of our ethical thought – both religious and secular, deriving from philosophy as well as tradition – lies the principle that one may not degrade an individual human life by treating it as an instrument for the benefit of others rather than as something to be regarded and respected in its own right.'[71]

Human life is not something that ought to be created and manipulated primarily for the benefit of someone else. That cheapens and devalues the moral and ethical status of that individual, which damages both them and also harms society as well. Thus, if we deviate from that principle by manipulating human life, that would be crossing the ethical Rubicon, and descending down the ethical slippery slope.

7.84 Baroness O'Cathain was quite specific about what is meant by a saviour sibling and by what is entailed in its design:

'...it is a case of having a particular child only if it is compatible physiologically with the tissue of another. The designed child, for the duration of its life, will be witness to the intention of the designers and will always be vulnerable, both physically and psychologically, to further demands on its body.'

Their tissue-compatible status therefore renders them vulnerable to further tissue being mined or exploited from their bodies. Thus, she concluded by stating that:

'to manufacture a person in this way is to offend against the respect that is due to the integrity of that person, no matter how compelling the goal of trying to cure.'

---

70 *Hansard*, 15 January 2008, at col 1269.
71 Ibid, at col 1270.

Genie out

7.85   Lord Alton of Liverpool said that, despite a letter from Lord Darzi on 8 January 2008 providing an assurance that government amendment 31 would make clear that a decision to allow embryo testing on the basis of providing a future organ transplant for a sibling would not be allowed:

> 'the difficulty is that once we tissue-type in the first place we set these wheels in motion. When you tissue-type to test for umbilical cord or bone marrow, you have the genetic footprint of that child and then organs could be used after birth, even though this Bill does not set out to permit that.'[72]

He was still unhappy with the use of the term 'or other tissue':

> 'Doctors have put it to me that it could mean taking part of a liver – not a whole liver – or a lobe from a lung, which could be used and identified as 'other tissue'. Because it might be regenerative, it might qualify under 'other tissue'. Obviously, that has considerable implications for the child from whom those tissues have been taken. Morbidity, even mortality, rates can be high.'[73]

7.86   Lord Alton was not convinced that the role of the HTA was an effective safeguard and bulwark against organs or parts of organs being removed from saviour siblings at some future date:

> 'However, if this legislation is passed, the Human Tissue Authority will have seen the signal from Parliament that it is perfectly all right to create a child as an organ donor and therefore will be under strong pressure to agree.'[74]

He was also not convinced of the efficacy of the additional safeguard that the HTA will only authorise that an organ be transplanted if that is in the best interests of the child, here presumably the saviour sibling. As he argued:

> 'However [the best interests test] includes psychological, emotional and social best interests, as well as medical ones. Imagine that the saviour created as an organ donor is now utterly devoted to his older brother and does not want him to die. It could be argued that it would be much better for his psychological, emotional and social health to part with this or that part organ rather than to see his brother die.'[75]

Emotional and psychological blackmail are unedifying and not a sound ethical basis for legitimising this practice.

Pontius Pilate

7.87   Lord Alton was not happy either with the government for doing a 'Pontius Pilate' and washing their hands of responsibility for authorising an organ or part organ transplant in an individual case, by passing that decision over to the HTA, even though they had actually given the green light to the

---

72 Ibid, at col 1270.
73 Ibid, at col 1271.
74 Ibid, at col 1272.
75 Ibid.

creation of saviour siblings to help sick existing children by, inter alia, the transplantation of umbilical cord blood, bone marrow or other tissue. He said:

> 'The Government have repeatedly cited the Human Tissue Act, passing the buck to the Human Tissue Authority and implying that it would be the same for any child after birth ... It is not a comparable situation. Normal children are not deliberately created to be organ or part-organ donors for their older brother or sister.'[76]

Lord Alton, moreover stated that:

> 'It is an absolute sham to claim that a saviour sibling would be created for only umbilical cord blood and possibly bone marrow-and even for part organs. After birth, the child could be used for whole organs, as it would be immune-matched for the existing sick child.'[77]

The sick child might be partially helped in the short term by tissue from the saviour sibling, but the saviour sibling is a permanent insurance policy of matching tissue. The purpose for its creation after all was to be a tissue compatible/disease-free match after all.

Three words

7.88   Lord Alton concluded by stating that three words out of the 44,363 words in the Bill (ie 'or other tissue') could consign a child to being created deliberately as an organ donor. Government attempts to argue that saviour siblings will not be created to harvest 'whole' organs, but rather only 'part' organs were disingenuous:

> '[T]hat could consign a child to being deliberately created from the outset as a part-organ donor and to being available after birth as a whole-organ donor. Once the child has been tissue-typed, that possibility is inevitable.'[78]

Referring to Aldous Huxley's *Brave New World*, Lord Alton concluded by saying that, 'There is nothing brave and nothing good in breeding babies for the purposes proposed.'

Human rights

7.89   Lord Patten attacked the creation of saviour siblings from a different angle, raising the issue of the human rights of saviour siblings, 'on which the government have been strangely silent', but does not stipulate what human rights exactly are at issue here – possibly arts 3, 8 and 14 of the European Convention on Human Rights. He added:

> 'I have always believed that a child is a child is a child and I am fearful that the Government may well lead us down the route of setting up two classes of children: children and saviour children.'[79]

---

76   Ibid.
77   Ibid.
78   Ibid, at col 1273.
79   Ibid.

The implication is that children have more moral and legal status than saviour siblings. He invoked the argument of the saviour sibling being regarded as a mere commodity and tied it to the slippery slope argument:

'once tissue typing begins, a child once created for this purpose will rapidly be seen as a commodity. A child is not a commodity; a child is not a donor; at best a child is a patient.'

7.90 Also of profound concern to opponents of saviour siblings, including Lord Patten, is the issue of consent, or rather the lack of it here, and who gives that consent. 'Children are children and not organ banks.'

Commodification

7.91 Baroness Williams was concerned about, the danger of society drifting, 'towards the commodification of the individual':

'If we allow this we treat the second child essentially as a commodity to be used and exploited by the first child or the first child's parents. The parents are almost certain, understandably, to be overwhelmingly concerned about rescuing their child.'[80]

The sick child is in existence now, they may be an infant or a child who is greatly loved and valued by their parents, whose suffering is devastating for the parents, never mind the child. If they were to die, that too would be emotionally catastrophic for all of the family – those enormous emotional pressures have to be weighed in the scales against a tissue-compatible and disease-free designed saviour sibling embryo. For some this is an ethical or moral no-brainer.

7.92 Baroness Williams argued that a line had to be set to respect the 'sacramental nature' of the human being who is being asked to make this 'terrible sacrifice', to avoid the moral pressure to produce spare parts. The government must draw that line to say that 'we will not accept the commodification of children'. She added the fundamental objection was the 'deliberate' creation and use of that child as an 'instrument' for others and 'not being treated for itself'.

7.93 Concerning the accusation of instrumentality, namely that the saviour child has been only created to provide benefit for someone else, Baroness Deech stated that up until about 20 years previously '[C]hildren came along and people had them for whatever reason they thought fit.' She added that the Hashmis might have carried on having children naturally, which was possibly a worse ethical situation and certainly more of a stress on the family than having PGD. She stated:

'The only thing that worries me about the use of PGD for saviour siblings is that, while the use of the umbilical cord is fine, who will consent to the use of the tissue?'[81]

---

80 Ibid, at col 1274.
81 Ibid, at col 1276.

In answering her own question she stated that she would feel content if any donation other than umbilical cord blood had had to be sanctioned, as was the case in the past, by a family court judge.

Motives

7.94   Lord Harries of Pentregarth stated:

> 'The heart of the matter is the ethical issue ... when parents have children they have a mixture of motives. They are not having another child simply in order to aid a sick sibling; they still want another child anyway. All of us have a range of motives when we do things, and I do not think that this is simply a question of instrumentality.' [82]

Interestingly, Lord Harries wondered about possible bad consequences of permitting the creation of saviour siblings:

> 'if we allow this for the use of umbilical cord or bone marrow, it could create a culture in which people might think it more normal to use the organs of children and therefore there will be unfair psychological pressure on that child, perhaps even an infringement of its human rights.' [83]

Permitting the creation and use of saviour siblings might thus herald or signal a sea change in society's hitherto reluctance to use children as a source of organs and replace that ethos with a more liberal recourse to children as potential organ donors generally, which might be an ethically retrograde step down the slippery slope. Lord Harries wondered on that basis whether there were enough safeguards to ensure there would not be unfair psychological pressure on the child and its parents for its organs to be used. [84]

Snags

7.95   Lord Winston, one of the creators of PGD alongside Dr Alan Handyside, made the point that the first children created following the pioneering PGD, in April 1991, would be 17 years old in April 2008. He explained some of the potential technological snags and pitfalls of PGD/tissue typing:

> 'When you biopsy an embryo, you effectively take away one or at most two cells containing one or two molecules of DNA. What you are effectively doing is something which has been in the courts recently in Northern Ireland and is currently under scrutiny in the courts generally in the British [sic] – a form of low copy number DNA. [85]

> 'Essentially, you are trying to establish the genetics of an embryo based on the tiniest possible amount of tissue in very controlled circumstances, unlike in criminal circumstances or where the courts are looking at age DNA, but

---

82   Ibid, at col 1277.
83   Ibid.
84   Ibid, at cols 1277–1278.
85   For an analysis of some of the problems associated with low copy number DNA, See S Burns, 'Low copy number DNA on trial' (2008) 158 NLJ 919.

none the less subject to all sorts of problems regarding the gene amplification and the risk of contamination of that DNA.'[86]

Lord Winston referred to some of the problems further:

'At present, that technology is by no means entirely safe. There are risks of making a wrong diagnosis – thinking that you have a particular tissue type when you have not, or getting a gene defect right when you have not. The history of PGD shows that from time to time mistakes have been made and an embryo affected by a disease for which there has been screening has been transferred to the uterus.'

The science is not therefore foolproof. Lord Winston added:

'Most of these cases will be in families where there is a gene defect already and therefore the scientists involved will not just be screening for one specific gene but for the gene which causes the defect and the series of genes which make up the tissue type of that embryo. Therefore, there is the very real risk of not making a correct diagnosis.'

The more genes being examined, the greater the propensity for error.

Odds

7.96   Regarding the alleged 1 in 16 chance 'of getting it right', ie having a tissue compatible/disease-free saviour sibling, Lord Winston observed:

'I am not sure what the mathematics are, but I imagine that the chances of getting it right every time are really quite low and even if it is correct, you still have the recognition that if that child grows up, its stem cells will be capable of being taken up by that embryo.'[87]

Lord Winston, with the benefit of considerable practical experience in the matter, cautioned the House against regarding PGD and tissue typing as being some sort of panacea, warning of the serious risk of unreasonably raising the hopes of couples by a technology which was then very rare, unlike IVF.[88] He also noted that requests to the HFEA for this type of reproductive technological intervention were exceptional:

'They are very unusual and it is interesting to notice that over the years they have not increased' and that if the practice is legalised in an Act, 'I do not think will make a huge difference to the practice of in vitro fertilisation in actual issues.'[89]

Slippery Slopes

7.97   Lord Winston said he feared the risk of being on a kind of slippery slope in that:

---

86   *Hansard*, 15 January 2008, at col 1279.
87   Ibid.
88   1% of all babies are now born by this procedure.
89   *Hansard*, 15 January 2008, at col 1280.

'even if we do establish a child who is compatible with its elder sibling and free of the gene defect, the problem is that if the initial stem cell transplant does not work, there is then the increasing pressure to consider what you might do next as the child grows up.'[90]

Lord Winston was not convinced about the distinction between regenerative and non-regenerative organs, stating that a number of organs are regenerative that are solid tissues, such as the liver. He felt that this definition was not very clear, and gave rise to a medical problem. Lord Winston does not pull his punches, adding: 'There is a real risk that children might be used, and therefore abused, with this technology, so we must consider this very carefully.' Theoretically the courts can protect such a child:

'but in practice such children who are at risk cannot be protected, because even if the courts decide against a particular procedure for that child as a donor, there is still the family pressure and the notion that that child has in some way failed its elder sibling and therefore its parents.'[91]

Choice

7.98 Baroness Tonge argued that it was surely the woman's choice as to whether she subjected herself to this procedure for the sake of an existing child. Baroness Knight of Collingtree was concerned that that decision or choice put the mother in a terrible dilemma. Earl Ferrers speculated on what a child would feel if it thought that it had been brought into the world solely in order to provide a donor for a sibling, saying:

'you do not necessarily have to be a butcher to smell when the meat is bad. It seems to me that this is taking science too far. In many respects it might be described and considered as grotesque.'[92]

Reform

7.99 Baroness Royall summed up the existing law on saviour siblings:[93]

'The HFEA currently licences, on a case-by-case basis, the screening of embryos where the intention is that the resulting baby's umbilical cord blood stem cells, or bone marrow stem cells, will be used to treat an existing sibling, who has a life-threatening, or serious illness.'[94]

Fundamentally:

'The Bill clarifies the scope the HFEA has to make such decisions by setting out five purposes for which embryos can be tested, including one that specifically enables testing embryos for tissue type where there is a seriously older sibling.'

---

90   Ibid.
91   Ibid.
92   Ibid, col 1282.
93   Ie as it was prior to the coming into force of the 2008 Act on 1 October 2009.
94   *Hansard*, 15 January 2008, at col 1282.

She reiterated that up until then the HFEA had licensed tissue typing for three conditions. She noted an important safeguard in that, in practice, tissue typing was only ever considered when all other options for successful treatment are exhausted; in other words, when there were no matched donors on the worldwide bone marrow registry or within the family. These are tangible and effective safeguards and the fact that as at 15 January 2008 the HFEA had only granted three such licences is strong evidence that the practice of authorising saviour sibling creation has not become a free-for-all under the watch of the statutory regulator.

7.100 The Baroness added:

'we should remember that parents making this decision are often in a difficult situation with one very sick child and no other option. It is highly unlikely that any further child who happened to be born to such parents as a result of treatment would be anything other than loved and cherished.'[95]

She categorically stated that the decision of parents to create such a child would unquestionably not be taken lightly: 'I am sure that the parents would have reflected long and hard on such a difficult decision, and they will certainly be aware of all the risks involved.' The decision to create a saviour sibling by the parents is autonomous and fully informed.

7.101 The Baroness agreed that cord blood could be collected at the time of birth with minimal impact on the child born. Concerning bone marrow, if this is used:

'the Human Tissue Authority would oversee the transplants from children. The Human Tissue Authority and an independent assessor would have to be satisfied that the child's best interests have been properly considered and that the regulations and the Human Tissue Authority's codes of practice have been properly followed. Where a child donor is involved, the courts may also be involved to authorise what is in the donor's best interests.'[96]

Therefore, said the Baroness, the Government concluded that:

'on balance … the creation of embryos where the intention was to collect bone marrow for the treatment of a seriously sick sibling was appropriate, subject to these safeguards. Protection is in place by two regulatory authorities – the HFEA to licence the creation of embryos for this purpose and the HTA to oversee transplants of bone marrow taken from children.'[97]

Thus there is a double-lock provided in the form of two separate statutory authorities both at the creation and use stage of the saviour sibling to ensure full and proper consideration of ethical issues.

7.102 Baroness Royall gave an assurance that 'other tissue':

'is intended to capture regenerative tissue other than whole organs. An example of such tissue would be the actual cells of the umbilical cord.'

Furthermore, concerning the safety of removing two cells from the embryo for tissue typing and checking for the disease status of the embryo, she said that

95   Ibid, col 1283.
96   Ibid.
97   Ibid.

there had been no evidence of harm to date from thousands of children born worldwide following PGD.

7.103   Finally Baroness Royall addressed the concerns of some peers regarding the human rights of the saviour sibling, stating:

> 'It would not be lawful to remove any tissue from a child if that would be incompatible with the rights of the child under the European Convention on Human Rights. A parent could consent on behalf of a child, but only where that would be in their best interests, subject to final determination by the courts. Any decision in a child's best interests would have to comply with the convention.'[98]

The Baroness elaborated on safeguards for children where solid organs are proposed to be removed (presumably applicable also to saviour siblings). The HTA panel making such a decision must consist of no fewer than three members and the HTA Code of Practice advises that before the removal of a solid organ from a child, whether competent or not, it is good practice for court approval to be obtained.

Votes

7.104   The House of Lords voted 62 in favour of Amendment 29, preventing saviour sibling creation and use, but 180 peers voted against the amendment, almost 3–1 in favour of the government Bill permitting saviour siblings.

---

98   Ibid, col 1283.

Chapter 8

House of Commons Debates

INTRODUCTION

8.1   The House of Commons debates covered broadly the same terrain and arguments as those of the House of Lords.

SECRETARY OF STATE'S VIEW

8.2   In introducing the Bill in the House of Commons for its second reading Alan Johnson MP, Secretary of State for Health, stated:

'The Bill introduces explicit regulations on embryo screening. Embryo screening and selection will be allowed only for the purpose of detecting serious genetic diseases or disorders.'[1]

Mr Johnson was emphasising that the government were now passing specific and clear legislation regulating this controversial procedure of embryo screening. The government was showing its commitment and determination to set out clearly the parameters for permitting this contentious procedure and not merely leaving it to the HFEA to sort out, or alternatively passing unsatisfactory secondary legislation to regulate embryo screening. He made the point that the HFEA has licensed screening in a number of cases since 1990, including for single-gene disorders, eg muscular dystrophy and sickle cell disease.

Clarification

8.3   He added that the Bill would clarify the powers of the HFEA to license embryo screening to enable parents to have a child who is a genetic match for an older brother or sister who is seriously ill. He noted that that had been permitted by the HFEA in a handful of cases (eg the Hashmis) as a last resort. This is an important safeguard and reassurance for the public against abuse and frivolous recourse to the procedure. The Secretary of State noted that this had been permitted where there are no other donors and all other medical avenues have been exhausted (eg cord blood banks, other family members as donors etc).

8.4   Mr Johnson challenged the argument that permitting the creation of saviour siblings is akin to creating a child just for spare part, as a misrepresentation. Creating saviour siblings occurred, he said, when there was no other medical avenue to pursue. All such cases involved the treatment of very rare blood disorders, and the tissue taken was from the umbilical cord. He added that the Bill would support such screening as a last resort, and it was expected that tissue used would be confined to cord blood and bone marrow.

---

1   *Hansard*, 12 May 2008, col 1069.

However, the 2008 Act specifically refers to 'or other tissue', as well as cord blood and bone marrow.

Ethical rubicons

8.5   Mr Johnson added:

'The Bill makes it clear that it would not be possible to test an embryo where the intention is to remove an organ from a child to treat a sick sibling'.[2]

That would seemingly be crossing the ethical Rubicon. He went on:

'Nor will the Bill permit parents to screen embryos in order to include, rather than exclude, a particular disability.'

What the Health Secretary is referring to here is, eg, deaf parents having IVF or PGD to deliberately choose and create an embryo with deafness. Most people would find it unacceptable to permit this type of selection, ie deliberately creating a child with a disability. Besides which, how could such a choice be reconciled with s 13(5) of the 1990 Act, ie the welfare of the child principle? It is surely right for Parliament to limit such parental autonomy/choice. This sort of reproductive liberty if permitted might undermine confidence and the general support for most of the activities permitted by the regulatory regime.

DEBATES

Balances

8.6   Andrew Lansley MP, the Shadow Health Secretary, agreed with the Secretary of State:

'the testing of embryos to prevent the implantation of an embryo with an inherited or genetic condition will, in many cases, be in the best interests of that child if the condition is life-threatening or would severely impair their quality of life'.[3]

However he had prefaced this by saying:

'We understand that the interests of the child to be born must be paramount. The dignity of life demands that a life should not be created simply to serve the interests of another.'

This is recognition of the intrinsic and inherent value of the saviour sibling for itself, that life should not be valued or that persons should not be used solely or simply as a means toward an end, but should be valued as an end in themselves.

8.7   Mr Lansley added that:

'Likewise, we believe that the so-called "saviour sibling" permission should be tightly restricted to life-threatening conditions and those that would seriously impair the life of the sibling. The Bill says "serious medical condition", but it does not specify in sufficient detail the criteria to be applied.'

2   Ibid, col 1070.
3   Ibid, col 1078.

The implication being unclear law equals bad law. He then added:

'The balance of advantage against ethical constraints must be judged case by case, and we need to provide strong language in the legislation to ensure that the Human Fertilisation and Embryology Authority does not allow the boundary of what is to be permitted under the "saviour sibling" provision to be stretched too far over time.'

The HFEA should not be given too much discretion here or the danger is that saviour siblings will be permitted to be created too easily and quickly.

Signals

8.8   Kevin Barron MP welcomed the Bill, because it spelt out for the first time in law a number of rules relating to the screening and selection of embryos and gametes.[4] Acts of Parliament can 'spell out' the law in a way that courts cannot, and the Act sends signals out to society as well.

Negative selection

8.9   Norman Lamb MP, speaking on genetic testing of embryos, supported negative selection, which involves testing IVF embryos for serious inherited diseases and selecting those that are free from disease.[5] Mr Lamb disagreed with some disability rights campaigners who argue that screening out was tantamount to regarding an individual with a disability as less valuable in some way, and contended that avoiding babies being born with very serious disabling conditions was compatible with doing 'everything possible to avoid any discrimination against an individual who has a disability.'[6] Just because one tries to prevent babies being born with very serious disabilities, it does not mean, therefore, that one should discriminate and be intolerant to people who have been born and are living with very serious disabilities. However, opponents of this view would submit that making this distinction in practice in the real world is much more problematic than merely stating an aspiration or ideal. The reality is that people with very serious disabilities suffer very great discrimination and intolerance and lack of support in their daily lives. Mr Lamb also added that:

'There is also the potential to reduce the prospect of a termination at a later stage in pregnancy. For that reason, the negative selection seems entirely appropriate.'[7]

Positive selection

8.10   Concerning positive selection and saviour siblings,[8] Norman Lamb stated:

---

4   Ibid, col 1084.
5   Eg the Hashmi scenario, in contrast to the Whitaker scenario which did not involve an inherited serious disease.
6   *Hansard*, 12 May 2008, col 1087.
7   Ibid, cols 1087–1088.
8   Again the Hashmi case involved both negative and positive selection.

'By tissue typing IVF embryos, we can identify an embryo that is a tissue match for a sick older sibling suffering from a serious disease so that the transplant of umbilical cord or bone marrow would be a more effective treatment.'[9]

Here with positive selection one is screening for positive characteristics, ie the saviour sibling embryo being the same tissue type as the older sick sibling. For some though this is tantamount to sliding down the ethical slippery slope. Mr Lamb preferred the use of the wider expression 'serious' disease to merely a 'life threatening' one, arguing that it would be hard to argue that we should help only those with a life-threatening condition, leaving those with serious conditions without hope. He acknowledged moreover the ethical concerns about saviour siblings:

'How does a saviour sibling cope with the knowledge that that they were created for such a purpose? I do not dismiss that anxiety, but my judgment is that the benefits outweigh the concerns.'[10]

This is a classic utilitarian justification for an action – look at the consequences and outcome of that action. It will be ethically justifiable if the good consequences outweigh the bad, if one maximises utility, ie the greatest good for the greatest number. For others (deontologists), looking at the consequences of an action and maximising utility are inherently subjective and relative and not susceptible to quantification. Rather, one should act on the basis of duties or obligations and that some actions/activities are inherently ethically wrong. People should not be used simply or solely as a means toward an end. They should not just have instrumental value as a mere commodity to be manipulated for the benefit of others. Again this does not fit in to the Kantian concept of universalisation: do unto others as you would expect to have done unto you.

Rarity

8.11 Dr Brian Iddon MP made the point that creating and using saviour siblings is a treatment option of last resort:

'firstly because it is costly and secondly because the family would look for a match transplant from elsewhere first.'[11]

He notes that as at 12 May 2008 there had been only six cases of saviour sibling treatment in this country. Thus the practice was exceptionally rare. The ethical floodgates had hardly been breached here, if at all.

Causes

8.12 Dr Ian Gibson MP made the telling observation that:

'Many of the conditions that afflict humanity are caused by many genetic factors interacting with the environment. As we would not be able to provide

---

9   Ibid, col 1088.
10   Ibid.
11   Ibid.

that evidence, we would be able to facilitate and help only a low number of people.'[12]

The creation of saviour siblings is clearly not a therapeutic panacea for a vast multitude of patients. Most diseases that mankind suffers from are not caused just by a genetic problem. Many are caused by both a genetic predisposition, or disease or mutation and their interaction with the environment, which is why there is the huge complexity and intractable difficulties in dealing with many diseases, and of course the reality is that whilst much scientific progress has been made to cure or improve or manage diseases, much remains to be done.

Consent

8.13   Geraldine Smith MP, one of the most vehement critics of the creation and use of saviour siblings and indeed one of the leading opponents of many of the more controversial ethical issues contained in the HFE Bill generally, said:

'Deliberately leaving open the option for children to be created apparently for the sole and explicit purpose of providing any type of tissue for an existing sibling is appalling. What about the child's right? What about consent? That child has not agreed to be a donor, and it will not have the chance to do so until it is 18.'[13]

Consent, or the lack of it from the saviour sibling donor, is one of the main ethical and legal objections to the use of saviour siblings. The saviour sibling has not consented to, eg, subsequent bone marrow transplantation or the transplantation of 'other tissue' either, and moreover the procedure is arguably not benefiting them and is in fact harming them. Both procedures are invasive and involve physical pain or harm and risks to the saviour sibling.

Waste

8.14   Geraldine Smith stated she readily sympathised with the plight of parents who are desperate to save the life of a very sick child, but:

'The difference here is that we are legislators; we are supposed to make rational decisions based on the arguments. We should not put parents in the awful position of having to decide whether to create a child for the sole purpose of helping another child.'

Needless to say MPs are influenced and swayed by populism, emotions, gut reactions, etc in the same way as ordinary voters and the general public are. She also had concerns about the waste of embryos involved in the process. Only tissue-matched and disease-free embryos will be selected for implantation. The rest will not be fit-for-the-particular purpose for which their creation was intended, ie to benefit and save the life of another. Thus disease-free embryos will be discarded as a direct result of the process. She said:

'I have concerns about embryos being discarded because of the possibility of disability. Embryo selection could be classed as the ultimate form of

---

12   Ibid.
13   Ibid, col 1099.

disability discrimination. Saying that someone cannot be born because they would have a disability is terrible.'

Autonomy

8.15   John Bercow MP rejected the arguments that the bringing into being of an additional human being was for a purely utilitarian purpose, devaluing the individual and causing that person to suffer subsequently and that the process would be intrinsically wrong, because 'in the first instance that should be a judgment for the prospective parent or parents.' He added that if the parent or parents decided that this was something that they wanted to do because a sibling could be helped, a disease could be cured or a life could be saved and, as a consequence, extended, then that decision should be respected. Mr Bercow put great emphasis and weight on parental choice and autonomy here.[14]

Morality

8.16   Gary Streeter MP made the important point that the fact that children can be selected to generate a source of material to help sick relatives does not mean that it should be done. The fact that a therapeutic procedure can be done does not mean that it ought to be done. He added that the fact that a complaint is very serious does not mean that a research process that is wrong should continue. Again, he raised the psychological harm or damage done to the saviour sibling as an objection to it being undertaken, stating that 'We should not solve one problem by creating another.' Two wrongs don't make a right:

> 'Saviour siblings may be loved, cared for and wanted – indeed, only families who care desperately about their first child will have them, so of course they will be cared for – but they will always have a secondary purpose. They are a means to an end, and they will come to know that.'[15]

He concluded:

> 'We should not seek a physical cure for one child at the expense of possible additional mental challenges for others. As Immanuel Kant said, humans should be an end in themselves, never a means.'[16]

Critics might point out that Kant in fact said that humans should never be used solely as a means toward an end.

Safeguards

8.17   Chris McCafferty MP supported pre-implantation tissue-typing, arguing that in fact:

> 'Each application is considered on its own merits and a licence is granted only when the authority is convinced that the child will be a valued member

---

14   Ibid, col 1102.
15   Ibid, col 1108.
16   Ibid, col 1109.

of the family and that tissue from that child is the only means of treating the older sibling.'[17]

In other words quite a number of safeguards are built into the process before the treatment is permitted. She added that in practice, tissue-typing was only carried out for life-threatening blood conditions and had happened in only a small number of cases.[18] Moreover, she said that the courts had already confirmed the authority's power to license tissue-typing (see the *Quintavalle* litigation) and so one of the Bill's most important aims had to be to make that power explicit, which is in fact what the 2008 Act did.

Commodities

8.18   David Burrowes MP noted that the HFE Bill:

'hides within its laudable exterior proposals that strike at the heart of the value of human life and commodifies a child's life as an instrument for the benefit of another.'[19]

He was therefore worried that a child might be created who is not so much a saviour sibling as 'a spare parts sibling' which he felt was unacceptable.

8.19   Dawn Primarolo, a Junior Health Minister, agreed that it would be unacceptable for organs to be donated and removed from saviour siblings but as she correctly (strictly arguably) observed, that was why the Bill prohibits it – but of course the prohibition only applies to whole organs.

Concerns

8.20   David Burrowes MP retorted that the debates in the House of Lords showed that although whole organs are excluded, many other tissues are not. The implication was that we are potentially quite a distance down it the slippery slope, but not yet at the bottom. He complained too that there was no safeguard in the Bill concerning any age limit. The saviour sibling could theoretically be available for 'harvesting' tissue up to the age of 18.

Alternatives

8.21   Furthermore, Mr Burrowes argued that there are alternatives to creating saviour siblings, namely umbilical cord blood collection and banking:

'If the Government took umbilical cord blood collection and banking seriously, controversial parts of the Bill would not be necessary.'[20]

In other words, saviour sibling production is an unnecessary procedure. It is highly controversial ethically and there are viable alternatives to it that should be pursued instead. He made the point that:

17   Ibid, col 1118.
18   Ie six families as at 12 May 2008.
19   Ibid, col 1129.
20   Ibid, col 1132.

'Cord blood is producing more than 80 treatments in leukaemia and other areas of immune deficiency and moving into degenerative diseases [but] the valuable resource of cord blood … is simply treated as waste in 98.5 per cent of all cases.'

Safeguards

8.22 Dr Evan Harris MP, one of the leading advocates and supporters of many of the controversial and ethically significant features of the Bill, disagreed with the view that there were no or few safeguards in it for saviour siblings. He stated:

'Common law provides significant safeguards for children regarding non-therapeutic acts such as the donation of bone marrow and other interventions.'[21]

The HTA has to approve such transplants and it is good practice that courts are involved and give their approval too. He also stated:

'There is no prospect of children's bodies being raided for organs against their best interests, and there has never been any question of that happening. Children have always been able to donate tissue to siblings, and our having the ability to do tissue-typing in advance does not change that.'

Evidence

8.23 Concerning whether harm will be done to the saviour sibling who might ask why and for what purpose they were born, Dr Harris stated:

'there is no evidence that that will happen. There is, however, clear evidence that if we do not allow these changes, small numbers of children – the siblings who are ill –would die. It is therefore appropriate to give the benefit of the doubt in favour of that clear evidence, and to proceed on that basis.'[22]

Dr Harris is clearly favouring a utilitarian or consequentialist approach here, balancing the risks of harm against the benefits and looking at the overall outcome and consequences of either permitting or prohibiting the practice of creating saviour siblings. For him the balance tilts heavily in favour of permitting PGD and HLA tissue typing. In the Whitaker case, there was no harm, he claimed, as they ended up with two healthy children, but the alternative would have been that they ended up with none.

Cord blood

8.24 Dr Richard Taylor MP endorsed the comments made concerning the need to use cord blood in cord blood banks and to try and secure more of this wonderful resource after the birth of children. He argued:

---

21   Ibid, col 1139.
22   Ibid, col 1139–1140.

'The Anthony Nolan Trust ... estimates that 65,000 litres of cord blood are discarded every year. Cord blood is taken after the baby is born, so there is no risk to the baby. It is wasted, yet it can be an excellent source of stem cells.'[23]

This is a pragmatic objection to the terrible waste of an ethically non-controversial alternative to the creation and use of saviour siblings.

CONCLUSIONS

8.25   Not surprisingly the contributions from MPs (ie our democratically elected component and second limb of Parliament) on permitting the creation of saviour siblings reflected the sharp divisions between the views of those in favour of permitting a potentially hugely beneficial procedure to improve the quality of life of an existing child suffering great physical trauma and at the same time creating a new and valued human being, and the genuine and legitimate concerns of those opposed to this technology being applied, who were fearful it would lead to the commodification of certain types of children, negate the consent of those 'saviour sibling children to the subsequent use of their tissue and potentially be a step down the ethical slippery slope to the creation of designer babies. Again these verbal and intellectual jousts in the House of Commons reflected the views of many of the public. Arguably a majority of the public were strongly sympathetic to the plight of these sick children and to the necessity for helping them therapeutically by means of creating saviour siblings, but at the same time were concerned that tangible limitations and safeguards were built into HFEA 2008 to strictly limit the availability of this controversial new technology. Vigorous debate and forensic examination of proposed legislation (especially ethically controversial legislation with profound repercussions for future generations) by our elected representatives is surely indispensable for a representative legislature and to producing sound laws. These laws must be hammered out (by our MPs) in the anvil of Parliament.

---

23   Ibid, col 1142.

Chapter 9

New Beginnings – New Law?

INTRODUCTION

9.1   The 2008 Act amended the earlier and original 1990 Act considerably and significantly in a number of ways.

NEW LAW

9.2   The 2008 Act amends Sch 2, para 1 to the 1990 Act, by, inter alia, inserting new activities for which a licence may be granted. After para 1(1)(c), 'using gametes', is inserted a new activity for which a treatment licence may be granted by the HFEA:

> '(ca) using embryos for the purpose of training persons in embryo biopsy, embryo storage or other embryological techniques.'

Clearly in 1990 when the original Act had been passed PGD had just been invented by Dr Alan Handyside and Professor Robert Winston,[1] so the possibility of training doctors and embryologists in the use of the technique using embryos would have been far from the contemplation of most commentators. However in 2008 (and now 2012) that is precisely what the statute permits. Some would see the legalisation of this activity as further evidence of the inexorable slide down the feared ethical slippery slope. Now the law permits embryos to be created and used (manipulated) for the benefit not of alleviating a couple's infertility in, eg, IVF, or for a specific research project for one of the permitted research purposes for using human embryos, but merely to train embryologists. Human life has, it might be said, become a mere tool for training, thus further instrumentalising, commodifying and cheapening the intrinsic, inherent value and moral worth of human life. However, those in favour would obviously argue that the embryo is not a person, does not possess any rights and is being used for a valuable and legitimate purpose, namely training future embryologists in embryo biopsy and storage or for training for other embryological purposes, an expression which is arguably very wide in scope too. There is a safeguard built into new sub-para 4A of Sch 2, para 1 to the HFEA 1990, which provides;

> '(4A) A licence under this paragraph cannot authorise the use of embryos for the purpose mentioned in sub-paragraph 1 (ca) unless the Authority is satisfied that the proposed use of embryos is necessary for that purpose.'

Presumably, if animal embryos or computerised training will suffice for training, ie there are alternative and effective, efficacious methods of training, then it can be argued that the use of human embryos would not therefore be

---

1   Later Lord Winston.

necessary. The use of human embryos for training embryologists would notbe 'necessary' and, therefore, the HFEA would not grant such a treatment licence.

9.3   The 2008 Act then inserts a new paragraph 1ZA after para 1 of Sch 2 to the 1990 Act which governs 'Embryo testing and sex selection' and provides 5 grounds for testing embryos under the new paragraph 1ZA, namely;

> '1ZA(1) A licence under paragraph 1 cannot authorise the testing of an embryo, except for one of the following purposes—
>> (a) establishing whether the embryo has a gene, chromosome or mitochondrion abnormality that may affect its capacity to result in a live birth,[2]
>> (b) in a case where there is a particular risk that the embryo may have any gene, chromosome or mitochondrian abnormality, establishing whether it has that abnormality or any other gene, chromosome or mitochondrian abnormality,
>> (c) In a case where there is a particular risk that any resulting child will have or develop—
>>> (i)   a gender- related serious physical or mental disability,
>>> (ii) a gender-related serious illness, or
>>> (iii) any other gender-related serious medical condition,
>> establishing the sex of the embryo,
>> (d) in a case where a person ("the sibling") who is the child of the persons whose gametes are used to bring about the creation of the embryo (or of either of those persons) suffers from a serious medical condition which could be treated by umbilical cord blood stem cells, bone marrow or other tissue of any resulting child, establishing whether the tissue of any resulting child would be compatible with that of the sibling, and,
>> (e) in a case where uncertainty has arisen as to whether the embryo is one of those whose creation was brought about by using the gametes of particular persons, establishing whether it is.

9.4   Testing the sex of an embryo is, therefore, generally prohibited unless the testing is done under one of the three grounds listed in new paragraph 1ZA(1)(c)(i)–(iii). So sadly the Mastertons (see **para 23.13**) would still not be able to get a licence from the HFEA to use IVF and then do PGD to test the sex of embryos in order to implant female embryos in Mrs Masterton, so that she could have a female child following the loss of her daughter in a tragic accident. That would constitute sex selection for social purposes, which is not permitted under the 2008 Act, unless the scenario fits into one of the three permissible grounds above.

9.5   The passion of debates in both Houses of Parliament, engendered by the scope, meaning, legality and ethics of what exactly was meant by the terms 'a serious medical condition', 'umbilical cord blood stem cells', 'bone

---

2   This is similar to what Maurice Kay J says PGD could lawfully be used for, ie testing for the viability of an embryo, so giving the words in the 1990 Act a very restricted, narrow, limited meaning; see *R (on the application of Quintavalle) v Human Fertilisation and Embryology Authority* [2002] EWHC 3000 (Admin).

marrow' and particularly 'other tissue', as set out in sub-para 1ZA(1)(d), were abundantly evident throughout the passage of the 2008 Bill in Parliament.

9.6   The fifth type of testing of embryos using PGD, as set out in sub-para 1ZA(1)(e), is directed at addressing the terrible problem experienced in the case of *Leeds Teaching Hospital NHS Trust v Mr A, Mrs A and others*,[3] where a white woman undergoing ICSI with her white husband was mistakenly inseminated not by her husband's sperm but by a black man's sperm who had in turn being receiving treatment with his wife at the clinic. If the clinic or embryologists are uncertain as to the correct identity of gametes used to create an embryo, PGD can be used under a treatment licence to establish whose gametes were used. Clearly this type of embryo testing and biopsy has got absolutely nothing to do with creating a saviour sibling who is tissue compatible with an existing sibling or with whether the embryo is suffering from a serious genetic disease, etc.

9.7   Furthermore, new para 1ZA(2) provides that:

'(2) A licence under paragraph 1 cannot authorise the testing of embryos for the purpose mentioned in sub-paragraph (1)(b) unless the Authority is satisfied—
   (a)   in relation to the abnormality of which there is and particular risk, and
   (b)   in relation to any other abnormality for which testing is to be authorised under sub-paragraph (1) (b),
   that there is a significant risk that a person with the abnormality will have or develop a serious physical or mental disability, a serious illness or any other serious medical condition.'

Again it is not entirely clear what is meant by a significant risk as opposed to a mere risk. Subsequent litigation may clarify this term in the context of the 2008 Act.

9.8   New para 1ZA(3) provides:

'(3) For the purposes of sub-paragraph 1(c), a physical or mental disability, illness or other medical condition is gender-related if the Authority is satisfied that—
   (a)   It affects only one sex, or
   (b)   It affects one sex significantly more than the other.'

Clearly most cases of gender-related physical or mental disability, illness or other medical conditions will affect male embryos and children. Females tend to be carriers of these diseases, because they have more genetic material on their two x chromosomes, whereas males have less on their y chromosome.

9.9   Finally, new para 1ZA(4) provides the arguably vital safeguard and protection against exploitation of the saviour sibling:

'(4) In sub-paragraph 1(d) the reference to 'other tissue' of the resulting child does not include a reference to any whole organ of the child.'

However, whilst whole organs seemingly cannot be harvested from the saviour sibling, it is far from clear that part organs are included in this exemption. Thus,

---

3   [2003] EWHC 259.

a lobe of a liver, or alternatively a lung lobe could be theoretically harvested from the saviour sibling to save the life of the existing sick older sibling. These operations and transplants would be very invasive, serious and complex surgery, with major risks for the saviour sibling, clearly violating the non-maleficence and beneficence ethical principles. Again, the autonomy of the saviour sibling would arguably not figure here or alternatively be fatally compromised.

9.10   Under the terms of new para 1ZC, the so-called second level of control, ie a government minister being given power to pass secondary legislation (regulations), is conferred on the Secretary of State, giving power to add to or repeal any part of para 1ZA:

> '1ZC(1) Regulations may make any amendment of paragraph 1ZA (embryo testing).'

CONCLUSIONS

9.11   The creation and use of saviour siblings by PGD and HLA tissue typing generated enormous controversy when the HFEA initially permitted it in 2001, and the differences of opinion in the courts (certainly between initially the High Court on the one hand and the Court of Appeal and House of Lords on the other) on the legality of licensing tissue typing was a warning message to Parliament to send out a clear signal in primary legislation as to the exact parameters within which the procedure could be carried out. Parliament seems to have sent out such a clear signal in the 2008 Act, particularly in new para 1ZA of Sch 2 to the 1990 Act. The words 'a serious medical condition' were preferred over 'a life-threatening' illness, and the words 'or other tissue' remained in the final 2008 Act, although significantly Parliament made it clear that these words 'do not include a reference to any whole organ of the child'. Therefore, a kidney or lung for example cannot be harvested from a saviour sibling, but worryingly it is not clear whether part of an organ could be transplanted from a saviour sibling to save a sick older sibling, or what other types of tissue may be transplanted from that saviour sibling. Fears of saviour siblings being viewed as spare body part banks have not therefore fully dissipated.

9.12   The breadth and depth of the arguments in Parliament and the courts on the legality, ethics, morality, practicalities and assessment of the medical implications of precisely how to regulate this practice provides welcome reassurance that there is no, nor will there be any, 'free-for-all' when creating or using saviour siblings.

Part 3

Welfare of the Child versus the Wishes or Whims of the Parents

Chapter 10

Welfare of the Child in 2012

BACKGROUND

10.1 The original 1990 Act had enshrined in it, as a central overarching legal and ethical principle, the so-called 'welfare of the child' principle. Thus, before a couple or an individual (a woman) could receive eg IVF, ICSI, donated gametes or embryos (AID or DI), HFEA-licensed clinics were obliged to consider the welfare of any child that might be born as a result of this treatment, including controversially, and arguably unfairly and discriminatorily, the need of that child for a father. So, whilst the wishes of the desperate and potentially good, loving putative parents to have a much-wanted and loved child are a major consideration, and obviously a tangible reality given their presence at the clinic, nevertheless that consideration, under the 1990 legislation, is de jure subservient to the welfare of the child principle, as contained in s 13(5) of the 1990 Act, which provides:

> 'A woman shall not be provided with treatment services unless account has been taken of the welfare of any child who may be born as a result of the treatment (including the need of that child for a father), and of any other child who may be affected by the birth.'

Needless to say, perhaps not surprisingly if arguably regrettably, Parliament did not elaborate or specify in the primary legislation (the 1990 Act) what exactly was meant by the term 'the welfare of any child', still less what was meant by the term 'father' referred to in the brackets. This task or duty was left to the statutory and independent regulator, the HFEA, when it was drafting the Code of Practice (another major source of regulation in the sphere of assisted reproduction), which fleshed out the dry bones of the primary legislation in assisting to explain or further define what key terms and sections meant and how they ought to be interpreted in the real world of clinical practice when providing assisted reproductive treatments to patients.

Discretion

10.2 Both the 1990 and the 2008 Acts and the Code of Practice confer significant discretion to both the HFEA, and in turn clinics/clinicians, in interpreting and applying key parts of the regulatory regime. Stauch, Wheat and Tingle[1] commented that the 1990 Act 'is ... notable for its flexibility and its willingness to entrust the HFEA with large amounts of discretion' in reaching decisions. Montgomery added[2] that the way the debating 'forum', ie the HFEA, 'is structured' is by a complex web of discretion, restraints control and

---

1   Stauch, Wheat and Tingle, *Text, Cases & Materials on Medical Law* (Routledge-Cavendish, 2006), p 349.
2   J Montgomery, 'Rights, restraints and pragmatism' (1991) 54 MLR 524.

accountability. The HFEA would be given powers to oversee the activities of individual health practitioners, and would not be limited to applying standards established by parliament or government. Moreover, the HFEA would have considerable autonomy and indeed would be required to develop its own standards of what is acceptable and proper. In 2005, the HFEA produced guidance which Herring claimed, 'made it clear that clinics should only refuse treatment if the child is likely to be at risk of serious harm.'[3]

CRITICISMS OF 'OLD' S 13(5)

10.3   Critics have raised a number of concerns about the continuing 'fitness for purpose' of s 13(5) of the 1990 Act in 2007–2008. Herring outlines a number of objections that 'supporters of reproductive autonomy rights' have to the welfare of the child provision, (s 13(5)), including the need for a father clause.[4] These are:

(1) 'They require the clinic to assess the parental fitness of infertile individuals wanting to have children when we do not do this for couples who wish to have children by sexual intercourse.' Axiomatically, this is, therefore, 'an improper discrimination against infertile people.' However, clinicians do this because they can feasibly and practically do this with the infertile, 1.5 per cent of people, but not with the 98.5 per cent fertile population, which would be totally impractical. Equally, potential adoptive and foster parents are vetted rigorously but the vast majority of other parents are not subject to such vetting. Sometimes allocation of scarce resources is and must be part of practical ethics and legal and policy decisions.

(2) Herring then says that s 13(5) is based on an assumption, which some believe unfounded, that a child has a need for a father, and that this discriminates against lesbian couples and single women seeking treatment, it is claimed. Where is the evidence, as opposed to the assertions, of this alleged discrimination? Also, given that all children have a genetic father and that the vast majority have a social father for at least part of their existence, and that most have a legal father, then this 'assumption' has prima facie a justifiable basis.

(3) 'It requires the clinic to ask an unanswerable question: how can anyone know whether someone else will make a good parent or not? This is guesswork and the test is simply an invitation to prejudice.' Moreover, '[I]n any event clinicians are not social workers and have no training in assessing parenting skills. Even if they did have the skills, how are they to get evidence to make an effective decision?' However, could the same not be claimed equally legitimately about what makes for good 'supportive parenting'? Again, discovering what a supportive parent is and how clinics determine exactly what is meant by this elusive concept remains to be seen. Clinicians are not social workers, but then again are social workers necessarily better than anyone else at determining who makes a good parent? Some doctors do make social decisions every day

---

3   J Herring *Medical Law and Ethics* (Oxford University Press, 2010), p 336.
4   Ibid.

on whether women can have abortions under s1(1)(a) of the Abortion Act 1967.[5] Why the concern about them also making these difficult calls in the context of creating rather than ending human life?

(4) 'The test is meaningless. How can it not be in the interest of the child to be born?' Better to exist than not to exist, surely? Moreover the test 'states that the child's welfare need only be taken into account; it is not a "paramount consideration" as is often the case in child law.'[6]

(5) Herring noted that there appeared to be inconsistencies in the way that the provision is interpreted by clinics and that some used it to justify a policy of not offering treatment to single women, whilst others did not interpret it so. Surely this accusation could be equally levelled at a myriad variety of treatments offered by the NHS, eg access to abortion and to expensive life-saving drugs?

(6) Herring stated: 'The provisions appear to be rarely used to deny treatment. It has been reported that clinics have used this provision in between 0 and 0.3 per cent of cases to deny treatment.' (This was the figure given in evidence to the House of Commons Science and Technology Committee in 2005). If correct, why then the heightened concern over its deletion?

10.4   Herring submitted that the 'logic ... of reproductive autonomy would be ... there should be no restrictions on who can receive reproductive assistance.'[7] But autonomy, even reproductive autonomy, is not in fact, nor ought it to be an absolute ethical principle that can be legally enforced. Where IVF is offered, it is offered privately in 75 per cent of cases – the reality being that IVF treatment is inaccessible to most couples or individuals; reproductive autonomy is a meaningless mantra for many. Obviously the Code of Practice effectively prevents a range of individuals becoming parents, eg child abusers, alcoholics, drug users, violent persons, etc. The bottom line is that infertile couples or individuals who want to be parents can be scrutinised and policed under an Act of Parliament and an independent statutory regulator, but the fertile masses cannot practically be scrutinised or policed. That is unfair reality.

Treatment, not idealism

10.5   Bryan and Higgins[8] cautioned against 'restrictive notions' limiting medically assisted pregnancies to infertile heterosexual couples or even just to married couples, because it ignores 'the wide variety of families that are now common'. Moreover:

'Any medical system has to beware of imposing dogmatic or perfectionist criteria of selection, bearing in mind that in the wider society there is virtually no control on who conceives by whom, with what motives or in whatever conditions.'

---

5   As amended.
6   See, eg s 1 of the Children Act 1989.
7   Herring (above, fn 3), p 337.
8   E Bryan and R Higgins *Infertility: New Choices, New Dilemmas* (Penguin health books, 1995), p 194.

'[A doctor's] prime responsibility is to his or her patients and their would-be children, and not to possibly prejudiced notions about the moral condition of the nation at large.'[9]

Indeed, the GMC's *Good Medical Practice* states one of the duties of all doctors registered with the GMC is: 'Make the care of your patient your first concern.' Doctors ought to make clinical judgments about their patients – not moral ones.

Genesis of welfare of child?

10.6 Morgan and Lee[10] said, referring to Lord Mackay, that it was important that children are born into a stable and loving environment. The family is a concept whose health is fundamental to the health of society in general. Hence the fundamental principle of law relating to children, that their welfare is the paramount consideration, had a necessary place in legislation dealing with assisted conception. The concept of the welfare of the child being the paramount principle is of course enshrined in other legislation, notably the Children Act 1989,[11] Morgan and Lee also noted that Lord Mackay said: 'The concept of the welfare of the child is very broad and indeed all-embracing',[12] ie inclusive and not designed to be exclusive, and that he also said that a very wide range of factors would need to be taken into account when considering the future lives of children who may be born as result of the licensed treatment services. They noted that Lord Mackay, in explaining what was meant by the welfare of the child concept, referred specifically to a discussion of the 'welfare concept' by Hardie Boyce J in *Walker v Harrison*.[13] Morgan and Lee refer to Lord Mackay, citing Hardie Boyce J:

> 'Welfare is an all-encompassing word. It includes material welfare, both in the sense of an adequacy of resources to provide a pleasant home and a comfortable standard of living and in the sense of an adequacy of care to ensure that good health and due personal pride are maintained. However, while material considerations have their place, they are secondary matters. More important are the stability and the security, the loving and understanding care and guidance, the warm and compassionate relationships, that are the essential for the full development of the child's own character, personality and talents.'[14]

Morgan and Lee noted that the message from Parliamentary discussions bore all the hallmarks of a pro-family ideology. Assisted conception is to be, for the most part, for the married, mortgaged middle-classes; a conclusion which is entirely consonant with infertility services being unavailable on any scale through the NHS.[15] Is this the case with most privately funded IVF?

---

9   Ibid, p 195.
10 *Human Fertilisation & Embryology Act 1990 – Abortion & Embryo Research, The New Law* (Blackstone, 1991), p 144.
11 See s 1.
12 Morgan and Lee, p 144.
13 [1981] New Zealand Recent Law 257.
14 Morgan and Lee.
15 Morgan and Lee, p 146.

Double standards?

10.7   Professor John Harris highlighted the double-standards and hypocrisy being applied by society, by which parents are deemed 'morally unsound parents' and denied the right to be parents, by contrasting the contradictory and inconsistent approach taken to natural parents as opposed to adoptive or foster parents, stating:

> 'We, society, have never taken any care to scrutinise the suitability of natural parents for the role, while we have, on the other hand, for some time taken care to satisfy ourselves, as a society, that adoptive or foster parents be fit and proper persons to bring up children.'[16]

That is unfair, inconsistent and inequitable. A fortiori, it is equally unfair, inconsistent and inequitable that would-be 'IVF' parents are 'vetted' about whether they will make 'good' parents. Harris contends that a consistent policy would either scrutinise all parents or none, and challenges as a 'cop-out' the argument that the existing policy on who becomes a parent, inconsistent though it is, constitutes the best available policy since people, let alone people judged to be undesirable or unsuitable, cannot as a matter of fact be prevented from procreating:

> 'It is no more impossible to attempt to prevent people from procreating illicitly than it is to attempt to prevent them from making whisky, or using drugs or avoiding tax illicitly.'[17]

Fertility apartheid?

10.8   Harris also flagged up the manifest unfairness of preventing homosexual couples or single people from becoming parents and contended that this was wrong in three regards:

(1)   Most important, anyone denied the opportunity to have children which they want to have is effectively denied 'one of the most worthwhile experiences and important benefits of life', ie being a parent, and this is therefore a 'substantial wrong'.

(2)   To label homosexual or single people as unfit for one of the most important roles in life means '[A] second and separate wrong is done to people who are singled out as a class of second-class citizens or inferior beings, namely those deemed unfit to have children.' That is tantamount to, in the context of IVF availability, fertility apartheid.

(3)   The final 'separate, significant and identifiable wrong' inflicted on such individuals is, according to Harris, 'when and if such people do manage to have children, despite society's very best endeavours to prevent them, they are usually subjected to more careful and conspicuous scrutiny than are more "normal" parents ... To subject an individual or group of people to these wrongs and injuries without the weightiest and clearest of justifications for so doing is clearly unjustifiable.' He added that he knew of no evidence to show that homosexuals are or are likely to be

---

16   J Harris *The Value of Life* (Routledge & Kegan Paul, 1985), p 150.
17   Ibid, p 151.

worse parents that any other sort of person nor that any 'disadvantage' children brought up by single parents might have would justify our preventing them from rearing children.[18]

'Fit parent'?

10.9 Harris also argues that if we were to screen all would-be parents and license only those judged fit and proper persons to be parents that 'we have no clear idea of what it takes to be a fit and proper parent.'[19] What exactly a 'fit and proper' parent might be and who decides this or ought to decide this is contentious and debatable, yet that is what happens whenever whatever version of s 13(5) is used by clinics and clinicians.

'WELFARE OF THE CHILD' REQUIREMENT – PRE-OCTOBER 2009 – CRITICISED

10.10 There has been much impassioned debate about the wisdom and necessity of retaining the welfare of the child test or principle in s 13(5), or at least retaining a slightly altered version of the need for a father clause as part of it, or alternatively whether it should be scrapped and replaced with a more non-discriminatory, fairer, egalitarian clause such as the need for supportive parenting clause (although supporters of the existing need for a father clause would contend there is no tangible evidence that any lesbian couple or single woman has ever been refused IVF etc under the pre-October 2009 law merely because of their sexuality or marital status, and that removal is tantamount to political correctness gone mad). Professor Emily Jackson (the current deputy Chairman of the HFEA) was highly critical of the pre-October 2009 welfare of the child provision, stating that '[this] oddly worded provision amounts in theory, if not in practice, to a child-welfare filter upon access to treatment.'[20] Arguably the same criticism could be directed at the current, post-October 2009, welfare of the child provision, including the need for supportive parenting clause.

10.11 The historical reason frequently cited for the inclusion of the need for a father clause in the 1990 Act was that, without its inclusion, s 13(5) would not have been passed given the parliamentary arithmetic in the House of Commons in 1990 (arguably in a chamber and society with a much more sceptical and cautious outlook, with many members condemning the rapid developments in the field of assisted reproduction). Indeed there was an amendment to the original Bill which would have restricted access to assisted reproductive treatments to married couples, which was only defeated by a solitary vote. This is the historical context for the genesis of the need for a father clause. Jackson noted:

---

18 Ibid, pp 152–153.
19 Ibid, pp 153.
20 E Jackson *Medical Law, Text, Cases, and Materials*, 2nd ed (Oxford University Press, 2010), p 771.

'in order to shore up support for the Bill, an amendment was introduced which instructed clinicians to take account of the welfare of any child to be born *"including the need of that child for a father"*.' [21]

Jackson flagged up the apparently anomalous position of the need for a father clause in the context of other government legislation promoting equality and non-discrimination, eg the Adoption and Children Act 2002 which, inter alia, permits lesbian couples and single women to adopt children, and the Civil Partnership Act 2004, which, inter alia, permits same-sex couples to enter into civil partnerships and to obtain the same legal rights as married heterosexual couples. These anomalies were flagged up in Parliament too. As she observed:

'When the 2007 Bill came before Parliament, the government had assumed that deleting the "need for a father" clause would straightforwardly bring the 1990 Act into line with post-1990 family law reforms and with equality legislation.' [22]

Paradoxically, this was arguably completely out of alignment with various government policies and initiatives designed and aimed at emphasising the responsibilities of fathers to their progeny. She added,

'Single women and lesbian couples can adopt children, and same-sex couples can enter into civil partnerships and thereby acquire the same legal rights as married couples ... In the light of this, and of the prohibition of discrimination on the grounds of sexual orientation, it seemed anomalous for the statute governing fertility treatment to contain a statutory clause which, on the face of it, looks like an *invitation to discriminate* against women without male partners.'

One could counter by contending if this was indeed an invitation to discriminate against women without male partners, the invitation does not appear to have been taken up or accepted by anyone, given the paucity of evidence of actual, as opposed to alleged discrimination. Also is not the need for a 'father' clause aspirational only in nature, ie it is an ideal or optimal environment to bring a child into, but that does not mean bringing a child into a environment where there is no father, ie a single woman or lesbian couple, is a bad environment, much less that this should be prohibited?

10.12 Jackson categorically states: 'Nor is a presumption against treating women without male partners, on welfare grounds, supported by the evidence.' However, there is no such presumption against treating women without male partners actually contained expressly or implicitly in s 13(5) of the 1990 Act. Jackson then noted:

'While there are numerous studies which appear to show some correlation between single motherhood and poor outcomes for children, these reflect the poverty and greater mobility that often accompany divorce, separation, or unplanned single motherhood.'

Clearly living in poverty is bound to affect the outcomes for children, but poor outcomes for children are not just caused by poverty but also by broken families, which affects not just the unemployed or poor, but more affluent, middle-class families. She added:

21 Ibid, p 772.
22 Ibid.

'Women who seek treatment without men in licensed clinics are a very different cohort to those who have single motherhood thrust upon them, and this is reflected in the evidence, which in fact suggests that children conceived using donor insemination by women without male partners are, if anything, doing better than similarly conceived children who are being brought up by married couples.'

Jackson then referred to the research of Golombok and others to substantiate this contention. But is she referring to children created naturally or by IVF being brought up by married couples? One needs to compare like with like.

10.13 A further argument advanced by Jackson for the removal of the iniquitous and discriminatory need for a father clause is that if lesbian couples or single women are denied access to licensed treatment 'they could engage in casual, unprotected sex.' she said: 'Not only would this be less safe, but also it might mean that the resulting child would have no information about her genetic father.' Therefore, allegedly:

'For reasons of safety and to ensure that offspring have access to information from the register … there may be good reasons for *encouraging* women without male partners to make use of licensed services, rather than leaving them to try to find alternative ways to conceive.'[23]

However, this line of argument could again be challenged. Lesbian couples and single women may quite reasonably and legitimately be refused IVF, not because of their sexuality or marital status, but because of a variety of other reasons totally unconnected with their lesbian/single status. Again, in theory couldn't anyone, not just lesbian couples and single women, who was refused access to licensed treatments resort to 'casual, unprotected sex' as an alternative? Why necessarily the emotive 'unprotected' sex? They could and probably would use protection. Also, if this was the case, the lesbian woman or single woman would hardly have sex with a complete stranger immediately. They would know something about the father – probably more than about an anonymous sperm donor at a licensed clinic!

10.14 Jackson noted correctly:

'It is also, of course, true that the existence of a potential father-figure, when assisted conception services are sought, offers no guarantee of his presence, either when the child is born, or throughout her childhood.'[24]

However, exactly the same charge or accusation could potentially be levelled about the existence of a supportive parent or parents – there before IVF, but are they both still there throughout the childhood years of that child? There is equally no guarantee of that, as there is not if one were to substitute a married or cohabiting heterosexual couple for the supportive parent(s).

10.15 Jackson is also unhappy with the retention of the need for a father clause because clinicians and doctors are ill-equipped to be making assessments or judgments on the potential parenting skills of would-be-parents. As she comments:

23 Ibid.
24 Ibid.

'It must … be admitted that clinicians do not have access to all the information which might be relevant in attempting to judge prospective patient's parenting abilities.'[25]

They are making an ill-informed or not fully informed decision. She argued that, unlike adoption agencies, infertility clinicians do not make home visits, and nor do they undergo any specialist training in evaluating the capacity to be a good parent. The same criticism could, however, be directed at doctors involved in deciding whether a woman falls within s 1(1)(a) of the Abortion Act 1967, as amended (the so-called 'social ground' for abortion), regarding whether she fulfils the criteria for that ground. Again, the two doctors who make the decision that the woman satisfies this ground may take into consideration the woman's actual or reasonably foreseeable environment. This is surely a social judgment: how qualified, skilled, trained and suited are they to this task? Each year over 190,000 abortions are carried out under this social ground, far more than the, eg, under 12,000 children born in 2007 following IVF. To be brutally honest home visits and specialist training are no guarantee that a couple (same-sex or opposite-sex or a single woman) will necessarily make a 'good' parent, whatever a 'good' parent is.

10.16   Jackson further criticised s 13(5) and the need for a father clause, saying that it was:

'… placing an unfair burden upon infertile individuals who are, it must be admitted, not necessarily any more likely to pose a risk to their children than fertile people, who can reproduce without anyone scrutinising their parenting ability.'[26]

However critics would point out they are not contending that a single woman or lesbian couple pose any risk to the child, but rather that the welfare of the child is best promoted if there is a father or father figure or male role model, who will play some part in the bringing up of the child. It is correct that no one scrutinises fertile people about their parenting ability before they have children, but then again it would not be really practical to positively vet all would-be parents, both fertile and non-fertile, for their suitability and ability as parents. After all, only 1.5 per cent of all pregnancies are achieved through IVF – the rest are normal, fertile, non-assisted reproductive pregnancies.

10.17   Jackson noted that the evidence suggested that children born following fertility treatment, if anything, do better than children conceived naturally and cited a variety of sources to corroborate this assertion. Again this assertion is open to the rebuttal that like is not being compared with like. She went on to state:

'This should not be surprising since the pool of individuals who use assisted conception services are clearly very committed to having children and, due to restrictions on NHS treatment, will additionally often be fairly well off. In contrast, the pool of people who conceive naturally will include individuals who may find parenting difficult, such as children and drug addicts.'[27]

25   Ibid, p 774.
26   Ibid.
27   Ibid, pp 774–775.

Incontrovertibly the major factor limiting access to assisted reproductive technology treatments is money. Three-quarters of IVF is offered privately – a huge filter weeding out lots of potentially good parents. Another significant filter which limits and denies access is of course the NHS IVF postcode lottery.

10.18   In fairness to Jackson, she does admit that there is a difference between refraining from interfering with a fertile couple's right to conceive a child naturally and actively assisting an infertile couple. People who do not need help conceiving do not tend to come to IVF fertility clinics, whereas obviously those who are possibly infertile do. Also, how could society police the fertile, when policing the non-fertile generally proves so controversial and complex?

10.19   However Jackson does make a very telling and accurate observation, highlighting the difference between the need to apply the welfare of the child principle, including its need for a father clause to those seeking, eg IVF or DI or ICSI treatment on the one hand, to those who, eg need gynaecological surgery, fertility drugs or ovulation testing kits, to presumably help conceive and give birth to a child, where no such welfare of the child principle or need for a father clause is applied. That appears to show double standards, inconsistency and unfairness. Jackson argues:

> 'if we think that pre-conception assessment of parenting ability is necessary whenever positive steps are taken to help a couple conceive, we may need to draw a line between procedures that *do* require preconception parental assessment and procedures that *do not* ... Surely we would not want to suggest that a doctor should not carry out investigations into the causes of infertility, or even try to repair a woman's fallopian tubes, without first assessing the couple's fitness to parent?'[28]

The argument would be that if it is deemed unnecessary for certain procedures designed to help a woman or couple conceive, why is it deemed necessary for others? Jackson adds:

> 'Nor would it seem sensible to refuse to supply ovulation testing kits, which might help couples to conceive, unless consideration has first been given to the welfare of any child who might have been born ... If we think we need to judge parental fitness when doctors do *some* things which help women to become pregnant, but not others, we need to be able to explain why.'

10.20   Professor Margaret Brazier referred to s 13(5) of the 1990 Act, and the need for a father clause as:

> 'A compromise ... which provided, apparently innocuously, that a licence holder treating a woman must take into account the welfare of any child who may be born as a result of treatment, *including the need of that child for a father.*'[29]

She added that:

> 'Today, the notion that doctors should impose any sort of conditions about the form of family structure a child should be born into is seen by many people as outdated.'

---

28   Ibid, p 775.
29   Prof M Brazier *Medicine, Patients and the Law*, 4th edn (Penguin, 2007), p 324.

Of course if that is correct, it is the legislation passed by Parliament that is ultimately imposing this form of family structure that a child should be born into. The doctors are only applying the law of the land. Alternatively, one could legitimately contend that no one is imposing anything on any individual. Rather, Parliament is saying that part of the welfare of the child consideration entails clinicians considering if there is a father, father-figure or male role model who will have some involvement in the life of the child. This is not a ruse or method to bar lesbian couples or single women from accessing IVF.

10.21 Brazier pointed to the House of Commons Select Committee on Science and Technology Report,[30] which concluded that the requirement to consider the need for a father was unjustifiably offensive to many and constituted unjustified discrimination against unconventional families. She noted that the Report went further and recommended abolition of this welfare principle in its current form.[31] She then referred to the Government White Paper,[32] which, 'none the less proposes the retention of a modified welfare principle, but agrees that provisions insisting on consideration of the need for a father should be abolished.'

10.22 Furthermore Brazier asserted, concerning the need for a father clause, that the HFEA always sought to attenuate the effect of that provision, looking more to the mother's capacity to raise a child alone, and evidence of male role models in the child's life. The would-be mother did not have to be married or have a male partner, but merely that there was evidence of a male role model (very woolly and wide) in the child's life – not an exacting requirement, and arguably not a requirement at all. Brazier noted in addition that after extensive consultation of its own, the HFEA revised its guidance,[33] and that:

'Clinics should operate on a presumption of providing treatment to those seeking help to conceive whether they be heterosexual couples, lesbian couples or single women. Only if there is evidence of risk of serious harm to a future child should treatment be refused.'

10.23 Brazier observed that there were still some who would argue that it is not right to provide DI to help a woman have a child who will have no father,[34] and said:

'It is argued that society should not allow fatherless children to be born by assisted conception because children need a parent of either sex to develop properly.'

She countered correctly that countless children are born by natural means to women alone, and countless more lose contact with their 'legal' father.' but, just because something occurs 'naturally' or frequently, neither makes its occurrence a good or desirable thing, nor a fortiori is an ethically justifiable reason for deliberately creating that situation.

---

30 House of Commons Science and Technology Committee, *Human Reproductive Technologies and the Law,* (Fifth Report of Session 2004–05) (pub 24 March 2005), para 101.
31 Brazier (above), p 324.
32 *Review of the Human Fertilisation and Embryology Act* (2006, Cm 6989), paras 2.20–2.26.
33 HFEA, *Tomorrow's Children* (2005), and HFEA, *Welfare of the Child and the Assessment of Those Seeking Treatment Guidance* (2005).
34 Brazier (above) at p 774, citing Laing and Oderberg (2005) 13 Med L Rev 328, who advocated this view.

10.24 Brazier continued:

> 'If it is asserted that a woman unable to have children by the usual means must be denied help via assisted conception unless she has a male partner, a case must be made out that her child's welfare is likely to be imperilled by fatherlessness.'[35]

Again, is the woman being denied, eg, IVF merely because she is single or a lesbian, or rather for other more objectively legitimate reasons? Alternatively one could argue again that the need for a father clause is not designed to bar or deny single women or lesbian couples or anyone else from accessing IVF, and moreover there is no evidence of it having done so. It is aimed at emphasising the role and importance of fathers, father figures or male role models in the life of a child.

10.25 Brazier submitted that arguments calling for bans on assisted conception for women without a male partner needed to be analysed carefully, and that:

> 'banning women from licensed clinics does not prevent them practising self-insemination: it simply bars access to assisted conception in safer, supervised conditions.'[36]

This is correct. The same reasoning could be used to argue against banning lawful abortions. However, by the same token laws that ban murder, rape, GBH, assault, or even theft do not sadly prevent their occurrence and re-occurrence, but that is not a good reason for not having them on the statute book or at common law. At the end of the day, very few commentators favour banning any woman, be they single, married, cohabiting or lesbian, from access to clinics. More importantly, s 13(5) of the 1990 Act is not a ban or bar.

10.26 Lord Winston posed the question whether, eg, IVF should be made available to couples who are living together but not formally married (the same question could be posed substituting single or lesbian women), answering 'Most people would seem to think this entirely acceptable, but by no means everybody.'[37] He then posed a second question: 'If a couple is living together, should there be a minimum time-limit on how long they should cohabit in order to ensure that they are genuinely in a stable relationship?' He answered:

> 'At first glance this may seem rational and fair, but it is worth considering that the fertile members of the population do not have to go through any such assessment when they are considering a baby.'

Obviously the law does not insist on any minimum time-limit.

10.27 Concerning offering treatment, eg IVF, to single women or a lesbian couple, Winston commented:

> 'At first, it would seem that this is a perfect example of where a child is likely to be disadvantaged. No father figure exists and no male sex role model. It is widely believed that children brought up by a lesbian couple may exhibit some profound sexual disturbance.'

---

35 Ibid.
36 Ibid, p 325.
37 Prof R Winston, *Making Babies: A Personal View of IVF* (BBC Books, 1996), p 38.

However he dismissed this fear thus: 'As it happens, there is no serious evidence that children born from single women or to lesbian couples are in any way disadvantaged.'[38]

10.28 Concerning who merits eg IVF treatment, Winston applied a number of ethical principles in determining who to treat – as he stated, certain general ethical principles exist. These include, firstly, that there should be respect for the autonomy of the people seeking treatment. He gives the example of a desperate couple whose only chance to have a baby is receiving IVF, with very little chance of the IVF being successful. Attempting IVF will put an enormous financial and emotional burden on them, nevertheless:

> 'ultimately it would be wrong for me to refuse this couple treatment once they are in the position of knowing all the facts which surround their circumstances. They surely have the right to choose. If their autonomy is to be properly respected, the couple must be given all the information possible and then left free to decide for themselves whether or not they have treatment. This is the principle of informed consent.'

One can see how this ethical principle's application might favour single women and lesbian couples being provided IVF. Winston added:

> 'It would certainly be undesirable for the doctor, or for that matter a social worker or a nurse, to decide on a paternalistic basis whether or not a particular infertile couple merits the treatment. Neither the doctor, nurse, social worker nor anyone else can put themselves in the shoes of this couple and say that the distress they feel does or does not justify the gamble they are taking.'

Of course the obvious retort here would be that single women and lesbian couples are not suffering from infertility – they are generally fertile like 6 out of 7 couples. Why should a very scarce and costly treatment, aimed at the infertile, be offered to the fertile on the NHS, especially in the current economic climate?

10.29 Winston cited another principle of medical treatment (really two major ethical principles: non-maleficence, sometimes referred to as primum non nocere or 'first do no harm', and beneficence, ie the treatment should do good), that being, wherever possible, it does no harm and potentially it may do good, and notes: 'Doctors choosing which patients to treat by IVF must first consider the adverse consequences.'[39] Furthermore, Winston provided two examples where he would refuse IVF:

(1) where there would be a serious risk to a woman's life if she underwent treatment, eg if the woman had major venous thrombosis and had suffered a stroke that almost killed her; and

(2) where he, as the doctor, would have strong suspicions that any child born might be seriously at risk, for example, from child abuse.

He added, commenting on the welfare of the child provision in s 13(5) of the 1990 Act:

---

38   Ibid, p 39.
39   Ibid, p 42.

'To my mind, this is a rule which is practically very limited because most of the time it will never be possible to forecast the long-term outcomes in anyone's circumstances.'[40]

In other words a couple or a single woman might, at the interview or assessment, appear to be potentially very good parents, but there is no guarantee that this will be the case, and certainly not long-term. Winston does note, however, that when a child is likely to be in physical danger, it would certainly seem sensible to refuse treatment. He pours scorn on:

'... the concept that anybody, fertility expert or lay person, can actually decide whether or not a couple would make "perfectly good parents" – not only that, but presume to do so on the basis of possibly a 20-minute consultation in the highly artificial environment of an IVF clinic.'

Winston very fairly and honestly states:

'I have no idea whether...any of my patients will make good parents. In fact, I am not certain whether I would qualify for that accolade myself.'[41]

10.30 Winston concludes:

'What troubles me most about this arbitrary process, whereby we impose our values on other people – often perhaps those who are less articulate, knowledgeable, or well provided than ourselves – is that we are in a position to do so simply because they are suffering from a disease process. No other free member of society is vetted before he or she decides that they want to try for a baby.'[42]

The argument might be that infertility places doctors in a position of power and trust over infertile patients or those seeking IVF. They must not abuse either that power or trust. Winston concedes that people do not have a right to have a child, but citizens do have a right to fair and equitable treatment, ie the justice principle, by which all equals are treated equally and fairly and receive their just desserts.

10.31 Pattinson[43] was also sceptical about the logic and justification for retaining s 13(5) and the need for a father clause, stating that it prioritised the traditional family unit of a man and a woman in a stable, or even marital, relationship, and so reflected the Warnock Committee's view that 'as a general rule it is better for children to be born into a two-parent family, with both father and mother'.[44] It nudged fertility doctors towards a particular view of parenthood and family. Pattinson argued though that for some, by contrast, it constituted unjustified discrimination against the involuntary childless. However others would contend that if by involuntary childless one means lesbian couples and single women, they are in fact childless by choice, and secondly they are not generally infertile or sub-fertile.

10.32 Pattinson correctly observed s 13(5), even as amended, places considerable power in the hands of doctors, and that the factors to be taken

40 Ibid, pp 42–43.
41 Ibid, p 48.
42 Ibid.
43 S Pattinson *Medical Law and Ethics,* 2nd edn, (Sweet & Maxwell, 2009), p 275.
44 Warnock et al, (1984), para 2.11.

into account are not purely medical. However the same can be said about the two doctors' respective decisions under s 1(1)(a) of the Abortion Act 1967, as amended, concerning the woman's actual or reasonably foreseeable environment. He noted that, '[D]octors are expected to make decisions that are not strictly within their competence.' Does that mean they are contravening *Good Medical Practice* and their professional duties under it? Has the law medicalised access to assisted reproduction? Again, the same criticism can be levied at doctors regarding access to abortion under s 1(1)(a) of the abortion legislation, where the two requisite doctors perform almost a gate-keeping role under the Act. Pattinson asserted:

'Social judgments about the suitability of the involuntarily childless to be parents are not simply encouraged, doctors are required to make them.'

He also highlighted that the key term, 'welfare', is not defined in the Act. Pattinson voiced further concerns about the welfare of the child requirement raising conceptual difficulties insofar as it is concerned with the welfare of the child that will be born – as opposed to the welfare of an existing child – quite apart from the measure of speculation involved concerning a child not yet in existence. He also observed that reconciling s 13(5) with an interpretation that makes philosophical sense is no easy task, so that the upshot of the welfare of the child requirement is that clinicians have a great deal of discretion to decide whom to treat.

WARNOCK

10.33 Baroness Warnock, whose Report[45] famously laid the foundations for the 1990 Act, albeit 27 years ago in 1984, noted:

' … the various techniques for assisted reproduction offer not only a remedy for infertility, but also offer the fertile single woman or lesbian couple the chance of parenthood without the direct involvement of a male partner.'

So Warnock did not rule out this possibility in the future. IVF was not axiomatically confined to the infertile. That, said Warnock, nonetheless flagged up that:

'many believe that the interests of the child dictate that it should be born into a home where there is a loving, stable, heterosexual relationship and that, therefore, the *deliberate* creation of a child for a woman who is not a partner in such a relationship is morally wrong … On the other side some expressed the view that a single woman or lesbian couple have a right under the European Convention to have children even though those children may have no legal father.'

However Warnock concluded:

'We have considered these arguments, but, nevertheless, we believe that as a general rule it is better for children to be born into a two-parent family, with both father and mother, although we recognise that it is impossible to predict with any certainty how lasting such a relationship will be.'[46]

45 Warnock Committee *Report of the Committee of Inquiry into Human Fertilisation and Embryology,* (Cmnd 9314) (London: HMSO: 1984) (the Warnock Report),
46 Ibid, para 2.11.

DANGERS?

10.34 Herring[47] refers to alleged deleterious consequences to children born as a result of assisted reproductive treatments, which might compromise the welfare of the child requirement, including medical dangers, eg greatly increased chances of multiple births, and the danger that children will suffer psychological damage when they discover the unusual circumstances of their conception. – it is sometimes said to be harmful for children to be born with no clear familial identity or sense of kinship. However, Herring challenges these claimed dangers, saying that in fact it is far from clear what the dangers of IVF are, but the rather limited data to date does not prove that children born using assisted reproductive treatments suffer psychologically or physically.

10.35 Concerning whether a single woman should receive, eg, IVF and whether a child would suffer psychologically if they had one as opposed to two parents, Herring notes that such a question is difficult to resolve on the statistics. There is no conclusive evidence either way. He noted though:

'It does seem to be true that children raised by single parents do less well than children raised by two according to a variety of indicators.'[48]

But he entered the important caveat, that this may be simply due to the economic and social deprivations suffered by many lone parents. That unquestionably is partially correct, but it is submitted it fails to fully explain this disadvantage. Part of the problem lies in the fact that there is no good father, father figure or male-role model to help in the development and care and love of the child. The existence of poverty and social deprivation in many of these one parent families should not blind us to the loss of such a father figure to a young child. Herring contended also that there is clear evidence that children who are raised by a couple whose relationship is bad will suffer greatly. He adds:

'There are also those who are convinced that children will suffer without a clear male role model in their lives, although even if a couple are married there is no reason to assume that the marriage will survive and that the husband will continue to provide a role model.'[49]

This criticism could of course be levelled equally at cohabiting heterosexual partners, or a lesbian couple, or same-sex partnership or civil partnership. Interestingly in *In re D (A child Appearing by her Guardian ad Litem),*[50] Lord Walker stated that clinics were 'rightly cautious about providing assisted conception services for unmarried women.' In 2005 the Government said that as a general rule it was better that a child be brought up by two parents.

10.36 Concerning offering lesbian couples IVF, Herring notes when the 1990 Act was enacted the possibility of a lesbian couple receiving ART was a highly controversial issue, but that is less so now. However, IVF test-tube babies were a highly controversial issue in 1978 when the first test-tube baby, Louise Brown, was born, yet in 2012 it is arguably a routine, standard, ethically non-controversial procedure. Herring refers to the Adoption and Children

---

47 Herring, *Medical Law and Ethics*, 2nd ed. (Oxford University Press, 2008), p 321.
48 Ibid, p 337.
49 Ibid, pp 337–338.
50 [2005] UKHL 33, para 35.

Act 2002, which permits same-sex couples to adopt children, and the Civil Partnership Act 2004, which, inter alia, provides official recognition for same-sex relationships, as evidence of the sea-change in attitudes in society to the acceptability of homosexuality and to the greater tolerance and liberalisation of the law generally here. He notes that evidence suggests that children raised in lesbian households do not suffer as compared with children raised in opposite sex couples, citing Brewaeys (2003)[51] in support of this proposition, but interestingly he adds:

'That said, most of the studies have involved relatively small numbers of children and it would be wrong to suggest the case has been made beyond reasonable doubt.'

Or indeed even on the lower civil standard of the balance of probabilities.

10.37 Herring[52] cites one study by Brewaeys et al (1997),[53] which found that:

'children benefited from a greater degree of involvement from the mother's partner than on average a child raised by an opposite sex couple received from her or his father.'

This initially appears persuasive evidence, but on reflection, this is not surprising as fathers in the majority of cases are out working from 9–5pm or longer. The work and child-rearing roles are much more likely to be blurred and shared more equitably between a same-sex couple raising a child. Fathers are becoming more involved in the rearing of children and generally getting more involved in the life of their children, but this is a very gradual process.

10.38 Finally Herring says:

'Although it is clear that some clinics do offer lesbian couples ART, there is evidence that some lesbian couples are deterred from approaching clinics for fear of how they will be treated and prefer to use unregulated methods.'[54]

He adds, speculatively:

'In part this fear may spring from the existence of the HFE Act, section 13(5), which, it will be remembered, requires the clinic to consider the child's "need" of a father.'

10.39 Morgan and Lee rather provocatively talk of s 13(5) as 'Licensing Parents', adding:

'This section raises but does not address a fundamental question in respect of assisted conception ... If all the financial and counselling hurdles are surmounted, does every one have a right to "marry and found a family" (European Convention on Human Rights art 12), such that they can either

---

51 K Varifraussen, I Ponjaert, A Brewaeys, 'Family functioning in lesbian families created by donor insemination', American Journal of Orthopsychiatry, 0002–9432, January 1 2003, Vol 73, Issue 1.

52 At p 338.

53 A Brewaeys, I Ponjaert, E V Van Hall, and S Golombok 'Donor insemination: Child development and family functioning in lesbian mother families', 1997 Human Reproduction, Vol 12, No 6, pp 1349–1359.

54 Ibid, p 338.

demand the provision of treatment services or not be excluded on spurious grounds?'[55]

Concerning whether single or lesbian women ought to be able to access IVF, Morgan and Lee, in 1991, note, 'it has been suggested that only 200 single or lone women have been knowingly treated at clinics in the past 12 years. (from 1979–1991). They continue:

'It is possible to argue that lesbian couples who choose maternity and motherhood are those who have perhaps most clearly examined and rejected patriarchal notions of motherhood and the family with which western society is most totally suffused. For them, it is the lifestyle truly of choice rather than of convention and it is they who are most likely to be deprived by unsupported appeals to those conventions.'[56]

Morgan and Lee forthrightly state that:

'The extraordinary facet of this debate is that the evidence which would enable the negative conclusions to be drawn about single or lesbian couple parenting is in scant supply. While it is true that there is a high correlation between one parent families and emotional or behavioural deprivation, that does not lead straight to the conclusion that it is the single parenting which causes the poverty; rather it tells us about some of the priorities in social welfare spending.'

---

55   Morgan and Lee, *Human Fertilisation & Embryology Act 1990 – Abortion & Embryo Research, The New Law* (Blackstone, 1991), p 141.

56   Ibid, p 147.

Chapter 11

The Common Law Response: Case Law on the 'Welfare of the Child' and Suitability of Parents

INTRODUCTION

11.1   Given the importance of the 'welfare of the child' principle to the general scheme of the assisted reproductive treatment regulatory regime it is strange that there is a comparative paucity of cases examining, either directly or indirectly, the suitability of potential would-be parents to access, eg, IVF and promote the welfare of the child who might be born as a result of that medical intervention.

HARRIOTT

11.2   In *R v Ethical Committee of St Mary's Hospital (Manchester) ex p Harriott*,[1] the applicant, Ms Harriott, wanted to have a child but could not conceive naturally. She had applied a number of times to Manchester City's social services department to be allowed to foster or adopt children. In the High Court, Schiemann J stated:

> 'These applications have been uniformly unsuccessful, the authority taking the view that the applicant's criminal record (which includes allowing premises to be used as a brothel and soliciting for prostitution), and her allegedly poor understanding of the role of a foster parent and the social services department, precluded them from approving her applications.'

Frustrated in her desire to foster and adopt and to conceive by normal means, the applicant wished to be considered for IVF under the NHS. However the NHS decided to refuse to give her this treatment. She was refused IVF treatment as a result of advice given to her consultant by the Ethical Committee of St Mary's Hospital, Manchester. It was concerned that Ms Harriott and her husband had already been rejected as foster parents on the basis of her past convictions. Ms Harriott had then applied for judicial review of the decision of the Ethical Committee refusing her IVF, claiming that it was reached by the wrong body; alternatively that she was not given an adequate opportunity to make representations to the decision-maker before the decision was taken.

11.3   Significantly Schiemann J stated:

> 'This, I believe, is the first occasion when a decision to refuse treatment for an illness – and for present purposes infertility may be regarded as an illness – has been the subject of an application for judicial review.'

---

1   [1988] 1 FLR 512.

So the case was a precedent in that it marked the first occasion when a decision to refuse medical treatment was challenged by a patient seeking judicial review of that refusal decision, and also because the courts affirmed that infertility was an illness (the implication being it needed treatment), and not just some mere social condition or lifestyle whim that was being thwarted.

11.4   Schiemann J said that the Ethical Committee:

'submit[s] that the courts will not investigate the reasons behind a decision by the Health Service to refuse treatment nor ... will the courts investigate the procedures which have been followed in the decision making process'.

They also submitted that judicial review did not lie to review any advice given by the committee, but Schiemann J stated: 'As at present advised, I would be doubtful about accepting that submission in its full breadth.' However he added that:

'If the committee had advised, for instance, that the IVF unit should in principle refuse all such treatment to anyone who was a Jew or coloured, then I think the courts might well grant a declaration that such a policy was illegal.'

The point was that prima facie the decision of a clinic refusing eg IVF treatment is subject to court review but that this will be limited to a clinic or ethical committee eg acting illegally, presumably irrationally (in a non-*Wednesbury* reasonable manner), and if there is procedural irregularity. However Schiemann J observed that he did not need to consider that situation in this case because:

'Here the complaint is that the committee's advice was that the consultant must make up her own mind as to whether the treatment should be given. That advice was, in my judgment, unobjectionable.'

Ms Harriott was unsuccessful in her application for judicial review challenging the decision to refuse her NHS IVF.

SEALE

11.5   In *R v Sheffield Health Authority, ex p Seale*,[2] Mrs Seale, a 37 year old woman, was unsuccessful in getting the High Court to quash the decision of Sheffield Health Authority refusing her NHS IVF on the basis of her age. The Court held on the basis of limited resources available to the Health Authority and given the lower live birth rate achieved by women over 35[3] that Sheffield Health Authority's policy, inter alia, only to treat women below the age of 35 was not irrational (ie was not a decision that no reasonable Heath Authority could reasonably have taken).

EX P H

11.6   Again in *R v Human Fertilisation and Embryology Authority, ex p Assisted Reproduction and Gynaecology Centre and H*,[4] the applicants,

---

2   (1994) 25 BMLR 1.
3   Statistically women over 35 have less chance of conceiving or having a baby than women under 35.
4   [2002] EWCA Civ 20.

Ms H, a 46 year old woman, and the clinic treating her, namely the Assisted Reproduction and Gynaecology Centre, sought judicial review of the HFEA's policy of only permitting a maximum of three embryos to be placed in a woman during a single IVF treatment cycle (aimed at, inter alia, lessening the chances of multiple pregnancy and the problems associated with that), contending that policy was irrational. The clinic wanted to transfer five embryos into Ms H, who also favoured this number of embryos being transferred. The Court of Appeal upheld the trial judge's decision (Ousely J) to dismiss the action, because the court had no role to play in the scientific debate about the number of embryos that ought to be transferred and thus had no power to intervene in this decision. Judges and courts generally tend to be very reluctant at second-guessing the decisions of scientists and doctors about treatment decisions. The HFEA, in the latest Code of Practice,[5] say that normally only two embryos ought to be placed in a woman under 40, and a maximum of three for women over 40. Interestingly the HFEA is currently trying to get all clinics to reduce the number of multiple births and appear to be pushing ultimately in time for one embryo transfer per IVF cycle only.

BLOOD

11.7   A further concern is whether IVF should be provided to spouses or partners of deceased individuals using the deceased's gametes with or without the deceased's consent, and how does this equate with taking into account the welfare of any child who may be born as a result of that treatment? In *R v Human Fertilisation and Embryology Authority ex p Blood*,[6] Mrs Diane Blood had sought judicial review of the HFEA's decision to refuse to allow her to use her dead husband's sperm to be inseminated in a licensed clinic in the United Kingdom, because the sperm had been retrieved from Mr Blood whilst he was in a meningitis coma just before he died and he had not given his written consent to his sperm either being stored or used as required by Sch 3 to the 1990 Act. Both the High Court and Court of Appeal had held that the requirement of written consent was a clear legal necessity under the 1990 Act, so Mrs Blood was not permitted to use her dead husband's sperm in the United Kingdom to be inseminated, but partially because this was a one-off situation that was not likely to occur again. Arguably more importantly, the HFEA, in reaching their decision to refuse her treatment and allow her to export the sperm to an EU country where she could receive treatment, had failed to consider relevant EU law, notably arts 59 and 60 of the EU Treaty. The Court of Appeal asked the HFEA to reconsider its decision in the light of these EU articles. The HFEA then exercised its discretion under s 24(4) of the 1990 Act to grant an export licence to her and she used Mr Blood's sperm to be inseminated and had two children subsequently. But did deliberately creating two children, knowing there would be no father, promote their welfare? The fact that many children have no father 'naturally' because of bereavement or divorce or separation is no justification for the intentional creation of such a fatherless child. Is this personal autonomy and procreative freedom taken too far?

---

5   8th edn, October 2009.
6   [1997] 2 WLR 806.

'SHEILA'

11.8   Another case that starkly illustrated the dichotomy between the reproductive choice and wishes of a putative IVF parent and arguably promoting and safeguarding the welfare of the child was evident in the 'Sheila' case,[7] where Professor Winston's IVF team in Hammersmith, London, controversially decided to offer IVF treatment to an HIV-positive woman. The argument here was that, if the treatment were successful, any baby subsequently born ran a small risk of being infected by this virus, thus compromising its welfare. IVF treatment was offered to the woman but as it transpired was unsuccessful.

BUTTLE

11.9   In the Buttle case Liz Buttle, a 61 year old woman, had lied to a fertility clinic about her age, claiming she was only 49, in order to receive IVF. The IVF was privately funded and the clinic offered IVF to women up to 50. Regardless of the deceit involved here, this case raises wider issues about the ethics, wisdom and effectiveness of offering IVF to older woman. Does a child having a mother of 45, 50, 55, 60 or even older when the child is born potentially damage or undermine the welfare of the child?

RASHBROOK – THE AGE-OLD QUESTION

11.10   The issue of the age of an IVF mother was raised in the *Rashbrook* case. Here Dr Patricia Rashbrook, a child psychiatrist, had a baby at the age of 62, following IVF treatment involving using an egg donated in the former Soviet Union, thus becoming, in 2006, the UK's oldest mother.

11.11   The author highlighted some of the concerns with offering IVF to older women in the New Law Journal:

> 'Critics … contend motherhood at 62 is unnatural, selfish and potentially dangerous to mother and child; commodifies the child into a good desired by a parent consumer; and is harmful to the child, who will be brought up by an elderly mother/couple unable to physically cope with the childcare.'[8]

The 1990 and 2008 Acts and the Code of Practice do not, of course, specify any upper-age limit for women or men receiving IVF. In the 75 per cent of privately funded IVF cases, private clinics effectively determine any age-limits or fertility cut-off times, and individual PCTs decide on the maximum ages of women potentially treated for NHS IVF, albeit adhering to the NICE Guidelines – realistically no woman over 40 need apply – thus contributing to an IVF 'postcode lottery'.

11.12   However, arguably every woman should be treated and assessed individually for IVF. Some 62 year olds would be medically unfit to have a baby or mentally or physically unfit to cope with that child after it was born, but others by contrast would be in very good physical health and well able to cope

---

7   See Prof R Winston, *Making Babies: A Personal View of IVF* (BBC Books, 1996),
8   S Burns, 'The age-old question – who gets IVF?' (2006) 156 NLJ 1377.

with the demands of caring for that child after its birth and beyond. One size (one's age) does not necessarily fit all. Also, it is highly unlikely there will be a deluge of older (ie 45-plus) women coming forward and inundating private fee-paying clinics. As the author notes:

'Visions of an army of pensionable mothers pushing around buggies containing their IVF children, rather than their grandchildren, are precisely that, visions and illusions. The reality is that most women in their 60s do not have a burning desire to become mothers. The few that do may be unable to afford and realise their ambition to try and have a child. The even tinier number who are actually able to bear the considerable costs of IVF, and who are in sufficiently good health, may well be unsuccessful anyway, given the low-rate of live births for women over 45. Reports of slippery slopes and the cataclysmic repercussions of the phenomenon of a handful of geriatric mums are greatly exaggerated.'[9]

In *R v Human Fertilisation and Embryology Authority, ex p Seale*, where the High Court upheld a decision of the Sheffield Health Authority to offer a 37 year old woman NHS IVF treatment, the Sheffield Health Authority then having a cut-off point of 35 for women being offered IVF, the age of the potential mother was a highly significant factor.

POST-OCTOBER 2009: 'NEW' WELFARE OF CHILD PRINCIPLE, (INCLUDING THE 'NEED FOR SUPPORTIVE PARENTING')

11.13 Section 14 of the 2008 Act amends s 13 of the 1990 Act very significantly. Section 14 provides that:

'(1) Section 13 of the 1990 Act (conditions of licences for treatment) is amended in accordance with subsection (2) to (4).
(2) In subsection (5)—
    (a) omit ", other than basic partner treatment services,", and
    (b) for "a father" substitute "supportive parenting".'

11.14 So the new s 13(5) of the 1990 Act, as amended by s 14 of the 2008 Act, now provides that:

'A woman shall not be provided with treatment services unless account has been taken of the welfare of any child who may be born as a result of the treatment (including the need of that child for supportive parenting), and of any other child who may be affected by the birth.'

The replacement of a mere two words by two other words, namely replacing including the need for 'a father' with the words including the need for 'supportive parenting' was one of the most ethically controversial amendments made by the new 2008 Act and generated much heated debate in both Parliament and in academia. The author notes, however:

'that surely the real issue is not discrimination against lesbian couples or single women (the statistics would appear to provide strong – if not arguably compelling – evidence that there is none), but general availability of IVF/

9   S Burns, 'The age-old question – who gets IVF?', above.

assisted reproductive techniques across the country, and the reality of the all too evident and insidious postcode lottery. Moreover, three quarters of IVF is privately funded. Thus if you cannot afford to pay for IVF, a patient simply does not get it ... Parliament is convulsing and fulminating about symbolic, not instrumental, words in legislation, which leads to no actual discrimination against lesbian couples or single women, and is thus failing to see the wood (the bigger more pressing picture of the reality and unfairness of the postcode lottery allied to the IVF market unfairly discriminating against large cohorts of patients), from the trees (namely, alleged and perceived, but not apparently actual, discrimination against a much smaller cohort of patients – lesbian couples and single women).'[10]

However, the author sums up the diametrically opposed arguments of those in favour of scrapping the need for a father clause and replacing it with the allegedly fairer, non-discriminatory, more protective of human rights, need for supportive parenting clause, thus:

'Basically, the argument is that Parliament (national legislatures) should not be interfering in a fundamentally private matter, namely deciding who will make a suitable parent and be offered assisted reproduction, and imposing eligibility criteria which act as hurdles or brakes on certain classes of patient accessing those treatments, and which are unfair and unjustified. Laws should arguably only interfere in private lives of individuals if someone is being harmed (the classical John Stuart Mill approach). It is no business of the state to meddle in family life and favour one type of family as an ideal over another type, if there is no good reason for doing so.'[11]

CODE OF PRACTICE 2009 (8TH EDN)

11.15 The Code of Practice 'fleshes out' the words, or dry bones, of the 1990 and 2008 Acts. Basically it elaborates and expands on the bare words used in the legislation to help clinics further interpret, apply and indeed comply with the overarching statutory regime.

11.16 Part 8 of the Code of Practice deals with further guidance given to licensed clinics. This concerns primarily the interpretation of the amended, s 13(5) welfare of the child provision, with its new 'need for supportive parenting' clause. Paragraph 8.2 provides that licensed clinics should 'have documented procedures to ensure that proper account is taken of the welfare of any child who may be born as a result of treatment services', so tying in with the general Sch 3 legislative requirement that all consents be in writing.

11.17 Crucially, para 8.3 provides that:

'The centre should assess each patient and their partner (if they have one) before providing any treatment, and should use this assessment to decide whether there is a risk of significant harm or neglect to any child referred to in 8.2'.

---

10 S Burns, *Current Law Statutes Annotated* 'Human Fertilisation and Embryology Act 2008, Chapter 22' (Sweet & Maxwell, 2009), p 45.
11 Ibid, pp 50–51.

Since 1 October 2009, therefore, when the Code of Practice and indeed the 2008 Act became effective, there exists a presumption that an individual or couple will satisfy this welfare of child test, unless there is apparent a risk of significant harm or neglect to any child who may be born following the treatment.

11.18 Again, another highly significant feature of the latest version of the Code of Practice is the inclusion of para 8.7:

'Those seeking treatment are entitled to a fair assessment ... The centre is expected to consider the wishes of all those involved, and the assessment must be done in a non-discriminatory way. In particular, patients should not be discriminated against on grounds of gender, race, disability, sexual orientation, religious belief or age.'

This paragraph's inclusion and clarity underlines why the original need for a father clause in s 13(5) of the 1990 Act had to be scrapped. The argument was that the need for a father clause was, or could be perceived as being, discriminatory against eg lesbian couples or single women, and moreover that this was unfair and possibly unjustifiable when considered in the light of the Human Rights Act 1998.

11.19 In addition, para 8.10 helpfully sets out the factors clinics should take into account during the assessment process. Not surprisingly, given the earlier para 8.3, the centre should consider factors that, 'are likely to cause a risk of significant harm or neglect to any child who may be born or to any existing child of the family.' The factors include any aspects of the patient's or (if they have one) their partner's:

'(a) past or current circumstances that may lead to any child mentioned above experiencing serious physical or psychological harm or neglect, for example:
    (i) previous convictions relating to harming children
    (ii) child protection measures taken regarding existing children, or
    (iii) violence or serious discord in the family environment'

There are a number of criticisms of these factors, namely what exactly constitutes 'child protection measures taken regarding existing children'? The meaning of 'violence' is possibly clear, but the meaning of 'serious discord in the family environment' is far from clear. Again is this placing too onerous an assessment task on clinicians or clinics, who might be singularly untrained or inexperienced to discharge it? Worryingly too, para 8.10 says the factors 'include', ie this is by no means an exhaustive list. Does that mean individual clinics will add in their own factors arbitrarily and at whim?

11.20 Also under para 8.10 the factors include any aspect of the patient's and (if they have one) their partner's:

'(b) past or current circumstances that are likely to lead to an inability to care throughout childhood for any child who may be born, or that are already seriously impairing the care of any existing child of the family, for example:
    (i) mental or physical conditions
    (ii) drug or alcohol abuse
    (iii) medical history, where the medical history indicates that any child who may be born is likely to suffer from a serious medical condition, or

(iv) circumstances that the centre considers likely to cause serious harm to any child mentioned above.'

Equally with para 8.10(b), the initial criticism is that once again this is not an exhaustive list of factors, with the use of the words 'includes any aspect', with potentially much discretion and scope given to individual clinics to add to the list of factors included. 'Mental or physical conditions' could be construed incredibly widely, arbitrarily and inconsistently in various clinics. What is meant exactly by 'drug or alcohol abuse'? Does it include binge drinking or over-use addiction to prescribed drugs? Also what is a 'serious medical condition'? Do all, or even a majority of clinicians agree on a definition of this nebulous term? Again what is meant by 'circumstances ... likely to cause serious harm to any child' in para 8.10(b)(iv)? Is the latest incarnation of the Code of Practice simply likely to add to the phenomenon of the fertility treatment and IVF postcode lottery? Is it Parliament sending out a message in 2009 which is fundamentally different to the 1990 message sent out by the then Parliament, which makes no real difference to how individual clinics decide who gets infertility treatment and IVF? Or is it imposing a further pointless, bureaucratic procedure on clinicians and complicating, rather than simplifying the decision as to who gets treatment and why?

11.21 Paragraph 8.11 provides a definition of what is meant by 'supportive parenting':

'When considering a child's need for supportive parenting, centres should consider the following definition:

"Supportive parenting is a commitment to the health, well being and development of the child. It is presumed that all prospective parents will be supportive parents, in the absence of any reasonable cause for concern that any child who may be born, or any other child, may be at risk of significant harm or neglect. Where centres have concern as to whether this commitment exists, they may wish to take account of wider family and social networks within which the child will be raised."'

It is not entirely clear what relevance taking account 'of wider family and social networks' has, if the centre has concerns about whether the commitment to the child exists. Surely if there is doubt, ie 'concern', treatment should not be given, otherwise the centre is gambling on the child's future health, well-being and development?

11.22 Provision is made in paras 8.13–8.14 for centres to obtain further information during the assessment process.

11.23 Paragraphs 8.15–8.18 outline provision in the Code of Practice for refusing patients licensed treatments. Paragraph 8.15 provides:

'The centre should refuse treatment if it:
(a) concludes that any child who may be born or any existing child of the family is likely to be at risk of significant harm or neglect, or
(b) cannot obtain enough information to conclude that there is no significant risk.'

Individuals or couples therefore really do need to provide 'enough information' to satisfy licensed centres, otherwise they run the risk of being refused treatment.

Again the meaning of 'enough information' is not defined. Will licensed clinics interpret this term consistently?

11.24   Paragraph 8.16 provides:

'In deciding whether to refuse treatment, the centre should:
  (a)   take into account the views of all staff who have been involved with caring for the patient (and their partner if they have one), and
  (b)   give the patient (and their partner if they have one) the opportunity to respond to the reason or reasons for refusal before the centre makes a final decision.'

11.25   Paragraph 8.17, arguably provides a patient or patients who have been refused, eg, IVF some modicum of due process. It provides:

'If treatment is refused, the centre should explain, in writing, to the patient (and their partner if they have one):
  (a)   why treatment has been refused
  (b)   any circumstances that may enable the centre to reconsider its decision
  (c)   any remaining options, and
  (d)   opportunities for obtaining appropriate counselling.'

11.26   Finally para 8.18 provides for records of the assessment process to be kept. This could be important in the event of future litigation over a refusal of treatment decision. It provides that:

'In all cases, the centre should record in the patient's medical records the information it has considered during the assessment. If further information has been sought or discussion has taken place, the record should reflect the views of those consulted in reaching the decision and the views of the patient (and their partner if they have one).'

Time will tell how effective the new Code of Practice guidelines are and whether they generate any litigation in disgruntled would-be parents.

Chapter 12

House of Commons Debates

INTRODUCTION

12.1   The debates in the elected chamber of Parliament epitomised the depth of the divisions between those in favour of retaining the need for a father clause in s 13(5) of the 1990 Act (which was after all effective from 1990 up until 1 October 2009), and those pressing for its deletion and replacement by the 'need for supportive parenting' clause. The argument boiled down to preserving the legal status quo (arguably tried, trusted and not broken), or modernising s 13(5) to make it fit for purpose in the changed social, legal and political environment in 2009 (the contention being the need for a father clause was discriminatory, unfair, contrary to human rights laws and/or redundant and hence legally superfluous). Support for both retaining or scrapping the need for a father clause straddled the usual party political divisions in the House of Commons, which arguably was as it ought to be given that the matter is patently an issue of conscience.

DEBATES

Status quo maintained

12.2   Iain Duncan Smith, MP, the former Conservative Party Leader and currently the Secretary of State for Work and Pensions in the Liberal/Conservative Coalition government, set up following the General Election in May 2010, and the leading opponent of the deletion of the term '(including the need for a father)' from s 13(5) of the 1990 Act, and by the replacement of that term with the words '(including the need for supportive parenting)' in the proposed new 2008 Act, urged that the need for a father ought to be continued in this key section. Indeed, he proposed in his amendments[1] that, in relation to the new s 13(5):

'We propose to retain the wording "a father" and add "and a mother".'

He contended his suggested and favoured wording here was supported and endorsed by the public, stating that in the Government's consultation they had received an overwhelming amount of correspondence from the public in favour of a reference to fathers and mothers, so the case for deleting the old term, or at least not replacing it with his suggested new term, ie '(including the need for a father and a mother)', had not been made out. He claimed, moreover, that if the Bill permitted gay couples acting as fathers then, in the interests of balance, there should be a reference to mothers and the Bill ought to be amended accordingly.

---

1   Amendment Nos 21 and 22, in *Hansard*, 20 May 2008, col 166.

12.3 Mr Duncan Smith then highlighted the vital role of fathers to the development and general health and wellbeing of their children, the family and society generally:

> 'Since 1990 there has been a huge amount of research on the effect of absent fathers, demonstrating an increasing understanding of the importance of the role of that fathers play in the home. That is not to suggest that if a family breaks up and the father leaves, that is simply bad for the children: research that we published recently, which was drawn from more than 3,000 evidence sessions, showed that the effect on those broken families is remarkable – 75 per cent of the children are more likely to fail at school, 70 per cent are more likely to succumb to drug addiction, 50 per cent are more likely to have serious alcohol problems, and 35 per cent are more likely to experience some form of unemployment or welfare dependency.'[2]

Thus the corollary of broken homes and absent fathers is the creation of a raft of major social problems that bear most heavily on the children of those 'broken families', which detrimentally affect their future life chances and opportunities.

12.4 He continued: 'The research highlights the fact that fathers bring something more profound to the parenting process, which has for too long been taken for granted.'[3] Fathers are a vital part of the environment in which children of both sexes grow up and develop. Their presence is not an optional extra. It is fundamental. They are not just viewed as mere sperm donors, who subsequently play little or no role in the child's future life. He drew support for this proposition from, inter alia, the Joseph Rowntree Foundation (2007):

> '"Maternal 'inputs' are not consistently correlated with indices of their children's development once they enter secondary school, whereas paternal 'inputs' *are* so correlated. Indeed, there is an indication that teenagers' sense of self-worth is predicted by the quality of their play with their fathers some 13 years earlier."'[4]

He said:

> 'the report goes on to say that:
>
> > "has demonstrated links between parental reports of father's involvement at the age of seven and lower levels of later police contact as reported by the mothers."
>
> Obviously, that makes the strong and profound point that the effect of fathers on both sexes during the teenage years is important.'

12.5 Mr Duncan Smith argued that contrary to popular belief and wisdom the absence of fathers and male role models from the life of a child is not only detrimental to male children, but is equally damaging to female children. He contended therefore that the effect that absent fathers also have on young girls was often forgotten. He reiterated:

> 'We always hear of the effect of a father's absence on young boys in respect of the whole issue of role modelling and giving them a stable beginning.

2   Ibid.
3   Ibid, col 167.
4   Quoted by Alan Duncan Smith at ibid, col 167.

However, in Britain we have some of the highest levels of under-age sexual activity, particularly among young girls, and there is very strong evidence to suggest that the effect of an absent father is to distort that further.'

The argument would be that the constant presence of a good father and mother (ie two good parents and role models) in the life of a young and growing girl would stop or at least lessen the likelihood of her engaging in early sexual activities and possibly prevent her getting pregnant or contracting sexually transmissible diseases, both scenarios blighting her future life. Mr Duncan Smith's central argument was that the absence of a father is at least a contributing factor to the phenomenon of the spiralling number of teenage and younger pregnancies in the United Kingdom. He also claimed that the reason young girls need a father, and male role model figure, in their life is because:

'[they] more often learn empathetic and non-conditional love – something important and profound – from their fathers. They learn that it is possible to have a relationship that does not necessarily involve sex.'

In other words they learn that not all relationships with the opposite sex are sexual ones or conditional, maybe transient, in nature. According to Mr Duncan Smith, the absence of a father is equally harmful to a girl, albeit the harm manifests itself in a different regard from boys.

Bad dads?

12.6 George Howarth MP challenged Mr Duncan Smith on this line of argument for retaining s 13(5) of the 1990 Act, or at least retaining it with the addition of 'and a mother', stating the reality was 'not as rosy' as there are bad fathers who may have a bad influence. Mr Duncan Smith agreed that there were plenty of very bad fathers but contended, by contrast:

'on the whole, the absence of fathers has a detrimental effect on children; the vast majority of fathers are more likely to be positive influences if they are connected to and held to the family for various other reasons.'[5]

The fact that there are a few rotten apples (ie violent, abusive, neglectful, unsuitable fathers) in the barrel of fatherhood does not spoil the entire barrel – and the same argument is surely equally applicable to mothers.

Broken lesbian families?

12.7 Dr Evan Harris MP, one of the leading opponents of the existing s 13(5) provision of the 1990 Act, challenged Mr Duncan Smith, explaining that the House was dealing with the duty on clinics when they consider applications from lesbian couples and solo parents, and primarily the controversy regarding the application of the existing s 13(5) of the 1990 Act, and asked:

'Does he consider that lesbian couples with children are broken families, to some of which he attached the litany of concerns that he rightly has? If he does, what evidence does he have that children with lesbian parents are going off the rails?'[6]

5   Ibid, col 168.
6   Ibid.

His point was that a lesbian couple wanting a child cannot be equated with or compared to a 'broken' family with an errant, 'bad' father.

Broken families

12.8 Mr Duncan Smith replied that he did not consider them to be broken families, but that:

> 'We know that absent fathers have a detrimental effect on their children. That is found up and down the income scale – the percentage effect is exactly the same for people living in Chelsea as it is for people living in difficult parts of Lambeth.'

The detrimental and damaging effect of broken families, here ones without fathers or male role models, straddles class barriers. It is not just confined to lower income or unemployed families.

Married parents best?

12.9 Gerald Howarth MP agreed with the main thrust of Mr Duncan Smith's case for retaining and strengthening s 13(5), rather than replacing it, by referring to a study carried out by the Office for National Statistics about six or seven years prior to the debate (so around 2001–2002):

> 'It [the study] found that the incidence of behavioural disorder in 11 to 16-year old boys was up to three times higher in households where there was a single parent or where the parents were cohabiting than it was in those households where the parents were married. That is a real issue, facing our people day-to-day in our streets and cities throughout this land.'[7]

Again the clear implication is that children with married parents generally have better life prospects than those being brought up by one parent or even by two cohabiting parents. The former scenario is clearly the ideal situation accordingly.

12.10 Mr Duncan Smith concurred that the issue with regard to cohabiting was the scale of break-up, and added:

> 'We know from the reports that have been done ... that 50 per cent of cohabiting relationships are likely to break up. One in two will break up before the child is five. That is an enormously high figure – the highest level of divorce for married couples with a child is one in 12.'[8]

The argument would therefore be that marriage with two parents seems to be the favoured if not best arrangement to maximise the life chances of the child. He added that there was a particular problem with cohabitation, which posed a problem in the Bill as there was no recognition in it of family ties: 'as long as the people involved are considered to be "stable" or in loving relationships, treatment should be available.' That being the case he contended:

7   Ibid.
8   Ibid, cols 168–169.

'it is even more important that we introduce the recognition of the need for a father because we are dealing with the strong likelihood that that cohabiting couples want to undergo such treatment, and such a change would act as a strong reminder to them, much as it will do to lone parents.'[9]

Generalisations?

12.11 Dawn Primarolo MP, the Minister of State at the Department of Health, challenged him, however, saying he was making general points about single parents and asked what evidence did he have that his assertions applied to couples who approached IVF clinics and were in receipt of such treatment. She claimed: 'Research shows the contrary of what he is suggesting.'

Mr Duncan Smith countered by suggesting:

'the level of break-up for cohabiting couples will be higher, even for those receiving IVF, than it will be for married couples. That is the nature of such relationships … it is a fact. I do not think that that will change regardless of IVF.'

Where's the beef?

12.12 Mark Simmonds MP then made a very telling, and, if correct, highly significant intervention concerning whether the existing legislative formula and wording of s 13(5) of the 1990 Act should be replaced by the words '(including the need for supportive parenting)', by asking Mr Duncan Smith:

'Is he aware that despite the fact that it is necessary for clinics to consider the need for a father, there is no evidence that there has been any discrimination against same-sex couples or single mothers in accessing treatments?'

One of the main charges against the continued existence of s 13(5) of the 1990 Act was that clinics needed to consider the welfare of the child, including the need of that child for a father, before providing eg IVF treatment, and that that is discriminatory against gay and lesbian couples and so is also unfair and possibly contrary to a same-sex couple's human rights. However, Mr Simmond's point was that there was no hard, tangible evidence of any discrimination against same-sex couples in clinical practice as a result of s13(5) , so what is the problem with deleting it? To paraphrase Ronald Reagan, where's the beef (ie where is the evidence of actual discrimination, as opposed to alleged or asserted discrimination)? Not surprisingly, Mr Duncan Smith agreed, saying: 'I do not believe that there is any such evidence; I agree with him on that.'

Fathers not necessary?

12.13 Regarding cohabiting parents Mr Duncan Smith contended that recognising in the Bill that it was important for people to understand the importance of the father in a relationship would be beneficial for potential parents. The implication is that not having a father is not a bar to receiving, eg, IVF if you are a same sex couple, but those seeking IVF nevertheless need to

9   Ibid, col 169.

be aware of the need for a child to have a father or male role model before they embark on IVF. Regarding the deletion of the need for a father, he stated:

'We cannot promise anything, but taking it away will have exactly the opposite effect. It is as though we are saying to couples, especially in the heterosexual world, that fathers are less important than mothers and that, therefore, they do not need to be considered.'[10]

The deletion of the original need for a father clause was a signal from Parliament to society that fathers are not as vital to children as mothers, and can be viewed as an optional extra, or even maybe considered surplus to requirements. Mr Duncan Smith claimed that there was little research that anyone could claim one way or the other about outcomes for gay and lesbian couples and drew no inference from that other than that more research was needed on this, which he believed would come in time. He added that he wanted same-sex relationships to prosper and for any child to benefit in such 'stable, successful relationships', and that his amendments would help and not hinder that objective.

Political correctness

12.14 Mr Duncan Smith added that the Government's action was 'unnecessary' and that they had overreacted with the deletion of the need for a father clause. He said that the unease amongst some in the gay and lesbian community, which he was sympathetic to, did not mean that there was discrimination. Is the legislation symbolic only, or is it designed to be instrumental, ie would same-sex couples have to jump over another hurdle to access IVF which opposite sex couples would not have to? He contended the government wished to remove the need for a father clause 'because they perceived it as discriminating against gay or lesbian couples' – different of course to actual discrimination. Mr Duncan Smith rejected the contention that the original clause clearly contravened the European Convention on Human Rights, and moreover emphasised he had not heard 'about any couples who have gone to a clinic and been refused on the ground of the existing clause.'[11]

Actual discrimination?

12.15 Emily Thornberry MP challenged him on this, referring to the Birmingham women's hospital, where she claimed:

'the eligibility criteria for Birmingham-funded treatment and entry on the waiting list for assisted conception include:

"A stable, heterosexual relationship of two years minimum."

That is direct discrimination against lesbian couples and single women.'[12]

10 Ibid, cols 169–170.
11 Ibid, col 170.
12 Ibid, col 171.

Not a bar

12.16 Mr Duncan Smith countered that in reality his clause 14 'is an advisory clause' and that:

'It requires that account be taken of the welfare of the child, "including the need ... for a father" and, if our amendment were passed, a mother. Nowhere does the Bill say that if that situation does not pertain, people will not be allowed that treatment. Should anybody attempt not to allow such treatment after the Bill is passed, it would be illegal.'

A question of rights

12.17 Andrew Selous MP posed a number of supportive questions at Mr Duncan Smith: why did human rights law seem to look only at the view of the adult? What about the child's right to be born with a father, surely 'the most fundamental human right' a child could ask for?[13] He was emphasising that the debate on deletion of the so-called offensive existing clause focuses too much on the human rights of the putative same sex or single woman would-be parent(s), but not enough or at all on the human rights of the child, and implicitly the need for a father.

12.18 Dr Evan Harris MP retorted that the Parliamentary Joint Committee on Human Rights, in a unanimous report, stated that '"Without justification, such distinctions" – the distinctions that he [Mr Duncan Smith] wants to put into the Bill—

"May be in breach of the right to respect for private life without discrimination".'[14]

Dr Harris added:

'The report continued:

"Similarly, the Convention prohibits unjustified discrimination"

he has not shown justification for his position—

"between married and unmarried parents for the purposes of recognition of parental responsibility, or wider family law decisions on access and custody."'[15]

He then concluded by noting that the Committee went on to say that that needed to be removed in order for the provisions to comply.

12.19 Mr Duncan Smith replied: 'I simply do not agree' and that there were human rights lawyers out there who did not agree with those recommendations either. He also added:

'In reality, the Government have set themselves on siding wholly with the rights of the adult. The truth, however, is that the rights of the child must also be a paramount consideration.'

---

13 Ibid.
14 Seemingly this has not been decided definitively by the European Court of Human Rights.
15 *Hansard*, 20 May 2008, col 172.

At the end of the day, both the original and the amended version of s 13(5) of the 1990 Act refer to the welfare of the child, and not about the wishes or whims of the would-be parents. He also refers to the UN convention on Human Rights and the European Convention on Human Rights, both of which:

> 'make it clear that the rights of a child to have those parents is the paramount consideration and that no element can override that.'

Mr Duncan Smith added that the issue was the wellbeing of the child, not, in this case, the well-being of the adult concerned, and that fundamentally:

> 'this is a balance of rights, and in the end, in the case of human rights, the courts must place as paramount the rights of the child.'[16]

Common sense

12.20 Geraldine Smith MP, another leading advocate for the retention of the original s 13(5) need for a father clause said that doing so was just a matter of common sense, although critics might contend that talking in terms of common sense was a mask for common prejudice. She stated:

> 'To most people outside this House, the right hon Gentleman [ie Mr Duncan Smith] is simply talking common sense – they must wonder why we are even having this debate. Is it any wonder that people think politicians are out of touch with ordinary people when we have such debates?'

She then argued that 'the only thing we are saying is that there should be a father figure somewhere, who may be a grandfather, or another relative.' The father figure did not have to be a married man. Ms Smith wanted the term to be construed broadly, not narrowly, concluding:

> 'Many single parents depend on father figures, whether they are grandparents or other relatives. It is just pure common sense, and the fact that we are even debating it is ridiculous.'[17]

Again, not surprisingly Mr Duncan Smith agreed with Geraldine Smith, stating that 'we should not be dancing on the head of a legal pin, but recognising common sense and what most people would say.' Critics would counter again that appeals to common sense or what most people would say ignore unfairly the rights of minorities or those who do not adhere to common sense views, however that term is defined.

Supportive parenting

12.21 Emily Thornberry was adamant that binning the 'need for a father' clause and replacing it with the 'neutral' term 'supportive parenting', which is a legally watertight definition, simple and non-discriminatory, would obviate wrangling and litigation by lawyers in the future, and hence for all these reasons, the latter term was to be preferred over the former. Mr Duncan Smith demurred and dismissed this argument, stating it was not discriminatory to remind of the importance of the role of the father. Consideration did not automatically

---

16 Ibid, col 173.
17 Ibid.

translate into a prohibition. The fact that something should be considered (ie the need for a father) does not act as a bar or prevent same-sex/single would be parents applying for or receiving IVF.

12.22 John Hemming MP noted that the Human Rights Act 1998 took precedence in how legislation is interpreted, meaning that the HFEA legislation 'could not be properly interpreted as preventing lesbians or single women from receiving help in conceiving.'[18]

Balancing

12.23 Mr Duncan Smith concluded by saying that the matter hinged on 'a balance of judgments' by the Government concerning:

> 'the rights of the child versus the rights of adults, and to the importance of fathers and the demonstrable body of evidence regarding the effect of absent fathers on children and families.'[19]

He favoured the legal status quo, and said that the government had to make their case with legislative change. He continued: 'However, the case has not been made, and I do not believe that it exists.' He rejected emphatically the Government's argument and saw insufficient evidence that the existing s 13(5) of the 1990 Act contravened human rights.

Keep status quo

12.24 He described s 13(5) as 'the advisory section' and he submitted that in interpreting it:

> 'clinics should be sensitive to the needs of all parents ... We want people to recognise that fathers have a major role to play, and if they are not around, let us find a way of ensuring that their influence can still be felt.'[20]

Confusion

12.25 Emily Thornberry MP flagged up what she claimed was the confused and legally uncertain position created by s 13(5) of the 1990 Act, primarily in the guise of the need for a father clause, arguing:

> 'If there is a lack of clarity in the current law, we have an opportunity to sort it out today. If we were to confirm the need for a father, to add the need for a mother or to move away from the carefully thought out wording proposed by the Government, there would be increased confusion – or, worse, no clear law at all.'[21]

Her argument would be that unclear law is bad law. The meaning of '(including the need for a father)' is, inter alia, far from clear, and this position is logically

---

18   Ibid, col 174.
19   Ibid.
20   Ibid, col 175.
21   Ibid, col 176.

untenable for clinicians and would-be parents, making the existing s 13(5) a bad piece of law.

Common sense equals discrimination?

12.26 In addition she wondered why in the 21st century were we putting ourselves in such a position:

> 'Why are we saying, "We are not really overtly discriminating against lesbians or single women, but if we are, the Human Rights Act will sort it out, even though the Human Rights Act does not apply at the moment"?'[22]

She then confronts the 'common sense' argument of those in favour of retaining the 'need for a father' clause or need for a father or mother, by stating:

> 'I always worry when people say they are applying only common sense, because all too often common sense is a cover for discrimination, narrowness and an inability to face the 21st century.'

John Bercow MP strongly supported Ms Thornberry asking:

> 'Is she aware of another example of a lesbian couple who went to an IVF clinic in pursuit of treatment and were told in terms that their best option would be to go to the pub and find themselves a man? If that is not discrimination, it is not entirely obvious what is.'[23]

Legal confusion?

12.27 Ms Thornberry suggested that lesbian couples or single women wanting children would be influenced by the current confusion, that they would believe the law to be that lesbians or single women need not apply for IVF, because there needs to be a father or father-type figure or male role model under the existing law to access, eg, IVF. She said that they would continue to be confused and would end up believing that IVF is not for them. In that case she said 'they may well go out to a pub and get pregnant or try other informal means of doing so.' Not a desirable position to be forced into. The disadvantage of this was that:

> 'there will be no details of the biological father on the register, yet that will become increasingly important as time goes on ... As a result of the amendment, no more fathers will be brought into any more families. That is the central point.'[24]

Two better than one

12.28 She believed strongly in giving equal rights here regarding accessing IVF etc to lesbian and single women, and noted: 'As far as lesbian couples are concerned, we will then at least have two legally recognised parents instead of just one. What is wrong with that?'

22   Ibid.
23   Ibid.
24   Ibid, col 177.

Father equals good

12.29 Ms Smith challenged Ms Thornberry, stating that she was displaying a very patronising attitude towards lesbian women's ability to understand a simple concept that if they went for IVF treatment they would have to take into consideration the welfare of the child and the need for a father. Surely, she said, it was good to have a father figure in a child's life?

Patronising

12.30 Ms Thornberry replied that she hoped before deciding to have children people appreciated that those children must be brought up in loving households. Nevertheless, she said:

> 'In my experience, based on the lesbian mothers whom I know, before they make the very serious decision to have children in what is not, in all circumstances, the most liberal of worlds, they look to the welfare of the child and to how they can best bring that child up. They do not need a doctor who is not trained in and has no particular experience of these matters to give them counselling on what sort of father figure they should seek, how long that father figure should be involved in their lives, and exactly what 'father figure' means in what circumstances. It is not for a doctor to make that sort of decision.'[25]

Having said that, doctors, under s 1(1)(a) of the Abortion Act 1967, as amended (the so-called 'social ground' for having an abortion), determine on a daily basis if a woman satisfies that ground and can have an abortion under it and are frequently called upon to make an equally controversial decision considering the woman's 'actual or reasonably foreseeable environment' in deciding whether that ground is satisfied. Again, how qualified are they to reach such a decision?

12.31 Ms Thornberry, (implicitly emphasising the autonomy of the would-be mother or parents), urged that it is the would-be parents who need to consider the welfare of the children before they decide to embark on having children, whether they are a heterosexual couple or homosexual couple or single, and that the good sense of parents and of women who do not need to be patronised by anyone should be trusted. The parent or parents are the best judge or judges of who will promote the welfare of the child.

Balance

12.32 Tim Loughran MP took issue with what he called Ms Thornberry's 'common sense-free world' (as opposed to the common sense world of children needing a father), by asking what takes precedence, 'the supposed right of adults to have children or the actual right of a child to have access to and enjoyment of both parents during his or her upbringing?'[26]

---

25 Ibid.
26 Ibid.

One size does not fit

12.33 Ms Thornberry seized on this comment as an attack on children with single parents, saying:

> 'many role models are available to children ... Members should not make blanket judgments about children and families, and they should not demonise such a large number of children.'[27]

The argument would be that one size does not fit all, in the sense that countless number of children have been brought up very successfully and in happy homes by one parent, albeit the counter-argument would be that even more children in more families have been brought up successfully and happily by two parents (generally opposite sex parents, ie by a mother and a father).

Back to basics revisited?

12.34 Sandra Osborne MP agreed that what purported to be common sense was reminiscent of the 'back to basics' campaign of the previous Conservative Government, and queried whether the insistence on a male role model for lesbian couples was tantamount to saying that lesbian families are not proper family forms? This encapsulates the battle between conservative, traditional notions of what constitutes a family and the alleged best environment to bring up children, ie ideally a happily married heterosexual couple or at least a stable cohabiting heterosexual couple, versus the more liberal and progressive view that gay or lesbian or single parents are equally suitable parents for would-be children.

No ideal family

12.35 George Howarth MP stated that there was no 'ideal version' of right parents or family model. Arguably both sides in the debate fall into the trap of being overly prescriptive, judgmental or politically correct, depending on your point of view, concerning their preferred type or model parent or family. It is certainly true that society's views about what is socially permissible regarding certain matters changes over time. If that is the case, then the law needs to reflect that change. The major differences of opinion about what are 'normal' or 'acceptable' families in the United Kingdom in 2008 surfaced in the verbal joust between Sir Patrick Cormack MP and Ms Thornberry, when the former observed:

> 'Whatever may be the case in Islington, in Staffordshire it is actually thought normal for a child to have a mother and father. Does [Ms Thornberry] think it is equally normal for a child to have two mothers?'[28]

Ms Thornberry countered, 'I think it is wrong to make judgments about families, and to tell one family that they are normal and another family that they are abnormal.' To be fair to Sir Patrick, he does not in fact say a family comprised of two mothers and one child is 'abnormal', but that it is not 'equally normal' to one with a father and mother.

---

27   Ibid, col 178.
28   Ibid.

Vilification

12.36 Ms Thornberry then stated, 'I think it wrong to vilify single parents.' However, s 13(5) of the 1990 Act with its inclusion of the need for a father does not in fact 'vilify' single parents or indeed same-sex parents. It can be interpreted as being aspirational in substance, rather than being prescriptive, or arguably as being informative, by alerting would-be parents to the need for a child, to promote their welfare, to have a father figure or male role model in the family or extended family set-up. Ms Thornberry added, 'I think it is wrong for the law to discriminate against lesbian couples.'

Joint Committee

12.37 Robert Key MP referred to the recommendation of the Joint Committee (of which he was a member), made when considering the Human Tissue and Embryos (Draft) Bill, as it then was in 2007: 'it would be detrimental to remove entirely the requirement to take into account the "need for a father".'

He said, however, that he had changed his mind during the submission of evidence:

> 'The first point was that both Houses of Parliament should set the legal framework and be the de facto bioethics commission for this country, and then once we have set the legal framework it should be for the Human Fertilisation and Embryology Authority to regulate … We also made it clear that the final decision on an individual case of in vitro fertilisation treatment should be taken between the mother, the clinician and the husband or partner – that the decision should be taken at the lowest possible level.'[29]

However, ultimately it is the doctor initially in the clinic who takes the decision whether someone gets, eg, IVF treatment, or the person responsible, or ultimately the ethics committee of the clinic in difficult, controversial cases – it is not the would-be mother, or her husband or partner. He noted that the Committee took into account civil partnerships and that the current law did not prevent single-sex couples adopting or fostering children or accessing IVF, and that they could provide a warm background that was stable and loving, ie potentially better than an unhappy heterosexual family. Few would challenge or disagree with that, but does this compare like with like? Would a child brought up by a same-sex couple, one of whom at least is not his biological father, in a loving home be in as good a position as a child brought up by a married couple, where each parent being his biological parent, in a loving home? That is not as easy a question to answer.

Redundant?

12.38 Seemingly *the* answer, according to Mr Key, or at least *an* answer had been provided to the Committee on 7 June 2007, by Mr Ted Webb, the deputy director of scientific development and bioethics at the Department of Health who crucially revealed:

---

29   Ibid, col 179.

"'From a legal point of view the legislation at the moment'"—

the new clause that takes out the need for a father—

"does not actually seem to achieve anything. So we have looked at it from a legalistic point of view more than anything else. It does not prevent treatment being provided to single women or same-sex couples, and also does not seem to fit too comfortably with the Government's wider civil partnership policy. So I think that is really our starting point for recommending that the need for a father reference is taken out of the legislation'"[30]

Therefore, according to this high-ranking civil servant, the main reason for the scrapping of the need for a father clause is that it was not serving any practical purpose in 2007. The civil servant also conceded it did not serve as a bar preventing gay and lesbian couples or single women from receiving, eg, IVF. The other reason for the deletion of the clause is that seemingly it fitted very uneasily with the Government's broader approval of recognising civil partnerships.

Need for a father supported by experts

12.39 Mr Key then referred to 'pretty convincing' evidence from specialists and academics in the field, including Professor Ann Buchanan of Oxford University (who had conducted two major studies), who, when asked about the need for a father, had said that the evidence for the roles of fathers is important and that father involvement was strongly related to children's later educational attainment, as well as noting a number of other beneficial consequences, eg better life chances, mental health and well-being of the child. He also drew support, interestingly, from Professor Susan Golombok of Cambridge University, who, when asked about the need for a father said, surprisingly using Mr Duncan Smith's terminology of the need for a father being 'common sense':

"'in a way, it is common sense ... so that fathers who are highly involved with their children ... have better adjusted children".'

The converse follows:

"'in families where fathers are not very involved ... the outcomes for their children can be negative".'[31]

Most people would agree and find most of these comments unobjectionable, although Professor Golombok flags up what is meant in fact by the term a 'good parent'. The term is bandied about by lots of commentators and critics on all sides of the debate, but what exactly it means is never nailed down, less agreed. Professor Golombok added: 'Really, it all comes down to the quality of parenting offered by fathers which makes a difference to outcomes for children.'

Dangers of generalisation

12.40 However Dr Evan Harris, by contrast, flagged up that Professor Golombok had also said:

---

30 Ibid.
31 Ibid, col 180.

"'Families are all very different and you find very good relationships in single-parent families and you find two-parent families with bad relationships so I do not think that you can really generalise in that way".'[32]

Again these comments are unobjectionable and accurate. He added:

'She continued:

"in lesbian mother families where two women are heading the family, the presence of two parents seems to be more important than the fact that one parent is male. It is the relationship rather than the gender".'

Again, the counter argument might be: are two lesbian parents as good as two opposite sex parents, both in happy, stable relationships? To argue that one is better than the other is not tantamount to saying one is normal, the other abnormal, that one is good the other bad, still less to prevent children being brought up, following IVF, in a loving same-sex relationship. However, Mr Key in turn retorted that Professor Golombok also stated:

"'To my mind, it suggests that the idea that a mother and a father are both a good thing on the whole for children, and also some basic assumption about the structure of family life is undeniable".'

Supportive parenting

12.41 However Phil Willis MP added that the overwhelming evidence the Committee had got from Professor Golombok, the leading expert on lesbian couples, and from other academics was that the 'supportive family unit was important', hence the need for changing s 13(5) of the 1990 Act. Interestingly, the vote to replace the 'need for a father' clause with the 'need for supportive parenting' was 7–7, with the Chairman, Phil Willis, having the casting vote to permit the legislative change.

12.42 Mr Key challenged the argument that if the 'need for a father' clause was not replaced all single mothers would be discriminated against, by referring to the words of the Archbishop of York, Dr John Sentamu:[33]

"'However, there is all the difference in the world between children who find themselves in a single-parent family through bereavement or breakdown of parental relationship, and those who find themselves in that situation by design…If discrimination is indeed the issue here, surely the greater discrimination is in ensuring that a child will never have any chance of knowing its natural father".'[34]

The fact that something happens naturally is no reason to deliberately manufacture it.

Benefits of regulation

12.43 Dawn Primarolo MP asked if Mr Key accepted that:

32 Ibid.
33 From *Hansard,* 19 November 2007, cols 705–706 (HL).
34 *Hansard,* 20 May 2008, col 181 (HC).

'if single women and lesbian couples are driven away from regulated IVF clinics to other methods in order to have children, their children will never know who their natural father is because they will be outside the protection of the regulation of IVF services?'[35]

The argument here would be better to have regulated parenting under the aegis of the HFEA, rather than unregulated backstreet parenting.

Equality

12.44 Dr Desmond Taylor MP viewed the issue rather differently: it was an equalities issue because the provision only affected lesbian couples. If the 'need for a father' clause were retained, it would be a legislative step backwards, and would clearly be in contravention of HRA 1998. Geraldine Smith pointed out that the provision did not just affect lesbians; it also affected heterosexual single women who may wish to have a child. Dr Turner referred to potential hurdles, eg producing 'a token father', and the real danger of women being compelled to enter informal arrangements, 'such as going to the pub to look for a likely temporary partner or receiving unlicensed, unregulated sperm, which carries all sorts of hazards.' A single woman or lesbian couple would have to surmount these obstacles to satisfy the amendments which retain the 'need for a father' clause in various guises, or indeed the current law. Mr Duncan Smith asked how s 13(5) of the 1990 Act acted as an absolute device to refuse treatment. Dr Turner responded:

'the need to take account of something strongly implies the requirement to produce a father figure, and that would be interpreted by many ... to mean that a father, real or otherwise, would be required.'[36]

'Janet and Jane' world challenged

12.45 However, Dr Turner endorsed retaining the much more realistic and much more important wording about supportive parenting:

'We no longer live in a "Janet and John" world where everybody has an ideal father and an ideal mother ... Let us be honest and admit that many fathers have been damaging.'[37]

One could counter that the vast majority of fathers have been beneficial, that the vast majority of children are in families headed by a father and a mother, and that equally some mothers have been damaging. Again he does not quantify what is meant by 'many'. He then continued:

'How many single parents are left without a supportive father for their child because that natural father has deserted them, often with associated domestic violence? I know of far more cases in which that is true than of lesbian couples having IVF.'

Then again there are far more heterosexual cohabiting couples than lesbian couples receiving IVF.

---

35   Ibid.
36   Ibid, col 182.
37   Ibid, col 183.

Why change?

12.46 Dr Turner favoured the term 'supportive parenting' because it provided a child with a parental insurance policy; if one parent dies there is a second one provided in certain family scenarios under the new Act. It was almost assured that the child would have two parents, which was entirely logical. Furthermore, he noted: 'We do not apply such strictures to same-sex adoption.' His argument was that the law in relation to accessing IVF needed to be brought into line and harmony with the existing law on adoption, ie permitting same-sex couples to adopt.

Anomalies

12.47 Dr Gibson MP flagged up another inconsistency:

> 'If a woman has tubal or hormonal therapy for infertility problems, no one asks questions about parenthood. That only happens when it comes to IVF, which suggests that there is an element of discrimination behind this.'[38]

That is correct, but Parliament deliberately chose to have this 'inconsistency' enshrined in primary legislation in 1990. Tubal therapy involves surgery, whilst hormonal therapy involves administering hormonal drugs. Neither therapy involves creation or manipulation of embryos outside the body, so both procedures are qualitatively and arguably ethically different from IVF.

IVF and adoption analogies

12.48 Mr Duncan Smith challenged the accuracy of comparing IVF with adoption:

> 'adoption is a spurious example, because to go and adopt a child requires huge amounts of exhaustive enquiry into one's background, social position, and what one does.'

However, Dr Turner was adamant that the situations were entirely analogous, 'because they both involve the creation of a family with a child and two parents – in this case, with supportive parents.'

The real deal-real discrimination

12.49 Dr Brian Iddon noted the very significant words of Baroness Deech[39] that: '"in the last year of statistics, over 2,000 women who were single or lesbian accessed IVF treatment".'[40] He added (perhaps sadly incontrovertibly) that there was postcode discrimination in the country, a point with which Dr Turner agreed.

---

38 Ibid.
39 Quoted from *Hansard,* 21 January 2008; col 60 (HL).
40 *Hansard*, 20 May 2008, col 184 (HC).

12.50 Phil Willis made a telling contribution to the debate on discrimination by suggesting that the real discrimination took place in the primary care trusts, which limit the number of treatments for IVF in different ways across the country. He continued:

'If we had proper access to IVF treatment that was fair and equitable across the whole of Great Britain, that would achieve more than our spending hours debating angels dancing on the head of a pin, as we are at the moment.'[41]

The real discrimination is that in reality 75 per cent of IVF is provided privately, with the other 25 per cent available notionally on the NHS, depending largely on the PCT of the would-be recipients, leading to the so-called post code lottery. This might be considered the real scandal, rather than alleged discrimination against same-sex couples, in a tiny minority of cases, for which there is no hard evidence.

12.51 Dr Turner did not disagree and deplored the 'postcode discrimination' on carrying out NICE recommendations on the provision of IVF, but he considered that a different problem. He concluded that the 'need for a father' clauses and variants on them, 'are discriminatory in practice, whether that is the intention or not, and would perhaps lead to a worse situation than the Bill would.' Mark Simmonds MP agreed with Dr Turner:

'The one issue on which he was absolutely correct is the disparity in PCT provision of IVF treatment, which causes a lot of angst and concern across the country.'

He added that, 'Those Labour Members who have tried to defend the Government's position are skating on very thin ice and dancing on the head of a pin.' He agreed that the 1990 Act had worked well, but noted that it was agreed at the time that the need for a father was an important factor in the welfare of a child. He argued that the welfare of the child principle should not be ignored, but rather 'should always be the cornerstone of this aspect of the Bill.'[42]

Covering every angle!

12.52 Mark Simmonds said his amendments would not remove the phrase 'supportive parenting' from the Bill:

'My amendments would retain the phrase "supportive parenting". Reinstate the need for a father and add a requirement for a "male role model".'[43]

He said his amendments recognised that supportive parenting needs to be provided, and that various types of family unit existed. 'The amendments would emphasise the importance of father, while at the same time reflecting what happens in practice in clinics now.' In support of this he referred to John Parsons, lead consultant at the assisted conception unit at King's College hospital, who said:

---

41 Ibid.
42 Ibid, at col 185.
43 Ibid.

'"We like to know there will be men in these children's lives. They don't have to have a father, but they should at least have a male influence in their lives".'

Covert discrimination?

12.53 Andy Slaughter MP disagreed and was concerned that:

'As proposed, the need for a father or for a male role model is an additional requirement to the 1990 Act. It is clearly aimed at single women or lesbian couples and is therefore an additional burden on them. How can that not be discriminatory?'[44]

Mr Simmonds replied that first, the evidence was that that requirement was sought in clinics already, so his amendments were not altering the law or existing clinical practice. Secondly, he said that there was no evidence that same-sex couples and single mothers were not accessing IVF treatment, and no evidence on that point had been produced in the debate. Indeed, according to Baroness Deech in January 2008, there were figures showing that in the previous year over 2,000 single or lesbian women had accessed IVF. Mr Simmonds said that these women were accessing IVF and that his amendments proposed that clinics look for a male role model, as distinct from just a female one.

Evidence

12.54 Mr Simmonds stated there was a considerable amount of evidence pointing to the positive contribution of a father or male role model for a child. They contribute in a variety of positive ways to the health and general well-being of the child. He went further, stating, '[I]ndeed, the importance of the father is now almost uncontested in social research.'[45]

Familial breakdown

12.55 Furthermore, he noted:

'Social research has found that the involvement, or lack of it, of the father, not the mother, is the key determinant of teenage behavioural problems. Unbelievably, 24 per cent of children in this country are growing up in families without a live-in father.'

This is a shockingly high and worrying statistic. Mr Simmonds agreed that society and social attitudes have moved on between 1990 and 2008, but nevertheless, in practice, the need for a father condition has made no difference to access to treatment for same-sex couples and single mothers.

---

44 Ibid, at col 186.
45 Ibid.

Burden of change

12.56 Mr Duncan Smith submitted that supporters of retaining the clause were not removing something, but were in favour of the 'status quo'. The onus of proof was therefore on the Government to prove that the existing law is broken and needed fixing as it is they who were claiming the 'need for a father' clause was unfair, discriminatory, contrary to human rights and redundant. Mr Burrowes agreed, saying that the government had failed to discharge this burden, ie none of those things had been proved. So why drop the 'need for a father' clause?

Ineffective?

12.57 Mr Edward Vaizey MP queried the logic of retaining the 'need for a father' clause: 'If ... the provision on the need for a father has not worked, what is the point of keeping it in the Bill?' In other words what is the point of keeping a legislative provision if it does not work or serve any purpose? This again suggests that the provision is more symbolically important than instrumentally effective. Mr Simmonds contended:

> 'The need for a father or a male role model ensures that the welfare of the child can be maximised, by enabling access to the benefits of having a male role model or a father figure.'[46]

A male role model or father figure, it is argued, maximises the welfare of the child and is the optimum scenario.

Licence to encourage fraud?

12.58 Mr Vaizey challenged Mr Simmonds again, contending:

> '[W]ould not the male role model part of his proposal encourage fraud? ... Numerous lesbian couples could attend clinics with their hired male role model for the day. Surely, that would be totally counter-productive?'[47]

However, if that is true, fraud may be occurring too (except more of it) in the larger heterosexual cohort seeking IVF.

Statistical evidence

12.59 Mr Simmonds disagreed strongly with that analysis 'because at present, when there is no direct father figure, a male role model such as a grandfather may be used.' In 2006, he stated there were only 775 IVF treatment cycles, and fewer than two per cent of them were for single women or single-sex couples. He then referred to further statistics from the King's College Hospital NHS Foundation Trust which show that:

> 'of the 6,000 patients treated between 1995 and 2004, 500 gave rise to "welfare of the child" considerations, and 28 were refused treatment. Eight of them were refused treatment because of psychiatric problems, four

---

46   Ibid, col 188.
47   Ibid.

because of virus infections, and two because previous children were wards of court.'[48]

He noted that:

'There were other issues, too, such as drug or alcohol abuse, or the fact that partners were in prison. There was only one case in which a single woman was refused treatment, and that was because of physical problems.'

On that basis, there does not seem to be any hard evidence of any discrimination against single women by virtue of the fact that they are merely single women. He added that there had been two cases in which same-sex couples were refused treatment because of concerns about their relationships but, importantly, none of the refusals had allegedly been due to the fact that individuals were single or in same-sex relationships. Seemingly, therefore, the refusals were not attributable to their same-sex relationship but due to concerns about their particular relationship. He concluded, therefore, that those statistics would be replicated across the country, showing that single women and same-sex couples did not face barriers to accessing treatment under the 1990 Act.

Why legislate?

12.60 Dr Tony Wright queried whether the exchanges in the House showed only that in practice it would make no difference at all what wording is used in the welfare of the child clause in s 13(5) of the 1990 Act. Mr Simmonds responded that:

'it is important that, through the Bill, we send a message to the country that fathers are important to the welfare of the child, as we have done since 1990.'[49]

He then claimed that the existing 'need for a father' clause had not caused any harm, (adopting the John Stuart Mill approach that harmful things and harm should be avoided). He referred to the Joint Committee on the Human Tissue and Embryos (Draft Bill), which:

'concluded that there was "little evidence that the existing provisions have caused harm" – a point that I made – and it said that it may be "detrimental to remove ... the 'need for a father'."'

Inconsistencies with existing policies

12.61 Mr Simmonds then raised one of the strongest arguments of those who favour the retention of the existing 'need for a father' clause, namely that its deletion ran directly contrary to a whole raft of government policies and initiatives designed to get fathers more involved and responsible in the lives, care, health and well-being of their children. This is seemingly a clear case of government policy and legislation sending out totally contradictory messages to society and not acting holistically for the general good –a recipe for confusion. He gave the following examples:

48 Ibid.
49 Ibid, col 189.

'There is to be an end to anonymity for sperm donors; divorce courts are to ensure that contact with both parents is seen as beneficial; donor children are to have every opportunity to establish their origins; the Government have a policy to extend, promote and encourage paternity leave; and the Department for Work and Pensions has said:

"Fathers and mothers matter to children's development. Father-child relationships ... have profound and wide ranging impacts on children".'

Yet he claimed:

'It is odd, inconsistent, incompatible and paradoxical that the Government are promoting those policies on the one hand but wish to remove the need for a father to be considered prior to IVF on the other.'[50]

Male role models

12.62 Pete Wishart MP speculated as to who would qualify for that 'lofty position' of male role model. Mr Simmonds had mentioned grandparents, he said, and queried who else qualified as a male role model, suggesting celebrities such as David Beckham, Andy Murray, or pop stars. The same argument could be advanced for who qualifies as 'supportive parents'. Mr Simmonds replied that it was not for Parliament to detail such a list – that would be up to clinicians on the ground. This ties in with the notion that Parliament sets out the overarching legislative, regulatory and ethical framework and the clinics interpret it, tailored to the individual circumstances of each case, ie they fill in the detail as well as making a decision about whether the couple (same or opposite sex) or individual accesses, eg, IVF. He suggested that the role model should be a close family member. Moreover, he submitted that his amendments were not discriminatory and applied to all patients. Lesbians and single sex women were not being targeted or singled out for criteria that only apply to them. He added that in his opinion it was right for clinics to be able to refuse treatment under such circumstances, whether it be mental instability or a history of child abuse or drug abuse. He refuted the argument that the retention of the reference to a father would drive people away from regulated services and the quality and safety assurances that those provide, and reiterated that single women and same-sex couples have not faced barriers.[51]

Impediment

12.63 Ms Primarolo saw the issue of retaining the need for a father from a fundamentally different perspective, claiming that it could be a practical impediment to obtaining treatment. She also noted that it had never prevented people from receiving treatment and issued a warning (or was it a veiled threat?) that if the Committee were 'to reaffirm' the continuance of the 'need for a father' clause, it would be reasonable to expect that position to continue and, most likely, worsen if it became the current endorsed view of Parliament (a variation of the slippery slope argument). Moreover: 'It is a question not just of access, but of equitable access.'

---

50 Ibid.
51 Ibid, col 190.

No to legislative signals

12.64 Concerning how the House defined 'supportive parenting', Ms Primarolo added that it should not include wording which would have no meaning or practical effect in IVF legislation. This would send a wider message to the whole population about family structures. The HFE Bill was not the right place to do that.

Research

12.65 Gerald Howarth asked what research had been carried out by the government or others into the likely effect on children of being brought into the world in what some would regard as an unnatural relationship, ie by same-sex couples. Ms Primarolo answered that Mr Duncan Smith had made assertions about behaviour in all families on the basis of evidence from families that had broken down. Additionally:

'With no support or evidence [Mr Duncan Smith] sought to advance the argument that the children whom we are discussing would suffer a certain fate.'[52]

By contrast, she said, the evidence was available that far from suffering harm or detrimental consequences, children brought up by same-sex couples thrived. She noted:

'Social research from Murray, Golombok and Brewaeys shows that children of same-sex couples develop emotionally and psychologically in a similar way to children born of heterosexual donor-inseminated couples. What counts is the quality of parenting ... Quality of parenting will make the difference to the child's development.'

12.66 In response, Mr Duncan Smith observed that the body of evidence on that issue was not yet good enough for her to make any judgment. Furthermore, he said, a huge burden was being placed on clinicians to construe the term 'supportive parenting', rather than the, ease and 'simplicity' of interpreting 'the role of a father'. He contended that there was no real body of evidence on same-sex couples:

'However, in respect of the vast bulk of couples – heterosexual couples – who have IVF, there is a huge amount of evidence concerning the absence of fathers and its effect on families ... The body of evidence shows that the absence of fathers has a detrimental effect on children, regardless of family income.'[53]

All parents prima facie presumed supportive

12.67 Ms Primarolo countered, arguing that the government's stance was that all parents prima facie will be presumed to be supportive parents unless there is evidence to the contrary. It was the view of the Government that all parents

---

52 Ibid, col 191.
53 Ibid, col 191.

assessed for treatment would be assumed to be supportive parents unless there were evidence to the contrary. In rather delphic terms, Ms Primarolo said that a supportive parent would be willing and able to make a commitment to safeguard and promote the child's health, development and welfare and to provide direction and guidance in a manner appropriate to the age and development of the child.[54] She compared this to the view taken Mr Duncan Smith, who, she said, wanted to start with the proposition that they should be considered bad parents unless they are given an additional test.

Access

12.68 Regarding support mechanisms to ensure children have access to their father, Ms Primarolo reassured the House that the Bill introduced a provision to ensure that the child has access at the age of 18, or 16 if necessary, to the details of their natural father. She argued that if couples were driven away from the regulated service, the child would never know those details. She also added:

> 'The parents have the responsibility to make clear to that child their relationship with either parent and the possibility of an absent natural father.'[55]

Good parenting

12.69 Bernard Jenkin MP challenged the Minister on her interpretation of good parenting and asserted the traditional approach that men and women were different and provided different role models to children, both of which were necessary for the upbringing of children. Ms Primarolo was emphatic though that the need for the supportive parenting clause was not about doing away with fathers. Fathers had an important role in the upbringing of children. Rather, the government was ensuring that the law reflected current practice and family set-ups, and current legislation on human rights and discrimination. The wording was designed to reflect changed family structures and a legal framework altered by equality and human rights legislation, and to ensure that IVF children had quality parenting and support. Iris Robinson, the DUP MP for Strangford, commenting on the Minister putting great importance on the quality of parenting, and asked whether Ms Primarolo could envisage, in the future a child being collected from primary school by two females or two males, and the bullying and abuse to which those children would be exposed, or going into their parents' bedroom, as is natural for a child to do, and finding two women or two men making love? Ms Primarolo did not think this important to the debate and responded that children were loved by many adults in families, extended families and neighbourhoods and that it was crucial to consider their safety and nurture.

---

54 See also the Code of Practice.
55 *Hansard*, 20 May 2008, col 193.

Evidence

12.70 Ms Dari Taylor said the House needed to get it right because the welfare of the child was so crucial. She added that there has been much research,[56] and that the conclusions were clear:

> Being without a resident father from infancy does not seem to have had negative consequences for children. There is no evidence that the mother's sexual orientation influences parent-child interaction or the child's socio-emotional development. Those statements are clear and made by people who are not pushing a line. They are conducting research and reporting fairly and objectively.'[57]

Ms Primarolo added to this that the Committee was not saying that fathers are not needed. The quality of parenting and the impact on the child, which should be paramount at all stages, was being recognised thanks to a broadened understanding.

Fairness

12.71 In addition, Ms Primarolo claimed the amendments of Mark Simmonds and Ian Duncan Smith would have a wide-ranging, discriminating effect on access to treatment for single women and same-sex couples and drive them away from the safety of the regulated services, which would be a retrograde step. Ensuring the safety and nurture of the child was paramount and the legislation should be fair to all people who seek treatment. Ms Primarolo was emphasising the important principle of equality (before and under the law) as being a major consideration or driver in changing the 'need for a father' clause. All equals should be treated equally, so same-sex couples and single women should get the same fair and equal opportunity to access, eg, NHS IVF as their counterparts, married or cohabiting heterosexual couples.

Ms Primarolo said the government's amended need for supportive parenting clause recognised the fact that it was the quality of parenting that made the most difference, not the gender of the parents per se. The Bill struck 'the correct balance between protecting the interests of the child to be born by requiring that their welfare is considered and the right to supportive parenting.'[58]

Quality parenting

12.72 Ms Primarolo emphasised again that the need for supportive parenting clause is designed to promote and value 'quality parenting' to enhance and respect the welfare of the child. She added that the government intended to strike the correct balance between protecting the child and providing those supportive arrangements. Furthermore she claimed that Mr Simmonds' amendments more or less said that any man would do, which did not fit with the considerations of quality parenting. Two loving and caring lesbian parents are better for the child

---

56 Ie MacCallum and Golombok.
57 *Hansard*, 20 May 2008, col 194.
58 Ibid, col 195.

than a woman and any father or male role figure would be her contention, and who would argue to the contrary? But was her understanding of Mr Simmonds' argument correct? He would definitely not have thought so. She then asked whether women who were not being treated with a man would have to bring one along for the sake of it? Ms Primarolo referred to evidence that had been provided to the Select Committee on Science and Technology, of women having to bring along a letter signed by a man – any man. However a counter-argument might be that using deception to obtain certain types of treatment exists in many types of medicine, eg accessing drugs, abortions, getting organ transplants, etc. She was adamant that:

> 'This issue is about reflecting the concept of quality of parenting, recognising the diversity of families and judging clearly whether individuals can provide the necessary parenting. That has to be right.'[59]

Discriminatory

12.73 She dismissed Mr Duncan Smith's amendments (Nos 21 and 22), which, inter alia, require clinicians to take into account the need of any resulting child for a father and a mother, as being discriminatory, because, as with the existing 'need for a father' clause, they would create an additional hurdle for female couples and single women seeking treatment. Given the position of the House and the Government on civil partnerships and on adoption by same-sex couples she said 'it was wholly inappropriate to retain that additional, discriminatory burden.'

Dog whistles?

12.74 She again flagged up the alleged inconsistencies in the arguments of those in favour of the 'need for a father' clause or variations basically retaining it, arguing:

> 'Those who oppose the removal of the need for a father provision talk about it not making any difference anyway. They want a provision in the Bill to send a signal about family structures.'

Is this the legislative equivalent of the dog whistle, ie it does not matter about the efficacy of the law, the important thing is whose law is it? She commented that that could not be right.

Signals

12.75 Ms Primarolo was strongly of the opinion that including a reference to the need for a father or for a male role model would send the message from Parliament that it wanted to return to the position when the 1990 Act was introduced, when additional tests were imposed on certain groups of people. Such a provision would not be so harmless or meaningless if it were reintroduced.

---

59   Ibid, col 196.

Key question?

12.76 Gary Streeter MP then asks a number of crucial and pertinent questions in seeking clarification of the Government's position, which at least get to the crux of the matter regarding whether the 'need for a father' clause should be deleted and replaced by the need for supportive parenting clause:

> 'Does the Minister believe that a child in a family unit containing a mother and a father has any advantage compared with a child in a family unit with two mums – supposing that all the parents are loving? Are the Government really saying that there is no advantage in having a loving mother and father compared with two loving parents who are both female?'[60]

Ms Primarolo answered that that was not the Government's position. She accused Mr Streeter of seeking to use a particular provision on access to IVF treatment to argue a general position that he knows full well is not universally accepted by everyone. She suggested that, 'it is the duty of the House to ensure that we reflect all those who make up our communities and all the family units.' However, if there is no hard evidence that any lesbians have been denied access to IVF under the 'need for a father' clause, then how does the law of the land not reflect all our communities? She added:

> 'When deciding whether people can have access to IVF treatment, the absolute cornerstone must be the quality of the parenting. That is precisely what the Government are seeking to take into account.'[61]

Ms Primarolo then said, 'It is nonsensical to say that it is better for a child to have a mother and father, while also arguing that the amendments would not prevent people from accessing treatment.' However, the latter does not logically follow from the former. What evidence is there of lesbians being denied access to IVF? Just because a lesbian couple or single woman has been denied treatment, it does not mean that they have been denied it by virtue of that status. A myriad of legitimate factors and considerations could have led to the decision to deny them IVF treatment.

Justification

12.77 Ms Primarolo concluded the government's defence of why the existing 'need for a father' clause needed replacing with the expression 'supportive parenting', by claiming the former was discriminatory and the latter clause was fair, offered equitable access and recognised the complexities of the Britain we live in today.

No unjustified discrimination

12.78 Dr Evan Harris MP told the House that the Liberal Democrats had a party policy against unjustified discrimination, such as the inclusion of a provision in the Bill for the need for a father, which, he claimed, was both discriminatory and unjustified. Concerning lesbian parents, he said that the evidence was clear that children in such families do very well. He stated, moreover, that the removal

---

60   Ibid, col 197.
61   Ibid.

of the 'need for a father' provision had nothing to do with attacking fathers or fatherhood, or not wanting to tackle the problem of broken homes. Dr Harris added that he recognised the problem of broken homes, and the consequences of such homes for children, but that the legislation was not about broken homes:

'in fact, it is about precisely the opposite. It is about a couple or an individual seeking to create a family and a home, and taking a serious decision to undergo treatment, which is not a decision to be undergone lightly.'[62]

The argument here would be that the lesbian couple are utterly committed to starting a family, unlike some of their heterosexual counterparts. As Dr Harris correctly notes, many children are brought into the world in an unplanned moment, but the provision dealt with people who were making a specific decision to create a family. 'It is astonishing that it should be seen as some kind of an attack on families.'

Unnecessary

12.79 Dr Harris asserted that the need for a father provision, 'has not brought a single extra father into a family, or retained a man in a family' (although proving this would be difficult). He added:

'I do not understand why anyone believes that young men who act irresponsibly and abandon their partners and families are suddenly going to read the statute on IVF treatment – these men are usually fertile – and decide to mend their ways. I have to say that I cannot see that happening.'[63]

Mixed messages

12.80 Sammy Wilson, the DUP MP for East Antrim, queried whether rather than being about bringing more fathers into families, this was instead about state recognition of the importance of fatherhood within families. He added:

'If this provision goes through unamended, we will send out the message that it does not matter whether there is a father, while at the same time Government policy says that it does.'

His comment highlights again the unclear and contradictory policy messages the government might have been sending out regarding the necessity of, involvement of and role and responsibilities of fathers in the bringing up of their children. Dr Harris's response was that he took the view that statute should not be used simply to send out a message, and reminded the House that Geraldine Smith had stated that the amendment would affect not only lesbian families, but those of solo parents as well. Ms Smith challenged this robustly:

'The intention behind the amendment is to ensure that the welfare of the child, rather than the desires of adults, is paramount.'[64]

Her argument would be the welfare of the child prevails over the wishes and whims of the heterosexual or homosexual couple, or single person to have a child, or at least access eg IVF with a view to hopefully getting a child.

---

62 Ibid, col 198.
63 Ibid.
64 Ibid, col 199.

Origins

12.81 Dr Harris explained the genesis of the 'need for a father' provision:

'In 1990, when this provision was put into the Bill, one of our Houses had voted by a majority of just one not to ban unmarried couples from accessing regulated IVF therapy. The sort of thinking going on at that time [by some MPs and peers] was entirely different from that of today. It would be unthinkable for us to pass legislation to prevent unmarried couples from accessing IVF.'[65]

Times change, as do social attitudes about what behaviour is acceptable. Concerning Mr Simmonds' amendments, Dr Harris agreed that if the provision had any effect, it would be a bad one, and that if it did not have an effect, it would be pointless.

Representative

12.82 Dr Harris argued that it was sensible to look at consensus medical opinion on the need for male role models, rather than individual medical opinion, and referred to the British Medical Association (which represents doctors) and the British Fertility Society (which represents doctors working in that particular area of medicine). The latter wanted to get rid of the 'need for a father' provision, because it felt the provision was anachronistic and it would tempt doctors to discriminate, 'which they do not want to do'.

Out of the frying pan!

12.83 Mr Duncan Smith said that the government's new clause on the need for supportive parenting, far from clarifying or simplifying the interpretative task of clinicians under s 13(5), made it even more difficult:

'their proposals now ask doctors to interpret in a way that they did not have to under the 'father' provision … Now they have to interpret what the definition of supporting parenting really means for them.'[66]

Dr Harris addressed this by confirming that doctors would have to do that, which was why the HFEA had produced a Code of Practice which was set out in a non-discriminatory, light-touch way.

Unfair hurdles

12.84 Dr Harris then raised objections to unfair hurdles being set for certain people, stating that fertile individuals were not required to pass a parenting test by the state before becoming pregnant, so why should the infertile? This is of course correct, but such a test for all would-be-parents would be totally impractical. He added that the BMA were even unhappy with the Government's wording – another hurdle – and that many or almost all of the unsatisfactory

---

65 Ibid.
66 Ibid.

families come from the fertile part of the population, not from infertile people seeking infertility treatment. Again, this is true, but then most children are brought up in a heterosexual couple family, and most of those (ie 98 per cent in 2006 of those who seek IVF) are themselves heterosexual. Perhaps a note of caution therefore needs to be sounded before one takes these arguments at face value.

Two questions

12.85   Dr Harris stated that there were really only two questions to be asked.

(1)   Is the discrimination – or the measure – justified?
(2)   Is there discrimination?

Is the measure justified?

12.86   In answering whether the measure was justified, Dr Harris said that the research was clear and was summarised by the BMA which said that there was no evidence that children do badly in families of that kind. He cited the BMA as saying that the emotional and psychological development of those children was comparable to children born of donor insemination to two heterosexual parents. Dr Harris also referred approvingly to Murray and Golombok's research and made the very telling point that solo parents were often well-resourced, given that they often had to obtain private treatment. They often had established careers, and did not have partners. Such parents are thus entirely different from families of the kind Mr Duncan Smith has been considering in his Social Justice Foundation examining broken families.

12.87   Dr Tony Wright MP queried the use of the word 'treatment', which, he said, usually suggested the existence of an illness. It was unclear to him whether the absence of a child constituted an illness in the case of single-sex couples. Dr Harris replied that the National Institute for Health and Clinical Excellence recognised that infertility was a condition that requires treatment, and he thought that donor insemination for lesbian couples should be allowed, particularly because it was cheaper than in vitro fertilisation. He continued:

'In the evidence session on 27 June [2007] Professor Golombok said

"these greater difficulties for children in one-parent homes are very much associated with the circumstances of being in a one-parent family rather than just whether or not there is a father present. For example, a drop in income, lack of social support for the family, a disrupted relationship with the father with whom they had often spent many years and separation from that father, and moving into stepfamilies."'[67]

So there certainly seem to be a host of reasons underpinning why children in one-parent families appear to be disadvantaged. Dr Harris commented that 'if a child has a father and that father goes, it is a different scenario from being brought up without a father in the direct household.'

---

67   Ibid, col 201.

Is there discrimination?

12.88 Regarding the second question, Dr Harris observed that the HRA 1998 was about ensuring that there was a framework for legislation and the behaviour of the state that did not intrude into private matters in breach of individual liberties. He also emphasised the importance of restraining the state and its unreasonable intervention in private matters, and referred to the Equality and Human Rights Commission:

'[The Commission] has issued this statement:

"The central issue here is not fatherhood; it is fairness. The current legalised discrimination in the provision of IVF services is something that we should be ashamed of as a country."

Dr Harris commented that even if single women and lesbian couples received that treatment, it should be received on the same basis as everyone else. He cited Trevor Phillips[68] who had said that the Commission understood the importance of male role models for children, but believed it to be a matter for the parents themselves, and not an issue for legislation. He also said that an 80 per cent male House of Commons shouldn't instruct women as to how and with whom they bring children into the world, akin to an 'authoritarian society'.

12.89 Dr Harris concluded:

'Fortunately, the code of practice currently enables the need for a father provision to be dealt with in a relatively moderate way, but if we voted for a requirement for clinics to observe a need for a father provision, they would have to apply the test to every single group of people in order not to discriminate.'[69]

He suggested that would turn out to be a logistical nightmare and prove totally impracticable, unfair, ineffective, bureaucratic and unfeasible for busy doctors and health care professionals to implement.

Hard evidence

12.90 Geraldine Smith said advocates of the retention of the 'need for a father' clause were by no means belittling or attempting to undermine the enormously valuable role of same-sex parents to a minority of children, and s 13(5) of the 1990 Act was not designed for that purpose. She added that the House had heard some third-hand evidence of cases where there may have been discrimination, but that she had never been presented with the name of a woman or a specific case where someone had been refused treatment because of the 'need for a father' clause. No hard evidence of actual discrimination had been presented. The only evidence is evidence by assertion, or by third-hand hearsay. She added that witnesses had been called to the Joint Committee, but none had said they have been discriminated against and that only vague third-hand examples had been put forward.

---

68   Chair of the Equality and Human Rights Commission.
69   *Hansard*, 20 May 2008, col 203 (HC).

Possible explanations

12.91 Ms Dari Taylor countered that there was a very good reason why no such evidence of discrimination against same-sex couples existed. She had asked such infertile women and couples 'time and again' to write to their MP, and to speak loudly about the fact that they are discriminated against but on the whole, they would not do so, because they were shy and they were seriously concerned. Geraldine Smith responded:

> 'If people suffer discrimination, usually someone is willing to speak out and say, "I've been discriminated against," so I find it very strange that no one has.'[70]

Mr Slaughter replied that he did not think any MP was going to get up and start naming names.

Child's interests are paramount

12.92 Geraldine Smith was adamant, that:

> 'In IVF treatment, the interests of the child must be paramount. IVF must not be about the potential parents; it must be about what is best for that child.'[71]

The parental cart (ie the wishes of the parent(s)), must not be put before the child horse (ie welfare of the child)! Ms Smith failed to see what harm was done by saying to a lesbian couple or single woman going for IVF treatment: 'For the welfare of the child, can you consider the need for a father? If there is not a father, is there a potential father figure?' In her opinion even having that discussion would do some good, and make people think. She continued that she suspected that there was no problem, or rather 'no one has come forward and said there is a problem and they have been affected – because most lesbians and single women going for IVF treatment are responsible.'

Common sense

12.93 She then stated that: 'Most people will think that [retaining the 'need for a father' clause] is about not discrimination, but common sense.' Again some would contend for 'common sense' read the 'dog whistle' of prejudice, intolerance, unfairness and discrimination. However she submitted that the apparent angst concerning the clause was more to do with vocal lobby groups making points. The argument would be that a vocal and unrepresentative lobby were hijacking the issue and creating an issue and alleging an injustice where none exists. The vast majority of same-sex couples have no issue with the 'need for a father' clause or are indifferent to its presence. Chris Bryant MP challenged her, saying if she talked to most lesbians in this country about the amendment she would discover that they found it profoundly offensive. Geraldine Smith countered that she did talk to many lesbians, 'and quite a few of them have a great deal of common sense and would not find any problem with this.' Summing up, she said that this was about common sense and the

---

70 Ibid, col 204.
71 Ibid.

best interests of the child, and it was also about saying that fathers have a role to play:

> 'women need a man if they are to bring a child into the world ... That is a fact of life at the moment; science has not changed that yet, so there is nothing we can do about it. Therefore, fathers are pretty important.'[72]

She added that it was a fact of life that men and women were different and brought different things to parenthood.

> 'Sometimes when there are two same-sex parents, it is a good idea also to have someone who can act as a male role model. That is not discriminating against anyone. That is just enhancing the upbringing of the child; it is just helping. At the end of the day, this is not about discrimination; it is about the child.'[73]

Traditionalist

12.94 Sir Patrick Cormack MP said he had listened to the debate 'with profound depression' and observed:

> 'When I entered this House in 1970, if somebody had told me that nearly 40 years thence, the House would debate the need for a father, I would have thought that that person had taken leave of his senses.'

He was firmly of the opinion that deletion of the 'need for a father' clause is a thoroughly bad and retrograde step. For him, preserving the legal status quo, as witnessed by the 'need for a father' clause and the desirability and necessity of retaining it, 'is the natural order of things'. He said it was one thing to stand up for the human rights of those in, eg, Burma, but:

> 'another thing entirely to extend and distort that concept of human rights, so that some people in this place, and many outside this place, are afraid to say – that it is a natural thing for a family to consist of a man and a woman who have children, and who give those children a natural and proper home.'[74]

He added that some of the 'surreal exchanges' that took place in the House on the clause reminded him of Mr Bumble, who said 'If the law supposes that ... the law is an ass.'

12.95 Sir Patrick clearly and forthrightly stated that he did not believe that a lesbian couple or two gay men could provide the same degree of balance, harmony and domestic comfort as parents of the opposite sex could, but also admitted that there were many parents – men and women, married and unmarried – who were very bad parents and were cruel to children. He asserted that: '[i]f we are intent on promoting the concept of the family, why do we run away from the importance of the role of the father?' He was unapologetic for stating his belief that the natural family unit was the man, woman and children. 'We should not out of a misguided concept of equality and fairness, pretend that there is an automatic right for anyone to have a child, regardless of sex,' he said, and continued that no one had the right to a child:

72 Ibid, col 205.
73 Ibid, col 206.
74 Ibid, col 207.

'I happen to believe that a child is God-given … A child who is deliberately brought into the world with no desire that there should be a man and a woman as the parents is brought into it with a disadvantage.'[75]

Quality counts – not gender

12.96 Ms Dari Taylor firmly stated that for her the quality of parents was much more relevant than their gender in determining and delivering the emotional, social and educational achievements of their children.

12.97 David Blunkett MP then posed a number of very telling questions to Ms Taylor:

'[W]ould she concede that there is a difference between the issue of same-sex couples being suitable to foster a child at a particular point in that child's life in the interests of the child … and the creation of a child, and the belief that the creation of that child is somehow a right, in circumstances outwith the normality of how we would proceed were we not able to implement IVF? That is quite different from the situation of those seeking a child through the course of a marriage or a separate relationship. Would she therefore agree that this is not about equality or rights, and that it is about the nature of procreation and the way in which we proceed in respect of a policy in the nation, rather than an individual right for a human being?'[76]

Ms Taylor unsurprisingly disagreed, arguing that whatever was appropriate for children who were adopted or fostered was equally appropriate for any who produced by IVF.

Real injustice

12.98 Ms Taylor correctly and very wisely noted that the debate in the House was not just about whether every child needs a father or a stable home; it was about the IVF treatment available to couples or women. The great majority of women and couples were having to access private clinics (75 per cent), 'and in so doing they have to stump up between £5,000 and £10,000.' The real injustice with IVF is that 75 per cent is offered privately, for those who can afford it, and that the remaining 25 per cent is offered on the basis of a postcode lottery. These are real instances of unfairness, discrimination and injustice, not the alleged instances of unfairness and discrimination against same-sex couples and single women, which supposedly come about because of the need for a father clause. Are the real targets of discrimination being missed because of the politically correct myopia blinding some of the protagonists in the debate? Ms Taylor added that it was inconceivable to her that couples or women, 'would not love, cherish, protect the child and provide it with a stable home.'

Access

12.99 Ms Taylor objected to the amendments laid down by Mr Duncan Smith and Mr Simmonds because they would make what was an emotional and

---

75   Ibid, col 208.
76   Ibid, col 209.

prolonged process and ordeal of accessing IVF even more fraught and lengthy and, give the doctor a further qualification and responsibility. The amendments were discriminatory and did not make sense.

Undermining

12.100 Tim Loughton MP said he was concerned about the undermining of the role of fathers, 'the message that that sends out about fatherhood and the resulting effect on our children's welfare.' He argued that the need for supportive parenting clause, 'is not about the power of scientists; it is about a misconceived notion of equality and fairness, which has been behind many of the objections'.[77]

Analogies

12.101 Moreover he argued that analogies with same-sex adoption are misplaced. Legislation on same-sex adoption 'dealt with children in care who were born of, and may have spent time with, two parents but then needed to be given the opportunity for a stable upbringing.' By contrast, it was children who would, by design, never have a father who were under discussion here and there is no comparison. These children's only connection with a father will have been 'a momentary collision of gametes in a test tube at the point of conception.'

Welfare of the child

12.102 Mr Loughton added:

'My primary concern is for the welfare of the child, as we are all bound to take into account under clause 1 of the Children Act 1989 and in practice because it is the right priority to have.'[78]

He was not concerned with the wishes of would-be-parents, but was concerned about the constant emphasis on the rights of adults to have a child – not the rights of a child – 'as if they are the latest must-have accessory'. He repeated the 'indisputable' enormous contribution of the father to the health, wellbeing and life prospects of the child:

'Statistically, depriving children born by IVF of the need to take account of a father's role when considering the creation of that child is to condemn that child to a much greater likelihood of underachievement and unhappiness.'[79]

Need for a father

12.103 Mr Loughton then said, slightly less dogmatically, that the amendment:

'does not specify that the father has to be there, but regard must be given to the benefits that a father or the alternative father figures that have been mentioned can bring to bear for the good of the child.'

---

77 Ibid, col 210.
78 Ibid, col 211.
79 Ibid.

In addition he claimed that fathers brought something distinctive to the parenting process, and were 'the forgotten contributor to child development,' but the Bill sent out another damaging message, which threatened to undermine fatherhood. References during the debate to absent fathers ignored the issue. Many absent fathers are denied access to their children because they are the non-resident parent:

> 'They would like to be the resident parent or to have access to their children, but have been denied that by the courts. Let us not vilify all fathers who happen not to be resident parents.'

Mr Loughton continued this theme, noting that many fathers lose contact with their children unintentionally after the break-up of a marriage, and urged the need for some balance in the debate 'because many fathers feel aggrieved and undermined.' That feeling maybe reinforced by legislation that says that fathers are no longer necessary to the nucleus of a family. He noted this view was supported by the organisation Fathers Need Families, and finished by stating:

> 'At a time when fathers are spending more time than ever with their children – eight times as much as they did 30 years ago – when fathers in families in which women work carry out a third of parental care, and when fathers are more eager than ever to play a central role in the daily lives of their children, is it not ironic that this Bill would undermine that important role?[80]

Mixed messages

12.104 Again the government are sending out very mixed messages. Mr Loughton continued that he supported the amendments retaining the need for a father clause because they were balanced, and sent out an important message to cohabiting couples as well as to same-sex couples and anybody else interested in IVF. He added that it was not discriminatory, it was supported by the public and was the right thing to do because it is in the best interests of the child, and was common sense.

Illogical

12.105 Chris Bryant MP did not agree:

> 'Either the original clause in the 1990 Act has had some effect, in which case the logic is that the status quo should preclude lesbians or single women from receiving IVF treatment, or the clause has had no effect and the amendment is just a declaratory gesture'.[81]

Those in favour of the clause can't have it both ways. He said that the various amendments would send the message out to lesbians and single women that they should not apply for IVF. He also contended that the 1990 Act should not be restated, making the HFEA tell all clinics that they should start discriminating against people on grounds of their sexuality.

80   Ibid, col 212.
81   Ibid.

Natural

12.106 Mr Bryant added that the reality was that IVF is not strictly natural. It is assisted conception, and it is 'one of the great joys that doctors have been able to bring to many families around the country,' a joy that should be made available to same-sex couples and single women. He concluded:

'When we start to impose our understanding of what is normal or natural on others, we are treading a very dangerous path. I for one was taught as a child, "Judge not that ye be not judged."'[82]

Airbrushing out

12.107 Iris Robinson MP stated she was saddened by MPs who wished to 'airbrush out' the role of fatherhood, and said that she stood by her faith:

'the word of God that man was created in the image of God and that woman was created from the rib of Adam to be his helpmate and companion. That is the natural progression of procreation ... We are moving mountains to facilitate immorality and to bring the rights of lesbians above all others in this country. It is a shame, and hon Members ought to hang their heads in shame.'[83]

Part of the tapestry

12.108 Mr Duncan Smith concluded the Committee deliberations by stating that the 'need for a father' clause 'has been part of the tapestry that has allowed people to understand the need to take a balanced judgment about the importance of a father.' He added that the Government's position was far more complicated than that which was in existence until they introduced the Bill because it was asking clinicians to make a judgment, after they have gone through a long list of criteria, about which group of parents is supportive or not supportive. Mr Duncan Smith said that was far more complicated and judgmental than current practice and would, in his view, lead to a large number of problems. Doctors will still be judging patients, except the judgments they will be making under the new supportive parent clause may well prove to be much more difficult and demanding than under the old 'need for a father' clause. He concluded by saying:

'[Dr Harris] said that the matter is about fairness, not fatherhood – but if the clause does not say that fatherhood is important, there will be no fairness in the Bill ... [The Government] will tear up a reasonable guidance and substitute a mess.'[84]

---

82 Ibid, col 213.
83 Ibid.
84 Ibid, col 214.

Votes

12.109 In a series of votes, the House first voted 217–292 that Mr Duncan Smith's amendment be made, voting by a majority of 75 that the need for a father (and mother), clause be scrapped. This was not a huge majority given that over 140 MPs did not vote. Then the House voted 290–222, a smaller majority of 68, to reject Mr Simmonds's amendment, basically inserting 'and a father or male role model.'

Chapter 13

House of Lords Debates

INTRODUCTION

13.1 The debates in the second chamber mirrored in parts those in the House of Commons, albeit with the advantage of more expertise in science, law, philosophy and religion informing discussions.

BREADTH OF VIEWS

13.2 Baroness Deech[1] warned peers of the risks in the proposed new law deleting the 'need for a father' clause, and found it extraordinary that the government, through the Houses of Parliament were prepared to make a statement that, in welfare, there is no need for a father. She said:

> 'we know from research in this country and abroad that a special contribution is made by fathers to the raising of their children, which is not replicated by the contribution made by mothers.'

Mothers and fathers bring something unique to the upbringing of their child. She added that:

> 'We know that it is said that children lack male role models and that some of the violence and disorder in society is created by the lack of a fathers.'

She was vexed that there was also a risk that the role of men had generally been downplayed in reproduction. Women have been increasingly legitimately having their reproductive autonomy respected, but men by contrast were, she said, in danger in this field of being reduced to a sort of genetic contributor and nothing more. The vital role of the father should not be relegated to that of a donor of sperm.

13.3 Baroness Deech said that the HFE Bill would supposedly 'ensure non-discrimination between family units and persons, at the expense, it could be argued, of the welfare of the child.' Hence the wishes of would-be-parents to have a child seemingly prevail over the welfare of the child. She noted:

> 'Current government and judicial policy is that fathers have a vital role to play. We should not be afraid of being labelled politically incorrect in standing up for the welfare of the child, as we best understand it in current conditions.'[2]

However, she insisted that the current welfare of the child requirement, including the 'need for a father' clause would continue not to be a barrier to treatment.

---

1   *Hansard*, 8 November 2007, col 211 (HL).
2   Ibid, col 212.

Guidance

13.4   However Lord Adonis, the Parliamentary Under-Secretary of State at the Department for Children, Schools and Families, concerning the 'need for a father' clause, whilst admitting that there was currently no ban on access to assisted reproduction in cases where there would not be a father,[3] nevertheless referred to the 2005 Guidance of the HFEA which states, inter alia:

> 'Where the child will have no legal father the treatment centre is expected to assess the prospective mother's ability to meet the child/children's needs and the ability of other persons within the family or social circle willing to share responsibility for those needs.'

Implicit in this is that there will be cases where there is no father and women will still be offered, eg, IVF. In those cases an assessment will be made of the mother and other people in the family or social circle to collectively meet that child's needs. On that basis, Lord Adonis and the government contended:

> 'Therefore, the current situation is unclear and the Government, having carefully considered whether research evidence supported the continued reference in primary legislation to a duty on clinicians to give specific attention to the need for a father, concluded that the findings of research in that area tend to show that the factor of prime importance is the quality of parenting, rather than the gender per se.'[4]

13.5   Thus, the government have decided to remove the 'need for a father' clause, 'but to retain in primary legislation a general duty to take account of the welfare of the child.' Lord Adonis concluded by referring to the House of Commons Science and Technology Committee Report of 2005, 'which says:

> '"The requirement to consider whether a child born as a result of assisted reproduction needs a father is too open to interpretation and unjustifiably offensive to many. It is wrong to imply that unjustified discrimination against 'unconventional families' is acceptable".'[5]

Fit for purpose

13.6   Lord Darzi, the Under-Secretary of State at the Department of Health, stated 'that the law', the proposed 2008 Act, was designed so that it 'remained effective and fit for purpose in the 21st century.'[6] What was acceptable in 1990 may not necessarily be acceptable in 2008–09. As he stated, the Bill included clear recognition of same-sex couples as legal parents of children conceived through the use of donated sperm, eggs or embryos. Therefore, a lesbian couple can clearly apply for IVF.

Keep old law

13.7   Lord Mackay, one of the architects of the 1990 Act, said the 'welfare of the child' section with the 'need for a father' clause:

3   Ibid, col 231.
4   Ibid.
5   Ibid, col 232.
6   *Hansard*, 19 November 2007, cols 663–664.

'was negotiated here in the House with considerable care and it was accepted unanimously [in both Houses] … male material is still necessary for the procreation of human life … If it is necessary, it seems extraordinarily undesirable, the very moment when the child comes into existence, to leave that out of account altogether.'[7]

He thus appealed to the natural order of things, ie that both male and female material is needed to make a child. Moreover he submitted that s 13(5) of the 1990 Act was a very general provision, 'and does not prescribe anything.' It does not insist there must be a father, still less a married father, or that a woman will be prevented from having, eg, IVF. Rather, 'It just says that the need for a father has to be kept in view.' Lord Mackay is clear that it is a 'very innocuous provision.'

Social networks

13.8 Baroness Tonge agreed 'that of course every child needs a biological father … but children can be brought up well without either parent in some circumstances.'[8] She said that a network of support for any future child was more important than either parent; 'there must be a social network and an extended family.' Moreover, what this debate was really about was that gay people should never be discriminated against.

Dilution

13.9 Baroness Deech expressed her concerns that as the science of assisted reproduction develops certain fundamental pillars of ethics may be disregarded or diluted. Thus she claimed:

'There is a risk in the unfolding of IVF and the consequent science that our humanity and the respective roles of men and women are ignored. It would be extraordinary if this House were to ignore the contribution made by half of the human race towards the upbringing of the next generation. It is important that this House should reaffirm the importance of parenting; both mothering and fathering.'[9]

Compromise

13.10 Baroness Deech hoped that the need for supportive parenting clause could be removed 'so that we can revert to the law as it stands – the careful and sensitive compromise worked out in 1990 … which has held firm for all that period'(ie 17 years).[10] She added:

'The requirement is, after all, only to consider the need; it is not an absolute ban on treatment by any means, and it is well known that many single women and gay couples receive IVF treatment at clinics and have children.'[11]

---

7   Ibid, col 669.
8   Ibid, cols 671–672.
9   Ibid, cols 672–673.
10   Ibid, col 673.
11   Ibid, cols 673–674.

She said that:

> '[the] argument for removing it is that it is now public policy to treat all families equally and to avoid any discrimination between persons on grounds of gender and sexual orientation and because there are inconsistencies and unknowns in the way that the provision is applied. There is no need for a father ... given that there is provision ...for two women to be the legal parents of a child.'[12]

Need for a father

13.11 Baroness Deech queried whether a child really does not need a father and answered first, that the need for a mother clearly remained unchallenged, saying that it was implicit in the way that the law worked. Secondly, however, she stated that it was her view that a child needs a father. She said, 'First, we are where we are,' ie the law requires a father, with the implication that the onus is on those who want to change the status quo to do so. She continued:

> 'To remove the requirement that a child needs a father is to make a fresh statement to the effect that a child does not need a father. It sends a message to men, at a time when many of them feel undermined as providers and parents, contrary to government policy in this field.'[13]

Mixed messages

13.12 Baroness Deech then listed government policy which emphasises a father's responsibilities for their children, in marked contrast to the removal of the 'need for a father' clause:

(1) It is government policy is that men should pay for their children after divorce and separation and that they should take responsibility.

(2) Divorce law judges hold that contact with a father after divorce is a good thing.

(3) The Government had recently tried to encourage single women to name the father of their babies on the birth certificates.

(4) It was thought that children who find out that they were adopted or created by donor insemination need to know their fathers.

(5) According to the United Nations Convention on the Rights of the Child, every child has the right to know and to be cared for by both parents.

(6) Finally, anonymity had been removed from sperm donors,[14] which, said the Baroness, must mean that they are important.

Meaning

13.13 Baroness Deech, in defending the existing 1990 law, said:

---

12 Ibid, col 674.
13 Ibid.
14 For those donating sperm after April 2005, arguably with the bad consequence of reducing the number of sperm donors.

'The current law does no more than require that a doctor checks whether there is a male in the social circle – for example, a grandfather – and causes parents to reflect on how to cope with the situation.'[15]

It is, therefore, not a case of no father, no treatment. Referring to the HFEA Code of Practices after 2005, which have arguably diluted the 'need for a father' clause anyway, she said the requirements had been much watered down by the HFEA Code which had done as much as possible to ensure that there was no discrimination without good reason. She was emphatic that the current law does not in fact discriminate:

'I would argue that the present law is not discriminatory. It applies to men and women: heterosexual couples, homosexual couples, married, cohabiting and others.'

The present law therefore applies equally to all and does not discriminate unfairly against anyone. Her other powerful argument is that, concerning the 'need for a father' clause, even if it had been discriminatory, it was justified on the ground that the welfare of the child is paramount.

Evidence

13.14 In addition Baroness Deech added

'There is a wealth of research showing that children need fathers, not just a parent. Children need to see complementary roles, the relationship between the sexes, a microcosm of society as they grow up.'[16]

She flags up the limited scope of the research on lesbian parents, which had been mostly carried out by one researcher in this country, and of necessity the children were very young. She claims there are three weaknesses or limitations with the research:

(1) it is research carried out by one researcher only, and not repeated by many others;
(2) the research has only been done in this country; and
(3) the children are very young in this research.

Baroness Deech claimed that some research showed that those children suffered from the inevitably confused and secretive family relationships that occur. She added that:

'Recent reports had placed Britain at the bottom of the international league tables for the welfare of children and we know that boys without parents fail at school, that they turn to worse role models and that fathers play a great part in the upbringing of their children as well.'

Error

13.15 Lord Alton described the government's decision to delete the reference in s 13(5) of the 1990 Act to the need for a father as 'a huge error'. He conceded that:

---

15   Ibid, col 674.
16   Ibid.

'Women should not be interrogated at IVF clinics about their sexual orientation or their marital status and many single women are loving and exceptionally good mothers, but the need for a father, and the right to know who he is, are the issues.'[17]

He referred with approval to Lord Warner: '"children are not accessories to adults' preferences".'[18]

Unique contribution

13.16 Baroness Williams strongly supported Baroness Deech in urging the retention of the 'need for a father' clause, albeit she agreed that a pair of men or women, or indeed a woman on her own, could be marvellous parents. Few would deny that reality, but that in itself is not an argument for writing out of the legislation and effectively downplaying the crucial role fathers play in the life of their children, nor the desirability of protecting and promoting their vital role. She said that her main concern was that:

'research shows conclusively in fields such as education and educational achievement that a child who has a male model as well as a female model is likely to do considerably better than one who does not have that male model, because...our society is made up of men and women.'[19]

Both bring something unique to bringing up a child. As Baroness Williams added: 'They often have rather different approaches, even rather different language.'

Marginalised

13.17 Baroness Williams boldly forecast the potential long-term deleterious consequences of marginalising the role of the father, as evidenced here by deleting the 'need for a father' clause. The vital role of the father needs to be supported, encouraged and celebrated, not airbrushed out of the child's life, as suggested here. There is potentially a ticking timebomb being primed under the fabric of society if the signal is sent out in legislation that fathers are surplus to requirement or optional extras in the upbringing of children. The ultimate health and wellbeing of future society may hinge on that not being the case.

Disconnect

13.18 Dr John Sentamu, the Archbishop of York and second most senior Anglican Bishop in England and Wales, initially flagged up his concerns about the disconnect between the laws of the land and morality and religion, which he considered immensely regrettable and indeed harmful to society. Thus he asserted unequivocally that the severance of law from morality and religion had gone too far:

---

17 Ibid, cols 681–82.
18 Quoted from *Hansard*, 8 November 2001, col 157 (HL).
19 *Hansard*, 19 November 2007, col 687.

'Religion, morality and law were once intermingled, which helped to shape both the common law and the statutes of this land, and greatly influenced the way in which judges interpreted them.'

This was presumably a good thing, but now:

'However, the law is now regarded purely as an instrument for regulating our personal affairs and as being completely severed from morality and religion.'[20]

This sweeping statement would be challenged by some who would argue that it is incorrect, that law is not completely severed from morality and religion, but rather both are integral parts of law, or at least shape the final form and content of law. Others would argue if law and morality and religion are completely severed that is no bad thing at all. Law ought to be completely separate from both. Dr Sentamu claimed, moreover, that provisions in the HFE Bill demonstrated just how far the severance had gone and its unintended consequences.

False dichotomy

13.19 Archbishop Setamu regarded the removal of the 'need for a father' clause as a thoroughly retrograde step and contended:

'[it] creates a false dichotomy at the heart of the Bill which places the welfare and needs of the child against their need for a father. Since when did they become competing requirements?'[21]

The answer would appear to be from 1990 to 2007. He then posed a second question: 'Is it not self-evident that the welfare and needs of a child are enhanced and met when there is a father present, as against there being no father at all?' Intuitively the answer in the vast majority of cases must be a resounding yes. However, in a small minority of cases it probably is better for the child to have no father present, if that father is violent, an alcoholic, drug addict, or has no interest or concern whatsoever for his child. However, that said government policy and ultimately the law of the land should not be constructed on the fears or concerns about a tiny minority of bad fathers, and this should not be a pretext for jettisoning the long-established 'need for a father' clause. Dr Sentamu claimed that holding to the view that a father should be present:

'... is surely not controversial and would be shared by many who find themselves, through bereavement or relationship breakdown, as the single parents of children. However, there is all the difference in the world between children who find themselves in a single-parent family through bereavement or breakdown of parental relationship, and those who find themselves in that situation by design. That is precisely what the Government propose in the Bill: the removal, by design, of the father of the child.'[22]

Confusion

13.20 Dr Sentamu noted that not all absent fathers wanted to be absent from their child's lives and referred to the confusion in the government's approach

---

20 Ibid, cols 704–705.
21 Ibid, col 705.
22 Ibid.

generally to the importance of fathers as evidenced by the mixed messages their various policy and legislative initiatives were sending out:

> 'First, in 2004, they made regulations to encourage parental responsibility and visibility by removing donor anonymity and allowing donor-conceived children to access the identity of donors involved in their conception. Secondly, they have rightly emphasised in their policies the need for male role models for social cohesion, to reduce underachievement, and to avoid increasing violent crime and gang culture. We are now faced with a Bill which seeks formally to remove in its entirety the need for the ultimate male role model, that of the father.'[23]

He directed swingeing criticism at the government's decision to remove the 'need for a father': 'Such is the value placed on a father by this legislation; it is reduced to a role where any substitute will do.'

Unjustifiably offensive

13.21   Dr Sentamu robustly challenged the argument of the Science and Technology Committee in 2005 that the need for a father is unjustifiably offensive, querying to whom it was unjustifiably offensive – to the child who would be dependent upon the love and care of the father? He said the 2005 Report also concluded that consensus on this issue could not be expected because, 'on the one hand, we are a multi-faith society and, on the other, we are largely secular.' However, he noted that the previous population census in 2001 had indicated that 85 per cent of the population described themselves as 'people of faith'. He stated:

> 'However, statistics aside, it is far from clear to me that my brothers and sisters of faith, and indeed of no faith, feel less keenly than me about the importance of a father's role in the life of a growing child.'[24]

Instead of having an ethical framework with the highest ethical standards at the heart of the Bill promoting the welfare of the child, Dr Sentamu noted that such a framework was sadly missing:

> 'What we have in the Bill, rather than those high ethical standards, is, on the contrary, a signal being sent that everyone has a right to a child and that this right overrules consideration of the child's welfare.'

The demands of the consumer (would-be parent) trump those of the welfare of a would-be child – or is it a product? He added:

> 'The rationale given in the White Paper for removing the need of a child for a father was so as to appear not to discriminate against same-sex couples or single mothers who wanted to have a child through IVF. The Government's response is based not on the welfare of the child but on the desire of those who feel that they should have a child as of right, without the need of a father.'[25]

23   Ibid.
24   Ibid, col 706.
25   Ibid.

Limitations

13.22 He very firmly stated that:

'The right of a prospective parent to have a child by any means necessary must not triumph over the welfare of children brought into the world as a result of the treatment authorised under the current legislation.'

The fact that single people and gay and lesbian couples could now adopt did not mean they should be able to 'commission' a child using IVF. He said:

'That is a non-sequitur, because the situations are markedly different; in adoption, the hospitality of a home is being offered to already existing children who have had the misfortune, through circumstances or necessity, to lose or be removed from the constant love of their own parents. Bringing the care of an adoptive home to a needy child is a wholly different circumstance to deciding in advance to use IVF technology to bring into the world a child who will, by design, never have a father. If discrimination is indeed the issue here, surely the greater discrimination is in ensuring that a child will never have any chance of knowing its natural father.'[26]

Tesco ergo sum

13.23 Dr Sentamu clearly stated:

'if we are serious about the paramount place of child welfare in this Bill, that means such welfare taking precedence over the desires of those who want a child as of right. The child's right not to be deliberately deprived of a father is greater than any right to commission a child by IVF.'

Moreover he sharply criticised the Government who:

'have often championed the slogan of "rights and responsibility" and the need to recognise the duty and responsibility that goes alongside any talk of rights.'

Dr Sentamu then very forthrightly and powerfully complained:

'There is an unhealthy theme of rampant indifference at the heart of this Bill, rooted in a consumerist mentality in which the science that allows something to happen is transformed into the right to have it. The "cogito ergo sum" of Descartes—"I think therefore I am"—becomes the consumerist mantra, "I shop therefore I am" or "Tesco ergo sum". The competing individualist arias of "I, I, I" and "me, me, me" provide the mood music for an individualism that posits the right of a wannabe parent over the welfare of a child. This virus of individualistic consumerism which informs a rights-based mentality is alien to those of us who come from another place – Africa – where they say, "I am because we are; I belong therefore I am".'[27]

Dr Sentamu concluded by stating that the laws that are passed in Parliament were more than mere regulation. The law is a statement of public policy.

---

26 Ibid.
27 Ibid, col 707.

'This is not about messages which are sent out about what is or is not acceptable in terms of family arrangements, but more fundamentally about the roles of parents, and in particular the need for a father where possible.'

The Government's new welfare of the child requirement with the need for supportive parenting, rather than the need for a father ran the risk of:

'... fundamentally altering the paramount importance of the welfare of the child, as set out in legislative terms almost 20 years ago in the Children Act 1989, and to place the interests of adults, in the form of prospective parents, above those of the child.'

Changed times?

13.24 Baroness Warnock, arguably the midwife of the original 1990 Act and the entire assisted reproduction regulatory regime, and the designer of the ethical, legal and moral framework which has arguably stood the test of 20 years of rapid scientific development in this medical sphere, noted that since 1990 there had been huge changes not only in knowledge and technology but in social and moral attitudes among people at large, and that the passage of the Human Rights Act may be taken as symbolic of those changes. Concerning whether the 'need for a father' clause ought to be deleted she observed that:

'There has certainly been a change in the readiness of society and government to countenance a variety of different forms of family, including same-sex partnerships. It seems consistent with such attitudes to remove from the Bill the requirement that, for assisted conception to be offered, account must be taken of the need of the child for a father. However, this is already highly controversial.'[28]

Most commentators would agree with her on the latter point. She added that it was a clause that could be interpreted as discriminatory, a view with which she admitted a certain, rather mild, sympathy. She noted however that for some the removal of the old clause had been taken to be a statement that the old forms of family were no longer necessary and, particularly, 'that men have no use in the procreation of children.' She continued,

'That does not seem the intention of the Government, but if that is how it is widely interpreted it ought to stay in the Bill, partly because it has always been a pretty ineffective bit of legislation.'

Does this imply it is symbolic rather instrumental legislation? She noted further:

'That and the reference to the welfare of the child seemed pretty wishy-washy in 1990 and still do now, and I doubt whether that consideration has ever caused a change in a decision on whether to offer in vitro fertilisation.'

She said the Warnock Committee thought of some scenarios where it would be wrong to allow IVF for a couple, eg known child abusers or people who were more interested in their own careers, for whom the child would be an accessory. On that basis, the committee had included their thoughts about the welfare of the child in the report, and she felt it had done no harm. Also, she importantly stated:

---

28   Ibid, col 720.

'I do not think the bit about the need for a father has done any harm either, but I very much doubt it has made any difference. Therefore, I would be quite happy to see it still there.'

Double standards

13.25 Lord Turnberg correctly highlighted a number of 'gross' anomalies which have arisen with assisted reproductive treatments. The first concerned the welfare of the child principle, which he said was very laudable in principle, but in practice the obstetrician was required to assess the suitability of potential parents for parenthood, which was difficult to fulfil. He also felt it illogical to single out this form of fertility treatment from the other forms, eg tubal surgery, gamete intrafallopian transfer (GIFT), or providing super-ovulatory drugs. However, this assessment process would continue, if not become more bureaucratic or lengthy, with the replacement 'need for supportive parenting' clause. Also, he said there were double standards and inconsistent practice afoot given that if there was an insistence on assessing the suitability of would-be IVF parents, why confine the assessment there? Why not extend it to all would-be parents, embracing the vast majority who can conceive naturally? As Lord Turnberg said, 'If you go along that route, you might in logic need to assess every couple wanting to have a child.' That throws up, 'some stark illogicalities'.[29]

Writing out

13.26 The Lord Bishop of Newcastle was perplexed by the decision to airbrush out the need for a father clause from s 13(5) of the 1990 Act, saying:

'We hear it said again and again that children lack good male role models today, yet we are writing fathers out of the script.' [30]

Lord Elton referred to the benefits of a male role model, and endorsed the stance that it was:

'an extraordinary thing to try to write fathers out of the lives of children before they are born. It seems to me grotesque and unpleasant. The sensibilities of those who may be bringing children up after they are born must come second to the interests of the child'[31]

The wishes of an individual or couple to have a child, therefore, should not take precedence over the welfare of that child. Lord Ahmed, a Muslim peer, emotively but very powerfully and sincerely argued that the Bill robbed a child of a father, and that no Parliament had that right, and nor did any law. He found these proposals, 'utterly repellent and repugnant.'[32]

Undermining

13.27 Lord Northbourne also found it very depressing that the words used by the Government in the Bill would undermine the role of fathers and families. He

---

29 Ibid, col 723.
30 *Hansard*, 21 November 2007, col 840–1.
31 Ibid, cols 842–3.
32 Ibid, col 845.

felt that the Bill had major social implications, and pointed out the many alleged worrying consequences of deletion of the 'need for a father' clause. Fathers should be written into the life of children more, rather than, as here, seemingly written off and written out. Parliament should be striving to encourage fathers, 'to be more responsible for their child or children.'[33]

Why important?

13.28   He said there was an accumulation of evidence which demonstrated the importance of a father in bringing up children. The father had four roles:

(1)   to give physical, financial and emotional support to the mother;
(2)   to be a secondary, but still very important, attachment figure for the child, adding to its self-esteem and sense of security;
(3)   to be a role model, showing a boy what it means to be a man, building his self-esteem, encouraging him to work at school and developing by example his social skills; and
(4)   to be a role model to both boys and girls, showing them how a man and a woman can live and work together in a loving relationship.

Commenting on these four roles, he submitted:

'It is possible, but not proven, that a second mother can perform the first two of the roles that were traditionally those of the father, but she certainly cannot substitute for the father as a male role model.'

Lord Northbourne said that boys 'instinctively' seek out male role models:

'With so few male teachers in primary schools today, he may have little alternative but to find a role model in his computer game or, as he grows up, in a gang leader on the street.'

Again, he noted:

'that the statistics show that, across the board, children who grow up with a dad, or with a committed surrogate dad, such as a grandfather, are likely to have better chances in life, both at school and later.'[34]

Meaningless

13.29   Baroness Hollis emphasised that the 'need for a father' clause had currently become 'meaningless, vacuous, empty rhetoric'. The reality was that single women received IVF. Their single status is an irrelevant consideration and the 'assessment' as to whether or not they receive IVF:

'is made on whether the woman is in sound physical and emotional health – or, in more conventional parlance, not "flaky" – and has family support.'[35]

She summed up that:

'Either the wording is meaningless, as it is now, in which case it should not be there; or it is meaningful but the answer ignored, in which case it is irrelevant; or it is meaningful but got around and manipulated, and we

33   Ibid, col 850.
34   Ibid.
35   Ibid, col 857.

end up with doctors deciding which families are desirable and which are undesirable, with some families and some children being judged second-class but perhaps smuggled under the ropes. If it is meaningful and upheld, it is utterly discriminatory.'[36]

Basically for all these myriad reasons it would be logical to jettison the clause.

Social need

13.30 Baroness O'Neill made the telling and correct observation that 'this legislation does not in any way abolish the biological reality of fathers.' The question concerned the social need for a father and she thought that children needed about five parents. She added that:

'Fathers are needed. Biological fathers are not touched by this legislation but we must face the reality that the social father is very often not the biological father.'[37]

This is of course one of the consequences of the IVF revolution. The whole concept of a father has been irrevocably altered by the 33-year-old technology. As she contended, social fathers could be a stepfather, close friend of the family or an uncle: 'The role of the father is indisputably essential and it must be fulfilled for every child ... especially so for young boys, also for young girls.' That said the 'need for a father' is:

'[a] highly ambiguous phrase which has not proved practical in the way in which IVF clinics operate ... Fatherhood is not something that is up for legislative redefinition.'[38]

Changing fatherhood

13.31 Baroness Barker referred to the approach taken by the Joint Committee on the HFE Bill, which was, 'moving towards the concept of parenthood as a legal responsibility rather than a biological relationship.' This is partially as it should be viewed, but dismissing the role of the father as a mere 'biological relationship' to the child is absurd – fathers are not just sperm donors. She commented that the dichotomy 'is a reflection of modern life, but perhaps it is more a reflection of family life, which is, and always has been, complex and messy.'[39]

13.32 Times and attitudes have changed since the Warnock Report publication in 1984 and the enactment of the 1990 Act, and Baroness Barker noted 'not only science and scientific knowledge has changed, but families have changed.' She urged equal treatment and consideration for all potential parents embarking on 'the physical and emotional trauma of fertility treatment'. Yet double standards are applicable when single or gay people embark on the same traumatic journey. She said children then become 'accessories' and 'nobody has the right to a child', adding:

---

36 Ibid.
37 Ibid, col 858.
38 Ibid.
39 Ibid, col 860.

'Of course nobody has the right to a child, but nothing in the Bill suggests that they do. All that is suggested is that people are given the same consideration as potential parents.'[40]

EVIDENCE

13.33 Earl Howe said that Parliament needed to be guided by the evidence. There was some evidence that the presence of a second parent rather than the gender of that parent counts more in terms of a child's welfare. However, he balanced those comments by noting:

'At the same time, many of us are instinctively uncomfortable with the notion that the presence or absence of a father in a child's life should be completely irrelevant to any assessment of its likely welfare.'[41]

Signals

13.34 Lord Darzi, for the Government, noted that many of the concerns raised by opponents of removal of the 'need for a father' clause:

'appear to be motivated not by any practical effect that the clause may have in relation to assisted reproduction but by a general concern for the perceived signal or message that may be derived from its removal.'[42]

He said that he understood that concern and reassured the House:

'Let me say at the outset that the proposal is not motivated by any attack on fathers or on the concept of fatherhood. Nor is it motivated by a simplistic desire for political correctness. The Government recognise clearly the extremely important role that fathers can and do play in their children's lives and the consequences that can follow where a relationship breaks down. Many measures taken by this Government are aimed at strengthening the role of fathers and ensuring that they are aware of their responsibilities.'

The issue

13.35 Lord Darzi said that the debate dealt, however, with a very specific context, ie a fraction of the fewer than 1.5 per cent of assisted reproductive births – a few hundred children. The issue was what duties did the state impose on clinicians regarding who they may or may not treat, or whether access to services, including those purchased privately, should be easier or harder for certain groups of people. In answering that, he said that unless the law was to be purely rhetorical, the intended outcome must be considered and whether it was justified by evidence. Therefore, the test is first, what is the aim or objective of the law, here the 'need for a father' clause, and secondly is there evidence its deletion would be harmful to, presumably, children and families or society?

---

40 Ibid.
41 Ibid, col 864.
42 Ibid, col 868.

No ban

13.36 Lord Darzi further noted that there was no ban on single women or same-sex couples receiving assisted conception treatment. Nor did the law require that there must be a father or any man involved in the upbringing of the child. Therefore, he said:

'The outcome intended to be achieved by the current law is therefore extremely unclear – or, as … Lady Warnock, said, ineffective and wishy-washy.'[43]

Consideration

13.37 He agreed fully that people contemplating having children should think through the implications, but that given the nature of the procedures in question, we are talking about people (the infertile), be they straight or gay, single or couples, who desperately want children:

'who will almost invariably have considered very carefully their decision to approach treatment services and who will have decided to act responsibly. In addition, the law requires the provision of information and an offer of counselling.'[44]

Regulation

13.38 He warned:

'We must be careful that there is no perverse incentive for some people to avoid regulated services and the quality and safety assurances that they provide. The Government propose to retain the overarching requirement to consider the welfare of the child, which in practice, following consultation by the HFEA, focuses on the likelihood of serious harm to the child.'[45]

Quality

13.39 Finally he concluded that:

'In relation to fathers, there is clear evidence of poorer outcomes for children where a marriage or partnership breaks down and the father is then absent. It is right and proper that that should be addressed. However, in the context that we are discussing today, the available research evidence suggests that it is the quality of parenting that is the factor of prime importance, not the gender of the parent per se'.[46]

Litmus test

13.40 Baroness Deech argued strongly that an ethical principle 'so basic that it is a litmus test of the ability of this nation to agree on ethical principles' is

43   Ibid, col 869.
44   Ibid.
45   Ibid.
46   Ibid.

s 13(5) of the 1990 Act, with its 'need for a father' clause, 'which has held firm and worked well for the last 17 years'.[47] The new 'need for supportive parenting clause', which replaces it, 'calls for the wisdom and natural practice of the centuries to be disregarded.' Her view was that the public needed reassurance that science was not leaping ahead to the detriment of future generations. Science must not be too far ahead of the law and, a fortiori, not be too far ahead of the public. Importantly she said that no one had a right to a baby. She then warned that care was needed, that:

> 'the science is great but that there is a risk in all that we do of dehumanisation, commercialisation and loss of identity.'[48]

She then highlighted the positive policies of the government to emphasise the importance of fathers and their roles and responsibilities to their children on the one hand, whilst contrasting these with the anomalous deletion of fathers from s 13(5) of the 1990 Act. She listed those policies:

(1)   paternity leave in order that a father can bond with his child;
(2)   encouragement for single women to name the father on the birth certificate;
(3)   ensuring contact between father and child after divorce;
(4)   ensuring that fathers pay maintenance for their children; and
(5)   ending the anonymity of sperm donors in order that they can be known if necessary at some time in the future.

She commented that all these policies were about enabling the child to discover who his or her father is. 'Why should that be if there is no point in having a father?'[49]

13.41 In addition she noted that the pre-legislative scrutiny committee concluded that children need two parents:

> 'The need for a mother is implicit in the direction to consider the welfare of the child, because it is the would-be-mother who presents herself for treatment.'[50]

One could imagine, she said, the reaction of the public were the Bill to say that the need for a mother was to be deleted from the law.

Inconsistencies

13.42 Not only is government policy inconsistent on the need for a father, but the Bill also remained full of inconsistencies, claimed Baroness Deech, in that it promoted truth about origins, but provided for birth certificates to name two parents of the same sex. (Some might claim it therefore promotes lies about who parents are.) It also, she said, ensured non-discrimination between family units and persons at the expense, it could be argued, of the welfare of the child. The notion that all families have equal status might therefore be considered false:

---

47   *Hansard*, 10 December 2007, col 22.
48   Ibid.
49   Ibid.
50   Ibid, col 23.

'After all, British law does not treat all families the same. It still rightly discriminates against underage marriage, which is not possible, and polygamous and incestuous unions, which are not legalised, so why should a child not have its family welfare considered before the mother undergoes IVF?'[51]

Realities

13.43 She furthermore argued that:

'Current government and judicial policy is unanimous that fathers have a vital role to play, and research … shows that children need fathers as role models. We should not be afraid of being labelled discriminatory or politically incorrect in standing up for the welfare of the child and for its right to have two parents of different sexes, even though that requirement has not been and will continue not to be a barrier to treatment.'

That said, she pointed out that the number of single women being treated by IVF had gradually risen, and she had no quarrel with that.

Discrimination?

13.44 Baroness Deech added that it was alleged that the factor that a child needs a father is discriminatory, but vehemently rebutted that allegation:

'It is not discriminatory because it applies to all patients regardless of sex and marital status. If it is discriminatory, it is justified by the welfare of the child, and it is proportionate; it is not an absolute bar.'

She claimed to be supported by the rest of Europe in this.

13.45 The argument that lesbian and single women are refused treatment is spurious and false. She noted that HFEA figures showed that treatment was regularly provided to single and lesbian women, and the number was rising, not decreasing. She claimed that clinics were looking for stability and a male role model, and that they considered the risk of harm in deciding who gets treatment. She added:

'I have a list of about 80 research papers listing the unique contribution made by fathers to the upbringing of girls and boys in terms of social and academic success and psychological and physical health. The father's input to the upbringing of girls is as vital as it is to the upbringing of boys. A household of two parents of different sexes is a microcosm of society. It gives children the chance to see the complementariness of roles, to hear adult conversation, to see two perspectives, to see the adjustment between the sexes, to have two sets of grandparents and a wider family, and to have respect for the opposite sex, not the denigration of it.'[52]

51 Ibid.
52 Ibid, cols 23–24.

Comparative position

13.46 Baroness Deech then considered the beneficial comparative positions in other countries that put great emphasis on the need for a father, stating:

> 'In keeping the law as it is, we will be in line with the rest of Europe; our law is already more liberal than the laws in the rest of Europe. Single people cannot be treated by IVF in France, Italy, Sweden, Norway, Switzerland, Portugal and Germany. That limitation is not therefore confined to the more deeply religious societies. If we say that there is no need for a father in any circumstances, we will be in a group of countries that includes Romania, Bulgaria, Venezuela, Mexico, Belgium and Finland …it is the hallmark of a civilised society that for the welfare of the child some restraints are put on who may reproduce when the matter is in the hands of clinics and the law.'[53]

13.47 She challenged the applicability of the existing studies on same-sex parenting, which are largely directed towards the existence of two parents of the same sex when the children are very young, but noted that in Norway and Sweden, where same-sex partnerships have been legal for very much longer, the risks of breakdown are considerably higher:

> 'Female partnerships have a divorce risk that is double that for males. The median length of male relationships in the UK is only 25 months. Thirty per cent of Swedish female unions and 20 per cent of male unions end within five years.'[54]

The Baroness's conclusion was that it was right to consider the child's need for a father. Also Parliament needed:

> '… to signal to men that we are all partners in the health of the next generation and that none of us is worthless or to be written out of reproduction or valued only for the money that we can contribute – that is, if we are men. If we maintain the existing law on the child's need for a father, that will do more to reassure the public about the advances in science than anything we can do … in its way, it is the bedrock for confidence in going forward in the in vitro fertilisation and stem cell field.'

She concluded that the current law does not prohibit many single women and lesbian couples being treated.

New families

13.48 Baroness O'Cathain was scathing in her criticism of the government, who were refashioning the architecture of the traditional family, ie mother and father, and extending it to include mother and parent. As she stated, the Bill was intended to create a separate category of parent for those who did not fit the description of either mother or father, thereby creating in law 'a family that could never exist in nature'. She agreed with Baroness Deech that there were over 100 pieces of research demonstrating the distinctive and important value and benefits of fathers to children, rendering this legislative change 'foolish.'

---

53 Ibid, col 24.
54 Ibid.

Adoption

13.49 She commented that analogies between adoption and IVF were wholly fallacious and inappropriate and that the context of the two was entirely different. Children who are 'adoptable' at least have a chance of having a father, whereas IVF children with lesbian parents do not. As she noted, 'adopted children are not purposively conceived on the basis that they should never have a father.' She continued:

'the decision of the state to facilitate the deliberate creation of children who would be prevented from having a father is morally wrong. That is a clear example of the Government prioritising the interests and desires of adults – in this case, would be-same-sex parents – above the welfare and rights of the children.'

Welfare of child paramount

13.50 Very interestingly, Lady Saltoun of Abernethy said she was 'concerned only with the best interests of the children.' Section 13 of the 1990 Act was the response of Lord Mackay, the then Lord Chancellor, to her amendment which would have made illegal the provision of IVF services to unmarried women. This was defeated by the House by one vote on a free vote. She said:

'The point about Section 13 is that it puts the interest of any children resulting from those services first and above the interests of the woman who wants a baby, where those interests conflict.'[55]

She was adamant too in stating that she was not aware that the child's interests had ceased to be paramount in the previous 17 years. She also submitted:

'It is widely acknowledged…that it is the best interests of a child to have two parents, one of each sex. Many unfortunate children do not, but they have been born without the use of artificial processes, often paid for by the taxpayer.'[56]

Deconstruction

13.51 Lord Patten was clear that: 'It is axiomatic that fathers should be as visible and present as possible.' He was struck by the fact that definitions in the Bill were sometimes inexact. Furthermore, he took the simplistic, non-expert view that 'one should not legislate about that which one cannot define.' He said the government could define the meaning of 'mother', but that, led into a magical mystery tour about what on earth the word 'father' might mean in different times and places, as a sign:

'This leads me to the conclusion that the Government, either by design or, as I suspect, by a muddled series of accidents, have ended up attempting to deconstruct the meaning of fatherhood in the Bill, divorcing male parenthood from biological reality as well as from practical and moral responsibilities.'[57]

---

55   Ibid, col 25.
56   True of 25 per cent of cases.
57   Ibid, col 30.

Statistical generalities

13.52 He said that he knew:

'... of no expert who gainsays the statistical generalities – to which of course there are many splendid exceptions – that there are close links between fatherless families without consistent male role models and the following factors; children living in poverty; children enjoying poorer health; children subject to a higher risk of abuse; children subject to a higher risk of offending ... [and] the close link between the likelihood of offending and the lack of a father or male role model; and poor school performance.'[58]

In short the HFE Bill was likely to lead, whether intentionally or not, to the deconstruction over time of fatherhood in the United Kingdom, and to 'the incipient devaluation, by the signs that the Government are giving, of the very idea of fatherhood in the United Kingdom.'

Evidence

13.53 Lord Warner disagreed with the deletion of the 'need for a father' clause for the simple reason that he considered it to be inconsistent with the Government's own family policy. He added:

'The great majority of people in the debate accept the research evidence strongly supports the view that children in general – although not necessarily in all individual cases – do much better in later life across a wide range of measures, including education, employment and offending, when a father is involved.'[59]

Why keep?

13.54 He also referred to the Joint Committee on the draft Bill, which had concluded, inter alia;

(1) it would be detrimental to remove entirely the requirement to take account the 'need for a father';
(2) it had little evidence that the existing provisions have caused harm; and
(3) it recognised that in an area such as this, the law has symbolic value, a point with which Lord Warner agreed.

Why scrap?

13.55 He addressed the three arguments against retaining the need for a father clause thus;

(1) it is difficult to administer;
(2) it brings fertility treatment into line with adoption policy;
(3) the wording discriminates against single women and gay couples.

---

58   Ibid.
59   Ibid, col 31.

He conceded that some doctors were uncomfortable applying the 'father test', but that the legislation, even after the Government's amendments on fathers, still required those providing treatment to 'pick and choose'.

Difficult to administer

13.56 Addressing the first argument that the clause is difficult to administer, he pointed out that fertility treatment was not an NHS service on demand, which is why some people went elsewhere and would probably continue to do so. The legislation now required those providing NHS fertility treatment to satisfy themselves on the likely welfare of an unborn child. This would continue to be the case even after the Government's wording. The reality, he said, was:

> 'Some people will be rejected and probably should be … That is the requirement that Parliament is making of doctors as part of the licensing system. It is inescapable that that requirement remains in place.'[60]

Consistency

13.57 Regarding the second argument, he contended that the consistency with adoption policy issue was a poor argument, given that the adoption agency is confronted with a child who already exists. In contrast, said Lord Warner, a person who is licensed to offer fertility treatment must decide whether the person seeking help is in a set of social circumstances in which the unborn child's welfare is likely to be protected: 'For 17 years, the law has rightly asked them to have regard to the need for a father.'

No discrimination

13.58 Thirdly, he contended, the 'need for a father' clause has not discriminated against, nor has it prohibited single or gay couples from accessing IVF on the NHS as long as they can convince a licence-holder with regard to the welfare of the child. So, there already exists no absolute discrimination against them. He added, as is the case with a heterosexual couple:

> 'if a single woman or a gay couple's circumstances call into question their capacity to protect the welfare of the prospective child, a licence holder … would still be required to reject that because of the welfare of the child requirements.'[61]

Hence all would-be parents or applicants are treated the same way – equally, fairly and on a non-discriminatory basis. Lord Warner concluded that the deletion of the 'need for a father' clause gave an 'ambiguous signal' to licence holders that they do not have to take as seriously the welfare of the child requirements in the 1990 Act and it is, therefore, a diluted version of the 1990 Act.

---

60 Ibid, col 32.
61 Ibid, col 33.

Detrimental consequences

13.59 Lord Northbourne resisted the removal of the 'need for a father' clause, and flagged up a number of alleged detrimental social problems that might subsequently ensue. He noted that 24 per cent of the nation's children were growing up in families without a live-in father. Whilst admitting that some of these single parent families arose from the death of the father, and others from family breakdown, he noted that in many cases the father simply did not accept that he had any responsibility for the child or children he has brought into the world, and often moved on. He stated:

> 'If the Government carelessly give the impression in this Bill that they are downgrading the importance of a committed father in the family, there will certainly be more single-parent families in the future than there are today.'[62]

Messages

13.60 Baroness Butler-Sloss, a former President of the Family Division of the High Court, was emphatic that by removing the requirement in the 1990 Act the government was sending a very important message to the public that 'fathers are not at all important – that they do not matter.' She said that the Government may say that they did not intend that to be the effect, but, intentionally or not, the message would go out to fathers, and the Government could not ignore that. She also highlighted the inconsistent messages of the Government here:

> 'It is also contrary to the ethos of the child legislation and the ethos of this Government ... concerning the importance of fathers in the life of children.'[63]

She concluded that s 13(5) of the 1990 Act recognised the vital contribution of fathers, although not to every family – and here she acknowledged that single-sex couples and single parents brought up many children successfully – but to many families. She said what message was being sent out was critical and that the government must not allow some groups to prevail over the welfare of children.

Illogicalities

13.61 Lord Turnberg disagreed, saying fatherhood was of course extremely important, but nevertheless the question was whether it should be made a legal obligation in the Bill in relation to IVF, which leads into a series of illogicalities, in that other forms of fertility treatments should be considered in the same light, when it is clear they are not. No one asks about the welfare of the child, still less the need for a father, when a woman is getting fertility drugs, or having surgery to unblock fallopian tubes, nor when a man has surgery to allow him to produce sperm. That is logically inconsistent. However, by contrast, when would-be parents seek IVF they are suddenly faced with having to answer questions about whether they are suitable parents and whether a father should be involved. 'That puts an illogicality into a system,' said Lord Turnberg. He concluded, 'Of course fatherhood is important but should it be part of the Bill?'[64]

---

62   Ibid, col 34.
63   Ibid.
64   Ibid, col 35.

Symbolic

13.62 Lord Harries criticised references to the symbolic effect of the clause and the message that would go out if it were deleted, saying:

'But symbols can, of course, be interpreted in different ways, and they can be interpreted in very different ways by different constituencies.'

Lesbian couples, single women and quite a lot of heterosexual couples and individuals would be very pleased by the signal the new, fair, non-discriminatory s 13(5) of the 2008 Act is sending out. He said that there was no doubt that everyone agreed that fatherhood brought a huge amount to a family, but studies showed the even more important effect of a stable and loving environment and of supportive relationships, whatever the sex. The symbolic effect of the law on the wider public and on those desperate for IVF and to have the chance to be a loving parent needs to be taken into account.

Workable

13.63 Baroness Hollis said that neither the Bill nor the new 13(5) clause (the 'need for supportive parenting' clause) was seeking to abolish fatherhood, rather that the question was whether the words 'the need for a father' are workable if they are in the Bill, and if they are workable – which the Baroness believed they were probably not –whether they were also fair. If they were workable, they were not fair. The Baroness said: 'If the words are meaningless then they should not be in the Bill'. Legislation should not be used to send out messages to carry personal views in that way:

'We are operating by the law of the land, which has to be administered by clinicians in their day-to-day dealings ... empty rhetoric is not part and process of what those clinicians should be engaged in dispensing when dealing with their patients.'[65]

She said if the 'need for a father' clause was not mere rhetoric and symbolic, but meant to have practical effects, then, when a single woman presented without an obliging male in tow she was, presumably, to be refused treatment while a heterosexual woman presenting with an obliging male in tow is allowed to become pregnant she knows that 'the average time that a woman spends as a lone parent is not a lifetime sentence, but two and a half years. She is likely to re-partner – for good or bad'.

Crystal balls

13.64 She also claimed:

'We also know that when a heterosexual woman comes with an obliging partner in tow, if that is the husband then 50 per cent of those marriages will end in divorce and if they are cohabiting then two-thirds will break up.'

Being in a heterosexual relationship is no guarantee of a couple's permanence, or its benefit to the child. The Baroness said that what happened at the point of presentation for IVF treatment bore little connection or correlation to whether

---

65 Ibid, col 36.

a man or a male partner would, as a result, play a long-term role in the life of a child. IVF clinics and doctors and Parliament cannot fashion legislation to predict uncertain human behaviour in the future. If the woman is single, a male partner may come on to the scene, and if that woman is partnered, it is unfortunately more than likely that their relationship will break up before that child even reaches their teens. She added that using IVF treatment as the litmus test of whether the man who was there at that point would continue to be an active, engaged father in that child's life was not certain – indeed 'the facts are that the odds against that are more than even.'[66]

13.65 She added that Parliament should not be engaged in high-flown rhetoric about the need for a father, and that something stating this should not be added to the Bill, when in practice whatever was said in the Bill would not affect human behaviour. This presupposes laws do not change human behaviour. Humans behave in a certain way regardless of what the law says. Does this mean law has only symbolic significance? She concluded that retaining the 'need for a father' clause would not change that behaviour at all:

> 'It will send out a message that all families without fathers, whether the children were conceived through IVF or, even more widely, naturally, are second-class and second-rate. Those children face the reality of stigma.'[67]

No harm

13.66 Lord Mackay countered that an important aspect of the welfare of the child was the need for a father. He also stated that the inclusion of the phrase, when interpreted in the light of the HFEA Code of Practice, had not harmed anyone.

> 'What the doctor looks for, as the evidence shows, is some person who can be a role model – a model of male thought as distinct from female thought – in the life of the child.'[68]

He conceded that no one can predict how much and for how long a father or parent or mother will be involved in the life of any child, but even women who bear children by IVF may not necessarily live all that long. 'Nobody can tell.' He added:

> 'I thought that this was a very reasonable thing to include in 1990. It is not prescriptive in any sense. It does not debar people from getting IVF when no father is in the offing but it requires the child's need for a father to be considered as a factor in the welfare of the child ... a father is an important factor in the welfare of the child. That is what the 1990 Act stipulates and asks should be considered, without imposing any sanction if, for some good reason, that aspect of the welfare of the child cannot be provided.'[69]

He commented too that in assessing the welfare of the child there must be an element of future judgment with very variable factors is involved, but the doctor makes the best judgment they can and then acts on it. He concluded that the

---

66   Ibid, cols 36–37.
67   Ibid, col 37.
68   Ibid, col 38.
69   Ibid.

welfare of the child and 'need for a father' provision had been in place since 1990, and had had no detrimental effect:

'... the wisdom of 1990, which I believe prevailed unanimously in Parliament at that time, is still pretty wise today.'

Old law not working well

13.67 Lord Winston challenged Baroness Deech's claim that the law has worked well in regard to s 13(5) of the 1990 Act and said that he did not think that it had worked particularly well or that it was a workable law. He said it was not appropriate for doctors to police infertile patients who wanted to have treatment, and that it was dangerous and led to problems:

'It is one of the reasons why doctors recently have sometimes got into trouble, because they have tried to interpret what is in the interests of society rather than understanding above all the autonomy of the patient sitting in front of them.'[70]

Research

13.68 Lord Winston said that the research was fundamentally important to the argument concerning retaining the 'need for a father' clause. He referred to the Golombok research:

'In Britain we have only one good study of lesbian couples bringing up children in a controlled fashion; the study compares those children with children born naturally, by in vitro fertilisation and artificial insemination ... [and] shows that after nine or 10 years the children brought up by these couples are showing signs of being better parented, are better adjusted to their peers at school and have better relationships with other children than many others in her study.'[71]

He added that looking at studies of single women in our society was not enough, because these women have a whole range of other issues:

'Most women in our society are single because they are poor, because they have been abandoned or because they have been threatened, and they are in an environment that is very much below the standards that we would desire for ourselves.'[72]

Evidence challenged

13.69 The Earl of Listowel correctly stated that there was not much research in this area, and only one longitudinal study in this country. He asked Lord Winston if he agreed that the sample for that research was quite small and, at about 16 or 17 years old, the young people going through this were quite young, meaning it was not possible to say what the results of the experience of having same-sex parents were. He did point out that of the sample of 25

---

70   Ibid, col 39.
71   Ibid.
72   Ibid, col 40.

children growing up in lesbian families, six had had a same-sex relationship while growing up, whereas in the heterosexual sample none had had such a relationship. He admitted that that may not mean very much, but it suggested that the Golombok research was perhaps more controversial than one might at first think.

Evidence supported

13.70 Lord Winston disagreed. He did not think that the research was at all controversial and noted that it was widely accepted around the world, that Professor Golomobok was frequently invited to meetings around the world to show her work, and that her work had been published by peer review in various journal 'as being the best evidence that we have available'. He conceded that it was not perfect evidence, but no research ever is. He pointed out that generally, unfortunately, governments too often make policy without research evidence. 'It is far better to have research evidence when you are making social policy.'[73]

Small sample

13.71 Baroness Deech, however, responded that whilst Golombok's work was frequently cited, she was one alone in this country with a very small sample. Her work was vastly outweighed by the work of many others. She referred to one example from the Department of Works and Pensions which says:

> "'Fathers and mothers matter to children's development. Father-child relationships … have profound and wide-ranging impacts on children.'"

She concluded that Golombok's work was known simply because it stood out from of the much larger amount of evidence showing that children received different inputs from fathers and mothers.

Evidence supported

13.72 Lord Winston accused Baroness Deech of citing anecdotal evidence.[74] He thought that information published by peer review after a proper study would be preferable, and as far as he was aware the Golombok studies in this country were the only ones that had been published on that basis.

Other problems

13.73 Lord Winston flagged up two other potential consequences of retaining the 'need for a father' clause:

> 'First, there is a risk of a racist attitude in certain clinics. If I am a doctor in South London and I am dealing with a black patient who has a different social and cultural background where it is regular for fathers to leave mothers pregnant after these kinds of treatments, I could easily find justification for

---

73 Ibid.
74 It is debatable whether the evidence from the Department of Work and Pensions can be dismissed merely as anecdotal evidence.

refusing that treatment. That is not just an airy-fairy idea; that is a practical proposition that really can and does happen.'[75]

Secondly he said the House needed to think much more seriously about a major problem in society:

'As women get educated, gain skills, increasingly pay taxes and contribute to our society, they grow older, getting more and more infertile, without finding a partner. That is not anecdotal; it is well known and published.'

One consequence of this was that older women often seek help for their infertility without a male partner. It was not desirable or practical to refuse treatment to those women. He concluded that removal of the 'need for a father' clause would not undermine at all:

'our collective recognition that there is a desire to look after, nurture and, above all love children. Love is the key issue here, but it is something that we as practitioners and we as members of society who are looking on cannot measure.'[76]

He later said that it was very difficult to judge what the interests of the welfare of the child would be.

Stigma always bad?

13.74 Lord Tebbitt confessed he did not believe that stigma is necessarily a bad thing, but Baroness Hollis replied that s 13(5) of the 1990 Act was stigmatising policy that would lead to the stigmatisation of children.

Technologists

13.75 Lord Tebbitt countered that he was one of those males according to Baroness Hollis's description who is an 'obliging' partner 'in tow' with his wife. He said he thought that was a pretty sneering, cheap and stigmatising remark to husbands who go around with their wives and support them. He then importantly and legitimately stated that the House had to be careful about making policy on the basis of the views of the technologists, ie the doctors, scientists, embryologists and researchers working in the sphere of assisted reproduction – the so called experts and informed opinion lobby. He said that on the moral use of the technology, every peer has an equal standing in expressing a view. Why should the medical establishment's views in this field have automatically more weight than anyone else's?

13.76 He added that legislators and doctors, 'as the technologists', had the same responsibility as a man and woman who create a child naturally. The important point is that about the discussion concerns the creation of a life that does not exist. So the considerations should include whether they have the means to sustain the child, their own health and the possibility that the child might inherit ill health, or whether one of the partners is very old and therefore likely to die when the child is young. All must be considered when a life that does not exist is going to be created.

---

75   Ibid, col 41.
76   Ibid.

Rights and responsibilities

13.77   Lord Tebbitt correctly restated the point that there is no right to a child, but that a child has a right to a parent. In fact, he said, a child has a right to two parents, preferably one of each sex. He concluded:

> There is a responsibility here: the responsibility to ensure that, on balance – for there are no certainties in these matters – we give the child whose life we create the best possible chance. A child is not a consumer accessory ... A child is a great gift and a great responsibility; those who create that life carry the responsibility for ever.'[77]

Lord Winston countered querying whether Lord Tebbitt agreed that a patient seeking help had the right to be listened to without prejudice.

Fathers important

13.78   Lord Alton agreed that 'children can never be accessories,' and that 'the law has a symbolic value.' He said that to add deliberately to the vast numbers of families that had no men involved in the upbringing of their children would be 'ludicrous'.

> 'For the law to send a signal – not to stigmatise others – that we do not think men are very important in this equation plays into the arguments of male redundancy ... Men are not redundant.'[78]

He added that men and fathers had a unique role to play in the upbringing of children. He said it was estimated that that some 800,000 children in Britain did not have access to their fathers, and Parliament should think very carefully before unravelling and unpicking the very careful sentiments Lord Mackay had put together in 1990.

Onus of change

13.79   Lord Alton cited questions which came up at the Joint Committee where it had been asked whether there were any examples of anyone who had been unable to receive IVF on grounds of sexual orientation. The answer was no. He also referred to Professor Golombok, who said that there were no cases that she was aware of. Baroness Hollis queried what the point of the provision is if there were no cases, but Lord Alton countered:

> 'That is the reverse of the argument. If the law has not been used to discriminate against people having IVF, why change it? ... we send out messages if we change the law in a way that is not helpful.'[79]

Lord Alton said that the House was getting into 'quite a muddle' on the duties and responsibilities of a father. He asked whether the heart of the problem was that it would suit a lot of men to be told that they had no duty or responsibility, and warned finally against reducing the role of men to the provision of gametes

77   Ibid, col 43.
78   Ibid, col 44.
79   Ibid, col 45.

in fertility tests: 'It is important that we recognise the social role that men have to play as fathers as well.'

Interrogation

13.80 Baroness Howarth said that she favoured interrogation of every family who has a child to ensure that the child has a stable family, and did not much mind how that stable family is constituted. However she added that there were many men who do not make good fathers. Concerning assessing the welfare of the child requirement and the need for a father, she said her experience was that families often break down when children become difficult or when there was economic stress or sickness. These were all things that could not be predicted when facing that moment in the clinic. In reality no-one can be certain of the future. She added that many of the families that would rather not have children are the ones that will have the children anyway. She said that ultimately the only thing that mattered was the welfare of the child, but many adults would not have that in mind when looking to have a child. She asked why a person should be interrogated about their family when they go to a clinic when it will not be done that in a million other families across the nation? The answer possibly is that 'we do it because we have the opportunity' (which is correct). She then controversially argued that the criteria and questions asked at the welfare of the child assessment would be middle class. Those would be moral judgments from a particular, stereotyped set of moral views. She concluded that fathers were important, and were one bit of the stability in families. 'However, our nation is extraordinarily complex and family trees are sometimes totally unbelievable.' Lord Tebbit challenged her asking why it was 'assume(d) that middle-class morals and middle-class families are somehow better than working-class morals and working-class families?'

Rights

13.81 Lord Elystan-Morgan contended that when speaking of a child having a right to a father, we are speaking not about one right but about two. One is the right to know who the father is. The second is the right to have the prospect of a relationship with the father if possible, as there are practical difficulties:

> 'for all the furore about fathers being denied rights of contact, hundreds of thousands of fathers have no wish to have contact at all and are depriving their children of that second, massive right.'[80]

Value judgments

13.82 Baroness Finlay noted that because there were problems for healthcare professionals making so-called value judgments, and because different parents come before them in 'all shapes and sizes,' it is very easy for healthcare professionals working in a clinic naturally to gravitate towards people who are a little bit more like them and to empathise a little more with them. In other words we give IVF people to 'nice' people like us.

---

80 Ibid, col 48.

Judgments

13.83 Baroness Barker agreed that in areas of social policy, 'it is extremely important to work from an evidence base,' and referred to the UNICEF report which showed that the United Kingdom was in a bad way regarding children's well-being. However, the report showed conclusively that 'economic status of a family had a great impact on the well-being of children in a number of different aspects of their life chances.'[81] She also added that she trusted that clinicians used the same basis to judge any person who presented to them for that treatment, ie every patient is treated equally and fairly and not treated as belonging to a category or class. Clinicians should not make sweeping judgments about groups within the population, but they should rather look at the needs of the person presenting to them. Single women and gay couples are entitled to 'equality of consideration'.

Valued

13.84 Lord Darzi wound up the debate by saying that the removal of the 'need for a father' clause was not motivated by any attack on fathers or the concept of fatherhood. Nor was it an attempt at political correctness. He also said the Government recognised clearly the extremely important role played by fathers in their children's lives and the serious consequences that can follow where a relationship breaks down. Also the legislation did not in any way abolish the biological reality of fathers, and nor would it change the social reality of fathers for the overwhelming majority of families in this country, either now or in future. He was adamant that:

> 'The idea that the Bill in any way sounds the death knell for fathers is very far removed from the truth.'[82]

Duties

13.85 He said that the issue was the duties placed on clinicians by law to examine and judge their patients. He added that as a clinician himself he was well aware of the difficulty of making such judgments about people's circumstances and predicting with certainty what may happen at a later date. Thus the Government had 'on balance' decided to remove the 'need for a father' clause and keep the general duty to consider the welfare of the child in a broad sense.

Why amend?

13.86 Importantly Lord Darzi stated;

> 'There is no ban on single women or same-sex couples receiving assisted-conception treatment. There is no requirement in law that there must be a father or any man involved in the upbringing of the child. Nor is it a matter

---

81   Ibid, col 49.
82   Ibid, col 50.

of policy that single women or same-sex couples should not be able to access clinics.'[83]

On that basis, he submitted that the outcome intended to be achieved by the wording of the 1990 Act was therefore unclear. He referred to Baroness Warnock's description of it as 'wishy-washy', and said that to retain the provision would be to perpetuate a confusing and potentially discriminatory situation. He said:

'fathers belong in children's lives but that the phrase does not belong in the Bill. Either the question is meaningless, or the answer is ignored, or both are meaningful and therefore discriminatory.'

The phrase either serves no purpose or it serves a potentially bad purpose!

Quality of parenting

13.87 He added:

'By removing the requirement to consider the need for a father, we are recognising the existence of a wider range of family arrangements.'

The argument was that social attitudes as to what consititued an acceptable family in 2007 was different from what was deemed acceptable in 1990. He contended that it was vital that children be raised in a loving and supportive family environment:

'The evidence suggests that the quality of parenting is the factor of prime importance and not necessarily the gender, or even the size, of the family.'[84]

Quality of families, not quantity or gender of parents is the crucial determinative regarding promoting the welfare of the child. The need to enshrine in law and therefore give special legal sanctity or pre-eminence to the need for a father or father figure has become obsolete and unnecessary with the passage of time and in view of these alleged changed social attitudes. He stated:

'The Government fully recognise the important role that fathers play in their children's lives. The proposal does not detract from that role but it does recognise the crucial role played by all parents.'

Interestingly, Lord Darzi said that he doubted that any clinician would take responsibility for that assessment, including the need for a father, if the Bill remained with the provision on the need for a father.

No right to a baby

13.88 Baroness Deech challenged some of the Government's arguments in favour of deleting the need for a father clause, stating again that there was no such thing as a right to a father, or indeed the right to a baby. She referred to Hohfeld:

83   Ibid, col 51.
84   Ibid.

'who said that there is no right to a baby and there is no duty to give anyone a baby; it is a privilege. There is a need for a father, not a right to a father or a right to a baby.'[85]

She conceded that the law was discretionary here, and that the rates of IVF for single women and gay and lesbian couples were going up, 'probably with no harm done at all, but this is about the symbolism of the law, which is very important.'

Love – not all you need

13.89 She concluded that things should be looked at through a child's eyes:

'Do we not call it a tragedy for a child if his or her father is killed, especially during pregnancy? Does the baby appreciate that his fatherlessness is planned rather than accidental?'[86]

She continued:

'The need for a father goes back millennia. It is a very modern phenomenon indeed, as yet unproven, that there is no need for parents of both sexes ... the removal of the statement that a child needs a father – the view that a father is a discretionary factor-sends a message.'[87]

She said that love was not all in the upbringing of children, but rather was only the beginning, presumably be it a heterosexual couple, same sex couple or single woman. Seemingly love is not all you need to be a good parent and maximise the welfare of the child.

Patient first

13.90 Lord Winston reiterated that IVF doctors (and doctors generally) need to put the interests of the patient in front of them first.[88] He said:

'When doctors forget that the most important person is the person in front of them whom they are treating, they forget their responsibility to that person ... There is a risk in doctors thinking about their responsibility to society; they can forget why they are doing medicine.'[89]

Baroness Deech deprecated the liberalisation of IVF treatment, which was continuing and had continued since 1990: 'it would be best if the law were left untouched. It gives clinicians the discretion to do as they see fit at the time.'

Functional

13.91 Lord Northbourne agreed that:

---

85 Ibid, col 54.
86 Ibid, col 54–55.
87 Ibid, col 55.
88 Indeed the GMC emphasise in *Good Medical Practice* that doctors must, '[M]ake the care of your patient your first concern'. Available at www.gmc-uk.org/guidance/good_medical_practice.asp
89 *Hansard*, 10 December 2007, col 55.

'Expert opinion and modern research tells us … that, on average, a child who grows up in a single-parent family is likely to be less successful in school and later life than a child who grows up in a functional two-parent family.'[90]

Critics would say the word 'functional' is critical, in that if a child grows up in a non-functional two-parent family that argument is invalid. He readily conceded that this was not true in every case. but added:

'None the less, for the majority of children who grow up in a single-parent family, there are real disadvantages, which can easily last for life – and often do.'

Parental expectations

13.92 He also said that the contributions made by the mother and father might be different, but both were important, and he observed that the time might have come, indeed he suggested it was long past, when society should define more clearly what it expects of our parents. Finally he noted that too many families were affected by domestic violence, drug addiction and many other failures that are extremely damaging to the children, and he could see no reason why an IVF clinic should not be required to satisfy itself that 'the child it manufactures will not be entrusted to a dysfunctional family of that kind.'[91]

13.93 Baroness Finlay said she felt strongly:

'that we have reached a point where we need somewhere in a Bill to state what parents are expected to do. We brandish the term around, based on biological definitions, rather than ongoing duty.'[92]

She added it was not just a long term commitment, because the commitment is lifelong, for as long as the parent is alive.

Inconvenient truths

13.94 The Earl of Listowel said the debate highlighted three inconvenient truths:

'first, that boys need fathers or, failing that, a proxy for a father; secondly … parents are driven to have children and over-prescription may drive prospective parents away from licensed provision into the arms of we know not who … and thirdly … that current legislation in respect of the importance of fathers is largely ignored by clinicians.'[93]

He added that lone mothers spoke to him about the need of their sons for a father figure, and that 'not having an interested male in one's life is often a contributory factor to failure.' He thus challenged the popular fallacy that:

'children do just as well without interested and responsible fathers. That boys need fathers may be an inconvenient truth but it must not be ignored.'[94]

90 Ibid, col 56.
91 Ibid, col 57.
92 Ibid.
93 Ibid, col 58.
94 Ibid.

Distinctions

13.95 Earl Howe distinguished between married couples and couples in a civil partnership on the one hand, and unmarried couples, same-sex couples and single women on the other hand seeking IVF, stating:

> 'it is perfectly sensible for the welfare assessment to make an assumption – all things being equal – that the marriage or the civil partnership will provide the basis of a stable upbringing for the child.'[95]

Whilst the future cannot be predicted with certainty, he said, the fact that two people committed to live the whole of their lives together was a strong a priori indicator of their long term relationship. Regarding the latter categories of people seeking IVF, he said that it could not reasonably be assumed that statistically people who cohabit are at a far greater risk of breaking up than those who marry. He emphasised that unmarried couples or single women should not be ineligible for IVF. Rather:

> 'for these people there is an additional dimension of the welfare assessment that must be covered and an extra box to be ticked before the test is satisfied.'[96]

Condoning dishonesty

13.96 Lord Winston was concerned that keeping the 'need for a father' clause would lend itself to encouraging a degree of dishonesty among some couples that was surprisingly difficult to detect, eg women bringing 'a male in tow who was not actually their partner,' seeking IVF and attempting to satisfy the need for a father clause. Baroness Hollis claimed that 'the real litmus test of whether a child will flourish is income – at least as much as what type of parent and family structure the child has.'[97]

Clinical enforcement

13.97 Lord Warner said although clinicians may not like the welfare of the child assessment, they may find it difficult to do and they may find it uncomfortable to have these conversations with the people in front of them, 'it is the will of Parliament to have that provision.' Lord Winston countered that, 'if Parliament makes laws that cannot be enforced, it is bound to be the case that the doctors will struggle.' Baroness Hollis added that the House should be concerned about what was practicable and workable, not saying merely what serves their own moral high ground. Lord Warner responded that Parliament makes legislation that may, on occasion, be difficult to administer:

> 'That is why we often have secondary legislation, guidance, advice and codes of practice: to help the people who must implement parliamentary legislation to do so.'[98]

---

95 Ibid, col 59.
96 Ibid, col 60.
97 Ibid, col 61.
98 Ibid, col 63.

Baroness Tonge agreed with Lord Winston, questioning how a responsible doctor ensured that a genuinely responsible male adult was involved, ie not 'a male in tow' just to satisfy the 'need for a father' clause? She asked whether the doctor would interrogate him in the surgery or clinic, and 'How could the doctor ensure that 'this is not a guy the woman has just met in a bar or at a party who said that he would do this for her?'

The bottom line

13.98 Interestingly, Lord Darzi stated:

'that there is no legal definition of parents but our intention is that someone who is recognised as a parent under this Bill will have the same parental rights and responsibilities as other parents.'[99]

CONCLUSIONS

13.99 Some might contend that it beggared belief that the deletion of two apparently small, simple words from the 1990 Act, ie 'a father', and their replacement by two other words, namely 'supportive parenting', could generate such intense angst, denunciation and impassioned and informed recourse to principle, yet that is precisely what happened in Parliament. Was the 'need for a father' clause in s 13(5) of the 1990 Act broken, superfluous, discriminatory, unfair, not human-rights compliant, symbolic or instrumental? There certainly was no consensus on that question. Equally unclear was whether the new 'supportive parenting' clause contained in the new version of the 1990 Act, as amended by s 14 of the 2008 Act, would be any improvement on the 'need for a father' clause. Was it a more nebulous and potentially more difficult clause for clinics to interpret and apply and did it undermine the crucial role of fathers in families and in the wider society? Was the legislative change an example of government in thrall to the god of political correctness, or did the change make no difference at all? Time will tell.

99 Ibid, col 65.

Part 4

The Case for Abortion Reform

Chapter 14

The Abortion Controversy

BACKGROUND

14.1 The legalisation of abortion and the scope of the permitted grounds and gestation periods within which abortion may be lawfully permitted has generated much debate and argument across society over many years. These ongoing debates and arguments have been intense and no consensus has been reached, or is likely to be reached by those on either side of the debate. That said, Parliament has passed legislation[1] which attempts to regulate abortion. The topicality and continuing controversial nature of the abortion issue can be gleaned from the recent urging of the British Pregnancy Advisory Service (BPAS), which carries out 50,000 abortions each year for the NHS, to 'reclassify women's homes as places where terminations could be done.'[2] The article reported that under existing law all abortions must be carried out in a hospital or clinic. But after an earlier challenge by BPAS in 2011, a High Court judge ruled that the Secretary of State had the power to approve women's homes as a 'class of place' where abortion drugs can legally be taken.[3] This is a further liberalisation of the law on abortion.

14.2 Another example of the war of attrition on the existing law on abortion was the unsuccessful attempt by Nadine Dorries MP to include an amendment in the Health and Social Care Bill 2011 that required women seeking abortions to be informed of the availability of independent, non-directive counselling prior to being permitted an abortion. Her argument was that the BPAS, the biggest non-NHS abortion provider, was itself offering this counselling yet at the same time making huge sums of money from abortion procedures. The counter-argument would be that the doctors working at the BPAS provide independent non-directive counselling anyway, that it is a woman's right to choose, and that the so-called informed consent requirement was a ruse by pro-lifers to make access to abortion slower and more cumbersome for women, thereby reducing the number of abortions occurring and restricting indirectly the woman's right to choose.

BATTLELINES DRAWN

14.3 In *Life After Death: Britain's Tragic Abortion Story, 1967–1997 – Looking Beyond a Culture of Death*,[4] David (Lord) Alton very powerfully sets out his pro-life credentials and the essence of the pro-life arguments – our 'Judaeo-Christian belief in the sanctity of life, the dignity of the human person,'

---

1   The Abortion Act 1967, as amended by the Human Fertilisation and Embryology Act 1990.
2   As reported in *The Sunday Times,* 15 May 2011.
3   Ibid.
4   (The Christian Democrat Press, 1997), p 1.

come from Judaism. He notes that since the passage of the Abortion Act 1967, four million children have been 'savagely' aborted, and that one in five of all pregnancies ends in abortion. Furthermore:

'All forms of life are now subject to genetic manipulation. We select out. We distort, practising an unnatural selection on our own ... species ... [and] 100,000 human embryos are destroyed in laboratories each year.'

Alton's view is that this constitutes 'terrible destruction' which goes 'to the very heart of our humanity.' Our society has slid down the ethical slippery slope:

'The abortion mills have replaced the Satanic mills, and the laboratories, their terminations and experiments have replaced the nursery and the cradle. Human life has been reduced to a commodity: bought or bartered, experimented upon, tampered with, destroyed or disposed of at will.'

14.4 Pro-choice campaigners argue with equal conviction that it is a fundamental right of a woman to exercise her autonomy to control her fertility. She alone, advised by her doctors, determines her own reproductive choice and destiny. Her condition, circumstances and wishes are unique to her. Pattinson notes that, regarding the abortion issue, 'The whole area is beset with terminological difficulties.'[5] So describing an unborn baby or child as a foetus may be seen as automatically dehumanising it, making the abortion procedure much easier to justify and condone, given this entity is merely a foetus rather than a human, and so stripped of its moral and ethical value.

HISTORICAL OVERVIEW

14.5 Abortion, like suicide, has existed and occurred for millennia. That is despite various legislative attempts at proscribing or alternatively limiting its availability and also regardless of social pressure from myriad sources seeking to stigmatise the practice and ostracise those participating in abortion procedures, be they women seeking terminations or the practitioners assisting those women. Greenwood and Young[6] noted that '[A]bortion has always existed,' and women have used 'various substances, objects and instruments' to help them abort. Eskimos used carved walrus rib, and, women in 10th century Persia used sharpened marrow root. Old wives' tales of abortion in Britain over the centuries spoke of using herbal concoctions and chemical solutions. They note however:

'Many of these methods involved extreme risk. Some of the substances were lethal. Others seriously damaged the woman's or child's (if the abortion failed) health.'

Laws may outlaw abortion and criminalise those who provide it or undergo it, but they do not prevent its occurrence. Some counter that legalising abortion and liberalising the grounds for its availability encourages the practice by legitimising it and draw support for this argument from the huge numbers of abortions that take place each year in England and Wales.

14.6 Historically at common law, abortion prior to 'quickening' (about 12 weeks' gestation, when the soul supposedly entered the foetus) was not deemed

---

5   *Medical Law and Ethics,* (Sweet & Maxwell, 2009), p 235.
6   *Abortion in Demand,* (Pluto Press, 1976), p 19.

a crime, whereas abortion after quickening was a misdemeanour. In 1803, the Lord Chief Justice Lord Ellenborough introduced a Bill into Parliament, which eventually became the Malicious Shooting or Stabbing Act 1803. This was popularly known as Lord Ellenborough's Act, and significantly altered the existing common law on abortion. It distinguished clearly between aborting a 'child' before and after quickening, the latter being a felony punishable on conviction by death. The punishment for abortion prior to quickening was not quite so draconian, merely being, inter alia, 'publickly or privately whipped,' or transportation 'beyond the sea' (probably to Van Diemen's land (Tasmania) for up to 14 years – hardly a light sentence). Therefore, prima facie, abortion was historically regarded as a very serious crime, and the criminalisation of abortion was a major feature underpinning the practice of abortion and remains so. In 2012, if an abortion is not carried out in accordance with the Abortion Act 1967, as amended, that abortion will become a criminal offence under either s 58 or s 59 of the Offences Against the Person Act 1861 (OAPA 1861), so the stigma and rigour of criminal law has not entirely vanished from our allegedly progressive, liberal abortion laws today.

14.7 Interestingly, 25 years after Lord Ellenborough's Act, the distinction between abortion of a child before and after quickening was scrapped. Also abolished, by the Offences Against the Person Act 1828 (OAPA 1828), was the death penalty for abortion.

14.8 The latest incarnation of the Offences Against the Person Act was OAPA 1861, which further modified the law on abortion by making abortion a misdemeanour. Thus, anyone procuring the miscarriage of a woman (ie an abortion) under s 58 of OAPA 1861 could be sentenced to life imprisonment. Also, under s 59 of OAPA 1861, anyone found guilty of supplying any instrument, poison or noxious thing for an abortion could, if convicted, be imprisoned for up to three years – again quite a draconian penalty. This Victorian legislation governing illegal abortions (ie abortions not covered and protected by the Abortion Act 1967, as amended), albeit 150 years old, remains. From 1861 until 1929 doctors nevertheless performed abortions where this was necessary to save the woman's life.

14.9 The next legislative milestone in abortion regulation was the Infant Life (Preservation) Act 1929, which made a number of important changes to the regulatory regime governing abortion. Section 1(1) created the new offence of child destruction. Anyone who intentionally destroyed 'a child capable of being born alive' was guilty of a felony and liable on conviction to life imprisonment unless it was proved the child destruction 'was ... done in good faith for the purpose only of preserving the life of the mother.' Very significantly s 1(2) provided that if a woman was pregnant for 28 weeks or more that was 'prima facie proof' that the child was capable of being born alive. So from 1929 up until the enactment of the Human Fertilisation and Embryology Act 1990, a child or foetus was presumed capable of being born alive (ie viable) if there had been 28 weeks' gestation.

14.10 The common law effectively extended the availability of lawful abortion to women in 1938 with the seminal case of *R v Bourne*,[7] where a 14-year-old

---

7   [1939] 1 KB 687, [1938] 3 All ER 615.

girl was violently raped by a man and became pregnant. The defendant Aleck Bourne, an obstetric surgeon, after examining the girl and informing her of all the relevant facts, believing that the continuance of the pregnancy 'would probably cause serious injury to the girl,' and if she gave birth it was 'likely' she 'would become a mental wreck,' performed an abortion operation with the consent of her parents. He was then charged with unlawfully using an instrument with intent to procure the miscarriage of the girl contrary to OAPA 1861, s 58. As the trial judge Mr J MacNaghten in directing the jury noted, this case did not involve a back-street abortionist plying his dangerous trade for money, rather it was very different.

> 'A man of the highest skill, openly, in one of our great hospitals, performs the operation … as an act of charity, without fee or reward, and unquestionably believing that he was doing the right thing, and that he ought, in the performance of his duty as a member of a profession devoted to the alleviation of human suffering, to do it.'

These two types of abortion are like comparing chalk and cheese. He also directed the jury that the legal burden rested on the crown to satisfy the jury 'beyond reasonable doubt that the defendant did not procure the miscarriage of the girl in good faith for the purpose only of preserving her life.' Concerning how to interpret the words 'for the purpose of preserving the life of the mother,' he directed the jury that these words should not be given a restricted or narrow or literal construction, but rather should be construed more purposively, ie not just be confined to danger to life but include danger to health, 'since life depends on health, and it may be that health is so gravely impaired that death results.' He favoured the latter construction that 'you should take a reasonable view of those words,' and they were not confined to 'mean merely for the purpose of saving the mother from instant death.' Thus he directed the jury:

> 'those words ought to be construed in a reasonable sense, and, if the doctor is of the opinion, on reasonable grounds and with adequate knowledge, that the probable consequence of the continuance of the pregnancy will be to make the woman a physical or mental wreck, the jury are quite entitled to take the view that the doctor who, under those circumstances and in that honest belief, operates, is operating for the purpose of preserving the life of the mother.'[8]

The jury found Dr Bourne not guilty under OAPA 1861, s 58, thereby effectively creating a new common law exception to illegal abortion.

14.11 Greenwood and Young[9] furnish some useful statistics about the prevalence of abortions performed in the 1960s prior to the passage of the Abortion Act 1967. By 1961 about 2,300 abortions were taking place in the NHS. The number rose to 9,700 in 1967. 'The market for private abortions also expanded. At least 10,000 a year took place prior to 1968 in that sector. Hence according to their figures at least 20,000 lawful abortions (NHS and private) were already taking place in the country prior to the enactment of the Abortion Act 1967. The original Abortion Act 1967 (prior to the significant amendments made to it by the 1990 Act) could be viewed as either a major liberalisation of the law, socially just and respectful of women's reproductive rights and right to

---

8   [1939] 1 KB 687, at 693–694.
9   Above, fn 6.

choose on the one hand, or alternatively as being a hugely damaging piece of legislation to society, leading to the deaths of innumerable innocent children. Section 1 of the Abortion Act was the pivotal section and provided, inter alia, that a woman would not be guilty of an offence under abortion law (ie OAPA 1861) if the pregnancy was terminated by a registered medical practitioner, if two doctors formed an opinion in good faith that either:

- the continuance of the pregnancy would involve risk to the life of the pregnant woman, or of injury to her physical or mental health or any existing children of her family, greater than if the pregnancy were terminated;[10] or
- that there was a substantial risk that if the child were born it would suffer from such physical or mental abnormalities as to be seriously handicapped.

Section 1(4) provided that the normal requirement or safeguard of two doctors' opinions did not apply where a doctor was of the opinion in good faith that a termination was 'immediately necessary to save the life or to prevent grave permanent injury to the physical or mental health of the pregnant woman.' Section 1(4) is still good law in 2012, its justification being that saving the woman's life in these exceptional circumstances ought to prevail over the usual safeguards for all other abortions in s1(1).

CURRENT LAW

14.12 The current law governing abortion is located interestingly and paradoxically in ss 37 and 38 of the Human Fertilisation and Embryology Act 1990 (the 1990 Act), which substantially altered the original Abortion Act 1967. Rather than have a new Act of Parliament governing abortion the government opted by contrast to amend significantly the existing abortion law by means of including two sections (ss 37 and 38) in the 1990 Act, primarily aimed at regulating the creation, keeping and use of embryos outside the body, and specifically helping infertile individuals have babies, an aim fundamentally at variance with terminating a pregnancy. It was not surprising therefore that in 2008–2009 many MPs and peers wanted to tighten up and restrict the availability of abortion or alternatively further relax and liberalise the law on abortion, again equally paradoxically by using the vehicle of assisted reproduction legislation (ie the Human Fertilisation and Embryology Act 2008 (the 2008 Act)).

14.13 Section 1 of the Abortion Act 1967, as amended by s 37 of the 1990 Act, provides that a person will not be guilty of 'an offence under the law relating to abortion' (ie OAPA 1861) when the pregnancy is terminated by a registered medical practitioner, if two doctors form the opinion in good faith that one or more of the grounds set out under s(1)(a)–(d) is applicable.

14.14 The most important ground for a lawful abortion to occur since the 1990 Act is s1(1)(a), the 'social ground', quite simply because 98 percent of all abortions take place under this ground. In 2010 no less than 186,926 abortions were carried out under this ground. Section 1(1)(a) provides that the pregnancy

---

10 Nb the doctors could under s 1(2) take account of the 'woman's' actual or reasonably foreseeable environment.

must not have exceeded 24 weeks (foetal viability in 1990 – a reduction of four weeks from the 28-week presumption of gestational viability contained originally in the Infant Life (Preservation) Act 1929), and the continuance of the pregnancy would involve risk, greater than if the pregnancy were terminated, of injury to the physical or mental health of the pregnant woman or any existing children of her family. The two doctors are hence required to engage in a balancing exercise of the respective risks of continuing with or terminating the pregnancy. This exercise may have been appropriate in 1967 when abortions were far less frequent and more dangerous procedures, but it appears anachronistic and unnecessary both in 1990 and certainly in 2012, when early, legal abortions are virtually risk-free procedures, certainly in terms of women's mortality. Indeed Ann Furedi of BPAS noted that the risk of death from a safe, early legal abortion was 0.7 women per 100,000 abortions, compared to seven women dying for every 100,000 births. However, pro-life advocates would point out that s 1(1)(a) fails to adequately consider the potential morbidity consequences of abortion which may harm the woman if she has an one or several abortions, namely post-abortion traumatic syndrome, greater chances of subsequent infertility, and an increased risk of developing breast cancer later in life. Clearly pro-choice advocates vehemently contest the existence of these risks. Importantly, the two doctors can take account of the pregnant woman's actual or reasonably foreseeable environment. This ground is incredibly broadly and widely framed, giving further ammunition to those who claim that the reality is that in the United Kingdom in 2012 (and arguably since 1967) we have de facto abortion on demand, although de jure the two doctors act as the gatekeepers of the Act.

14.15   The second ground for a lawful abortion is s 1(1)(b), the first therapeutic ground, which provides 'that the termination is necessary to prevent grave permanent injury to the physical or mental health of the pregnant woman.' Of critical importance with this ground is that there is no gestational time limit for accessing it. Also the doctors can, as with s 1(1)(a), take account of the woman's actual or reasonably foreseeable environment in assessing the applicability of the ground. This ground would, inter alia, cover the *Bourne* scenario. Only 317 abortions were performed under this therapeutic ground in 2010.

14.16   The second therapeutic ground, which again has no gestational time limit, entails the two doctors undertaking a balancing exercise, similar to the social ground, except here crucially it is in respect of the life and not merely the physical or mental health of the pregnant woman. Section 1(1)(c) provides 'that the continuance of the pregnancy would involve risk to the life of the pregnant woman, greater than if the pregnancy were terminated.' Fortunately, like s 1(1)(b), very few abortions occur under this ground – the figure for 2010 was 41 abortions carried out under s 1(1)(c).

14.17   The fourth ground, s 1(1)(d), is the 'eugenic ground', which again has no gestational time limit so fully viable foetuses can be, and in fact are aborted under this ground. It very nebulously and unclearly provides 'that there is a substantial risk that if the child were born it would suffer from such physical or mental abnormalities as to be seriously handicapped.' Worryingly the terms 'substantial risk', as opposed to a mere risk, and what constitutes, 'such physical or mental abnormalities as to be seriously handicapped' are not defined in the Act, nor in any case law. Pro-life opponents of the Act state that this provision allows doctors and parents to abort unborn children for minor conditions that would be easily correctable by surgery, eg cleft lip, hare lip, club foot or polydactylis, and could be considered eugenics by the back door. In 2010, 2,290 abortions (ie 1 per cent) were carried out under this ground, a small percentage by comparison to the total number of abortions, but not a small number in and of itself.

14.18 Under s 1(4), in certain situations one doctor's opinion suffices for a lawful abortion.

SAFEGUARDS

Central role of doctors

14.19 The fact that the statute specifies that two doctors must form an opinion in good faith that one or more of the abortion grounds are satisfied and that generally a doctor must perform the abortion procedure is intended as a safeguard for the pregnant woman to avoid an unqualified backstreet abortionist plying their trade and possibly killing, mutilating or harming the woman who wants the pregnancy terminated. It also acts as a safeguard to reassure the general public that whilst abortions are lawful they can only be sanctioned and generally performed by registered medical practitioners.

It takes two!

14.20 The second safeguard built into the legislation is that generally two registered medical practitioners must form the opinion in good faith that one or more of the grounds (s 1(1)(a)–(d) or s1 (4)) are applicable, although only one opinion is needed for s 1(4). The fact that generally two doctors' opinions are necessary for a lawful abortion is again protection against the potential misuse of the legislation by doctors too readily permitting abortions to be performed. Critics however might contend that the requirement to obtain a second opinion from a doctor that one of the grounds is applicable is no safeguard at all. Indeed it could be contended the requirement to get any opinion at all is itself a meaningless gesture. Other critics by contrast would contend there should be only one opinion needed and yet others that no opinion is needed, that fundamentally abortion is a private matter between the doctor and woman and no one else. The law should not therefore interfere in this private matter.

Forming an opinion in good faith

14.21 Again the fact that two doctors must form their opinion 'in good faith' is further protection against potential abuse of the abortion legislation. The leading case on the interpretation of these words is *R v Smith*,[11] and is the only case in over 44 years where a doctor has been convicted under the criminal law relating to abortion (OAPA 1861, s 58) of not forming an opinion in good faith, in accordance with the Abortion Act 1967. In this case a normal healthy girl of 19, Miss Rodgers, became pregnant by a man she did not want to marry. She was referred by her GP to Dr Smith, who saw her for 15 minutes. According to

---

11   [1974] 1 All ER 376.

the girl, Dr Smith made no internal examination of her and asked no questions about her medical history. Scarman LJ, the trial judge, stated that the doctor:

> 'asked for £150 in cash and said that, if she could get it that day, he would operate the following morning. There was no suggestion of the need for a second opinion or for further enquiries.'

Scarman noted that no arrangements appeared to have been made for a second doctor to see Miss Rodgers and she in fact saw none. Furthermore there was no indication that any enquiries or investigations were made into her personal history, her family background, or her actual or future environment, in accordance with s 1(2) of the Abortion Act 1967.

14.22 Dr Davis, the anaesthetist, testified he gave the second opinion required by law and then administered the anaesthetic to Miss Rodgers, but Miss Rodgers said she saw no doctor other than Dr Smith before the operation, denied that she ever saw Dr Davis before the operation and asserted that the anaesthetic was given her by somebody quite different; allegedly the general driver and porter employed at the nursing home. When he was first questioned by the police, Dr Smith said he had no records, but later produced two documents (his case note and Certificate A – this certificate must be completed before an abortion is performed and is the certificate of the opinion of the two doctors as required by the Act). As Scarman LJ added:

> 'Because of [Dr Smith's] prior assertion that he had no records and his belated production of certificate A after questioning by the police, he was charged with its forgery; but the jury acquitted him.'

Dr Smith was found guilty of performing an illegal abortion under OAPA 1861, s 58 and sentenced to 12 months' imprisonment suspended for two years and also fined £1,000. Scarman had directed the jury that concerning the good faith of the doctor it was 'essentially one for the jury to determine on the totality of the evidence.'

ABORTION NUMBERS

14.23 The most recent figures available on abortions carried out in England and Wales in the year 2010[12] reveal the large number of abortions that took place legally. The Report's summary noted that the total number of abortions was 189,574 for women resident in England and Wales, ie 8 per cent more than in 2000 (175,542). In addition, the Report noted that 96 per cent of abortions were funded by the NHS, and over half (59 per cent) took place in the independent sector under NHS contract, up from 2 per cent in 1981. Not surprisingly, 91 per cent of abortions were carried out at under 13 weeks gestation, and 77 per cent were carried out at under 10 weeks, compared to 58 per cent in 2000. Also, significantly, in 2010 the Report found that 2,290 abortions (1 per cent) were carried out under risk that the child would be born handicapped. There were a further 6,535 abortions for non-residents of England and Wales carried out in hospitals and clinics in England and Wales, bringing the total number of abortions carried out in 2010 to 196,109.

---

12 *Abortion Statistics, England and Wales: 2010*, (Department of Health, May 2011), (DoH Report).

ETHICAL ISSUES

14.24 Clearly a myriad of ethical and moral issues and principles, quite often conflicting and virtually impossible to prioritise or rank, arise in the abortion debate. Traditionally these are subdivided into what are usually referred to as pro-choice and pro-life arguments. Those broadly in favour of a pro-choice stance believe it is fundamentally the woman's right to choose whether she wants to get pregnant or not, and if she is pregnant whether she wants to continue with the pregnancy or alternatively terminate it. By contrast those who are pro-life broadly believe that the foetus, or as they describe it, the unborn child, is a person from the moment of conception, and has the same moral, legal and ethical status, value and worth as a 2, 20 or 60-year-old person. Thus, laws should not generally permit termination of the innocent life of a vulnerable human being in the womb.

14.25 These two stances are irreconcilable polar opposites but nevertheless it is worth highlighting that most people do not inhabit either extreme position on abortion, but would be located somewhere between these two diametrically opposed views. The law on abortion is arguably pitched in between these two extremities, and the debates in Parliament demonstrate that the current battles in the abortion war are being fought in the middle, eg cutting the gestational time limit to 20–23 weeks or less, rather than at the poles, eg prohibiting abortion outright or alternatively permitting it on request with no statute regulating it.

Dworkin

14.26 Ronald Dworkin[13] argues that depicting the abortion debate in these polarised terms is based on a widespread intellectual confusion. He contends that opponents of abortion object to it on the basis of two very different ideas:

(1) 'the *"derivative"* objection to abortion'. This holds it 'is wrong in principle … because abortion violates someone's right not to be killed', ie the foetus, in the same way as killing an adult is 'normally wrong'. He calls it the *derivative* objection to abortion because it presupposes and is derived from rights and interests that it assumes for all human beings, including foetuses, and that someone who accepts this and believes the government should prohibit or regulate abortion for this reason 'believes that government has a derivative responsibility to protect a fetus.'

(2) the '*detached*' objection to abortion. The argument here runs:

> 'that human life has an intrinsic, innate value; that human life is sacred just in itself; and that the sacred nature of a human life begins when its biological life begins, even before the creature whose life it is has movement or sensation or interests or rights of its own.'

According to this idea, 'abortion is wrong in principle because it disregards and insults the intrinsic value, the sacred character, of any stage or form of human life.' He calls it the *detached* objection to abortion, 'because it does not depend

---

13 *Life's Dominion: An Argument About Abortion, Euthanasia and Individual Freedom* (Vintage Books, 1994), p 10.

on or presuppose any particular rights or interests,' and someone who accepts '*this* objection, and argues that abortion should be prohibited or regulated by law for *this* reason, believes that government has a detached responsibility for protecting the intrinsic value of life.'

14.27 Dworkin believes that this confusion has 'poisoned' the abortion debate and made it more confrontational and less open to argument, and contends that the pro-life movement seems to presuppose and presumably endorse the derivative claim. He argues that the real disagreement is about how best to respect a fundamental idea which is shared by almost everyone: that individual human life is sacred, and contends that '[A]lmost everyone who opposes abortion really objects to it … on the detached rather than the derivative ground.' He also states that the question of whether a foetus is a person is 'multiply ambiguous.' And:

> 'is an even more treacherous question, because the term "person" has a great many uses and senses that can be easily confused.'

Woman's right to choose

14.28 One of the most powerful and cogent arguments in the pro-choice arsenal justifying a woman being permitted to undergo an abortion is that the woman has a right to choose what happens to her body. Choosing to abort her foetus is her legitimate exercise of her right to choose and exercise her bodily autonomy. Her choice ought to be and must be respected by the law. Autonomy is one of the four key ethical principles underpinning medicine and medical treatment, according to Beauchamp & Childress.[14] Autonomy originates from two Greek words, 'auto' meaning 'self' and 'nomos' meaning 'rule', so literally autonomy is self-rule. Singer defines autonomy as, 'the capacity to choose, to make and act on one's decisions.'[15] Autonomy is a fundamental but not an absolute ethical principle. Pro-life advocates would counter the woman's wish to terminate her pregnancy cannot possibly be more important and prevail over the unborn child's right to life. One person's choice ought not to be respected at the expense of another's very existence.

Foetus not a person

14.29 Pro-choice advocates also frequently state that a foetus is not a person, and, a fortiori, an unviable foetus incontrovertibly is not a person. Therefore, how can it be unethical or immoral to terminate an unwanted pregnancy, given that no person or human being with moral status is being harmed or killed? Only persons have rights to life and possess all the attributes and rights of a person. As noted already, Dworkin commented that the term 'person' was 'multiply ambiguous'. Singer says the term 'human being' or 'person' can be given a precise meaning as equivalent to 'member of the species Homo sapiens', ie give it a narrow definition, but he prefers an alternative definition, following Joseph Fletcher's list of indicators of humanhood that includes the following:

---

14 Beauchamp and Childress, *Principles of Biomedical Ethics*, 5th Edn (Oxford University Press, 2001).
15 P Singer, *Practical Ethics*, 2nd ed (Cambridge University Press, 1993), p 99.

'self-awareness, self-control, a sense of the future, a sense of the past, the capacity to relate to others, concern for others, communication and curiosity.'

This is a wider definition. For Singer, human beings characteristically possess certain qualities – listed beforehand. However, he says that the embryo or the later foetus, whilst 'indisputably' human in the former narrower sense, are not self aware, do not have a sense of the future or the capacity to relate to others, and so are not persons in the wider sense and therefore do not warrant the rights or protections afforded to persons.

14.30 Harris asks two distinct questions: 'when does human life begin?' and 'when does life begin to matter morally?'[16] He says that the moment of conception is the 'obvious answer' to the question of when life begins. But he argues that life is a 'continuous process' and it cannot be proven that a new *individual* begins at conception, because fertilisation can result in a tumour (hydatiform mole), not an embryo, and also because the fertilised egg divides into two major components with one becoming the foetus and the other the placenta and umbilical cord. Also the embryo can split up to 14 days after fertilisation. In answering the second question, when does life matter morally, Harris suggests that it is when that life is accorded 'the social and moral status of a person' and 'be any being capable of valuing its own existence.'

14.31 However, pro-life advocates insist that abortion is immoral and unethical because it causes the death of a human being, ie the unborn child. They contend that when fertilisation and the moment of conception occurs the entity created has the same moral and ethical status as, eg, an adult human being.

Doctors

14.32 Strictly speaking, while a woman effectively has a right to choose to abort a foetus, doctors are the gatekeepers and sentinels under the 1967 Abortion Act. Access to abortion for the woman is determined by the decision of the two doctors that one or more of the permissible grounds exist. The rhetoric and actual reality might be that it is a woman's right to choose, but in law two doctors must give the legal green light before an abortion can be lawfully carried out, hence circumscribing her autonomous right to choose. Pro life supporters would contend that the sheer breadth and vagueness of the words used in the Abortion Act 1967 reflect ethically muddled and morally woolly thinking on the part of the legislators and form the background to the high number of abortions occurring annually, sanctioned by members of the medical profession.

Utilitarian support

14.33 Retaining our permissive abortion laws could be justifiable on the basis of the good consequences of having abortions, ie the ending of unwanted, unplanned or difficult pregnancies and avoiding bringing a child into the world in unfavourable circumstances, and avoiding a woman having to bring up a child she does not want or cannot care for. Legalisation of abortion also has the good outcome that abortions are carried out in hygienic, safe locations

16   J Harris, *The Value of Life: An Introduction to Medical Ethics*, (Routledge, 1985), p 10.

(hospitals or clinics) by qualified professionals, rather than carried out by backstreet abortionists in unhygienic, unsafe locations as had previously happened. The potential risk of harm to the woman is thereby minimised. The benefits of the abortion greatly outweigh any harmful consequences. However, pro-lifers would counter that abortion rather than being an option of last resort has instead become for many an easy option of first resort. The very high number of abortions that occur each year tend to confirm this. The pro-life view would be that abortion has effectively become a type of contraception, which is damaging to society.

Outlawing?

14.34 Outlawing abortion is ineffective and futile. Even restricting its availability is pointless, because outlawing or restricting it does not prevent desperate or determined women from travelling to jurisdictions with more permissive abortion laws to obtain abortions, or even sadly accessing backstreet abortions. Several thousand women travel every year from both Northern Ireland and the Republic of Ireland to England to get abortions.

PARLIAMENTARY DEBATES – HOUSE OF LORDS

Terminology

14.35 The subject of abortion in the context of the HFE Bill was discussed in a number of debates in both the House of Lords and the House of Commons. In the Lords, Earl Howe[17] highlighted the unsatisfactory and unclear nature of the terms used in s 1(1)(d) of the Abortion Act 1967, like 'substantial risk' and 'seriously handicapped' (which are defined neither in the Act nor in case law). This criticism is equally valid in respect of the incredibly wide and broad words used especially in the 'social' ground for abortion (s 1(1)(a)) and indeed the two therapeutic grounds (s 1(1)(b) and (c)). He noted 'Everything is left to the subjective decision making by the doctor and mother.'

14.36 However Lord Darzi disagreed,[18] saying:

'Parliament chose not to define "serious handicap" in the Act. Parliament chose to leave this to the expert judgment of the two doctors, based on the merits of each individual case. The doctors must form their own opinion of the seriousness of the handicap the child would suffer if born, taking account the facts and circumstances of the case.'

Flexibility was what was important, not constructing a one-size-fits-all provision.

Reproductive choice

14.37 Baroness Tonge starkly noted:

---

17 *Hansard*, 12 December 2007, col 307 (HL).
18 *Hansard* 28 January 2008, col 530.

'In the end, it is the woman who has to be pregnant for nine months, go through childbirth and be primarily responsible for the child, whether it is disabled or not. We have to give her the right to choose.'[19]

Gillian Douglas stated the woman was the 'central actor' in abortion. The woman's autonomy must prevail.

14.38 Lord Steel, the architect of the original Abortion Act 1967, observed that 'all the abortion law does is to lay down the boundary of the criminal law. It is not a law that says what doctors or parents should do.'[20] Clearly the law does not compel, dictate or direct women to have abortions, but arguably it encourages them to do so, given the very wide, vague terminology employed in the legislation. Also, given that over seven million abortions have occurred since 1967, arguably there exists a culture of acceptance of abortion as a routine, ethically uncontroversial and demonstrably widely occurring medical procedure.

14.39 Lord Darzi said the idea behind pre-natal screening was to ensure that women and their partners had accurate information about the foetus.[21] Parents should be making their decisions on a fully informed basis after receiving balanced information.

Sanctity of life

14.40 Lord Alton was adamant regarding disabled babies and persons that the medical imperative must always be to heal, to comfort and preserve life. He added 'there is a very important principle at stake: we may not intentionally kill.'[22] Abortion violates the sanctity of life principle.[23]

14.41 Baroness Hollis contends an unborn foetus does not possess rights: 'I am not convinced that a foetus as such carries rights; we have responsibilities to it, but I think that humans grow into rights.'[24] By this argument, foetuses are not created possessing rights, but only start acquiring these when born. Saying we only have responsibilities to foetuses accords the foetus less moral status and worth than a human being. The notion that 'humans grow into rights' signals the belief of many that acquisition of rights is dependent on development; it is a gradual incremental process, rather than something that occurs suddenly, eg at the moment of fertilisation.

14.42 Lord Darzi was emphatic on the legal status of the foetus: both domestic and European law on discrimination, including the ECHR, apply only to living persons. The foetus is not classified as a living person:

'The foetus is not regarded as a living person in domestic law and has no rights independent of its mother until it is born alive. The courts have

---

19 Ibid, col 316.
20 *Hansard* 28 January 2008, col 518.
21 Ibid, col 530.
22 *Hansard*, 12 December 2007, col 311.
23 See also Baroness Paisley of St George's, at *Hansard*, 21 November 2007, cols 836–838 (HL), and Lord Ahmed, at ibid, cols 845–846.
24 *Hansard* 28 January 2008, col 526.

consistently held that a foetus is not recognised as being a separate person from its mother.'[25]

Eugenics

14.43   In calling for a tightening of the abortion laws, Lord Alton cited the huge numbers of abortions occurring: 'We have laws that have allowed 7 million abortions in the past 40 years, some 600 every day, and thus 200,000 every year.'[26] He also referred to a three-year period in the south-west of England where 100 babies were aborted with minor disabilities, eg cleft palate, club foot, hare lip, webbed fingers and webbed feet, albeit he correctly noted that '99 per cent of abortions have nothing whatever to do with disability'.[27] Is the eugenic clause the human equivalent of BS 5750 (the British Standard on 'Quality Systems'), determining what human life is fit for purpose, or alternatively can be discarded? Baroness Masham contended that use over 20 years of s 1(1)(d) of the Abortion Act 1967 'has "normalised" this brand of eugenics,' and that the principles of equality and non-discrimination were being violated too.[28]

14.44   Baroness Gould countered that the British Medical Association (BMA), the Royal College of Obstetricians and Gynaecologists (RCOG) and the Royal College of Nurses (RCN) all believed the current eugenic ground should be retained, and added that only 1 per cent of abortions carried out in England and Wales took place under s 1(1)(d).[29] She also said that the eugenic ground is very beneficial to both women and doctors, given that there needs to be sufficient flexibility to take account of individual cases. Parliament in 1990 tied 216–216 on a vote defining the term 'seriously handicapped' and the status quo (the existing law not defining the term) was retained. She added that women in these difficult decisions about aborting seriously handicapped foetuses are given real choice:

> 'All pregnant women are offered some kind of antenatal screening. It is always presented as optional and designed to enable women to make reproductive choices.'[30]

These decisions, especially to abort, are not taken lightly or easily by women. Generally they are informed choices.[31] As Baroness Emerton states, terminations occur:

> 'after careful consideration, advice and counselling of what the diagnosis may mean for their baby, the child's quality of life and what it might mean for themselves and their family's future.'[32]

She noted that 25 out of 27 EU countries enable women to end a pregnancy legally after a notice of foetal impairment. She denied that s 1(1)(d) was

---

25   Ibid, col 531.

26   *Hansard*, 19 November 2007, col 680. See also Baroness Emerton at col 715.

27   *Hansard*, 12 December 2007, col 309.

28   See *Hansard*, 11 December 2007, cols 726–727, and also *Hansard*, 12 December 2007, cols 301–302. See also Baroness Wilkins, ibid, cols 305–306 and Baroness Campbell of Surbiton, ibid, cols 306–307 and Lord Alton, ibid, cols 309–311.

29   Ibid, col 302, and generally see cols 303–305.

30   Ibid, col 303.

31   See also Baroness Tonge, ibid, col 316.

32   Ibid, col 304.

underpinned by eugenic principles, given that 'a eugenics policy demands public coercion'. However the choice here is the woman's, not the state's.

14.45 Baroness Emerton noted that regrettably:

'European statistics on social abortions show that we have the highest rate in Europe, where the average upper limit is 13 weeks. Ours is 24 weeks.'[33]

It should be noted that several EU countries have abortion on request for the first 13 weeks, whereas here two doctors must sanction abortions.

14.46 Baroness Williams stated it was 'right and proper that the same laws should apply to people who are disabled as those who are not.'[34] The seriously handicapped unborn child is discriminated against with the ultimate act of discrimination, ie being singled out and terminated. She correctly added that many of us will be disabled, not because we were born with a genetic disability but because we have suffered an accident that has heavily disabled us. Equally, many of us will become disabled by naturally occurring illnesses. She said that we all have to be accepted in society. 'Society has to make changes to ensure our lives are worth living.'[35] Lord Darzi, however, said that terminations under the eugenic clause were usually complex. 'There may be multiple anomalies rather than one.'[36]

Risks?

14.47 Lord Ahmed detailed a large number of risks and harmful consequences for women associated with having abortion. These included:

'more depression, suicide and future obstetric problems, including premature births and miscarriages ... serious risks of haemorrhages, infections and pain from medical abortions carried out in the home ... The evidence of association between early abortion and breast cancer is a growing concern'.[37]

He continued, noting the deleterious psychological condition of post-abortion syndrome, a form of post-traumatic syndrome, and was also concerned about the large amount of anecdotal evidence that showed that women, once they attended an abortion clinic, find themselves on 'a virtual conveyor belt'. Alternatives to abortion are not adequately discussed and abortion is the only effective available option, and Lord Ahmed queried whether women were always being given independent non-directive counselling.

Foetal survival rates

14.48 Several peers pushed for a reduction in the gestational time limit of 24 weeks based on research and evidence from a variety of sources. Lord Clarke

---

33 *Hansard*, 19 November 2007, col 715. See also Lord Alton, *Hansard*, 12 December 2007, col 307.

34 *Hansard*, 28 January 2008, col 528.

35 See also Baroness Masham, ibid, col 516, Baroness Knight of Collingtree, ibid, col 520 and Lord Alton, ibid, cols 522–524.

36 Ibid, col 530 and generally cols 530–531. See Baroness Hollis of Heigham, *Hansard*, 12 December 2007, col 313–314, Lord Steel of Aikwood, *Hansard*, 28 January 2008, cols 517–519, Baroness Gould, ibid, cols 521–522 and Baroness Tonge, ibid, col 530.

37 *Hansard*, 21 November 2007 col 845 (HL).

of Hampstead referred to an article in the *British Journal of Obstetrics and Gynaecology* published in May 2007 which considered a large population-based cohort of births that occurred in a ten-year-period from 1995–2004 in the West Midlands, which found that of 3,189 cases of termination for foetal anomaly, 102 – 3.2 per cent – of the babies were born alive, and the live births at different gestation periods were:

- 14.7 per cent at between 16 and 20 weeks;
- 65.7 per cent between 20 and 24 weeks; and
- 19.6 per cent at or after 24 weeks.

He referred to Millie McDonagh, who was born in Manchester in October 2007, at 22 weeks gestation, and also referred to Minneapolis, Minnesota where, 'we are told that 66 per cent of babies born at 23 weeks survive.'[38] However the RCOG, the BMA, the then government, the Science and Technology Committee and many others contended that survival rates across all hospitals need to be aggregated to get the 'correct' survival rate, rather than selectively and misleadingly looking at a small number of hospitals globally with the best or higher survival rates as some sort of gold standard or yardstick.

14.49   Baroness Tonge urged peers to be cautious about restricting or cutting the gestational time limit, stating that flexibility in the law was needed for certain hard cases to be dealt with. She gave as an example aborting foetuses with cleft palate, a condition that can be associated with some 'pretty gross abnormalities' as well, ie holes in the heart.[39]

Foetal pain

14.50   Lord Clarke objected to later abortions on the basis that post-16 week foetuses feel pain, claiming that, from 16 weeks, babies will recoil from a noxious stimulus in the womb and pre-24 week gestational babies will, if stabbed in the heel with a needle, pull their foot away and cry. He said: 'It seems reasonable to assume that they are feeling pain.'[40] RCOG do not accept this, arguing a foetus does not feel pain until 26 weeks gestation. However Lord Clarke referred to the research of Professor KJ (Sunny) Anand, from the University of Arkansas, who said that RCOG's understanding is based on an outdated understanding of physiology and that foetuses do have the apparatus to feel pain down to 18 weeks. Lord Darzi referred to the RCOG 1997 report which, he said:

'concluded that before 26 weeks' gestation the nervous system has not developed sufficiently to allow the foetus to experience pain … I am not aware of any new evidence that has changed that conclusion.'[41]

4-D Foetal imagings

14.51   Lord Alton said that the research and work of Professor Stuart Campbell in developing his 4-D foetal imagings had 'opened a vivid window into the

---

38   Ibid, cols 852–853 at col 853.
39   *Hansard*, 12 December 2007, col 316.
40   *Hansard*, 21 November 2007 col 853.
41   *Hansard*, 28 January 2008, col 530.

womb', and along with Professor Anand's research on foetal pain 'have completely changed the terms of the debate.'[42] Lord Darzi disagreed contending that, 'from a scientific perspective they [4-D Foetal Imagings] do not change the current knowledge about foetal viability or foetal pain.'[43]

PARLIAMENTARY DEBATES – HOUSE OF COMMONS

14.52 Despite the obvious demand by a considerable number of MPs to tighten up or alternatively further relax the law on abortion, the government signalled that they had no intention of altering it. As Alan Johnson MP, the then Secretary of State for Health, stated: 'The Government have no plans to change the abortion laws'.[44] Furthermore, abortion is viewed as a matter of conscience for individual MPs, not a matter of government policy or whipping, and it was up to MPs on a free vote, as a matter of conscience, to change the law.

Repeat abortions

14.53 Andrew Lansley MP, the then Shadow Health Secretary, as well as noting that 'there continue to be far too many abortions', and that the UK had the highest rate of teenage pregnancy in Western Europe, arguably symptomatic of a 'wider malaise' and our 'broken society,' added that: 'far too many abortions – about a third – are repeat abortions.'[45] This suggests that for many women abortion has become an option of first resort and effectively another type of contraception.

Timing of abortions

14.54 Mr Lansley flagged up the desirability of earlier abortions:

'if a woman needs an abortion [it] must surely be better for it to be an early, medical abortion than a later, surgical one.'[46]

He also urged MPs to 'take a more restrictive view of late abortions'. This is arguably consistent with the gradualist approach to a foetus acquiring protection, if not rights.

Survival rates

14.55 Mr Lansley referred to the research of Field and others published in the *British Medical Journal*,[47] which was based on a study of the survival of extremely premature babies in the former Trent Health Region and to the survival rates for babies at 23 weeks gestation and claimed that 18 per cent of those babies admitted to neonatal intensive care did survive – out of a total of 510 babies a year born at 23 weeks' gestation, that meant approximately 100 of those babies would live and go home. These figures (if accurate) and replicated

---

42   *Hansard*, 12 December 2007, col 312.
43   *Hansard*, 28 January 2008, col 531.
44   *Hansard*, 12 May 2008, col 1066.
45   Ibid, col 1080, and generally cols 1079–1081.
46   Ibid,
47   5 May 2008.

across the UK in other hospitals, provide powerful evidence for those calling for a reduction in the gestational time limit from 24 to 23 weeks.

14.56 Norman Lamb MP believed that the research evidence (ie Field's study above) showed that there appeared to be no real advance in the survival rates of babies born before 24 weeks, and that that appeared to be the scientific consensus.[48] Clearly pro-life and other commentators would fiercely contest this consensus. Mr Lamb continued: 'If we are making legislation on the basis of evidence, we should not be persuaded that there is a case for changing the current 24-week limit.' Laws should be made on the basis of evidence (medical, scientific, research, surveys, etc.) and not on the basis of hunch, prejudice, religion, gut feeling etc. Evidence-based medicine is widely followed. Evidence-based laws should be equally encouraged.

Comparing like with like?

14.57 It should also be noted that the pregnancies referred to in the survey relate to pregnancies where there were clearly problems with the mother or foetus or both, yet the vast majority of abortions are carried out on healthy foetuses and on women who have had no problems with their pregnancy (apart from not wanting to be pregnant or have a baby). If the survival rate for these premature births is so high, it might be argued that the survival rate for the 198,000 unwanted, healthy foetuses, if they were born at 23 weeks, would arguably be as high, if not slightly higher.

Forced pregnancies

14.58 Chris McCafferty MP submitted that the solution to reducing the high abortion figures was not cutting the gestational time limit, because 'any reduction in the time limit would force a small number of vulnerable women to continue a pregnancy against their will.' Rather, good sexual health education is the best way to reduce the numbers. Forced pregnancies and birth completely violates the woman's right to choose and her procreative liberty.[49]

Definitions

14.59 Dr Evan Harris MP argued that the term 'viability': was:

'not the earliest point at which babies might survive when prematurely born, but the point at which a premature baby – a foetus – alive at the onset of labour would have a decent chance of surviving, without serious abnormality, independently of the woman's body.'[50]

Fundamental right

14.60 Edward Leigh MP emphatically asserted that there was 'just one overwhelming, fundamental right' involved in the abortion issue – the right to

---

48 Ibid, col 1091, and generally cols 1090–1091.
49 Ibid, col 1118, and generally cols 1118–1119. See also Dr Desmond Turner MP, ibid at col 1129 and Jacqui Lait MP, ibid at cols 1136–1137.
50 Ibid, col 1140.

life of the unborn child.[51] He contended that the 'pro-choice lobby dominates the establishment' and, regarding private abortions, 'we are talking about a multi-million pound industry.' Abortion is not just a social policy but also a lucrative commercial business for some clinics and doctors who offer it privately for paying customers. He also claimed that, 'some women have multiple abortions – 4,000 women have had four abortions, and scores have had eight.'[52]

Informed consent

14.61 Claire Curtis-Thomas MP urged MPs to enhance the informed consent requirements before a woman could have an abortion. Building in robust informed consent requirements would protect the woman from acting precipitously in obtaining an abortion and regretting this later, and would provide indirectly some degree of protection for the foetus. She very disturbingly contended: 'Consultations at the hairdresser's have taken longer than the time it took to make a decision to have an abortion.'[53]

Consensus

14.62 Dawn Primarolo MP highlighted that there was no evidence that the 'clear consensus' of all the professional bodies, that a foetus was viable at 24 weeks, has changed, and 'all concur with that view.'[54]

Inconsistencies?

14.63 Nadine Dorries MP referred to the RCOG guidelines on a new way to abort babies after 19 weeks gestation. The baby was given a lethal injection of potassium through the mother's abdominal wall, into the baby's heart, and the baby died and was then removed from the mother's body. Ms Dorries then asked the pertinent question: 'If babies do not live below 24 weeks' why does the RCOG provide guidelines, to guarantee that they do not. Do they live or not?'[55]

Survival rates

14.64 Ms Dorries flagged up University College hospital as an excellent example of high foetal survival rates. Between 1996 and 2000, 50 per cent of babies born at 22–23 weeks survived.[56]

VOTING ON AMENDMENTS

14.65 Clause 3, which proposed cutting the gestational time limit from 24 to 16 weeks, was defeated 387–84. Clause 5, which proposed cutting the time limit

---

51 *Hansard*, 20 May 2008, col 224, and cols 224 – 227.
52 Ibid, col 225.
53 Ibid, cols 227 – 231.
54 Ibid, col 245.
55 Ibid, col 259.
56 Ibid, col 260.

in s 1(1)(a) of the Abortion Act 1967, as amended, to 20 weeks, was defeated 332–190. Clause 8, which was the neutral extra information and counselling clause, was defeated 309–173. Clause 9, which proposed cutting the time limit to 22 weeks, was defeated 304–233 (this was only a majority of 71, and could have been closer, bearing in mind 112 MPs did not vote).

CONCLUSIONS

14.66 The law on abortion has been settled for the past 21 years, although it is far from being universally accepted. The votes in the House of Commons not surprisingly signal a clear majority in favour of legalised abortion, although where the gestational time limit is set from 22 weeks on is not as clear cut. Arguably if there had been a vote to cut the gestational time limit to 23 weeks the vote would certainly have been much closer, if not won by those wanting the reduction to 23 weeks. The vote on expanding the informed consent requirement for lawful abortions highlights concerns about the apparent ease of obtaining abortions and the huge numbers of abortions taking place. However pro-choice advocates also tried unsuccessfully to amend the existing abortion law by, eg, getting rid of the 'two doctor' requirement, allowing nurses to be more involved in decisions about abortions, and extending the 1967 Act to Northern Ireland. The abortion issue is likely to remain an ethical hot-potato periodically resurfacing in different guises for many years to come.

Part 5

Human Fertilisation and Embryology Act 2008 – The New Order of Parents

Chapter 15

The Birth of the New Parenthood Regime

INTRODUCTION

15.1 Part 2 of the Human Fertilisation and Embryology Act 2008 ('the 2008 Act') radically, and for many controversially, alters fundamental family structures and units in the UK, albeit for a minority of the 1 per cent of children born following certain types of assisted reproductive treatments (eg IVF) using donated gametes and embryos. For others, the 2008 Act is just taking note of and following other legislation by recognising in law the existence of civil partnerships and 'non-traditional' relationships, in the context here of certain fertility treatments.

HUMAN FERTILISATION AND EMBRYOLOGY ACT REFORM

15.2 Part 2 of the 2008 Act is titled 'Parenthood in Cases Involving Assisted Reproduction' and the new s 33 provides for 'Meaning of "mother"', in other words who is the lawful mother in cases involving assisted reproduction, eg IVF. Section 33(1) provides:

'The woman who is carrying or has carried a child as a result of the placing in her of an embryo or of sperm and eggs, and no other woman, is to be treated as the mother of the child.'

This provision mirrors exactly s 27 of the earlier Human Fertilisation and Embryology Act 1990 (the 1990 Act). It is much easier to determine who the mother of a child produced by assisted reproduction is than who the father is, or indeed who the other parent is. The mother of, eg, the IVF-created baby is quite simply the woman who has carried the child inside her – the 'carrying woman'. The author comments:

'Thus the genetic, social (and possibly subsequent legal) mother, and gestational/carrying mothers may not necessarily be the same person. That is undeniably one of the possible consequences of the legalisation of the phenomenon of test-tube babies. That said, the law here is incontrovertibly clear and certain. The old adage that one can always be certain who one's mother is would appear to have received statutory reinforcement (albeit the corollary being one cannot entirely be sure who one's father is!).'[1]

15.3 Furthermore the author observed that:

'This section [s 33] curiously starts with the heading *Meaning of "mother"*, replacing the heading in the 1990 Act, which was merely *Status*. Critics of

---

1   *Current Law Statutes Annotated,* 'Human Fertilisation and Embryology Act 2008, Chapter 22', (Sweet & Maxwell 2009), p 134.

the legislation would point to the absurdity of defining the patently obvious and clear in an Act of Parliament, namely what is a mother, as evidence of the corrosive effect the legalisation of assisted reproduction, the use and creation of human embryos, especially in research, and now the advent of the creation of human admixed embryos is having on the ethical and moral compass of both our legislators and the medical establishment.'[2]

15.4   Section 33(2) provides that:

'Subsection (1) does not apply to any child to the extent that the child is treated by virtue of adoption as not being the woman's child.'

The author notes:

'There are a number of cases where the woman who has carried the child following the placing in her of an embryo or of sperm and eggs will not be the legal mother of that child. The first situation is where that child is subsequently adopted, thus extinguishing the carrying mother's legal motherhood (specifically covered by s 33(2)). The second scenario is where a parental order has been obtained, thereby transferring parenthood to another person.'[3]

15.5   Interestingly too, s 33(3) provides that s 33(1) – that the woman who is carrying or has carried a child as a result of the placing in her of an embryo or sperm or eggs, and no other woman, is to be treated as the mother of the child – 'applies whether the woman was in the United Kingdom or elsewhere at the time of the placing in her of the embryo or the sperm and eggs.' Thus, woman inseminated overseas, eg Diane Blood in Belgium, are the mother of any children born as a result of that insemination, in the same way as if they were inseminated in the United Kingdom.

15.6   Section 34 of the 2008 Act is concerned with the application of ss 35–47, and s 34(1):

'Sections 35 to 47 apply, in the case of a child who is being or has been carried by a woman (referred to in those sections as "W") as a result of the placing in her of an embryo or of sperm and eggs or her artificial insemination, to determine who is to be treated as the other parent of the child.'

This section and the subsequent sections in the Act, especially ss 35–38 and ss 41–45, signal a major shift enshrined in primary legislation by Parliament from the arguably more narrow and conservative definition of the traditional family structure of married father and mother, or alternatively cohabiting father and mother, towards a more inclusive all-embracing redefinition of what is an acceptable family unit where the child has been created, eg, as a result of IVF, from October 2009 onwards. As the author stated, the general effect of these provisions is that:

'[T]he "other parent" can be her husband or partner if that woman is heterosexual, or her civil partner or female partner if she is homosexual.'[4]

---

2   Ibid.
3   Ibid.
4   Ibid.

15.7   The next sections, in particular ss 35–38, address the thorny and more intractable question of the meaning of 'father' under the 2008 Act. Section 35, 'Woman married at time of treatment', deals with the scenario where the woman, referred to as 'W', is married at the time of, eg, the IVF treatment. Section 35(1) provides:

> 'If—
> (a)   at the time of the placing in her of the embryo or of the sperm and eggs or of her artificial insemination, W was a party to a marriage, and
> (b)   the creation of the embryo carried by her was not brought about with the sperm of the other party to the marriage,
> then, subject to section 38(2) to (4), the other party to the marriage is to be treated as the father of the child unless it is shown that he did not consent to the placing in her of the embryo or the sperm and eggs or to her artificial insemination (as the case may be).'

The author comments:

> 'This section is virtually identical to s 28(2) of the 1990 Act. Thus there is still this legislative presumption that the husband is the legal father if the wife is inseminated with, eg someone else's sperm, unless he can rebut this presumption by showing that he did not consent to the sperm being placed in his wife, as was the case in *Leeds Teaching Hospital NHS Trust v Mr A, Mrs A and Others* [2003] EWHC 259; [2003] 1 FLR 1091.'[5]

15.8   Additionally, s 35(2) stipulates:

> 'This section applies whether W was in the United Kingdom or elsewhere at the time mentioned in subsection (1)(a).'

Interestingly too, the Explanatory Notes to the 2008 Act add:

> 'This provision (and others which operate to determine legal parenthood) is subject to the common law presumption that a child is the legitimate child of a married couple.'

15.9   Section 36, titled 'Treatment provided to woman where agreed fatherhood conditions apply', might be considered a radical, significant and controversial provision. It covers the scenario where a woman, unmarried, receives treatment, eg IVF, where the agreed fatherhood conditions are applicable:

> 'If no man is treated by virtue of section 35 as the father of the child and no woman is treated by virtue of section 42 as a parent of the child but—
> (a)   the embryo or the sperm and eggs were placed in W, or W was artificially inseminated, in the course of treatment services provided in the United Kingdom by a person to whom a licence applies,
> (b)   at the time when the embryo or the sperm and eggs were placed in W, or W was artificially inseminated, the agreed fatherhood conditions (as set out in section 37) were satisfied in relation to a man, in relation to treatment provided to W under the licence,
> (c)   the man remained alive at that time, and

---

5   Ibid, p 135.

(d)   the creation of the embryo carried by W was not brought about with the man's sperm,

then, subject to section 38(2) to (4), the man is to be treated as the father of the child.'

15.10   Four conditions, therefore, need to be satisfied before the unmarried father will be considered the lawful father of, eg, the child born by the mother as a result of IVF:

(1)   The embryo or sperm/eggs were placed in the woman (mother), or the woman was artificially inseminated in the course of licensed treatment services in the United Kingdom. This is not so problematical,

(2)   More problematically and arguably controversially, when the embryo or sperm/eggs were placed in the woman, or when the woman was artificially inseminated, the agreed fatherhood conditions set out in s 37 were met.

(3)   Less controversially, that man remained alive at that time

(4)   The creation of the embryo carried by the woman was not in fact created with that man's sperm.

Then, subject to s 38(2),[6] (3)[7] and (4),[8] that unmarried man is to be treated as the father of the child.

The author comments:

'Thus s 36 replaces s 28(3) of the 1990 Act, which basically permitted an unmarried father to be treated as the child's father if, "the embryo or the sperm and eggs were placed in the woman, or she was artificially inseminated, in the course of treatment services provided for her and a man together by a person to whom a licence applies".'[9]

Again one could illustrate the application of s 28(3) by reference to the *Leeds* case, where the white man was not deemed the legal father as he was not being treated together with his wife using donor sperm (ie he never agreed or consented, and nor did his wife or the black man, that his wife be treated, ie inseminated with the black man's sperm).

15.11   Concerning the reference to s 42 in s 36 above, the author notes:

'The reference to s 42 above covers the situation where at the time of the placing in her of the embryo or the sperm and eggs or of her artificial insemination, W was in a civil partnership, then subject to s 45(2)–(4), the other party to the civil partnership is to be treated as a parent of the child unless it is shown that she did not consent to the placing in W of the embryo or the sperm and eggs or to her artificial insemination. Section 42 replicates exactly almost s 35 (the provision concerning when a husband will be the

---

6   'In England, Wales and Northern Ireland, sections 35 and 36 do not affect any presumption applying by virtue of the rules of common law, that a child is the legitimate child of the parties to a marriage.'

7   'In Scotland, sections 35 and 36 do not apply in relation to any child who, by virtue of any enactment or other rule of law, is treated as the child of the parties to a marriage.'

8   'Sections 35 and 36 do not apply to any child to the extent that the child is treated by virtue of adoption as not being that man's child.'

9   *Current Law Statutes Annotated,* 'Human Fertilisation and Embryology Act 2008, Chapter 22', (Sweet & Maxwell 2009), p 136.

legal father of the child) – same sex couples in a civil partnership being put on the same footing as heterosexual married couples, thus ending an anomalous discriminatory practice.'[10]

15.12 Section 37, 'The agreed fatherhood conditions', deals with these innovative and potentially far-reaching agreed fatherhood conditions:

'The agreed fatherhood conditions referred to in section 36(b) are met in relation to a man ("M") in relation to treatment provided to W under a licence if, but only if,—

    (a) M has given the person responsible a notice stating that he consents to being treated as the father of any child resulting from treatment provided to W under the licence,

    (b) W has given the person responsible a notice stating that she consents to M being so treated,

    (c) neither M nor W has, since giving notice under paragraph (a) or (b), given the person responsible notice of the withdrawal of M's or W's consent to M being so treated,

    (d) W has not, since the giving of the notice under paragraph (b), given the person responsible—

        (i) a further notice under that paragraph stating that she consents to another man being treated as the father of any resulting child, or

        (ii) a notice under section 44(1)(b) stating that she consents to a woman being treated as a parent of any resulting child, and

    (e) W and M are not within prohibited degrees of relationship in relation to each other.'

Significant too, and arguably a formal procedural requirement that acts effectively like a safeguard or protection evidentially is that s 37(2) specifies:

'A notice under subsection 1(a), (b) or (c) must be in writing and must be signed by the person giving it.'

Therefore, both the woman (mother) and the man (prospective father) must have each given the person responsible a notice, in writing and signed respectively by them, stating that they consented to the man being treated as the father of the child born as a result of, eg, IVF treatment at a licensed clinic. Also, any purported notice from either the woman/mother or the man/prospective father withdrawing the woman or man's consent to the man being treated as the father of the child must also be in writing and signed by either the man or woman/mother. These requirements of course tie in with Sched 3, para 1 of the 1990 Act concerning consent and how it is manifested and required under the HFEA legislation:

'A consent under this Schedule must be given in writing and, in this Schedule, "effective consent" means a consent under this Schedule which has not been withdrawn.'

The extra safeguard is that the notice must not only be in writing, but must also be signed by the party giving the notice to the person responsible. Again this is an extra responsibility or potential duty placed on the person responsible under the 2008 Act.

---

10 Ibid.

15.13   The author elaborated on this, stating:

> 'A procedural requirement and a safeguard is that notice under subss (1)(a),
> (b) or (c) must be in writing and must be signed by the person giving it. This
> is in keeping with the requirement in the Act that all consent must be in
> writing to be legally effective. This was witnessed in *R v Human Fertilisation
> and Embryology Authority, Ex p Blood* (1997) 2 WLR 806, where the Family
> Division court of the High Court, and then subsequently the Court of Appeal,
> upheld the decision of the Authority denying Mrs Diane Blood permission to
> use her dead husband's sperm to inseminate her in a clinic in the United
> Kingdom because he had not given his consent in writing to his sperm being
> kept or used (albeit that the appellate court ruled that the Authority should
> consider granting her an export licence to use the sperm in another EU State,
> given that the Authority had not considered arts 59 and 60 in reaching their
> decision, and given also that the tragic circumstances in the *Blood* case were
> unlikely to occur again – was this a classic illustration of hard cases making
> bad law?).'[11]

In addition the Explanatory Notes to the 2008 Bill point out:

> 'After the transfer of the gametes or embryo, neither the man nor the woman
> can withdraw their consent to the man being treated as the child's father
> unless the woman does not conceive and a new cycle of treatment has to
> begin.'

15.14   The author comments on this:

> 'Clearly once the gametes/embryos are transferred the consent then becomes
> irrevocable.'[12]

The Explanatory Notes continue:

> 'Changes to the conditions which must be included in all treatment licences,
> which are made by clause 14(3), will require that, if the man withdraws his
> consent at an earlier stage, the woman must be told before the treatment
> proceeds. She will therefore have the opportunity to decide whether she
> wishes to go ahead in these circumstances. If the woman withdraws her
> agreement to the man being the father, he must be told as soon as possible
> but he would not, through these provisions, be able to stop her going ahead
> if she wished to do so. Notices may not validly be given by two people who
> are within the prohibited degrees of relationship. This is defined in clause
> 58(2) to include parents and children, siblings and uncles or aunts and their
> nephew or nieces. Close relatives of this kind may not jointly be treated as a
> child's parents.'

15.15   In addition the Explanatory Notes sounded a warning of caution:

> 'The Bill will maintain the situation that if an unmarried couple carry out
> self-insemination with donor sperm at home or elsewhere, not as part of
> licensed treatment, the male partner would not be the legal parent. He would
> have to take steps to acquire formal parental responsibility, for example by

---

11   Ibid, p 138.
12   Ibid.

adopting the child. An unmarried man cannot become a parent where donor sperm is provided under a licence under para 1A of Sch 2 to the 1990 Act (non-medical fertility services) unless also used in treatment services.'

The author commented on the new agreed fatherhood conditions, therefore, that:

'The inclusion of the innovative, agreed fatherhood conditions in the legislation is one of the salient major changes made to the assisted reproduction regulatory landscape by the 2008 Act. Section 37 sets out the meaning and scope of the agreed fatherhood conditions. The agreed fatherhood conditions are met in relation to a man "M" in relation to treatment provided to W under a licence if, but only if, five conditions are met.'[13]

The five conditions are set out in s 37(1)(a)–(e) respectively.

15.16 Section 38 is headed 'Further provision relating to sections 35 and 36'. Section 38(1) provides:

'Where a person is to be treated as the father of the child by virtue of sections 35 or 36, no other person is to be treated as the father of the child.'

If a man is deemed to be the legal father of a child created, eg, by IVF, under either s 35 or s 36, that precludes any other man being treated as the father of that child. So there appears to be some finality on this issue of who legally is the father by virtue of these two sections.

Section 38(2) states:

'In England and Wales and Northern Ireland, sections 35 and 36 do not affect any presumption, applying by virtue of the rules of common law, that a child is the legitimate child of the parties to a marriage.'

15.17 The new statutory provisions in the 2008 Act do not, therefore, alter longstanding presumptions and rules of common law in three countries of the United Kingdom, that a child is the legitimate child of a married couple. The Explanatory Notes to the 2008 Bill give some illustrative examples to explain the import of this subsection:

'If for example, a woman marries between the conception of the donor-conceived child and its birth, it will be presumed that her new husband is the father of the child, even if the agreed fatherhood conditions were satisfied in relation to a different man at the time when the gametes were transferred. This presumption may, however be rebutted by evidence (for example a DNA test) showing that the husband is not in fact the child's father. In that case, the provisions of clause 36 would apply and the man in respect of whom the agreed fatherhood conditions were satisfied would be the child's father. There is no parallel presumption at common law for people who enter a civil partnership. So the provisions which would otherwise apply to determine parenthood will not be affected by the mother entering into a civil partnership after the transfer of the embryo or gametes.'

---

13   Ibid, p 137.

15.18   Section 38(3) is the equivalent subsection for Scotland, a separate legal system heavily influenced by civil law, as opposed to common law, and provides:

> 'In Scotland, sections 35 and 36 do not apply in relation to any child who, by virtue of any enactment or other rule of law, is treated as the child of the parties to a marriage.'

Finally, s 38(4) provides that:

> 'Sections 35 and 36 do not apply to any child to the extent that the child is treated by virtue of adoption as not being the man's child.'

15.19   Section 39 is headed 'Use of sperm, or transfer of embryo, after death of man providing sperm'. Section 39(1) provides:

> 'If—
>
> (a)   the child has been carried by W as a result of the placing in her of an embryo or of sperm and eggs or her artificial insemination,
>
> (b)   the creation of the embryo carried by W was brought about by using the sperm of a man after his death, or the creation of the embryo was brought about using the sperm of a man before his death but the embryo was placed in W after his death,
>
> (c)   the man consented in writing (and did not withdraw his consent)—
>
>   (i)   to the use of his sperm after his death which brought about the creation of the embryo carried by W or (as the case may be) to the placing in W after his death of the embryo which was brought about using his sperm before his death, and
>
>   (ii)   to being treated for the purpose mentioned in subsection (3) as the father of any resulting child,
>
> (d)   W has elected in writing not later than the end of the period of 42 days from the day on which the child was born for the man to be treated for the purpose mentioned in subsection (3) as the father of the child, and
>
> (e)   no-one else is to be treated—
>
>   (i)   as the father of the child by virtue of section 35 or 36 or by virtue of section 38(2) or (3), or
>
>   (ii)   as a parent of the child by virtue of section 42 or 43 or by virtue of adoption,
>
> then the man is to be treated for the purpose mentioned in subsection (3) as the father of the child.'

15.20   This quite convoluted and complex provision is geared to cover the scenario arising in the *Blood* case,[14] discussed earlier. In the *Blood* case Mrs Diane Blood intended to be inseminated with her dead husband Stephen Blood's sperm, that had been extracted from him by means of electro-ejaculation whilst he was in a meningitis-induced coma, and was in an incompetent state, thus clearly unable to exercise his autonomy and give consent in writing to the storage and use of his sperm to inseminate his wife. Mrs Blood obviously intended her husband's sperm to be placed in her after his death also. However the glaring problem for Mrs Blood, if her scenario were to arise post the 2008 Act, would be that under s 39(1)(c) the man, ie Stephen Blood, had not

---

14   *R v Human Fertilisation and Embryology Authority ex p Blood,* [1997] 2 WLR 806.

consented in writing to use of his sperm after his death under s 39(1)(c)(i), nor had he equally and also consented, under s 39(3), to the purpose of enabling his 'particulars to be entered as the particulars of the child's father in a relevant register of births'. On that basis he would unfortunately not qualify as the father of the child under s 39.

15.21 Even if the man had given his consent in writing to the use of his sperm after his death to inseminate his wife, he would not be deemed the father of the child unless a further safeguard or restriction were satisfied: the woman must have elected 'in writing', again reinforcing the general requirement that all consents and agreements must be in writing under the Acts, within 42 days – effectively a six-week 'cooling-off' period – of the birth of the child, for that man to be treated as the father of the child for the purposes of enabling his particulars to be entered as the particulars of the child's father in a relevant register of births. Also, the final condition that needs to be satisfied is that no one else is to be treated as the father of the child under ss 35, 36, 38(2) or 38(3), or alternatively no one else is treated as a parent of the child under ss 42 or 43 or as a result of adoption. The author adds:

> 'Hence if the *Blood* case were to arise in 2009, Mrs Blood, as well as needing the consent in writing from her dead husband (before he died), would need to write to the Authority within 42 days of the birth of the child, that her dead husband was to be treated as the father of her newly born child. This section replaces the provisions inserted into the 1990 Act by virtue of the Human Fertilisation and Embryology (Deceased Fathers) Act 2003.'[15]

15.22 Section 39(2) adds that:

> 'Subsection (1) applies whether W was in the United Kingdom or elsewhere at the time of the placing in her of the embryo or of the sperm and eggs or of her artificial insemination.'

The author observes:

> 'Thus, again, using the *Blood* case as an analogy, Mrs Blood was inseminated with her dead husband's sperm in Belgium, so she would satisfy this part of the section.'[16]

15.23 Section 39(3) explains the purpose referred to in s 39(1):

> 'The purpose referred to in subsection (1) is the purpose of enabling the man's particulars to be entered as the particulars of the child's father in a relevant register of births.'

Interestingly, the 42-day period from the birth of the child, for the woman having to elect in writing that the man be treated as the father of the child for the purpose of s 39(3), discussed earlier and referred to as applicable in England, Wales and Northern Ireland, is cut in Scotland to the much less generous period of 21 days. This might be considered anomalous and arbitrary, but the contrary view might be that it reflects and acknowledges a separate devolved region, with a separate legal tradition, north of the border.

---

15   *Current Law Statutes Annotated,* 'Human Fertilisation and Embryology Act 2008, Chapter 22', (Sweet & Maxwell 2009), p 140.
16   Ibid.

15.24 Section 40 is headed 'Embryo transferred after death of husband, etc who did not provide sperm'. Section 40(1) states:

> 'If—
>
>   (a) the child has been carried by W as a result of the placing in her of an embryo,
>
>   (b) the embryo was created at a time when W was a party to a marriage,
>
>   (c) the creation of the embryo was not brought about with the sperm of the other party to the marriage,
>
>   (d) the other party to the marriage died before the placing of the embryo in W,
>
>   (e) the other party to the marriage consented in writing (and did not withdraw the consent)—
>
>   (i) to the placing of the embryo in W after his death, and
>
>   (ii) to being treated for the purpose mentioned in subsection (4) as the father of any resulting child,
>
>   (f) W has elected in writing not later than the end of the period of 42 days from the day on which the child was born for the man to be treated for the purpose mentioned in subsection (4) as the father of the child, and
>
>   (g) no-one else is to be treated—
>
>   (i) as the father of the child by virtue of section 35 or 36 or by virtue of section 38 (2) or (3), or
>
>   (ii) as a parent of the child by virtue of section 42 or 43 or by virtue of adoption,
>
> then the man is to be treated for the purpose mentioned in subsection (4) as the father of the child.'

This scenario is very similar to s 39 with two major exceptions. First, s 40(1) is specifically aimed at married couples. Secondly, and more fundamentally here, unlike in s 39(1), the creation of the embryo was not brought about with the partner's or here husband's sperm, but rather was brought about with donor sperm. As the author noted:

> '[s 40(1)] applies to embryos transferred after the death of the husband, etc, who did not provide the sperm. Its provisions are similar to s 39 but with some significant differences.'[17]

15.25 The second scenario dealt with in s 40 is s 40(2):

> 'If—
>
>   (a) the child has been carried by W as a result of the placing in her of an embryo,
>
>   (b) the embryo was not created at a time when W was a party to a marriage or a civil partnership but was created in the course of treatment services provided to W in the United Kingdom by a person to whom a licence applies,
>
>   (c) a man consented in writing (and did not withdraw the consent)—
>
>   (i) to the placing of the embryo in W after his death, and
>
>   (ii) to being treated for the purpose mentioned in subsection (4) as the father of any resulting child,

---

17 Ibid, p 142.

    (d)   the creation of the embryo was not brought about with the sperm of that man,

    (e)   the man died before the placing of the embryo in W,

    (f)   immediately before the man's death, the agreed fatherhood conditions set out in section 37 were met in relation to the man in relation to treatment proposed to be provided to W in the United Kingdom by a person to whom a licence applies,

    (g)   W has elected in writing not later than the end of the period of 42 days from the day on which the child was born for the man to be treated for the purpose mentioned in subsection (4) as the father of the child, and

    (h)   no-one else is to be treated—

        (i)   as the father of the child by virtue of section 35 or 36 or by virtue of section 38 (2) or (3), or

        (ii)   as a parent of the child by virtue of section 40 or 42 or by virtue of adoption,

then the man is to be treated for the purpose mentioned in subsection (4) as the father of the child.'

This second scenario covers the situation where the child carried by the woman following the placing of the embryo in her, when she was not married or in a civil partnership, was created in treatment services offered in a licensed clinic, where a man (her unmarried partner) consented in writing to the placing of the embryo (not created from his sperm, but from donated sperm) in the woman after his death and to his particulars being entered as the particulars of the child's father in the relevant register of births, that the man died before the embryo was placed in the woman, that immediately before the man's death the s 37 agreed fatherhood conditions were met, that also the woman had elected in writing within 42 days of the birth of the child that the man would be treated as the father of the child for the purposes mentioned in s 40(4), and that no other person would be treated as the father by virtue of ss 35, 36, 38(2) or s 38(3), or that no other person would be treated as a parent of the child by virtue of ss 42 or 43 or by adoption. Then, and it is only then after this rather long list of requirements are satisfied, will that man be treated for the purposes of s 40(4) as the father of the child. As the author observed on this:

'Hence the additional requirement (arguably safeguard or unnecessary bureaucracy depending on your particular view), means that in order for an unmarried man to qualify as the father, an additional hurdle has to be surmounted, namely the satisfying of the agreed fatherhood conditions immediately before the man's death.'[18]

15.26 Like s 39(2), s 40(3) provides:

'Subsections (1) and (2) apply whether W was in the United Kingdom or elsewhere at the time of the placing in her of the embryo.'

Again, the purpose referred to in s 40(4) is identical to that referred in s 39(3), ie:

'The purpose referred to in subsections (1) and (2) is the purpose of enabling the man's particulars to be entered as the particulars of the child's father in a relevant register of births.'

---

18 Ibid.

Finally, Scotland (unlike England, Wales and Northern Ireland, where the period is 42 days) favours a shorter period (21 days) after the birth of the child for the woman to elect in writing for the man to be treated, for the purposes mentioned in s 39(4), as the father of the child.

15.27 The next provision, s 41, is headed 'Persons not to be treated as father'. Section 41(1) provides:

'Where the sperm of a man who had given such consent as is required by paragraph 5 of Schedule 3 to the 1990 Act (consent to use of gametes for purposes of treatment services or non-medical fertility services) was used for a purpose for which such consent was required, he is not to be treated as the father of the child.'

This section is aimed at covering sperm donors in licensed clinics. As the author states:

'Thus, eg a sperm donor who donates sperm for the benefit of, eg an infertile couple at a licensed clinic and signs the pertinent consent forms, will not be the father of any child born as a result of the subsequent use of his sperm. If this were not the case, the current very limited pool of sperm donors would probably evaporate completely.'[19]

The section clarifies that sperm donors who donate their sperm at licensed clinics to help those less fortunate than themselves (ie infertile couples or individuals), and who sign the requisite consent forms, will divest themselves of any legal responsibility as the father of any child born subsequently.

15.28 Section 41(2) states that:

'Where the sperm of a man, or an embryo the creation of which was brought about with his sperm, was used after his death, he is not, subject to section 39, to be treated as the father of the child.'

Furthermore s 41(3) provides that:

'Subsection (2) applies whether W was in the United Kingdom or elsewhere at the time of the placing in her of the embryo or of the sperm and eggs or of her artificial insemination.'

15.29 Sections 42–47 deal with cases in which a woman will be the other parent, so the child born as a result of, eg IVF will have a mother and a parent, as opposed to having a mother and a father, like the vast majority of other children. Section 42 deals with the first scenario where another woman will be the 'parent' of the child and is headed 'Woman in civil partnership at time of treatment'. Section 42(1) provides:

'If at the time of the placing in her of the embryo or the sperm and eggs or of her artificial insemination, W was a party to a civil partnership, then subject to section 45(2) to (4), the other party to the civil partnership is to be treated as a parent of the child unless it is shown that she did not consent to the placing in W of the embryo or the sperm and eggs or to her artificial insemination (as the case may be).'

---

19   Ibid, p 143.

15.30 Section 42 mirrors exactly s 35, which applies to heterosexual married couples. Civil partnerships, ie unions recognised by the state between homosexual couples, are treated equally on exactly the same basis and footing as heterosexual marriages from the point of view of children born as a result of, eg, IVF. Equality before the law was of course was one of Professor Dicey's three elements in his classic definition of the rule of law. The author commented too that;

'This section is virtually identical to s 35 (the section setting out who will be the father of the child, if the woman is married). Thus, here again, there is a presumption that the woman's civil partner will be the other parent unless she can show that she did not consent to W having, eg the embryo placed in W. The woman's (W's) civil partner is thus effectively placed on the same legal footing as a woman's husband re being the parent of the child.'

15.31 Section 42(2), like its equivalent s 35(2), which applies to heterosexual married couples, provides:

'This section applies whether W was in the United Kingdom or elsewhere at the time mentioned in subsection (1).'

15.32 The next provision, s 43, headed 'Treatment provided to woman who agrees that second woman to be parent', is the equivalent same-sex couple provision to s 36 (its opposite-sex couple provision). Section 43(1) stipulates:

'If no man is treated by virtue of section 35 as the father of the child and no woman is treated by virtue of section 42 as a parent of the child but—
  (a) the embryo or the sperm and eggs were placed in W, or W was artificially inseminated, in the course of treatment services provided in the United Kingdom by a person to whom a licence applies,
  (b) at the time when the embryo or the sperm and eggs were placed in W, or W was artificially inseminated, the agreed female parenthood conditions (as set out in section 44) were met in relation to another woman, in relation to treatment provided to W under that licence, and
  (c) the other woman remained alive at that time,
then, subject to section 45(2) to (4), the other woman is to be treated as a parent of the child.'

The author comments that yet again:

'This section largely replicates s 36 (the section relating to unmarried men being deemed the father of the child). Hence same sex female couples are put on effectively the same legal footing (regarding parentage) as their equivalent opposite-sex unmarried couples.'

15.33 Section 44 of the 2008 Act proceeds to then set out 'The agreed female parenthood conditions'. Unsurprisingly, these are virtually identical to the agreed fatherhood conditions in s 37, except instead of a man, "M" (in s 37), the legislation in s 44 refers to 'another woman ("P")' instead, much to the consternation and upset of some critics of this excessively liberal and libertarian provision. Section 44(1) thus reads:

'The agreed female parenthood conditions referred to in section 43 (b) are met in relation to another woman ("P") in relation to treatment provided to W under a licence if, but only if,—

(a) P has given the person responsible a notice stating that P consents to P being treated as a parent of any child resulting from treatment provided to W under the licence,

(b) W has given the person responsible a notice stating that W agrees to P being so treated,

(c) neither W nor P has, since giving notice under paragraph (a) or (b), given the person responsible notice of the withdrawal of P's or W's consent to P being so treated,

(d) W has not, since the giving of the notice under paragraph (b), given the person responsible—

    (i) a further notice under that paragraph stating that W consents to a woman other than P being treated as a patient of any resulting child, or

    (ii) a notice under section 37 (1) (b) stating that W consents to a man being treated as the father of any resulting child, and

(e) W and P are not within prohibited degrees of relationship in relation to each other.'

Again, as with the five conditions (the agreed fatherhood conditions) that need to be satisfied under s 37(1) of the 2008 Act, so too with this section all five conditions need to be satisfied before the other woman is to be treated as a parent of the child, and again like s 37(2), s 44(2) provides that:

'A notice under subsection (1)(a), (b) or (c) must be in writing and must be signed by the person giving it.'

Finally s 44(3) stipulates that:

'A notice under subsection (1)(a), (b) or (c) by a person ("S") who is unable to sign because of illness, injury or physical disability is to be taken to comply with the requirement of subsection (2) as to signature if it is signed at the direction of S, in the presence of S and in the presence of at least one witness who attests the signature.'

15.34 Section 45 deals with 'Further provision relating to sections 42 and 43'. This section is virtually identical to s 38 (concerned with opposite sex relationships). Section 45(1) provides:

'Where a woman is treated by virtue of section 42 or 43 as a parent of the child, no man is to be treated as the father of the child.'

The author comments:

'A child can thus have two opposite sex parents or two same sex parents, but not two same sex parents and one opposite sex parent. This would appear to be the Parliamentary equivalent approval of the old adage that two's company, three's a crowd.'[20]

Section 45(2) states:

'In England and Wales and Northern Ireland, sections 42 and 43 do not affect any presumption, applying by virtue of the rules of common law, that a child is the legitimate child of the parties to a marriage.'

This is similar to s 38(2).

---

20 Ibid, p 146.

Then s 45(3) provides:

> 'In Scotland, sections 42 and 43 do not apply in relation to any child who, by virtue of any enactment or other rule of law, is treated as the child of the parties to a marriage.'

Again, this is virtually identical to s 38(3).

Finally s 45(4) says:

> 'Sections 42 and 43 do not apply to any child to the extent that the child is treated by virtue of adoption as not being the woman's child.'

Once again, this is broadly similar to s 38(4).

15.35 Section 46 of the 2008 Act, headed 'Embryo transferred after death of civil partner or intended female parent' corresponds broadly with the equivalent earlier ss 39 and 40. The first scenario dealt with in s 46 covers an embryo transferred after the death of a civil partner in s 46(1):

> 'If—
> - (a) the child has been carried by W as the result of the placing in her of an embryo,
> - (b) the embryo was created at a time when W was a party to a civil partnership,
> - (c) the other party to the civil partnership died before the placing of the embryo in W,
> - (d) the other party to the civil partnership consented in writing (and did not withdraw the consent)—
>   - (i) to the placing of the embryo in W after the death of the other party, and
>   - (ii) to being treated for the purpose mentioned in subsection (4) as the parent of any resulting child,
> - (e) W has elected in writing not later than the end of the period of 42 days from the day on which the child was born for the other party to the civil partnership to be treated for the purpose mentioned in subsection (4) as the parent of the child, and
> - (f) no one else is to be treated—
>   - (i) as the father of the child by virtue of section 35 or 36 or by virtue of section 45(2) or (3), or
>   - (ii) as a parent of the child by virtue of section 42 or 43 or by virtue of adoption,
>
> then the other party to the civil partnership is to be treated for the purpose mentioned in subsection (4) as a parent of the child.'

15.36 The second scenario is covered by s 46(2) of the 2008 Act, namely an embryo transferred after the death of an intended female parent. This section provides:

> 'If—
> - (a) the child has been carried by W as the result of the placing in her of an embryo,
> - (b) the embryo was not created at a time when W was a party to a marriage or a civil partnership, but was created in the course of treatment services provide to W in the United Kingdom by a person to whom a licence applies,

    (c)   another woman consented in writing (and did not withdraw the consent)-

        (i)   to the placing of the embryo in W after the death of the other woman, and

        (ii) to being treated for the purpose mentioned in subsection (4) as the parent of any resulting child,

    (d)   the other woman died before the placing of the embryo in W,

    (e)   immediately before the other woman's death, the agreed female parenthood conditions set out in section 44 were met in relation to the other woman in relation to treatment proposed to be provided to W in the United Kingdom by a person to whom a licence applies,

    (f)   W has elected in writing not later than the end of the period of 42 days from the day on which the child was born for the other woman to be treated for the purpose mentioned in subsection (4) as the parent of the child, and

    (g)   no one else is to be treated—

        (i)   as the father of the child by virtue of section 35 or 36 or by virtue of section 45(2) or (3), or

        (ii) as a parent of the child by virtue of section 42 or 43 or by virtue of adoption,

then the other woman is to be treated for the purpose mentioned in subsection (4) as a parent of the child.'

15.37 The author commenting on these provisions states:

'Section 46 of the 2008 Act covers the situations respectively where an embryo has been transferred after the death of the civil partner or intended female parent. Yet again, this provision closely resembles ss 39 and 40 of the 2008 Act. Yet again, same sex civil partners and partners are given parity of esteem and afforded the same legal protection/rights as their equivalent opposite-sex married and unmarried couples. Arguably this is a seismic change wrought by the 2008 Act to reflect the massive changes in society's attitude to acceptable parenting.'[21]

15.38 Section 46(3) provides that:

'Subsections (1) and (2) apply whether W was in the United Kingdom or elsewhere at the time of the placing in her of the embryo.'

This is again similar to s 39(2) and s 40(3).

15.39 Section 46(4) notes that:

'The purpose referred to in subsections (1) and (2) is the purpose of enabling the deceased woman's particulars to be entered as the particulars of the child's other parent in a relevant register of births.'

This is equivalent to s 39(3) and to s 40(4).

15.40 Finally s 46(5) provides that there is substituted a 21-day period in Scotland for the 42-day period referred to in the rest of the United Kingdom in s 46(1)(e) and s 46(2)(f).

---

21 Ibid, p 147.

15.41 The next section, s 47, is headed 'Woman not to be other parent merely because of egg donation'. Section 47 provides:

'A woman is not to be treated as the parent of a child whom she is not carrying and has not carried, except where she is so treated—
   (a) by virtue of section 42 or 43, or
   (b) by virtue of section 46 (for the purpose mentioned in subsection (4) of that section), or
   (c) by virtue of adoption.'

Section 47 is effectively the female gamete donor equivalent of s 41, concerning male gamete donors. Thus, egg donors or women who donate eggs under egg sharing schemes, whereby they get free or reduced cost IVF, will not be deemed the 'other parent' of any child born as a result of the treatment. The author observes that:

'This short section of the 2008 Act deals with women who will not be the other parent merely because of egg donation. The section provides that a woman is not to be treated as the parent of a child whom she is not carrying and has not carried, except where she is treated as the parent of a child by virtue of ss 42, 43 or 46 of the 2008 Act, or alternatively by virtue of adoption. Thus again, egg donors will not be the parent of a child created from those donated eggs at a licensed clinic carried by another woman. This is in keeping with the equivalent provisions concerning sperm donations, both activities being regarded as not only philanthropic/altruistic acts by the donors, but ones which will not lead to them assuming any parental responsibilities for any resulting children, if the gamete donation is done under the aegis of the 1990 and 2008 Acts.'[22]

Interestingly the Explanatory Notes to the 2008 Bill point out:

'Parenthood could however be conferred by other legal provisions in this case (for example, if a woman donated an egg to her female partner, and the agreed female parenthood conditions were met in relation to her).'

15.42 Section 48 is headed 'Effect of sections 33 to 47'. Section 48(1) provides:

'Where by virtue of section 33, 35, 36, 42 or 43 a person is to be treated as the mother, father or parent of a child, that person is to be treated in law as the mother, father or parent (as the case may be) of the child for all purposes.'

This subsection covers all three of arguably the child's closest relatives, namely the mother and father or alternatively the mother and other parent. Thus, under s 48(1) if you are deemed a mother, father or parent, you are deemed one for all purposes, period.

15.43 Section 48(2) – effectively the corollary of s 48(1) – therefore, not surprisingly, states:

'Where by virtue of section 33, 38, 41, 45 or 47 a person is not to be treated as a parent of the child, that person is to be treated in law as not being a parent of the child for any purpose.'

---

22 Ibid, p 148.

Hence the sperm or egg donor, or woman who donates eggs for the benefit of another infertile woman or couple as part of an egg share scheme, will not be considered a parent of any child born for any purpose.

15.44 Section 48(3) and (4) cover the scenarios regarding deceased men and women respectively. Section 48(3) stipulates:

'Where section 39(1) or 40(1) or (2) applies, the deceased man—
  (a) is to be treated in law as the father of the child for the purpose mentioned in section 39(3) or 40(4), but
  (b) is to be treated in law as not being the father of the child for any other purpose.'

Then s 48(4) states:

'Where section 46(1) or (2) applies, the deceased woman—
  (a) is to be treated in law as a parent of the child for the purpose mentioned in section 46(4), but
  (b) is to be treated in law as not being a parent of the child for any other purpose.'

So the deceased man or deceased woman is only treated as the father or as a parent respectively of the child for the purposes of enabling either the deceased man or the deceased woman's particulars to be entered as the particulars of the child's father or other parent respectively in a relevant register of births.

15.45 Section 48(5) provides;

'Where any of subsections (1) to (4) has effect, references to any relationship between two people in any enactment, deed or other instrument or document (whenever passed or made) are to be read accordingly.'

Section 48(6) is applicable only in relation to England, Wales and Northern Ireland and therefore does not apply to Scotland. It provides:

'In relation to England and Wales and Northern Ireland, a child who—
  (a) has a parent by virtue of section 42, or
  (b) has a parent by virtue of section 43 who is at any time during the period beginning with the time mentioned in section 43(b) and ending with the time of the child's birth a party to a civil partnership with the child's mother,

is the legitimate child of the child's parents.'

Also s 48(7) adds:

'In relation to England and Wales and Northern Ireland, nothing in the provisions of section 33(1) or sections 35–47, read with this section—
  (a) affects the succession to any dignity or title of honour or renders any person capable of succeeding to or transmitting a right to succeed to any such dignity or title, or
  (b) affects the devolution of any property limited (expressly or not) to devolve (as nearly as the law permits) along with any dignity or title of honour.'

A similar provision to s 48(7) above, namely s 48(8), applies to Scotland. This stipulates:

'In relation to Scotland—

(a) those provisions do not apply to any title, coat of arms, honour or dignity transmissible on the death of its holder or affect the succession to any such title, coat of arms or dignity or its devolution, and

(b) where the terms of any deed provide that any property or interest in property is to devolve along with a title, coat of arms, honour or dignity, nothing in those provisions is to prevent that property or interest from so devolving.'

15.46 The next two sections, ss 49 and 50, explain and elaborate what is meant by the various references to parties to a marriage and civil partnership respectively. Thus, s 49(1) provides:

'The references in sections 35–47 to the parties to a marriage at any time there referred to—
(a) are to the parties to a marriage subsisting at that time, unless a judicial separation was then in force, but
(b) include the parties to a void marriage if either or both of them reasonably believed at that time that the marriage was valid; and for the purposes of those sections it is to be presumed, unless the contrary is shown, that one of them reasonably believed at that time that the marriage was valid.'

Hence the marriage must be subsisting at that time. A marriage will not be subsisting for the purposes of the 2008 Act if an order for judicial separation was in force. Interestingly, by contrast, for the purposes of competence and compellability of witnesses spouses will still be deemed married even if there is an order for judicial separation or even if a decree nisi has been made. It is not until the marriage is over, ie when the decree for divorce has become absolute, that the marriage will be deemed to have ended.

15.47 Section 50 is the same-sex couple equivalent of s 49 of the 2008 Act, and defines what is meant by references in the Act to a civil partnership. It provides:

'The references in sections 35–47 to the parties to a civil partnership at any time there referred to—
(a) are to the parties to a civil partnership subsisting at that time, unless a separation order was then in force, but
(b) include the parties to a void civil partnership if either or both of them reasonably believed at that time that the civil partnership was valid; and for the purposes of those sections it is to be presumed, unless the contrary is shown, that one of them reasonably believed at that time that the civil partnership was valid.'

Section 50(2) adds:

'The reference in section 48(6)(b) to a civil partnership includes a reference to a void civil partnership if either or both of the parties reasonably believed at the time when they registered as civil partners of each other that the civil partnership was valid; and for this purpose it is to be presumed, unless the contrary is shown, that one of them reasonably believed at that time that the civil partnership was valid.'

Finally, the term 'separation order' is defined in s 50(3):

'In subsection (1)(a), "separation order" means—

(a)   a separation order under section 37(1)(d) or 161(1)(d) of the Civil Partnership Act 2004 (c 33),

(b)   a decree of separation under section 120(2) of that Act,

(c)   a legal separation obtained in a country outside the United Kingdom and recognised in the United Kingdom.'

15.48   Section 51, headed 'Meaning of "relevant register of births"', inter alia, explains what is meant by the expression 'relevant register of births'. Section 51 provides:

'For the purposes of this Part a "relevant register of births", in relation to a birth, is whichever of the following is relevant—

(a)   a register of live-births or still births kept under the Births and Deaths Registration Act 1953 (c 20),

(b)   a register of births or still-births kept under the Registration of Births, Deaths and Marriages (Scotland) Act 1965 (c 49), or

(c)   a register of live-births or still births kept under the Births and Deaths Registration (Northern Ireland) Order 1976 (SI 1976/1041 (NI)).'

Basically in England, and in the devolved parliament and assemblies in Wales, Scotland and in Northern Ireland, the relevant register of births is the register of live-births and still-births kept under the relevant legislation concerning births and deaths in each jurisdiction.

15.49   Section 52 is headed 'Late election by mother with consent of Registrar General'. Section 52(1) provides:

'The requirement under section 39(1), 40(1) or (2) or 46(1) or (2) as to the making of an election (which requires an election to be made either on or before the day on which the child was born or within the period of 42 or, as the case may be, 21 days from that day) is nevertheless to be treated as satisfied if the required election is made after the end of that period but with the consent of the Registrar General under subsection (2).'

Thus the normal 42- or 21-day period for the woman to make her election that, eg, a man is to be treated as the father for the purpose of being registered as such in the relevant register of births, can be effectively disregarded and ignored and thus also be satisfied if the required election is made after that period with the consent of the Registrar General.

15.50   The power of the Registrar General to consent to the making of an election after the normal 42-day period (or 21 days in Scotland) is articulated in s 52(2), which states:

'The Registrar General may at any time consent to the making of an election after the end of the period mentioned in subsection (1) if, on an application made to him in accordance with such requirements as he may specify, he is satisfied that there is a compelling reason for giving his consent to the making of such an election.'

What actually constitutes 'a compelling reason' is not defined or explained in the Act. Finally s 52(3) explains who the Registrar General is, namely the Registrar General for England and Wales, the Registrar General of Births, Deaths and Marriages for Scotland or (as the case may be) the Registrar General for Northern Ireland.

15.51 The next section is s 53, headed 'Interpretations of references to father etc'. This technical provision clarifies the meaning of references to certain terms. Section 53 (1) provides:

'Subsections (2) and (3) have effect, subject to subsections (4) and (6), for the interpretation of any enactment, deed or any instrument or document (whenever passed or made).'

Section 53(2) adds:

'Any reference (however expressed) to the father of a child who has a parent by virtue of section 42 or 43 is to be read as a reference to the woman who is a parent of the child by virtue of that section.'

Section 53(3) states:

'Any reference (however expressed) to evidence of paternity is, in relation to a woman who is a parent by virtue of section 42 or 43, to be read as a reference to evidence of parentage.'

Section 53(4) provides that;

'This section does not affect the interpretation of the enactments specified in subsection (5) (which make express provision for the case where a child has a parent by virtue of section 42 or 43).'

Section 53(5) sets out 14 enactments which are not affected by s 53(2) and (3), and s 53(6) sets out two further pieces of legislation also unaffected.

15.52 The next two provisions deal with parental orders. Section 54 sets out the procedure for a couple applying for a parental order that a child be treated in law as the child of that couple, ie 'the applicants'. Thus s 54(1) provides:

'On an application made by two people ("the applicants"), the court may make an order providing for a child to be treated in law as the child of the applicants if—
   (a) the child has been carried by the woman who is not one of the applicants, as a result of the placing in her of an embryo or sperm and eggs or her artificial insemination,
   (b) the gametes of at least one of the applicants were used to bring about the creation of the embryo, and
   (c) the conditions in subsection (2) to (8) are satisfied.'

Interestingly s 54(1) refers to the application for a parental order being made 'by two people', so seemingly a single person could not, therefore, make an application for a parental order. Applications for parental orders presumably are made in surrogate mother type situations where the commissioning couple cannot have or carry a child themselves and commission a surrogate mother to carry the embryo, created from their gametes, or be inseminated using the husband's sperm. Clearly, under s 33 the surrogate mother is the lawful mother of the child, so the commissioning couple need the surrogate mother to 'give up' the child to them, and then they can apply for parental orders regarding the child. The conditions that need to be satisfied under s 54(2) are that:

'The applicants must be—
   (a) husband and wife,
   (b) civil partners of each other, or

> (c)   two persons who are living as partners in an enduring family relationship and are not within prohibited degrees of relationship in relation to each other.'

Yet again arguably the law here reflects the fundamental change in society's attitudes as to what constitutes an acceptable family structure in the context here of children created using certain assisted reproductive techniques. Significantly, s 54(2) does not define what is meant by 'an enduring family relationship' in the context of what amounts to 'two persons who are living as partners in an enduring family relationship'. This may generate litigation in the future, because the meaning is far from clear of this nebulous term. Section 54(2) clearly covers same-sex partners, as well as opposite-sex partners.

15.53   The time limit for applying for a parental order is within six months of the child being born – arguably quite a generous time-frame. Thus, s 54(3) states:

> 'Except in a case falling within subsection (11), the applicants must apply for the order during the period of 6 months beginning with the day on which the child is born.'

15.54   Section 54(4) deals with a further condition that needs satisfying before a parental order may be made by the court:

> 'At the time of the application and the making of the order—
> (a)   the child's home must be with the applicants, and
> (b)   either or both of the applicants must be domiciled in the United Kingdom or in the Channel Isles or the Isle of Man.'

Importantly, the child must be with the applicants at both the time of the application and at the time of the making of the order, and one or both of the applicants must have been domiciled in the UK or Channel Isles/Isle of Man. Also, under s 54(5): 'At the time of the making of the order both the applicants must have attained the age of 18.' The applicants must therefore be adults legally.

15.55   Furthermore, under s 54(6), before the court grants a parental order:

> 'The court must be satisfied that both—
> (a)   the woman who carried the child, and
> (b)   any other person who is a parent of the child but is not one of the applicants (including any man who is the father by virtue of section 35 or 36 or any woman who is a parent by virtue of section 42 or 43), have freely, and with full understanding of what is involved, agreed unconditionally to the making of the order.'

Hence under s 54(6) the woman who carried the child (ie the surrogate mother), and any other person who is deemed a parent of the child (but not one of the applicants for the parental order), must have freely (presumably with no coercion, duress, undue influence, or misrepresentation/fraud involved), and with full understanding (the fully informed consent requirement, essential here for such a final, monumental step) agreed unconditionally to the making of the order. So if the agreement of the woman or any other person who is a parent of the child contains caveats, exceptions, or elements of wishing to retain, eg, some contact with or influence over the child, then presumably the court will not make the irrevocable parental order. The court really needs to be sure and certain that the agreement to 'give up' the child is totally freely made, fully informed of what is involved (ie the consequences of the agreement for them and the child), and that moreover it is an unconditional agreement. In short these are very demanding criteria that need satisfying. The author notes:

'The inclusion of these stringent and rigorous requirements in the legislation acknowledge the fundamental significance of a parental order being made in favour of parties who are not the genetic/gestational or legal parents of the child.'[23]

15.56 In addition the next condition is s 54(7) which provides that:

'Subsection (6) does not require the agreement of a person who cannot be found or is incapable of giving agreement; and the agreement of the woman who carried the child is ineffective for the purpose of that subsection if given by her less than six weeks after the child's birth.'

Critically the final condition specified in s 54(8) provides:

'The court must be satisfied that no money or other benefit (other than for expenses reasonably incurred) has been given or received by either of the applicants for or in consideration of—
  (a) the making of the order,
  (b) any agreement required by subsection (6),
  (c) the handing over of the child to the applicants, or
  (d) the making of arrangements with a view to the making of the order, unless authorised by the court.'

Court orders, especially parental orders vesting parental rights on would-be parents, should not be subject to an auction. More importantly still, children should not be bought or sold. That is ethically, morally and legally wrong. Surrogates can be paid for expenses reasonably incurred, but cannot be paid on a commercial basis. Markets, or the creation of markets in the buying and selling of children, cannot be countenanced under the law. If money or other benefit is to be given to, eg, the woman who carried the child, that can only be done if specifically authorised by the court. Again the author notes here that this is:

'[A] very important provision enshrined in the Act ... Yet again, Parliament is stating categorically and unequivocally that children are not commodities to be bought and sold in the marketplace. That would be morally repugnant and legally outrageous.'[24]

15.57 Section 54(9) outlines and defines what types of courts can hear applications for parental orders under s 54 of the 2008 Act, in the four constituent parts of the United Kingdom.

15.58 Section 54(10) states that:

'Subsection 1(a) applies whether the woman was in the United Kingdom or elsewhere at the time of the placing in her of the embryo or the sperm and eggs or her artificial insemination.'

23 Ibid, p 155.
24 Ibid, p 156.

15.59   Finally s 54(11) provides that:

'An application which—
   (a)   relates to a child born before the coming into force of this section, and
   (b)   is made by two persons who, throughout the period applicable under subsection (2) of section 30 of the 1990 Act, were not eligible to apply for an order under that section in relation to the child as husband and wife,
may be made within the period of six months beginning with the day on which this section comes into force.'

15.60   The author concludes regarding the potential import and impact of s 54 that:

'The cumulative effect of s 54 is the further liberalisation of the law on assisted reproduction to extend the range of individuals who can now apply for a parental orders to reflect the concomitant changes in majority opinion in the United Kingdom about who can be suitable parents. Section 30 of the 1990 Act had arguably narrowly restricted the persons who could apply for a parental order to married couples. Under the new dispensation, civil partners, and both unmarried opposite-sex couples and same sex couples not in a civil partnership may also apply for a parental order, thereby promoting equality of opportunity, and ending arguably irrational discrimination against a large swathe of potential parents.'[25]

15.61   Finally, the Explanatory Notes to the Bill note that:

'The other provisions relating to parental orders remain the same as the existing provisions of the 1990 Act. A single person remains unable to apply, but would be able to apply to adopt the child from the surrogate mother.'

15.62   Section 55, headed 'Parental orders: supplementary provision', is again a highly technical section dealing with supplementary provision concerning parental orders. Section 55(1) states:

'The Secretary of State may by regulations provide—
   (a)   for any provision of the enactments about adoption to have effect, with such modifications (if any) as may be specified in the regulations, in relation to orders under section 54, and applications for such orders, as it has effect in relation to adoption, and applications for adoption orders, and
   (b)   for references in any enactment to adoption, an adopted child or an adoptive relationship to be read (respectively) as references to the effect of an order under section 54, a child to whom such an order applies and a relationship arising by virtue of the enactments about adoption, as applied by the regulations, and for similar expressions in connection with adoption to be read accordingly.'

Then, s 55(2) adds that the regulations made by the Secretary of State:

---

25   Ibid, p 156.

'may include such incidental or supplemental provision as appears to the Secretary of State to be necessary or desirable in consequence of any provision made by virtue of subsection 1 (a) or (b).'

15.63 Section 55(3)(a)–(d) outlines the legislation concerning, 'the enactments about adoption' in the four jurisdictions of the United Kingdom covered and affected.

15.64 Section 56 headed 'Amendments relating to parenthood in cases involving assisted reproduction' simply and concisely provides that Sched 6 of the 2008 Act, 'contains amendments related to the provisions of this Part.'

15.65 Section 57, headed 'Repeals and transitional provision relating to Part 2' makes a number of repeals of sections in the 1990 Act and transitional provision concerning Part 2 of the 2008 Act. Thus, s 57(1) provides:

'Sections 33 to 48 have effect only in relation to children carried by women as a result of the placing in them of embryos or of sperm and eggs, or their artificial insemination (as the case may be), after the commencement of those sections.'

Secondly, s 57(2) provides that;

'Sections 27–29 of the 1990 Act (which relate to status) do not have effect in relation to children carried by women as a result of the placing in them of embryos or of sperm and eggs, or their artificial insemination (as the case may be), after the commencement of sections 33 to 48.'

Section 57(3) of the 2008 Act provides that:

'Section 30 of the 1990 Act (parental orders in favour of gamete donors) ceases to have effect.'

Finally, s 57(4) stipulates that:

'Subsection (3) does not affect the validity of any order made under section 30 of the 1990 Act before the coming into force of that subsection.'

15.66 The last section in Part 2 of the 2008 Act is s 58, headed 'Interpretation of Part 2'. It defines some of the terms used in Part 2, Section 58(1)(a)–(d) defines what is meant by an 'enactment', namely an Act of Parliament, an Act of the Scottish Parliament, a Measure or Act of the National Assembly for Wales, or Northern Ireland legislation. Then s 58(2) provides:

'For the purposes of this Part, two persons are within prohibited degrees of relationship if one is the other's parent, grandparent, sister, brother, aunt or uncle; and in this subsection references to relationships—
(a) are to relationships of the full blood or half blood or, in the case of an adopted person, such of those relationships as would subsist but for adoption, and
(b) include the relationship of a child with his adoptive, or former adoptive parents,
but do not include any other adoptive relationships.'

The author comments here:

'The significant subsection here is s 58(2), which provides clarification of the circumstances when two persons will be deemed to be within the prohibited degrees of relationship for the purpose of the legislation.'[26]

CONCLUSIONS

15.67   Again one could contend the changes made in the 2008 Act to parenthood will not affect the vast majority of people, given only 1 per cent of all births are, eg, IVF births, but they do send out very clear Parliamentary signals that since October 2009 the law of the land (eg via birth certificates) recognises same-sex couples, whether in civil partnerships or not, as potentially equivalent legally to their heterosexual counterparts in the context of children born by certain assisted reproductive treatments using donated gametes or embryos.

---

26   Ibid, p 158.

Chapter 16

Naming but not Shaming?

INTRODUCTION

16.1   The Human Fertilisation and Embryology Act 2008 (the 2008 Act) permitted and legalised same-sex couples being named on birth certificates as the legal parents of children born from, eg, IVF treatment for the first time. Some saw this as a welcome liberalisation of the law, taking account of the many changes in society and public attitudes to parenting since 1990 and that it was in essence the law catching up with what was happening in real life. For others, this represented an unacceptable legal development, putting parental wishes above the best interests of their children, acquiescing in a legislative trick (the argument being that lesbian or gay partner was not biologically or genetically the other parent of the child), and condoning actions potentially harmful to the IVF child.

16.2   On 20 April 2010, the *Daily Mail* reported that Natalie Woods and Elizabeth Knowles had become the first two same-sex parents in Britain to jointly sign a birth certificate, and that the baby, Lily-Mae Betty Woods, who Ms Woods gave birth to, would not have a mother and father, but rather a mother and also a parent. It noted that the birth certificate left the father off the birth certificate for the first time in nearly 200 years. It showed only a mother and a 'parent – also a woman' for the baby. The article continued:

> 'There is no mention of the father, or donor, as the couple prefer to call the anonymous man whose sperm provided half of Lily-May's genes through IVF treatment.'

It also reported that the couple had been together for 15 years, were engaged and expected to have a civil partnership in the near future. Ms Woods said:

> 'We knew we wanted a child and that we were going to be together for ever. The only option was either through a donor or adoption, but it felt important to me to have a biological child.'

To critics who claimed a child needs both a mother and a father, Ms Woods countered '[A] child needs unconditional love and that is what Betty and I offer Lily-Mae in spades.'

PARLIAMENTARY PERSPECTIVES – HOUSE OF LORDS

16.3   Lord Darzi[1] emphasised that since 1990 technology had moved on and so had attitudes, and that therefore one of the key changes made by the

---

1   *Hansard*, 8 November 2007, col 141 (HL).

HFE Bill was that there would be a legal recognition for different family forms, particularly to recognise same-sex couples as legal parents of children conceived through the use of donated sperm, eggs or embryos.[2] In other words Parliament was giving effect to the principle of equality (an aspect of the ethical principle of justice), ie treating all equals as equals from the point of view of legal protection, rights and recognition. Lesbian and gay individuals would not be unfairly differentiated from heterosexuals and discriminated against from the point of view of becoming the lawful parent of an IVF-created child. The argument would be that in 2007 (or October 2009 when the 2008 Act became effective) it was ethically, morally and legally wrong to deny a couple IVF or prevent both of the same-sex couple from being named on the birth certificate of that IVF-created child as its lawful parents.

16.4 Later Lord Darzi added, to reinforce the points made by him earlier, that the Bill included clear recognition of same-sex couples as legal parents of children conceived through the use of donated sperm, eggs or embryos, and that in essence that would mean, eg, that the woman who gives birth and her civil partner will both be recognised as the parents of a child conceived via assisted reproduction. Instead of the legal position with IVF children up until October 2009, where the lesbian partner had to adopt the child to be a parent, or the gay partner and father of the IVF child had to obtain a parental order under s 30 of the 1990 Act, the same-sex partners will be the legal parents of that IVF child – a radical change in the law. As Lord Darzi noted:

> 'the woman who gives birth and her civil partner will both be recognised as the parents of a child conceived via assisted reproduction … At present, the partner would have to apply to adopt the child … Similarly, two men will be able to apply for a parental order to become parents of a child conceived through a surrogacy arrangement.'

He also said: 'At present, parental orders are open only to married couples.'

Truth

16.5 Baroness Deech was worried by the implications and damaging repercussions of legalising, eg, the naming of two women as the parents of an IVF child on its birth certificate, considering it 'another risk',[3] and adding it was 'strange' the law could permit a birth certificate to show two women as the parents of the child. Whilst that was to avoid discrimination, 'at the same time we all respect the truth, and to have a birth certificate listing two women as parents is an odd way of pursuing the truth.' The argument would be that the law should be based on the truth, not on legal fiction at the whim of individuals who want to become parents. Laws based on untruth or fictions are, if not bad laws, not based on solid foundations and thereby inherently weakened laws. Baroness Deech flagged up the mixed messages being sent out by the government

> 'The pre-legislative scrutiny committee was very anxious to ensure that donor-conceived children should be given every opportunity to discover the truth about their origins, but it believed that children need two parents, preferably including a father … The Bill will promote the truth about origins

2   Ibid, col 142.
3   *Hansard*, 8 November 2007, col 211 (HL).

[however totally contradictorily] so why should it also provide for birth certificates naming two parents of the same sex?'[4]

The government appear to be running with the hare and hunting with the hound at the same time, which is logically untenable. Baroness Deech also added that 'The Bill will ensure non-discrimination between family units and persons,' at the expense, it could be argued, of the welfare of the child.

Legal fiction

16.6   Lord Alton also objected strongly to the HFE Bill permitting lesbians or gay men to be named as the other parent on birth certificates: 'I would also like all references in the Bill that seek to create a legal fiction around parenthood to be deleted.'[5] He referred in support for this contention to the Joint Committee who:

'rightly said, to deny to a child that he or she had a real biological father would be nothing short of the state colluding in a deception. An estimated 800,000 children in Britain already have no contact with their father. To deliberately add to that number is downright irresponsible.'

Mixed messages

16.7   The Archbishop of York, Dr John Semtanu, also highlighted 'some confusion in the mind of the Government over the importance of fathers,' by referring to the fact that:

'First, in 2004, they made regulations to encourage parental responsibility and visibility by removing donor anonymity and allowing donor-conceived children to access the identity of donors involved in their conception. Secondly, they have rightly emphasised in their policies the need for male role models for social cohesion, to reduce underachievement, and to avoid increasing violent crime and gang culture.'[6]

However, he pointed out how the government was at the same time sending out mixed messages by means of the HFE Bill: 'We are now faced with a Bill which seeks formally to remove in its entirety the need for the ultimate male role model, that of the father.'

Truthfulness

16.8   This theme was also taken up by the Lord Bishop of Newcastle, who stated that it was surely very odd that the law might provide a birth certificate showing two women as parents of the child, and noted:

'I well understand that comes from a desire not to discriminate, but to have two women, or, indeed for that matter, two men on a birth certificate as parents is a very odd way to put things.'[7]

---

4   Ibid, col 211–12.
5   *Hansard*, 19 November 2011, col 681 (HL).
6   *Hansard*, 19 November 2011, col 705 (HL).
7   *Hansard*, 21 November 2011, col 841 (HL).

He emphasised the importance of truthfulness as the key consideration here rather than non-discrimination, saying:

'We have come to see that donor-conceived children should be able to discover the truth about their origins, and of course we all commend the Bill's desire to promote the truth … So why provide a birth certificate naming two persons of the same sex, when it is simply not true? If the well-being of the child is a key principle, and if truthfulness is a key principle, then above all we have to be honest.'

The Bishop was, therefore, elevating the principle of truthfulness and honesty to a position of ethical primacy over other ethical and conflicting principles. It could be countered that IVF, inter alia, has altered permanently and profoundly our concepts of parenthood by separating the concepts of genetic, social and legal parents. Parenting has ceased being an indivisible concept. Therefore sperm donors, if they donate at a licensed HFEA clinic and complete the requisite consent forms, will clearly not be the father legally of any children created by, eg, IVF. By contrast the woman who carries a baby for nine months and gives birth to that baby will be the lawful mother of that child, even though the embryo was created from a commissioning couple using that commissioning couple's genetically created embryos.

Principles

16.9   Earl Howe, in moving an Amendment (No 63) to the HFE Bill, that birth certificates should indicate the fact that a person has been born as a result of treatment involving non-partner donated sperm, said he believed very firmly that birth certificates should carry this information and, moreover, he believed it was in the best interests of every donor-conceived child to be told of their donor conception, preferably at an early age.[8] He also argued that human rights were involved in children knowing their genetic origins, stating:

'The fundamental issue underlying it concerns human rights. One of the main reasons why, some three years ago, we decided to lift donor anonymity in this country was the recognition, at European level, that every child has the right to know or to find out who his or her parents are.'

Earl Howe conceded that since the ending of sperm donor anonymity there had been a marked drop in the number of sperm donors but that 'we cannot credibly argue that the relations were wrong in principle.' He was adamant that for the birth certificate of a donor-conceived person to omit any mention of the donor conception is equivalent to the state being complicit in a lie. He also added that whilst the truth might be difficult to confront and might cause pain, it should not be withheld:

'A person's sense of identity is bound up in very large measure with their personal history and a knowledge of where they came from … A birth certificate that omits any mention of donor conception falsifies that history in a profound way.'

He conceded that as well as the issues of principle (ie the necessity of truthfulness about genetic origin on birth certificates), there was a practical issue, namely the donor child possibly being embarrassed about revealing to

8   *Hansard*, 10 December 2007, col 91.

the outside world the fact that they were donor-conceived, eg when opening a bank account or having to prove their identity, etc. However, this difficulty and potential embarrassment could be overcome by, eg, a person having a shorter birth certificate and a longer one:

'the fuller form of the birth certificate of a donor-conceived child should contain a note indicating the fact of the donor conception. The shortened form would not.'[9]

Genetic origin

16.10 Baroness Warnock, the architect of the ethical principles and legal parameters underpinning the 1990 Act, and arguably also the 2008 Act, strongly agreed with Earl Howe, stating that, as a matter of principle, it seemed to her 'profoundly immoral' to bring a child up without them knowing something fundamental to their well-being, ie their genetic origin. She added, furthermore:

'It is a sign of a kind of pettiness on the part of the parents to share a secret that they are not prepared to share with their child ... That is no way to bring up a child – among hidden secrets, about which he is not allowed to know.'[10]

Balance

16.11 Baroness Barker, on the issue of birth certificates, said:

'On the one hand, it is understandable that one would wish to record truth and to pass it on between generations ... Equally, it must be admitted that doing so via the birth certificate is clumsy [given that] Birth certificates are public documents – they are matters of public record – and the proposal would pass on what can be intensely private and personal information.'[11]

She noted the pragmatic problems with having two types of birth certificate, especially a shorter one:

'times are changing – for example, we live under threats of terrorism, and questions about identity are becoming more and more important – short birth certificates are not being used as much; or rather, officials increasingly ask for long birth certificates, which creates a problem.'

She also referred to the ethical considerations pushing in different directions, namely the right to privacy and the right to know and referred to the Joint Committee, which had set out that we have the right to know versus the right to privacy. She said that it was not possible to balance these two conflicting things, and suggested that some sort of 'symbol' be placed on a birth certificate showing that there had been no donor conception.[12]

16.12 Lord Harries of Pentregarth said whilst he had great respect for family privacy and did not think that everything should be 'blazoned abroad', nevertheless added that over the years he had come to realise the importance of

---

9   Ibid, col 93.
10 Ibid.
11 Ibid, col 94.
12 Ibid, col 95.

truthfulness and transparency, and so agreed with both Baroness Warnock and Earl Howe about:

> '[striking] the balance about right between the importance of truthfulness and transparency, on the one hand, and, on the other, a proper and very important respect for family privacy and the parents' roles and responsibilities in revealing to children the circumstances of their birth in their own proper way.'[13]

Pragmatism

16.13   Lord Jenkin of Roding also agreed that it was highly desirable that the donor-conceived person should be told about their genetic origin as soon as they were able to understand, which would happen at different ages for different people. He said that 'it is highly undesirable that the authorities should appear to connive at deception,' and added that furthermore there were a number of practical reasons for that, quite apart from the moral one:

> 'How does a person know that they can go to the HFEA and find out their parentage unless they know that they have been donor conceived? …When young people begin to engage in relationships or even contemplate marriage, there is a risk that the relationship might be consanguineous or even worse … There are all sorts of reasons why it is highly desirable for people to know.'[14]

Knowledge is, therefore, power, but particularly here knowledge of their genetic origins might prevent the child and others being harmed in the future.

Deception

16.14   Baroness Warnock reiterated that the need for truthfulness concerning the genetic origins of children born following gamete and embryo donation was vitally important. She said it had long been her view that not perpetrating official lies and almost compelling the child to be told of his origins are overriding considerations and, moreover, contended that 'one of the greatest immoralities is to keep up a long-term deception of a child as to his origins.'[15] Her practical 'preferred' solution as to what was recorded in the birth certificate of, eg, a child created from sperm donation was simply to have 'by donation' on the birth certificate. She believed that there ought not be any stigma attached to children born from donation:

> 'Times will change and it will become recognised that being a child by donation is an honourable thing to be and casts no aspersions on the social father whatsoever. In fact it shows his generosity.'

16.15   Viscount Craigavon sensibly seemed to be wondering why some peers were concerned about the accuracy and truthfulness of birth certificates concerning the genetic origin of the child, given that between 5 and 10 per cent (or possibly more) of fathers named on birth certificates were not actually the genetic fathers. He added that that was an important thing to bear in mind if

---

13   Ibid, col 96.
14   Ibid, col 97.
15   Ibid, col 99.

the integrity of the register of birth certificates was being considered, and he put that down to 'the imperfection of human nature,' leading to an imperfect register of births.[16] Lord Mackay of Clashfern was also worried about the state being seen to be a party to the false presentation if donor conception is not mentioned. Lord Alton agreed that fake identities were not something that should be promoted and added that he suspected 'that it will be a matter of litigation in the future if we do not make information of this kind available to children who have been donor conceived.'[17]

Squaring circles

16.16 Baroness Hollis of Heigham referred to the problem, on the one hand, of the increasing worry that sperm donors were now limiting themselves in number and not coming forward precisely because of the tracking problem, and on the other hand, equally, that people needed to know their medical history. But the question is how this circle can best be squared. Baroness Finlay of Llandaff felt there were two separate things happening. One was about 'deceiving the infant, child or adolescent – at whatever stage they are – because they are carrying a piece of paper which is not reasonably truthful.' She added,

'I say "reasonably truthful" because we know that between 10 and 40 per cent – I have heard 25 per cent – of children believe that somebody is their dad, and genetically he is not.'[18]

However she noted:

'There is a difference between the state colluding in a deception and a deception which has arisen either because the woman was unaware of it or because she did not want to face the consequences of having been off with someone else, or whatever. The problems relate to a child who has been lied to.'

Openness

16.17 Baroness Royal of Blaisdon, for the government, said that the Government fully recognised the importance of donor-conceived children being told about their origins and that government policy was one of openness in this area. She also said that the government:

'have long believed that it is of prime importance that donor-conceived children are made aware from a young age, of their background and are committed to encouraging that.'[19]

Functions

16.18 Baroness Deech continued her criticisms of the new proposed law on birth certification involving same-sex couples later on in the House of Lords' Committee stage of the HFE Bill by stating that with regards to the fundamental purposes of birth registration:

16   Ibid, col 100.
17   Ibid, col 102.
18   Ibid, col 103.
19   Ibid, col 104.

> 'We are talking about a birth registration in these clauses, not a record of the legal relationship between the adults ... It is the welfare of the child that is paramount in English law, not the formal benefits that might accrue to the parents. Using birth certificates to record the adult relationship is not the way to certify the relationship between two people of the same sex or to secure their obligation to the child.'[20]

Birth certificates are primarily meant to cover the birth of the child, not to cover, detail or legitimise the parent's particular relationship. She added a further pragmatic objection to the changes:

> 'Now that everything these days is globalised – another way of saying that we travel a lot – the certificate with two parents of the same sex on it will divulge facts like that in parts of the world which, unlike us, might treat the situation with considerable disfavour.'[21]

She also referred to birth registration being used to gain nationality, in circumstances where fraud is all too easy. It could also be used where the mother had conceived naturally and wanted to exclude the natural father. Crucially too, the birth certificate:

> '[with] two same-sex parents will give insufficient information to help towards identifying antecedents and will give rise to unnecessary anxiety about possible medical problems which could not be resolved ... The child might not even know which of, say, two women on the birth certificate is actually physically the mother.'

She also noted that the tendency of the entire Bill and its thrust was towards greater truth in IVF for children about their origin, 'and this is not the way to do it.' In addition, she contended, nor was the birth certificate the way to formalise a particular link that exists between two parents of the same sex, and added:

> 'Perhaps a special domestic cohabitation certificate should be devised instead to fulfil that need rather than the distortion of the birth register for all time.'

Adults first?

16.19 Baroness Deech was concerned that, overall, the provisions put the demands of adults ahead of the rights of children to know and benefit from both sides of their genetic makeup and they sat uneasily with the ending of donor anonymity. She also noted that:

> 'not all unions between two adults can be the same, or must be treated the same, for all purposes. UK law still does not recognise, for example, underage, incestuous or polygamous marriages ... It is the hallmark of a civilised society to set boundaries around mating and conception to control, for example, abortion laws, the age at which children may consent to sex, marriage and the prohibited degrees.'[22]

She stated the matter was not a moral issue: 'it is about disguising true facts, and the birth certificate is the record for generations to come.' She concluded that the new law confused biological genetic parenthood and legal social

---

20 *Hansard*, 12 December 2007, col 289 (HL).
21 Ibid, col 290.
22 Ibid, col 291.

parenthood, and that there was a risk of creating a 'legal and social quagmire of adult claims and counterclaims over the children's status.' It would:

'mark a shift in the function and purpose of birth certificates. Instead of providing for all time permanent and available information about biological parentage, birth certificates would be used to assign legal and financial responsibility to non-related individuals.'

Facts

16.20 Baroness Barker pointed out a number of facts concerning birth certification. First, there can only ever be one mother registered on a birth certificate – the mother who carries the child – not two mothers. Secondly, since the passage of the 1990 Act, the name of a father on a birth certificate is not the name of a donor and it never has been. Other certificates record the relationships of the adults to each other, eg marriage, divorce or civil partnership certificates. Birth certificates are about registering the relationships of the parents to the children, but they are not foolproof or always necessarily truthful or accurate about the parentage of children, because people have lied on birth certificates ever since they have been around. She refuted the argument about the change in the law putting the needs of adults above those of children, saying rather:

'Many of us believe that it is in the best interests of children that they are born into and lie in secure and loving families and that those families, however they are made up, are recognised.'[23]

She also repudiated the argument that the new law sets up a 'quagmire'; rather, she believed it brings clarity for those families who have existed for a long time, and the new law represented a 'test of whether this House can demonstrate that it understands and keeps pace with the way in which modern life is changing, and changing for the better.'[24]

Meaning

16.21 The Lord Bishop of Winchester said he was very troubled by what he saw as 'an untruthful widening of the meaning of "parent",' Which he understood to be a 'progenitor':

'It means a mother or a father in the strictest physical sense, whether by donation or whatever. It means, in the generic sense, a mother or father.'[25]

Equality

16.22 Baroness Royall noted that since December 2005 same sex couples had been able to have their relationships legally recognised:

'From that time, couples registering as civil partners have had the same rights and responsibilities as married couples in most areas of their lives, including the ability to apply for a parental responsibility order for a partner's child … However, while the Civil Partnership Act provided for the

---

23 Ibid, col 292.
24 Ibid, col 293.
25 Ibid, col 294.

acquisition of parental responsibility, it did not provide for civil partners to be joint legal parents following assisted conception with donor sperm, for both partners to be legal parents of that child or for that fact to be recorded on birth certificates.'[26]

Hence, the need for change in the law by means of the 2008 Act. As she added:

'The Bill allows that same-sex couples, whether in civil partnership or being treated together, can both be legal parents of a child born through assisted conception.'

She added that she understood that some saw as a fallacy recording on a birth certificate that a child has a mother and a second parent who happens to be female. However, she said, a child born to a married couple by the use of donor sperm has recorded on their birth certificate that the husband is their father, although he is in fact not their biological father. She also noted that:

'Currently, if a same-sex female couple have a child as a result of assisted conception, only the mother's name will go on the birth certificate … If the second parent then goes through the process of adopting the child, a new birth certificate will be produced that has the mother's name and the name of the second parent. Therefore, having the name of a mother and a second female parent on a birth certificate is not a new concept in birth registration.'[27]

Why the concern then? She concluded, therefore, that under the HFE Bill the mother and another parent were the two people responsible for the child:

'Legal rights and responsibilities flow from the names cited as parents on the birth certificate … Those rights and responsibilities are in the best interests of the child.'

Confusion

16.23   Baroness Deech was concerned about confusion about the purpose of a birth certificate and repeated that it was not to legitimise or recognise in any way the union of the two adults who are on it, and it should not be used in that way. She said her earlier point about polygamous and incestuous marriages not being allowed was that if a child were born of such a union no doubt the names of the two parents would be on the birth certificate and that is all that it means: the child's origins. She added that it was not in the interests of the child to list two people on a birth certificate, which that child will carry for the rest of his life and will have to produce all over the world, who are plainly not both his genetic parents. Birth certificates should be focusing on the child's origins, not the situation of the parents, she said, and concluded that she was simply pointing out that whatever union the parents have is a separate issue from what goes on the birth certificate.[28]

State deception

16.24   Baroness Williams of Crosby was also concerned about effectively deceiving the child herself, or himself, on the birth certificate. She added:

26   Ibid, col 296.
27   Ibid, cols 296–297.
28   Ibid, col 298.

'The child will know that you cannot be the biological child of two parents of the same gender. Therefore, the child is bound to keep asking questions about who the father was. The issue is about the biological origin of the child.'[29]

She submitted that the analogy of birth certificates being the same as adoption certificates was a false one, given an adoption certificate was clearly not a statement of biological origins, but of responsibility toward the child. She said that when people adopted children there is no deception involved and that this was perfectly legitimate. That is a key difference with what is proposed by the new law. She concluded by saying she was 'terribly troubled' about a legal acceptance of something that is not a fact suddenly becoming a fact because Parliament says so.[30]

16.25 Baroness Barker was adamant though that a birth certificate was not a certificate of someone's genetic identity: 'We do not have such a thing and never had,'[31] and added that: 'it is a record of who a child's social parents are at any time … It is not about trying to deceive people; on the contrary, it is a different kind of truth.'

16.26 Baroness Deech was emphatic that a birth certificate was not a social record but a historical record. Her objection to the new law was 'simply a plea not to include a deliberate biological lie on a birth certificate.'

Misconception

16.27 Baroness Warnock argued that if Parliament:

'[was] serious about the welfare or the good of the child being the most important consideration in offering treatment to women or couples who want it, we must try to ensure that children are not brought up under a misconception about their genetic parenthood.'[32]

She warned that was one of the most obvious cases of immoral treatment of a child and it could only be embarked on by parents who were thinking more of themselves than of the good of their child. She referred to adoption where nearly all people who adopt children nowadays tell their children at a very early stage that they are adopted, and thought the same practice should be followed with children born following donation. She strongly believed that 'the child's interests come first.'

Honesty

16.28 Baroness Finlay referred to the need to uphold the fundamental principle of being open and honest with the child, and that:

'it is essential to reinforce the principle of honesty in all that we do, particularly when medical technology is used to intervene in what could be called processes of nature.'[33]

---

29   Ibid.
30   Ibid, col 299.
31   Ibid.
32   *Hansard*, 21 January 2008, col 104 (HL).
33   Ibid, col 106.

This sentiment was also taken up by Lord Alton, who urged that 'we should never try to conceal from someone the truth of their identity.' He referred to the risks of consanguinity or even of incest if people's genetic identity is not accurately and truthfully recorded on birth certificates, and added that every child, whether born naturally or by IVF, should have a true record of their identity. He cautioned:

'Without absolute knowledge of your genetic profile, the possibility of unwitting consanguineous or incestuous relationships is obvious.'[34]

He welcomed the fact that, from April 2005, the donor anonymity that previously existed had been lifted and children were given the right to know the identity of their biological parents, but regretted that 'We gave the right to inquire, but created no duty to tell.'

16.29 Lord Patten agreed that:

'absence of knowledge of the natural origins of a person's life can have profound consequences on an individual's emotional, social and spiritual development.'[35]

He went further, arguing that knowing one's genetic origins was a human right. The state must not 'connive in a falsehood.'

16.30 Lord Winston observed that:

'Everyone has said ... that it is important to be open with children, to be as honest as we can about their origins and explain to them as early as possible that they come from a donor parent of one or the other sort.'[36]

But his impression, albeit anecdotal and not based on solid research, was that an increase in the number of men and women who want to keep the origin of their children secret had been seen.

Two best?

16.31 Lord Darzi, in justifying the new law in the HFE Bill, said:

'At present, we have the invidious situation where the female partner of a woman who gives birth following assisted reproduction treatment is not recognised as a parent of the child.'[37]

It was invidious not only because it causes a disparity between same-sex couples and heterosexual couples, but because this means that the child would have a 'legal' relationship with only one parent and not two. So not only do the same-sex couple suffer and lose out thereby, but also more importantly the child loses out too. As he noted:

'The Civil Partnership Act 2004 allowed for the acquisition of parental responsibility, but it did not provide for joint legal parenthood following assisted conception treatment. The Bill now addresses this.'

---

34 Ibid, col 108.
35 Ibid, col 109.
36 Ibid, col 111.
37 *Hansard*, 28 January 2008, col 476.

He said the HFE Bill allowed for female couples, whether they are in a civil partnership or are being 'treated together', to both be legal parents of a child born through assisted conception, and allows for the second female parent to be registered on the child's birth certificate under UK law.[38] He highlighted a number of consequences which flowed from the information recorded in the birth register: 'Birth certificates are used as prime evidence of status as well as rights to benefits, passports, inheritance, and parentage'. He gave the example that where parents are not married to each other, the father will acquire parental responsibility by registering the child jointly with the child's mother under the Children Act 1989. A father named on a birth certificate is evidence for liability for child support payments.

16.32 Lord Darzi noted that when the 1990 Act came into force it allowed for fathers to be recorded on a child's birth certificate, following assisted conception treatment, where they were not in fact the genetic father of the child because donated sperm was used. Arguably that equally could be termed state deception in genetic origins. Thus,

'the 1990 Act specifically excludes the sperm donor from being the father of any child born through assisted conception as a result of his donation. Therefore, where donated sperm or eggs are used, the birth certificate does not record the donor as a parent, and therefore is no longer a record of genetic parentage'

On that basis the 2008 Act is really just building incrementally on the ethical foundations laid by the 1990 Act.

16.33 Lord Darzi noted that at the time, where a single woman received infertility treatment at a licensed centre only one name went on the child's birth certificate, but he contended that 'where there would not be a father, but there would be a same-sex partner, surely it must follow that having two legal parents recorded is better than only having one.' The argument is that it is better to have two parents than one. He also argued that allowing same-sex couples legal responsibility for a child born through assisted conception treatment also safeguarded the welfare of the child. A child's welfare is more likely to be advanced with two same-sex parents named on a birth certificate as having parental responsibility, rather than having just the mother named on it. He added:

'By allowing them to go to a licensed centre and both register as the child's parents we hope we would dissuade same-sex couples from carrying out unlicensed self-insemination at home ... It also means that, in the event that something happened to the mother, there is another person who is the legal parent of that child.'

Parents

16.34 Lord Darzi reaffirmed that birth certificates would not record that a child has two mothers: 'The Bill sets out that the woman who gives birth to the child will be the mother and her female partner will be recorded as a parent.' He added that was not a wholly new concept, as:

---

38   Ibid, col 477.

'Currently, if a same-sex female couple have a child as a result of assisted conception treatment, only the mother's name will go on the birth certificate. If the second parent then goes through the process of adopting the child, an adoption certificate will be produced that has the mother's name and the name of the second parent.'[39]

He also noted that birth certificates could not necessarily be relied on to trace one's genetic heritage. The current 'disparity' in the law needs to be addressed.

No consensus

16.35 Lord Jenkin of Roding noted that whilst there was general support for telling the child they were donor conceived there was far less agreement about recording the fact on birth certificates. He also stated:

'the organisations primarily representing donor-conceived people differ: the International Donor Offspring Alliance [IDOA] takes a quite different view from the Donor Conception Network [DCN] a self- help group that primarily represents families.'[40]

He pointed out that, the IDOA felt strongly that the fact of donor conception should be recorded on the birth certificate, whereas the DCN took the opposite view:

'It warmly welcomes the objective and believes that donor-conceived children should be told, but believes that recording the fact of donor conception on the birth certificate is not the right way to achieve that and, indeed, would not be an effective way of doing so.'

Lord Jenkin examined the arguments for the two opposing stances taken by the two bodies. He said the argument of the IDOA, which represents donor-conceived people, that the genetic and biological parents as well as social parents should be recorded was based on six propositions:

'First, genetic heritage has existence. It is a fact, and has meaning and value in itself. Secondly, everyone has a moral right to know. While it cannot be universally enforced, the state should not connive in abrogating that right. Thirdly, because the state intervenes in assisted reproduction, it has a duty to give legal protection to that moral right and should not deceive the child or withhold information about its genetic parents. The genetic regulations give the donor-conceived child the right to find a donor's identity, but this is meaningless if many parents continue to conceal the fact of donor conception. Fourthly, the truth must be put in the hands of the offspring for reasons of avoiding consanguinity or even incest. Fifthly, and this is an important fact, falsifying a birth certificate is illegal, so it is discriminatory if the state connives at concealing the fact of donor conception. Finally, only honest and accurate birth certificates would be consistent with the rest of UK law, the UN Convention on the Rights of the Child and case law under the European Convention on Human Rights.'[41]

---

39 Ibid, cols 477–478.
40 Ibid, col 502.
41 Ibid, col 503.

16.36 Lord Jenkin commented that the Joint Committee had found these to be strong and persuasive moral and legal arguments. However he said there were also practical arguments too:

'how are children to find out if they were donor conceived if no one tells them? How can they find out about the medical history of a biological parent? … How can these children be sure of avoiding the risk of consanguinity, or even incest, if they do not have the knowledge that would prompt them to seek assurances from the HFEA?'[42]

By contrast he said the DCN carried out a survey of their members which had showed that the overwhelming majority of respondents were against the birth certification proposal.

'Many said that they would be prepared to lie to the registrar to protect the privacy of their children or would consider going abroad for a further child in order to avoid appearing on the HFEA register.'

He said the DCN also pointed out that the law on assisted reproduction required absolute confidentiality, on the part of both the clinic and the HFEA:

'Putting a note or … some sort of code on a baby's birth certificate would be a complete break with this protection of a family's privacy and would broadcast to the world how the parents had set about securing the birth of their child.'[43]

Change

16.37 Baroness Warnock said she had a strong feeling that the 'proper thing to do' was to 'put "by donor" on the birth certificate, because that would be honest and it would virtually compel parents to tell their children the truth.'[44] She said that the attitude to donor conception that it was something to be kept desperately secret was changing and placed her faith in the changing attitudes of society. People's attitudes had already changed towards donor conception. The default position of doctors of secrecy and protecting the sensitivities of the parents has been replaced by more emphasis on the rights of the child to know its genealogy. As she noted:

'[doctors] are now more inclined to think of the interests of the child who may be the result of the birth by donation. There is no doubt whatever that it is in the child's interest to know, or to be able to know eventually, something about their wider family.'[45]

She concluded that 'our genealogy' was an important part of everybody's individuality and sense of their own personality.

Truth emphasised

16.38 Baroness Knight of Collingtree agreed, taking a slightly different tack, saying, 'you cannot have two women who are parents,' and the House had

42 Ibid.
43 Ibid, col 504.
44 Ibid, col 505.
45 Ibid.

'tried to turn a lie into the truth.' The truth, she said, should not be distorted for people's feelings. She agreed that it was an offence to put down a lie on an official document such as a birth certificate. Lord Alton also agreed that everyone needed to know about our genealogy, not just because of the dangers of consanguinity or incest, but because of the danger of not knowing about hereditary diseases and of not being able to take early decisions about healthcare because of ignorance of one's origins.

16.39 Earl Ferrers, in addition, noted:

> 'If you have put on the record that somebody else is the father, that must be a complete untruth ... One ought not to permit an untruth to happen.'

He added:

> 'Birth certificates must tell the truth. If it is a donor, surely it must say that it is a donor. It cannot say that it is somebody it is not.'[46]

Baroness Butler-Sloss stated that she also shared the disquiet that many peers had expressed about the fact that a birth certificate 'will not show the honest position.'

16.40 Baroness Barker stated that the DCN and IDOS organisations did not represent all shades of opinion on the matter regarding what went on the birth certificates of donor-conceived children, and that:

> 'this is an intractably difficult problem to which there is no answer that satisfies both the desire of donor-conceived people to have a right to know and those who say that the matter should be handled with the privacy of the family.'[47]

Education

16.41 Baroness Royall accepted that 'the same culture of secrecy is no longer the case' but said that the issue of donor-conceived children being told about their origins was a sensitive area that involves delving into intimate family relationships. Whilst everyone agreed on the value of donor-conceived children knowing about their origins, nevertheless this must be weighed against inappropriate interference from the state and the best method for achieving openness worked out. The Government were committed to encouraging openness by way of education rather than enforcement.[48]

16.42 Lord Mackay asked if the Government was 'content with the discrimination that involves the fact of donor conception being registered for some children but not for others who are donor-conceived?' Baroness Royall, for the Government, replied that it was trying to modernise the legislation, 'so that heterosexual and homosexual couples are treated in the same way and the same information is on the birth certificate of their children.' Earl Ferrers countered by querying the point of a birth certificate – should it not record

---

46 Ibid, col 507.
47 Ibid, col 509.
48 Ibid, col 510.

who the parents are, who the mother and father are? Baroness Royall said the important issue was that, 'children should be informed of their real parenthood, as it were, at an appropriate time.'[49]

Dilemmas

16.43 Baroness Hollis noted three dilemmas to deal with. First, there were very diverse and probably irreconcilable views whether birth certificates should reflect the biological or social parentage of children. Secondly, there was the issue of which of those things any child at any point in their life might wish that public document to reflect. Finally, there was the right of the child to know and the right of the family to have the privacy to teach their children what their origins are according to their own values and mores, knowing that parents can withhold that information.[50]

Informing

16.44 At the Third Reading of the HFE Bill on 4 February 2008, Baroness Royall reiterated that:

'The Government recognise the importance of ensuring that prospective parents understand the importance of telling a child at an early age that they were donor-conceived. A child who grows up with this knowledge will be better informed and is likely to have a better family relationship. They would receive the information from their parents in the most sensitive, constructive and least distressing way.'[51]

She repeated that it was the Government's view that this was best achieved by education rather than enforcement, and that encouraging openness in this way was the best way forward. She said the HFE Bill requires that the HFEA produced, in its Code of Practice, guidance for clinics about the provision of counselling and information, in addition to requiring that all patients be offered counselling and provided with information. Furthermore, the Bill ensured that:

'it is a condition of all licences that people being treated using donor gametes, or embryos taken from a woman who is not being treated, must be provided with information about the importance of telling their child that they were donor conceived, as well as information about the best way to do this.'[52]

She concluded that the combined effect of the HFE Bill provisions would mean that:

'clinics are obliged to provide patients with information about the importance of talking to children about their donor conception, and that the code of practice should provide details of what information should be provided, as well as how the offer of counselling should be made.'

---

49 Ibid, col 511.
50 Ibid, col 512.
51 *Hansard*, 4 February 2008, col 865 (HL).
52 Ibid, col 866.

Inconsistencies

16.45 Baroness Deech flagged up the inconsistencies in the Bill in the Committee stage:

'The Bill remains full of inconsistencies. It promotes truth about origins, but it will provide for birth certificates to name two parents of the same sex.'[53]

Clearly this interpretation is correct if one defines a parent biologically or genetically. Whether it is correct if one defines the term 'parent' more purposively to embrace the individuals charged with looking after and loving the child as it grows up, even if they are not the biological or genetic parent, remains a moot ethical point.

Two parent policy

16.46 Lord Darzi countered the argument that the changes made by the HFE Bill concerning who is deemed a parent on birth certificates were not writing fathers out of legal parenthood when their sperm was used to create a child because:

'Recognition of a same-sex couple as the parents of the child born following treatment with donor sperm does not take the parenthood from the father or oust him from the birth certificate, because there is no legal father. On the contrary, it enables the child to have two legal parents. Surely that must be in the interests of the child.'[54]

Sperm donors who donate sperm at licensed clinics after completing the requisite consent forms simply are not the legal parents of children born as a result of their donation, but what the new law does is permit a second individual to be named as the legal parent on the child's birth certificate and that 'parent' may be a same-sex individual. Having ideally two legal parents rather than just one would command universal support probably, but having a same-sex couple as parents (either lesbians or gay men) would not patently command such widespread approval with the public. Lord Darzi firmly believed that 'the proposals in the Bill recognise society as it exists and value all parents.'[55]

HOUSE OF COMMONS

16.47 The Secretary of State for Health, Alan Johnson, noted and commended the changes made to birth certification, stating that the HFE Bill would, inter alia, give same-sex couples who have children through assisted conception the same parenting rights as heterosexual couples.[56] The law, therefore, promotes equality and non-discrimination, based on sexual orientation. He noted that:

'The current law recognises the woman who carries the child following assisted conception as that child's mother. If the woman is married her husband, unless it is shown that he did not consent to treatment, is recognised as the child's legal father.'

---

53   *Hansard*, 10 December, 2007, col 23 (HL).
54   Ibid, col 52.
55   Ibid, col 53.
56   *Hansard*, 12 May 2008, cols 1071–1072.

But sadly the law in 2008 is anomalous and unfairly discriminatory against homosexuals. He noted:

'However, at present, the female civil partner of a woman who gives birth following assisted conception has no legal status. She is not recognised as the parent of the child, and her name would not appear in the birth certificate.'

He added that the Civil Partnership Act 2004, which he noted had been widely supported in the House, had recognised the joint parental responsibility of same-sex couples. Essentially, therefore, the HFE Bill:

'would mean that the non-birth woman in a civil partnership would have the same recognition as a husband whose wife underwent treatment using donor sperm. It would also mean that male couples and civil partners could apply for a parental order, in line with married couples.'

The bottom line is that these legislative changes in the 2008 Act would bring this area of law into line with national legislation prohibiting discrimination on the grounds of gender or sexual orientation – legislation which was also widely supported in the House. Arguably the changes here are a logical, incremental legislative follow-up to the earlier 2004 legal changes. For some though this represents a further slide down the ethical slippery slope.

16.48 Norman Lamb MP stated that there was considerable force behind the argument that the individual has the right to know, and that the birth certificate of a donor-conceived child should have that fact recorded on it.[57]

Anomalies

16.49 Emily Thornberry MP referred to the anomalies and inequities in the law prior to the 2008 Act by citing the example of three couples who become parents with the help of a sperm donor.[58] These were;

(1) *A heterosexual married couple* – In this case both people will be on the birth certificate, even if the father is not the biological father.
(2) *A heterosexual unmarried couple* – in this case, if the couple have a child through sperm donation, both people can be on the birth certificate, even if the father is not the biological father, so long as he goes to register the birth.
(3) *A lesbian couple* – in this case, if they were refused a donor, they might enter into informal arrangements which would mean that only one of them – the biological mother – would be on the birth certificate. Ms Thornberry noted that the child would then be unlikely ever to know their father or find out any details about them. Also, the lesbian partner would have absolutely no rights, even though she was in practice a parent. Ms Thornberry commented: 'That is not fair or right, and it is not 21st century.' The law should be guided by changing ethical values and social acceptability, if not dictated by these.

16.50 Emily Thornberry continued very critically concerning the law prior to 2008. If this third lesbian couple managed to get a donor, eg by bringing along a male friend:

57 Ibid, col 1090.
58 Ibid, col 1123.

'As the law currently stands, only the biological mother would be on the birth certificate, although the biological father would be on the register held by the authority. Again, that is not fair, it is discriminatory and it has negative effects on the child.'[59]

She added:

'Until the non-biological mother adopts, she has absolutely no rights as a parent, even though the child was born into a stable, loving relationship that had been legally endorsed through a civil partnership. That is not right.'

Again arguably it is enshrining inequality and discrimination in legislation. Ms Thornberry added that if the non-biological mother's partner died when the child was 18 months old, the second parent would have absolutely no rights over the child:

'In fact, the biological mother's parents could take away the child and not give the other parent any access at all to the toddler. Is that fair? No, it is not.'[60]

16.51 Mrs Claire Curtis-Thomas MP took a fundamentally different ethical stance, contending:

'Opposition to the creation of same-sex parented families does not imply a fear of homosexuals or rejection of homosexual relationships; it is the simple assertion of the rights of a child.'[61]

By contrast Dr Evan Harris MP was opposed to discrimination against lesbian couples, such as making them jump over extra hurdles. He said:

'[It] is not justified by the evidence we have heard about. That evidence comes from research into how well children do when they are born to lesbian parents and solo parents – women who specifically seek to become single parents.'[62]

Family changes

16.52 Dawn Primarolo MP, a Minister at the Department of Health, stated in conclusion:

'On the question of birth certificates, and of telling children that they are donor-conceived, we have made it clear [in the House of Lords] that we would carry out a review within four years of the Bill coming into force.'[63]

However she added that recognition that family structures had changed was needed, and stated that the proposed legislation was about 'introducing regulation that takes us into the 21st century. Not to do so would be a lost opportunity.'[64]

Addressing some critics who might counter that the new law is political correctness enshrined in legislation, she rebutted this accusation: 'What I am

---

59 Ibid.
60 Ibid, col 1124.
61 Ibid, col 1134.
62 Ibid, col 1140.
63 Ibid, col 1160.
64 Ibid, col 1161.

saying is not political correctness, or if it is, I do not care. It is just correctness. It is basic justice; it is what is right.'[65]

16.53 She then raised another important argument: that not recognising a same sex partner as a parent on the birth certificate would not prevent either the desire for a same sex partner to be a parent, nor a same-sex couple in fact becoming parents. She emphasised that those women would still become mothers and they would not be stopped from doing so. She continued that if the legislation was not passed, 'hundreds of children of lesbian parents will be denied the opportunity to have a second loving parent at the heart of their family. We should do the right thing.'

HOUSE OF LORDS

16.54 When the HFE Bill went back to the House of Lords from the House of Commons with the latter's amendments, Baroness Thornton noted that the HFE Bill was seeking to ensure that civil partners and other same-sex couples are recognised as the legal parents of children conceived through the use of donated sperm, eggs, or embryos, in line with married couples and unmarried heterosexual couples.[66] The 2008 Act is, therefore, designed to promote and ensure equality and equal treatment between same-sex and opposite sex couples. She added that additionally the Bill amended the Births and Deaths Registration Act 1953 enabling the second female parent to be named on the birth certificate. She said this was:

'consistent with the wider government policy on promoting equality, as evidenced by the Civil Partnership Act 2004 and the national legislation prohibiting discrimination on the grounds of sexual orientation.'

She argued that the provisions in the HFE Bill which enabled a child born to a same-sex couple to have two legal parents must be in the best interests of the child. The basic argument would be that the 2008 Act is merely realigning and recalibrating the law on assisted reproduction, specifically on who is named as the legal parents on the birth certificates, into line with other earlier existing legislative measures doing the same thing, eg the Civil Partnership Act 2004.

Good parents

16.55 Fundamentally the Bill protected the interests of the child by ensuring it has two parents named on its birth certificate. Baroness Thornton elaborated on this:

'Noble Lords may not approve of same-sex couples being parents but the fact is that they are parents, and they are good parents. The suggestion which has run as an undercurrent through this debate, that same-sex parents are of less value than mixed-sex parents, is quite offensive and incorrect ... it is sad to suggest in this day and age that having two women as loving parents is somehow to deny a human right to a child.'[67]

---

65   Ibid, col 1124.
66   *Hansard*, 29 October 2008, col 1643.
67   Ibid, col 1644.

Baroness Thornton, concluded by extolling the virtues of the new legal changes made by this legislation by referring to the evidence presented to the Joint Committee of both Houses, which demonstrated that the emotional well-being and other aspects of development of children growing up in lesbian families are comparable to those in heterosexual families. She concluded:

'what is important is that children are brought up in loving, supportive families. It is unrealistic to suggest that that is an undesirable situation when that is what happens. We need to make sure that such children are not disadvantaged by the legal process through not having legitimate parents entered on their birth certificates.'

That was what the new law was about.

THE NEW LAW

16.56 As discussed in Chapter 15, the law on parenthood was radically and, for some, controversially redrawn by Parliament in Part 2, ss 33–58 of the 2008 Act. The most fundamental change was that a lesbian woman's partner in a civil partnership (referred to in s 42 as 'the other party to the civil partnership') would be the lawful parent of that lesbian woman's IVF baby, for example. Furthermore, in a same sex relationship, if a number of conditions including the agreed female parenthood conditions (s 44) were satisfied, the lesbian partner of the woman who gave birth to the IVF baby would be the legal parent of that child.

16.57 Schedule 6 of the 2008 Act, inter alia, deals with the amendments relating to parenthood in cases involving assisted reproduction. For example, paras 2 and 3 make amendments to the Births and Deaths Registration Act 1953, in the light of ss 42 and 43 of the 2008 Act. Paragraph 2 provides;

'In section 1 of the Births and Deaths Registration Act 1953 (particulars of births to be registered) after subsection (2) insert—
    "(3) In the case of a child who has a parent by virtue of section 42 or 43 of the Human Fertilisation and Embryology Act 2008, the reference in subsection 2 (a) to the father of the child is to be read as a reference to the woman who is a parent by virtue of that section."'

Paragraph 3 provides:

'In section 2 of the Births and Deaths Registration Act 1953 (information concerning birth to be given to registrar within 42 days) renumber the existing provision as subsection (1) of the section and at the end insert—
    "(2) In the case of a child who has a parent by virtue of section 42 or 43 of the Human Fertilisation and Embryology Act 2008, the references in subsection (1) to the father of the child are to be read as references to the woman who is a parent by virtue of that section."'

CONCLUSION

16.58 The very small – in terms of statutory provisions – yet very large and significant – in terms of recalibration and restructuring of the family unit – changes made by the 2008 Act, in formalising state recognition and legitimacy of same-sex couples being named expressly on birth certificates as the legal parents of children born from, inter alia, IVF incontrovertibly sent out signals to society that Parliament was widening the legal net to include and recognise a broader, more inclusive variety of family type. The State, via Parliament, was further extending the parameters and definition of a family beyond the traditional, nuclear family comprising legally married opposite-sex couples. Parliament was arguably also merely accepting social reality in the United Kingdom in 2009, and that this reality logically ought to extend to the sphere of assisted reproduction. This further de-stigmatising of same-sex couples acting as legal parents of, eg, IVF-created children by Parliament was obviously a welcome legislative development for many, not just same-sex couples, but at the same time others felt this development undermined and diminished the value and worth of the conventional family (opposite-sex couples), was tantamount to state connivance in a legal lie on the birth certificate, was potentially damaging to the welfare of the child and flew in the face of other government initiatives and legislation emphasising the importance, role and responsibilities of fathers in family life, especially for their children. Families in 2012 come in all shapes and sizes, but then again this was equally true in 1990, and indeed in earlier eras. The 2008 Act now legally permits the naming of same-sex parents as the legal parents of, eg, IVF-created children and has arguably ended the injustice of their shaming.

Part 6

The Impact of Human Rights

Chapter 17

Human Rights and Reproductive Medicine

INTRODUCTION

17.1   Since the passage of the Human Rights Act 1998 (HRA 1998), which became effective on 1 October 2000, the impact of human rights on a huge range of activities in the United Kingdom has become more pronounced. Interestingly, Sir Nicholas Bratza, the British judge sitting at the European Court of Human Rights (ECtHR) at Strasbourg since November 1998, and one of its vice-presidents since January 2007, was elected to take over as President of the Court in November 2011. However, as the *Belfast Telegraph* of 5 July 2011 commented:

> '… the choice of a Briton is unlikely to calm increasing political concerns in the UK that the court is passing judgments seen as imposing human rights policy on the Government, from prisoners' voting rights to the rights of illegal asylum seekers to stay in the UK despite incurring serious criminal convictions.'

An area that is incontrovertibly being affected by human rights is medical law and ethics generally including the specific sphere of assisted reproduction.

17.2   Basically the HRA 1998 'brought home', to paraphrase the words of the then Labour Home Secretary, Jack Straw, the human rights contained in Arts 2–12 and 14 of the European Convention on Human Rights (ECHR). In other words those human rights contained in the ECHR could be directly enforced and relied on by citizens in our domestic courts, without the need to enforce them by going all the way to the ECtHR in Strasbourg, which was potentially a slow and costly process, quite apart from *locus standi* considerations and surmounting our domestic courts first. Instead of human rights being contained merely in an international agreement (the ECHR), from 1 October 2000 these human rights were specifically included and referred to in an Act of Parliament and henceforth they could be used effectively as both a shield and a sword by a citizen who believed one or more of their human rights had been violated by, eg, a public body. What had, up until October 2000, been merely an international obligation for our government to comply with and adhere to, became transformed into directly enforceable rights for UK citizens in UK domestic courts. For a country like the United Kingdom with an unwritten constitution, and with no culture of human rights, but who relied on the courts to protect citizens' residual freedoms, as opposed to their human rights, the enactment and ultimate effectiveness of the HRA 1998 in October 2000 was indeed seismic in consequence. It signalled a transformation, if not a constitutional revolution or legal tsunami, that swept over vast tracts of UK common law. It might also be argued that the repercussions and resonance of the HRA 1998 affected medical law and reproductive medicine profoundly.

17.3 However the considerable impact of ECHR rights on UK citizens and on UK law has not occurred without dissent. That was abundantly evident in the debate in the House of Commons on 10 February 2011 concerning whether convicted prisoners should have the right to vote, and following the ECtHR ruling that the United Kingdom's blanket ban on prisoners voting was contrary to the ECHR. Many MPs objected strongly to what they saw as unelected, unaccountable, foreign judges imposing objectionable judgments contrary to the wishes and views of a democratically elected and sovereign Parliament. In the debate, Jack Straw MP had noted that convicted prisoners had been deprived of the vote since 1870 and that there had been a consensus in Parliament since then that that would remain the case, stating that the ban 'is part of the mix of penal policy and the subject of wide consent by the public.' He furthermore warned, regarding the ECtHR:

'By extending their remit into areas way beyond any original conception of fundamental human rights the court in Strasbourg is, I suggest, undermining its own legitimacy and its potential effectiveness in respect of the purposes for which it was established.'

David Davis MP urged MPs to defy the ECtHR ruling that the UK ban was illegal, saying it was not unjust to deny the prisoners this right, given that they had 'broken their contract with society,' ie if one acts lawfully, one gets the rights that all lawful citizens of the state enjoy. He further added: 'The concept is simple. If you break the law, you cannot make the law,' and he contended that Parliament must assert itself on an issue of great democratic importance. Permitting potentially thousands of convicted criminals who had perpetrated serious criminal offences to vote was something the public would 'recoil from'. This seemingly is a continuation of the ECtHR's extension of the human rights of prisoners as manifested in the earlier *Dickson* case.[1]

17.4 Interestingly too, the impact of the enactment of the HRA 1998 has, not surprisingly, been felt directly professionally by the medical profession. The General Medical Council (GMC) highlighted very early on in their draft Review of the *Good Medical Practice* consultation document entitled *Good Medical Practice – A draft for consultation* the pivotal nature of respecting and upholding a patient's human rights, by providing that regarding the duties of a doctor registered with the GMC:

'Patients must be able to trust doctors with their lives and health. To justify that trust you must:
Respect human rights …'

Interestingly, and arguably bizarrely, express reference to respecting human rights and the specific duty to respect human rights does not actually appear in *Good Medical Practice* itself.[2] However, para 13 nevertheless provides that doctors registered with the GMC 'must keep up to date with, and adhere to, the laws and codes of practice relevant to your work.' One such law relevant to all doctors working in the NHS is s 6 of the HRA 1998, which provides:

'(1) It is unlawful for a public authority to act in a way which is incompatible with a Convention right.'

---

1 *Dickson v United Kingdom* (no 44362/04).
2 Available at http://www.gmc-uk.org/guidance/good_medical_practice.asp

Several other parts of *Good Medical Practice* specifically refer to protecting the rights of patients. *Good Medical Practice* (effective on 13 November 2006) now provides, concerning the duties of a doctor registered with the General Medical Council: 'Patients must be able to trust doctors with their lives and health.' Significantly, *Good Medical Practice* provides: 'To justify that trust you must show respect for human life'. Article 2 of the ECHR, inter alia, provides: 'Everyone's right to life shall be protected by law.' Furthermore, *Good Medical Practice* provides that doctors must '[T]reat patients as individuals and respect their dignity' (strongly overlapping with art 8 of the ECHR), and must '[R]espect patient's right to confidentiality' (again art 8 is involved). *Good Medical Practice* also provides that doctors must '[R]espect patients' right to reach decisions with you about their treatment and care'. Again, this duty involves, inter alia, art 8. Finally, *Good Medical Practice* provides that doctors must '[N]ever discriminate unfairly against patients or colleagues.' Discriminating fairly against patients, eg, seeking IVF is perfectly in keeping with a doctor's GMC duties. Article 14 of the ECHR is obviously relevant to this GMC duty. It is, therefore, a professional duty of a doctor, including doctors working in various capacities in licensed clinics and research laboratories if undertaking research on human embryos or admixed embryos, to respect human rights.

THE HUMAN RIGHTS ACT 1998: OPENING THE FLOODGATES?

17.5   The short title to the HRA 1998 states, inter alia, that it is:

'An Act to give further effect to rights and freedoms guaranteed under the European Convention on Human Rights'

It does not, therefore, expressly or implicitly state that it is an Act that means human rights contained in the ECHR now have precedence or invalidate sections of Acts of Parliament which conflict with those convention rights. Section 1(1) provides:

'(1) In this Act 'the Convention rights' means the rights and fundamental freedoms set out in—
  (a) Articles 2 to 12 and 14 of the Convention,
  (b) Articles 1 to 3 of the First Protocol, and
  (c) Articles 1 and 2 of the Sixth Protocol,
  as read with Articles 16 to 18 of the Convention.'

Significantly too s 1(2), also provides that:

'Those Articles are to have effect for the purposes of this Act subject to any designated derogation or reservation (as to which see sections 14 and 15).'

Hence not all of the ECHR human rights are directly enforceable in UK courts. Only 12 are – Arts 2–12 and 14.

17.6   Section 2 of HRA 1998 sets out how domestic courts and tribunals interpret Convention rights when reaching decisions involving human rights. Under the terms of s 2, courts or tribunals must take into account, inter alia, judgments and decisions of the ECtHR when determining questions which have arisen in domestic courts regarding ECHR rights. Section 2(1) stipulates:

'A court or tribunal determining a question which has arisen in connection with a Convention right must take into account any—

(a) judgment, decision, declaration or advisory opinion of the European Court of Human Rights,

(b) opinion of the Commission given in a report adopted under Article 31 of the Convention,

(c) decision of the Commission in connection with Article 26 or 27 (2) of the Convention, or

(d) decision of the Committee of Ministers taken under Article 46 of the Convention,

whenever made or given, so far as, in the opinion of the court or tribunal, it is relevant to the proceedings in which that question has arisen.'

A major weakness and drawback of this section is that it only states that domestic courts and tribunals 'must take into account' ECtHR judgments, decisions etc. It does not state domestic courts or tribunals are bound by ECtHR judgments and decisions etc. Arguably this is the Achilles heel of HRA 1998 – indeed it could be further submitted it is one of several such Achilles heels contained in the Act – and Ewing says 'to sever the jurisprudence from the treaty is like severing the limbs from a torso,'[3] that is, given that the ECtHR supposedly gives definitive interpretations as to what the various ECHR articles mean, surely domestic courts ought to follow strictly and fully to the letter the decisions of the ECtHR, and not merely be obliged to take them into account in reaching a decision. That appears to show a half-hearted commitment to upholding human rights by the UK government. Clearly, a huge amount of UK law is judge-made law, ie common law, so s 2 should fashion, or at least influence, decisions made by our domestic courts or tribunals in the future where human rights are invoked and come into play in a case being heard. This section is of significance when one considers various cases concerning reproductive medicine involving human rights, discussed later.

17.7   Of major significance too is s 3, which concerns the interpretation of domestic legislation, including primary legislation. Section 3 provides:

'(1) So far as it is possible to do so, primary legislation and subordinate legislation must be read and given effect in a way which is compatible with the Convention rights.

(2) This section—

(a) applies to primary legislation and subordinate legislation whenever enacted;

(b) does not affect the validity, continuing operation or enforcement of any incompatible primary legislation; and

(c) does not affect the validity, continuing operation or enforcement of any incompatible subordinate legislation if (disregarding any possibility of revocation) primary legislation prevents removal of the incompatibility.'

Arguably our domestic courts and tribunals have, therefore, been furnished with another new rule of statutory interpretation when construing and interpreting both primary and secondary domestic legislation, namely that insofar as it is possible to do so they must read and give effect to it (ie interpret it) in a way that is compatible with and complying with the ECHR. Clearly the use of the words 'So far as it is possible to do so,' implies that sometimes domestic courts

---

3   K D Ewing, 'The Human Rights Act and Parliamentary Democracy' (1999) 62(1) MLR 79 at 86.

or tribunals will not be able to read and give effect to domestic legislation in a way compatible with or complying with the ECHR. They simply will not be able to stretch the words used in a domestic Act in a way compatible with a specific ECHR right.

17.8 Crucially, s 3 applies to primary legislation and subordinate legislation whenever passed. Thus its effect is not limited to primary or secondary legislation enacted post-1 October 2000, but rather it extends to all legislation, primary and secondary, *whenever* enacted, so it is applicable to the 1990 Act and of course the 2008 Act. It is potentially very far-reaching indeed therefore. Also, importantly, s 3 and its use does not affect the validity, continuing operation, or enforcement of any incompatible legislation. Thus if, for example a section in a domestic Act cannot be read and given effect in a way compatible with the ECHR, our courts and tribunals are not then given *carte blanche* to strike down, invalidate or declare unlawful and null and void that section in the Act of Parliament. Parliamentary supremacy and sovereignty is thus preserved and remains intact, despite the new legal dispensation created in s 3.

17.9 The next important provision in HRA 1998 is s 4, which concerns the power of the courts to make a declaration of incompatibility. Section 4(1) and (2), which are aimed at primary legislation, provides that:

'(1) Subsection (2) applies in any proceedings in which a court determines whether a provision of primary legislation is compatible with a Convention right.

(2) If the court is satisfied that the provision is incompatible with a Convention right, it may make a declaration of that incompatibility.'

This declaration is effectively the judicial equivalent of a yellow card being given to a provision in primary legislation. It is a formal declaration by a court that a provision in an Act is not compatible with the ECHR and with our human rights obligations, so in that sense it is a very serious step. However, the fact that the court has made a declaration of incompatibility does not invalidate that statutory provision. As s 4(6) provides:

'A declaration under this section ("a declaration of incompatibility")—

(a) does not affect the validity, continuing operation or enforcement of the provision in respect of which it is given; and

(b) is not binding on the parties to the proceedings in which it is made.'

Our courts do not therefore enjoy or exercise the same powers as the Supreme Court in America, which, under their written Constitution, are able to strike down as unconstitutional legislation passed by Congress which violates and is contrary to the provisions of the American Constitution. Our courts cannot give a provision in domestic primary legislation the equivalent of the judicial red card, thereby invalidating it as being unconstitutional – another manifestation of parliamentary supremacy and the sovereignty of our Parliament.

Section 6: public authorities offering IVF beware!

17.10 Section 6 of HRA 1998 is incontrovertibly of fundamental importance in protecting and safeguarding the human rights of patients refused, eg, IVF treatment by a clinic offering IVF, or by a Primary Care Trust (PCT) or Strategic Health Authority (SHA) offering IVF. It also effectively provides the basis for an aggrieved patient challenging such a refusal by a public authority under HRA 1998, and it furnishes aggrieved patients with a fourth ground for judicially reviewing such a decision (the other three grounds being irrationality, procedural impropriety and illegality or *ultra vires*), namely that a decision has been reached by the public authority which does not comply with and has violated the ECHR. Section 6 provides:

> '(1) It is unlawful for a public authority to act in a way which is incompatible with a Convention right.'

However, s 6(2) provides some leeway for the public authority and stipulates:

> 'Subsection (1) does not apply to an act if—
> (a) as the result of one or more provisions of primary legislation, the authority could not have acted differently; or
> (b) in the case of one or more provisions of, or made under, primary legislation which cannot be read or given effect in a way which is compatible with the Convention rights, the authority was acting so as to give effect to or enforce those provisions.'

Then s 6(3), (4) and (5) of HRA 1998 defines (not terribly felicitously and arguably very nebulously and opaquely) what is meant by a 'public authority':

> '(3) In this section 'public authority' includes—
> (a) a court or tribunal, and
> (b) any person certain of whose functions are functions of a public nature, but does not include either House of Parliament or a person exercising functions in connection with proceedings in Parliament.
> (4) In subsection (3) 'Parliament' does not include the House of Lords in its judicial capacity.
> (5) In relation to a particular act, a person is not a public authority by virtue only of subsection (3) (b) if the nature of the act is private.'

Finally, s 6(6) of HRA 1998 provides, inter alia, '"An act" includes a failure to act'.

17.11 Section 7 of the HRA is significant if, for example, a patient were to challenge a decision of a public authority (eg a PCT or SHA) refusing him or her IVF treatment and the patient was arguing that the PCT or SHA had acted in contravention of HRA 1998 and one or more of the Convention rights. Section 7(1) provides:

> 'A person who claims that a public authority has acted (or proposes to act) in a way which is made unlawful by section 6 (1) may—
> (a) bring proceedings against the authority under this Act in the appropriate court or tribunal, or
> (b) rely on the Convention right or rights concerned in any legal proceedings,
> but only if he is (or would be) a victim of the unlawful act.'

This section thus confirms that the claimant or aggrieved citizen is given both a sword (ie is able to bring proceedings against the erring public authority under the HRA 1998, so using the Convention offensively to assert the claimant or patient's rights), and a shield (ie they are able to rely on Convention rights in any legal proceedings, so using the Convention as a defence).

17.12 Section 7(2) of HRA 1998 defines what an 'appropriate court or tribunal' is under s 7(1)(a) and provides that it:

'means such court or tribunal as may be determined in accordance with rules; and proceedings against an authority include a counterclaim or similar proceeding.'

Then s 7(3) stipulates:

'If the proceedings are brought on an application for judicial review, the applicant is to be taken to have a sufficient interest in relation to the unlawful act only if he is, or would be, a victim of that act.'

Litigants under HRA 1998 must, therefore, be 'victims' of an unlawful act under the Act, as opposed to interested parties.

17.13 With regard to when, eg, an aggrieved party or claimant must commence proceedings under the HRA 1998, s 7(5) provides generally proceedings must be brought within:

- one year of the 'act complained of'; or
- 'such longer period as the court or tribunal considers equitable having regard to all the circumstances ... but that is subject to any rule imposing a stricter time limit in relation to the procedure in question.'

This means that a claimant or aggrieved patient who contends that his human rights under the ECHR have been violated must generally, subject to s 5(2)(b), commence proceedings within one year of the date on which the act complained of took place. This is a considerably shorter limitation time than, eg, that for commencing proceedings in tort (three years) or in contract (six years). So the patient claimant needs to be very quick out of the legal block to uphold and vindicate his human rights.

17.14 Section 7(6) of HRA 1998 partially explains what constitutes 'legal proceedings':

'In subsection (1)(b) "legal proceedings" includes—
(a) proceedings brought by or at the instigation of a public authority; and
(b) an appeal against the decision of a court or tribunal.'

So under s 7(6)(a) if a public authority brings or instigates proceedings against a patient, that patient can rely on the Convention rights as a possible available defence in the legal proceedings.

17.15 Section 7(7) of HRA 1998 provides also that:

'For the purposes of this section, a person is a victim of an unlawful act only if he would be a victim for the purposes of Article 34 of the Convention if proceedings were brought in the European Court of Human Rights in respect of that act.'

Importantly too, s 7(8) provides that:

'Nothing in this Act creates a criminal offence.'

17.16 Of patent significance to the patient or claimant is what legal and judicial remedies can be obtained under the Act. Section 8 provides, inter alia:

> '(1) In relation to any act (or proposed act) of a public authority which the court finds is (or would be) unlawful, it may grant such relief or remedy, or make such order, within its powers as it considers just and appropriate.'

However, the award of damages to the patient or claimant for a violation of their ECHR rights is not straightforward, as is seen in s 8(2), (3) and (4).

17.17 Section 8(2) stipulates:

> 'But damages may be awarded only by a court which has power to award damages, or to order the payment of compensation, in civil proceedings.'

Also under s 8(3):

> 'No award of damages is to be made unless, taking account of all the circumstances of the case, including—
> (a)   any other relief or remedy granted, or order made, in relation to the act in question (by that or any other court), and
> (b)   the consequences of any decision (of that or any other court) in respect of that act,
> the court is satisfied that the award is necessary to afford just satisfaction to the person in whose favour it is made.'

Basically no damages will be awarded to the patient claimant unless the court is satisfied that the award of damages is necessary to afford just satisfaction to that claimant.

17.18   Finally, s 8(4) provides:

> 'In determining—
> (a)   whether to award damages, or
> (b)   the amount of an award,
> the court must take into account the principles applied by the European Court of Human Rights in relation to the award of compensation under Article 41 of the Convention.'

Again, a further criticism would be that the domestic court must only take into account the principles applied by the ECtHR in relation to awarding compensation under Art 41 of the ECHR, but the domestic UK court is not bound by those principles, which could again be considered a half-hearted commitment to the protection of human rights.

REPRODUCTIVE MEDICINE: THE SALIENT ECHR ARTICLES

17.19 Several Articles of the ECHR theoretically impact on the sphere of human reproductive medicine and specifically, eg accessing infertility treatments.

Article 2: right to life

17.20 Article 2 is a fundamental human right but it is not absolute. There are exceptions to it recognised and indeed explicitly built into the ECHR itself in

Art 2(2)(a), (b) and (c) (see below), namely the right to life does not have to be protected necessarily where deprivation of life occurs when it results from the use of force which is no more than absolutely necessary, for example in defence of any person from unlawful violence (ie this would include a self-defence scenario), in order to effect a lawful arrest or prevent the escape of a person lawfully detained, or in action lawfully taken for the purpose of quelling a riot or insurrection. In the United Kingdom self-defence has been accepted as a defence to a murder charge for centuries. Art 2 provides:

> '(1) Everyone's right to life shall be protected by law. No one shall be deprived of his life intentionally save in the execution of a sentence of a court following his conviction of a crime for which this penalty is provided by law.' and
> '(2) Deprivation of life shall not be regarded as inflicted in contravention of this Article when it results from the use of force which is no more than absolutely necessary:
>> (a) in defence of any person from unlawful violence,
>> (b) in order to effect a lawful arrest or to prevent the escape of a person lawfully detained;
>> (c) in action lawfully taken for the purpose of quelling a riot or insurrection.'

17.21 Article 2 – the 'right to life' – might at first glance be viewed as being significant in protecting the right to life of the embryo to be experimented on in human embryonic research. But the human embryo does not appear to have a right to life, nor certainly one that is protected by the ECHR. An embryo is not therefore included in the term 'Everyone's'.

Article 6: right to a fair trial

17.22 The salient part of this article in the context of human reproductive medicine is:

> '(1) In the determination of his civil rights and obligations or of any criminal charge against him, everyone is entitled to a fair and public hearing within a reasonable time by an independent and impartial tribunal established by law.'

This article could arguably be relied upon by an aggrieved patient claimant, arguing that, eg, a decision to refuse them fertility treatment (IVF) resulted from an unfair hearing by a licensed clinic.[4]

Article 8: right to respect for family and private life

17.23 This Article is potentially, and in fact has proven to be, highly significant in the context of persons seeking access to infertility treatment. It states:
> '(1) Everyone has the right to respect for his private and family life, his home and his correspondence.
> (2) There shall be no interference by a public authority with the exercise of this right except such as is in accordance with the law

---

4   See HFEA Code of Practice.

and is necessary in a democratic society in the interests of national security, public safety or the economic well-being of the country, for the prevention of disorder or crime, for the protection of health or morals, or for the protection of the rights and freedoms of others.'

17.24 Again, this article is fundamental in nature, but it is not absolute. Part of someone's private and family life would arguably include trying to have children by, eg, IVF if a couple had difficulty conceiving, but is this a negative right? Are the state or public authorities only obliged not to deny people this right? Or is it a positive right, namely they are obliged to take steps to facilitate this right being achieved, and if yes, what steps? Clearly, under the terms of Art 2(2) this human right to respect for private and family life can be interfered with (ie limited or restricted) if it is done in accordance with domestic law, and is necessary in a democratic society for a number of reasons, including in the interests of national security (very wide and arguably vague), public safety (equally wide and vague), or the economic well-being of the country, for the prevention of disorder or crime (yet again very broad and unclear), for the protection of health or morals (incredibly wide), or for the protection of the rights and freedoms of others (very wide too, and of course the upholding of the rights of one person has to be balanced and weighed against equally upholding other persons human rights – not an easy task). Also, Art 2(2) means the rights of the individual have to be balanced and weighed up against the wider interests of society too. Human rights of the individual are therefore not always absolute. Again, if there is interference with a human right here, the right to respect for family and private life by a public authority, or indeed in national legislation, that interference must also be for a legitimate aim and moreover the interference must not be disproportionate, ie greater than necessary.

Article 12: right to marry

17.25 This Article could again be potentially invoked by an aggrieved patient claimant or person denied, eg, IVF treatment by an NHS IVF clinic. It states:

'Men and women of marriageable age have the right to marry and to found a family, according to the national laws governing the exercise of this right.'

However, once again this right is arguably a negative right; the state or a public authority cannot prevent men and women from founding a family, but does that mean that they have to positively help them to found a family by providing costly infertility treatments like IVF and ICSI? Surely the state does not have to sign a blank cheque for the individual or couple to fund their treatment?

Article 14: prohibition of discrimination

17.26 The final right relevant to reproductive medicine and accessing infertility treatments is Art 14, which prohibits various forms and types of discrimination. It states:

'The enjoyment of the rights and freedoms set forth in this Convention shall be secured without discrimination on any ground such as sex, race, colour, language, religion, political or other opinion, national or social origin, association with a national minority, property, birth or other status.'

Did the old, s 13(5) of the Human Fertilisation and Embryology Act 1990 discriminate unfairly and contrary to the ECHR and HRA 1998, by including the 'need for a father' clause? According to the then Government (and others), it did, and that was why, inter alia, it was replaced by the 'need for supportive parenting' clause (see Chapters 12 and 13).

Chapter 18

ECHR Square Pegs in Common Law Round Holes

INTRODUCTION

18.1 There have been several cases involving reproductive medicine where human rights, inter alia, have arisen. Some of the decisions in these cases have not surprisingly generated considerable controversy and, for some, reinforced their conviction that the ECHR is being inappropriately and erroneously extended to afford protection to individuals in circumstances not warranting their applicability.

CASES

Dickson

18.2 In *Dickson v United Kingdom (Application 44362/04)*,[1] the Grand Chamber of the ECtHR held that the Home Secretary's refusal to provide a convicted murderer in jail with facilities for artificial insemination violated Art 8 (the right to private and family life) of the ECHR. The applicant, Kirk Dickson, had been convicted of murder and sentenced to life imprisonment in 1994 with a tariff of 15 years set. In prison he had met the second applicant, Lorraine Dickson, via a prison pen-pal network, while she was in prison serving a 12-month sentence. Lorraine Dickson had three children from previous relationships. She was released from prison and in 2001 the applicants married.

18.3 In December 2002 they both applied for facilities for artificial insemination on the basis that it was unlikely they would be able to have a child together without artificial insemination, given that Kirk Dickson's earliest release date was 2009 and that Lorraine Dickson was then aged 51. The Home Secretary refused their application in a letter in which he set out the government's policy regarding provision of artificial insemination facilities and why he had refused their application in applying the government policy.

Government policy

18.4 Government policy, inter alia, stated that 'requests for artificial insemination by prisoners are carefully considered on individual merit and will only be granted in exceptional circumstances,' and that in reaching a decision 'particular attention' should be given to a range of considerations, including whether:

---

1   [2007] All ER (D) 59 (Dec).

(a)   the provision of artificial insemination facilities is the only means by which conception is likely to occur;

(b)   the prisoner's expected day of release is so distant that he would be unable to assume the responsibilities of a parent;

(c)   the couple were in a well-established and stable relationship before imprisonment which is likely to subsist after the prisoner's release;

(d)   there is any evidence to suggest that the couple's domestic circumstances and the arrangements for the welfare of the child are satisfactory, including the length of time for which the child might expect to be without a father or mother; and

(e)   having regard to the prisoner's history, antecedents and other relevant factors there is evidence to suggest that it would not be in the public interest to provide artificial insemination.

18.5   The Home Secretary justified his decision to refuse the applicant's artificial insemination stating in a letter to Kirk Dickson that he:

'... had particular regard to the likely age of your wife at the time that you will become eligible for release ... and therefore the likelihood of her being able to conceive naturally is small.'

The minister conceded that the applicants were in total agreement about conceiving artificially and were also fully committed to each other. However, the minister maintained that given their relationship had been established in prison, axiomatically it had therefore yet to be tested in the normal environment of daily life. 'A reasoned and objective assessment cannot be made as to whether your relationship will subsist after your release.'

18.6   The minister also stated in the letter that he was 'concerned that there seems to be insufficient provision in place to provide independently for the material welfare of any child which may be conceived.' Furthermore, 'there seems to be little in the way of an immediate support network in place for the mother and any child which may be conceived' and that, 'it also remains a matter of deep concern that any child which might be conceived would be without the presence of a father for an important part of his or her childhood years.' The minister, whilst noting Kirk's good behaviour in prison, 'nevertheless notes the violent circumstances of the crime for which you were sentenced to life imprisonment' (kicking a man to death), and that:

'it is considered that there would be legitimate public concern that the punitive and deterrent elements of your sentence of imprisonment were being circumvented if you were allowed to father a child by artificial insemination while in prison.'

18.7   The applicants then proceeded unsuccessfully to seek leave to apply for judicial review of the Home Secretary's refusal in the High Court and also, unanimously, in the Court of Appeal, before going to the the European Court of Human Rights. The Chamber of the ECtHR held there was no violation of Art 8.[2]

2   ([2006] All ER (D) 219 (Apr).

18.8 The Grand Chamber cited and relied on *Hirst v United Kingdom (No2) (Application 74025/01),*[3] concerning the potential scope of restrictions on prisoners' rights while incarcerated. In *Hirst*, which concerned a prisoner's right to vote, the ECtHR said:

'prisoners in general continue to enjoy all the fundamental rights and freedoms guaranteed under the Convention save for the right to liberty, where lawfully imposed detention expressly falls within the scope of Art 5'.

In other words prisoners legitimately and in compliance with the ECHR lose and expect to lose their liberty, but they do not thereby lose the full gamut or panoply of other human rights enshrined in and protected by the ECHR. Indeed in *Hirst* the ECtHR stated;

'There is, therefore, no question that a prisoner forfeits his Convention rights merely because of his status as a person detained following conviction... nor is there any place under the Convention system, where tolerance and broadmindedness are the acknowledged hallmarks of democratic society, for automatic disenfranchisement based purely on what might offend public opinion.'

18.9 Governments and public authorities must avoid playing to the gallery of public opinion, but rather must concentrate on singing from the ECHR songsheet and basically complying with the human rights set out in the Convention. As the author observed:

'Enforcement of Convention rights, therefore, must not depend on populist whim and avoidance of giving offence to the fickle, shifting sands of public opinion.'[4]

The Grand Chamber, therefore, stated:

'Accordingly, a person retains his ... Convention rights on imprisonment, so that any restriction on those rights must be justified in each individual case.'

The author noted that:

'The state, therefore, can legitimately justify restrictions on a prisoner's Convention rights based on the necessary and inevitable consequences of imprisonment, or alternatively from an adequate link between the restriction and the circumstances of the prisoner in question, but it cannot automatically disenfranchise, based purely on what might offend public opinion.'[5]

18.10 The Grand Chamber stated that the question concerning whether the refusal of the requested facilities was essentially a positive or negative state obligation was arguably a distinction without a difference in that:

'the boundaries between the state's positive and negative obligations under Art 8 do not lend themselves to precise definition. The applicable principles are nonetheless similar ... in both instances regard must be had to the fair balance to be struck between the competing interests.'

In addition the ECtHR emphasised that:

---

3   [2005] All ER (D) 59 (Oct).
4   S Burns, 'The killer question' (2001) 158 NLJ 362–363, at 362.
5   Ibid, at 363.

'[the] core issue in the present case ... is precisely whether a fair balance was struck between the competing public and private interests involved'.

Yet again the human rights of the individual are crucial but not absolute. They have to be weighed in the scales against sometimes competing and conflicting public interests, never mind the conflicting interests of other individuals.

18.11 The ECtHR accepted that artificial insemination remained the only realistic hope of the applicants having a child together, given the woman's age (then 51), and the man's release date in 2009. Then the ECtHR proceeded to consider the three main objections of the UK government to providing the applicants with artificial insemination and rejected all three.

Inability to have a child – inevitable consequence of imprisonment?

18.12 The ECtHR said that:

'while the inability to beget a child might be a consequence of imprisonment, it is not an inevitable one, it not being suggested that the grant of artificial insemination facilities would involve any security issues or impose any significant administrative or financial demands on the state.'

This was particularly true since the Dicksons would be paying privately for the facility.

Maintaining public confidence in the penal system and punishment

18.13 The ECtHR conceded that whilst maintaining public confidence in the penal system had a role to play in the development of penal policy and that punishment was a legitimate aim of imprisonment, these were not the only important considerations. It emphasised:

'There is no place under the Convention system, where tolerance and broadmindedness are the acknowledged hallmarks of democratic society, for automatic forfeiture of rights by prisoners based purely on what might offend public opinion'.

Put bluntly, the views of the public (but how representative are these so-called views?) should not dictate that convicted murderers necessarily should forfeit all or some of their human rights other than forfeiting their liberty (deprivation of a key human right which is after all protected by Art 5 of the ECHR) and being incarcerated. Prisoners are not lost souls. Some attempt ought to be made at rehabilitation. The court, therefore, stated that at the end of a prison sentence evolving European penal policy should rather focus more on the 'rehabilitative aim of imprisonment'.

Concerns for the welfare of the child

18.14 Here the court conceded that the UK authorities, when developing penal policy, 'should concern themselves, as a matter of principle, with the welfare of any child,' and ensure the effective protection of children. However, the court said that as laudable an objective as ensuring the effective protection of children was, that:

'... cannot go so far as to prevent parents who so wish from attempting to conceive a child in circumstances like those of the present case, especially as the second applicant was at liberty and could have taken care of any child conceived until such time as her husband was released'.

At the end of the day there are lots of children being brought up 'naturally' by effectively one parent, be it as a result of death, divorce, separation, desertion etc.

Margin of appreciation

18.15 Under the ECHR, and as evident in many cases involving the ECHR, Member States are normally given a margin of appreciation regarding the assessment of where a fair balance lies in a case, between the public and private interests involved, and the Grand Chamber emphasised this 'will also usually be a wide margin,' in a case like this in particular given there is no consensus in Member States. The author noted: 'However, the UK legislature and judiciary had failed to weigh the competing interests or assess the proportionality of the relevant restriction on prisoners.' Hence, the restriction was tantamount to 'a blunt instrument', which:

'indiscriminately stripped a significant category of prisoners of their Convention rights and it imposed a blanket and automatic restriction on all convicted prisoners irrespective of the length of their sentence, the nature or gravity of their offence or of their individual circumstances'.[6]

The Grand Chamber admitted that more than half of the Member States (who were signatories of the ECHR) permitted conjugal visits for prisoners, thereby arguably obviating the need for the authorities to provide additional facilities for artificial insemination, but that in the final analysis the UK policy as structured:

'effectively excluded any real weighting of the competing individual and public interests, and prevented the required assessment of the proportionality of a restriction, in any individual case'.

18.16 The author also noted:

'The court was concerned that the UK policy set the threshold so high against the applicants from the outset that it did not allow a balancing of the competing individual and public interests and a proportionality test by the secretary of state or by the domestic courts because the applicants had to demonstrate as a condition precedent to the application of the policy, that the deprivation of artificial insemination facilities might prevent conception altogether. More significantly, they had to then demonstrate that the circumstances of their case were "exceptional" within the meaning of the remaining criteria of the policy. The court was clear, therefore, that the policy placed an inordinately high "exceptionality" burden on the applicants. Finally, since the policy was not embodied in primary legislation, the various competing interests were never weighed, nor were issues of proportionality ever assessed by Parliament.'

---

6   Ibid.

In essence the policy appeared to be a very crude blunderbuss or instrument designed to achieve a dubious aim contrary to human rights.

Bottom line

18.17 The court concluded that while the government policy was not a blanket ban, as was the case in *Hirst*,[7] since a quarter of similar applications had been granted, these statistics did not 'undermine the above finding that the policy did not permit the required proportionality assessment in an individual case.' Furthermore, as the author has noted: 'The court also rejected the spurious defence of justification, ie the minimal number of people adversely affected by the government policy.'[8] The Grand Chamber held, therefore, that Art 8 was violated by this government policy.

18.18 The author commented on the significance of the case:

'Populist opinion might be outraged by the proposition that a convicted murderer in prison should have the right in prison to artificial insemination facilities, and for some this might appear the thin end of the wedge of unelected judges bestowing preposterous rights on a category of undeserving citizens, but others would welcome this decision as being tangible evidence of an enlightened ECtHR in action, vigorously championing human rights for all. For them the litmus test of a civilised society is how it treats its most vulnerable, vilified and marginalised members. Some might see the ECtHR, with considerable adroitness in this case, lending credence to the rule of law, namely that the law applies equally to everyone.'[9]

The case was certainly a huge fillip to infertile couples attempting to use the ECHR and the deployment of human rights as a sword to advance the cause of greater access to infertility treatments, albeit paid for privately here.

18.19 The scope and extent of the human rights of prisoners has been of very recent topical concern following the ruling of the ECtHR in the *Hirst* case, which inter alia held that the United Kingdom's blanket ban on a prisoner's right to vote in elections was contrary to the ECHR. The ECtHR did not rule or specify that all prisoners must be allowed to vote, but merely that the blanket ban on all prisoners voting violated the ECHR. The ruling needless to say incurred the wrath of many in the United Kingdom, including the Prime Minister David Cameron, who said that giving prisoners the vote made him feel 'physically ill'. In the *Hirst* case, John Hirst, who had been convicted of manslaughter, had successfully argued before the ECtHR that his human rights had been violated by being barred from voting in elections. The government, in response to the ECtHR ruling, had indicated they were contemplating giving voting rights to all prisoners serving under four years. However, as BBC News reported on 20 January 2011,[10] if all prisoners serving less than four years' imprisonment were granted the right (and privilege) of voting, that would:

---

7   *Hirst v United Kingdom (No2) (Application 74025/01)*, fn 3 above.
8   Ibid.
9   Ibid.
10   www.bbc.co.uk/news/uk-politics-12233938

'involve granting the vote to up to 28,000 prisoners, including 6,000 jailed for violent crime, more than 1,700 sex offenders, more than 4,000 burglars and 4,300 imprisoned for drug offences.'

For many law-abiding voters this scenario would be unconscionable and morally repugnant.

18.20 However, Hirst himself, arguably correctly, said that the law applied equally to all, including prisoners, and that law included rulings by the ECtHR. He contended: 'If I'd have gone to court and said I'm not accepting a judge's life sentence where would that put us?' and added, 'You have to accept that the law applies to everybody and it applies to the government, and David Cameron is not above the law and he'll find out that very shortly.' However following the House of Commons free vote, which is not binding on the government, on 10 February 2011, when MPs voted overwhelmingly to reject giving prisoners the right to vote, the government intimated that they are inclined to possibly limit the right to vote to prisoners sentenced to a year or less imprisonment. Sadiq Khan MP, the Shadow Justice Secretary, welcomed the government's U-turn and stated:

'The government should be standing up for the victims of crime but instead they are slashing police numbers and giving dangerous convicted prisoners the vote.'

Interestingly, Ministry of Justice figures for England and Wales at the end of 2010 show that 1,551 inmates convicted of violence against the person are serving less than one year in prison and that there were 229 people convicted of sexual offences in the same bracket – as David Davis MP, arguably correctly, noted: 'People serving one year have committed quite serious offences.'

Evans

18.21 In *Evans v United Kingdom (Application 6339/05),*[11] the ECtHR rejected Ms Evan's appeal and argument that her Art 8 rights (respect for private and family rights) were violated. In this case, Natalie Evans, following a diagnosis of pre-cancerous tumours, had both of her ovaries removed. Before this surgery, 11 of her eggs were harvested from her ovaries and mixed with the sperm of her then partner, Howard Johnston. The resulting six embryos created were then frozen for subsequent implantation.

18.22 At the consultation at the IVF clinic, before the collection of the gametes, in accordance with the 1990 Act, both parties signed a written form consenting to the IVF treatment. The nurse at a meeting with the couple explained that it would be possible for either of them to withdraw their consent at any time before the embryos were implanted in Ms Evan's uterus. Significantly too, the respective consent forms for the couple also stated: 'You may vary the terms of this consent at any time except in relation to sperm or embryos which have been already used.'

18.23 Sadly, in May 2002, the couple's relationship broke up. Ms Evans' cancer treatment was successful and her cancer went into remission. She was now in a

---

11 [2006] All ER (D) 82 (Mar).

position to try and get pregnant with the frozen embryos being implanted in her. Unfortunately Mr Johnston wrote to the IVF clinic revoking his consent to the use and storage of the embryos and furthermore asked that they be allowed to perish under the 1990 Act, Sch 3, para 8(2). If unchallenged, Ms Evans would thereby lose her last chance to have a child that was biologically hers. Ms Evans unsuccessfully sought an injunction in both the High Court and the Court of Appeal requiring Mr Johnston to restore his consent, and a declaration that he had not varied and could not vary his consent.

ECtHR judgment

18.24   The ECtHR rejected Ms Evans' appeal, by a 5–2 majority, emphasising the fundamental importance of consent enshrined in the 1990 Act, and 'the primacy of continuing bilateral consent…' up until the implantation of the embryos. Consent and the need for consent in a certain form, ie in writing, effective and not withdrawn, as per Sch 3, para 1 of the 1990 Act is one of the central legal pillars and ethical foundations supporting and underpinning the assisted reproductive regulatory regime. The author has noted:

'HFEA 1990, s 12(c) – applicable to storage, treatment and research licences – states that HFEA 1990, Sch 3 "shall" be complied with, ie there is a mandatory or "bright-line" requirement.'[12]

In addition, Sch 3, para 3(1) says, inter alia:

'A consent … must be given in writing and … [effective consent] means a consent … which has not been withdrawn, by notice given by the person who gave the consent to the person keeping the … embryo'.

The author has commented:

'The legal importance of consent was manifest in two earlier cases. In *R v Human Fertilisation and Embryology Authority, ex p Blood* [1997] 2 FCR 501 Diane Blood was refused permission to use her dead husband's sperm in the UK because he had never given his written consent to the procedures. In *Leeds Teaching Hospital NHS Trust v A* [2003] EWHC 259 (QB), [2003] All ER (D) 374 (Feb) a white woman was mistakenly inseminated with a black man's sperm resulting in the birth of mixed-race children, and it was held that the white man was not the legal father of the children as he had not consented in writing to his wife being inseminated by effectively a sperm donor.'[13]

18.25   The ECtHR noted that several other EU countries, including Denmark, France, Greece and Switzerland, mirrored the UK position of giving either party the right to withdraw consent up to the moment of implantation. In addition, significantly, the Council of Europe Convention on Human Rights and Biomedicine, Art 5 provides: 'The person concerned may freely withdraw consent at any time.'[14]

---

12   S Burns, 'Is a bright-line the right line?' (2006) 156 NLJ 565.
13   Ibid, at 565.
14   Note that the United Kingdom is not a signatory of this Convention.

18.26 The ECtHR held that there was no violation of ECHR, Art 2 (the right to life) since 'in the absence of any European consensus on the scientific and legal definition of the beginning of life … [the issue was] within [each state's] margin of appreciation,' and that this margin 'must be a wide one'.

18.27 Regarding Ms Evans' argument that her Art 8 right to private and family life was violated by the decision to permit her former partner to revoke his consent, given that use of the frozen embryos 'represented her only chance to have a child to whom she was biologically related', the court said:

> '[it did] not accept that the Art 8 rights of the male donor would necessarily be less worthy of protection than those of the female; nor [did] it regard it as self-evident that the balance of interests would always tip decisively in favour of the female party'.

The ECtHR thus held that the UK consent requirements encapsulated in the 1990 Act were accordingly valid and compliant with human rights. The consent requirements cut both ways. If the man had testicular cancer and had his sperm mixed with his partner's eggs, as a reproductive insurance lifeline, before embarking on cancer treatment, and the partner split up with him in the meantime and then like Mr Johnston revoked her consent to the continued storage of the embryos in writing, the embryos would equally have to be allowed to perish. Hence Art 8 applied to the couple equally ('the fair balance').

18.28 Finally the ECtHR was adamant that 'strong policy considerations' entitled Parliament to enact a bright-line rule to 'produce legal certainty and … maintain public confidence in the law in a highly sensitive field'. They noted also that the 1990 Act 'was the culmination of an exceptionally detailed examination of the social, ethical and legal implications of developments' in the field, and the 'primacy of the continuing consent…' of both parties to treatment was a fully legitimate bright-line to be drawn.

The author remarked:

> 'The decision demonstrates the lack of consensus in European countries about if and when a party can revoke their consent once embryos have been created and stored for future use. The glimmer of hope for Ms Evans is that Parliament may in the future decide to exercise its margin of appreciation and redraw its bright-line, by "making the consent of the male donor irrevocable…" or by moving it to the "point of creation of the embryo…". Alternatively Ms Evans may decide to appeal the decision to the ECtHR's Grand Chamber (consisting of 17 judges), which could offer her the life-line she seeks.'

18.29 This is in fact the route Ms Evans did in fact take. Parliament has indeed subsequently, in the 2008 Act, redrawn its legal and arguably ethical bright-line. Now, since October 2009, the 2008 Act has amended the 1990 Act by inserting a new para 4A(1) after para 4 of Sch 3 of the 1990 Act. New para 4A(1) provides:

> '(1) This paragraph applies where—
>> (a) a permitted embryo, the creation of which was brought about *in vitro*, is in storage.
>> (b) it was created for use in providing treatment services,
>> (c) before it is used in providing treatment services, one of the persons whose gametes were used to bring about its creation

('P') gives the person keeping the embryos notice withdrawing P's consent to the storage of the embryo, and

(d)   the embryo was not to be used in providing treatment services to P alone.

(2)   The person keeping the embryo must as soon as possible take all reasonable steps to notify each interested person in relation to the embryo of P's withdrawal of consent.

(3)   For the purposes of subparagraph (2), a person is an interested person in relation to an embryo if the embryo was to be used in providing treatment services to that person.

(4)   Storage of the embryo remains lawful until—

(a)   the end of the period of 12 months beginning with the day on which the notice mentioned in sub-paragraph (1) was received by P, or

(b)   if, before the end of that period, the person keeping the embryo receives a notice from each person notified of P's withdrawal under sub-paragraph (2) stating that the person consents to the destruction of the embryo, the time at which the last of those notices is received.

(5)   The reference in sub-paragraph (1)(a) to a permitted embryo is to be read in accordance with section 3ZA.'

18.30   The new law arguably expressly covers and addresses the *Evans* scenario. So, if an *Evans* type scenario were to occur in 2012, Mr Johnston could still write in to the clinic storing the former couple's embryos withdrawing his consent to their storage. The person keeping the embryos would then have to contact Ms Evans as soon as possible notifying her of Johnston's decision to withdraw his consent, *but* the embryos would not be de-thawed and allowed to perish for a *further* 12 months from the day on which the notice withdrawing his consent was received by the person keeping the couple's embryos, ie from Johnston. This reform of the law does not entirely address the wishes or claims of Ms Evans or someone in a similar position to her, but arguably it is a fairer re-casting and recalibration of the law to meet the alleged harshness of the old law contained in the original, un-amended 1990 Act.

The Grand Chamber decision

18.31   Ms Evans appealed the decision of the ECtHR to the Grand Chamber of the ECtHR, comprised of 17 judges, which delivered its judgment on 10 April 2007. As well as seeking an injunction requiring Johnston to restore his consent to the use and storage of the embryos and a declaration that he could not vary his original consent, she also sought a declaration of incompatibility under the HRA 1998, that the 1990 Act, s 12 and Sch 3 (basically requiring bilateral consent) breached her Arts 8, 12 and 14 ECHR rights, and also that the embryos were entitled to protection under Arts 2 and 8 of the ECHR.

18.32   The Grand Chamber referred to the deliberations of the Warnock Committee Report of 1984,[15] the precursor to the 1990 Act, which recommended that if a couple separated, since there was no right of ownership

---

15   Warnock Committee *Report of the Committee of Inquiry into Human Fertilisation and Embryology,* (Cmnd 9314) (London: HMSO: 1984) (the Warnock Report), para 10.11.

in a human embryo, one party to the disagreement could not require use of the embryo contrary to the wishes of the other party. In addition further support for Johnston's submission could be found in the white paper report, *Human Fertilisation and Embryology: A Framework for Legislation,*[16] which stated (at para 57): 'Donors would have the right to vary or withdraw their consent before the gametes/embryos were used.'

18.33 The court referred specifically to para 2(2)(b) of Sch 3 to the 1990 Act which, inter alia, provides: 'The terms of the consent may be withdrawn, in accordance with this schedule either generally or in relation to a particular embryo or particular embryos.' Also, para 4(1) stipulates that:

'The terms of any consent under this schedule may from time to time be varied, and the consent may be withdrawn, by notice given by the person who gave the consent to the person keeping the gametes or embryo to which the consent is relevant.'

The author has noted here:

'Unless there is effective consent from a gamete's owner (see paras 5(1) and 6(1)), then it cannot be used. The requirement of continuing consent from both parties up until implantation of the embryos is viewed as one of the two central pillars of HFEA 1990 – the other being the welfare of the child.'[17]

18.34 The court also held that, relying on *Vo v France (Application 53924/00)*:[18]

'in the absence of any European consensus on the scientific and legal definition of the beginning of life, the issue of when the right to life begins comes within the margin of appreciation which the court generally considers that state should enjoy in this sphere'.

Therefore the 'embryo does not have independent rights or interests and cannot claim … a right to life under Art 2'.

18.35 In addition, Evans's argument that her Art 8(1) rights were violated by virtue of the 1990 Act, effectively preventing her from using the couple's embryos and thereby denying her the opportunity permanently of having a child that was genetically hers, was also rejected. The author has also noted:

'To further complicate the situation, the *Evans* case does not merely involve a conflict between individuals, but there are equally weighty public policy/ public interest dimensions that must be considered too. As the court said;

"The legislation in question also served a number of wider, public interests, in upholding the principle of the primacy of consent and promoting legal clarity and certainty, ie domestic legislation promoting and enshrining 'bright-lines'".'[19]

18.36 In marked contrast to the domestic courts in this case, which regarded the 1990 Act as interfering in Evans's Art 8 rights, the Grand Chamber held

---

16 November 1987 (Cm 259).
17 S Burns, 'Terms of law' (2007) 157 NLJ 736–737.
18 [2004] 2 FCR 577.
19 S Burns, 'Terms of Law' (fn 17 above), p 736.

that the case concerned a positive obligation 'whether the legislative provisions as applied in the present case struck a fair balance between the competing public and private interests involved'. Next, the question arose: 'What did Johnston give his consent to?' The court answered that it was sure he had, 'never consented to the applicant using the jointly created embryos alone – his consent being limited to undergoing 'treatment together' with the applicant'. The Grand Chamber examined a number of other jurisdictions and did a very useful comparative analysis of these other countries' approaches to the vexed issue of withdrawing of consent, and noted, as did the ECtHR, that in five countries, ie Denmark, France, Greece, the Netherlands and Switzerland, the right of either party freely to withdraw their consent 'at any stage up to the moment of implantation of the embryo in the woman is expressly provided for in the primary legislation'. Hence, the adoption of a crystal clear legal rule or ethical bright-line is not therefore confined to the United Kingdom. The author has noted that:

> 'The position in the US is understandably more complex, given there are 50 states. The federal legislatures, and indeed the state legislatures, have not regulated in this area of consent, and have abdicated this responsibility to the courts, from which unclear guidance has emerged on the question of which party's consent prevails.'[20]

18.37 In favour of Ms Evans' arguments is the position in Israel. As the author has noted:

> 'The most favourable precedent for Evans was the Israeli Supreme Court decision in *Nachmani v Nachmani* (50 (4) PD 661 (Isr)). The facts were broadly similar to *Evans*, except a surrogate mother was involved. A majority (7–4) found the woman's interests and her lack of alternatives to achieve genetic parenthood outweighed those of the man. This case is of course only of persuasive, not binding authority as a precedent.'[21]

18.38 The Grand Chamber, like the ECtHR, considered the margin of appreciation and set out several factors to be considered concerning the extent of the margin of appreciation that was permissible for states in framing domestic legislation which was compatible with Art 8. The court said:

> 'Where ... there is no consensus within the Member States of the Council of Europe, either as to the relative importance of the interest at stake or as to the means of protecting it particularly where the case raises sensitive moral or ethical issues, the margin will be wider.'

This is arguably stating the obvious and sensible.

18.39 The court also stated that the margin of appreciation afforded to individual Member States will be a 'wider margin if the state is required,' as here, 'to strike a balance between competing private and public interests or Convention rights'. In addition, the court also held that the issues in the *Evans* case were undoubtedly of a morally and ethically delicate nature and that there was no consensus in Europe as to the stage in IVF treatment when the gamete

---

20 Ibid, p 737.
21 Ibid.

providers' consent becomes irrevocable. Therefore, they held that the relevant provisions in the 1990 Act did not violate Art 8.

18.40 The author has noted that the Grand Chamber felt that decisions about the principles and policies to be applied in this sensitive field must primarily be for each state to determine.[22] The EU principle of subsidiarity appears to be evident here. The individual Member States are frequently best placed to assess and weigh up crucial priorities and then translate these into appropriate legislation. In passing legislation enshrining the principle of continuing bilateral consent the court held:

> '… the 1990 Act was the culmination of an exceptionally detailed examination of the social, ethical and legal implications of developments in the field of human fertilisation and embryology, and the fruit of much reflection, consideration and debate.'

The Grand Chamber concluded that Evans knew as a matter of law Johnston would be free to withdraw consent to implementation at any moment. The author has commented: 'This is harsh for Evans, but on the basis of the evidence, probably the correct decision.'[23] In fact the decision was incredibly harsh for Evans, but unfortunately for her, the UK legislation was patently clear and unambiguous and sadly human rights compliant, ie it did not violate the ECHR. Fortuitously though, Parliament re-considered the law on this issue and changed it.

18.41 Finally the court held that since Evans' claim under Art 8 failed, so did her claim under Art 14. A finding of a breach of Art 14 hinges on there being a breach of another article. The author commented on the Grand Chamber decision:

> 'One can only have sympathy for Evans' plight in losing her last chance to have a child that is genetically hers, and also it is difficult not to harbour concerns at the waste of scarce embryos, given the levels of infertility in the UK. That said, the Grand Chamber's decision upholds the importance of obtaining effective consent generally as underpinned in HFEA 1990, and to respecting the legal validity of the HFEA 1990 principle of continuing bilateral consent of both gamete providers right up to the moment of implementation. The written terms of the consent form – akin to a legal agreement between the parties – prevail over Evans' terms of endearment, ie her despair at being thwarted in her natural inclination to parent her own biological child, despite her assurances to her former partner that she will forego any maintenance from him for the child's upbringing.'[24]

18.42 The UK Parliament chose deliberately to insist on written consent and effective consent and consents that were not withdrawn by either party. That was not done lightly or by mistake or in error. As the author has commented:

> '"Bright –lines", ie clear rules regarding consent in domestic legislation, are not inconsistent or disproportionate with Convention rights, especially if they strike a fair balance between the parties to IVF treatment.'[25]

22 Ibid.
23 Ibid.
24 Ibid.
25 Ibid.

Finally, the author has also observed:

> 'As the Grand Chamber said, it was spared having to weigh up the merits of one party's respective wishes against the other to calculate which party prevails, an impossible task in an emotionally fraught scenario, because the absolute nature of the rule [on consent] served to promote legal certainty and to avoid the problems of arbitrariness and inconsistency inherent in weighing, on a case by case basis, what the Court of Appeal described as "entirely incommensurable" interests.'[26]

Leeds Teaching Hospital

18.43   Another key case involving reproductive medicine where human rights figured prominently was *Leeds Teaching Hospital NHS Trust v A*.[27] In this case two couples, a white couple, Mr and Mrs A, and a black couple, Mr and Mrs B, were undergoing infertility treatment (ICSI) at the Leeds Teaching Hospital NHS Trust. Mrs A consented to her eggs being used and mixed with her husband's sperm, and equally Mr A, consented to his sperm being used to treat his wife. Neither Mr A nor Mrs A consented to the use of anyone else's eggs or sperm as part of the treatment. Again Mr B consented to his wife, Mrs B, being inseminated by his sperm (as did Mrs B), and did not consent to anything else. Tragically, Mrs A's eggs were inseminated in error by Mr B's sperm, rather than her husband Mr A's sperm, and then implanted in Mrs A. Mrs A then gave birth to mixed race twins.

18.44   Although it had been agreed that Mr and Mrs A would raise the twins, it was necessary to determine who the legal father was. There was no issue who the legal mother was. It was Mrs A, since s 27 of the 1990 Act (now s 33 of the 2008 Act) clearly provides:

> '(1)   The woman who is carrying or has carried a child as a result of the placing in her of an embryo or of sperm and eggs, and no other woman, is to be treated as the mother of the child.'

Arguably, the two main issues in the case were:

(1)   did ss 28 and 29 of the 1990 Act apply to the facts of the case – if they did then Mr A would be the legal father; and

(2)   whether the ECHR, in particular Art 8 (the right to respect for private and family life), had an impact on the statutory regime.

18.45   The Court of Appeal, held, inter alia, that whilst Mr A had given his consent to the placing in his wife of an embryo, the embryo which was placed in his wife was a fundamentally different embryo from the one that might have been created using his own sperm. Thus Mr A clearly had not consented to effectively the sperm of an anonymous donor being mixed with the eggs of his wife, and the embryo that had in fact been created had been created equally clearly without the consent of Mr and Mrs A. Thus s 28(2) of the 1990 Act did not apply, because Mr A wanted his wife to be only inseminated with his sperm and thus should not be treated as the father of the children because 'it is shown that he did not consent to the placing in her of the embryo or the sperm'.

---

26   Ibid
27   [2003] EWHC 259.

18.46 Also, the court held that s 28(3) was inapplicable to Mr A being the legal father of the children, because her eggs were meant to be fertilised with her husband, Mr A's sperm, not by Mr B's sperm, and the embryos that were subsequently meant to be implanted in Mrs A were supposed to be ones created using her eggs and her husband's sperm. They were not, so how could it be contended the embryos were implanted in her or she was artificially inseminated, 'in the course of treatment services provided for her and a man together'. Quite clearly she was not being treated *together* with Mr B. Therefore Mr A was not the legal father of the children under the terms of s 28(3) of the 1990 Act, and Mr B was clearly the biological/genetic father of the children.

18.47 Dame Elizabeth Butler-Sloss, the President of the Family Division of the High Court as she then was, stated, inter alia, that all the parties were agreed that the twins should remain with the family into which they were born, with Mr and Mrs A, that furthermore 'Mrs A gave birth to the twins and is their biological mother. It is equally clear from the DNA tests that Mr B is their biological father.' She also referred to the tragic mix-up blunder as a 'mistake' (which term she said she would use despite its inadequacy as a description of what occurred), and added:

'Behind the legal arguments which occupied the court for three days lies a tragic human story of two families trying to come to terms with the consequences of the mistake.'

She held that at common law Mr B had the status of an unmarried father and would not have parental responsibility by virtue of s 2(2)(b) of the Children Act 1989.

18.48 Butler-Sloss was adamant that, regarding s 28(2) of the 1990 Act not being satisfied:

'On the clear evidence provided in the consent forms Mr A plainly did not consent to the sperm of a named or anonymous donor being mixed with his wife's eggs. This was clearly an embryo created without the consent of Mr A and Mrs A.'

The Court also rejected the argument that using Mr B's sperm was just a simple or mere mistake that did not vitiate the consent of Mr A. Butler-Sloss repudiated this argument stating:

'[it] was entirely contrary to the written consents given by Mr A. This mistake went to the root of the whole process and has had irreparable consequences.'

Section 28(2), therefore, 'did not apply'.

18.49 Concerning s 28(3), Butler -Sloss stated:

'Subsection (2), although limited to husbands, appears to be broader than subsection (3). The husband is to be treated as the father, unless it is shown that he did not consent, that he "opted out". However in subsection (3), by contrast the boot is on the other foot, in that the acceptance of fatherhood has to be shown, which clearly it is not regarding both men in fact. Neither Mr A nor Mr B agreed to or consented in writing to the creation of mixed race children. Under s 28(3), the man has to show commitment and that commitment has to be demonstrated by his active involvement in the treatment together with his wife, which again it patently was not. Mr A must basically "opt in". He did not "opt in".'

Butler-Sloss was, therefore, emphatic that:

'A fundamental error resulting in the use of the sperm of another in place of the use of sperm of the man taking part in the treatment must vitiate the whole concept of "treatment together" for the purposes of the 1990 Act.'

Section 28(3), therefore, 'cannot cover the present facts'. Equally, Mr B did not consent to his sperm being used to fertilise the eggs of Mrs A or anyone else other than his wife. That was evident and could be gleaned easily from the consent forms signed by Mr B. As Butler-Sloss stated: 'His gametes were therefore not used in accordance with the terms of the consent given by him.'

Article 8

18.50 Butler-Sloss stated, concerning Art 8 (right to respect for private and family life), when considering its applicability to the two couples, that, inter alia:

(1) Mrs B 'has no blood relationship with the twins', and 'had no de facto relationship with the twins' – here Art 8 rights were not engaged at all.

(2) Mr B 'is the biological father of the twins in circumstances in which he has had no opportunity to forge any relationship with them'. Family life, 'as understood under art 8 implies close personal ties in addition to parenthood', and Mr B's contact with the twins had been non-existent. Mr B, therefore, does not have a right to respect to family life which has been breached.

(3) Mrs A 'is the natural, biological mother of the children and it is beyond argument that her rights under article 8(1) are clearly engaged in this case.'

(4) Mr A 'is in the position of the father and has established a close relationship with the twins whom he regards as his children, His rights are therefore also clearly engaged under article 8(1)'.

18.51 Butler-Sloss added that the interpretation given to s 28(2) and (3) constitutes an interference with Mr and Mrs A's rights under Art 8(1), but that there are other legal remedies under Art 8(2) which could nonetheless underpin and protect the position of Mr A with regard to the twins. For example, Mr and Mrs A could apply for a residence order giving Mr A parental responsibility, or, if he wants to be the legal father of the twins, Mr A could apply to adopt the twins. The legal remedies would be decided with reference to the welfare and best interests of the children. Butler-Sloss added that 'the interference with the exercise of the rights of Mr and Mrs A under article 8(1) is in accordance with the law.' Moreover:

'It can be properly cured by the legal remedies in our domestic law. The interference is necessary in a democratic society and pursues the legitimate aim of protecting the rights and freedoms of others, in this case the twins. It is proportionate in its aim to provide the necessary protection of the twins whose rights and welfare must predominate'.

In short, in particular Mr A's Art 8 human rights are not violated, nor are his wife's (Mrs A).

The twins' Art 8 rights

18.52 Butler-Sloss stated:

> 'The twins unquestionably have rights ... They are clearly entitled to respect for their family life with their mother, Mrs A, and with Mr A whom they regard as their father ... They have inherited two cultures but, in reality, can only gain real benefit from one during their childhood ... Of all the parties who have undoubtedly suffered from this mistake, the twins, who at present know nothing of it, have had their human rights most obviously and seriously infringed.'

She added that the twins' rights to respect for their family life with their mother and Mr A can be met with appropriate family and adoption orders, and that these orders would be proportionate to the infringements of their rights. Also, Butler-Sloss emphasised the importance both of guaranteeing that the twins 'remain within a loving, stable and secure home' and also 'retain the great advantage of preserving the reality of their paternal identity.' Both of these components are an integral part of the twins' private and family rights under Art 8. Butler-Sloss added that 'truth' is more important here to the twins than 'fictional certainty', and that:

> 'To refuse to recognise Mr B as their biological father is to distort the truth about which some day the twins will have to learn through knowledge of their paternal identity.'

It is surely better that the children are told this earlier in their life rather than discover it in adverse circumstances later on in their lives. She also noted:

> 'The requirement to preserve the truth will not adversely affect their immediate welfare, nor their welfare throughout their childhood. It does not impede the cementing of the permanent relationship of each of them with Mr A, who will act as their father throughout their childhood.'

Butler-Sloss held that the infringement of the twins' Art 8(1) rights is met by the application of Art 8(2), and it is proportionate to those rights for the court not to apply s 28(2) or (3).

18.53 This case again highlights the importance of Art 8 in the context of human reproductive medicine, and signals how crucial for the courts are the human rights of the child or children born following the use of infertility treatment. They mirror the importance of s 13(5) (the welfare of the child principle) of the 1990 Act, when considering whether to offer, eg IVF, ICSI or DI, before offering infertility treatment to a person or couple.

CONCLUSIONS

18.54 The almost daily media coverage on how human rights legislation is being manipulated and interpreted, and arguably abused and misapplied to give human rights protection to allegedly spurious recipients like illegal immigrants, dubious asylum seekers, deviants and even criminals (eg murderers like Dickson), undermines the whole basis of human rights and confidence in them for many people. The rights of the wrongdoer and criminal are seemingly more important than the rights of the victims and general law-abiding population.

That cannot be right, runs the argument. Hence the clarion call for our Parliament to adopt a British Bill of Rights, to pull out of the ECHR, and to ignore the decisions of unelected, unrepresentative foreign judges who have no understanding of the rich legal traditions built on the common law in this country.

However, for the foreseeable future Parliament and British courts cannot ignore ECtHR judgments, or the provisions of the ECHR. Their pivotal role was abundantly clear in the *Dickson*, *Evans* and *Leeds* cases, both as swords and as shields for the litigants and indeed other parties. For would-be-parents or a parent refused eg IVF, recourse to violation of their human rights effectively gives litigants a fourth ground for judicial review when challenging the decision of a PCT or licensed NHS clinic. That must be a good thing.

Part 7

The Human Fertilisation and Embryology Authority – Fit For Purpose In 2012?

Chapter 19

Warnock: The Ethical Compass

BACKGROUND

19.1 The Human Fertilisation and Embryology Authority (HFEA), created in August 1991 in the United Kingdom, was the first body set up in the world to regulate, police and monitor certain treatments to help the infertile have children in the sphere of assisted reproductive medicine. This was perhaps not surprising given that the first IVF, or 'test tube', baby, Louise Brown, was born in 1978 in the United Kingdom following the pioneering work over many years of Professor Robert Edwards and Patrick Steptoe, a Consultant Obstetrician and Gynaecologist. Four years later, in July 1982, the Warnock Committee was set up by the government with the following terms of reference:

'To consider recent and potential developments in medicine and science related to human fertilisation and embryology; to consider what policies and safeguards should be applied, including consideration of the social, ethical and legal implications of these developments; and to make recommendations.'

19.2 In setting the scene and explaining the context for the setting up of the Warnock Committee and its terms of reference, Baroness Warnock observed that:

'The birth of the first child resulting from the technique of *in vitro* fertilisation in July 1978 was a considerable achievement. The technique, long sought, at last successful, opened up new horizons in the alleviation of infertility and in the science of embryology ... It was now possible to observe the very earliest stages of human development, and with these discoveries came the hope of remedying defects at this very early stage.'[1]

The new science, therefore, promised much in medicine's enduring war against disease, suffering and disabilities that perpetually afflict mankind. However Warnock also sounded a cautionary warning:

'However there were also anxieties. There was a sense that events were moving too fast for their implications to be assimilated. Society's views on the new techniques were divided between pride in the technological achievement, pleasure at the new-found means to relieve, at least for some, the unhappiness of infertility, and unease at the apparently uncontrolled advance of science, bringing with it new possibilities for manipulating the early stages of human development.'[2]

---

1   M Warnock, *A Question of Life: The Warnock Report on Human Fertilization and Embryology* (Blackwell, 1995) p 4.
2   Ibid.

19.3 Implicit in this was the recognition that regulation of the new science by primary legislation of Parliament, and, allied to this, policing and monitoring and fundamentally creating a licensing jurisdiction operated by the HFEA, would address directly the concerns about 'unease at the apparently uncontrolled advance of science' and possible 'manipulating' of early human life. The dangers of science advancing rapidly beyond the reach of laws and the safety net of ethical and moral constraints and failing to gain the acceptance or acquiescence of the public was thus a real issue.

19.4 Concerning the scope of the inquiry, Baroness Warnock stated:

> 'In considering our terms of reference, we recognised that we were being asked to examine a sphere of activity still developing, and rapidly changing.'[3]

Assisted reproduction medicine and research is a moving target, and one moving fast. Warnock emphasised:

> 'A common factor linking all the developments, recent or potential, medical or scientific, was the anxiety which they generated in the public mind.'

A flavour of this public anxiety can be gleaned by perusal of some of the tabloid newspaper coverage of developments in embryology, which at times verges on the sensationalist and lurid and also occasionally misrepresents the scientific developments in the sphere and/or their repercussions for society. Warnock added that:

> 'The issues raised [by the Warnock Inquiry] reflect fundamental moral, and often religious, questions which have taxed philosophers and others down the ages.'[4]

The issues covered in the Warnock Report regarding the then (1982–1984) relatively new science of assisted reproductive medicine and research are not actually new, although the science is, but have been argued about in different guises and in different contexts for many years.

19.5 The inquiry delivered its Report in 1984. The Report[5] is popularly and commonly known as the Warnock Report, named after its Chairman, Dame Mary Warnock (now Baroness Warnock). She was a distinguished Professor of Philosophy and Mistress of Girton College, Cambridge and a Senior Research Fellow at St Hugh's College, Oxford University.

THE WARNOCK REPORT: SETTING THE ETHICAL, LEGAL AND MORAL BOUNDARIES OF THE NEW SCIENCE

19.6 One of the key recommendations of the Warnock Report was the creation of a statutory licensing authority (ultimately to become the HFEA) charged with regulating the new infertility services (eg IVF and DI) and research using human embryos. That was because:

---

3   Ibid.
4   Letter from Mary Warnock to the government, 26 June 1984.
5   Warnock Committee, *Report of the Committee of Inquiry into Human Fertilisation and Embryology,* (Cmnd 9314) (London: HMSO: 1984).

'Public concern about the techniques we have discussed need to be reflected in public policy [ie in legislation] ... all the techniques require active regulation and monitoring, even though, as we realise, such restrictions may be regarded by some as infringing clinical or academic freedom.'[6]

Warnock added that whilst:

'It is not our intention to interfere with the duty of the doctor to exercise clinical judgement in treating patients ... Indeed we accept and expect the doctor to be the person who makes the final decision about whether a treatment is likely to succeed, and whether it should be used [nevertheless] ... doctors and scientists work within the moral and legal framework determined by society.'[7]

Moreover Warnock said that they did not and should not depart radically from that framework. Doctors and scientists must operate within a framework broadly acceptable to society. Therefore, they will not be permitted to work in an ethical, moral or legal vacuum or free-for-all. Warnock emphasised that the interests of those directly concerned (presumably infertile patients, or patients keen that embryonic research will yield positive results and eventually hopefully treatments or drugs for their diseases or disabilities), as well as those of society in general, demand that certain legal and ethical safeguards should be applied.

HUMAN FERTILISATION AND EMBRYOLOGY AUTHORITY

19.7   One way to apply 'certain legal and ethical' safeguards was to set up the Human Fertilisation and Embryology Authority (the HFEA), arguably a legal and ethical safeguard itself, but certainly a body designed to ensure that the legal and ethical safeguards set out by Parliament in the 1990 and 2008 Acts respectively are upheld and complied with by doctors and scientists. Warnock stated:

'The protection of the public, which we see as the primary objective of regulation, demands the existence of an authority independent of Government, health authorities, or research institutions.'

The argument is that, unless it is actually independent of government, health authorities, doctors, scientists, researchers, etc and also, perhaps more crucially, it is viewed as separate, it will not command the respect of the public. It will be just viewed as an agency of government which rubber-stamps government edicts and applies government whitewash when necessary. Warnock continued:

'[this] authority should be specifically charged with the responsibility to regulate and monitor practice in relation to those sensitive areas which raise fundamental ethical questions.'[8]

Critically therefore, Warnock recommended,

'the establishment of a new statutory licensing authority to regulate both research and those infertility services which we have recommended should be subject to control.'

6   The Warnock Report, para 13.1.
7   Ibid, para 13.2.
8   Ibid, para 13.3.

Later on, Warnock reinforced the fundamental recommendation underpinning all its other recommendations:

> 'But of all the recommendations we have made, by far the most urgent is the recommendation that a statutory body should be established, within whose powers would fall the licensing and monitoring of provision for infertility treatment and of research on the human embryo. None of our other recommendations can have any practical impact until such a body is set up.'[9]

Composition

19.8   The Warnock Report, whilst at pains to point out that it was not its function to specify the precise size and detailed composition of the new body, noted, nonetheless, that the new body would need access to expert medical and scientific advice. It therefore envisaged a significant representation of scientific and medical interests among the membership.[10] The Report, therefore, readily acknowledged the wisdom of having doctors and specifically experienced gynaecologists/obstetricians and scientists with expertise in research in the sphere as members of the proposed authority. The need for expert and informed input from the medical and scientific communities was obvious, but not dominance by them, and certainly not an authority comprised exclusively of them. However, Warnock also said that the statutory licensing authority would also need to have members experienced in the organisation and provision of services. Also, to emphasise the latter points, Warnock stated that the authority was not exclusively, or even primarily, a medical or scientific body, but that it was concerned essentially with broader matters and with the protection of the public interest:

> 'If the public is to have confidence that this is an independent body, which is not to be unduly influenced by sectional interests, its membership must be wide-ranging and in particular the lay interests should be well represented.'

Thus Warnock unsurprisingly recommended:

> 'there should be substantial lay representation on the statutory authority to regulate research and infertility services and that the chairman must be a lay person.'

In fact the 1990 Act went further, requiring both chairman and deputy chairman to be lay persons and the majority of members of the authority to be lay persons.

Functions

19.9   Warnock set out two particular, 'distinct' functions of the HFEA, one advisory and one executive.

Advisory

19.10   Concerning its advisory function Warnock said the HFEA:

---

9   Ibid, para 13.14.
10   The exact number was not specified by Warnock, nor was the actual total number of authority members specified either.

'should issue general guidance, to those working in the field, on good practice in infertility service provision and on the types of research which, without prejudice to its view of any individual project, it finds broadly ethically acceptable.'[11]

In addition, the authority should also offer advice to Government on specific issues as they arise, and be available for Ministers to consult for specific guidance. The standing expert body therefore advises the theoretically here-today gone-tomorrow politician or government, providing continuity of experience and expertise and importantly an independent informed viewpoint on controversial ethical issues in the area. Accountability of the authority to Parliament is secured by the need to report to Parliament annually. The Warnock Report recommends:

'As part of its responsibility to protect the public interest, it should publish and present to Parliament, an Annual Report, setting out the facilities for infertility treatment currently licensed and the research currently in progress, its purpose and scope, including an indication of the number of embryos being used, and their type, so that this knowledge may be publicly available.'

Accountability, transparency and openness of the authority are therefore advocated by Warnock. This was enshrined effectively in ss 6 and 7 of the 1990 Act.

Executive

19.11 Regarding the HFEA's executive function, Warnock, stated this would be twofold:

'to grant licences to those wishing to offer the kinds of infertility treatment we have discussed, whether in the NHS or in the private sector; and to grant licences to researchers wishing to work with human gametes and embryos.'[12]

Both NHS and private clinics offering infertility treatment come under the radar or net of regulation. Furthermore:

'The licensing body would be supported by an inspectorate, who would undertake regular inspections of premises where such work was carried out, to ensure that licence holders were keeping to the terms of their licences and meeting the prescribed conditions.'

Licensing

19.12 Concerning the licensing of infertility services, Warnock recommended that:

'all practitioners offering the services that we have recommended should be provided under licence [eg IVF, DI, and later including ICSI] and all premises used as part of any such provision, including the provision of fresh semen and banks for the storage of frozen human eggs, semen and embryos should be licensed by the licensing body.'

---

11   The Warnock Report, para 13.5.
12   Ibid, para 13.6.

Again this was the 'green light' by Warnock for treatment and storage licences respectively. Importantly, Warnock stated that:

'Licensed infertility services should be run by a qualified medical practitioner with appropriately qualified supporting staff and adequate facilities.'[13]

This again has been effectively implemented into both primary legislation, by inter alia ss 12, 16, 17 and 18 of the 1990 Act, and into the HFEA Code of Practice,[14] Parts 1 and 2.

19.13 In relation to research, Warnock recommended that:

'research conducted on human *in vitro* embryos and the handling of such embryos should be permitted only under licence ... any unauthorised use of an *in vitro* embryo would in itself constitute a criminal offence.'[15]

This demonstrably does not give the *in vitro* embryo any rights, still less state it is a person or potential person, nor that it has the same legal or moral status as either an adult or child human being, but it does implicitly give the *in vitro* embryo indirect protection in that certain activities (eg research using embryos) cannot be undertaken unless licensed by the HFEA, and if not so authorised, constitute a serious criminal offence.

WARNOCK: STATUS OF EMBRYO

19.14 The Warnock Report states:

'Although the questions of when life or personhood begin appear to be questions of fact susceptible of straightforward answers, we hold that the answers to such questions in fact are complex amalgams of factual and moral judgements.'[16]

Arguably Warnock avoids actually answering this critical question. Rather, it contends:

'Instead of trying to answer these questions directly we have therefore gone straight to the question of *how it is right to treat the human embryo* [and have] considered what status ought to be accorded to the human embryo, and the answer we give must necessarily be in terms of ethical or moral principles.'

Arguments against using human embryos

19.15 Warnock noted that the main argument and the central objection to the use of human embryos as research subjects was a fundamental objection, based on moral principles:

'the use of human embryos for research is morally wrong because of the very fact that they are human ... The human embryo is seen as having the same status as a child or an adult, by virtue of its potential for human life.

---

13 Ibid, para 13.8.
14 8th ed, (2009).
15 The Warnock Report, para 11.18.
16 Ibid, para 11.9.

The right to life is held to be the fundamental human right, and the taking of human life on this view is always abhorrent. To take the life of the innocent is an especial moral outrage.'[17]

Embryo research, therefore, thwarts the fulfilment by an embryo of its potential for life and so ought to be prohibited. Opponents of embryonic research also submit that:

'since it is unethical to carry out any research, harmful or otherwise, on humans without first obtaining their informed consent, it must be equally unacceptable to carry out research on a human embryo, which by its very nature cannot give consent.'[18]

19.16   Furthermore, Warnock pointed out that many people feel an instinctive opposition to research which they see as tampering with the creation of human life, ie manipulation and almost the commodification of life, which to them is ethically abhorrent. Also:

'There is widely felt concern at the possibility of unscrupulous scientists meddling with the process of reproduction in order to create hybrids, or to indulge theories of selective breeding and eugenic selection.'[19]

In other words the spectre or shadow (or is it a mirage or delusion?) of the mad and bad hubristic scientist looms large in the imaginations of opponents and some of the public.

Arguments in favour of use

19.17   Warnock asserted that those in favour of research do so for a wide range of reasons:

'At one end is the proposition that it is only to *human persons* that respect must be accorded. A human embryo cannot be thought of as a person, or even as a potential person. It is simply a collection of cells which, unless it implants in a human uterine environment, has no potential for development. There is no reason therefore to accord these cells any protected status. If useful results can be obtained from research on embryos, then such research should be permitted.' [20]

Quite simply if the embryo is not a human person and human persons alone deserve respect, protection, etc then there is no ethical problem using them for research purposes.

19.18   Warnock said that the more widely held justification for their use was that:

'though the human embryo is entitled to some added measure of respect beyond that accorded to other animal subjects, that respect cannot be absolute, and may be weighed against the benefits arising from research.'

---

17   Ibid, para 11.11.
18   Ibid, para 11.12.
19   Ibid, para 11.13.
20   Ibid, para 11.15.

In other words this approach rejects the absolutist stance of according the embryo the same full ethical and legal status as an adult or child. It rather says the embryo is entitled to some respect, but this must be weighed or balanced against using it for research that may benefit mankind by, eg, discovering new treatments or drugs. The use of human embryos must be necessary, so Warnock noted:

> 'Although many research studies in embryology and developmental biology can be carried out on animal subjects, and it is possible in many cases to extrapolate these results and findings to man, in certain situations there is no substitute for the use of human embryos.'

This is reflected in law in Sch 2, para 3(2) of the 1990 Act. Warnock cites several examples of the desirability and necessity of using human embryos, as opposed to animal embryos, for research:

> 'This particularly applies to the study of disorders occurring only in humans, such as Down's syndrome, or for research into the processes of human fertilisation, or perhaps into the specific effect of drugs or toxic substances on human tissue.'

19.19 In considering the legal position of the *in vitro* embryo Warnock initially considered the current position of the *in vivo* embryo in law and found:

> 'The human embryo *per se* has no legal status. It is not, under law in the United Kingdom accorded the same status as a child or an adult, and the law does not treat the human embryo as having a right to life. However, there are certain statutory provisions[21] that give some level of protection in various aspects.'[22]

Warnock therefore concluded:

> 'Although, therefore, the law provides a measure of protection for the human embryo *in vivo* it is clear that the human embryo under our definition of the term[23] ... is not, under the present law in the UK accorded the same status as a living child or an adult, nor do we wish it to be accorded that same status.'[24]

Presumably then, post-six weeks after fertilisation one talks of a foetus rather than an embryo. Warnock added:

> 'Nevertheless we were agreed that the embryo of the human species ought to have a special status [Singer would dispute this] and that no one should undertake research on human embryos the purposes of which could be achieved by the use of other animals or in some other way. The status of the embryo is a matter of fundamental principle which should be enshrined in legislation.'

Therefore Warnock recommended that 'the embryo of the human species should be afforded some protection in law.'

---

21 Eg the Congenital Disabilities (Civil Liability) Act 1976.
22 The Warnock Report, para 11.16.
23 Set out at para 1.4 of the Report: 'While the term "embryo" has been variously defined in considering human embryology, we have taken as our starting point the meeting of egg and sperm at fertilisation. We have regarded the embryonic stage to be six weeks immediately following fertilisation which usually corresponds with the first eight weeks of gestation counted from the first day of the woman's last menstrual period.'
24 The Warnock Report, para 11.17.

19.20 However, a majority of the Warnock Committee (a minority of three members dissented) stated: 'That protection should exist does not entail that this protection may not be waived in certain specified circumstances.'[25] Again, respect is shown for the human embryo, but not absolute respect like that owed to an adult or child. The majority, therefore, held that such research should not be totally prohibited. The majority set out the broad sweep of the ethical framework and ethical bright lines:

> 'We do not want to see a situation in which human embryos are frivolously or unnecessarily used in research but we are bound to take account of the fact that the advances in the treatment of infertility … could not have taken place without such research; and that continued research is essential, if advances in treatment and medical knowledge are to continue. A majority of us therefore agreed that research on human embryos should continue.'

This research, however, would be strictly regulated and policed. There will be no research free-for-all. The Report continued that, nevertheless, 'because of the special status that we accord to the human embryo', such research must be subject to stringent controls and monitoring, these stringent controls being contained in the 1990 and 2008 Acts and the Code of Practice, all policed by the HFEA. Finally, the Committee 'see these controls as essential to safeguard the public interest and to allay widespread anxiety.'

19.21 Another ethical bright line to safeguard the public interest and allay widespread anxiety was setting a time limit for keeping embryos alive *in vitro*. Warnock settled on the formation or development of the primitive streak as this time limit and accordingly recommended:

> 'that no live human embryo derived from *in vitro* fertilisation, whether frozen or unfrozen, may be kept alive, if not transferred to a woman, beyond fourteen days after fertilisation, nor may it be used as a research subject beyond fourteen days after fertilisation. This fourteen day period does not include any time during which the embryo may have been frozen. We further recommend that it shall be a criminal offence to handle or to use as a research subject any live human embryo derived from *in vitro* fertilisation beyond that limit.'[26]

Again this was enshrined in s3 (3), (4) and s41 (1) of HFEA 1990.

19.22 Other significant recommendations of Warnock were that:

> 'AID should be available on a properly organised basis and subject to the licensing arrangements [outlined in the report] to those infertile couples for whom it might be appropriate. Consequently we recommend that the provision of AID services without a licence for the purpose should be an offence.'[27]

AID therefore, like IVF and later ICSI, must only be undertaken if licensed by the HFEA. If undertaken without a licence it will be a criminal offence. Following on from this Warnock recommended that:

---

25   Ibid, para 11.18.
26   Ibid, para 11.22.
27   Ibid, para 4.16.

'the AID child should in law be treated as the legitimate child of its mother and her husband where they have both consented to the treatment.'[28]

19.23   Concerning children born as a result of AID, Warnock recommended that:

'on reaching the age of eighteen the child should have access to the basic information about the donor's ethnic origin and genetic health and that legislation be enacted to provide the right of access to this.'[29]

Furthermore they recommended a 'change in the law so that the semen donor will have no parental rights or duties in relation to the child.'[30] Additionally, Warnock recommended that 'it should be presumed that the husband has consented to AID, unless the contrary is proved.'[31]

19.24   Warnock also made a number of other recommendations, namely 'for the present a limit of ten children who can be fathered by donations from any one donor,'[32] and that, regarding payment for semen donors, 'there should be a gradual move towards a system where semen donors should be given only their expenses.'[33]

19.25   Not surprisingly, Warnock recommended also, inter alia, that:

'the service of IVF should continue to be available subject to the same type of licensing and inspection as we have recommended with regard to the regulation of AID [and that] IVF should continue to be available within the NHS.'[34]

19.26   Concerning egg donation, Warnock recommended it be:

'accepted as a recognised technique in the treatment of infertility subject to the same type of licensing and controls as we have recommended for the regulation of AID and IVF. The principles of good practice we have already considered in relation to these other techniques should apply, including the anonymity of the donor, limitation of the number of children born from the eggs of any one donor to ten, openness with the child about his genetic origins, the availability of counselling for all parties and informed consent.'[35]

As with semen donors, Warnock also recommended that:

'legislation should provide that when a child is born to a woman following donation of another's egg the woman shall be regarded in law as the mother of that child, and that the egg donor should have no rights or obligations in respect of that child.'[36]

19.27   Concerning embryo donation, Warnock recommended that:

28   Ibid, para 4.17.
29   Ibid, para 4.21.
30   Ibid, para 4.22.
31   Ibid, para 4.24
32   Ibid, para 4.26.
33   Ibid, para 4.27.
34   Ibid, para 5.10.
35   Ibid, para 6.6.
36   Ibid, para 6.8.

'embryo donation involving donated semen and egg which are brought together *in vitro* be accepted as a treatment for infertility, subject to the same type of licensing and controls as we have recommended with regard to the regulation of AID, IVF and egg donation.'[37]

19.28 Warnock sought to address the vexed issue of surrogacy by recommending that:

'legislation be introduced to render criminal the creation or the operation in the United Kingdom of agencies whose purposes include the recruitment of women for surrogate pregnancy or making arrangements for individuals or couples who wish to utilise the services of a carrying mother; such legislation should be wide enough to include both profit and non-profit making organisations. We further recommend that the legislation be sufficiently wide to render criminally liable the actions of professionals and others who knowingly assist in the establishment of a surrogate pregnancy.'[38]

Significantly, the Committee also recommended that 'it be provided by statute that all surrogacy agreements are illegal contracts and therefore unenforceable in the courts.'[39]

19.29 Regarding the transmission of hereditary disease, Warnock recommended that 'it should be accepted practice to offer donated gametes and embryos to those at risk of transmitting hereditary disorders.'[40]

19.30 Finally Warnock made a number of recommendations on the freezing and storage of human semen, eggs and embryos, namely that 'the use of frozen semen in artificial insemination should continue,'[41] and that:

'the use of frozen eggs in therapeutic procedures should not be undertaken until research has shown that no unacceptable risk is involved. This will be a matter for review by the licensing body.'[42]

Clearly in 1984, and for many years after, egg freezing was a problematic and scarcely available procedure because of the technical problems involved in freezing and thawing eggs.[43] Although strides have been made to address this problem since, embryo and sperm or semen freezing and thawing are still easier and more successful. Again Warnock recommended that 'the clinical use of frozen embryos may continue to be developed under review by the licensing authority.'[44] They also recommended that there should be automatic five-yearly reviews of semen and egg deposits,[45] and furthermore 'a maximum of ten years for storage of embryos after which time the right to use or disposal should pass

---

37 Ibid, para 7.4.
38 Ibid, para 8.18.
39 Ibid, para 8.19.
40 Ibid, para 9.3.
41 Ibid, para 10.1.
42 Ibid, para 10.2.
43 One of the problems in the *Evans* case was that her eggs could not be frozen: *Evans v United Kingdom (Application 6339/05)* [2006] All ER (D) 82 (Mar).
44 The Warnock Report, para 10.3.
45 Ibid, para 10.8.

to the storage authority.'[46] The Report also recommended that, 'legislation be enacted to ensure there is no right of ownership in a human embryo.'[47]

CONCLUSION

19.31 The ethical parameters and regulatory landscape mapped out by Baroness Warnock and her Committee in 1984 have stood the test of time and much of them remain largely intact, as evident in the 2008 Act. Despite the Coalition's commendable and imperative economic objective of cutting waste and addressing the UK financial deficit, it is submitted that jettisoning an effective, expert independent statutory regulatory body like the HFEA, a key feature of the Warnock assisted reproductive roadmap, may weaken legal and ethical regulatory oversight in this field with no discernible, tangible financial saving. That would not make sense and be regrettable.

---

46   Ibid, para 10.10.
47   Ibid, para 10.11.

Chapter 20

The Human Fertilisation and Embryology Act 1990 – the Birth of the Human Fertilisation and Embryology Authority

INTRODUCTION

20.1   The Human Fertilisation and Embryology Act (HFEA 1990, referred to here as the 1990 Act) was passed on 1 November 1990. The short title to the Act stated it was:

> 'An Act to make provision in connection with human embryos and any subsequent development of such embryos; to prohibit certain practices in connection with embryos and gametes; to establish a Human Fertilisation and Embryology Authority; to make provision about the persons who in certain circumstances are to be treated in law as the parents of a child; and to amend the Surrogacy Arrangements Act 1985.'

Hence the original 1990 Act was very ambitious in scope regarding the raft of areas covered in the regulatory net, and also in its legislative intent.

THE REGULATORY NET

20.2   Brazier pertinently notes:

> 'The Human Fertilisation and Embryology Act 1990 sets out to regulate selected parts of reproductive medicine in the United Kingdom.'[1]

So, for example surgery to unblock fallopian tubes and giving a woman drugs to produce more eggs (eg the Mandy Allwood case) is left unregulated by the 1990 Act and the 2008 Act. She adds that the 1990 Act also:

> 'subjects fertility specialists to constraints on their practice and their research quite separate from, and over and above, those legal and ethical constraints generally applicable to all medical practitioners.'

So whilst generally doctors need to obtain the consent of a patient prior to treating them, the law generally does not insist that that consent be in writing. Consent is equally valid if implied (the majority of consents) or oral. However, all consents under the 1990 and 2008 Acts need to be in writing to be effective (see Sch 3 to the 1990 Act).

20.3   As is apparent from the short title to the 1990 Act, one of the key aims and objectives of the Act was to establish this new, innovative, pioneering and potentially ground-breaking Authority (the Human Fertilisation and

---

1   M.Brazier, 'Regulating the Reproduction Business' (1999) 7(2) Med L Rev 166–193, at 166.

Embryology Authority (HFEA)). Brazier notes that the 1990 Act created the HFEA:

'an apparently powerful regulatory body with powers to control the practice and development of embryology and certain fertility treatments ... Reproductive medicine is singled out as special, as a part of medicine of such particular social concern and significance that the state should have a direct stake in its evolution.'[2]

Brazier adds that 'the British model of regulating fertility treatment and embryo research has undoubted strengths,' and that 'those strengths benefit patients and promote British reproductive medicine as a success story.' She cites in support of this claim that the British model of regulation:

'ensures a degree of public accountability in the development and delivery both of new treatments and research procedures ... It promotes high standards of medical practice and offers those lucky enough to benefit from the advances made in reproductive medicine assurances that their treatment is not likely to be marred by gross misadventure, delivered by maverick doctors, or rank "amateurs." ... Because the British system is built on consensus, regulators, clinicians and scientists work well together.'[3]

However critics might contend this relationship built on consensus between regulators and regulated leads to, or potentially at least to, too cosy and complacent a relationship between both, to the detriment of protecting and safeguarding the interests of both the patient and the embryo. Also, a sizeable chunk of the HFEA running costs come directly from licence fees and fees from every IV and DI treatment cycle carried out in HFEA licensed clinics. Might this appear as a conflict of interest?

Pragmatism

20.4 Brazier concedes:

'The price paid for consensus however is that all too often crucial issues of individual rights, the balance between individual rights and public policy, and issues of conflicting rights are skated over.'[4]

She asserts that our reproductive regulatory regime's foundations are based on pragmatism (not an infirm basis arguably), that:

'British law too displays contradictions, no single, coherent, philosophy underpins the law's response to reproductive medicine. Yet a regulatory system is in place and perhaps suggests that pragmatism has its advantages.'

MEMBERSHIP

20.5 Section 5(1) of the 1990 Act set up the HFEA, and s 5(2)(a) and (b) provided, inter alia, that the HFEA comprised a chairman, a deputy chairman, and other members appointed by the Secretary of State (see also para 4(1) of

---

2   Ibid, at 166.
3   Ibid, at 167.
4   Ibid.

Sch 1). Also, importantly, s 5(3) stated Sch 1, which deals with the membership of HFEA, 'shall have effect'. Schedule 1 covered a range of issues pertaining to the HFEA, including, inter alia, the status and capacity of the HFEA, expenses, appointment of members, tenure of office, disqualification of members of the HFEA, remuneration and pensions of members, staff, proceedings and various other matters.

20.6   Critically, the Secretary of State for Health, a senior member of the Cabinet and government and a politician, appoints the chairman, deputy chairman and the membership of the HFEA. Currently, as at April 2012, the Chair of the HFEA is Professor Lisa Jardine CBE,[5] and the Deputy Chair is Professor Emily Jackson.[6] As at April 2012, there are 16 other members of the HFEA, including a Professor of Philosophy and Public Policy, a retired senior Manager at the BBC, an accountant, a journalist, a former IVF patient and of course a number of medical practitioners or persons who have kept or used gametes and embryos outside the body or who have commissioned or funded research on such embryos or gametes.

20.7   Paragraph 4 of Schedule 1 of the 1990 Act critically sets out the parameters for appointing members of the HFEA. Paragraph 4(1) reiterates essentially s 5(2) and states that:

'All members of the Authority (including the chairman and deputy chairman who shall be appointed as such) shall be appointed by the Secretary of State.'

Furthermore para 4(2) adds that:

'In making appointments the Secretary of State shall have regard to the desirability of ensuring that the proceedings of the Authority, and the discharge of its functions, are informed by the views of both men and women.'

The HFEA is not meant to be a bastion of male only, nor more pertinently male doctor only, members. The current Chair and Deputy Chair of the HFEA, arguably the two most important positions in the regulatory authority, are in fact both women, and in addition currently (as at January 2011) 12 of the other 16 members are women. Over 75 per cent of the HFEA members are therefore women, so by no stretch of the imagination could the accusation be levelled of the HFEA, as it is by some feminist critics, that it is a male body comprised and dominated by men controlling and restricting a woman's procreative and reproductive liberty – quite the reverse is true. Indeed, three of the last four Chairs of the HFEA, if one includes Lord Harris (an interim Chair) in the calculations, have in fact been women.

20.8   Perhaps of much more significance than the gender balance of the HFEA, certainly arguably from the point of view of reassuring the general public, is the requirement enshrined in the legislation that fewer than half of the members (ie excluding the Chair and Deputy Chair) can be medically qualified doctors or have been involved in the keeping or use of gametes or embryos, or been involved in commissioning or funding research on embryos

---

5   Director of the Centre for Editing Lives and Letters and the Centenary Professor of Renaissance Studies at Queen Mary, University of London.
6   Professor of Law at the London School of Economics.

or gametes. The HFEA cannot be, nor be perceived to be, a cabal of doctors policing doctors, possibly in the interests of doctors and to the detriment of the general public.[7] The HFEA, if its membership was comprised entirely of doctors, including a Chair or Deputy Chair who both were doctors, would not necessarily command the general respect of the public for its decisions and policies in often highly controversial ethical, moral and legal issues in areas of rapidly developing science and research. Two highly germane sub-paragraphs concerning the appointment and composition of the HFEA membership are therefore evident in paras 4(3)(a) to (c) and (4) respectively.

20.9   Concerning who definitely cannot be either the chairman or deputy chairman[8] of the HFEA, paragraph 4(3)(a)–(c) provides that any person who is or has been 'a medical practitioner registered under the Medical Act 1983,' or 'concerned with keeping or using gametes or embryos outside the body,' or 'is or has been directly concerned with commissioning or funding any research involving such keeping or research' is disqualified. The two leading figureheads and members of the HFEA, therefore, cannot be registered medical practitioners, or have been involved in storing embryos or gametes, or performing IVF, ICSI, or DI, or have been involved in embryonic research and experimentation using human embryos or, since October 2009, human admixed embryos.

20.10   Equally significantly, para 4(4) provides:

> 'The Secretary of State shall secure that at least one-third but fewer than half of the other members of the Authority fall within sub-paragraph (3)(a), (b) or (c) above, and that at least one member falls within each of paragraphs (a) and (b).'

Again, considering the current HFEA (as at April 2012) which, excluding the Chair and Deputy Chair, consists of 16 members, therefore at least 5 of those members must be medically qualified doctors, or have been involved in keeping or using embryos or gametes or commissioned or funded embryonic and human admixed embryonic research. At least 5 and up to 7 of the other members therefore must have practical clinical and research expertise and knowledge effectively in the field of assisted reproduction. It would be foolish if the regulator of IVF had no practical and expert knowledge of what was involved in IVF. However, the regulator is not dominated or controlled by those with that expertise, knowledge and training.

20.11   HFEA members are appointed (para 5(2)) for a three-year term which is renewable; for example, Ruth Deech (now Baroness Deech) was appointed as Chair of the HFEA in 1994 and remained as Chair till 2002.

ACCOUNTABILITY

20.12   A duty is imposed under s 6(1) requiring the HFEA to keep proper accounts and records each year and under s 6(3) to send a copy of the statement of accounts to the Secretary of State and to the Comptroller and Auditor

---

7   To paraphrase George Bernard Shaw, all professions are conspiracies against the laity.
8   Chairman and deputy chairman are the terms used in the 1990 Act, although not adopted by the current incumbents of the post, who use Chair and Deputy Chair.

General. The Authority is, therefore, legally obliged to keep proper accounts and records which must in turn be made available to the Secretary of State for Health (ie political accountability of the HFEA to the government) and the Comptroller and Auditor General (ie financial and fiscal accountability). Ultimately, the HFEA accounts are laid before both Houses of Parliament, where they can be considered and scrutinised by MPs and peers, promoting transparency, openness and accountability concerning the workings and cost of the HFEA to Parliament and particularly to our elected representatives, ie our MPs.

20.13 An additional vehicle of accountability of the HFEA to Parliament is that the HFEA must, under s 7, submit a yearly report to the Secretary of State, setting out what the HFEA has done in the last year and what it proposes to do in the following year. This report is, under s 7(3), also laid before Parliament, thereby hopefully promoting further scrutiny and accountability of HFEA.

FUNCTIONS OF THE HFEA UNDER THE 1990 ACT

20.14 The original 1990 Act stipulated under s 8 that the general functions the HFEA was tasked with were fourfold. First, under s 8(1)(a), it must keep under review information about embryos and any subsequent development of embryos and about the provision of treatment services and activities governed by the 1990 Act, and advise the Secretary of State. The HFEA is after all the independent, expert, statutory body on the regulated matters and areas. Government ministers come and go, for short or longer periods of office, with little or no knowledge or experience of, eg, IVF or embryonic research, so they need all the help they can get from such a body as the HFEA in this complex and rapidly developing field of medicine. Secondly, under s 8(1)(b), the HFEA must publicise the services provided to the public by the HFEA or under licenses. Clearly this will embrace publishing, eg, live birth rates at the various licensed clinics for different types of treatment, and generally providing information about all the licensed UK clinics. Thirdly, under s 8(1)(c), it must provide appropriate advice and information to licensed clinics, to persons receiving treatment services, or providing gametes or embryos for use under the 1990 Act. The HFEA, therefore, has an important role to advise and provide information to licensed clinics, infertile patients and embryo or gamete donors. Finally, under s 8(1)(d), the HFEA shall perform such other functions as may be specified in regulations – secondary legislation may specify additional functions in the future for the HFEA.

20.15 However, the primary function and responsibility of the HFEA is that it is fundamentally a licensing authority or body, that grants, varies, revokes, suspends, monitors and polices licensed premises to ensure that they comply with the 1990 and 2008 Acts and comply with the requirements of the Code of Practice.[9] Basically the HFEA was empowered to grant three types of licence:

- treatment licences;
- storage licences; and
- research licences.[10]

---

9   Eighth edition, effective from 1 October 2010.
10   See s 11 of the 1990 Act.

Licence committees

20.16 Section 9 of the 1990 Act covered licence committees (the committees established under the 1990 Act to grant/revoke/suspend/etc licences) and set out some of the functions of these committees. Section 9(5) stipulates that, inter alia, these are comprised solely of HFEA members, of whom at least one is not a person falling within para 4(3)(a)–(c) of Sch 1. That licence committees must consist entirely of HFEA members is a clear indication of the importance Parliament attaches to the licensing process under the legislation. A licence committee of three, therefore, would have to have at least one non-medically qualified member or a member who is not involved in, eg, IVF or embryo research. Again this 'lay' member requirement is designed to reassure the general public that the critical licensing process is not carried out exclusively by the doctor members of the HFEA, and thus can be regarded as another safeguard or protection built into the regulatory regime.

Inspections

20.17 Another critical safeguard in the architecture of the 1990 Act regime is that before any licence is granted by the HFEA it will, via the licence committee, inspect any proposed clinic that will be subject to a licence to see if it is suitable for such a licence (s 9(7)). As well as carrying out a preliminary inspection of premises before even considering an application for a licence, the HFEA supervises and monitors existing licensed clinics too. Under s 9(8), therefore, licensed clinics are inspected annually and a report on that inspection is made. Clearly though, if a licensed clinic is fully complying with the Acts and the Code of Practice, this annual inspection requirement may be relaxed and clinics can be inspected every two or three years (s 9(9) and (10)). These sections promote a lighter touch approach, hence avoiding unnecessary inspections and rewarding compliance and adherence to the regulatory regime. Finally, s 9(11) provides that inspections do not have to be carried out by licence committee members. The HFEA employs a considerable number of part-time inspectors to discharge its licensing inspection regime.

Raison d'etre

20.18 As stated already the fundamental function of the HFEA is that it is a licensing authority. Its raison d'etre is to grant licences, and of course then to supervise, renew, vary or possibly revoke or suspend licences. Section 11(1) (a)–(c) empowers the HFEA to grant three types of licence, namely treatment, storage and research licences.

20.19 Secondly, s 11(2) states that para 4 of Sch 2 has effect in the case of all licences, and para 4(1) crucially stipulates that a licence:

'can only authorise activities to be carried on premises specified in the licence and under the supervision of an individual designated in the licence.'

These two requirements can be viewed as essential and axiomatic safeguards. Clearly, if the HFEA licensing committee or members or inspectors have visited premises 1 and deemed it satisfactory for, eg, treatment purposes and then granted it a treatment licence, logically the treatment licence is and ought only to be applicable to the premises that have been duly inspected and not to premises 2, which have not been visited, inspected and approved. Again, the second critical safeguard is the accountability one, namely that a licence can only authorise activities to be carried out under the supervision of an individual designated in the licence. All licences must, therefore, have a person responsible or individual designated to supervise the licensed activities under the licence. Again this reassures the general public of the probity of licensed activities, protects vulnerable patients from potential exploitation and ensures that the likelihood of a maverick scientist or doctor engaging in illegal or unethical actions contrary to the HFEA legislation and Code of Practice is hopefully lessened.

20.20 Paragraph 4(2)(a)–(d) also adds additional safeguards and protections, for example that a licence cannot authorise both research and treatment services or apply to premises in different places. A separate treatment and research licence will need to be applied for from the HFEA for the treatment services and for the research project. Again, if the clinic has two research projects it wants to embark on it needs to apply for two separate research licences. One research licence for both research projects will not suffice legally, under para 4(2)(b). Also a licensed clinic cannot have more than one person responsible or person to supervise the designated activities under the licence. One person alone is responsible. Sharing this duty between two individuals might blur responsibilities and lead to confusion or a poorly managed clinic. Again, a further problem might be: what would happen if supervisor one disagreed with supervisor two on an issue? How would the disagreement be resolved? Finally para 4(2)(d) states that a licence cannot apply to premises in different places. There may be good practical and logistical justifications for this safeguard, ie the worry that split sites are tantamount to potentially less effective scrutiny or supervision of the licensed activities.

General conditions: s 12

20.21 Another critical area that the HFEA is given supervisory power over is in policing the general conditions (s 12) for all three licences, including s 12(1)(a):

'that the activities authorised by the licence shall be carried on only on the premises to which the licence relates and under the supervision of the person responsible'.

Secondly, and importantly, under s 12(1)(b), any member or employee of the HFEA is permitted at all reasonable times to enter those premises and inspect them, which includes inspecting any equipment or records and observing any activity. This general condition permits HFEA members and HFEA inspectors to enter and inspect all licensed clinics, in order to inspect any equipment used on those premises, examine any records, eg consent forms or donor information, and observe activities on those premises, ie what actually takes place at the licensed clinic. Presumably 'all reasonable times' would mean during normal business hours, ie 9.00am–5.30pm, Monday to Friday. This power in the general condition of every licence keeps the clinics on their toes and provides a strong incentive for their compliance with the Acts and Code of Practice. It is yet another tangible example of the real enforcement powers given to the HFEA by Parliament. Again, these are powers are designed to have real bite, even though they will be used very sparingly.

20.22 Thirdly, s 12(1)(c) states 'that the provisions of Schedule 3 to this Act shall be complied with'. All the requirements for consent under the Act must be complied with, so all consents must be in writing and be 'effective', ie be consents that have not been withdrawn.

20.23 Next, s 12(1)(d) states 'that proper records shall be maintained'. Again, the requirement to keep proper records, whether it be regarding consent forms or details about donated gametes or embryos etc would appear to be stating the obviously sensible, never mind a legal obligation. The terrible and disastrous consequences of mistakes were too apparent in the *Leeds* case, when a white woman's egg was inseminated by a black man's sperm, resulting in the birth of two mixed-race children.[11]

20.24 Finally, a further general condition is s 12(1)(e):

'that no money or other benefit shall be given or received in respect of any supply of gametes or embryos unless authorised by directions.'

Basically only the HFEA has the power to authorise payment (or other benefits) for the supply of gametes or embryos. They may authorise such payment by issuing directions applicable to all clinics or, eg, to one named clinic. Clinics or individual doctors cannot, therefore, unilaterally pay donors for the supply of gametes or embryos.

Specific conditions

20.25 Sections 13–15 of the 1990 Act relate to the specific conditions for treatment, storage and research licences respectively.

Section 13

20.26 Section 13(1) specifies that conditions of every treatment licence include that certain information must be recorded (s 13(2)), including (s 13(2) (a)–(e)) information about:

- the persons who are provided licensed services;
- the services provided;
- the persons whose gametes and/or embryos are kept or used;
- any mixing of sperm and eggs; or
- acquisition of embryos from a woman; or
- any other matter the HFEA specify in directions.

Also, crucially, all consents as per Sch 3 must be recorded. This is vitally important information that needs to be recorded and moreover recorded accurately.

20.27 Section 13(5) of the 1990 Act is the welfare of the child provision, arguably one of the most important provisions legally and ethically in the legislation, which has been fundamentally altered by the 2008 Act (the 'need for a father' clause having been replaced by the need for supportive parenting

---

11 *Leeds Teaching Hospital NHS Trust v Mr A, Mrs A and others* [2003] EWHC 259.

instead). The next provision is s 13(6), the so-called 'informed consent' provision.

Section 14

20.28 Section 14 of the 1990 Act governs storage licences and the specific conditions pertaining to these licences. Section 14(1)(a)–(d) include that a person's gametes or an embryo taken from a woman can only be stored in licensed premises. This provision highlights again the vital role of the HFEA in ensuring that gametes and embryos that are stored can only be stored in premises licensed by the HFEA. Section 14(c) stipulates that no gametes or embryos shall be kept in storage for longer than the statutory storage period and, if stored at the end of the period, shall be allowed to perish. Again the independent statutory regulatory authority, the HFEA, is charged with monitoring compliance with this requirement by the clinics that possess a valid storage licence. A further specific condition is s 14(d), that all consents necessary under Schedule 3 need to be recorded. Again, the importance of getting and keeping all the necessary consents and ensuring these are recorded for possible inspection by the HFEA and their inspectors is emphasised here.

Section 15

20.29 Section 15 contains the specific conditions for all research licences under the Act. Again, s 15(2) emphasises the need to record certain information specified by the HFEA. Also, s 15(4) stipulates that embryos appropriated for a particular research project cannot be used instead for some other purpose.

The licensing procedure

20.30 Section 16 is the key provision governing the granting of licences by the HFEA. Section 16(1) stipulates that a licence committee may grant a person a licence when an application is made and an initial fee paid to the HFEA if the requirements in s 16(2) are met. An application form and initial fee need to be forwarded to the HFEA before they will even consider granting a licence. Under the requirement in s 16(2)(a), the application must designate an individual as the person who will supervise the licensed activities. This requirement, as already stated, is critical to the licensing regime implemented by the HFEA. All licensed activities must be supervised by 'the person under whose supervision the activities to be authorised by the licence are to be carried on,' or as they are also called, 'the person responsible'. This person carries all the supervisory responsibilities for all staff employed and all activities undertaken in the licensed clinic. The person responsible can be the applicant (s 16(2)(b)) or (s 16(2)(b)(i) and (ii)) the application can be made with the consent of that individual if the 'licence committee is satisfied that the applicant is a suitable person to hold a licence'. The person responsible, therefore, must either be the applicant for the licence, or alternatively the application must have been made with the consent of that individual. Also, a significant pre-requisite and safeguard is that the licence committee must be satisfied that the applicant is a suitable person to hold a licence, although the term 'a suitable person' is not actually defined in the legislation.

20.31   Thirdly, s 16(2)(c) provides that the committee must be satisfied that individual has the required 'character, qualifications and experience' to supervise the licensed activities and 'discharge' their s 17 duties. Again the HFEA licensing committee may require more information from the applicant before granting a licence and provision is made for this eventuality in s 16(4). Also of some significance is that (s 16(5)):

> 'The licence committee shall not grant a licence unless a copy of the conditions to be imposed by the licence has been shown to, and acknowledged in writing by, the applicant and (where different) the person under whose supervision the activities are to be carried on.'

Duties of the person responsible

20.32   The duties of the person responsible are set out in s 17 of the 1990 Act. These are critically important and surely must feature very prominently when the HFEA members and inspectors are inspecting licensed clinics. Section 17(1)(a) states it is the duty of the person responsible to secure that:

> 'persons to whom the licence applies are of such character, and are so qualified by training and experience, as to be suitable persons to participate in the activities authorised by the licence'.

Clearly this first duty is of fundamental importance to the workings of the Act and more importantly to ensuring that proper and ethical standards are adhered to in licensed clinics, which minimise or prevent exploitation of desperate, vulnerable patients by clinics, three-quarters of whom operate on a commercial basis in the IVF marketplace.

20.33   Secondly, the person responsible must ensure (s 17(1)(b)) that proper equipment is used, and that proper arrangements are made for the keeping of gametes and embryos and for the disposal of gametes or embryos that have been allowed to perish (s 17(1)(c)). Also, crucially, the person responsible is charged with ensuring (s 17(1)(d)) 'that suitable practices are used in the course of the activities,' and (s 17(1)(e)) 'that the conditions of the licence are complied with.' These are in fact quite demanding duties.

Revocation and variation of licences

20.34   As well as granting licences, the licence committee of the HFEA can also revoke and vary licences. Under s 18(1)(a), the HFEA may revoke a licence if 'any information' on it 'was in any material respect false or misleading'; there is, therefore, a premium placed on applicants being truthful in their application forms. Secondly, a licence may be revoked if the licensed premises are no longer suitable for the activities authorised by the licence (s 18(1)(b)), and thirdly, if the 'person responsible has failed' or is unable because of incapacity to discharge the duty under s 17 of the Act or has failed to comply with HFEA directions (s 18(1)(c)). Again, this emphasises how vital it is that the person responsible discharges and carries out their s 17 duties. Failure to do so potentially carries a very heavy price, namely revocation of the licence. Of course, if the person responsible has their clinic's licence revoked they cannot lawfully undertake the licensed activity any longer. So if they were to continue to operate the clinic, now unlicensed due to the licence being revoked, they would be committing a serious criminal offence under s 41(2)(a), by not having a licence under s 3(1) of the 1990 Act, and could, on conviction of the indictment, be imprisoned for up to two years. A licence may be revoked if (s 18(1)(d)) 'there has been any other material change of circumstances since the licence was granted.' In addition a licence committee may revoke a licence if they are not satisfied that the character of the person responsible or the nominal licensee remains suitable to supervise and hold a licence (s 18(2)(a)), or if they die, or are convicted of an offence under the Act (s 18(2)(b)). Under s 18(3), a licence committee is vested with equivalent powers to vary, instead of revoking, a licence.

Procedure for refusal, variation or revocation of licence

20.35 Section 19(1) of the 1990 Act sets out the procedure for the refusal, variation and revocation of licences. Basically under s 19(1) a licence committee must give notice of their proposal to refuse or refuse to vary a licence, the reasons for it, and the effect of s 19(3) to the applicant. Equally, the licence committee must give the same notice etc if they are proposing to vary or revoke a licence under s 19(2). Under s 19(3) of the 1990 Act, the applicant has 28 days to make representations about the proposal to revoke the licence before the licence committee makes its final decision. These representations may be basically either oral or written (s 19(4)). Furthermore, under s 19(5), the licence committee have to basically give notice of their determination to the person responsible regarding granting, refusing, refusing to vary or revoking a licence. Also, reasons must be provided in this notice for that decision.

20.36 Again, further provision was made under s 20 of the 1990 Act concerning appeals from determinations (refusals, revocations or variations of licences) made by licence committees to the HFEA. These appeals to the HFEA must be made within 28 days of the notice of determination being served on the applicant. These appeals are (s 20(3)) a 'rehearing' by different HFEA members (ie different from the HFEA members making the original decision). This subsection ensures there is no conflict of interest by expressly stipulating that HFEA members who have taken part in the deliberations and determinations of licence committees cannot also be party to any appeal proceedings resulting from the original determination. This provision merely states what ought to be obvious. Under s 20(4), at the appeal the appellant can appear themselves or be represented, as can the licence committee, and the HFEA can consider any written representations from these parties, before it makes 'such determination on the appeal as it thinks fit.' Again, importantly, under s 20(5) the HFEA must give notice of its determination to the appellant and the reasons for the decision. The HFEA is crucially required to give the reasons for its decision to, eg, refuse a licence. A bald and bare decision to refuse the licence will not suffice legally under this subsection. Finally s 20(6) provides that this appeal must be heard by HFEA members with a quorum of at least five.

Appealing from the HFEA to the High Court or Court of Session

20.37 Section 21 governs appeals from the HFEA determinations made under s 20. Appeals 'on a point of law' are to either the High Court or, in Scotland, to the Court of Session.

Suspending licences: s 22 of the 1990 Act

20.38   Potentially very significant powers were given to HFEA licence committees to temporarily suspend licences in certain circumstances (s 22(1)(a) and (b)). The first circumstance is if there are reasonable grounds to suspect that there are grounds for revoking the licence under s 18, eg the licensed premises to which the licence relates are no longer suitable for the activities authorised by the licence or alternatively, eg, that the person has failed to discharge their s 17 duties, ie ensuring that the other staff in the licensed clinic are sufficiently qualified by training and/or experience to work in the clinic and that proper equipment is used in the clinic. The second circumstance is if the licence committee is of the opinion that the licence should immediately be suspended. In either circumstance the licence committee can suspend the licence for up to three months by serving a suspension notice on the clinic. Again, this section gives the HFEA real, tangible policing and enforcement powers to effectively deal with non-compliant licensed clinics. Needless to say, suspending a licence for three months would be disastrous for the errant clinic, person responsible or applicant, so the existence of this power in the 1990 Act signals the commitment of the government and Parliament to police the assisted reproduction field rigorously and effectively.

20.39   Again, the notice procedure required under s 22(1) is outlined in s 22(2), and significantly the licence committee of the HFEA could theoretically suspend a licence for longer than three months (ie 'for such further period not exceeding three months') if they serve a further suspension notice on the person responsible.

20.40   Clearly, as stated earlier, if a licence has been suspended the person responsible cannot lawfully carry out the formerly licensed activities on the formerly licensed premises. They are out of business. If the person responsible were to ignore the suspension notice and continue to, eg, provide IVF or experiment on human embryos, they would of course be committing a criminal offence under s 3(1) of the 1990 Act.

Directions: s 23 of the 1990 Act

20.41   The HFEA are given the power to issue directions 'for any purpose', eg varying or revoking licences, and guidance to, inter alia, licensed clinics under s 23 of the 1990 Act. This is potentially a very wide and far-reaching power. Directions from the HFEA must be complied with. They are mandatory and not optional. Section 23(2) states: 'A person to whom any requirement contained in directions is applicable shall comply with the requirement.' Furthermore, if a clinic is directed to do anything by the HFEA, the direction effectively renders the directed activity lawful under the licence. So, s 23(3) states: 'Anything done by a person in pursuance of directions is to be treated for the purposes of this Act as done in pursuance of a licence.'

20.42   Section 23(4) and (5) concerns how directions are to be given to various parties. Therefore, s 23(4) provides that where directions are to be given to a particular person, they shall be given by serving notice of the directions on the person. In other cases, in respect of any licence, s 23(5) adds that directions may be given by serving notice of the directions on the person responsible.

Directions can, therefore, be given to a particular person, presumably eg a person working in or a person responsible in a particular clinic, or directed at, eg, a specific, designated erring clinic, or alternatively general directions can be aimed at all licensed clinics or maybe a section of licensed clinics, eg just aimed at clinics with treatment licences. Significantly, s 24(4) additionally provides that directions may authorise, eg, a licensed clinic to receive gametes or embryos from outside the United Kingdom or send them outside the United Kingdom. Section 24(4) was invoked by the HFEA in the *Blood* case,[12] where the HFEA exercised its discretion to grant an export licence to Mrs Blood to take her husband's sperm to Belgium with her in order that she be inseminated with it.

20.43 Section 24(5) and (6) empower a licence committee to give such directions as are also mentioned in s 24(7) of the 1990 Act.

Code of Practice: s 25 of the 1990 Act

20.44 One of the central functions of the HFEA is to maintain a Code of Practice (CoP) to give guidance to licensed clinics about acceptable conduct and standards in licensed clinics and, inter alia, about how the person responsible and persons who work in licensed premises discharge their various functions and duties. This CoP fleshes out in much greater detail the requirements of the primary legislation regulating the field, namely the 1990 and 2008 Acts respectively. In essence both statutes provide the dry bones, the general principles and broad brushstroke of regulation. The CoP by contrast provides the detail. The CoP is now in its eighth edition, so this task has been an ongoing and evolutionary process, perhaps totally understandable in this rapidly developing area of medicine. Section 25(1) provides that the HFEA must:

> 'maintain a code of practice giving guidance about the proper conduct of activities carried on [in licensed clinics] and the proper discharge of the functions of the person responsible and other persons to whom the licence applies.'

20.45 Section 25(2) very significantly adds that the CoP shall include, for those providing treatment services, guidance about the 'need for a father' clause in s 13(5). Furthermore, s 25(4) confers on the HFEA very wide powers to revise all, not just parts of the CoP: 'The Authority may from time to time revise the whole or any part of the code.' In addition, s 25(5) provides that the HFEA shall publish the code. It does this by publishing paper versions of the CoP and by making it available on the web.

20.46 A very important part of s 25 is s 25(6)(a) and (b), which provides that a failure by anyone to 'observe' the CoP is not a criminal offence, but a licence committee shall, when considering failure to comply, particularly with conditions requiring anything to be 'proper' or 'suitable', take account of any relevant provision of the code, regarding revoking or not varying a licence. Crucially, a breach of the CoP, or a failure to comply with its terms, is not a criminal offence. However, it does not follow that clinics can simply ignore provisions of the CoP at their leisure. Failure to comply with the requirements

---

12   *R v Human Fertilisation and Embryology Authority ex p Blood* [1997] 2 WLR 806.

of the CoP does have potentially very serious consequences. So, if a licensed clinic fails, eg, to comply with the conditions of a treatment licence, eg regarding the qualification of professional staff in the licensed clinic, or fails to comply with conditions requiring anything to be 'proper' or 'suitable', then a licence committee of the HFEA may 'take into account any observance of or failure to observe the provisions of the code' when it comes to considering whether or not to revoke or vary a licence. Clearly, if it revokes the licence because of these failures to adhere or comply with CoP, the clinic is out of business.

20.47 Significantly, from the point of view of the HFEA's ongoing duty to update the CoP, and given the expertise of many of its membership in the sphere of assisted reproduction, s 26(3) states:

> 'Before preparing any draft, the Authority shall consult such persons as the Secretary of State may require it to consult and such other persons (if any) as it considers appropriate.'

Again, the idea underpinning this is that there should be a consultation process regarding updates and changes to the CoP. Interested parties, bodies or organisations need to be consulted before a new draft CoP is prepared, so that they can contribute meaningfully and in an informed way to the process of laying the foundations of a new edition of the CoP. As mentioned earlier, Parliament ultimately considers the draft new CoP, after the Secretary of State approves it.

HFEA Register of Information

20.48 Sections 31–35 of the 1990 Act cover the register of information which the HFEA is required to keep. This is another major responsibility and function of the HFEA. Section 31(1) provides that HFEA must keep a register containing information obtained by HFEA, including information about the provision of treatment services for any identifiable individual (s 31(2)(a)), or about the keeping or use of the gametes of any identifiable individual or of an embryo taken from an identifiable woman (s 31(2)(b)), or if it shows that an identifiable individual was or may have been born following treatment services. Significantly too, under s 31(3), a person aged 18 can request information from the HFEA about whether a person other than the parent of the applicant would have been the applicant's parent but for ss 27–29 of the 1990 Act, and the information about that other person will be non-identifying. Also, information may be disclosed to the applicant concerning whether the applicant and a person whom the applicant is proposing to marry are related. Theoretically two persons created, eg, from the same sperm donor could inadvertently propose to marry each other and s 31(4)(b) is specifically aimed at stopping this unlikely scenario from materialising. A safeguard is that the applicant be offered counselling about the implications of their request (s 31(3)(b)).

20.49 Section 31(6) similarly permits a 'minor' (ie a person under 18) to serve a notice on the HFEA asking if the intended spouse of that minor was or may have been born following licensed treatment services. The HFEA is required to answer this request, once the minor has been given a proper opportunity to receive counselling about the implications of compliance with that request. Also, under s 31(7), the minor may request that the HFEA give the minor notice if the information contained in the register shows that, but for ss 27 to 29 of this Act, the minor and the intended spouse are related.

Enforcement powers of the HFEA

20.50 Two key provisions of the Act concerning the enforcement powers of the HFEA are ss 39 and 40.

Section 39

20.51 Section 39 empowers HFEA members or HFEA employees, on entering licensed premises or clinics during normal business hours (presumably 9.00am–5.00pm, Monday–Friday), to take possession of anything they have reasonable grounds for believing may be required for any of their licensing functions, or which may be used in evidence for any criminal offence under the 1990 Act. Anything taken 'possession of' may be retained, 'for so long as it may be required for the purpose in question'. Both HFEA members and HFEA employees (ie HFEA inspectors and other HFEA employees) are given the power here to enter and inspect any licensed premises and importantly are able to take possession of anything – incredibly wide words – which they have reasonable grounds to believe may be required either for the various licensing functions of the HFEA (ie granting, revoking, suspending and varying licences), or for the purpose of being used in evidence for any of the many and varied criminal offences that may be committed under the 1990 Act, and furthermore that 'anything' taken possession of may be retained for as long as is required for the purpose in question (ie until the end of the criminal trial or licence committee hearing).

20.52 The potentially quite extensive scope of 'anything' that may be taken into possession by the HFEA members and employees is outlined in s 39(2), and includes 'information recorded in any form'. If information is, eg, not recorded in legible form, then the Act requires that any person having the power to do so to produce a copy of the information in legible form and take possession of the copy. So, however information is recorded in a licensed clinic, under this subsection the HFEA are empowered to take possession of it if they have reasonable grounds for believing it may be required in relation to either their licensing powers or alternatively in connection with a criminal offence under the Act. Also, if the clinic carelessly or intentionally records information in an illegible form, then the HFEA members or employees can require the offending clinic to produce that information in a legible form. Finally, s 39(3) provides that:

> 'Nothing in this Act makes it unlawful for a member or employee of the Authority to keep any embryo or gamete in pursuance of that person's functions as such.'

So it is not illegal for the HFEA member or employee to subsequently keep, eg, embryos or gametes taken possession of by them under s 39.

Section 40

20.53 Section 40 of the 1990 Act, headed 'Power to enter premises', relates to the enforcement powers of the HFEA where they have reasonable grounds for suspecting that an offence is being or has been committed on any licensed premises or clinic. Section 40(1) provides:

'A justice of the peace (including in Scotland, a sheriff) may issue a warrant under this section if satisfied by the evidence on oath of a member or employee of the Authority that there are reasonable grounds for suspecting that an offence under this Act is being, or has been committed on any premises.'

This section confers on the HFEA member or employee a very useful enforcement power to go to a Justice of the Peace or sheriff and seek to obtain a warrant from them, if there are reasonable grounds for suspecting that one or more of the criminal offences set out under the 1990 Act is being or has been committed in those licensed premises or clinic. The scope of the warrant to enter the licensed clinic or premises is set out in s 40(2) and provides that such a warrant authorises any named member or employee of HFEA together with any constables to enter the premises specified in the warrant, using such force as is reasonably necessary for the purpose, and to search the premises and take possession of anything which they have reasonable grounds to believe may be required to be used in evidence in any proceedings for an offence under the 1990 Act, or to take such steps as are necessary for preserving any such thing or preventing interference with it, including 'requiring any person having the power to do so to give such assistance as may reasonably be required.'

20.54 Section 40 confers a fundamentally wide and arguably draconian power on a named member of the HFEA and police constables (following the granting of a warrant from a Justice of the Peace or sheriff), authorising them to enter the licensed clinic using such force as is reasonably necessary for the purpose and then to search the licensed premises and take possession of 'anything' (again incredibly wide words) which the HFEA member or employee has reasonable grounds to believe may be required as evidence in any criminal offence covered by the 1990 Act. Alternatively, the warrant authorises them to take such steps as appear necessary to preserve anything in the licensed premises from being interfered with. Section 40(3) provides that such a warrant is effective for 1 month (quite a lengthy duration), and, furthermore, s 40(4) stipulates that anything taken possession of under s 40 can be retained for up to six months, or the end of proceedings against that person. Again, s 40(5) makes similar provision to s 39(2) regarding recorded information.

Chapter 21

Changes to the HFEA following the 2008 Act

INTRODUCTION

21.1 A number of changes were made to the HFEA concerning various matters arising out of the Human Fertilisation and Embryology Act (the 2008 Act).

CHANGES

21.2 Section 5 of the 2008 Act provides:

'Schedule 1 contains amendments of Schedule 1 to the 1990 Act (which are about disqualification for appointment to membership of the Authority and the tenure of office of members).'

The main amendment to the existing Sch 1, para 4 is the inclusion of the new para 4A(1) to (5). The most significant change is para 4A(1), which states that after para 4 of Sch 1 of the 1990 Act (ie appointment of members) is inserted;

'A person ("P") is disqualified for being appointed as chairman, deputy chairman or as any other member of the Authority if—
    (a) P is the subject of a bankruptcy restrictions order or interim order,
    (b) a bankruptcy order has been made against P by a court in Northern Ireland, P's estate has been sequestered by a court in Scotland, or under the law of Northern Ireland or Scotland, P has made a composition or arrangement with, or granted a trust deed for, P's creditors, or
    (c) in the last five years P has been convicted in the United Kingdom, the Channel Isles or the Isle of Man of an offence and has had a qualifying sentence passed on P.'

As the author states, the essence of these amendments in the new para 4A(1) to (5) is that:[1]

'Quite simply, persons who have certain criminal convictions or been subject to bankruptcy orders cannot be appointed to the Authority.'

21.3 Section 6 of the 2008 Act outlines a number of additional functions of the HFEA. Initially s 6(1) amends s 8 of the 1990 Act:

'In section 8 of the 1990 Act (general functions of the Authority), renumber the existing provision as subsection (1) of that section.'

Then s 6(2) provides that in subsection (1) of s 8 of the 1990 Act:

'(a) omit the word "and" immediately after paragraph (c), and
(b) After that paragraph insert-—

---

1   *Current Law Statutes Annotated,* 'Human Fertilisation and Embryology Act 2008, Chapter 22', (Sweet & Maxwell 2009), pp 1–210, at p 76.

> "(ca) maintain a statement of the general principles which it considers should be followed—
>> (i)   in the carrying-on of activities governed by this Act, and
>> (ii) in the carrying-out of its functions in relation to such activities,
> (cb) promote, in relation to activities governed by this Act, compliance with—
>> (i)   requirements imposed by or under this Act, and
>> (ii) the code of practice under section 25 of this Act, and".'

Commenting on this the author states:

> 'Thus the 2008 Act gives the Authority two extra functions, ie essentially to maintain a statement of general principles and secondly to promote compliance with the statutory requirements in the 1990 Act and with those contained in the Code of Practice, which basically fleshes out the dry bones of the statute.'[2]

21.4   Then finally s 6(3) provides that after s 8(1)(c) of the 1990 Act is inserted a new subsection (2) which stipulates that;

> 'The Authority may, if it thinks fit, charge a fee for any advice provided under subsection (1)(c).'

The author observed here:

> 'Thus now the Authority is given a discretionary power to charge a commercial fee for the advice and information it provides to licence holders, or to persons receiving treatment services, or persons who are providing gametes or embryos for use for the purposes of activities governed by the 1990 Act. Whether this new fee-charging power conferred on the Authority will deter persons from seeking hitherto free advice from the Authority on matters within their expertise regarding assisted reproduction – and may have detrimental consequences – remains to be seen.'[3]

21.5   Section 7 of the 2008 Act is headed 'Duties in relation to carrying out its functions' and provides that after s 8 of the 1990 Act, concerning the general functions of the HFEA, is inserted a new s 8ZA. It provides:

'8ZA Duties in relation to carrying out its functions
> (1)   The Authority must carry out its functions effectively, efficiently and economically.
> (2)   In carrying out its functions, the Authority must, so far as relevant, have regard to the principles of best regulatory practice (including the principles under which regulatory activities should be transparent, accountable, proportionate, consistent and targeted only at cases in which action is needed).'

The author has noted that:

> 'Section 8ZA(1) is consistent with the Government's desire and aim that statutory bodies and organisations operate and deliver services on a cost-effective basis. Subsection (2) is the general stricture that applies to all

---

2   Ibid, p 77.
3   Ibid.

public bodies or authorities exercising regulatory functions, namely that in doing so they must have regard to the principles of best regulatory practice.'[4]

This avowed government policy of quangos delivering services on a cost-effective basis has been accelerated and made arguably more compelling and pressing by the UK government deficit of £162 billion and the zeal of the new Coalition Government, created in May 2010, to tackle and cut dramatically this huge deficit. It aims to do so by, inter alia, wielding the axe to public spending, including culling certain quangos and reallocating the responsibilities of other quangos to other healthcare regulators, as is the case with the HFEA, which will effectively vanish as a separate, free-standing regulator.

21.6   Section 8 of the 2008 Act is headed 'Power to contract out functions etc'. It effectively inserts three new provisions for the HFEA to contract out certain functions it undertakes. It provides:

'After section 8A of the 1990 Act (duty of Authority to communicate with competent authorities of other EEA states) insert—

"8B Agency arrangements and provision of services
(1)   Arrangements may be made between the Authority and a government department, a public authority or the holder of a public office ('the other authority') for—
(a)   any functions of the Authority to be exercised by, or by members of the staff of, the other authority, or
(b)   the provision by the other authority of administrative, professional or technical services to the Authority.
(2)   Arrangements under subsection (1)(a) do not affect responsibility for the carrying-out of the Authority's functions.
(3)   Subsection (1)(a) does not apply to any function of making subordinate legislation (within the meaning of the Interpretation Act 1978)."'

21.7   The author has commented:

'Thus, under the new s 8B powers the Authority can make arrangements with any government department, a public authority or the holder of a public office, for any of the functions of the Authority, as outlined in the amended s 8 of the 1990 Act (s 8(1)(a), (b), (c), (ca), (cb)). This power extends to the Authority making arrangements with the other agency for that agency to provide administrative, professional or technical services to the Authority. This will hopefully allow the Authority to discharge its statutory responsibilities in a more flexible, responsive manner. As the Explanatory Notes to the Bill of February 5, 2008 state:

"This new flexibility will, for example, permit the Authority to arrange with another public body for that body to conduct inspections on behalf of the HFEA."'[5]

However, that said, the author also commented:

'However, even though the Authority is now empowered to contract out its functions to various agencies, Parliament is nonetheless clear that this

---

4   Ibid, p 78.
5   Ibid, p 79.

definitely does not mean that the Authority can wash its hands, in Pontius Pilate fashion, of its statutory responsibility for carrying out its functions under the 1990 Act. That much is explicit from the wording of s 8(2), which provides that:

> "Arrangements under subsection (1) (a) do not affect responsibility for the carrying-out of the Authority's functions."[6]

21.8 In addition s 8 of the 2008 Act inserts new s 8C into the 1990 Act. Section 8C provides:

'8C Contracting out functions of Authority

(1) This section applies to any function of the Authority other than—
  (a) any function which, by virtue of any enactment, may be exercised only by members of the Authority,
  (b) a function excluded from this section by the Secretary of State by order.
  (c) a function excluded from this section by the Secretary of State by order.

(2) A function is excluded from this section if—
  (a) it relates to the grant, revocation or variation of any licence,
  (b) it is a power or right of entry, search or seizure into or of any property, or
  (c) it is a function of making subordinate legislation (within the meaning of the Interpretation Act 1978).

(3) The Authority may make arrangements with any person ("the authorised person") for the exercise by that person, or by the employees of that person, of any function of the Authority to which this section applies.

(4) Any arrangements made by the Authority under this section—
  (a) may be revoked at any time by the Authority, and
  (b) do not prevent the Authority from exercising any function to which the arrangements relate.

(5) Subject to subsection (6), anything done or omitted to be done by or in relation to the authorised person (or an employee of the authorised person) in, or in connection with, the exercise or purported exercise of any function to which the arrangements relate is to be treated for all purposes as done or omitted to be done by or in relation to the Authority.

(6) Subsection (5) does not apply—
  (a) for the purposes of so much of any contract between the authorised person and the Authority as relates to the exercise of the function, or
  (b) for the purposes of any criminal proceedings brought in respect of anything done or omitted to be done by the authorised person (or any employee of the authorised person).

(7) Section 38A(2) of this Act (which relates to the keeping of embryos, human admixed embryos and gametes) applies in relation to the authorised person or any employee of the authorised person, when exercising functions of the Authority, as it applies in relation to

---

6   Ibid, p 80.

any member or employee of the Authority exercising functions as member or employee.'

21.9 Commenting on the new s 8C the author noted:

'Under s 8C of the 2008 Act, the Authority can now contract out functions to a body that is not a government department, public authority or to the holder of a public office. However, the functions that can be contracted out to a body that is not a public body are more limited than those that can be contracted out to public bodies/authorities. Hence the functions of the Authority that cannot be contracted out are listed in s8C (1) (a)–(c),

[…]

'The logic here, being if Parliament insists and is clear in an Act that a certain function can only be exercised by members of the Authority, then so be it. The Authority cannot ignore the clear intent of Parliament. Equally, if the Secretary of State explicitly states in secondary legislation that a function cannot be contracted out to a body that is not a public authority, then that too is the end of the matter. Certain functions of the Authority are specifically excluded from contracting out to a body that is not a public body, as stated in s 8C (b), and these are listed in s 8C(2) (a)–(c),

[…]

'This important safeguard ensure that ultimately it is only the Authority who can exercise the vital licensing jurisdiction under the Act, including granting/revoking and varying licences. This is crucial given the fact that a clinic cannot operate lawfully without a valid licence, whether it is storing or researching on embryos, or using them for treatment services – indeed it is a criminal offence to do any of the latter activities without possessing a licence from the Authority.'[7]

The author also noted:

'Equally importantly, the Authority cannot contract out its policing or enforcement powers under ss 39 and 40 of the 1990 Act, these being the potentially pivotal powers or right of entry, search or seizure into or of any property in the event the Authority believe a clinic is committing criminal offences or breaching their licence.'[8]

21.10 Section 8 of the 2008 Act inserts the new s 8D into the 1990 Act, covering the disclosure of information where functions of the HFEA are exercised by others. Section 8D provides:

'8D disclosure of information where functions of the HFEA are exercised by others
    (1)   This section applies to—
        (a)   the Authority,
        (b)   any public authority or other person exercising functions of the Authority by virtue of section 8B,
        (c)   any member of staff of any person falling within paragraph (b),

---

7   Ibid.
8   Ibid.

(d) any person exercising functions of the Authority by virtue of section 8C,

(e) an employee of any person falling within paragraph (d), or

(f) any person engaged by the Authority to provide services to the Authority.

(2) No obligation of confidence is to prevent the disclosure of information by a person to whom this section applies to another such person if the disclosure is necessary or expedient for the purposes of the exercise of any function of the Authority.'

21.11 Then, s 9 of the 2008 Act provides:

'After section 8D (inserted by section 8 above) insert—

"8E Power to assist other public authorities

(1) The Authority may if it thinks it appropriate to do so provide assistance to any other public authority in the United Kingdom for the purpose of the exercise by that authority of its functions.

(2) Assistance provided by the Authority under this section may be provided on such terms, including terms as to payment, as it thinks fit."'

Again, the author observed here:

'Section 9 adds a new s 8E, which is inserted after s 8D and confers another new power on the Authority to provide assistance to any other public authority in the United Kingdom regarding the exercise of that authority's functions, and furthermore that the Authority will be permitted to charge the other authority fees to reimburse it for the assistance rendered. Again, the notion of statutory bodies availing of opportunities to charge for some of its services and pay for its keep, if not make a profit, seems to underpin this section.'[9]

21.12 Finally, s 10 of the 2008 Act substitutes a new s 9A for s 9 of the 1990 Act. Section 10 is headed 'Power to delegate and establish committees' and provides:

'For section 9 (licence committees and other committees) of the 1990 Act substitute—

"9A Power to delegate and establish committees

(1) The Authority may delegate a function to a committee, to a member or to staff.

(2) The Authority may establish such committees or sub-committees as it thinks fit (whether to advise the Authority or to exercise a function delegated to it by the Authority).

(3) Subject to any provision made by regulations under section 20A (appeals committees), the members of the committees or sub-committees may include persons who are not members of the Authority.

(4) Subsection (1) has effect subject to any enactment requiring a decision to be taken by members of the Authority or by a committee consisting of members of the Authority."'

---

9   Ibid, pp 80–81.

21.13 The author noted:

'Section 9A(1) provides that the Authority may delegate an Authority function to a committee, a member of the Authority or to staff of the Authority, thus presumably permitting more flexibility for the Authority in its workings. Also, under s 9A(2) the Authority can also now, if it wants to, set up such committees/sub-committees as it deems fit, to advise the Authority, or even to exercise a function delegated to it by the Authority, and moreover, quite significantly, the members, respectively of these committees/ sub-committees do not now have to be members of the Authority. A practical example of the change that this section has made is that licence committees can now include non-Authority members. As the Explanatory Notes state:

"These new provisions will enable the HFEA to delegate any function, apart from those which can only be exercised by members, to its staff or to a committee. These functions can include licence decisions and development of the Code of Practice."

Section 9A(4) adds the significant caveat that the new powers of the Authority to delegate its functions is subject to any enactment which requires a decision to be taken by members of the Authority, or alternatively by a committee consisting of members of the Authority.'[10]

THE SAD DEMISE OF THE HFEA?

21.14 The announcement in late 2010 by the new Coalition government that they wanted, inter alia, to scrap the HFEA before the end of this Parliament (2015), and seemingly by as early as 2013,[11] and to transfer its functions to other healthcare regulatory bodies, has certainly unleashed a bureaucratic cutting cat amongst the regulatory pigeons. As the author contends[12], the government's 'cull and bonfire of many quangos or Arms Length Bodies, (ALB's), including the Human Fertilisation and Embryology Authority, (HFEA), whose functions will be allocated to other existing, retained health ALB's by the end of this current Parliament, (i.e. May 2015), signals the demise of arguably one of the more effective and respected quangos' in the UK.'

21.15 The author has noted that the HFEA has been monitoring and supervising a booming assisted reproduction industry and business over the last two decades. Three quarters of IVF is offered privately so the use of the commercial terms 'industry' and 'business' are apt descriptions of what essentially is being regulated. The author adds that the HFEA:

acting under the auspices and aegis of the HFEA 1990 and now the HFEA 2008, has incontrovertibly regulated and policed a burgeoning assisted reproduction industry over the past almost 20 years.'[13]

Indeed a HFEA press release on 1 November 2010, noted the success and effectiveness of the HFEA in regulating this expanding industry, stating that:

---

10 Ibid, p 81.
11 The author had noted this, saying the HFEA was on the government's hit list of public bodies: see S Burns, 'Seeds of change', (2010) 154(38) S J 16.
12 S. Burns, '*HFEA-RIP-OK?*' Family Law Journal, (forthcoming)
13 S Burns, 'Looking back' (2011) 12 (Mar) Family Law Journal 19.

'more than 200,000 babies have been born as a result of IVF treatment to those who would otherwise not have been able to have children.'

21.16 Also, by way of illustrating the scale of the infertility business being regulated by the HFEA, the HFEA document *Fertility Facts and Figures 2007*, which has the latest available figures, discloses that no less than 13,672 babies were born through IVF in licensed clinics in 2007, up from 11,262 in 2005, and that, furthermore, 472 babies were born through DI in licensed clinics in 2007, making a grand total of 14,146 babies born in 2007 as a result of the infertility techniques regulated by the 1990 Act. Putting these figures into the context of the total number of births in the United Kingdom, the HFEA stated:

'Around 1.5% of all births and 1.8% of all babies born in the UK were the result of IVF or donor insemination that occurred in 2007.'

Clearly, therefore, the vast majority of babies born in the United Kingdom (98.2 per cent) are born as a result of 'natural' conception, ie without the assistance of IVF, ICSI or DI, but 1.8 per cent is far from an insignificant percentage or total. As the author has noted, what had been the highly controversial in 1978 (when Louise Brown, the world's first IVF 'test tube' baby was born), and 1990–91 (when the 1990 Act was proceeding through Parliament, again the first legislation regulating the new assisted reproductive technologies in the world):

'...has in 2010/11, become for many the norm or conventional medical treatment, in no small measure due to the overseeing, monitoring role of the HFEA which has engendered and promoted the confidence and trust of the general public largely.'[14]

21.17 The HFEA press release of 1 November 2010, to mark the anniversary of the original 1990 Act receiving the Royal Assent on 1 November 1990, noted also that: 'there are 138 licensed centres and research establishments across the UK'. These clinics, licensed by the HFEA, provide, inter alia, a range of treatments to help infertile couples and individuals to have children, and some of them undertake research using human embryos and, since 1 October 2009, human admixed embryos for a range of research activities, permitted by Parliament and licensed, monitored and policed by the HFEA. The HFEA press release referred also to the 'huge advances in the field of assisted reproduction giving hope to many thousands of people otherwise unable to have children,' and that 'the HFEA has been at the heart of the licensing process as well as ensuring research is both ethical and of potential benefit to patients.'

21.18 Professor Lisa Jardine, the current Chairman of the HFEA, highlighted the huge benefits to mankind yielded by the infertility treatments and other activities regulated and supervised by the HFEA:

'In the last twenty years the world of fertility treatment has improved enormously and tens of thousands of families have benefitted directly as a result of IVF.'

She noted:

14   Ibid.

'Many of the issues that were debated twenty years ago such as the treatment of older women, compensation to donors and the risks of multiple births are still relevant today.'

Prof Jardine also asserted that the HFEA 'is the public body that the public looks to, to regulate these highly charged issues.'

21.19 Baroness Deech was one of several individuals highly critical of the new government's decision to include the HFEA on a hitlist of superfluous, expensive and excessively bureaucratic quangos ready for the chop, or at least reallocation of their regulatory role to other arm's length bodies (ALBs). On 9 August 2010 she challenged the HFEA being equated and likened to a superfluous, bureaucratic, expensive and pointless health 'regulator', stating that the HFEA is different:

'It was a world first and it remains a world model and leader ... It has enabled the UK to lead the way in issues connected to embryology; its record was a major factor in persuading Parliament to legislate in 2001 to extend the areas of permitted embryo research and again in 2008 in the renewed [2008 Act]'.

Baroness Deech emphasised the role of the HFEA as almost an ethical public shock-absorber, and referred to the Department of Health which found the HFEA 'useful in deflecting the embarrassment or blame that could result if anything went wrong in IVF treatment' (eg the tragic mix-up in Leeds when a black man's sperm was mistakenly inserted into a white woman's egg, and not into his wife's egg). She specifically gave the example of the HFEA 'giving reassurance that ... animal-hybrid embryos or the growth of eggs from tissue will be responsibly monitored.' Importantly, she observed:

'For 20 years the device of the HFEA has served to capture the ethical elements of new discoveries and the proper delivery of those treatments in the largely private clinics that it monitors.'

21.20 Scrapping of the HFEA, she claimed, made little financial sense either. She contended that:

'[the] current costs of the HFEA are approximately £5 million, most of it recovered from the clinics, with a small grant in aid [from the DoH, and that] This is minor; but the cost of doing away with it will be enormous.'

She also referred to the Report of the Parliamentary Joint Committee on the Human Tissue and Embryos (Draft) Bill (the abandoned precursor to the HFE Bill), which had, inter alia, recommended the merging of the HFEA and the Human Tissue Authority, but fortuitously the Committee recommended strongly against merging these two ALBs, and the government saw sense and backed down from their proposed merger of the two bodies. The Joint Committee stated that the HFEA had a distinct and expert job to fulfil; that no matter where its functions were situated, the same amount of money and the same quantity of expertise were going to be necessary; and that more money, allegedly in the region of £2 million, would be wasted in physically shifting the functions, creating a merged operation and losing experience. Baroness Deech commented: 'How much stronger are those arguments when it is contemplated submerging the HFEA in much wider health bodies?'

21.21 However the HFEA, and indeed how its membership is comprised, is not without its critics too. One vehement and persistent critic is Josephine

Quintavalle, Director of CORE. On 6 September 2010 she stated that the HFEA 'is an unelected body set up to implement the regulations of the 1990 [HFEA legislation] and no more than that', and that rather than the HFEA, National Parliaments should be in the vanguard making 'ethical decisions' on assisted reproduction issues and developments. Furthermore, she contended that:

> 'Decisions on complex ethical issues in the field of assisted reproduction should ultimately be taken by Parliament, but in the first instance should be deliberated by a democratic "National Bioethics Committee", acting in a purely advisory capacity. This would have the standing of an independent statutory body, with a membership encompassing professionals, patient groups, major religious and ethical groups, fairly representing the diverse positions within society. ... CORE believes that the creation of such a committee would bring the UK into line with most of the democratic world.'

The author has commented that the clear implication was that the HFEA is undemocratic and unrepresentative, thus undermining the legitimacy and authority of its decisions and policies. Interestingly Dr Evan Harries, a former MP who is generally very supportive of embryo research, stated on 2 August 2010 that 'those opposed to embryo research on principle are currently effectively prevented from serving on the HFEA.' He contended, therefore, that 'it's far better to have someone upfront about a contrary – albeit minority – view than to allow a subterranean fear of adverse tabloid over-reaction to distort decision-making [of the HFEA]'.

21.22 Some leading consultants in gynaecology (John Parsons and Michael Savvas at King's College Hospital, London) stated on 11 October 2010 that the 'dismembering' of the HFEA was a 'retrograde step and should be resisted'. They said that the HFEA played an important role in actively improving standards by, for example, being responsible for several public consultations on issues of best practice. They gave the example of reducing multiple pregnancies by limiting the number of embryos transferred. Also, from January – March 2011, the HFEA are consulting about increasing payments or expenses to egg donors and lifting the limit of families created from a sperm donor (currently set at 10 families per donor).[15] Parsons and Savvas added that the HFEA also:

> '... collates results and other data from clinics providing assisted conception services. These data allow patients to compare clinics where they might go for treatment and make decisions based on reliable information.'

The author noted:

> 'Thus the informed consent of the patient could be undermined if the HFEA is scrapped, if this vital source of information and role were lost or diluted, (ie 'submerged') in other ALB entities.'

Savvas and Parsons thus concluded on the epitaph of the HFEA that it 'plays a valuable role greater than the sum of its statutory obligations. Far better to prune it than uproot it.' That would be a fundamental error because:

> 'The public has learned to trust the HFEA which acts as a bulwark between the sensational headlines in the less responsible press and those working in the field.'

---

15   For a discussion of this See S Burns, 'Seeds of change', fn 11 above.

CONCLUSIONS

21.23 The very fact that the HFEA has overseen the creation of nearly 200,000 assisted reproduction births since 1991 in licensed clinics would for many be ample testimony to the success and effectiveness of its regulatory role. That there have been comparatively few, extremely rare disasters or accidents or mix-ups etc in licensed clinics must be in some small way directly attributable to the oversight of the HFEA in these particular spheres of assisted reproductive medicine.

The author has concluded:

'Regulation of some assisted reproductive techniques (not all, because surgery to help/overcome infertility problems, and administering of eg super-ovulatory drugs to increase fertility are not covered by the HFEA or the HFEA legislation), and strict but effective and sensible monitoring and policing of licensed clinics by an independent, expert, but not doctor dominated regulator (with respectively research/treatment and storage licences), are much preferable to prohibition (ineffective, unsafe, uncontrolled, unethical), or total permissiveness, ie letting scientists/doctors research on human embryos at will, or treat patients at will, eg implant five or six embryos in patients, (again unethical, dangerous). The demise of the HFEA may well be regretted by future generations. Is it a case of penny-wise pound foolish? Time will tell.'

Thus, it is a case of watch this space as to what actually materialises to replace the soon-to-be-defunct HFEA, or at least where its functions are to be relocated.

Part 8

The Lottery of Certain Lives

Chapter 22

The Lottery of Accessing Assisted Reproduction

INTRODUCTION

22.1   Incontrovertibly there exists a lottery in accessing certain assisted reproductive treatments in the United Kingdom. Three quarters of IVF treatments are offered privately to fee-paying customers. Accessing IVF in this largest percentage of treatment depends on the patient(s) fundamentally and principally being able to afford the cost of the IVF treatment. If the potential patient(s) cannot afford to pay for the IVF treatment, either directly out of their own pocket, with a bank loan, or thanks to a generous donation from a family member or relative or friend, quite simply they do not get private, fee-paid IVF. The ability to pay the fees at the private IVF clinic determine whether one can have the treatments offered by that clinic. Money talks and is crucial as to whether the patient is able to walk into the clinic and get help for their infertility. This must be unfair to the huge number of patients who quite simply do not possess the financial resources to pay for IVF privately. Some of course would contend that infertility is not a disease, and given a huge national debt, and with much more pressing and compelling competing demands on a finite budget, as well as a growing UK population, why should money be directed towards alleviating infertility? The argument might run: why direct money at a treatment (eg IVF) with a 25–35 per cent success rate at best, when that money could be more sensibly, profitably and beneficially be directed at treatments with better success outcomes, or treatments needed to alleviate diseases that kill, like cancers, heart-disease, strokes, or progressive neurological diseases like Alzheimer's disease, senile dementia or Parkinson's disease, or other progressive diseases like MS or motor neurone disease that cause immense physical suffering, pain and debilitation? For some this is an ethical no-brainer and merely stating the obvious. Indeed Kitzhaber noted that in Oregon in the United States over 700 medical services were ranked and prioritised and, given a limited public health Medicaid budget, infertility services were given a low priority. Also, given that IVF was an expensive treatment option, it was ranked 696 out of 709 services and treatments.[1]

22.2   Yet for the infertile and their families, and doctors wishing to treat them, the enormous pain and desperation to have a child is real, tangible and pressing. The emotional, psychological and mental pain, loss and feeling of exclusion, alienation and isolation are incalculable but no less real for that. Some commentators appear to be dancing on the head of ethical pins in either supporting or rejecting the claims of the 'deserving' or 'undeserving' infertile or those who merely wish to have a child, whilst completely ignoring the masses of people who are denied fertility treatment because they cannot afford it or because they fall foul of the vicissitudes of the IVF postcode

---

1   J A Kitzhaber, 'Prioritising health services in an era of limit: the Oregon experience' (1997) 307 BMJ 373–7.

lottery. This theme is endorsed by Bryan & Higgins who lament: 'We hear a great deal from politicians and commentators about who they think should not receive infertility treatment,' but that '[W]e hear much less about the far greater number of ordinary, desperate couples who should get treatment but don't.'[2] Our moralistic or ethical and legal arsenal and intellectual energies are directed at the periphery (eg should post-menopausal mums get IVF?; was s 13(5) of the 1990 Act theoretically discriminatory against a tiny minority of patients?) at the expense of letting the government off the hook in unfairly ignoring the NICE guidelines and more fundamentally not properly funding fertility treatments on the NHS, thus permitting the growth of a large private fertility industry, and effectively disenfranchising tens of thousands of potentially excellent candidates from becoming loving parents of much wanted children.

A BUSINESS

22.3 Brazier observes that the 1990 Act 'places limits on what patients seeking certain treatments for infertility may ask for and receive.'[3] Furthermore: 'What was until very recently seen as a couple's private business has become in many cases the business of the state', although arguably it ought to be the business of the state given that 25 per cent of all IVF treatment cycles are performed in NHS licensed clinics, that most consultants in human reproductive medicine, obstetricians and gynaecologists were trained and paid for at great tax-payer expense, and that children born prematurely following IVF will generally be treated in NHS facilities and paid for again at great expense by the tax-payer:

> 'An area of medicine, treatment of infertility, which was not long ago a "speciality" which offered little more than minor surgery, advice and tender loving care has grown into a multimillion pound international business.'

Brazier observes too 'the transformation of reproductive choices from the private to the public arena and the growth of such a profitable new medical business', ie reproductive medicine.[4]

22.4 Brazier also poses the question: is reproductive medicine a 'profession or market'? In attempting to answer the question, she noted that the most profound change in regulating reproductive medicine since the Warnock Report was the dramatically increased role of commerce. She also noted in 1984 that Warnock based its recommendations in relation to both fertility treatment and research on the supposition that fertility services would be integrated into the NHS and that research was essentially an 'academic' endeavour and not a business, as three-quarters of it currently is. She added:

> 'The enormous commercial potential of developments in reproductive medicine was hardly foreseen, and opposition to commodification of reproduction was almost a given.'

By contrast in 1999 (and arguably now in 2011), 'debate on commodification and commercialisation is at the forefront of debate today.' Brazier flagged

---

2   E Bryan and R Higgins *Infertility: New Choices, New Dilemmas* (Penguin Books, 1995) p 197.
3   M. Brazier, 'Regulating the Reproductive Business' (1999) 7 Med L Rev 166.
4   Ibid, at 168.

up that a fertility 'industry' has developed to provide treatment on a profit-making basis both to British citizens and 'procreative tourists' escaping more prohibitive regimes elsewhere in Europe, and 'Pressure to pay gamete donors and surrogates continues.'[5]

22.5   Brazier asserted that:

'Difficult questions confront regulators.
  (1)   Whatever the pros and cons of recognising a reproduction market, is a covert market more dangerous than an overt market?
  (2)   Given the diversity of regulation worldwide can any single jurisdiction continue to enforce its own rules?'

In other words firstly it is much better to have a strictly regulated or policed (by the HFEA) reproductive medicine business than an unregulated, free-for-all, open market in reproductive medicine, and secondly global health tourism, here specifically eg IVF tourism, or egg or sperm or embryo-buying tourism, render academic national strict regulation of these activities in the United Kingdom.

THE WARNOCK REPORT

22.6   The Warnock Report,[6] arguably the foundation stone and pioneering moral and ethical compass underpinning the whole edifice of assisted reproductive regulation as manifested in 1990 in the guise of the 1990 Act, had a number of pertinent and sensible views on eligibility and accessing the new assisted reproductive treatments. That said, the Warnock Report was published in 1984 (27 years ago!) and incontrovertibly times and social attitudes to a wide range of matters have changed beyond recognition in the United Kingdom since then.

22.7   The Warnock Report noted that whilst:

'[I]t is sometimes suggested that infertility treatment should be available only to married couples, in the interests of any child that may be born as a result [and] While we are vitally aware of the need to protect these interests, we are not prepared to recommend that access to treatment should be based exclusively on the legal status of marriage.'[7]

Moreover the Warnock Report helpfully elaborates on the definition of a couple for the purposes of accessing treatment, giving the term a wider, purposive, more modern construction, rather than interpreting it narrowly and restrictively, as connoting and being therefore applicable and available to only married couples. Warnock states that;

'In discussing treatment for infertility, this report takes the term *couple* to mean a heterosexual couple living together in a stable relationship, whether married or not …We use the words *husband* and *wife* to denote a relationship,

---

5   See the latest HFEA consultation on paying sperm or egg donors more compensation, at http://www.hfea.gov.uk/6285.html and see SBurns article too).

6   *Report of the Committee of Enquiry into Human Fertilisation and Embryology* ('The Warnock Report'), Cmnd 9314, July 1984.

7   Warnock, para 2.5.

not a legal status (except where the context makes differentiation necessary, for example in relation to legitimacy).'[8]

Clearly in 2012 even this then (1984) liberal interpretation of what constituted a 'couple' would appear terribly outdated, antediluvian, narrow and conservatively prescriptive, never mind arguably unfair, unjustifiable and discriminatory.

22.8   Warnock flagged up the importance of the interests of the child (ie the welfare of the child) in determining who accesses the new range of fertility treatments, noting:

> In the evidence, concern was expressed that infertility treatment may be provided for couples without due regard for the interests of any child that may be born as a result.'

It cited as an example permitting a couple who have a previous conviction for child abuse to access treatment, and therefore:

> 'It has been argued that the greater the degree of intervention in the creation of a child, the more responsibility must be taken for that child.'

Warnock addresses that point by correctly observing that:

> 'However the evidence also drew attention to the absence of any restrictions on procreation by fertile couples, whatever their circumstances.'

Perversely, the fertile can in sadly too frequent and unsuitable occasions procreate and bring children into the world without restrictions or scrutiny before birth and with flagrant disregard for their progeny's welfare. Warnock also touched on the impact of human rights in the sphere of who can access infertility treatment, noting that:

> 'Indeed, some of the evidence referred to the fact that Articles 8 and 12 of the European Convention on Human Rights guarantee a respect for family life and the right to found a family … It has been argued that these provisions create a right to take full advantage of the techniques which are available to alleviate infertility.

22.9   In addition, the Warnock Report referred to:

> '… other considerations which many believe should be taken into account. For example, a woman may seek treatment when she has herself, at an earlier stage, been sterilised at her own request. Perhaps because of a new marriage, she now very much wants children. The question may be raised whether, if she has children, albeit from another marriage, she should be eligible for infertility treatment.'

Warnock also notes the case of, again, a woman who has had children who may subsequently become infertile. 'Opinions may be divided about whether she should be eligible for treatment.' Interestingly the Primary Care Trust Survey highlights clearly that there is no uniformity on this consideration or non-clinical criteria necessarily automatically debarring a woman from accessing IVF.

---

8   Ibid, para 2.5.

22.10 Warnock then evaluates whether infertility treatments should be available and offered to single women or lesbian couples, noting:

'Furthermore, the various techniques for assisted reproduction offer not only a remedy for infertility, but also offer the fertile single woman or lesbian couple the chance of parenthood without the direct involvement of a male partner.'[9]

Lesbian couples and single women are generally fertile. There is no evidence to suggest more than one in seven of them are infertile, if the accepted guesstimate for general infertility is replicated in these two specific categories. Why allow the generally fertile to access equally a scarce, costly treatment for a condition (ie infertility) that they do not suffer from? Is that not an unethical and unjust use of resources? Warnock concluded:

'We … believe that as a general rule it is better for children to be born into a two-parent family, with both father and mother, although we recognise that it is impossible to predict with any certainty how lasting such a relationship will be.'

22.11 Warnock then states that the Committee considered very carefully whether there are circumstances where it is inappropriate for treatment which is solely for the alleviation of infertility to be provided, and answered that question:

'In general we hold that everyone should be entitled to seek expert advice and appropriate investigation. This will usually involve referral to a consultant. However, at the present time [ie in 1984] services for the treatment of infertility are in short supply, both for initial referral and investigation and for the more specialised treatments considered in this report.'[10]

That being so, the report continues that in this situation of scarcity some individuals (who and how?) will have a more compelling case for treatment than others:

'In the circumstances medical practitioners will, clearly, use their clinical judgment as to the priority of the individual case bearing in mind such considerations as the patient's age, the duration of infertility and the likelihood that treatment will be successful. So far this is not contentious.'

With great respect it is indeed contentious, as controversial decisions to provide IVF to post-menopausal women graphically demonstrate.

22.12 Warnock continued:

'However, notwithstanding our view that every patient is entitled to advice and investigation of his or her infertility, we can foresee occasions where the consultant may, after discussion with professional health and social work colleagues, consider that there are valid reasons why infertility treatment would not be in the best interests of the patient, the child that may be born following treatment, or the patient's immediate family.'

Warnock correctly, it is submitted, stated:

---

9   Ibid, para 2.9.
10   Ibid, para 2.12.

'This question of eligibility for treatment is a very difficult one, and we believe that hard and fast rules are not applicable to its solution.'[11]

Warnock did not provide a rosetta stone to decipher criteria for accessing scarce and costly infertility treatments. It therefore added:

'We recognise that this will place a heavy burden of responsibility on the individual consultant who must make social judgments that go beyond the purely medical, in the types of case we have discussed. We considered whether it was possible for us to set out the wider social criteria that consultants, together with their professional colleagues, should use in deciding whether infertility treatment should be provided for a particular patient. We decided it was not possible to draw up comprehensive criteria that would be sensitive to the circumstances of every case. We recognise however that individual practitioners are on occasions going to decline to treat a particular patient and we recommend that in cases where consultants decline to provide treatment they should always give the patient a full explanation of the reasons.'

A blank and bald refusal of infertility treatment without any reasons given for the refusal was, for Warnock, unacceptable. As Warnock concluded:

'This would at least ensure that patients were not kept in ignorance of the reason for refusal, and would be able to exercise their right to seek a second opinion.'

22.13 Warnock considered also the relative priorities of offering infertility treatment versus other arguably more compelling life preserving treatments, and noted:

'... with concern the lengthy hospital waiting lists for gynaecological treatment and the tendency in some places for infertility patients to be given the lowest priority on waiting lists for both in-patient and out-patient treatment.'

Cynics might argue that little has changed in 2012, given that some PCTs in the NHS do not even offer one IVF treatment cycle. Is infertility treatment regarded as a 'Cinderella' service by some?

THE BRITISH FERTILITY SOCIETY

22.14 The British Fertility Society (BFS), a multi-disciplinary organisation representing professionals with an interest in reproductive medicine, in their submission responding to the Department of Health publication,[12] inter alia, noted that:

'There is good published epidemiological evidence that identifies that the incidence of infertility varies across the United Kingdom, affecting approximately 1 in 6 of the population.'[13]

---

11 Ibid, para 2.13.
12 Department of Health, 'Liberating the NHS: Commissioning for patients' (2010).
13 British Fertility Society, 'Submission to Department of Health on "Liberating the NHS: Commissioning for patients"' (2010), p 3.

Although these figures need to be treated with caution and circumspection because a lot of these defined infertile couples or persons may not want children or alternatively may not in fact be infertile. Basically the quoted 1 in 6 figure must be a guesstimate, albeit an informed one. The BFS state that since 1983 the NHS has commissioned more advanced infertility treatment, such as in vitro fertilisation, and that in 2004 the National Institute for Health and Clinical Excellence (NICE) recommended that all eligible couples should be offered up to three complete IVF cycles. Furthermore, the response continued that an IVF cycle was clearly defined by the last Labour Government, as 'one fresh stimulated cycle plus the replacement of all spare embryos generated during this stimulated cycle'.

22.15 The BFS in addition were quite emphatic and sure that:

'Since the inception of NHS IVF funding there has been considerable variation in availability of service throughout the United Kingdom. This has been clearly outlined in a number of reports commissioned both by Government and performed independently. Unfortunately this has lead to a great inequality in the service, often described as a "post code lottery".'[14]

In other words whether you get NHS IVF depends totally, or at least largely, on your postal address (ie what part of the country you live in). If you have the good fortune to be in an area where the PCT funds IVF in accordance with NICE guidelines you are fortunate and at least get the opportunity to receive IVF, whereas by contrast if you are in an area where the PCT does not follow the NICE guidelines, because of lack of resources or different priorities, then you may well be unfortunate and not be offered IVF, even though your circumstances and burning desire or desperate need for a child are of equal measure to your more fortunate counterpart in the area that funds IVF. That is arguably unfair and unjust given that the NHS is a national health service and your needs are every bit as legitimate, compelling and essential for you as they are for your more fortunate counterpart.

22.16 The BFS furthermore adds:

'Currently there are 84 clinics licensed to provide IVF in the UK, some offering only NHS or private treatment, and other offering a mixture of both. Only around one third of the current figure of 46,000 IVF cycles performed annually in the UK, are funded through the Health Service.'[15]

The BFS in addition are not happy with the devolving of commissioning of NHS IVF, believing this leads to inequalities and iniquities in provision, which are unfair to infertile patients. They contend that devolved commissioning has not been shown to be effective for this service, and point out to illustrate this criticism how vulnerable fertility/IVF services are to cuts, citing Warrington, Bury, and central Manchester as having had to either withdraw or severely restrict services. They appear to be suggesting that a move to devolved commissioning of IVF might accentuate the lack of availability of NHS IVF. It might translate into divide and rule, in that more bodies deciding who and how one gets IVF might also make it easier for decisions being made to jettison

14 Ibid.
15 Ibid.

completely or at least severely restrict the availability of IVF. Thus the BFS warn:

'A move to devolved funding for IVF services poses a great threat to what many PCTs perceive as an easy target to save money in these testing financial times. This would downgrade a service which is still one of the most poorly state funded services in Europe.'[16]

Provision of NHS IVF is arguably one of the 'Cinderella' services therefore available in our NHS. The current climate of financial and spending cuts aimed at tackling the huge national debt does not augur well for its likely transformation into a 'beautiful princess' service.

22.17 The BFS therefore concluded by stating:

'The British Fertility Society firmly believes that licensed fertility treatment should be provided through the National Commissioning Board as a National Specialised Service, which would facilitate a uniform, transparent and fair service for all suffering from infertility, throughout the UK, eradicating the post-code lottery. Financially, this would allow a clear budget to be identified nationally, based on sound national statistics ... By adopting this approach the UK could redress the imbalance currently evident in the UK and provide a comprehensive and fair service for this vulnerable group of patients.'[17]

THE NICE GUIDELINES

22.18 The NICE Guidelines[18] are designed to help doctors reach decisions about the best treatment for certain conditions. The NICE Guidelines state at the outset that:

'Clinical guidelines have been defined as "systematically developed statements that assist clinicians and patients in making decisions about appropriate treatment for specific conditions."'

'The aim of this guideline is to offer best practice advice on the care of people in the reproductive age group who perceive that they have problems in conceiving.'[19]

Clearly the NICE Guidelines are just that, ie they are guidelines to assist doctors and patients in reaching decisions about the most suitable treatment for a condition. They are not meant to be a straitjacket designed to be rigidly enforced without the slightest deviance. That said, they are not meant to be blithely ignored.

22.19 The Introduction to the NICE Guidelines then sets out some interesting facts and figures concerning the prevalence of infertility in the United Kingdom. Infertility can be primary, in couples who have never conceived, or secondary, in couples who have previously conceived (presumably with a former partner). It

---

16 Ibid.
17 Ibid, pp 3–4.
18 The National Collaborating Centre for Women's and Children's Health, 'Fertility: assessment and treatment for people with fertility problems' Clinical Guideline commissioned by the National Institute for Clinical Excellence (February 2004) ('NICE Guidelines').
19 NICE Guidelines, p 1.

is estimated that infertility affects one in seven couples in the United Kingdom and that a typical primary care trust, health board or strategic health authority may therefore expect to see around 230 new consultant referrals per 250,000 head of population per year. The Guidelines also state that it would appear that there has been no major change in the prevalence of fertility problems but that more people now seek help for such problems than did so previously. In other words infertility rates are not necessarily or probably increasing in 2012 compared to 10, 20 or 30 years ago. It is just that more people are coming forward seeking help for infertility and more diagnoses of infertility or sub-fertility are being made by doctors. What had been frequently a hidden, socially embarrassing, or even in extremes cases shameful problem that was not viewed as a medical condition or illness warranting medical intervention is now routinely treated, and for most people arguably without any ethical controversy. The NICE Guidelines add that a cause of infertility is not identified in 30 per cent of couples – hence the scientific imperative for research into these unknown causes and the further need to use either human embryos or human admixed embryos for that research. In a further 27 per cent of couples the cause is attributed to ovulatory disorders, in 14 per cent of couples tubal damage, whilst a low sperm count or quality is thought to contribute to infertility in 19 per cent of couples. Finally the Guidelines state that the presence of disorders in both the man and the woman has been reported to occur in about 39 per cent of cases.

22.20   Crucially the Guidelines state:

'NHS funding for investigation of fertility problems is generally available but there is wide variation and often limited access to NHS-funded treatment, particularly assisted reproduction techniques.'

They proceed to categorise fertility treatment thus:

'There are three main types of fertility treatment: medical treatment (such as use of drugs for ovulation induction); surgical treatment (for example, laparoscopy for ablation of endometriosis); and assisted reproduction. Assisted reproduction relates to all treatments that deal with means of conception other than normal coitus.'

The Guidance flags up that assisted reproduction, moreover:

'frequently involves the handling of gametes or embryos and includes one or more of the following: ovarian stimulation; oocyte collection; sperm preparation; in vitro fertilisation (IVF)* embryo transfer;* intrauterine insemination (IUI); donor insemination;* intracytoplasmic sperm injection (ICSI);* gamete inrafallopian transfer (GIFT); zygote intrafallopian transfer (ZIFT); pronuleate stage tubal transfer (PROST);* cryopreservation* and other related procedures.* Those procedures which involve the handling of embryos or donated gametes (indicated by* above) are regulated by the Human Fertilisation and Embryology Authority.'

22.21 The NICE Guidelines, inter alia, highlight the biological reality that there is no guarantee that a couple even in the general population will conceive immediately or very soon after having normal, unprotected sex, so *a fortiori* couples with infertility problems will take even longer. This fact must be weighed up by patients and clinicians in deciding access to treatment. It notes:

'People who are concerned about their fertility should be informed that about 84% of couples in the general population will conceive within 1 year if they do not use contraception and have regular sexual intercourse. Of those who do not conceive in the first year, about half will do so in the second year (cumulative pregnancy rate 92%).'[20]

Hence only 8 percent of couples will not have conceived after two years of regular unprotected sexual intercourse. These are the potential market for assisted reproduction treatment. Again the NICE Guidelines further note that:

'People who are concerned about their fertility should be informed that female fertility declines with age, but that the effect of age on male fertility is less clear. With regular unprotected sexual intercourse, 94% of fertile women aged 35 years, and 77% of those aged 38 years, will conceive after 3 years of trying.'

22.22   The NICE Guidelines helpfully define the term 'infertility':

'Infertility should be defined as failure to conceive after regular unprotected sexual intercourse for 2 years in the absence of known reproductive pathology.'[21]

Again a definitive definition of what 'infertility' is arguably concentrates the minds of and focuses the response of those who are providing and those who fund assisted reproductive treatments. The Guidelines add that:

'People who are concerned about delays in conception should be offered an initial assessment. A specific enquiry about lifestyle and sexual history should be taken to identify people who are less likely to conceive.

[…]

'People who have not conceived after 1 year of regular unprotected sexual intercourse should be offered further clinical investigation including semen analysis and/or assessment of ovulation.'[22]

22.23   Chapter 4 of the NICE Guidelines relates to the principles of care expected when patients are undergoing assisted reproduction treatment:

'Couples who experience problems in conceiving should be seen together because both partners are affected by decisions surrounding investigation and treatment.

'People should have the opportunity to make informed decisions regarding their care and treatment via access to evidence-based information. These choices should be recognised as an integral part of the decision-making process.'[23]

Of fundamental importance too is that couples who suffer from fertility problems need to be offered counselling. This is viewed as giving couples a critical safeguard and protection against mental and psychological distress. Thus the Guidance provides:

---

20   NICE Guidelines, Chapter 2, 'Summary of recommendations and practice algorithms', p 8.
21   NICE Guidelines, p 9.
22   Ibid, p 10.
23   Ibid.

'People who experience fertility problems should be offered counselling because fertility problems themselves, and the investigation and treatment of fertility problems, can cause psychological stress.'[24]

The net of counselling potentially available is cast very widely:

'Counselling should be offered before, during and after investigation and treatment, irrespective of the outcome of these procedures.'[25]

22.24 Finally, sensibly given the insatiable demands on medical treatment and care, the Guidance favours and endorses treatment by specialist as opposed to generalist care for those who have fertility needs, urging that:

'People who experience fertility problems should be treated by a specialist team because this is likely to improve the effectiveness and efficiency of treatment and is known to improve patient satisfaction.'[26]

22.25 There are useful chapters and recommendations on treatments for a range of causes of infertility including:

- Chapter 6: Medical and surgical management of male factor fertility problems;
- Chapter 7: Ovulation induction;
- Chapter 8: Tubal and uterine surgery;
- Chapter 9: Medical and surgical management of endometriosis; and
- Chapter 10: Intrauterine insemination.

22.26 Chapter 11 covers 'Factors affecting the outcome of in vitro fertilisation treatment'. The summary of the NICE recommendations flag up female age as being significant, stating:

'Women should be informed that the chance of a live birth following in vitro fertilisation treatment varies with female age and that the optimal female age range for in vitro fertilisation treatment is 23–39 years.'[27]

This age band is critical as that is the age range in which theoretically PCTs will provide NHS IVF treatment to infertile women. It adds:

'Chances of a live birth per treatment cycle are:
- greater than 20% for women aged 23–35 years
- 15% for women aged 36–38 years
- 10% for women aged 39 years
- 6% for women aged 40 years or older.'

Unsurprisingly, the chances of a live birth per treatment cycle drop dramatically with the woman's age; the older she is the less likelihood that the IVF will result in a baby. Clearly a 45-year-old woman will have a very tiny chance of having a live birth by IVF (indeed a 45-year-old woman trying to have a baby naturally, without IVF, will also have a smaller chance of having a baby too). Then the Guidelines explain, at least partially, why the age range is set at a lower limit of 23 years:

---

24 Ibid.
25 Ibid.
26 Ibid.
27 Ibid, p 23.

'The effectiveness of in vitro fertilisation treatment in woman younger than 23 years is uncertain because very few women in this age range have in vitro fertilisation treatment.'

The woman's reproductive clock naturally starts ticking against her around the age of 35, continues to accelerate to her detriment from 35–45 and generally stops ticking totally with the menopause around the age of 45–48. So the NICE Guidelines are aimed generally (certainly from age 23–35) when most women will be trying to have children and trying most successfully naturally.

22.27   The summary regarding the number of embryos to be transferred and multiple pregnancy states:

'Couples should be informed that the chance of multiple pregnancy following in vitro fertilisation treatment depends on the number of embryos transferred per cycle of treatment. To balance the chance of a live birth and the risk of multiple pregnancy and its consequences, no more than two embryos should be transferred during any one cycle of in vitro fertilisation treatment.'[28]

Statistically the chances of having a live birth do not rise significantly by placing three rather than two embryos in the infertile woman, but the chances of multiple births by contrast rise sharply. In other words the risks or burdens exceed the benefits, so ethically and medically this procedure should generally not occur.

22.28   The general requirement for informed consent is manifest in the recommendations concerning number of previous treatment cycles.

'Couples should be informed that the chance of a live birth following in vitro fertilisation treatment is consistent for the first three cycles of treatment, but that the effectiveness after three cycles is less certain.'[29]

Again, a further wise recommendation is that:

'Women should be informed that in vitro fertilisation is more effective in women who have previously been pregnant and/or had a live birth.'

There are also sensible warnings to couples and women about the potential hazards and risks to conceiving and to an IVF pregnancy from alcohol, smoking and caffeine consumption, and a woman having a body mass index greater than the ideal range of 19–30.

22.29   The critical recommendation of NICE regarding access to NHS IVF is contained in para 1.10.8, which is headed 'Clinical effectiveness and referral for in vitro fertilisation treatment':

'Couples in which the woman is aged 23–39 years at the time of treatment and who have an identified cause for their fertility problems (such as azoospermia or bilateral tubal occlusion) or who have infertility of at least 3 years' duration should be offered up to three stimulated cycles of in vitro fertilisation treatment.'

28   Ibid.
29   Ibid, p 24.

NICE are basically contending that women in the 23–39 age category who have an identified cause for their fertility problems (presumably the 25 per cent of patients where the cause of infertility is unknown could legitimately and lawfully be denied IVF on that basis), including, eg, conditions like the male not being able to produce sufficient sperm in sufficient quality, or the female having blocked fallopian tubes, or alternatively who have been infertile for a period of three years, should be offered up to three stimulated cycles of IVF treatment. In essence this is how NICE believes the scarce resource of IVF treatment should be allocated in the NHS to maximise its effectiveness.

22.30 In addition the NICE Guidelines recommend that:

'Embryos not transferred during a stimulated in vitro fertilisation cycle may be suitable for freezing. If two or more embryos are frozen then they should be transferred before the next stimulated treatment cycle because they will minimise ovulation induction and egg collection, both of which carry risks for the woman and use more resources.'[30]

Therefore NICE are sensibly recommending that spare or excess frozen embryos created after the initial IVF treatment cycle are used before embarking on and subjecting the woman to the process of further invasive, worrying IVF treatment cycles, which needless to say involve greater financial costs and potentially attract various risks for the woman.

22.31 The NICE Guidelines make a number of recommendations concerning the treatment of patients with HIV, hepatitis B or hepatitis C. It recommends concerning medical assessment and screening that:

'People undergoing in vitro fertilisation treatment should be offered screening for HIV, hepatitis B virus and hepatitis C virus; people found to test positive should be managed and counselled appropriately.'

Also, in managing couples with viral infections it adds:

'In considering the decision to provide fertility treatment for couples with HIV, hepatitis B or hepatitis C infections the implications of these infections for potential children should be taken into account.'

Presumably this includes considering the small risk of the IVF child being infected with HIV, hepatitis B or hepatitis C and of the parent being ill or dying, or unable to care for the child in the (imminent) future. The decision to offer IVF treatment to, eg, an HIV positive woman or couple is for some totally unacceptable ethically and morally, although Professor Robert Winston and his team did offer IVF treatment to a woman dubbed 'Sheila'.[31]

22.32 Concerning the use of intracytoplasmic sperm injection (ICSI), a variation on conventional IVF, the NICE Guidelines state that the 'recognised indications' for treating by ICSI include severe deficits in semen quality, obstructive azoospermia or nonobstructive azoospermia. If any of those occur in the male patient, treatment by ICSI is thus indicated. In addition the Guidelines recommend:

30 Ibid, p 25.
31 Prof R Winston, *Making Babies: A Personal View of IVF Treatment* (BBC Books, 1996).

'In addition, treatment by ICSI should be considered for couples in whom a previous in vitro fertilisation treatment cycle has resulted in failed or very poor fertilisation.'[32]

The importance of genetic issues and counselling are also emphasised by NICE, who recommend, inter alia, that:

'Before considering treatment by intracytopasmic sperm injection couples should undergo appropriate investigations, both to establish a diagnosis and to enable informed discussion about the implications of treatment.'

Furthermore, before treatment by ICSI:

'consideration should be given to relevant genetic issues ... Where a specific genetic defect associated with male infertility is known or suspected couples should be offered appropriate genetic counselling and testing.'

Interestingly regarding which treatment (IVF versus ICSI) is preferable, the guidance recommends:

'Couples should be informed that intracytoplasmic sperm injection improves fertilisation rates compared to in vitro fertilisation alone, but once fertilisation is achieved the pregnancy rate is no better than with in vitro fertilisation.'[33]

Fertilisation of an egg is not the same thing as a pregnancy, still less a successful 9-month pregnancy or a healthy baby.

22.33   Next, regarding donor insemination (DI), the NICE Guidelines flag up the indications for DI, that the use of DI is considered effective in managing fertility problems associated with a number of conditions, namely obstructive azoospermia, nonobstructive azoospermia, infectious disease in the male partner (eg HIV), severe rhesus isoimmunisation and severe deficits in semen quality in couples who do not wish to undergo ICSI. It adds that DI should also be considered in certain cases where there is a high risk of transmitting a genetic disorder to the offspring. In relation to information and counselling, the guidance recommends:

'Couples should be offered information about the relative merits of intracytoplasmic sperm injection and donor insemination in a context that allows equal access to both treatment options.

'Couples considering donor insemination should be offered counselling from someone who is independent of the treatment unit regarding all the physical and psychological implications of treatment for themselves and potential children.'[34]

In accessing assisted reproductive treatments informed consent and availability of counselling are seen as vital safeguards for the patient, which is reflected in the NICE Guidelines.

22.34   Finally the guidelines deal with the indications for oocyte donation. This is considered effective in managing fertility problems associated with a number

---

32   NICE Guidelines, p 28.
33   Ibid, p 29.
34   Ibid, p 30.

of conditions: premature ovarian failure; gonadal dysgenesis including Turner syndrome; bilateral oophorectomy; ovarian failure following chemotherapy or radiotherapy; and certain cases of IVF treatment failure. It should also be considered in certain cases where there is a high risk of transmitting a genetic disorder to the offspring. Furthermore, the Guidelines states that before donation is undertaken, oocyte donors should be screened for both infectious and genetic diseases in accordance with guidance issued by the HFEA.

22.35 Concerning oocyte donation and egg sharing, which arguably increases access for other infertile couples wanting to have the chance to get a child themselves, the guidance recommends:

'Oocyte donors should be offered information regarding the potential risks of ovarian stimulation and oocyte collection … Oocyte recipients and donors should be offered counselling from someone who is independent of the treatment unit regarding the physical and psychological implications of treatment for themselves and their genetic children, including any potential children resulting from donated oocytes.'[35]

The oocyte donor's oocytes may result in the birth of a child to another woman or couple. Also, importantly, the guidelines recommend that everyone who is considering participation in an egg-sharing scheme should be counselled about its particular implications.

PRIMARY CARE TRUST SURVEY

22.36 The Department of Health document *Primary Care Trust survey – provision of IVF in England 2007*[36] sheds some light on the availability and non-clinical access criteria for providing NHS IVF treatment in England in 2006/07 and that planned for 2007/08. This comparatively recent survey details the number of IVF cycles offered to each patient, and also gives the number of patients provided with IVF in 2006/07 and the number of patients planned to be provided IVF in 2007/08 (or in some cases the number of IVF cycles provided or to be provided, respectively) to those patients, and critically the so-called 'non-clinical access criteria' employed by the PCTs. The survey covers the ten Strategic Health Authorities (SHAs) in England,[37] and the 151 PCTs within those SHAs. The results do not make good reading from a number of perspectives.

22.37 First, only 8–9 PCTs offer three full cycles of IVF treatment. Concerning what is meant by a 'full cycle', NICE state:

'In defining a *full* cycle, the NICE fertility guideline includes both the replacement of fresh embryos *and* the subsequent replacement of any good quality embryos not transferred as part of the fresh cycle but frozen and stored for future use.'[38]

35 Ibid, p 32.
36 Department of Health (2008): available at http://www.dh.gov.uk/en/Publicationsandstatistics/ Publications/PublicationsPolicyAndGuidance/DH_085665
37 Note that these will be scrapped under proposals announced by the Coalition government in late 2010.
38 DoH Survey, p 2.

Also NICE further define the term, 'one fresh cycle':

> 'The term "one fresh cycle" does not include the transfer of frozen embryos recommended by NICE.'

Only 5.29 per cent – 5.96 per cent (ie 8–9) of all PCTs in England actually follow the NICE Guidelines which recommend patients be offered three full cycles of IVF treatment. So much for the relevance of NICE recommendations on the provision and availability of treatments to patients being followed by PCTs, and so much also for NICE's attempt to reduce the development and continuance of the postcode lottery concerning who gets certain costly, controversial treatments and drugs.

22.38 Secondly, in addition 35–36 PCTs (ie 23.17 per cent–23.84 per cent) in 2006/07 offered two full (mainly) or fresh cycles of IVF treatment, ie less than one quarter of PCTs in the survey of English PCTs offered even two such cycles. Thirdly, and not surprisingly, 97 PCTs (64.23 per cent), ie nearly two-thirds, offered only one full cycle (mainly) or fresh cycle of IVF treatment. Nearly two-thirds of all English PCTs therefore were effectively offering the minimal possible number of IVF treatment cycles, in flagrant disregard of the NICE Guidelines.

22.39 Interestingly, the best SHA for a patient to be living in from the point of view of being offered the NICE-recommended three full cycles of IVF treatment was the North West Region, where 8–9 of the 24 PCTs offered the requisite number of treatment cycles, ie three. A further 11–12 PCTs offered at least two full or fresh IVF treatment cycles. Very worryingly, in six PCTs the number of IVF treatment cycles had either not been confirmed for 2006/07 (in two PCTs, ie 1.32 per cent), or had actually been suspended (in four PCTs, ie 2.64 per cent). In these four PCTs, NHS IVF would simply be unavailable and not offered to patients.

22.40 In addition the survey listed the non-clinical access criteria they used in reaching decisions about whether IVF treatment should be offered. The most frequently occurring non-clinical access criteria included, inter alia, NEC (ie no existing children), defined by NICE as meaning that the couple being treated have no children from their relationship or from any previous relationship, no previous sterilisation (this was referred to in the Warnock Report as being a justification by some for denying infertility treatment) and no smoking. Several PCTs included a maximum age limit for the woman seeking IVF, or alternatively an age range for availability of IVF. Some referred to the existence of a stable relationship of two years' duration. There was no consistency between the SHAs or PCTs regarding these non-clinical access criteria, which again is further cogent evidence of the existence of IVF by postcode lottery.

22.41 Even if one considers a single SHA on its own, there appears equally to be no consistency or uniformity in the non-clinical access criteria applicable in each PCT in the SHA. For example in Yorkshire and Humber SHA there are 14 PCTs and nine have NEC listed (ie 64.2 per cent), eight have a stable relationship listed (ie 57.1 per cent), but it is not clear that all eight interpret what is meant by a 'stable relationship' with any degree of consistency, one refers to non-smoking (ie 7.1 per cent) and five refer to no previous sterilisation (ie 35.7 per cent). One PCT refers to a financial contingency for patients on waiting list reaching the age of 39 who are deemed exceptional; in this PCT exceptionally, therefore, a woman aged 39 or over may be offered NHS IVF, but again it is not clear what is deemed 'exceptional'. Another PCT lists 'no children from current relationship', slightly more generous than NEC, and furthermore states that the male should be 47 or under. Another PCT states that the male must be under 46. In Sheffield the non-clinical access criterion listed is 'no children living with couple'. This is replicated in Barnsley, but that PCT more generously adds that the men must be under 55, as opposed to under 47 or 46 respectively.

22.42 The PCT survey provides clear evidence of the existence of an IVF postcode lottery in relation to accessing NHS IVF. As stated previously, approximately one-quarter of IVF only is offered and performed publically and for free on the NHS. The other three-quarters is only available if one can afford the cost of purchasing it from a private clinic. Money fundamentally determines access to IVF in private fee-paying clinics. Probably in no other area of medicine or the provision of medical treatments is the justice principle more obviously challenged than in the provision of infertility treatments, especially IVF. All equals are not treated equally. Why should an infertile woman or couple seeking, eg, IVF with Barnsley PCT be treated differently from a woman or couple in Sheffield with similar circumstances, regarding whether they can access IVF on the NHS? Equally why should the Barnsley woman or couple be denied IVF because she or they cannot afford to pay for it privately, whilst her Sheffield counterparts will be offered it if they by contrast can afford IVF treatment. That surely is contrary to and violates the justice principle.

PARLIAMENTARY CRITICISM

22.43 On 7 June 2011 the All Party Parliamentary Group on Infertility (APPGI) published their report into NHS IVF provision in the United Kingdom as at March 2011, *Holding back the British IVF revolution?*,[39] which basically, inter alia, highlighted, as Ann Milton MP, Parliamentary Under Secretary of State for Public Health, stated in the foreword to the report, 'some of the difficulties that infertile couples can face in accessing treatment,' and how successful PCTs were in implementing the 2004 NICE recommendations on the provision of NHS IVF treatment. The Minister added that:

'I am aware, however, that a small number of PCTs with historical funding problems have temporarily suspended provision of IVF services. I have already expressed my concerns about this approach and would encourage all PCTs to have regard to the current NICE guidance.'

22.44 In its Introduction, the Report stated:

'The aim of this report is to provide a snapshot of IVF provision across the UK and to assess the extent to which the National Institute for Clinical Excellence (NICE) guidelines are being implemented "on the ground".'

Interestingly, it noted that the information on which the report was based was collected through Freedom of Information (FoI) requests to Primary Care

39 Available at http://www.infertilitynetworkuk.com/uploadedFiles/InfertilityAwareness/appg%20IVF%20report.pdf

Trusts. These FoI requests were made to 177 PCTs, from whom information was obtained from 171. Obviously PCTs are at liberty to increase or decrease their level of funding for IVF treatment in the future.

22.45 The APPGI report noted that the HFEA figures for the number of babies born as a result of IVF in the UK in England from 1991 to 2008 revealed, eg, that 6,184 patients sought IVF in 1991, and the live birth rate was only 14 per cent. In 2000, 27,544 patients sought IVF and the birth rate had risen to 19.4 per cent. The most recent figures for 2008 revealed 39,879 patients had sought IVF and the live birth rate had risen further to 24.1 per cent. The APPGI report observed that:

'The two general trends that have been identified above (an increase in the number of couples seeking IVF, and improving success rates) are undoubtedly interlinked, and together have placed increasing pressure on NHS IVF provision.'

The demand for IVF has grown in tandem seemingly with the comparative and publicly perceived success of the IVF procedure as witnessed by the improved live birth rates. The APPGI report furthermore contended on the basis of its findings that:

'It can also be suggested from this data that as more IVF procedures are performed then success rates improve. Therefore we should be seeking to develop this great British innovation further.'

The argument is that more IVF treatments means an even higher live birth rate – hence the imperative for PCTs to follow the NICE guidelines and not treat NHS IVF treatment as a 'Cinderella' service operating on a postcode lottery basis, arguably sadly the reality in practice.

22.46 The APPGI report stated that the criteria for the provision of IVF for infertile couples contained in the 2004 NICE guidelines had been adopted by PCTs across the country in varying degrees, and that the NICE guidelines:

'do not suggest that IVF should be offered only to non-smokers or to those with a certain BMI, instead they suggest that patients should be encouraged to remain a healthy weight and to undergo smoking cessation where applicable.'

The APPGI report also notes that the NICE guidelines:

'also suggest that caffeine and alcohol consumption should be limited for patients wishing to undergo IVF which very few PCTs set down as criteria for treatment. This therefore illustrates how much of the content of the NICE guidelines has been taken out of context by PCTs and used to place arbitrary restrictions on the provision of IVF.'

The implication is that PCTs in a highly selective manner pick and choose which elements of the NICE guidance they actually incorporate into their own criteria for accessing IVF treatments – a very discretionary 'hit-and-miss' approach and inimical to ending the phenomenon of the IVF postcode lottery.

22.47 The APPGI report also cites with concern the inconsistent ways PCTs have interpreted and construed the NICE guidance concerning infertile couples who have children from previous relationships, noting that this was perhaps one of the most contentious areas of the NICE guidelines: 'According to the NICE guidelines if a woman has a child from a previous relationship she should not be eligible for publicly funded IVF.' By contrast, and seemingly unjustifiably and even discriminatorily:

'However if a male partner has children from a previous relationship this should not be taken into account. Again different PCTs have varying interpretations of this guideline.'

Very worryingly for advocates of the merits of having a body like NICE, and even more worryingly for those who spuriously believe those who ought to be subscribing and complying with NICE's recommendations (ie the 177 PCTs) are in fact actually doing so, the APPGI found that:

'Of the PCTs offering IVF to patients, 39% only offered one cycle of treatment. 26% of PCTs offered two and a further 27% offered three cycles. Therefore 73% PCTs are offering less than the three cycles recommended by NICE.'

Alarmingly therefore, a full seven years after the NICE recommendation that infertile couples should be provided with three free NHS IVF treatment cycles, only a minority of PCTs (27 per cent, or just over a mere quarter of them) in fact do so as at March 2011. Also of great concern was the fact that five PCTs did not offer NHS IVF at all. A further six PCTs had not responded to the information request.

22.48 Regarding the age of those receiving NHS treatment, APPGI found that the majority of PCTs offer IVF to those between the ages of 23 and 39, but some PCTs set the cut off at a lower age, such as 35, which is devastating for women between 36 and 39 years old who are effectively thereby barred from consideration for NHS IVF. By contrast the report pointed out that only a small number of PCTs placed restrictions on a male partner's age and of the ones that did, the limit was commonly 54 years of age. This appears unfair for women.

22.49 Whilst the majority of PCTs complied with the NICE guidelines age range (23–39), some of the PCTs offered IVF in a very narrow timeframe, eg where the female had a minimum age of 38.5 and a maximum age of 40, only an 18-month window of opportunity. On the face of it this is utterly absurd and indefensible given the clear evidence of the marked decline in female fertility after 35. These women really ought to be given the IVF treatment at an earlier age when the chances of maximising the likelihood of a successful pregnancy and live birth are greatest. Others by contrast had no minimum age for the woman but insisted still on a maximum age of, eg, 38 or 39. The bottom line was that there was no uniform compliance with the NICE guidelines.

22.50 Also of concern is that, as the Report notes:

'these age restrictions only portray part of the true picture. Most PCTs will only offer IVF to those who have been trying to conceive with a known cause of infertility for two years. This means that in many cases, the *effective* upper age limit for beginning the process of seeking treatment for infertility is two years lower than the stated figure (in most cases 37).

Furthermore, varying waiting times in different parts of the country can lower this *effective* upper limit even further.

'... this increased waiting time does not just cause emotional distress to the couple involved. As a woman gets older the chance of IVF procedures being successful is greatly reduced.'

After the age of 35 a woman's fertility decreases significantly naturally, so sadly the biological clock is conspiring with the vagaries and manifest unfairness inherent in the way the PCTs are deciding who gets IVF to militate against certain individuals getting NHS IVF.

22.51   A further unfair anomaly is flagged up by the APPGI Report in that the NICE guidelines recommend that if a woman already has a child she should not be eligible for IVF, but the guidelines do not stipulate that neither partner should have a child from a previous relationship. So the man can presumably have a child with a former partner or wife and not be precluded from accessing NHS IVF. The Report also found that many PCTs stipulated that neither parent can have a living child, but that this could be extremely restrictive to those wanting to have IVF as they may in fact have no contact with their partner's child. It cites the example of an infertile woman having a partner with a grown-up child who she has little or no contact with, adding that few would describe circumstances such as these as being a parent, yet a number of PCTs choose to interpret these as such. The report says:

'This also illustrates the impact that IVF provision can have on families as it can mean that couples are not eligible for IVF because of the existence of step-children. Arguably this can put a huge strain on families and relationships between step-parents and step-children.'

22.52   The APPGI report criticises other arbitrary, self-created criteria of PCTs (not included in the NICE guidelines), which further deter and restrict, if not preclude, certain individuals from NHS IVF treatment:

'Many PCTs also put other restrictions on the provision of IVF including ones that are contrary to the NICE guidelines. For example, the NICE guidelines do not specify that those undergoing IVF should be non-smokers, yet many PCTs stipulate this as a requirement.'

PCTs are effectively airbrushing individuals from accessing IVF on arguably very flimsy pretexts. The report continues that:

'Indeed, many PCTs require not only the female partner but also the male to be non-smokers for treatment to be offered, even if there are no fertility issues with the man.'

The same is true for BMI which several PCTs specified both male and female limits for IVF provision.

22.53   Furthermore the APPGI report noted that there were 595,000 babies born in the United Kingdom, of which 8,337 (1.4 per cent) were born as a result of IVF. Of concern was the fact that:

'It was shown that the UK was falling behind our Northern European counterparts with the amount of fertility treatment we provide, and consequently, the proportion of babies born as a result of ART.'

The report also stated that during the year 2000 in the United Kingdom there were 580 cycles of fertility treatment per million people, compared to an average of 1057 per million in other Northern European countries. In other words the United Kingdom considerably lags behind some comparable Northern European states in providing fertility treatment to those who need it. That cannot be right. The report cites Denmark as a good example, where the proportion of babies born following ART was 3.7 per cent of the national total births, whereas in the United Kingdom over the same period this figure was 1.0 per cent. The report concedes that:

'Whilst Britain is not the lowest provider of IVF in Europe it can be seen that it is by no means topping the league tables … we should be doing more to provide this great British innovation.'

22.54 The Chairman of the APPGI, Gareth Johnson MP, concluded in the report that there was little consistency in IVF availability on the NHS, and that he was not prepared to discover the existence of so many conditions and restrictions that are placed upon couples even in PCT areas that offer IVF treatment. He continued:

'In order for IVF treatment under the NHS to be truly available for infertile couples PCTs need to uphold not only the letter of the NICE guidelines but also the spirit.

'The NICE guidelines provide a good basis upon which IVF treatment should be offered to infertile couples. Many PCTs have used the guidelines as a basis for their own policy and allow infertile couples up to three cycles of IVF treatment within certain restrictions. This is exactly how the guidelines should be used.

'However some other PCTs have used the guidelines as a mechanism of adding their own more stringent restrictions on who is eligible for treatment.'

The criticism is that certain PCTs are using the NICE guidelines as a springboard for imposing their own additional criteria for restricting the availability of NHS IVF and that flies in the face of the NICE guidelines and the desirability, if not need, to increase the availability and access to NHS IVF in this country.

22.55 Mr Johnson emphasised that IVF is one of Britain's greatest innovations, and that, given that we created the first 'test-tube' baby, Louise Brown in 1978, created the first statutory regime and specialist regulatory authority (the HFEA) in the world, and given that Britain is leading many of the advances in the field, Britain more than any other country should be championing the use of IVF treatment. He admits that in a world with limited resources, and bearing in mind the huge budget deficit the United Kingdom has, the stark reality is that there will always be limits on the amount of infertility treatment that can be given on the NHS. Nonetheless:

'The NICE guidelines achieve a fair balance between the needs of infertile couples and the limits that have to be placed on funding. It is therefore vital that PCTs adhere to them.'

OTHER EVIDENCE

22.56 The APPGI Report of June 2011 followed two earlier reports: *The Messy Business of Conception: How the Postcode Lottery in NHS IVF Treatment is* *creating 'Baby boundaries' for childless couples,*[40] and *All your eggs in one basket: A comprehensive study into the continuing postcode lottery in IVF provision through the NHS.*[41] In both reports, Grant Shapps MP flagged up the anomalies and iniquities of the 'postcode lottery' concerning who obtains NHS IVF treatment.

MBC Report

22.57 The MBC report noted that prior to 2004 the supply of fertility treatment on the NHS was an entirely local decision: some Trusts offered it, some didn't. Furthermore, 'Following reports of inequality in the provision of in vitro fertilisation (IVF) treatment', NICE published a new national guidance about the way the NHS should provide IVF and other forms of fertility treatment. One of the ideas, inter alia, behind the February 2004 NICE guidelines was very noble and commendable, namely to rid the NHS system of this reprehensible and arguably unethical IVF postcode lottery which meant that the decision about whether, eg, a couple got NHS IVF or not hinged largely on their postal address and more fundamentally on which PCT they fortunately or unfortunately lived in. Referring to one of the key recommendations of the NICE guidelines, which states that you should be offered up to three cycles of IVF if the woman is between 23 and 39 years old at the time of treatment,[42] the MBC report commented that:

> 'Essentially, by stating this clearly in their guideline NICE are recommending that it is appropriate to fund IVF treatment where the chances of success are 10% or greater.'[43]

That ties in with the statistics relied on by NICE in 2004 that for every 100 women aged 39, around 10 will get pregnant after one cycle of IVF treatment. Clearly after the age of 39, the woman's chances of getting pregnant decrease even further. However as stated already the Secretary of State for Health, John Reid MP, diluted the NICE recommendation of three free NHS IVF treatment cycles to one, and the Department of Health asked all PCTs rather to offer all women aged 23–39 who meet the NICE clinical criteria a minimum of one full cycle of IVF from April 2005 and to give priority to couples who do not already have a child living with them.

22.58   The MBC report stated that:

> 'Two years after the date by which the Secretary of State for Health promised that the guidelines would be implemented throughout the NHS, [ie March 2007] there has been a worrying failure to implement the NICE recommendations ...

> 'In fact this research has found that it is still as complicated as ever to obtain NHS funded fertility treatment. In some parts of the country there continue to be a never-ending series of hoops to jump through for couples trying to prove themselves eligible.'

40   Survey undertaken by Grant Shapps MP in March 2007, (referred to as MBC report).
41   Report from Grant Shapps MP published in June 2009, (referred to as AEOB report))
42   NICE Guidelines, App A, p 149
43   MBC Report, p 1

The additional criteria respective PCTs adopt on an arbitrary basis (ie on top of the NICE guidelines) further impede would-be parents availing themselves of NHS IVF. The report also noted that:

'Elsewhere, even when couples are technically eligible, meeting all the necessary criteria, funding still prevents the treatment from actually taking place.'

Money appears to be the real critical criterion driving access to NHS IVF treatment, although individual PCTs are coming up with their own individual criteria, on top of the NICE criteria, to determine who gets this limited resource. The report adds that, 'the current rules mean that your chances of conceiving depend more on the county you live in than your need.' Location appears more crucial than patient need or desperation for a child. It also notes:

'Inconsistencies in the implementation of the guideline have created "baby boundaries" where couples are effectively being told that they cannot have a baby while their friends on the other side of the street, who might have a similar set of circumstances are able to obtain three cycles of IVF provided for them by the NHS.'

22.59 Again, like the later APPGI report, Mr Shapps and the MBC report based the research for the report on FoI requests to every PCT in the country. The MBC report stated that the results of the research showed glaring inconsistencies in the services on offer to couples who are having difficulty conceiving. Some of its findings were that with NHS finances under severe pressure there were some PCTs refusing to fund IVF, IUI or ICSI at all, and three local PCTs in Staffordshire were cited as examples.[44] It added that assisted reproductive treatments were viewed and treated as 'marginal' services and were 'being squeezed out' of Trust budgets. Concerning the NICE guidelines on the recommended age range of 23–39 for women being offered IVF, the report highlighted:

'the astonishing situation ... where a female may be too old to qualify for NHS funding in one locality while the same woman would be considered ineligible for free treatment in another part of the country on the grounds that she is too young.'

The Report gives as an example Wiltshire PCT, where a particularly narrow age range is evident in the criteria and IVF is only available for women aged 31–35, whereas in Isle of Wight and Hampshire PCT women must be aged between 36 and 39. It also cites Somerset PCT and Bath and North East Somerset PCT where the female partner must be 35 or over before being referred to a specialist. Commenting on these examples, the MBC report states:

'In short, the system is messy and insensitive to couples already experiencing the stressful experience of infertility. Furthermore it appears that financially unstable local NHS organisations are being forced to invent their own eligibility criteria in order to ration their increasingly scarce resources. The NICE recommendations are in large part being ignored.'[45]

22.60 The report also flagged up the 'bizarre' situation in Somerset where:

---

44 Ibid, p 3.
45 Ibid, p 4.

a woman in her early thirties must wait until she is over 35 before gaining access to services that could provide her with a family. This is despite medical opinion stating that the success rates of IVF diminish after the female partner passes 35.'

It further added: 'It therefore seems strange that many Trusts are restricting treatment to couples for whom it is less likely to succeed,' and continued:

'Where one PCT has the same minimum age criterion as another PCT's maximum age, this appears to defy medical logic and the system runs the risk of failing to serve everyone. To an extent PCTs are in a position of playing God; deciding who has the right to a child and who does not, based largely on the state of their annual budgets and deficit.'[46]

Previous children

22.61 Regarding the effect of a couple having a child already in relation to eligibility for IVF the MBC report was very critical, stating that once again the situation, even with regard to children from previous relationships, lacked clarity, and that around half of the Trusts would offer IVF to couples where a partner had living children from an earlier relationship:

'The results show that 51 PCTs [46.8 per cent] will exclude couples where one of the partners already has a child. 54 PCTs [49.5 per cent] have criteria that do not reject those couples while 4 of them [3.7 per cent] do not explicitly mention previous children as a factor in their policies.'[47]

The MBC report highlights the glaring anomalies between even PCTs in the same county (Essex) on the eligibility of couples to IVF in which a partner already has a child. In Essex, two of the five PCTs (West Essex and South East Essex) have policies rendering ineligible for IVF couples in which a partner already has a child, whereas three other PCTs (Mid Essex, North East Essex and South West Essex) have policies stating such couples are eligible for IVF. As the report contends:

'Essex serves as a perfect snapshot of the problem across the country ... the lack of any semblance of consistency is absurd. Couples in West and South East Essex are being locked outside the 'baby boundaries' of the county.'[48]

Previous fertility treatment

22.62 The MBC report noted that:

'More than half of the Trusts that are currently providing specialist fertility treatment reject any couples who have previously attempted treatment on the NHS.'

The worry is that less than half do not reject on this basis which again is arguably inconsistent and exasperatingly unfair for would-be parents seeking IVF. Indeed the report adds that a minority of PCTs will allow couples to go for IVF, ICSI or IUI even if they have tried on an earlier occasion using public

---

46 Ibid, p 5.
47 Ibid, p 6.
48 Ibid, p 7.

money. Also, the report stated that many PCTs would bar couples from IVF if they had ever had fertility treatment in the past at all, and '14.5% of PCTs will not consider for referral couples who have had treatment in the past, whether NHS or self-funded.'[49] Seemingly 'one strike' (previous attempt) at IVF and you, the patients or couple, are 'out', ie effectively precluded from being eligible ever again, which is potentially a very blunt criterion of denial in many circumstances. As the MBC report noted:

'Couples who decide to opt out of the NHS, perhaps because of waiting lists or, as discussed above the odd age limits in existence, are then being permanently excluded from the NHS.'[50]

That is totally unfair and arbitrary.

22.63 The MBC report flagged up other inconsistencies and anomalies evident in how the various PCTs decide who gets NHS IVF. Like the later 2011 report, the MBC report found discrepancies and variations between how many IVF treatment cycles were offered in each PCT, with some offering only one, others two and some, eg Central Lancashire, offering three. Couples desperate for a chance to have a baby and obtain IVF cannot understand the existence of such a postcode lottery system of being eligible for NHS IVF, nor indeed can many people who are not would-be-parents either.

22.64 The Report also noted that there were slight nuances in the Body Mass Index (BMI) parameters that Trusts insisted must be met, while some did not even give a passing mention to BMI. Again there is no consistency or uniformity here, and yet again it begs the question of whether some PCTs are using such criteria as mechanisms for filtering and weeding out applicants from being eligible for IVF.

22.65 In addition further disparities occur in criteria adopted by PCTs. For example, the Report stated:

A similar level of non-conformity cann be seen in the length of relationship of the couple. Many Trusts do not specify a period that the couple should have been together for. The most common request is a union of two years.'[51]

Again this is a very arbitrary and 'hit-and-miss' way to decide who gets IVF. In Gloucestershire PCT, for example, it was asked that couples be together for three years before seeking treatment, whereas Kensington and Chelsea PCT identified a relationship length of just one year. Also cited are Hartlepool PCT, where the relationship is 'stable' and Haringey PCT which likes 'couples to be in a "long term relationship".' Of considerable concern is that neither explicitly defined these terms.

22.66 Finally the report noted that:

'Other social criteria have been muscled into the IVF rules of Trusts ... for instance Birmingham East and North PCT ask that both partners are non-smokers ... Devon PCT only requests that the female partner is a non-smoker.'

49   Ibid, pp 7–8.
50   Ibid, p 8.
51   Ibid.

Plymouth Teaching PCT went further and extended this principle by specifying a period of six months as the length of time the female partner has been nicotine free. The MBC report not surprisingly therefore damningly concludes that:

'A muddled approach by the Department of Health and a failure to follow the NICE guidelines, combined with growing PCT deficits in many parts of the country, have created entirely arbitrary borders that decide which couples can start a family and which couples cannot.'[52]

It noted that, regrettably, starting a family was still regarded as a 'marginal' treatment in the NHS. The report scathingly stated that, despite the hype:

'In reality cash strapped NHS Trusts are being forced to flout the clinical guidance on offer and, as a result, millions of couples are facing even more anxiety during what is often a hugely stressful period in their lives. Indeed, couples who are desperate for comprehensible, unambiguous guidance are being given precisely the opposite.'

22.67 The report also deprecated the deplorable 'evidence' which suggested that even where a couple met the detailed criteria of the PCT that might potentially fund their treatment, they frequently discovered that the budget simply didn't exist to actually access IVF:

'The detailed work which has gone into producing criteria and guidelines is thereby entirely irrelevant to a couple in this position.'

The report was emphatic in its conclusion that as at March 2007:

'the situation is cryptic, confused and inconsistent; in 2007 the business of conception is nothing short of a mess.'

This is a pretty devastating, but accurate critique of the existing IVF postcode lottery.

AEOB Report

22.68 In the Introduction to the 2009 AEOB Report it was noted that:

Treatment for infertility is allocated based on the commissioning policies of the Primary Care Trust in which the female partner's General Practitioner's surgery is located.'[53]

FoI requests were sent out to all PCTs in England, using the Freedom of Information Act 2000, asking them 'to release details of the eligibility criteria they employ when deciding on eligibility for assisted conception techniques, specifically, IVF, IUI and ICSI.' The report made a number of key findings. Following an 80 per cent response rate from PCTs, it was found that more than eight out of ten PCTs were still failing to offer the full three cycles of IVF treatment recommended by the 2004 NICE guidelines. Indeed, furthermore two PCTs confirmed that they had, in the previous two years, refused to provide IVF. The Findings section of the report helpfully elaborated on the detail, by pointing out sadly:

---

52 Ibid, p 9.
53 AEOB Report, p 6.

'it would appear that the scope of fertility treatment is in retreat in 2009 as just over 18 per cent of Primary Care Trusts responding to Freedom of Information requests offered the full three-cycle treatment.'[54]

It was also found that 28 per cent of PCTs offered just two IVF cycles, and very worryingly 44 per cent only offered one cycle. A further 10 per cent of PCTs funded no IVF cycles at all or alternatively it was unknown how many cycles, if any, they funded.

22.69 The Report also noted:

'One in every eight PCTs are failing to comply with NICE guidelines with regards to the age of the female partner meaning the continuation of the bizarre scenario which sees the same woman being too old for treatment in one area and too young in another.'

The Report discovered that 12.5 per cent of the PCTs in 2009 were failing to follow the national NICE guidelines on the age of the woman (ie 23–39) regarding eligibility for treatment. Again, that is cause for great concern.

22.70 Equally worryingly, widespread variations between regions and within regions continued in 2009. The report cites the fact that in the East Midlands all Trusts would offer just one full cycle of treatment, whereas in London PCTs 39 per cent offer one cycle per couple, 26 per cent will provide two and a further 26 per cent fund the full three cycles. Thus in London PCT's region alone there exists an IVF postcode lottery. The report also flagged up that consistency was evident in the East Midlands, and two other regions, albeit not consistency in complying with the NICE guidelines, adding:

'Indeed, the East Midlands is one of three regions, along with the South East and Yorkshire & Humber, in which not one of the Trusts taking part in the survey offers the full treatment advocated by NICE.'

22.71 It was also noted that 41 per cent of South East PCTs responding confirmed that they were not providing IVF to women aged 23–39, as instructed to do so by NICE. This was again an alarming non-compliance rate with supposedly national guidelines, which ought to be complied with. These five PCTs had policies which only made eligible couples in which the female partner was between the ages of 34 and 37. Nearly as bad was the South West where six of the PCTs responding offered eligibility criteria which did not conform to national guidance. The survey found that overall around 86 per cent of PCTs offered IVF in 2009 to couples where the woman was aged 23–39, in accordance with the NICE guidelines, but that unfortunately more than 1 in 8 were still restricting access based on age. Glaring and quite frankly illogical policies in Southampton, Portsmouth and the Isle of Wight were flagged up in the report, where:

'access is restricted by PCTs until the female partner reaches the age of 36 even though the most expert of medical opinions estimate that the chances of conceiving through IVF diminish by between 16 per cent and 35 per cent after the age of 35.'

---

54 Ibid, p 12.

22.72   A further anomaly was flagged up. The Report noted that in the East Midlands no responding PCT would offer treatment to couples in which one partner already had a child, whereas by marked contrast in the North East 70 per cent said they *would* provide treatment in such circumstances. The report noted that unfortunately the differing policies adopted by officials in each locality had created a situation in which the split was almost 50:50. One may as well toss a coin here to determine whether a couple get IVF using this criterion!

22.73   A further anomaly was noted:

'Of the 92 Trusts with a properly defined minimum length of relationship or period in which the couple must have been attempting to conceive naturally, 9 felt that one year was a reasonable restriction; 38 set the barrier at two years; and 45 Trusts (49 per cent) required that couples be together for at least three years prior to accessing NHS-funded fertility treatment.'[55]

This is a complete mess and a recipe for increasing the frustration and sense of exasperation of couples at the vicissitudes of the IVF postcode lottery.

22.74   In the report's opening summary, it was stated that the inequality in infertility treatment was persistent, and that in June 2009, more than five years after the 2004 NICE guidelines, 'thousands of couples are still suffering the agony of being prevented from the chance of a family based on arbitrary restrictions or NHS financial constraints.' The report added that:

'The level of variation in criteria both between and within regions is surprising and proves that rather than being a regional lottery, in most cases, IVF provision boils down as a genuine postcode lottery.'[56]

These are scathing and condemnatory words. However the AEOB report welcomed the fact that just over half of the PCTs included in the survey (62 of the 120 responding PCTs) had updated their individual eligibility criteria since the MBC report of 2007. The report concludes by urging that:

'some degree of national, or even regional, standardisation would be fairest for all concerned, even if that means an effective tightening of the criteria in some areas. The continuation of this lottery means that couples are going so far as considering moving to areas in which their dreams of having a baby can be realised. Clearly that is an unfair situation for what should be a *national* health service.'[57]

22.75   One of the five PCTs not offering IVF treatment at the time of the AEOB survey was reported by BBC News on 7 June 2011[58] as stating that the decision not to fund treatment was 'not taken lightly' and that it understood the decision would be very distressing to presumably those affected. It added that it had to make 'increasingly difficult decisions' about which treatments it should commission. The PCT also stated: 'We know that infertility is a condition which causes great distress to the couples concerned,' but added, for some controversially, 'but it does not affect general physical health or life expectancy and as such is not scored, by a clinically-led panel, as one of our health

---

55   Ibid, p 16.
56   Ibid, p 4.
57   Ibid, p 17.
58   www.bbc.co.uk/news/uk-england-stoke-staffordshire-13690436

priorities.' This is strictly speaking correct, but does not pay sufficient regard to the enormous mental, emotional and psychological damage and harm caused to, eg, infertile couples by their infertility. The PCT emphasised the need for it to prioritise local needs when allocating limited budgets in North Staffordshire PCT, stating it had to focus on 'the health of the people of North Staffordshire and on the need to maintain financial stability to be able to provide high quality local healthcare.' The reality, it said, was that the NHS:

'... will never have the resources to fund every service, treatment, therapy or procedure which every individual may want ... We will continue to work with clinicians to review the health of the population to ensure our limited funding best matches the overall needs of North Staffordshire.'

22.76 Interestingly, on 18 June 2011 BBC News reported that:

'A decision to refuse NHS-funded IVF treatment to women in Stockport is to be reviewed after the local PCT [Stockport PCT] was merged into NHS Greater Manchester'.[59]

This new trust had been formed out of an amalgamation of the ten former PCTs from across Greater Manchester, and apparently needed to make £400m savings over the next four years. It said that it must have a 'consistent' policy on funding IVF treatment. Stockport PCT had taken the decision in December 2010, as a cost-cutting measure, to withdraw NHS IVF treatment and was the only PCT in Greater Manchester to withdraw it out of the 10 former PCTs in Greater Manchester. The new Chief Executive of NHS Greater Manchester PCT stated that:

'We want to make sure that the NHS offer to all people who live in Greater Manchester is a consistent offer and I accept the point that for a variety of reasons different approaches have been taken.'

This appears to be an endorsement of the justice ethical principle, namely treating all equals equally. He added that he knew that there was an issue in Stockport and 'IVF funding will be one of the issues which I'm sure we'll want to be looking at.'

22.77 Tony Rutherford, Chairman of the British Fertility Society, welcomed the publication of the AEOB Report and commented on 7 June 2011 that the findings that the majority of PCTs did not provide eligible patients with three 'free' cycles of IVF treatment in accordance with the 2004 NICE guidelines and often implemented their own criteria for eligibility with no evidence base 'unfortunately come as no surprise and bear witness to lack of funding and prominence that infertility is given by our healthcare system.' PCTs and government by their half-hearted commitment to implement NICE guidelines may be conveying their lack of certainty about whether infertility is a disease or condition that needs treating by finite resources, or whether it is a social condition not really needing NHS funding, and certainly not a priority one when compared to, eg, life saving treatments. Mr Rutherford added:

'Infertility is a devastating condition which affects one in six couples in the UK. The World Health Organisation recognises infertility as a physical illness that requires treatment; however, it can also cause significant emotional and psychological harm to patients. By not being given fair access to fertility treatment on the NHS, patients are effectively being denied the opportunity to start a family of their own.'

He was concerned too that PCTs had consistently failed to fulfil the evidence-based guidelines on infertility treatment set out by NICE, and that:

'This is unacceptable in a modern healthcare system and we owe it to patients to provide them with fair access to evidence-based treatment.'

22.78 The topicality and highly controversial nature of decisions about who receives IVF and how was amply demonstrated recently in two different instances. First, on 8 March 2012, BBC News reported that the Peninsula Health Technology Commissioning Group (PHTCG), which regulates NHS fertility treatment in the Devon and Cornwall region, had introduced a 'ruling' that couples could be denied IVF treatment in Devon and Cornwall if they were overweight or smoked. The BBC News also added that:

According to the regulations, introduced in 2004 [ie the NICE Guidelines], both men and women must not have smoked within the previous six months and must have a Body Mass Index of between 19 and 29.9 to be eligible for certain fertility drugs.'

The PHTCG chairman Dr Virginia Pearson noted that there was sound evidence that being significantly over or underweight can reduce fertility, and, furthermore, added that:

'Smoking may reduce fertility in women, while for men, there is a link between smoking and poorer quality sperm.'

22.79 Secondly, on 20 March 2012, the Health Committee of the Northern Ireland Assembly passed a motion calling on the Health Minister, Edwin Poots, in the Northern Ireland Executive to fund three cycles of IVF treatment for infertile couples wanting children. However Mr Poots regrettably indicated he would need more additional recurring funding to extend the current practice of funding just one cycle and that this funding was unavailable. He stated:

'In the absence of funding, to offer up to three cycles would result in other criteria being tightened and could limit the number of women who could access the service.'

However, the Chair of the Health Committee Sue Ramsey correctly countered that the 2004 NICE Guidelines clearly stated that a woman should be offered up to three cycles of IVF treatment, and this was necessary because one cycle was not likely to be successful. Mr Poots pointed out that from 1 April 2012 the Health and Safety Executive Board had agreed with the Regional Fertility Centre in Belfast to offer frozen embryo treatment to those women clinically suitable. The battle against the manifest injustices of the IVF postcode lottery remains fierce and unresolved despite the devolution of many legislative and executive powers to the devolved regions. Money still appears to be very much talking, even though politicians in devolved legislatures are talking passionately about ending the iniquitous postcode lottery.

22.80 The pivotal and fundamental role of financial resources to accessing IVF was evident too in a different context concerning the repercussions of increasing the payment to egg donors – presumably to increase the supply of egg donation to meet the demand for eggs from infertile women and couples desperate to have children. Interestingly and significantly, it was reported in the *Daily Mail* on 31 March 2012 that there was a 'five-fold jump' in the number of women inquiring about being potential egg donors. This follows the decision of the HFEA in October 2011 to increase from £250 to £750 the payment to women donating their eggs for use by other women/couples in licensed clinics. As a result of this change the egg donor is provided with free treatment to harvest the eggs, in addition to the £750, regardless of the number of eggs retrieved. The new figure of £750 for expenses/compensation, which became effective on 1 April 2012, is aimed at increasing the number of egg donors and eggs available for donation in order to address the acute shortage of eggs available for donation, which is forcing some women or couples to have to wait years for fertility treatment. The increased level of expenses for egg donation reflects not only the shortage of eggs and the regulator's laudable efforts to encourage further egg donors, but also recognises the medical difficulties of successfully harvesting viable eggs from a donor.

22.81 The *Daily Mail* reported that:

'CARE Fertility, which runs private IVF clinics across the country, said interest has increased five-fold, while Midland Fertility Services has seen a "noticeable increase" and the National Gamete Donation Trust a doubling in inquiries.'

The report referred to the positive comments of Dr Simon Thornton, Medical Director at CARE Fertility on the increase in expenses:

'Hopefully this change will reset the balance nationally so the requirement for donor eggs is going to match availability and waiting times will come down.'

He did, however, add the caveat that not all women who inquire at clinics will end up being donors. The *Daily Mail* also noted the comments of Dr Gillian Lockwood, of Midland Fertility Services:

'Most women donate eggs because they have experienced infertility themselves or know someone who has. The increase in compensation is recognition that donors go through a lot. There is extensive counselling and scrutiny, and the average donor cycle could involve six to eight visits to a clinic, daily injections, vaginal scans and some discomfort for the egg retrieval itself. Early counselling sessions would quickly identify women who were doing it purely for the money.'

However, the *Daily Mail* reported that other interested commentators were not so sanguine about the changes, for example Joyce Robins of the Patient Concern group cautioned that:

'For many women, £750 is worth having, especially if you are wondering how you are going to pay the mortgage. Increasing these payments will tempt the hard up, but women should give it proper thought.'

22.82 Desperate situations (ie an acute shortage of eggs in a society where women are putting off having children until their mid-30s and 40s, sadly forgetting that their reproductive biological clock cannot be put off) warrant and demand desperate remedies, such as permitting a substantial increase in the level of expenses or compensation (not payment or financial reward). In a global financial crisis and given a UK double-dip recession (as reported on 27 April 2012), some women in financially difficult circumstances may be very tempted to go down the egg donor route purely because of the financial inducement of £750. The HFEA and Parliament must guard zealously against this situation arising.

CONCLUSION

22.83 The development of a large private market in IVF treatment (75 per cent of all IVF) amply demonstrates and proves the unfairness of fertility provision in the United Kingdom in 2012, particularly when allied to the vicissitudes of the soon to be scrapped PCTs arbitrarily and inconsistently allocating at their discretion the remaining 25 per cent of NHS IVF treatments to individuals and couples happening despite the existence of NICE guidelines, supposedly in place to prevent that IVF postcode lottery. Sadly, given the parlous and precarious state of the UK economy, it is highly unlikely the government will be either willing or able to channel more of taxpayers' money to PCTs, or their successors, in order to either commit to complying fully with NICE guidelines, or more radically to finance the provision of greatly increased, or even universal NHS IVF provision.

Part 9

Randomness Rejected?

Chapter 23

Sex Selection under the Human Fertilisation and Embryology Act 2008

INTRODUCTION

23.1   Part of the joy, excitement, surprise and mystery of having children is that would-be parents do not plan, or cannot pre-ordain the sex of their future children. Clearly the sex of the child can be determined in the womb using scans after a certain period of foetal gestation, but the parents do not deliberately choose the sex of their child before conception or even before sexual intercourse.

23.2   Some parents want to be able to choose the sex of their child before implantation using IVF. This choice, arguably a manifestation of patient autonomy, can be for a variety of reasons. Couples might want, eg, a boy, because they have a girl already, or because they just want one child of a particular sex. Some parents might want a child of one sex for religious or cultural reasons (eg certain cultures and faiths may place more emphasis on having sons), others may do so for economic or employment or social reasons, ie a son is physically stronger to do hard, demanding, manual labour in a farm, or because there is a scarcity of daughters to have children to increase the population of a region or country. Others still may want, eg, to have a daughter because they prefer women to men. Yet others may want to have a daughter for medical or health reasons because if they have a son he may inherit some dreadful, debilitating and life-shortening gender-related disease or illness. Sadly too, a tiny minority may want a child of one sex to replace a child of that particular sex who has died tragically in their childhood. A fundamental ethical and legal question therefore arises: when is it permissible to allow would-be parents to select the sex of their would-be child? Should the law prevent sex selection outright, should it permit it freely, or should it permit it, but only under strict regulation and control, for certain specific reasons or purposes?

JUSTIFICATIONS

23.3   Bryan and Higgins argue that:

> '[for] couples to be allowed to select their child's gender for other than medical purposes, whether social, religious or economic, would be highly controversial and could have far-reaching consequences ... Many people think the world shows quite enough gender prejudice, indeed outright misogyny, without new "weapons" being added to its armoury.'[1]

---

1   E Bryan and R Higgins *Infertility-New Choices, New Dilemmas* (Penguin Books, 1995), p 191.

However, if sex selection was done by individual couples on the basis of choice, rather than state authorised or sanctioned or driven sex selection, objections to this may lessen. Procreative libertarian arguments could be raised to permit sex selection and arguments based on the autonomy and informed consent of the would-be parents deliberately selecting, eg, a female embryo. Bryan and Higgins contend:

'Has individual need and freedom no claim in such cases? What harm could this do provided overall numbers of both sexes were roughly even?'

This argument accords with John Stuart Mills' notion that people should be permitted to do actions and should not be prevented from doing them, presumably eg by laws preventing those acts, unless they are harmful to others. Put simplistically, Bryan and Higgins contend: 'The gender balance is not affected if "we" choose a boy and "they" choose a girl.' Indeed they say, the parents might even be happier at being given a choice, and look after the resulting children better, thereby maximising the good consequences of the sex selection.

23.4 One of the key features of the Human Fertilisation and Embryology Act 2008 (the 2008 Act) was a general ban, enshrined clearly and unambiguously in the Act, on sex selection of embryos and gametes, except for certain arguably tightly defined and limited health reasons.

23.5 One of the main advantages of sex selection of embryos following IVF and PGD is its very high success rate in determining the sex of the embryo. The Parliamentary Office of Science and Technology assessed this success rate and reliability as being, '[N]early all pregnancies are with a child of the desired sex.' By contrast, sperm sorting can only guarantee roughly that a child of the desired sex is produced in 70–90 per cent of pregnancies. The question concerning sperm sorting might be what effect it will have on the parents, the child, and the parents' attitude to the child if sperm sorting, with this far from foolproof success rate, results in a child of the wrong sex. Mason and McCall Smith note that:

'Opinions differ as to whether such methods are efficient and to what extent they can be relied upon but claims have been made to an accuracy of the order of 90 per cent.'[2]

However they add that they are more concerned with the 'ethical position' than with the 'efficiency of the method'. They also state that:

'Discussion is then at two levels – the practical and the deontological. The fact that both are highly culture-dependent – with a very evident East/West divide – deserves emphasis.'[3]

Regarding first the practical level, they note:

'it is probably fair to say that preconception sex selection would have, at most, a negligible effect on the distribution and status of the sexes in the United Kingdom. But this is essentially a western view and one which might well not be true of countries in the Far East – indeed, the gender balance

---

2 K Mason and G Laurie, *Mason and McCall Smith's Law and Medical Ethics,* 8th edn, (Oxford Univeristy Press, 2010), p 78.
3 Ibid, pp 78–79.

has become dangerously unstable in parts of India where health carers who practise a post-conception sex determination service are now liable to have their licences revoked.'[4]

23.6 Interestingly *The Times* reported on 1 April 2011 that a report by the UCL Centre for Health and Development said that sex-selective abortion, although illegal in India, was still carried out 'with impunity by medical personnel, usually qualified doctors, in hospitals and clinics, not in backstreet establishments,' and that four decades of public awareness campaigns and a raft of laws had failed to prevent a chronic and worsening gender imbalance in India. *The Times* alarmingly noted as well that:

'The first data from a census carried out earlier this year shows that for every 1,000 Indian boys under the age of 6 there are 914 girls. The equivalent figure in the last census a decade ago was 927; in 1991 it was 945.'

The cause appears to be sex-selective abortion and female infanticide. *The Times* also noted that campaigners said that cheaper and more mobile ultrasound technology and lax control over its illegal use was driving a 'genocide' of India's female population. And:

'Researchers in London estimated last month that, within two decades, there would be 20 per cent more males than females in India.'

23.7 Furthermore, *The Times* noted that:

'The preference for male children, reinforced by cultural traditions and economic factors, is found in many Asian countries'.

The 2011 Census revealed there were only 75,837,152 girls aged 0–6 in India, compared with 82,952,135 boys, again a portent of massive social, economic and health problems in the future. Also *The Times* referred to Sabu George, 'a public health activist,' who blamed the Government for failing to implement its own legislation to outlaw pre-natal sex determination, and complained that:

'The number of registered ultrasound clinics in India has grown ... to 40,000 today and yet the supervisory board supposed to enforce the law has not met for three years.'

This is a rather devastating indictment. Finally, as Francis Elliot commented in *The Times*,

'changing attitudes takes decades and, in the meantime, a technology [ie ultrasound] that is supposed to save lives is robbing India of millions of her daughters.'

A very bleak, but nevertheless accurate assessment.

23.8 Concerning the ethical plane, Mason and McCall Smith add that:

'very few, it is supposed, would oppose primary sex selection for the prophylaxis of X-linked disease. Similarly, even those concerned to minimise embryonic fetal rights would see "sperm sorting" as being morally preferable to secondary sex selection by way of embryo selection or abortion.'

---

4   Ibid, p 79.

To paraphrase the words of Professor James Rachels, there is less biological investment in sperm than in an embryo or foetus.[5] Mason and McCall Smith note:

> 'sex selection for non-medical or social reasons has been classed as anything from "playing God" to offering an acceptable new dimension to family planning.'

However, because it can never be 100 per cent accurate, and they state that they foresee a possibly disastrous outcome for some 30 per cent of children currently born using this technique:

> 'It follows that, in contrast to other forms of reproductive liberty, primary sex selection poses a real threat of harm to a resultant child; an equally distasteful increase in the number of 'social' abortions might also result. For these reasons alone, we advocate a legal limitation of "gender clinics" to those licensed to undertake the practice; the potential consequences for individual children – and, perhaps, for society by way of a "eugenic wedge" – are too serious for the process to be left unsupervised.'

23.9 Jonathan Herring notes that supporters of reproductive autonomy argue that sex selection should be permitted as an aspect of a person's right to control their reproduction.[6] However, he highlights five possible types of objection to the practice of sex selection: demographic impact, international implications, psychosocial impacts, sex discrimination and public opinion. He states regarding these:

(1) *Demographic impact:* Herring notes that the concern is that the ratio between male and female will be skewed, and he refers to India and China where the ratio is 107 boys: 100 girls, or even higher; this is said to be caused by the abortion of girls. However, as he pertinently remarks, 'there is no reason to believe that sex selection would lead to such askew in the UK. Indeed it is perfectly possible that couples would prefer girls to boys. In any event there would only be a noticeable demographical impact if a large number of parents engaged in sex selection, and that is unlikely.'

(2) *International implications:* Herring notes that there is concern that if sex selection were to be permitted in the United Kingdom it would make it difficult for the United Kingdom to object to the procedure in other countries where it was used in an unacceptable way, ie the moral high ground would be lost if the United Kingdom were to legalise the practice.

(3) *Psychosocial impacts:* Herring notes a concern that a child born as a result of sex selection will suffer psychological problems. In other words, she or he may fear that they were selected only on account of their sex. But Herring, in fairness, adds that it is simply not known if children would have these feelings, or if they did whether that would be harmful.

---

5   J Rachels, *The End of Life* (Oxford University Press, 1986).
6   J Herring, *Medical Law and Ethics* 2nd edn (Oxford University Press, 2007), p 354.

(4) *Sex discrimination:* Herring notes that there is an argument that allowing people to choose the sex of their child will pander to their sexist beliefs and attitudes, and he adds that people should be encouraged to accept children regardless of their sex.

(5) *Public opinion:* Herring states: 'The HFEA found widespread feeling among the members of public consulted against sex selection. Eighty per cent of those questioned thought that people should not be allowed to select on the basis of sex for social reasons. A common feeling was that parents should love their children whatever their characteristics.'

23.10 Brazier comments that:

'Sex selection is perennially controversial. In parts of the world, ante-natal testing and infanticide are used to abort or kill female foetuses and babies.'[7]

She furthermore notes: 'Opinion in the UK is divided.' Pattinson[8] observes that '[T]he 1990 Act does not allow prospective parents to use "any practice designed to secure that any resulting child will be one sex rather than the other" (Sched 2, para 1ZB(1))', and that provision 'is clearly wide enough to prohibit selecting embryos of a particular sex and selecting sperm samples for the purpose of sperm selection.' He adds that there was one key exception, namely allowing 'sex selection to avoid severe genetic conditions that are linked to a particular sex, so-called X-linked conditions (Sch 2, paras 1ZA(1)(c) and 1ZB(2), (3)).' Pattinson cites examples of X-linked conditions: Lescch-Nyhan syndrome, haemophilia, Duchenne's muscular dystrophy, and the milder colour blindness.

23.11 In justifying why some parents want to sex select for social reasons, Pattinson states:

'predictable harm to prospective parents is not limited to fears of serious X-linked conditions. In some circumstances having a child of one particular sex might cause the parents to be stigmatised or ostracised by their community.'[9]

This is what is happening in certain parts of India and China. Pattinson also states that;

'Some of the most powerful arguments against sex selection for social reasons have been presented using the metaphor of the slippery slope. Sex selection for social reasons will, so the argument goes, gradually lead us to a situation that is morally objectionable. That undesired outcome could be the treatment of an undesired sex as if it were a harmful trait, the re-enforcement of unacceptable gender-role expectations, or an imbalance in the sex ratio to the detriment of society.'

23.12 Professor John Harris makes a number of controversial and provocative comments about sex selection, or gender selection as he describes it. He argues that:

---

7 M Brazier and E Cave, *Medicine, Patients and the Law*, 4th ed (Penguin, 2007) at p 335.
8 S Pattinson, *Medical Law and Ethics* (Sweet & Maxwell, 2007), para 8.5.1.1.
9 Ibid, para 8.5.1.2.

'I assume no reasonable person thinks it could be *morally* better to have one colour of hair rather than another, nor for that matter to be one gender than another'.[10]

Although this is viewed as 'a difficult question' and he acknowledges that the notion of parents being able to make such a choice very often causes outrage, he states:

'I have found difficulty in seeing this question as problematic. It seems to me to come to this; either such traits as hair colour, eye colour, gender, and the like are important or they are not. If they are *not* important why not let people choose? And if they *are* important, can it be right to leave such important matters to chance?'

Harris also asserts:

'We should note that a pattern of preference for one gender amongst those opting for gender selection would not necessarily be evidence of sexual discrimination. There might be all sorts of respectable, non-prejudicial reasons for preferring one gender to another including just having a preference for sons and daughters ... A preference for producing a child of a particular gender no more necessarily implies discrimination against members of the alternative gender than choosing to marry a co-religionist, a compatriot, or someone of the same race or even class implies discrimination against other religions, nations, races or classes.'[11]

THE MASTERTON CASE

23.13 The tragic case of Alan and Louise Masterton is a classic illustration of the old adage that hard cases make bad law. Their harrowing case also exposes the limitations of confining the availability of sex selection of embryos to specific medical purposes, as opposed to extending its availability to non-medical purposes or social purposes.

23.14 The Mastertons had five children, four boys and a three-year-old daughter, Nicole. Tragically, in May 1999, Nicole was horrifically injured in a freak accident, suffering severe burns after a gas balloon fell onto a bonfire in the Masterton's garden, and died two months later. Mrs Masterton had been sterilised after Nicole's birth. The Mastertons wanted to try for another baby daughter but clearly needed IVF and then PGD to achieve their wish. Unfortunately the Mastertons were thwarted in their ambitions to receive IVF in all the licensed IVF clinics they tried. This was because the HFEA had a policy not to permit sex selection of embryos for non-medical reasons. The policy was contained in the HFEA Code of Practice,[12] and provided, at para 7.20, 'Centres should not select the sex of embryos for social reasons,' and added at para 7.21 that 'Centres should not use sperm sorting techniques in sex selection.' Moreover s 3(1) of the Human Fertilisation and Embryology Act 1990 (the 1990 Act) provides that:

---

10 J Harris, 'Rights and Reproductive Choice', in J Harris and S Holm (eds) *The Future of Human Reproduction* (Oxford University Press, 1998), at p 29.
11 Ibid, pp 29–30).
12 Fourth edition, published in 1998.

'No person shall—
  (a) bring about the creation of an embryo, or
  (b) keep or use an embryo,
except in pursuance of a licence'

Given that embryonic sex selection involves the prior creation and use of embryos, it is therefore regulated by the HFEA, under the 1990 Act and the CoP licensing regime.

23.15 The Mastertons were not selecting a female embryo to avoid, eg, a gender-related disease in a male embryo, but rather for social reasons, to have a female child to love and cherish, although some would contend as a replacement for their lost daughter. The HFEA's ethical bright line of only permitting sex selection of embryos for specific medical reasons (ie to avoid a serious, gender-linked genetic condition) was being put to the test by the Mastertons. Given their patent lack of success in the United Kingdom, the Mastertons decided to travel to the private Biogenesi clinic in Rome where they paid £6,000 for IVF and PGD. As Mr Masterton said:

'PGD was being denied to us in Britain for the most absurd reason and it would have been intolerable for us to live the rest of our lives knowing that there was treatment out there which could help us.'

This is one of the many problems with regulation of specific fertility treatments like IVF and PGD. The United Kingdom may be able to regulate the availability and access to IVF in the United Kingdom, but if the particular regulatory authority, the HFEA, takes a decision that is not favourable to a couple, as here, they can jump on a plane and go to a country with a more permissive regulatory regime if they can pay for the treatment in that country, hence the phenomenon of fertility tourism bypasses national laws and domestic regulation.

23.16 Their treatment in Rome unfortunately only resulted in the creation of one viable embryo, sadly for them a male one. The Mastertons very generously asked their doctors to donate their male embryo to another infertile couple. So some good came out of their misfortune, but obviously not for them personally.

23.17 For some this case represents yet another step down the ethical slippery slope. Parents, albeit in tragic circumstances, were desperately trying to 'replace' their dead daughter. In doing so they were commodifying human life, ie trying to buy a daughter. They were selecting and creating a baby selfishly to heal a wound – in essence a designer baby. The design had to be a female baby. However Mr Masterton refuted that allegation vehemently, saying:

'We are against so-called designer children and we are not seeking to replicate Nicole … What we are seeking to do is heal our family and return the female element to it.'

The reality after this was that the Mastertons were getting too old for successful IVF; both of them were 42 in 2001, when they travelled to Rome for the unsuccessful infertility treatment. Also, they simply could not afford any further private IVF and PGD treatment, given that Mr Masterton was unemployed and that a family friend had lent the couple the £6,000 needed for the original IVF and PGD.

23.18 After public consultation, the HFEA in November 2003 recommended that the current policy of only allowing sex selection of embryos for medical reasons should continue. Thus the ban on sex selection for non-medical or social reasons ought to continue. Family balancing would, therefore, fall into the category of a non-medical reason, as here with the Mastertons, or alternatively be categorised as a social reason, and hence be denied legitimately under the then HFEA policy for sex selection, or now under the 2008 Act.

23.19 The Masterton case, the HFEA policy on sex selection for non-medical reasons, and indeed the new law in the 2008 Act all share the same objective that sex selection can only be permitted for clearly defined, specific and limited medical purposes, and to avoid these medical conditions or disorders (ie negative selection) rather than selecting in order to eg balance a family (ie positive selection, or some might call it a type of designing babies). Currently there are over 200 known sex-related or linked diseases. The majority of these sex-related or linked diseases afflict males, the Y sex chromosome not being able to mask these diseases as effectively as the female X sex chromosome. Hence more males are sufferers of these diseases as opposed to females. These sex-linked diseases include Duchenne's muscular dystrophy, haemophilia (the 'royal' disease), and colour blindness.

OBJECTIONS TO SEX SELECTION

23.20 There are a number of objections to permitting sex-selection for non-medical reasons. These include that the practice is sexist, may cause a population sex imbalance, is harmful to the child, ie it may compromise the welfare of the child, it is only available to those who can afford it, ie a justice argument, and that there are limits to the individual autonomy of prospective parents. Also, it could be contended that sex selection is another method that commodifies children. Again, important questions arise about whether the law should intervene and prevent an activity if it is not harming anyone, although clearly some would argue the practice is intrinsically harmful and hence must be outlawed.

The practice is sexist

23.21 The House of Commons Select Committee on Science and Technology, flagged up, inter alia, their concern that the practice may well be sexist:

'it may be argued that permitting selection of embryos on the basis of their sex would lead to a demographic disaster or the reinforcement of sexist attitudes, both of which would be harmful to the wider society.'[13]

A sexist attitude might be: 'I am a man. Men are automatically better or superior than women. They are stronger physically, more intelligent and less prone to emotions.' If this attitude were to be translated into a couple choosing a baby by sex selection, that might mean the couple preferring a male embryo being implanted to a female one. Stereotyping comes into this as well. The argument

---

13 House of Commons Select Committee on Science and Technology, *Inquiry into Human Reproductive Technologies and the Law: Eighth Special Report of Session 2004–2005* (2005), p 20.

might be that females are, eg, more interested in fashion, image and having families than men, and not as interested in successful careers, therefore we ought to choose a male embryo. This is a crude stereotype and assumes that if true, this preference is due to the person's sex and no other reason(s).

23.22 However, it could be asked what is wrong with preferring a male or a female child if that preference is based, prompted and motivated by a desire of the couple to, eg, balance their family, rather than engage in blatant sexism (ie men are superior to females), or if the preference is underpinned by sexual stereotyping, ie making sweeping unsubstantiated generalisations about people's abilities and worth, based merely on their particular sex? Sex stereotyping is wrong and foolish too because it undermines the uniqueness and individuality of every person. Every person is different and unique. They cannot be categorised by reference to one attribute. They cannot be placed in one box as a result of that arbitrary classification. Their future life cannot be mapped out or predetermined on the basis of a stereotypical view made by reference to their sex. The person needs to have an open, not a closed future.

It may cause a population imbalance

23.23 Fears about sex selection leading to a population imbalance are greatly exaggerated. Certainly sex selection of embryos entails using IVF. Three-quarters of IVF treatment is offered privately, ie only to those who can pay. Also, even more significantly, only approximately 1 per cent of all births in the United Kingdom are in fact as a result of and following, eg, IVF treatment. The numbers, therefore, who will theoretically be able to opt for embryonic sex selection will be very tiny as a proportion of all births in the United Kingdom. The other imponderable and variable is, if one were to assume that couples or would be-parents were to make a choice, why would it necessarily be assumed they would choose one sex in an embryo, rather than the other? Why, for example, would all those couples necessarily choose to have a son? Even if they did opt for a boy, only 25–30 per cent of IVF treatment cycles result in a live birth anyway. Logically, therefore, permitting sex selection for family balancing purposes, or even relaxing the law to permit it for wider purposes (ie for social reasons) may not necessarily open the floodgates to creating a population sex imbalance crisis. Besides which, in the United Kingdom, we have had the benefits of the assisted reproductive regulatory regime, namely the 1990 Act, the HFEA, the Code of Practice, and now the 2008 Act, policing licensed clinics and safeguarding and protecting vulnerable and desperate patients from potential exploitation.

23.24 Critics however, and those worried about legalisation of sex selection for social reasons leading to a descent down the ethical slippery slope, might point to the Chinese policy of one child per family, aimed at tackling and attempting to curb the huge population explosion in China. The Parliamentary Office of Science and Technology, in 'Sex Selection',[14] noted that:

'Chinese census data shows that 20 years ago [presumably in 1973] there were 108 boys under the age of 5 for every 100 girls, and that by 2000 this ratio had shifted to 117 boys to 100 girls. This ratio varied across the country

---

14 In Parliamentary Office of Science and Technology, *postnote* (July 2003, No 198).

with some regions showing a normal 102–106 boys to every 100 girls and other, more prosperous, regions showing ratios of up to 135 boys for every 100 girls.'[15]

The report did note that those figures probably exaggerated the true situation because parents may be less likely to register the birth of a daughter so that they could then try for a son. They are fiddling with the system, but, of course they are doing so because of this one child policy which clearly operates against female babies and results in blatantly sexist consequences which are probably socially very detrimental too. The report continues that under Chinese law parents have the right to only one child, although since 2002 they have been able to apply to have a second under rules laid down on a regional basis. Needless to say, this example is open to the accusation that circumstances in the United Kingdom are fundamentally different to China. Comparisons are therefore odious and any lessons to be extrapolated from the Chinese one child policy in relation to UK policy on sex selection of embryos are wholly inapplicable to the United Kingdom, an allegedly liberal, Western democracy, operating under the rule of law and having to respect human rights in our courts. China by contrast is an undemocratic, totalitarian Communist dictatorship, with no apparent state respect for human rights.

23.25   Regarding India, another country with a huge and ever expanding population, the report notes:

'However, a similar trend has been reported in India, and again higher levels of education and affluence are directly associated with a greater imbalance in the boy: girl ratio. It appears that in both China and India there is easy access to ultrasound scanning for parents who can afford to pay and that females are being selectively aborted. A study carried out in a hospital in the Punjab, India found that the only girls born following sex determination by ultrasound had been incorrectly identified as male or had a male twin.'[16]

In other words, the females which had been born were mistakes.

23.26   The report did note:

'The use of ultrasound and abortion for sex *selection* has been banned since 1994 in India and 1995 in China. In neither case has the legislation been enforced.' [emphasis added]

Is this legislation merely designed to be symbolic or instrumental and effective? The report continues:

'While some observers argue that effective enforcement of the ban is essential, others believe that this would drive the practice underground where it would be unregulated and potentially unsafe. Instead, they believe that the priority should be to change attitudes so that parents no longer have a preference for sons. Such cultural change is likely to take a long time.'

The great beauty and advantage of the UK system, or at least one of them, is that currently sex selection of embryos is expressly and strictly regulated under our laws (ie the 2008 Act) and was regulated by the HFEA prior to the enactment

---

15   'Sex Selection', p 3.
16   Ibid.

of the 2008 Act, so there was no legal, ethical or social free-for-all in the United Kingdom, nor did the practice ever 'go underground'.

Sex selection is harmful to the child

23.27 The process of sex selection may be harmful to the child because the would-be parents are choosing this embryo totally or at least primarily because of its sex and for no other reason. The argument might be that that they are using this embryo and valuing it primarily as a means towards an end, their end, for example wanting a child of one sex to fulfil their wishes and desires, and not fully valuing the intrinsic value of the child regardless of its sex. They are not valuing the child as an end in itself and this is immoral. Consequently, the child has been harmed by this parental attitude and reason for its creation.

23.28 However critics of this view would counter that the child has not been harmed in any way, either physically, psychologically or emotionally, because parents who have children 'naturally' (ie not by IVF) have their children for a huge variety of reasons, good, bad and indifferent, or for no particular reason at all (ie unplanned and unwanted pregnancies), and no one (ie the law of the land, via a statute or regulatory regime) is judging them or preventing them from having their children here. That is logically inconsistent and unfair. Arguments about appeals to the harm that a process or activity may cause a potential child are of course currently dealt with directly by s 13(5) of the 1990 Act. There is law there specifically to deal with and cover this scenario if sex selection for social, non-medical reasons were ever to be permitted.

The justice argument

23.29 Another possible argument is that permitting and legalising embryo sex selection offends the ethical principle of justice. This justice principle basically states that all equals shall be treated equally and that there should be no unfair discrimination against anyone. Everyone should moreover get their just desert and entitlement. The argument might be that if sex selection of embryos were to be permitted the richer, more affluent citizens would be able to avail themselves of this facility much more easily in private clinics than their poorer, less affluent counterparts, and that that is unfair and unjust. Determining the sex of a child would hinge mainly on the ability to pay. Of course, currently, access to certain infertility treatments (eg IVF) depends in 75 per cent of cases on the ability of the patient to pay for the infertility treatment. The remaining 25 per cent of cases depend on the operation of what is in essence a 'postcode lottery'. Permitting embryo sex selection is just another manifestation or slight extension of what is an unjust and unfair system anyway.

Limits to autonomy?

23.30 Autonomy, here in the context of reproductive choice or procreative autonomy, is a fundamental ethical principle but it is not an absolute one. The Mastertons sadly discovered that when they unsuccessfully sought help from a number of UK licensed treatment clinics to help them get another female child. Clearly s 13(5) of the 1990 Act severely limits the full autonomy of parents in wanting to have a child because, before treatment can be given by a licensed clinic, account must be taken of the welfare of any child who might be born, including the need of that child for supportive parenting. The welfare of the child principle weighs heavily on clinicians before they agree to offer patients, eg, IVF.

Commodification of children

23.31   There is an argument that permitting sex selection of embryos is yet another example of the commodification of children. Children become products or must-have-items, to be bought off-the-peg. Their moral value and ethical worth is accordingly diminished appreciably. That is wrong. This argument, if accepted, could be extended to most IVF, 75 per cent of which is offered privately.

THE NEW LAW

23.32   The new law relating to embryo testing and sex selection is located in Sched 2 of the 2008 Act, titled 'Activities that may be licensed under the 1990 Act'. Introductory para 1 provides that: 'Schedule 2 to the 1990 Act (activities for which licences may be granted) is amended as follows.' Paragraph 3 of Sched 2 of the 2008 Act is headed 'Embryo testing and sex selection' and provides:

'3. After paragraph 1 [of the 1990 Act] insert—
"Embryo testing
   1ZA(1) A licence under paragraph 1 cannot authorise the testing of an embryo, except for one or more of the following purposes—"'

There are five permitted purposes for testing embryos. The third ground, referred to in paragraph 1ZA(1)(c), allows it for:

'in a case where there is a particular risk that any resulting child will have or develop—
   (i)   a gender-related serious physical or mental disability,
   (ii) a gender-related serious illness, or
   (iii) any other gender-related serious medical condition,
establishing the sex of the embryo,'.

Also importantly, para 1ZA(3) specifies that:

'For the purposes of sub-paragraph (1)(c), a physical or mental disability, illness or other medical condition is gender-related if the Authority is satisfied that—
   (a)   it affects only one sex, or
   (b)   it affects one sex significantly more than the other.'

Sex Selection

23.33   New paragraph 1ZB, inserted after para 1 of Sched 2 of the 1990 Act, relates specifically to sex selection and again very clearly and unambiguously states:

'(1) A licence under paragraph 1 cannot authorise any practice designed to secure that any resulting child will be of one sex rather than the other.'

Basically a clinic licensed by the HFEA cannot authorise sex selection. This appears to be a watertight, clear legal provision, and at the same time an ethical bright line.

23.34 Paragraph 1ZB continues that:

'(2) Sub-paragraph (1) does not prevent the authorisation of any testing of embryos that is capable of being authorised under paragraph 1ZA.'

Thus embryos can be sex-selected for one of the five permitted purposes under para 1ZA, ie for medical reasons. Also, new paragraph 1ZB (3) states that:

'Sub-paragraph (1) does not prevent the authorisation of any other practices designed to secure that any resulting child will be of one sex rather than the other in a case where there is a particular risk that a woman will give birth to a child who will have or develop—
(a) a gender-related serious physical or mental disability,
(b) a gender-related serious illness, or
(c) any other gender-related serious medical condition.'

This sub-paragraph future proofs the 2008 Act, and permits for new, innovative practices to be used in the future if they will secure that a child is of a particular sex where there is a particular risk that a woman may give birth to a child who will have or develop a gender-related serious physical or mental disability, or a serious illness or any other gender-related serious medical condition.

23.35 Then new paragraph 1ZB(4) provides:

'For the purposes of sub-paragraph (3), a physical or mental disability, illness or other medical condition is gender-related if the Authority is satisfied that—
(a) it affects only one sex, or
(b) it affects one sex significantly more than another.'

23.36 Finally new paragraph 1ZC empowers the Secretary of State to amend paragraphs 1ZA and 1ZB. It provides:

'(1) Regulations may make any amendment of paragraph 1ZA (embryo testing).
(2) Regulations under this paragraph which amend paragraph 1ZA may make any amendment of sub-paragraphs (2) to (4) of paragraph 1ZB (sex selection) which appears to the Secretary of State to be necessary or expedient in consequence of the amendment of paragraph 1ZA.
(3) Regulations under this paragraph may not enable the authorisation of—
    (a) the testing of embryos for the purpose of establishing their sex, or
    (b) other practices falling within paragraph 1ZB (1), except on grounds relating to the health of any resulting child.
(4) For the purposes of this paragraph, "amend" includes add to and repeal, and references to "amendment" are to be read accordingly.'

Again this regulation-making power given to the Secretary of State allows him to add to or even repeal new paragraphs 1ZA and 1ZB.

HOUSE OF LORDS

Banning

23.37   Lord Darzi, in setting out the key aims of the HFE Bill, flagged one important aim as being 'to impose a statutory ban on the sex selection of offspring for non-medical reasons.'[17] Later on he adds that such a ban 'will put on the face of the legislation something which is at present a matter of HFEA policy, giving Parliament the opportunity to fully debate the provisions.'[18] The clear implication is that whilst the independent, expert statutory regulator, the HFEA, has set its face against sex selection of offspring for social reasons, really it is such an ethically, morally, medically and legally important decision that the legislature ought to, inter alia, send out a clear signal to society, clinicians, scientists, etc that Parliament will not countenance it. The elected ethical and legal forum of the nation that passes the highest laws in the land ought to mark out the legal parameters and ethical bright lines here, not an unelected, albeit accountable body such as the HFEA.

Parameters

23.38   In addition Lord Darzi added that:

'The Bill will also make explicit the basic parameters for screening and selecting embryos. Again, the intention is that this should be undertaken only on the grounds of avoiding serious disease, and the Bill preserves some flexibility for how that is to be determined. The current situation, which has been the subject of legal challenge, is not sufficiently clear, and again the opportunity is presented for Parliament to give a clear steer for the future.'[19]

Parliament's role, inter alia, is to clarify the law if it is uncertain, which the law arguably was if legal challenges are being sought to the existing law, and to give a steer or sense of direction for researchers, scientists, doctors and patients regarding the road map for future developments.

23.39   Not surprisingly Lord Alton voiced his great concerns and objection to permitting sex selection of children for, inter alia, non-medical reasons:

'I am glad that the Bill unequivocally prohibits sex selection. We are absolutely right to do that. We have to guard against the mentality that can sometimes lead to wanting designer babies.'[20]

Baroness Royall emphasised what was actually involved in embryo testing, including sex selection for medical reasons:

'Embryo testing involves removing one or two cells of an embryo created in vitro at the eight-cell stage. The Bill introduces five principal purposes

---

17   *Hansard*, 8 November 2007, col 142 (HL).
18   *Hansard*, 19 November 2007, col 666 (HL).
19   Ibid.
20   *Hansard*, 4 December 2007, col 1645 (HL).

for which embryos can be tested. These are: ... to determine the sex of the embryo where there is a particular risk that any resulting child will have or develop a gender-related serious medical condition'.[21]

Choosing defective embryos: deliberately-designed handicap?

23.40 Section 14(4) of the 2008 Act amended s 13 of the 1990 Act (ie conditions of licences for treatment) by inserting new s 13(8)–(13), and, inter alia, also banned couples deliberately choosing an embryo with a disability or handicap because, eg, the couple were themselves handicapped, or alternatively because an existing child of theirs was disabled or handicapped. Baroness Deech, whilst welcoming generally the use of PGDs, nevertheless said that she hoped peers would be 'pleased that the deliberate choice of an embryo that is, for example, likely to be deaf will be prevented by Clause 14.'[22] One could argue that this prohibition merely confirms s 13(5) of the 1990 Act (the welfare of the child requirement). How could it conceivably be in the best interests of a child or promote its welfare to deliberately create it and design it with a major disability or handicap, ie deafness, built into its DNA? Avoiding creating deliberately and intentionally deaf children does not logically mean existing deaf people are condemned as being second-class citizens or as having any less moral worth or value, but rather does prevent the creation of rather unusual 'designer' children, an arguably dubious and ethically doubtful practice. There must be limits to autonomy and procreative freedom.

HOUSE OF COMMONS

23.41 In the Second Reading debate in the House of Commons, Alan Johnson MP, the then Secretary of State for Health, stated that the HFE Bill, inter alia:

> 'introduces explicit regulations on embryo screening. Embryo screening and selection will be allowed only for the purpose of detecting serious genetic diseases or disorders.'[23]

The government's modus operandi is therefore to combine clear laws, regulation, control and oversight with permitting embryo screening and sex selection in this tightly controlled regulatory environment.

Selecting disability

23.42 He added that the HFE Bill would not permit parents to screen embryos in order to include, rather than exclude, a particular disability.[24] Strictly controlled and defined negative screening would be permitted, but not positive screening. Parents cannot, therefore, choose to deliberately screen and subsequently select a handicapped or disabled embryo to produce a child who is, for example, deaf or blind. Creating so-called 'designer' children is effectively prohibited. Most people would find permitting this sort of manufacturing of children with certain

21   Ibid, col 1646.
22   *Hansard*, 19 November 2007, col 673 (HL).
23   *Hansard* 12 May 2008, col 1069(HC).
24   Ibid, col 1070.

attributes, here disabilities or handicaps, intuitively wrong. The autonomy and wishes of parents to have such a handicapped child with the positive assistance of a licensed clinic cannot be respected or allowed legally. Mr Johnson stated too that:

'Following the results of the public consultation, the Bill also outlaws sex selection for non-medical reasons.'

Catch-up

23.43 Kevin Barron, MP, welcomed the fact that:

'The Bill spells out for the first time in law a number of rules relating to the screening and selection of embryos and gametes. In broad terms, embryo screening and selection will be allowed only for the purpose of screening out serious genetic diseases or disorders.'[25]

He pointed out the reality that the independent regulator, the HFEA, has in any case 'licensed screening in a number of cases since 1990, including cases of single-gene disorders such as cystic fibrosis.' So the law here is just catching up with what is actually happening on the scientific ground. He also noted that:

'The Bill will ban selecting the sex of a child except when the intention is to avoid a serious sex-linked disease.'

CONCLUSIONS

23.44 In the 2008 Act, Parliament set out a very clear ethical and legal bright line concerning sex selection. It was clearly the correct line to set, but in individual cases like the Masterton scenario it appeared manifestly harsh and unfair. It did signal the aversion of Parliament to the creation of 'designer babies', ie embryos positively selected for social reasons at the whim and behest of would-be parents. That ethical slippery slope was cordoned off with a strong legal barrier.

---

25 Ibid, col 1084.

Part 10

In Search of the Best Ethical Compass

Chapter 24

The Role of Parliament: Our Ethical Compass

INTRODUCTION

24.1 Most of the legal, ethical and medical regulatory structure and framework for the assisted reproduction in the United Kingdom, and incontrovertibly its major salient features, are contained in the 1990 and 2008 Human Fertilisation and Embryology Acts (the 1990 Act and the 2008 Act), ie in Acts of Parliament. This is not accidental or a coincidence. It is only right and proper that regulation of this enormous developing area with such huge potential effects on future generations, let alone on society today, ought sensibly to be contained in primary legislation. Under the unwritten constitution of the United Kingdom, an Act of Parliament is the highest form of law in the country. This principle is known as parliamentary supremacy (or alternatively as parliamentary sovereignty) and is one of the dominant characteristics and features in our constitutional landscape. The classical definition of it is given by Dicey:

> 'The principle of parliamentary sovereignty means neither more nor less than this, namely that Parliament has, under the English constitution, the right to make or unmake any law whatever; and further that no person or body is recognised by the law of England as having a right to override or set aside the legislation of Parliament.'[1]

There are arguably two components to the theory: first, a positive aspect, that Parliament can make or pass any law it wants on any area, and secondly, a negative aspect, that no other body or person can override or set aside an Act of Parliament.

24.2 The sheer scope and breadth of the ethical, legal and technological terrain covered by both the 1990 and 2008 Acts amply demonstrate the efficacy of the first component of Dicey's theory and the primacy of Parliament's intent, as manifest in both Acts. Meanwhile, the necessity of the courts, HFEA, fertility clinicians and researchers having to comply fully with this overarching regulatory structure contained in the two Acts underlines the second component of the theory.

Alder

24.3 Alder contends there are three aspects to parliamentary supremacy:

> '1. Parliament has unlimited lawmaking power in the sense that it can make any kind of law.

---

1 A V Dicey, *Introduction to the Study of the Law of the Constitution*, (MacMillan & Co Ltd, 1915), pp 37–38.

2.   The legal validity of laws made by Parliament cannot be questioned by any other body.

3.   A Parliament cannot bind a future Parliament.'[2]

Alder's third aspect, that for example a Parliament in 1990 cannot bind a future Parliament in 2008, is most apposite in a rapidly developing area like assisted reproduction where the science is moving much faster than the laws supposedly regulating the science, so that what is scientifically possible in 2008 (cell nuclear replacement, creating human admixed embryos) was not possible in 1990, and so needs new laws to control and regulate it, demonstrating the necessity for the 2008 Act.

TESTING THE PRINCIPLE

24.4   The efficacy of the overarching constitutional principle has been tested on innumerable occasions in the UK courts and been endorsed by those courts. In several cases there have been a series of challenges, all unsuccessful, to the legal validity of an Act of Parliament, or a provision in such an Act. In *Cheney v Conn*,[3] the court held that a provision in an international treaty preventing the use of money being used for the construction of nuclear weapons could not invalidate a contrary provision in the Finance Act 1964. Indeed the judge in the case, Mr Justice Ungoed-Thomas, stated:

'What the statute itself enacts cannot be unlawful, because what the statute says and provides is itself the law, and the highest form of law that is known to this country.'

Also, in *R v Jordan*,[4] the court, inter alia, held that an Act of Parliament restricting racially motivated hate-speech prevails over the common law, even when the common law has sought to protect the freedom of speech of individuals as a fundamental right on many occasions. Furthermore, an Act of Parliament prevails over major constituent Acts (ie important constitutional Acts, as here the Act of Union 1800), as was demonstrated in *Ex P Canon Selwyn* (1872) 36 JP 54. Also, an Act of Parliament prevails over the exercise of prerogative powers, as was evident in *De Keyser's Royal Hotel Ltd* [1920] AC 508. Furthermore, Parliament does not have to expressly repeal earlier legislation – it can do so by implication. In other words a later Act or provision in an Act overrides an earlier contrary Act or provision in an Act. This occurred in *Vauxhall Estates Ltd v Liverpool Corporation* [1932] 1 KB 733. This doctrine of implied repeal is another illustration of the current validity of the theory of parliamentary supremacy.

24.5   Furthermore, Parliament can enact retrospective legislation and has done so on several occasions, eg the War Crimes Act 1991 and the War Damage Act 1965. By contrast, in the United States, the American written Constitution expressly forbids the enactment of retrospective legislation. Parliament is also unlimited as to the content of legislation it can pass. It has the legal power to pass Acts which have altered the succession to the throne, extended how long a Parliament can sit, abolished and reconstituted itself, altered its own power,

---

2   J Alder, *Constitutional and administrative law* 7th ed (Palgrave Macmillan, 2009), p 163.
3   (1968) 1 All ER 779.
4   [1963] Crim LR 124.

passed retrospective legislation, granted independence to former colonies, and passed Acts curtailing significantly citizens' basic freedoms and civil liberties. This rich seam of illustrative cases highlights the centrality of the principle in our constitution and in the United Kingdom generally. Acts of Parliament are, therefore, very important instruments and devices in our constitution.

24.6   So when Parliament legislates and passes primary legislation (ie an Act of Parliament), and particularly, for the purposes of this book, the 2008 Act and its earlier incarnation the 1990 Act in the highly controversial (legally, ethically, and medically) area of human reproductive medicine and embryonic research, that has huge significance and potentially very wide repercussions for society in the future.

24.7   Clearly though whilst Parliament can in theory enact any law it wants on any area, with any content it chooses, the political reality is that it frequently chooses not to do so. Public opinion, the media, its international obligations, and indeed its own members, be they MPs or peers in the House of Lords, rein it in. Proposed legislation must pass through both chambers of Parliament and is subject to a raft of scrutiny, review, consideration, debate and analysis by parliamentarians, hopefully to make the proposed legislation ultimately a better law. This was abundantly evident in the passage through Parliament of what ultimately became the 2008 Act.

CONCLUSION

24.8   There are many critics of both the effectiveness of Parliament and the role of members of both Houses of Parliament. This opprobrium was highlighted and exacerbated for many in the recent Parliamentary expenses scandal. That said, by complete and marked contrast the passage of the HFE Bill through Parliament, and its eventual enactment as the 2008 Act, showed Parliament in a much more favourable light generally, with the exception of the abortive legislative amendments concerning abortion. Parliament unquestionably subjected the HFE Bill to rigorous scrutiny and forensic examination, arguably culminating in better legislation in the final Act. Furthermore, as Alder stated: 'The traditional function of Parliament has been to represent the people,'[5] and the huge variety of opinions evident in both the Parliamentary debates and in the Committee and Report stages amply demonstrated this 'representativeness'. The Government were demonstrably held to account by both Houses of Parliament, especially by the House of Lords, in explaining and justifying the significant changes wrought by what ultimately became the 2008 Act. The legal and ethical foundations and basis of the 2008 Act were therefore tested and arguably strengthened by this process. This is surely no bad thing if regulatory oversight of assisted reproduction is thereby improved.

---

5   J Alder *Constitutional and Administrative Law* (Palgrave Law Masters) 8th edn, (Palgrave Macmillan, 2011), p 231.

Chapter 25

The View of the House of Lords

INTRODUCTION

25.1   The debates in the House of Lords on the passage of the HFE Bill, which ultimately became the Human Fertilisation and Embryology Act 2008 (the 2008 Act), demonstrated the importance of the role of the second chamber in the UK constitution and in our wider society. Alder noted that:

> 'The conventional justification for the existence of a second chamber in the UK is that it acts as a revising chamber to scrutinise the detail of legislation proposed by the Commons and to allow time for second thoughts, thus acting as a constitutional safeguard against the possible excesses of majoritarianism and party politics.'[1]

The argument would be that the House of Commons does not always possess the expertise, time, or possibly inclination to enact robust, fit-for-purpose primary legislation, and sadly may at times be concerned with populism, opinion polls and party politics or party advantage, with MPs increasingly being subject to whipping, and sometimes three line-whipping from their party machinery, whereas peers by contrast can cast a more critical, objective, dispassionate and expert eye over legislation. If not immune from whipping, they are at least less prone to it, and of course they do not have to worry about currying favour with the electorate (at least not yet in 2012) in order to get re-elected, unlike their lower House counterparts. The argument runs that a government's proposed legislation (and most of Parliament's proposed legislation are government bills) benefits from the active revision and scrutiny of our second chamber.

25.2   Interestingly the Wakeham Report in 2000[2] identified a number of functions of the second chamber of Parliament. These were, in no particular order:

(1)   To provide advice on public policy. On the HFE Bill, peers would bring a wide variety and range of informed views to bear that were broadly representative of British society. Leading scientists, doctors (including Lord Winston, Lord Patel and Lord Walton), lawyers (Lord Mackay, Baroness Deech), philosophers (Baroness Warnock), clerics (the Archbishop of York John Sentamu), former politicians (Baroness Williams and Lord Alton), and a variety of others, including cross-benchers and peers taking various party political whips, could contribute to the scrutiny, revising and debates on what eventually culminated in the 2008 Act. These various peers would hopefully be broadly

---

1   J. Alder, *Constitutional and Administrative Law* (Palgrave Law Masters) 7th edn (Palgrave Macmillan, 2009), p 207.
2   *A House for the Future: Royal Commission on the House of Lords* (Cm 4534, January 2000)

representative of the myriad views on the huge range of issues covered in the 2008 Act.

(2) To act as a revising chamber, to revise the Commons/government's bills, not to reject the elected chamber's bills.

(3) To provide a forum for general debate. The idea here is that matters of public concern are ventilated in the House of Lords.

(4) Introducing relatively uncontroversial legislation. This function was debatable in reference to the 2008 Act. It could hardly objectively be described as being 'relatively uncontroversial' legislation.

(5) To provide ministers – arguably, with Lord Darzi, very good and eminent ones!

(6) To provide Committees on general topics and issues. Obviously, in the context of the 2008 Act, the Science and Technology Committee would be the obvious example.

(7) To permit persons who have made a contribution to public life, other than party politicians, to participate in government. Again Lord Darzi, a leading surgeon, springs to mind as such a person.

(8) Critically, to act as a constitutional check on the government flexing its constitutional muscles and exercising its power unconstitutionally or improperly by, eg, bringing in bad, poorly thought-out legislation.

(9) To act more generally as a constitutional watchdog.

REVISING IN PRACTICE

25.3 In introducing the HFE Bill into the House of Lords Lord Darzi, the Parliamentary Under-Secretary of State at the Department of Health, stated that the HFE Bill represented 'an overhaul of the existing law', namely the Human Fertilisation and Embryology Act 1990 (the 1990 Act), 'taking account of developments both in technology and in attitudes, and will promote public confidence together with best regulatory practice.'[3] This is in keeping with the view of the Wakeham Report regarding one of the many functions of the second chamber, ie being broadly representative of the views of society and the public. These are views that had arguably changed since the 1990 Act, concerning the need for a father, the use of human admixed embryos for research, the creation of saviour siblings, and the banning of selection of embryos on the basis of sex for social reasons and abortion reform. He contended that whilst the government had kept to the fundamental underpinnings of the regulatory scheme based on the Warnock Report in the HFE Bill, it was noted that, nevertheless, technology and attitudes had moved on. He then cited:

'novel ways of creating embryos for research, a much-increased capacity to screen embryos for serious genetic diseases and, at the same time, a legal recognition for different family forms.'

Changes in technology, and to its subsequent use, demand corresponding changes in laws. There should not be a mismatch between the law and science. A function of Parliament, including the House of Lords, should be to make sure science does not proceed too far ahead of the law. He added:

---

3   *Hansard*, 8 November 2007, col 141 (HL).

'Those developments demand an examination of the legal and regulatory framework through parliamentary debate, and a resetting of the relevant parameters for the future.'

Was the 2008 Act essentially a fine-tuning exercise, or alternatively was it a radical rethink of the ethical parameters? Quite a few people would argue it was in fact the latter.

Robust

25.4   Lord Harries of Pentregarth, an Anglican Bishop, scientist and former interim chair-man of the HFEA, described the 1990 Act as 'a remarkably robust piece of legislation' that had stood the test of time and ensured that 'public confidence, so vital in the area of evolving research, has been retained'.[4] The 1990 Act was arguably enacted not because of concerns about infertility treatments primarily, but rather it was aimed at regulating maverick scientists and doctors (seen by some as latter-day Dr Frankensteins), and because a lot of people, not necessarily opposed to embryo research that helped, eg, find cures to dreadful diseases, were suspicious and did not fully trust some of the doctors and scientists who were advocating the research, or necessarily some of the motives allegedly underpinning that research. Lord Harries added that since 1990 (he was speaking in 2007):

'things have moved on most remarkably. Scientific advances, not envisaged by the framers of the 1990 Act, need to be regulated. In addition, social changes, already embedded in law, have taken place that Parliament will need to consider and evaluate in relation to this regulation.'

Parliament

25.5   Lord Harries referred to the wider question of the relationship between Parliament, regulatory bodies and those who worked in the field in relation to the possibility of cytoplasmic hybrids and stated:

'It is right that major issues of principle, about which the public are hesitant if not hostile, should be decided by Parliament.'[5]

In other words, decisions about permitting the creation and use of human admixed embryos, a huge decision and controversial step forward in research really needs to have to be approved by Parliament and not left to the HFEA, still less scientists or doctors on their own to decide if it should be permitted. He noted too that:

'A regulatory body regulates only on the basis of what Parliament has decided, making general decisions about good practice, while properly leaving other decisions to professional bodies and clinicians.'

The Code of Practice is of course where the general decisions about good practice are apparent. He referred to the legal advice to the HFEA that cytoplasmic hybrids were embryos within the meaning of the 1990 Act and,

---

4   Ibid, col 196.
5   Ibid, col 197.

therefore, 'were in principle within our remit to regulate.' Yet he argued that this was a development of such significance that it was absolutely right that it should be considered by Parliament. He said that fundamental issues like this 'should be so referred' to Parliament before being permitted.

Compromise

25.6   Baroness Deech, the Chairman of the HFEA from 1994 to 2002, was clear that the 1990 Act 'represented, and still represents a democratic compromise between strongly held views in society,'[6] as perhaps the debates in both Houses demonstrate. She said that the 1990 Act avoided the excesses of freedom and restriction in the United States and in Europe, and crucially noted that progress in this country had been largely in tandem with public acceptability – not totally or completely, but largely. She noted that other countries had run into trouble, citing the US ban on federally funded stem cell research then in place, while it left basic IVF unregulated.[7] She also sang the praises of the HFEA (now apparently to be scrapped in 2013 and its various functions transferred to other healthcare regulatory bodies (ALBs)), submitting that the HFEA worked to reconcile, to explain and to point to a way forward, and it was accountable to the public. She did not support the creation of a national ethical body alongside the regulator, arguing that 'the law already incorporates ethical issues that determine most matters'.

Second Chamber

25.7   Lord Adonis, Parliamentary Under-Secretary of State, Department for Children, Schools and Families, also observed that, since the passage of the 1990 Act, the House of Lords had made a very telling contribution to further regulating the burgeoning field of human reproductive medicine. He noted:

> 'the House has contributed expertise to help frame and improve the IVF legislative structure in a number of respects. Those include the 2001 regulations that extended the use of embryos to stem cell research, [and] the Human Reproductive Cloning Act 2001, which prohibited reproductive cloning'.[8]

THE HOUSE OF LORDS DEBATE

Clear boundaries

25.8   Lord Darzi, in the Second Reading debate, flagged up the many exciting developments in human reproductive medicine, noting:

> 'Alongside this enviable record of i[nnovation stands an equally pioneering history of effective regulatory oversight. The HFEA] was the first body of its kind in the world. The creation of the HFEA made for the first time an

---

6   Ibid, col 210.
7   President Obama lifted the federal ban on stem cell research in 2009.
8   *Hansard*, 8 November 2007, col 230 (HL).

area of medical practice subject to the control of an independent regulator, replacing professional self-regulation.'[9]

He added:

'Specialist regulation of reproductive technologies, together with clear legal boundaries, has united scientific breakthroughs with public confidence in their development and use.
'Among other things, this represents a considerable triumph for parliamentary debate.'

25.9   The role of Parliament and its debates over a huge area of scientific development and research, covering a myriad of legal, ethical, medical, social and moral issues, have shaped and influenced considerably the resulting legislation. However, arguably more importantly, Parliament has acted as the forum for discussing, analysing and resolving a wide range of arguments and views, representative of the many strands in UK society, and has reached a view on those issues which has ultimately been translated into the provisions in the 2008 Act. In extolling the significant part played by peers in shaping the Act, Lord Darzi said many peers had played, and continued to play, a direct role as legislators and experienced practitioners in the fields of philosophy, science and medicine, and that the HFE Bill provided a further opportunity for that expertise to be brought to bear.

25.10   So, in 1990, Parliament had set out the legal boundaries and parameters of a scheme of regulation, based on the principle of active monitoring of technologies that raised a range of profound social, legal and ethical questions, according to Lord Darzi. The huge importance of these questions cannot be underestimated. As Lord Darzi observed: 'Finding answers to those questions arguably goes straight to the heart of our existence as individuals, families and society.' He contended too that even though there were diametrically opposed views on many of the controversial issues that figure in the 2008 Act, nevertheless there was some inclination of parliamentarians to set out some broad principles and limits in the Act:

'Sincerely held views and opinions differ widely, and sometimes fundamentally, in this area. However, there was also in 1990 an evident desire for some principles and some defined limits. The 1990 Act represented a will to find common ground in a framework broadly acceptable to society.'[10]

Constant review

25.11   He described the 1990 Act as 'cutting-edge legislation,' but noted that it still needed to be reviewed from time to time by Parliament, the ethical, legal, social and moral forum of the United Kingdom. The government, through Parliament, were aiming to ensure that the law in the 2008 Act, and the 1990 Act, as amended, remained effective and fit for purpose in the 21st century. To that end, Parliament must effectively police the regulatory parameters of this cutting-edge science:

9   *Hansard*, 19 November 2007, col 663 (HL).
10   Ibid.

'These developments demand a rigorous examination in Parliament of the regulatory framework, and a resetting of the controls and boundaries for the future.'[11]

Baroness Deech impressed upon peers that the public did not take IVF for granted, despite 50,000 children per year being born as a result of the procedure. The public do not regard it as a procedure that should be left unregulated. She added that treatment rolled into new areas and blurred into research, and she hoped peers 'will resist the siren voices that say that IVF has become commonplace and there is no need to regulate it.' She was emphatic: 'In this field, the law is paramount'.

Religious perspectives

Letting rip?

25.12 The Lord Bishop of St Albans posed the question:

'does the kind of scientific endeavour and therapeutic treatment which this Bill allows need regulation at all and why not let scientific and therapeutic markets forces rip?'[12]

He rejected permitting leaving market forces to their own devices, ie to 'let rip', stating:

'Unregulated research and treatment could jeopardise our common understanding of what it means to be human; it could jeopardise our understanding of what we believe to be the meaning and purpose of human life; it could jeopardise our understanding of human relationships; and an unregulated free-for-all could and might lead to the unscrupulous treatment of the most vulnerable and could and might lead to some appalling abuses of power.'

Unless Parliament regulates this field, commercial and business interests will proliferate, and in a regulatory-free field of human reproductive medicine, sometimes at least, compliance with ethical principles will figure less prominently than maximising profit. The bishop also noted that the HFE Bill was not confined just to 'our generation', nor is it 'only about our place in the world scientifically and technologically. It is also potentially about generations of people yet to come.' Parliament's legislation can and does affect people for many years. Obviously the 1990 Act affected people from 1990 up until October 2009, and still affects them, even though considerably amended by the 2008 Act. The imperative for parliamentarians to try and get the law 'right' is all the greater in a fast-moving area of law, as are the difficulties too.

Severance

25.13 The Archbishop of York, Dr John Sentamu, complained that the severance of law from morality and religion had gone too far:

11 Ibid, col 665.
12 Ibid, col 665.

'Religion, morality and law were once intermingled, which helped to shape both the common law and the statutes of this land, and greatly influenced the way in which judges interpreted them.'[13]

The implication is that if law was underpinned by religion and morality that was a good thing, whereas the absence of religion and morality from being 'intermingled' was a bad development. The question could be posed: whose religion or morality is being talking about, never mind what they actually mean? He added that:

'the law is now regarded purely as an instrument for regulating our personal affairs and as being completely severed from morality and religion. Provisions in the [HFE] Bill demonstrate just how far the severance has gone and its unintended consequences.'[14]

The scientific and practitioner perspective

Inconsistency

25.14 Lord Winston was concerned about the inconsistency of regulating only certain assisted reproductive techniques but not others, and furthermore about heavy-handed regulation of the field. He stated:

'I have always had problems with regulation. I find it difficult to justify why a single medical practice should be singled out in this way for regulation … Therefore, for a regulatory authority to regulate clinical practice is questionable given that other aspects of infertility such as tubal surgery, the admission of drugs and other treatments that are routinely given are not subject in any way to this kind of regulation.'[15]

The full panoply of regulation, enforcement, policing, etc is being marched out to oversee one area of fertility treatment, despite the risks, ethical issues and sometimes identical or worse problems in other non-regulated fields of reproductive medicine, obstetrics or gynaecology. That seems to be both contradictory and untenable.

25.15 Lord Winston claimed, perhaps controversially, that the key things that affected patients were not and could not be regulated. The first was the transfer of multiple embryos leading to multiple births. With regard to this, it is interesting to note that the HFEA has a policy to aim for one embryo transfer in the future. Secondly he refers to infertility tourism, ie the phenomenon of infertile couples escaping 'tight' laws on, eg, IVF in the United Kingdom by travelling to other countries to benefit from laxer law or the lack of any laws in other jurisdictions. He also referred to 'exploitation of patients', which was 'burgeoning' largely because there had not been IVF under the health service from the start. Three-quarters of all IVF is offered privately. Lord Winston continued that as things stood, 'grotesquely inflated prices' were being charged in some clinics. Surely regulation might prevent or lessen this problem from

---

13   Ibid, col 704.
14   Ibid, cols 704–705.
15   Ibid, col 710.

occurring. The Code of Practice, which is after all a form of regulation, addresses this concern. It provides that:

> 'Before treatment, storage or both are offered, the centre should also give the person seeking treatment or storage, and their partner (if applicable) a personalised costed treatment plan. The plan should detail the main elements of the treatment proposed (including investigations and tests), the cost of that treatment and any possible changes to the plan, including their cost implications.'[16]

A Compromise

25.16 Baroness Neuberger, a former Member of HFEA, a rabbi, and former member of the Medical Research Council, as well as an honorary fellow of the Royal College of Physicians and Royal College of GPs, said by contrast that 'regulation is needed and I support it.' She pertinently noted that legislation axiomatically must be a compromise given the ethical gulf and moral chasm that exists between those on either side of the debates about embryo research, use of infertility treatments, etc, never mind the majority of people somewhere in between the two absolutist positions of prohibition and permissiveness and non-regulation. She stated that whatever Parliament did in this area would be a compromise. The compromise reached was to set an absolute limit of 14 days or the appearance of the primitive streak, whichever is earlier, with regard to experimentation and development, and to forbid implantation of cloned embryos – no reproductive cloning.[17]

The philosopher's angle

25.17 Baroness Warnock, who headed the Warnock Committee which laid the ethical, moral and legal parameters of the new order of regulation of the new technologies of human reproductive medicine, and most of whose recommendations formed the basis of the 1990 Act and the creation of the HFEA, welcomed the HFE Bill, saying it was timely and necessary to update the 1990 Act, that regulation had seemed necessary in 1990 precisely because of the novelty of creating an embryo outside the human body, which 'was wholly new to the lay public,' if not to scientists, and that regulation continued to seem necessary to many people. She agreed with Lord Winston that the regulation by Parliament should not be heavy-handed, but said it would be futile to suggest going back to having no regulation.

Utilitarianism

25.18 Baroness Warnock unapologetically said that utililitarianism underpinned and was the bedrock of the 1990 Act:

> 'At the centre of the moral thinking behind the 1990 Act was a broad utilitarianism. ... As legislators, parliamentarians have to be utilitarian in the broadest possible sense. They have to consider the consequences

---

16   HFEA Code of Practice, 8th edn (2008), para 4.3.
17   Ibid, col 717.

of any legislation they propose and carry through and, in considering the consequences, they have to weigh up the harms that may be done to society as a whole against the benefits to society as a whole. It is a morality that gives thought to the common good in so far as it can be ascertained.' [18]

She conceded that this underpinning philosophy of utilitarianism did not embrace or include respect for human rights, 'but in that moral thinking there was very little consideration of human rights.'[19] She then reiterates this point later, stating that the fact that there was no emphasis on human rights – there was none in the Bill – was a reason for not including abortion reform in the Bill.

25.19 Baroness Hooper commented that the role of peers and their job as politicians was to ensure that guidelines, safeguards and the necessary transparency and accountability were built in to the 2008 Act, so that scientists and clinicians were able to do good.[20]

Trust

25.20 The Bishop of Newcastle echoed some of the sentiments of earlier contributors by adding that the HFE Bill dealt with controversial matters:

'it permits research that much of the rest of the world would not allow; it tests ethical limits and where they should be placed in a number of ways. The Bill must continue to provide public trust in the system of regulation. That is not easy when it represents a compromise between passionately held and conflicting views.'[21]

Major issues

25.21 The Bishop noted that the HFE Bill transferred into legislation:

'certain issues hitherto left to the regulator and it is right that Parliament should decide the major issues of principle, for the regulatory body regulates only on what Parliament has decided.'[22]

Parliament ultimately has power over the HFEA. It created the HFEA. It can abolish it. In fact that is precisely what it has signalled it intends to do by 2013. He adds in doing so:

'many things need to be kept in balance. We need a balance between the pioneering work of our scientists and the benefits they will bring to many people; the key ethical principles we hold which determine where the boundaries are to be drawn; principles such as the utmost respect for the moral status of the embryo; the welfare and well-being of any potential child, which has to be paramount; the assurance of human dignity and worth; and the continuing confidence of the public in these hugely complex – indeed breathtaking – areas of research.'[23]

---

18 Ibid, col 721.
19 This is understandable given that the Human Rights Act 1998 was passed eight years after the Human Fertilisation and Embryology Act 1990 and was not effective until October 2000.
20 *Hansard*, 19 November 2007, col 725.
21 *Hansard*, 21 November 2007, col 839.
22 Ibid, col 840.
23 Ibid, cols 839–840.

Expertise

25.22 Baroness Barker emphasised the expert, dispassionate, independent (given the large number of cross-bench peers), considered and less overtly party-political contribution made by peers to setting the legal and ethical parameters in primary legislation, in moulding the ultimate content of the 2008 Act:

> 'The House with its scientific, ethical and religious expertise of the highest order has an unrivalled opportunity to go behind some of the simplistic and pejorative headlines to look at the legal and social evidence –I stress the word "evidence" – which should enable us to set the ethical boundaries for these matters.'[24]

She also flagged up one of the many weaknesses of legislation chasing bolting science and trying to regulate it, stating that the increasing rapidity with which scientific knowledge was being developed should be recognised, and that:

> 'Since 1984, legislation in this area has followed in the wake of scientific discovery and on each occasion it has been the responsibility of politicians to set the boundaries within which research is deemed necessary and acceptable.'

Changes

25.23 She also added, correctly, that since the Warnock Report in 1984 (23 years previously) not only had science and scientific knowledge changed, but families had changed. There have been scientific changes, major social changes and attitudinal changes. Primary law, contained in Acts of Parliament, must reflect this change and axiomatically our legislator and lawmakers must take cognisance of these seismic changes too.

Evolution

25.24 Earl Howe noted that whilst the HFE Bill may have broken important new ground, it was for all that an amending Bill, and as such it sought to build on an inherited corpus of thought and public policy embodied in existing legislation. In simple terms, the 2008 Act does not scrap or replace the 1990 Act, rather it amends it by building on the solid foundations laid by the Warnock Committee, as manifested in the 1990 Act itself. Those foundations and the superstructure of primary legislation built upon it have stood the test of time and proven remarkably resilient.

Balance

25.25 Earl Howe observed:

> 'Perhaps the defining feature of that underpinning was the balance which the Warnock committee sought to strike between utilitarian considerations about treatment and research and strongly held, often absolutist, beliefs

24   Ibid, cols 859.

about the sanctity of life and the status of the human embryo. The balance was struck by acknowledging on the one hand the legitimacy of the medical and scientific case, but on the other hand insisting on a system of strict regulation, tight codes of practice, an outright prohibition on certain sorts of activity and the adoption of a gradualist ethical position on the status of the developing human embryo, based on science.'[25]

Again, Earl Howe emphasised that the 1990 Act tried to reconcile as far as was possible two diametrically opposed camps. Full-scale consensus between the two camps was never going to be achievable. The 1990 and the 2008 Acts were both instances of the phenomenon of Parliamentary legal compromise. Neither side was going to get its way totally regarding the legal parameters in the Acts. Importantly he added:

'For Parliament there is no unequivocally right answer to the questions we are addressing, nor can we be reasonably expect to do other than debate those questions within the broad framework of principles laid down [in the Warnock Report] and the 1990 Act.'.[26]

Earl Howe also pertinently observed that another weakness of the HFE Bill was that it lacked the equivalent of a Warnock Report, establishing the ethical values and evidence-based pointers that should guide Parliament and the regulator in these novel areas of decision-making, citing the fluctuating and changing views of the government on the 'vague ethical' status of hybrid embryos, and about 'how rudderless they were'.

CONCLUSION

25.26 Alder pertinently observed regarding the role of the House of Lords in relation to the House of Commons that: '[T]he purpose of the second chamber is to act as a check on the main chamber by providing an opportunity for second thoughts [on legislation]'.[27] The calibre, expertise, intellect and passion of certain peers considering a wide array of legal, ethical, medical and social issues generated and included in the HFE Bill guaranteed that these 'second thoughts' were very informed and wise ones which improved the 2008 Act considerably. Primarily the House of Lords amends rather than rejects government bills and bills passed by the House of Commons, and tries to improve them. Bradley and Ewing:

'... noted that, "The distinctive procedures of the House, in contrast with those of the Commons, facilitate the submission and consideration of amendments".'[28]

The House of Lords' role and contribution in shaping and fashioning the 2008 Act, by its debates, scrutiny and a series of amendments, was immense.

---

25 Ibid, col 862.
26 Ibid.
27 J Alder *Constitutional and Administrative Law* (Palgrave Law Masters) 8th edn, (Palgrave Macmillan 2011), p 233.
28 A Bradley and K Ewing *Constitutional and Administrative Law* 13th edn, (Longman), p 191.

Chapter 26

The Case for an Alternative Ethical Forum

INTRODUCTION

26.1   The case for an ethical forum or decision-making body alternative to Parliament which would consider, debate and make decisions on the key ethical areas arising with the development of new scientific research, and use of that research in treatments, was canvassed by a number of peers in Parliamentary debates.

DEBATES

Justifications?

26.2   Several peers, including Lord Brennan, favoured and supported the creation of a National Bioethics Commission in the United Kingdom charged, inter alia, with the responsibility of setting an ethical framework in which scientific advances generally should be made, but especially in the areas covered in the HFE Bill, ie embryonic research. Lord Brennan and other peers contended that this forum would be much more appropriate and fit for purpose regarding assessing the morality and ethics of new scientific developments than leaving it to Parliament. He complained that:

> 'We are now at a stage where the speed of scientific advance is very fast indeed. It is outstripping the capacity of our people to understand what is happening. It thereby impairs our ability to set an ethical framework in which those advances should be made. That is not an acceptable state of affairs in a democracy. Science must speak and explain to us what it is doing and where it might go.' [1]

Underpinning these concerns is an implicit lack of trust in where certain research is leading us. Lord Brennan argued, therefore, that the public were:

> '... entitled to ... scientific social responsibility. With it we, the people, can understand better, be more aware and therefore be able to participate in the democratic processes about life sciences which so fundamentally affect us.'

Regulation not enough

26.3   Lord Brennan submitted that regulatory control (presumably the 1990 and 2008 Acts, the Code of Practice and the HFEA) 'is plainly necessary in this area, but it is not enough. Control may give people confidence, but an ethical framework will give them trust.' This contention could be vigorously challenged. It implies that regulation, as outlined previously, does not engender

---

[1]   *Hansard*, 19 November 2007, col 727 (HL).

trust. However surely one role of legislation is precisely that – to legitimise certain acts in the way that the HFEA legitimised IVF for many neutral observers. It made it acceptable, and arguably IVF is now a routine medical treatment. Also, it could be argued that effective regulations, primarily in the guise of Acts of Parliament, must themselves be ethical instruments, or reinforce ethical values and principles, in order to be legally valid, enforceable and obeyed by the general public. Ethics and morality are inextricably linked with valid laws and are not mutually exclusive from primary legislation. Lord Brennan argued for a vehicle which will provide both an umbrella or shelter for engendering confidence in the public and an ethical framework in which this cutting-edge science can operate, namely the creation of a national bioethics commission. He claimed that legislators do not already know what most people think about these issues.

Involvement

26.4   Lord Brennan, commenting on the function of any such putative commission, noted that Sir Ian Kennedy had proposed the setting up of such a commission 25 years ago, that such commissions exist in Austria, Denmark, Germany, France and other countries, and that they work. He added that:

'The societies there benefit from those communities. They do not determine or decide – they inform; they make one aware; one understands better and one plays one's democratic part more productively.'

Trust

26.5   Lord Brennan gave a practical illustration of the value of having such a commission, referring to the 2001 ban on reproductive cloning. He added that the HFE Bill inserted a clause banning this cloning that ran to nearly 40 lines, depended on definitions and introduced a regulation power. He was sure that the government wanted to maintain that prohibition but that clarity was needed – this was too much detail for such a plain point. He said that a commission would have clarified that as part of the general debate. Formation of a commission would serve to inform the debate, which would be highly beneficial in regaining or at least promoting trust by the public in science in general and particularly in research.

26.6   Lord Darzi, responding to the call for the creation of a national bioethics commission, said:

'The Government have considered the idea of an independent commission on several occasions and have expressed their view that the present system, whereby a number of bodies are able to consider and advise on various ethical issues, is preferable.'[2]

That said, he added that the Government agreed on the value of debating bioethical issues and the benefits of addressing complex issues in Parliament.

2   *Hansard*, 21 November 2007, col 866.

Acting ethically

26.7   Lord Alton, in the Committee Stage of the HFE Bill, set out the background as to why a National Bioethics Commission (NBC) ought to be set up:

'In Britain, as in other societies, we find ourselves in a situation in which those who make policy, who implement it and whose lives are influenced by it are all challenged by hitherto barely imaginable medical and technological advances. There are enormous opportunities for good ... but also risks and threats to individual and social well-being.

'In recent decades, we have become increasingly aware of the ethical dimensions of policy and practice. It is not enough to ask about what has been done in the past or what could be done in the future. We also need to address the question of what should be done.'[3]

Ethics is not just a question of what doctors and scientists in fact currently do or what they did, or even what they intend to do, but rather must surely include what they ought to do in the future. Lord Alton noted:

'That is in part a matter of prudence, effectiveness and efficiency, but it also has an important and ineliminable ethical aspect. Ethics comprises the identification of values and principles, but also surely the determination of their appropriate application in particular fields and cases.'

As Singer states:

'Ethics is not an ideal system that is noble in theory but no good in practice.' And he adds: 'An ethical judgement that is no good in practice must suffer from a theoretical defect as well, for the whole point of ethical judgements is to guide practice.'[4]

26.8   Lord Alton commented that applying ethical values and principles is no easy task:

'That is no easy matter, particularly given the diversity of moral, social and religious perspectives that characterises contemporary society. At the same time, however, there is widespread agreement on the importance of ethics. Among those who reflect on such matters, there is general agreement about the centrality of such values as welfare, autonomy and respect, and growing recognition that they cannot be reduced to a single value but must be maintained in some kind of balance.'

Is he arguing that the Warnock Report skewed too much towards a utilitarian approach in its recommendations and indeed in its underlying philosophical moorings at the expense of this balance? For Lord Alton, getting the correct balance is essential and imperative: 'It is important to get the balance between the conflicting questions right.'

3   *Hansard*, 12 December 2007, cols 258–259.
4   P Singer, *Practical Ethics*, 2nd edn (Cambridge University Press, 1993), p 2.

A broad church

26.9 Lord Alton noted that:

> 'Bioethics brings together philosophy, science, medicine and healthcare but increasingly recognises the need to have regard to broad social interests, as well as the needs and concerns of specialist groups.'

In other words, bioethics and an NBC should be a broad church with views from a wide range of diverse individuals representing professionals, special interest groups, etc. He also stated:

> 'The problems are pressing, the concerns widespread and the issues difficult, but resources can be brought to bear to provide policy-makers such as ourselves [ie peers and specifically Parliament] and others with information, advice and guidance.'

Rather than the ad hoc approach of individuals, organisations and institutions, directing their attention to bioethical issues, Lord Alton said that instead:

> 'surely it is time to establish a national resource, responsive to UK needs and, though independent of government, responsible to the nation through Parliament.'

26.10 Lord Alton, in selling the idea (or panacea?) of setting up an NBC, pointed to the fact that bioethics was well developed among academics, that patient and other service-user groups were also increasingly aware of the ethical aspect of their interest, and religious faiths, denominations and other value-based communities and organisations have also focused attention on various bioethical issues. He referred too to the 'good work done by small but committed groups' like CORE.[5]

Internationally

26.11 He also noted:

> 'In other parts of the world, it has come to be recognised that the scale, importance and difficulty of bioethical issues calls for the establishment of national committees within which these can be analysed, reviewed and debated with the purpose of informing society and policy-makers.'[6]

Indeed he referred to a conference of NBCs in March 2005 – the European Conference of National Ethics Committees, known as COMETH – which produced a report on the functioning of the 42 NBCs of its 42 members. He pointed out that there were established national bioethics committees in a number of EU countries, eg Austria, Belgium, Denmark, France, Germany, Italy, Holland, Portugal, Sweden, Switzerland and other countries.

Standing

26.12 Lord Alton asserted that an NBC would have the authority and standing of an independent statutory body, like the HFEA, and said:

5   Ibid, cols 259–260.
6   Ibid, col 260.

'Its membership should encompass relevant professional expertise, patients and other user-group interests, as well as major religious and ethical groupings.'

The fact that the membership of this UK NBC should include major religious groups might prove controversial. What is meant by a major religious group? Also why should a major or any religious group have seats on this NBC by virtue of being merely a major religious group or indeed just a religious group? Why not extend membership to the Law Society, Bar Council, National Union of Journalists, etc might be the retort.

Remit

26.13 Lord Alton advocated that membership should reflect the diversity of positions within society, and appointment procedures must be public and transparent. He added that:

'Although independent, such a committee would be responsible to Parliament through a Minister to whom it should deliver an annual report, including recommendations for policy and such additional reports as may be commissioned or submitted.'[7]

He added that the NBC would also, inter alia, monitor legislation and be able to evaluate its effectiveness: 'Its remit would be the entire range of bioethical issues, including, but not confined to those concerning reproduction.' Finally, Lord Alton noted that the creation of such a UK NBC did not preclude Parliament setting up a new in-house Westminster committee, if that would enhance the work of the existing Select Committees. He stated: 'Those two ideas are not mutually exclusive; indeed, they could complement one another very well.'

Existing alternatives

26.14 Lord Turnberg welcomed the creation of such an NBC noting that:

'It could take evidence and advice from a wide background of sources and produce well-informed and well-researched reports which set out the pros and cons of the issues.'[8]

However, he pointed out that there was already in existence the 'excellent Nuffield Council on Bioethics which produces valuable, informed and authoritative reports,' although he admitted it did not cover all the areas that might be needed or wanted, but 'it produces very good reports'. He also noted the existence of a tried and tested in-house mechanism (in Parliament) which has served holding UK government to account very effectively and which does not require a completely new and expensive bureaucracy – that in-house mechanism is the Select Committee structure. He suggested:

'A new standing all-party Select Committee of both Houses – or perhaps just the House of Lords – could be set up to examine specific ethical issues, to take all the evidence it needs and to produce reports which should be debated in Parliament.'

---

7   Ibid, cols 260–261.
8   Ibid, col 261.

Scepticism about the merits of creating a UK NBC

26.15 Baroness Deech voiced a number of concerns about setting up a UK NBC. Whilst she said that the idea was a good one in principle, she thought it had been oversold, and pointed out that the United Kingdom already had the Human Genetics Commission, the Nuffield Council, reports from the Wellcome Institute, and excellent reports from professional and learned societies. She favoured Parliament setting up a Select Committee 'because Parliament governs this field – the legislation passed by this House and the other place.'[9] In many ways Parliament is our national Select Committee, or NBC, as well as being our legislature, and it passes the highest laws in the country. It is also elected by all the electors in the United Kingdom, and so represents all of us.

Religious domination

26.16 Baroness Deech commented that the countries referred to by Lord Alton that have NBCs 'are all either deeply religious or totally unregulated, or both.' The United Kingdom is regulated, by inter alia the 1990 Act and now the 2008 Act. It is a moot question whether that regulation is too draconian, light touch or pitched just at about the right level. The clear implication too here is that the United Kingdom is not a deeply religious country, which is obviously true. The argument might be that one is not comparing like with like by comparing the UK 'secular' system of regulation with the unregulated, 'deeply religious' systems in other countries. She added:

> 'In my experience, the further south and east you go in Europe, the more these committees are dominated by religious people – not that there is anything bad in that, but they can be used to hold back the progress of the law.'

She referred to the United States with its bioethics commission, saying it had been alleged that it was filled with people who support the President of the day's view, whoever that is. Obviously, if correct that would mean in 2007 those individuals who supported President Bush's socially conservative, anti-abortion, anti-federal funding of embryonic research views would fill, ie be appointed to, the US bioethics commission. She also claimed: 'Its reports have regularly been ignored and they have been forward-looking.'

Parliament best

26.17 Of fundamental importance is that Parliament is ultimately the ethical regulator. Not the HFEA, or the 1990 or 2008 Acts, nor the Code of Practice, nor court decisions. That has become clear from Parliament's decision, initiated by the Coalition government, to scrap the HFEA by 2013. Baroness Deech added that this is a country governed by law, not by religion, ethics, morality or anything else, and so little can be achieved by a bioethics commission.

26.18 Baroness Deech added that:

---

9   Ibid, col 262.

'While a human bioethics commission may do no harm, if it is not used as a tool by those who might want to hold back progress – which is possible – I am not sure how much short-term good it can do by comparison with the committees we already have.'

Hence if the NBC does not actually cause harm, by blocking scientific, beneficial progress, what good will it do, certainly what additional good will it do over and above what existing ethical bodies and various committees in Parliament do? She also said that the choice of members would be extremely problematic, and also that the more experts there were on this topic, the more opinions there would be. The aim should be to avoid a proliferation of expert ethical bodies churning out a constant stream and deluge of reports and views. Less can be sometimes more. She stated: 'In the end, by negotiation through Parliament, these things have to be decided within a legal framework.'

26.19 Lord Northbourne, who favoured creating such a NBC, argued it was not designed as a device to hold back progress in science, nor as a Luddite wooden horse to undermine damage and trash scientific endeavour and progress. He countered: 'It is a question of whether progress is wise and whether it is, in fact, being made in the right direction.'[10] Lord Winston wondered whether the creation of such an NBC 'would carry far wider issues than the rather narrow issues that we are discussing in this Bill' (eg would it deal with euthanasia?)

Gap filling

26.20 Baroness Williams, a leading advocate of the creation of an NBC, said it appeared to her that there was an important gap in the present structure which a committee of this kind – possibly a parliamentary committee –would fill very successfully. She also pertinently remarked that:

'the question of how particular proposals [ie legislation] will work out lies in the future. By definition, that must be the case when we consider advanced research on the horizon of scientific knowledge.'[11]

The impact and repercussions of laws that are enacted, especially in science, cannot accurately, if at all, be gauged and evaluated until sometimes much later on. She complained:

'I am concerned that in this House we almost never assess the impact of what we decide to go ahead with, and that applies not only to scientific Bills but Bills in general.'

That accords with how Tony Wright MP caustically described Parliament as appearing to act, sadly too frequently, namely as a sausage factory churning out sausage meat (ie Acts), except that it is producing badly drafted legislation at times and that legislation is never, or rarely, subsequently evaluated by Parliament to assess the law's effectiveness. She added:

'We make decisions on the basis of the best information that we can get and the best projections that people can make, but necessarily we do not know

---

10   Ibid, col 263.
11   Ibid, col 264.

what the effects will be, and I am struck by how rarely we look later at what they are.'

26.21 One function of a putative NBC, said Baroness Williams, would be:

'to see precisely how far the predictions that we make in our debates, and which are embodied in Bills that become Acts of Parliament, are borne out by subsequent evidence.'

She furthermore emphasised it must be based on evidence, and that 'we need to rely heavily on facts and not simply on an exchange of opinion.' She continued:

'We would all be able to base our conclusions and our witness on much sounder ground if we knew that that follow-up would take place ... That is exactly the purpose for which I should like to see such a committee established.'

She also said that an NBC:

'should have the duty of reporting to Parliament on the discoveries made, how those have affected legislation that we have already passed and how they ought to guide legislation that we propose in future.'[12]

Superfluous?

26.22 Lord Harries of Pentregarth, a bishop, scientist and regulator, and former interim Chairman of the HFEA, referred to the various roles of other bodies with keen interest in this area, namely the Human Genetics Commission (HGC), the HFEA and the Science and Technology Committee of Parliament, which, he said, had strong ethical views. He pointed out that not every member of the latter body had the same ethical views. He also wondered whether the creation of an NBC was superfluous, saying 'what more would' this national bioethics commission add to the work already being done?' Would it be an expensive, pointless, white elephant? He noted, moreover, that the Nuffield Council on Bioethics was financed independently of government, and that appointments to the Nuffield Council were made in the usual manner for public appointments: members are unpaid and have a wide range of expertise, from scientific and philosophical to ethical. Reports by the Nuffield council are highly prestigious and authoritative and widely read, and there is no fear of addressing controversial issues.

Quick fixes

26.23 Baroness Finlay of Llandaff flagged up the fact that the law is at times a rather blunt, crude and simplistic tool for capturing the shades and colours of parliamentary debate and discussion of various competing and conflicting ethical principles and values:

'The law is asked to give absolute answers, yes or no ... Indeed research ethics committees are asked either to approve or reject applications before them.'[13]

---

12   Ibid, col 265.
13   Ibid, col 270.

Furthermore, regarding there being a gap that needs plugging in relation to the necessity of having some over-arching forum for considering ethical issues to advise and guide Parliament on future legislation, she agreed:

> 'There is certainly a call for plugging a gap and taking a longer-term view, rather than coming up with an absolute answer.'[14]

Quick fixes or simplistic solutions save time in the short run but may prove costlier long term. Baroness Finlay was clear that:

> 'Should such a committee be established in whatever format, some of the real difficulties that have been addressed, such as how people would be appointed to it and how balance would be achieved on the committee, would need to be addressed carefully in order for it to command confidence.'

26.24 Baroness Finlay concluded that:

> 'One difficulty for philosophers and ethicists is that they can debate and weigh up issues eternally but often not get to the so-called right or wrong decision whereas decisions in law and morality are either right or wrong.'

Laws need to be passed and final at a given date. They can always be amended or repealed by Parliament if found wanting, obsolete or defective in some way. She added: 'Many things happen that may be ethical but not legal or legal but, based on the individual situation, not ethical. That broader look might be called for.' Setting up a UK NBC, therefore, should not be dismissed out of hand.

Taking ethics seriously

26.25 Lord Patten was quite forthright in articulating the justification for setting up a UK NBC: 'We need it because it would send out the signal that the Government take ethical issues seriously, a signal that they should send out.' Concern for ethical issues ought not to be confined to experts or 'campaigners and committee rooms'. That would be folly in the extreme, given that:

> 'In the next few decades, these ethical issues will roar up the political agenda as the general population becomes aware of their implications and that which was a matter for the few – the well-intentioned and expert few whom I admire – will become something for the population as a whole.'[15]

Ethical issues and concern about them is not and ought not to be the preserve of the intelligentsia and the elite.

Speed

26.26 Lord Patten also stated that:

> 'Much as we need a forum for ethical issues at a national level ... we also need to be cautious about speed and the seductive idea that things are moving so fast that, even on a Friday afternoon, decisions have to be taken quickly.'[16]

---

14 Ibid, col 271.
15 Ibid.
16 Ibid, col 272.

Decisions may well need to be taken quickly on occasions, but that is not an excuse for bad decisions being reached, or unethical ones or ones of dubious ethicality. Act in haste, repent in leisure should be the legislative and ethical mantra.

Membership

26.27 Concerning the membership of the proposed new NBC, Lord Patten said:

'I would not like to see big pharmaceutical companies getting in and being in a dominant position to influence the commission, or biotech, medical, venturing industries getting an unnatural hold on the commission, important though they are … Nor would I like to see anything approaching a clear majority of doctors, scientists and technicians … and those in related fields, who might benefit, albeit inadvertently, from the commission's decisions, via everything from professional advancement through to profit from findings, product development, publication, media appearances and the rest.'

He said he would like to see a balanced membership, 'drawn from exactly that category of first-class researchers in the field, who are doctors, geneticists, biologists and others.' He said there should certainly be a strong representation of ethicists and philosophers, as well as a representative or so from the faith groups, 'shorthand to embrace those who might belong to secular, rather than religious, society and feel strongly in that direction.' Finally, he noted there was also probably a need for a competent statistician. Regarding a suitable candidate for chairing such an NBC, he said it would need to be chaired:

'by a woman or man who is above the fray of debate, whose views are as neutral as possible and who is not passionately in favour of anything or indeed passionately against certain things … someone who is passionate only about being dispassionate in the interests of the ethical issues that are raised and brought to such a commission.'

Talking shop

26.28 Baroness Warnock said that if the proposed NBC was intended above all to be neutral and non-political, the Nuffield committee fulfilled those criteria well, because it was independently funded. She added:

'To replicate the work of that committee would be wasteful, expensive and, in my experience of general ethics committees, probably counterproductive'.[17]

She referred to such a committee, set up by the European Commission to look widely at bioethics. It was:

'… an absolute disaster, because the discussions of fundamental moral issues were everlasting. It was very difficult to get on to the more practical points that we were meant to be discussing, because nobody was agreed about the basic ethical principles.'

---

17 Ibid, col 273.

Creating a glorified talking shop that never reaches decisions on practical ethical issues is futile.

26.29 Baroness Warnock said that one had to be realistic:

'Questions of ethics cannot be settled by a yes or a no; they are questions about which people feel very deeply. If what comes out of deliberation is going to have any effect, people must be prepared to compromise and see how a law governing a particular practice would work.'

She refuted the argument that the House of Lords did not take ethics seriously, citing the debates that preceded the passage of the 1990 Act, and those on Lord Joffe's euthanasia bill, as compelling evidence of the seriousness peers in fact attached to ethics. But she argued importantly:

'However, we learn that compromise has to be accepted, not only between different people's views, but also between the purpose of law and individual conscience. That is the most difficult thing of all when one is talking not about one's private conscience, but about something which might be incorporated in law, where we have to take into account a much more general consideration; namely, the good of society.'

She concluded:

'An ethics committee of the kind proposed would probably generate great excitement and passion.., but it would not have nearly as much practical utility as have the existing commissions, particularly the Nuffield committee.'

Reactive

26.30 Lord Tombs said that the debates on ethical issues in the House:

'are piecemeal; they are highly reactive; they do not tackle any issues before the time comes to address them. As a result, decisions based on them are made hurriedly.'

He added that the United Kingdom's ethical base, which had evolved over some thousands of years, was being challenged by a rapidly moving science, particularly medical science. Setting up a commission:

'would provide an opportunity for different groups to debate differences ... widely different groups can often reach an accommodation, given sufficient goodwill, time and information ... a number of the objections today have been territorially based; that is, for maintenance of existing territory.'[18]

Baroness Barker commented that there was, in fact, 'a strong ethical base to the Bill: it was set in 1990 and it has endured.'

Status quo

26.31 Baroness Royall of Blaisdon said that the Government rejected 'after careful consideration' setting up a national human bioethics commission:

---

18 Ibid, col 274.

'on the basis that the present distributed model of advisory bodies with more specific briefs remained the best option, as it enabled specific bioethical issues to be addressed by dedicated groups.'[19]

These bodies included the Nuffield Council, the HGC, the BMA medical ethics committee and the National Screening Committee. She said: 'They have the appropriate expertise and sufficient time to devote to complex issues within their fields.'

It ain't broken!

26.32 The Baroness also referred favourably to the work of Parliamentary Select Committees in the sphere of debating and promulgating ethical discourse, stating that they also played an important role in the current system. She continued that the government believe that:

'the "distributed" system of bioethical advice works well. It remains our view that a national human bioethics commission would not bring sufficient benefits in comparison. Indeed, it could lead to ethical issues being marginalised and ignored by committees that are responsible for guidance or policy on any number of aspects of medicine or the life sciences.'[20]

She also said: 'The Government takes ethical issues extremely seriously and we believe that there is no evidence that the current system is failing us.' Is this a case of if it ain't broke, don't fix it?

26.33 Regarding the argument of those who talk of the democratic necessity of a bioethics commission, she retorted 'but we have Parliament', and that it was for Parliament to consider such ethical issues: 'ethical issues are extremely important, but they are dealt with very well in this House specifically, and in Parliament generally.'[21]

Ethical gap

26.34 Lord Alton commended the breadth of opinion and expertise evident in the debates on the HFE Bill, but claimed this sadly was the exception, rather than the norm:

'It is precisely because we do not meet for four days in a Committee of this House on a regular basis other than when Bills are before us that there is … a gap. We need to plug that gap'

Setting up a NBC was, he said, one way in which that could be done. He challenged Baroness Deech, who stated that some of the countries with NBCs were religious and non-regulated, arguing by contrast:

'It is unfair to label them as either unregulated or religious because many countries have national bioethics commissions …France is secular and none of those countries could be described as a religious society.'[22]

---

19   Ibid, col 276.
20   Ibid, col 277.
21   Ibid, col 278.
22   Ibid, col 279.

He added: 'It would be disingenuous of us to suggest that we necessarily have this absolutely right in this country and everyone else has got it wrong.'

26.35 He added too, concerning the argument that it would be difficult for somebody to be appointed to the main body of the HFEA, the regulator, if they believed in the sanctity of human life from fertilisation:

'It surely cannot be very healthy in our society to exclude other opinion, even if it is dissenting or minority opinion. It would be far healthier to have a plurality of views.'[23]

However, Baroness Hollis countered that:

'if you go on to a body associated with embryo research, when you believe that that process is fundamentally wrong because you believe that a life is created at the point of procreation, that would be problematic.'[24]

Lord Patten contended that there was a slight danger of stigmatising people of a particular faith or view, or who care for the embryo. He continued that the suggestion they should be excluded from these great committees because they are not 'politically correct enough' to be on them makes the case for a national bioethics commission, which he hoped would be a broader body that could consider the broader ethical issues.

26.36 Lord Alton concluded that:

'It is not enough to suggest that existing parliamentary committees, or indeed outside bodies, frequently populated by the same people, are adequate to do the job'.[25]

CONCLUSIONS

26.37 Whilst there were powerful calls for the creation of a National Bioethics Commission in the United Kingdom to consider highly controversial ethical issues, including many that appeared in the 2008 Act, these fell on governmental deaf ears, and it has to be said were not met with fulsome support from independent expert peers in the field either. Parliament remains our primary ethical forum, albeit assisted occasionally by other specific ethical bodies, eg the Nuffield Council and the HFEA itself.

---

23   Ibid, col 280.
24   Ibid, col 281.
25   Ibid, cols 282–283.

Chapter 27

Stem Cell Research in the United States: the Ethical Civil War Battlelines Redrawn?

INTRODUCTION

27.1   The ethical debates and divides apparent in both legislative chambers in the United Kingdom concerning the myriad issues arising in the Human Fertilisation and Embryology Act 2008 (the 2008 Act), including the creation of saviour siblings, deleting the 'need for the father' clause in carrying out the welfare of the child assessment and replacing it with the 'need for supportive parenting' clause, the legalisation of the creation of human admixed embryos, the recognition of different, non-conventional families and proposed changes to abortion legislation, to name but some of the more significant proposed changes, were mirrored by, or were at least similar in nature to, those in the United States, in the context of whether federal funding should be made available for research on new embryonic stem cell lines. Sharp ethical bright battlelines were drawn between those who opposed funding being made available for such research and those who supported it.

MAGICAL STEM CELLS

27.2   Stem cells are vitally important in the workings of a functioning human being and body. They are the source of all other cells and tissue in the body, including blood, bones, muscles, nerves and organs. They are pluripotent and hence have the potential to become any of the aforementioned tissue or cells in the human body. Stem cells can be derived from a variety of sources. These include the umbilical cord and placenta of newborn babies, adult humans, and embryos, the latter being a procedure which many find ethically controversial. Scientists working in embryonic stem cell research strongly believe that harnessing this new and exciting research area will ultimately yield a variety of beneficial therapeutic advances for a range of debilitating conditions, including Alzheimer's disease, Parkinson's disease, paralysis, macular eye degeneration, etc.

27.3   Theoretically, one human embryo can provide a limitless supply of stem cells because stem cell lines can be grown indefinitely, thus generating a bountiful supply of blood/bone/muscle/nerve cells to be transplanted into the ailing patient, or used for developing or testing new drugs for those debilitating conditions. The promise of the new science is great. Therefore the need for it to be funded by the US federal government in Washington as opposed to merely permitting it to develop privately, ie without this federal financial support, is arguably compelling, as discussed later.

BLAZING THE STEM CELL RESEARCH TRAIL

27.4 A myriad of potential hoped-for treatments derived from stem cell research for patients suffering from a variety of debilitating diseases have been highlighted in the media over recent years. The promise of developing effective treatments/therapy/drugs from this stem cell research to help sick patients is obviously the key driver for this research, but the research teams are at pains to constantly emphasise that treatments resulting from this research will not be available immediately or in the short term, but rather will hopefully materialise in, normally, 5–10 years' time.

27.5 One such stem cell development with considerable potential is the research into induced pluripotent stem (IPS) cells. Mark Henderson, Science Editor of *The Times*, noted on 17 February 2010 that 'IPS cells are made by genetically manipulating adult skin cells to give them the versatile properties of embryonic stem (ES) cells.' The hope or promise, said Henderson, is that they might provide a limitless source of replacement tissue for treating conditions such as spinal paralysis, Parkinson's disease and diabetes, without the need to destroy embryos. For some that would be a considerable ethical plus. A second advantage was that as cells could be grown from a patient's own tissue they would be genetically matched, therefore minimising the risk of rejection by the immune system. Henderson noted too that the technology, ie IPS research, had been named as Breakthrough of the Year in 2008 by the journal *Science* and had caused some research funding to be diverted away from ES cell research. However, he said that Dr Thomas Okarma, the Chief Executive of Geron Corporation, whose company was expecting to begin the first patient trial of an ES in the summer of 2010, whilst welcoming that IPS research as science which was sound and very exciting, and noting that its ultimate potential would be in identifying the mechanisms and pathways of genetic disease and screening new treatments, which would be a huge success, nevertheless said that IPS cells had significant disadvantages compared to embryonic tissue if used in medical treatments.

27.6 According to Henderson, Dr Okarma, in his interview with *The Times*, said that the need to produce fresh IPS cells for every patient would make it uneconomical. He also said that regulatory issues would create further problems, given that under current European and American rules, every set of cells for each patient would have to be approved independently. 'ES cells remain a far more attractive option because they can be standardised and mass-produced for thousands of patients,' Dr Okarma stated. 'There is simply no business model for getting treatments based on your own cells into your body.' He continued: '[T]he degree of difficulty in getting regulatory approval is just too great when you're making new therapeutic cells from scratch every time,' and he highlighted the pragmatic reality that:

> 'The product, whether it's IPS or ES, has to be scaleable. You've got to have something that can be stored and frozen, to provide thousands of doses, each one standardised and as good as the last. It's a stretch to imagine you could do that with IPS cells, while with ES cells we are there already.'

27.7 On 13 July 2010, it was reported in the *Daily Mail* that scientists from the University of Keele were planning to carry out the first human trial of using stem cells retrieved from the patient's bone marrow, which were then transferred to the damaged cartilage of the infected joint of that patient with the aim that the transferred cartilage stem cells would encourage the growth of the patient's cartilage, so reducing the excruciating pain of osteoarthritis and obviously improving the patient's quality of life. According to the *Daily Mail*, there would be enormous financial benefits from this research if it reached successful fruition in the form of effective treatment, given that according to the *Daily Mail* eight million Britons suffer from this type of arthritis, and that each year around 60,000 hip replacements and another 60,000 knee replacements are carried out on the NHS, the majority due to osteoarthritis. Furthermore, it continued, the cost of surgery alone was £400 million but far more was spent on treatments, GP consultations and physiotherapy. However, Professor Sally Roberts, one of the leads for the research, noted that whilst stem cells certainly had huge potential 'we just need to learn how to harness it properly.' Nevertheless, it was important not to regard stem cells as a 'miracle cure'. She continued:

> 'Stem cells are portrayed as "wonder cells" that can do anything but they can't give you the joints of a 15-year-old. At the moment they are not the "magic bullet" and they don't solve the underlying problem of osteoarthritis which still needs to be addressed.'

Stem cells are not the elixir of youth for the aged or the therapeutic ambrosia guaranteeing health and vitality for the debilitated and those in pain.

27.8 On 2 August 2010, it was reported in the *Daily Mail* that clinical trials involving patients paralysed by spinal cord injuries, carried out by California-based biotech firm Geron, have been given the go-ahead in the United States. These trials used embryonic stem cells from discarded embryos which were injected into the patients' spines. Scientists hoped that these injected embryonic stem cells would trigger regrowth of damaged nerve cells and eventually allow the patients to recover feeling and movement.

27.9 On 12 October 2010, it was reported, again in the *Daily Mail*, that a partially paralysed patient had been injected with human embryonic stem cells in an attempt to help them walk again. Doctors hoped the stem cells would help nerves in a newly-damaged spinal cord[1] regenerate before the disability becomes permanent. However, once again eminent stem cell specialists, including Professor Sir Ian Wilmot (creator of Dolly the sheep), sounded sensible notes of caution, saying that the public should not be swept away on a tide of euphoria that embryonic stem-cell based treatments or medicine were available now or immediately imminent.

27.10 On 12 April 2011, it was reported in the *Daily Telegraph* that scientists at Edinburgh University had created human kidneys from stem cells in a breakthrough which could result in organs being grown from transplant patients' own cells. In this scientific breakthrough the scientists created artificial organs from adult stem cells using human amniotic fluid and animal foetal cell, thereby obviating the need to use stem cells derived from the ethically controversial source of human embryos. Needless to say the great advantage of potentially creating organs for transplantation from this ethically uncontroversial source would be that the major problem with transplanted organs would be overcome,

---

1   Apparently the injury occurred within the fortnight before the trial.

ie the recipient body's immune system rejecting the transplanted 'foreign' tissue. Clearly that would not occur here as the newly created organ was created from the patient's own stem cells. Also there would be no need to give the patient costly immunosuppressant drugs for the rest of their life, saving huge sums of money. Alternatively, if this new research could lead to the creation of human kidneys that could eventually be transplanted into humans successfully, it would also save money on keeping patients alive on kidney dialysis machines. The *Daily Telegraph* noted that there were about 7,000 people on the kidney waiting list in Britain, and many scientists believed stem cell technology could reduce shortages of organs. The use of this innovative research would, therefore, seemingly accord with the ethical principles of justice and beneficence.

27.11   On 4 April 2011, it was further reported in the *Daily Mail* that American scientists were growing human hearts in laboratories, 'offering hope for millions of cardiac patients.' This process involved the scientists stripping the cells from the dead hearts with a powerful detergent, leaving 'ghost heart' scaffolds made from the protein collagen. The ghost hearts were then injected with millions of stem cells, which had been extracted from patients and supplied with nutrients. The stem cells 'recognised' the collagen heart structure and began to turn into heart muscle cells.

27.12   On 5 June 2011, the *The Mail on Sunday* reported that a Glasgow-based company, Pharmacells, had been granted a licence by the Human Tissue Authority to extract stem cells from blood and then freeze them for storage, in the hope that they would one day help to cure fatal conditions. The practical ease of using blood collected in this ethically uncontroversial fashion is in marked contrast to the difficulty of extracting stem cells from adults as at present. Yet again cautionary notes must be sounded about the scientific promise of the new procedure running ahead of the present therapeutic reality.

27.13   On 6 July 2011, BBC News reported that a survey conducted by the Anthony Nolan charity, which questioned 2,049 members of the public online, found that most people (54 per cent) would consider joining the stem cell register, and of those who would not join, or were unsure, around a third (37 per cent) said they did not know enough about donating stem cells.

THE ETHICAL CHASM

27.14   In July 2006, the US Senate passed the Stem Cell Research Enhancement Act, which had earlier been passed by the US House of Representatives. This Act, inter alia, sought to expand embryonic stem cell research and to repeal the banning of federal funding for embryonic stem cell research imposed by executive order by President Bush in August 2001. This 2001 executive order had provided federal support (ie money) only for existing stem cell lines when the order came into effect, but not for any new lines.[2] The Senate voted 63–37 to pass the Act, rendering it susceptible to veto by the President, given it was not passed by a two-thirds majority of the Senate (ie 67 senators) in accordance

---

2   There were 60 such existing stem cell lines created from embryos destroyed prior to August 2001, but apparently, according to the BBC News Channel on 14 January 2009, 'scientists say only twenty eligible cell lines remain useful for research and many of these are problematic.'

with the US written constitution. Not surprisingly, President Bush promptly exercised his presidential veto (a power used very sparingly generally by most presidents) to derail the further progress of the Act into US law. President Bush, in justifying the exercise of his presidential vetoing of the Act, stated on 19 July 2006: 'It crosses a moral boundary that our decent society needs to respect, so I vetoed it.' He was opposed to the use of public funds for research involving the destruction of human embryos. He added that the Act 'would support the taking of innocent human life in the hope of finding medical benefits for others.' His argument would be that an early human embryo was a human being from the moment of conception, that such a human being could not be commodified and used instrumentally for the alleged benefit of others (ie be used as a means towards an end), and that anyway no demonstrable or tangible benefit (ie new therapy or treatment) could be shown to result from such embryonic stem cell research. In short such use was unethical. However, his opponents might argue that an early human embryo was not 'innocent human life' conferred with moral status warranting legal protection in this manner. The House of Representatives subsequently failed to reach the requisite two-thirds majority vote needed to overturn the President's veto. Interestingly, at the same time the Senate approved two other Acts, albeit ethically much less controversial Acts, which respectively aimed to promote stem cell research using cells from sources other than embryos, and to outlaw the creation and abortion of foetuses for research.

27.15 Following the mid-term congressional elections in November 2006, the House of Representatives, then back under the control of the Democrats, tried again to pass legislation permitting embryonic stem cell research. This time the Bill was passed by the House by 253–174 votes, but again President Bush vetoed this Bill and again the House did not have a two-thirds majority to override the Presidential veto. The then Speaker of the House, Nancy Pelosi, speaking on 11 January 2007, highlighted the significance of this proposed new law:

'Today, by passing legislation to expand stem cell research, the House gave voice to the hopes of more than 100 million Americans and their families.'

She challenged President Bush to join the bi-partisan support for the hope and promise anticipated from embryonic stem cell research.

27.16 President Bush, in justifying the use of his constitutional veto and in opposing the Democrat-inspired 'green light' to allowing federal funding of embryonic stem cell research, cautioned that permitting such a legislative change would effectively be to 'compel American taxpayers ... to support the deliberate destruction of human embryos,' and that scientists should rather be devoting their energies and directing their scientific expertise to 'pursue the possibilities of science in a manner that respects human dignity and upholds our moral values.' President Bush was saying that manufacturing human embryos for use solely as a research tool for experimentation in the hope of trying to garner new therapies for diseases fundamentally violates respect for the human dignity of that embryo and inherently undermines the moral status and value that human embryo inalienably possesses. It commodifies it and instrumentalises it. It is used for the potential benefit of others. It is not valued for itself. It has little or no moral status or worth.

27.17 The November 2008 presidential election proved pivotal with the election of a President, Barack Obama, who was seemingly less hostile to embryonic stem cell research and federal funding of such cutting-edge science, albeit a man who has described himself as 'a person of faith' with profound Christian beliefs. On 9 March 2009, President Obama signed an executive order lifting the Bush restrictions on federal funding for research on new embryonic stem cell lines. Signalling this major ethical and scientific u-turn, that 'so many scientists and researchers and doctors and innovators, patients and loved ones have hoped for and fought for these past eight years', President Obama cautioned: '[A]t this moment the full promise of stem cell research remains unknown and it should not be overstated,' but that nevertheless, 'scientists believe that these tiny cells may have the potential to help us understand and possibly cure some of our most devastating diseases and conditions.' He pledged to 'vigorously support' the new scientific research. Obama's approach and support for this innovative research full of promise signals the present triumph of science over religious objections, based on deeply held and sincere faith or superstition depending on your point of view. Obama also flagged up the deleterious consequences of the ban on federal funding of new embryonic stem cell research, namely the scientific 'brain-drain', whereby scientists, instead of working in the United States in the sphere of embryonic stem cell research, were relocating to more supportive, less inclement jurisdictions to pursue this cutting-edge research. He argued that 'medical miracles' did not occur overnight and that: 'When government fails to make these investments, opportunities are missed.'

27.18 However President Obama extended a fig leaf to the opponents of embryonic stem cell research, saying that many thoughtful and decent people were conflicted about, or strongly opposed this research, and that opponents could not all be categorised as blindly opposed to scientific development. For him, permitting embryonic stem cell research was the right and moral thing to do because the research aimed to relieve 'human suffering'. Moreover, strict guidelines and controls would cover such research. He balanced this fulsome backing for federal support for embryonic stem cell research with unequivocal denunciation and repudiation of permitting human reproductive cloning, stating:

> 'We will ensure that our government never opens the door to the use of cloning for human reproduction. It is dangerous, profoundly wrong, and has no place in our society, or any society.'

Also in the potential firing-line was the federal ban preventing federal support (taxpayers' money) for the creation of embryos for research purposes, as opposed to using 'spare' embryos (ie surplus embryos not used in IVF fertility treatment) for this research. This ban, which has been in place since 1996, (known as the Dickery-Wicker amendment), has been renewed by Congress every year. By marked contrast, John Boehner, the then Republican Minority Leader in the House of Representatives,[3] stated that President Obama's volte-face on this important ethical policy issue had undermined, 'protections for innocent life, further dividing our nation at a time when we need greater unity to tackle the challenges before us.'

---

3   Since January 2011, the Speaker of the House of Representatives in the now Republican-controlled House.

PITCHED ETHICAL BATTLE CONTINUES

27.19 Soon after President Obama lifted the ban on federal funding of research on embryonic stem cells using new stem cell lines in March 2009, US District Judge Royce Lamberth, in the case of *Sherley v Sebelius*[4] decided on 29 April 2011, issued a temporary injunction on the executive order pending a legal challenge to the order going ahead. However this suspension was itself overruled on appeal, pending a final decision. On Friday 29 April 2011, the US Court of Appeals in Washington DC ruled (2–1) that the 1996 US law against federal funding of embryo destruction was 'ambiguous' and 'did not prohibit funding a research project in which an ESC (embryonic stem cell) will be used.' Effectively the Court therefore overturned the earlier order suspending federal funding of embryonic stem cell research. It also said that opponents of embryonic stem cell research, who argued that the research was illegal because it involves the destruction of human embryos, were unlikely to succeed in their lawsuit to stop the funding.

SHERLEY V SEBELIUS: LEGAL BACKGROUND

27.20 The plaintiffs in this case, Dr James Sherley and Dr Teresa Deisher, were scientists who only used adult stem cells in their research. They contended that the National Institutes of Health (NIH), by funding research projects using human embryonic stem cells (ESCs), violated the Dickey-Wicker Amendment (DWA) passed by the US Congress in 1996, and renewed every year up until 2011. The DWA basically prohibits federal funding for research in which a human embryo is destroyed. It specifically, inter alia, prohibits the NIH from funding:

'(1) the creation of a human embryo or embryos for research purposes; or
(2) research in which a human embryo or embryos are destroyed, discarded, or knowingly subjected to risk of injury or death greater than that allowed for research on fetuses in utero under 45 CFR 46.204 (b) and section 498 (b) of the Public Health Services Act (42 USC 289g (b)).'

The Circuit Judge Ginsburg noted[5] that in 1996, when Congress passed the DWA, scientists had already taken steps to isolate ESCs (the science being in comparative infancy then) but had not been able then to stabilise the ESCs for research in the laboratory, and that:

'The historical record suggests that Congress passed the Amendment chiefly to preclude President Clinton from acting upon an NIH report recommending federal funding for research using embryos that had been created for the purpose of in vitro fertilisation.'

Ginsburg CJ noted also that the DWA became:

'… directly relevant to ESCs only in 1998, when researchers at the University of Wisconsin succeeded in generating a stable line of ESCs, which they made available to investigators who might apply for NIH funding.'

---

4   2011 WL 1599685 (CADC).
5   At p 6 of the judgment.

27.21 When that occurred, on 15 January 1999, the General Counsel of the Department of Health and Human Services issued a memorandum dealing with whether the DWA permitted federal funding of research using ESCs that had been derived before the funded project commenced. The General Counsel concluded 'such funding is permissible because ESCs are not "embryos".'[6] Subsequently the NIH issued funding guidelines consistent with this opinion in 2000, but the NIH did not fund any ESC research project while President Clinton was in office, ie up till January 2001. President Bush was elected in November 2000, took up office in January 2001 and proceeded to direct the NIH early in 2001 not to fund any project pursuant to President Clinton's earlier policy. As Ginsburg CJ observed: 'later that year he decided funding for ESC research would be limited to projects using the approximately 60 then-extant cell lines derived from "embryos that had already been destroyed".' President Bush's stance on embryonic stem cell research was diametrically opposed to that of his predecessor.

27.22 Following his election in November 2008 and taking office in January 2009, President Obama lifted the temporal restriction imposed by President Bush and permitted the NIH to 'support and conduct responsible, scientifically worthy human stem cell research, including human embryonic stem cell research to the extent permitted by law.' The NIH then issued the 2009 Guidelines on 7 July 2009, which are currently in effect. The NIH noted in the Guidelines that 'funding of the derivation of stem cells from human embryos is prohibited' by the DWA. The Guidelines also added:

'Since 1999, the Department of Health and Human Services (HHS) has consistently interpreted [Dickey-Wicker] as not applicable to research using [ESCs], because [ESCs] are not embryos as defined by Section 509. This longstanding interpretation has been left unchanged by Congress, which has annually reenacted [the DWA] with full knowledge that HHS has been funding [ESC] research since 2001. These guidelines therefore recognise the distinction, accepted by Congress, between the derivation of stem cells from an embryo that results in the embryo's destruction, for which Federal funding is prohibited, and research involving [ESCs] that does not involve an embryo nor result in an embryo's destruction, for which Federal funding is permitted.'

Therefore, according to the NIH and s 509, ESCs are not embryos, nor presumably do they have the moral, ethical, or indeed legal status accorded to embryos.

27.23 Ginsburg CJ noted that instead of President Bush's temporal limitation, by contrast, the 2009 Guidelines:

'instituted specific ethical restrictions upon ESC research funded by the NIH: Such research may be conducted only upon stem cell lines derived from embryos that "were created using in vitro fertilisation for reproductive purposes and were no longer needed for this purpose ... were donated by individuals who sought reproductive treatment ... who gave voluntary written consent for the human embryos to be used for research purposes," and who were not paid therefor.'[7]

---

6   At p 6 of the memorandum.
7   2009 Guidelines, p 6.

Moreover, the research may use stem cell lines derived from an embryo donated after the effective date of the Guidelines only if the *in vitro* clinic had fully informed the donor of all possible options for disposing of the embryo and had taken other specified procedural steps to separate reproductive treatment from donation.

27.24 After the 2009 Guidelines were issued, Congress re-enacted the DWA as part of the appropriations bill for the fiscal year 2010. Congress has adopted a series of continuing resolutions that have carried the DWA forward into 2011 and the present. This is the legal and policy context where the issue of the propriety of Dr Sherley's and Dr Deisher's preliminary injunction arises for consideration.

MAJORITY JUDGMENT: GINSBURG CJ

27.25 Ginsburg CJ delivered the majority (2–1) decision, and ruled on the substantive issue of when the court will make a preliminary injunction:

> 'A plaintiff seeking a preliminary injunction must establish [1] that he is likely to succeed on the merits, [2] that he is likely to suffer irreparable harm in the absence of preliminary relief, [3] that the balance of equities tips in his favor, and [4] that an injunction is in the public interest.'[8]

He then considered each of these four factors in turn.

Likelihood of success on the merits

27.26 Ginsburg CJ said, concerning whether the 2009 Guidelines are inconsistent with the limits upon funding in the DWA passed by Congress:

> 'We approach this issue under the familiar two-step framework of *Chevron USA, Inc. v Natural Resources Defense Council, Inc.*, 467 US 837, 842–43, 104 S Ct 2778, L Ed 2d 694 (1984), (*Chevron*): If the Congress has "directly spoken to the precise question at issue," then we must "give effect to the unambiguously expressed intent of Congress"; if instead the "statute is silent or ambiguous with respect to the specific issue," then we defer to the administering agency's interpretation as long as it reflects "a permissible construction of the statute".'[9]

27.27 This statement reflects the constitutional principle of the separation of powers, enshrined in the US written Constitution and evident in the UK unwritten constitution too, in the context here that Congress makes and passes the laws and the courts interpret them. A problem occurs, as here, where arguably Congress's law is unclear. What meaning do the courts give it? The answer according to the *Chevron* case is that they defer to the interpretation given to the Congressional law by the administrative agency (arm of government) charged with administering or controlling or policing that area of government, so long as that interpretation reflects a permissible construction of it – one could say so long as it is a reasonable construction or interpretation

---

8   *Sherley v Sebelius* 2011 WL 1599685 (CADC) at p 6.
9   Ibid, p 8.

of that law of Congress. The real question, initially at any rate, is whether the Congressional law is unambiguous or not. If the court rules the Congressional Act is unambiguous that is the end of the matter. The court must give effect to Congress's law and intent. If they rule it is ambiguous then the court can look further afield for assistance in interpreting the ambiguities, namely to see how the administrative agency in the field has interpreted the Congressional law or provision.

Step 1

27.28 Ginsburg CJ noted the terms of the DWA which bars federal funding specifically for 'research in which a human embryo or embryos are destroyed, discarded, or knowingly subjected to risk of injury or death greater than that allowed for research on fetuses in utero,' and the plaintiffs' argument that this provision unambiguously bars funding for any project using an ESC. They reason that, because an embryo had to be destroyed in order to yield an ESC, any later research project that uses an ESC is necessarily 'research' in which the embryo is destroyed. By contrast the Government argued:

> 'the "text is in no way an unambiguous ban on research using embryonic stem cells" because Dickey-Wicker is written in the present tense, addressing research "in which" embryos "are destroyed", not research "for which" embryos "were destroyed".'

Ginsburg was clear that the use of the present tense in a statute strongly suggested it did not extend to past actions. In other words, embryos created and destroyed to harvest ESCs prior to the DWA in 1996 are not covered or subject to the ban on federal funding, only those created after the DWA, or embryos created now in 2012. He added that the Dictionary Act provides 'unless the context indicates otherwise ... words used in the present tense include the future as well as the present,' and noted too that the Supreme Court had observed that that provision implied 'the present tense generally does not include the past.'[10] Also, Ginsburg CJ stated: 'The context here does not ... indicate a different understanding.' On the contrary, he argued, 'NIH funding decisions are forward-looking, requiring the NIH to "determine whether what is proposed to be funded meets with its requirements".'

27.29 Ginsburg CJ also rejected the 'primary' argument of the plaintiffs that because 'research' using an ESC included derivation of the ESC, the derivation did not predate but was an integral part of the 'research'. He stated that the conclusion did not follow from the premise; at best it showed Dickey-Wicker was open to more than one possible reading. The Congressional Act is, therefore, anything but clear and unambiguous, as claimed by the plaintiffs. Ginsburg CJ also rejected the plaintiff's argument that the court must read the term 'research' broadly because the Congress, had it intended a narrower reading, would have used a term identifying a particular action, as it did in subs 10 of Dickey-Wicker, which specifically bars the 'creation' of an embryo for 'research purposes'. He contended:

10 *Carr v United States*, US, 130 S Ct 2229, 2236, 176 L Ed 2d 1152 (2010).

'We see no basis for that inference. The definition of research is flexible enough to describe either a discrete project or an extended process, but this flexibility only reinforces our conclusion that the text is ambiguous.'[11]

Therefore, the courts are not bound by ambiguous words in Congressional Acts. The pivotal role of the judges and courts in interpreting legislation is graphically emphasised here.

Step 2

27.30 Ginsburg then addresses Step 2 of the *Chevron* test, 'under which we must uphold the NIH's interpretation [of the DWA] if it is but "reasonable".' As stated above, the DWA bars federal funding of ESC research in which a human embryo or embryos are destroyed. However, the administrative agency (the NIH):

'determined [the DWA] does not bar its funding a project using an ESC that was previously derived because a stem cell is not an "embryo" and cannot develop into a human being.'[12]

He adds that the plaintiffs did not dispute that. However they did contend that the NIH was not entitled to deference because it never offered an interpretation of the term 'research'. However, Ginsburg stated that their premise was not entirely correct. In the 2009 Guidelines the NIH expressly distinguished between the derivation of ESCs and 'research involving [ESCs] and research involving [ESCs] that does not involve an embryo nor result in an embryo's destruction'. According to Ginsburg CJ:

'Thus, although the Guidelines do not define the term "research", they do make clear the agency's understanding that "research involving [ESCs]" does not necessarily include the antecedent process of deriving the cells.'[13]

27.31 Ginsburg CJ rejected the plaintiff's assertion that 'the agency's [ie the NIH's] effort in this respect is insufficiently specific to warrant our deference.' He said, furthermore:

'[the] NIH has explained how funding an ESC project is consistent [with the DWA] ... The plaintiff's objection that the NIH has not explicitly defined a word in the statute – an important word [namely 'research'] to be sure – is mere cavil; it disregards the agency's use of the term, which implicitly but unequivocally gives "research" a narrow scope, thus ensuring no federal funding will go to a research project in which an embryo is destroyed.'[14]

Ginsburg CJ referred to the plaintiff's argument that the NIH had, by treating derivation as part of 'research', shown its understanding of the DWA was unreasonable. He contended that:

'because the standard definition of "research" requires some kind of scientific inquiry, and deriving ESCs, standing alone, involves no such inquiry, the act of derivation can be deemed "research" only if it is part of a larger project.'

11 *Sherley v Sebelius,* at p 9.
12 Ibid.
13 Ibid.
14 Ibid.

27.32 Ginsburg CJ stated:

> 'Although an understanding of "research" that includes the derivation of stem cells is not the ordinary reading of that term, it is surely as sensible as the plaintiff's alternative, in which the derivation of a cell line is deemed part of every one of the scores if not hundreds of subsequent research projects – although pursued by different scientists, perhaps many years later – to use one of the derived cells.'

He added:

> 'To define derivation as "research", in other words, makes at least as much sense as to treat the one-off act of derivation as though it had been performed anew each time a researcher, however remote in time or place, uses a stem cell from the resulting line.'[15]

He noted: 'The fact is the statute is not worded precisely enough to resolve the present definitional contest conclusively for one side or the other.' Very few pieces of legislation are in fact drafted in unambiguous terms. Ginsburg is really arguing that the Government and NIH interpretation of what constitutes 'research' is every bit as tenable and plausible as the plaintiff's is.

27.33 To further bolster the interpretation of 'research' in the DWA favoured by the NIH, Ginsburg stated:

> 'Broadening our focus slightly, however, we can see the words surrounding "research" in the statute support the NIH's reading ... [because] the Congress wrote with particularity and in the present tense – the statute says "in which" and "are" rather than "for which" and "were" – it is entirely reasonable for the NIH to understand Dickey-Wicker as permitting funding for research using cell lines derived without federal funding, even as it bars funding for the derivation of additional lines.'[16]

In other words it is an entirely reasonable and legitimate interpretation of the DWA that it permits federal funding for research using existing cells lines derived without federal funding, whilst simultaneously prohibiting and barring federal funding for the derivation of additional, new ESCs.

27.34 Ginsburg CJ also noted:

> 'Further, adding the temporal dimension to our perspective, we see, as the NIH noted in promulgating the 2009 Guidelines, the Congress has reenacted Dickey-Wicker unchanged year after year "with full knowledge that HHS has been funding [ESC] research since 2001," 74 Fed Reg 32, 173/2, when President Bush first permitted federal funding for ESC projects, provided they used previously derived ESC lines.'

The bottom line was that President Bush himself, at the end of the day, permitted federal funding for ESC research projects, provided those research projects used existing (previously derived) ESC lines. There never was a total prohibition of ESC research. Ginsburg CJ observes therefore that:

15 Ibid, at p 10.
16 Ibid.

'The plaintiffs have no snappy response to the agency's point that the Congress's having reenacted Dickey-Wicker each and every year provides "further evidence … [that it] intended the Agency's interpretation, or at least understood the interpretation as statutorily permissible".'

He therefore held that the plaintiffs had not shown they are more likely than not to succeed on the merits of their case.

Balance of the equities

27.35 Ginsburg CJ believed that the granting of a preliminary injunction to the plaintiffs 'would in fact upend the status quo,' and that the 2009 Guidelines merely 'inflict some incremental handicap upon the plaintiff's ability to compete for NIH money,' but do not in fact 'place a significant additional burden upon their ability to secure funding for their research.' However, he stated: 'The hardship a preliminary injunction would impose upon ESC researchers, by contrast, would be certain and substantial.' Indeed:

'The injunction entered by the district court would preclude the NIH from funding new ESC projects it has or would have deemed meritorious, thereby inevitably denying other scientists funds they would have received.'[17]

There is no doubt that a preliminary injunction would be enormously damaging to ESC research. It would effectively bring ESC research to a grinding halt. Adult stem cell researchers can still under the proposed NIH regime compete on an equal footing and level playing field for private research funding and indeed federal funding. How have they therefore been seriously disadvantaged by not getting their preliminary injunction? Ginsburg CJ highlighted further hugely deleterious consequences of granting the plaintiffs their injunction:

'Even more problematic, the injunction would bar further disbursements to ESC researchers who have already begun multi-year projects in reliance upon a grant from the NIH; their investments in project planning would be at a loss, their expenditures for equipment a waste, and their staffs out of a job.'[18]

In other words ESC researchers, doctors, scientists and companies would suffer a huge financial hit, if not 'meltdown' if this preliminary injunction were to be upheld (arguably a very unfair, unreasonable and ethical dubious decision). Ginsburg noted too that:

'The record shows private funding is not generally available for stem cell research but even if, as the district court thought, private donors or investors would provide a reasonable alternative source of funds for ESC researchers … it remains unclear why such donors or investors would not similarly support the plaintiff's research using adult stem cells and why the plaintiff's "very livelihood" instead depends upon obtaining grants from the NIH.'

He concluded that the balance of equities 'tilts against granting a preliminary injunction and that the district court abused its discretion in awarding preliminary injunctive relief.'

---

17 Ibid, at pp 11–12.
18 Ibid, at p 12.

DISSENTING MINORITY JUDGMENT

27.36 Henderson CJ rejected the majority interpretation of the DWA concerning ESC federal funding, saying the majority[19] 'perform linguistic jujitsu' and dissented from their interpretative approach and conclusions. He referred to the majority opinion, which had described 'derivation' of human embryonic stem cells (hESCs) from a human embryo – which destroys the embryo – and the subsequent use of the hESCs in the hope of remedying many serious, and often fatal, diseases and debilitating physical conditions. This hope or promise of remedying these diseases and conditions is, of course, one of the main 'sales pitches' for permitting the research. This is a utilitarian approach evaluating the ethics and morality of actions by the consequences produced by those actions (hopefully here beneficial, and certainly the good consequences will outweigh any alleged bad consequences – presumably here having to destroy human embryos in order to harvest, mine and exploit embryonic stem cells).

27.37 The minority dissenting judge agrees with the majority in applying the two-step approach adopted in the *Chevron* case:

'We start with the plain meaning of the text, looking to the language itself, the specific context in which that language is used, and the broader context of the statute as a whole.'

Henderson CJ stated she believed, 'we need go no further than *Chevron* step one here because the plain meaning of the Amendment is easily grasped' and cited from *Chevron* with approval the following: 'if the [statute] has a plain and unambiguous meaning, our inquiry ends so long as the resulting statutory scheme is coherent and consistent.' Accordingly, 'that is the end of the matter; for the court, as well as the agency, must give effect to the unambiguously expressed intent of Congress.'

27.38 She added that the district court had, moreover:

'correctly looked to the dictionary definition of "research" as "diligent and systematic inquiry or investigation into a subject in order to discover or revise facts, theories, applications, etc."'

She furthermore claimed that:

'The first sequence of hESC research is the derivation of stem cells from the human embryo. The derivation of stem cells destroys the embryo and therefore cannot be federally funded, as the Government concedes.'[20]

Of course, even President Bush permitted federal funding using the existing 60 stem cell lines, derived from embryos that were then obviously destroyed, so that would appear to undermine this minority contention or interpretation. Henderson CJ continued:

'I believe the succeeding sequences of hESC research are likewise banned by the Amendment because, under the plain meaning of "research," they continue the "systematic inquiry or investigation".'

---

19 Ibid.
20 Ibid, at p 13.

27.39 Henderson CJ was clear and adamant that:

'the intent of the 1996 Congress, in enacting the Amendment [ie DWA] is to prohibit all hESC research – not just research attendant on the derivation of the cells – is clear by comparing the language used to ban federal funding for the creation of an embryo with the language the plaintiffs rely on.'[21]

According to Henderson CJ, research was the express target of the ban the Congress imposed with respect to the destruction of a human embryo, and that according to her this made perfect sense because in 1996, according to the record, hESC research had barely begun. Congress, she said, recognising its scant knowledge about the feasibility or scope of ESC research, chose broad language with the plain intent to make the ban as complete as possible. She concluded:

'Because the meaning of research is plain, and the intent of the Congress to ban the federal funding of hESC research is equally plain, I would stop at *Chevron* step one and enjoin the Guidelines as violative of the Amendment to the extent they allow federal funds to be used for hESC research.'

27.40 Henderson CJ also added that:

'hESCs cannot be tested and evaluated unless and until they are derived from a human embryo, combined with the fact that derivation of hESCs is done solely as part of a "systematic investigation" of those cells, demonstrates that derivation is the necessary first sequence of hESC research. Because derivation of hESCs necessarily destroys a human embryo or embryos, and because derivation constitutes at least hESC research development under the Amendment, all hESC research is "research in which a human embryo or embryos are destroyed." Accordingly, the plaintiff's challenge to the Amendment is likely to succeed because the Amendment prohibits the expenditure of federal funds to engage in hESC research in all its sequences.'[22]

Not surprisingly, Henderson CJ therefore stated that 'the majority opinion strains mightily to find the ambiguity the Government presses.' Later on in her judgment she noted that it was not only the majority opinion's view of verb tenses that was wrong, but also their *Chevron* step two analysis on the transformation of 'research' into 'research project' in the Amendment's text. In other words, it read 'research' as if synonymous with 'research project'. However, she stated:

'But "research" is the overall "systematic investigation or inquiry" in a field – here, hESCs – of which each project is simply a part.'[23]

Henderson CJ concluded therefore that there was 'a strong likelihood' that the plaintiffs 'will prevail on the merits.'

27.41 Regarding the irreparable harm that the plaintiffs will suffer if the injunction they seek is not granted and upheld by the court, Henderson noted:

---

21 Ibid.
22 Ibid, p 14.
23 Ibid, p 16.

'We earlier held that these two plaintiffs do indeed suffer "an actual, here-and-now injury" from the Guidelines and that the probability they will "lose funding to projects involving [h]ESCs" is "substantial enough ... to deem the injury to them imminent".'

She noted too, that:

'As the district court noted, moreover, their injury is irreparable because we "cannot compensate [them] for their lost opportunity to receive funds".'[24]

CONCLUSIONS

27.42 The sharp division and interpretative chasm between the judgment of the majority and minority in this case is apparent for all to see. The majority judgment favours construing the Congressional legislation that is the DWA text very purposively, ie suggesting it is ambiguous, thus inviting the court to cast its interpretative net further and to consider a wider trawl of sources (primarily in the guise of an administrative agency's interpretations of the legislation, ie here the NIH in its 2009 Guidelines) in seeking to resolve the conundrum of the meaning of that legislation. By contrast, the minority endorse and subscribe to adherence strictly to the primary source of the law, what they perceive to be a completely unambiguous Act of Congress, without the need for consideration of a superfluous, wider context of sources, ie non-Congressional, administrative agencies, ie here the NIH.

27.43 Clearly the potential economic and financial importance of this decision, to both scientists who favour human embryonic stem cell research and scientists who are opposed to it and favour alternatively (ethically they would claim), eg, adult stem cell research, arguably underpins its significance. Which avenue of research promises the best results and which one is ethically most justifiable? Both are competing for both private and federal funding. But can the two types of stem cell research not complement each other, rather than compete with each other? The legal battle concerning the moral status of the embryo and its use in stem cell research may have been resolved legally in the case, albeit temporarily, but the ethical, moral, legal and political war on this issue is far from being settled in the United States.

24   Ibid.

Chapter 28

European Union and Research on Embryonic Stem Cells – the Door Closes?

INTRODUCTION

28.1   The opinion of Advocate General Bot, delivered on 10 March 2011 in case C-34/10, *Oliver Brüstle v Greenpeace eV*, would arguably, if upheld by the European Court of Justice (ECJ), have potentially major deleterious consequences for the emerging and developing embryonic stem cell research sphere. The ECJ generally follows the opinions of the Advocate General.

THE FACTS

28.2   Mr Brüstle was the holder of a German patent, filed on 19 December 1997, which concerned isolated and purified neural precursor cells, processes for their production from embryonic stem cells and use of neural precursor cells for the treatment of neural disorders. Brüstle's patent specification claimed that the transplantation of brain cells into the nervous system would permit the treatment of numerous neurological diseases and it was noted that the first clinical applications had already been developed, in particular for patients suffering from Parkinson's disease. The argument was that in order to remedy neural defects like Parkinson's disease it was necessary to transplant immune precursor cells. The patent specification stated, moreover, that these immature precursor cells exist only during the brain's development phase, with a few exceptions. However, clearly such use of cerebral tissue from human embryos raises major ethical issues. Also, the patent specification claimed that embryonic stem cells offer new prospects for the production of cells for transplantation.

28.3   In addition Brüstle's patent specification noted that embryonic stem cells are pluripotent, meaning they are able to differentiate and turn into any type of cell or body tissue necessary for the harmonious development of foetal organs, ie blood, bone, skin, organ, or brain cells, and that embryonic stem cells also had the advantage of maintaining this state of pluripotency for many passages, and of proliferating. The argument was that the invention Brüstle was seeking to protect by the patent would, inter alia, make it possible to resolve the technical problem of producing an almost unlimited quantity of isolated and purified precursor cells, possessing neural or other properties, obtained from embryonic stem cells.

28.4   However the environmental pressure group Greenpeace eV brought an action for the annulment of the patent filed by Brüstle insofar as certain claims under that patent concern precursor cells obtained from human embryonic stem cells; it considered Brüstle's invention unpatentable under Art 2 of the Law on Patents as applicable on 28 February 2005. The German Federal Patent Court allowed in part the application of Greenpeace and declared the patent filed by Brüstle invalid in so far as its claim relates to precursor cells obtained from human embryonic stem cells. Brüstle then appealed against that judgment at the referring court, the German Federal Patent Court. It considered that the outcome of its proceedings depended on the interpretation of certain provisions of EU Directive 98/44,[1] and decided to stay proceedings until the ECJ made a preliminary ruling on the meaning of those provisions in Directive 98/44. The German Federal Patent Court, therefore, made a preliminary reference to the ECJ asking them a series of questions.

28.5   The first question asked by the German Federal Patent Court was what was meant by the term 'human embryos' in Art 6(2)(c) of Directive 98/44, and did it:

> 'include all stages of the development of human life, beginning with the fertilisation of the ovum, or must further requirements, such as the attainment of a certain stage of development, be satisfied?'

Also, were the following organisms included in the term 'human embryos': unfertilised human ova into which a cell nucleus from a mature human cell has been transplanted, and unfertilised human ova whose division and further development have been stimulated by parthenogenesis? In addition are stem cells obtained from human embryos at the blastocyst stage also included?

The second question to the ECJ was: what was meant by the expression 'use of human embryos for industrial or commercial purposes'? Also, did it include any commercial exploitation within the meaning of Art 6(1) of Directive 98/44, especially use for the purposes of scientific research?

LEGISLATIVE FRAMEWORK

28.6   The Advocate General referred to the salient international legislative instruments dealing with, inter alia, patentability in this area, ie the Agreement on Trade-Related Aspects of Intellectual Property Rights (the TRIPS Agreement), the Munich Convention, the Charter of Fundamental Rights of the European Union (the Charter) and, critically, Directive 98/44.

28.7   The TRIPS Agreement, signed on 15 June 1994 importantly provides, inter alia, in Art 27(1), that:

> '...patents shall be available for any inventions, whether products or processes, in all fields of technology, provided that they are new, involve an inventive step and are capable of industrial application.'

This largely mirrors the UK law on patents. However, a significant departure and key difference is contained in Art 27(2) which provides;

> 'Members may exclude from patentability inventions, the prevention within their territory of the commercial exploitation of which is necessary to protect *ordre public* or morality, including to protect human, animal or plant life or health or to avoid serious prejudice to the environment, provided that such

---

1   Directive 98/44/EC of the European Parliament and of the Council of 6 July 1998 on the legal protection of biotechnological inventions [1998] OJ L213/13.

exclusion is not made merely because the exploitation is prohibited by their law.'

The meaning of the terms '*ordre public* or morality' are very elusive and unfamiliar to the UK legal system, and it is, therefore, conceptually difficult to determine and pin down their meaning or scope.

28.8　The Charter (part of European Union (EU) law, but not signed by the United Kingdom and so not part of domestic UK law), provides, inter alia, that under Art 1 human dignity is inviolable and must be respected and protected. Furthermore, Art 3 of the Charter adds that, in the sphere of medicine and biology, the prohibition on making the human body and its parts as such a source of financial gain must be particularly respected.

28.9　Directive 98/44, however, is the key legislative and regulatory provision protecting and controlling inventions in the EU. Indeed, the Advocate General (AG) stated that it aimed:

> 'not only to establish a framework for the legal protection of biotechnological inventions, in order in particular to maintain and encourage investment in the field of biotechnology, but also to remove differences in the laws and practices of the Member States.'[2]

One of its aims, therefore, is to ensure consistency and uniformity in EU Member States regarding the protection and control of biotechnological inventions under domestic patent law. As the AG states:

> 'Under Article 1(1) of the directive, Member States must protect biotechnological inventions under national patent law, which they must, if necessary, adjust to take account of the provisions [of Directive 98/44].'[3]

If, for example domestic law is not in tune with Directive 98/44, then domestic law must be adjusted accordingly, to ensure its compliance with EU law.

28.10　The AG proceeded to note that:

> 'In view of the special nature of the subject-matter to which patentability relates, namely living matter, the directive sets limits on what is patentable and what is not.'[4]

Scientists and researchers are not therefore given *carte blanche* to embark on any research on living matter they want and get that research, if it results in an invention, protected by EU patent law. Furthermore the AG observed that whilst Art 3(1) of Directive 98/44:

> 'provides that inventions which are new, which involve an inventive step and which are susceptible of industrial application are patentable even if they concern a product consisting of or containing biological material or a process by means of which biological material is produced, processed or used'[5]

nevertheless:

2　At para 15 of the *Brüstle* Opinion.
3　Ibid, para 16.
4　Ibid, para 17.
5　Ibid, para 18.

'On the other hand, under Article 5(1) of the directive, the human body, at the various stages of its formation and development, and the simple discovery of one of its elements ... cannot constitute patentable inventions'.[6]

The AG also noted, at para 6, that Article 6 laid down prohibitions on patentability and provided (at Art 6(1)) that:

'Inventions shall be considered unpatentable where their commercial exploitation would be contrary to *ordre public* or morality; however, exploitation shall not be deemed to be so contrary merely because it is prohibited by law or regulation.'

This is virtually identical to the terms of Art 27(2) of the Charter. Paragraph 2 of Art 6 then elaborates on this:

'On the basis of paragraph 1, the following, in particular, shall be considered unpatentable:
[...]
    (c)   uses of human embryos for industrial or commercial purposes;'

28.11   Based on these provisions of Directive 98/44, the German patent law effective on 28 February 2005 provided, according to the AG, that:

'patents may not be granted for inventions whose commercial exploitation would be contrary to *ordre public* or morality and that, in particular, patents may not be granted for uses of human embryos for industrial or commercial purposes.'[7]

Other relevant German law was the Law on the protection of embryos, effective on 13 December 1990, which, inter alia, prohibited and criminalised the artificial fertilisation of ova for a purpose other than inducing pregnancy in the woman from whom they originate, the sale of human embryos conceived *in vitro* or removed from a woman before the end of the nidation process in the uterus,[8] or their transfer, acquisition or use for a purpose other than their preservation, and the *in vitro* development of human embryos for a purpose other than inducing pregnancy. Furthermore, the AG stated this law defined an embryo as:

'a fertilised human ovum capable of development, from the time of karyogamy, and any cell removed from an embryo which is able to divide and develop into an individual provided that the other conditions necessary are satisfied.'[9]

This law added that cells capable of developing into an individual are totipotent cells, whilst stem cells which are capable of developing into any type of cell but which cannot develop into a complete individual are categorised as pluripotent cells. Also, the AG noted that under German law, namely the Law to ensure the protection of embryos in connection with the importation and use of human embryonic stem cells, effective on 28 June 2002, 'the importation and use of pluripotent embryonic stem cells are prohibited,' subject to some exceptions.[10]

---

6   Ibid, para 19.
7   Ibid, para 22.
8   The implantation process.
9   The *Brüstle* Opinion, at para 24.
10   Ibid, para 25.

AG ANALYSIS

28.12 The AG emphasised from the outset the extremely sensitive nature of the questions asked regarding patenting this type of research using embryonic stem cells in the hope of it yielding therapeutic benefits and treatments for very ill patients in the future. He also flagged up the centrality of 'the question of the definition of an embryo that the main points of different philosophies and religions and the continual questioning of science meet,'[11] but that he did not intend to decide between beliefs or to impose them. The ECJ is a court of law making legal decisions based on relevant EU law, and not a court of morals or beliefs, and that his opinion (the AG's opinion), which guides the ECJ, should also equally not be concerned about reconciling beliefs, still less choosing which beliefs ought to prevail or be given more weight.

28.13 The AG acknowledged explicitly the economic, financial and business repercussions and implications of the questions posed for the consideration of the ECJ by the German patent court, not just confined to Germany, but for all EU research on embryonic stem cell research. He referred to Brüstle's claim that 'a possible refusal of patentability would be liable to jeopardise research and the retention of researchers in Europe, so as to prevent them going to the United States or Japan.' This is the 'brain-drain' argument – if embryonic stem cell research-'friendly' laws and regulation are not in existence in the EU or United Kingdom, scientists will vote with their feet and gravitate and move to jurisdictions which do not inhibit their research work and their attempts to protect it using the vehicle of patent laws. By way of illustration, he cited Professor Yamanaka's protection by a patent in Japan of his research on obtaining pluripotent stem cells from mature human cells removed from an adult – research which clearly does not pose the same ethical concerns for many individuals as stem cells sourced from embryos.

28.14 Later on the AG stressed the nexus between patentability and research: 'Patentability and research do not appear to be indissociable from one another.'[12] Whilst conceding that EU Member States were 'obviously free' to regulate research however they felt was appropriate, authorising patentability was a completely different matter:

> 'patentability, ie placing on the market with the ensuing conditions relating to production, must be consistent with the requirements laid down by Directive 98/44 with a view to harmonisation which integrates ethical considerations so as to prevent the economic functioning of the market giving rise to competition at the cost of sacrificing the fundamental values of the Union.'

Directive 98/44 is all about harmonising the law in EU Member States to promote consistency and uniformity in both harnessing and regulating ethically, eg, patent law controlling embryonic stem cell research leading to new treatments for patients.

28.15 The AG repeated that whilst the question asked of the ECJ was certainly a difficult one, it was, however, exclusively legal in nature. Arguably inconsistently if not contradictorily, the AG then stated that the reference to

---

11 Ibid, para 39.
12 Ibid, para 44.

the notions of *ordre public*, morality and ethics in (primarily) Directive 98/44 'expediently illustrate that the Union is not only a market to be regulated, but also has values to be expressed,' and that one such value, the principle of human dignity, had been recognised by the Court as a general legal principle.[13] The clear implication is that harmonisation of patent laws in the EU concerning regulating embryonic stem cell research intrinsically involves regard being had to the principle of human dignity vis-à-vis the use of human embryos. He adds that:

> 'only legal analyses based on objective scientific information can provide a solution which is likely to be accepted by all the Member States.'[14]

However agreeing what constitutes 'objective scientific information' may not always be possible.

28.16 In defining the term 'human embryo' the AG stated he did not share the opinion that this concept must be left solely to the discretion of Member State law, but rather it ought to be defined 'autonomously specifically for Union law' in accordance with the words and purpose of Directive 98/44 and the ECJ interpretation of that law. Directive 98/44 is a harmonisation directive, and effective and harmonised protection throughout Member States 'is essential in order to maintain and encourage investment in the field of biotechnology.'[15] Whether a certain invention is patentable in the EU should not hinge on the vicissitudes of the domestic law that an EU citizen finds himself in. The whole *raison d'etre* of Directive 98/44 was to prevent such a regulatory lottery occurring or developing. As the AG observes, the Directive helps to promote research and development in the field of biotechnology by removing the legal obstacles within the single market that are brought about by differences in national legislation and case law. The EU is supposed to be a single economic market and unit, not 27 different national markets.

Human embryo – EU understanding

28.17 The AG was adamant that 'the concept of a human embryo must have a Community understanding.'[16] He gave three reasons:

(1) '... [A]ccording to settled case-law, the need for uniform application of Union law and the principle of equality require that the terms of a provision of Union law which makes no express reference to the law of the Member States for the purpose of determining its meaning and scope must normally be given an autonomous and uniform interpretation throughout the Union.'[17]
So unless the EU law expressly, and not merely implicitly, refers to domestic member state laws, that EU law must be give a uniform (without any allowances/note of domestic laws being made) interpretation throughout the EU, which is the case here with Directive 98/44 (i.e. no mention of member state law).

---

13 Ibid, para 46.
14 Ibid, para 47.
15 Ibid, para 54.
16 Ibid, para 61.
17 Ibid, para 58.

(2) Following *Netherlands v Parliament and Council*, with regard to Directive 98/44 the AG observed that 'by requiring the Member States to protect biotechnological inventions by means of their national patent law, Directive 98/44 in fact aimed to prevent damage to the unity of the internal market which might result from Member States deciding unilaterally to grant or refuse such protection.'[18]

(3) In relation to the scope accorded to Member States by Art 6(2) of the Directive, the AG held it allows Member States, 'no discretion with regard to the unpatentability of the processes and uses it sets out.' He added that:

> 'This binding aspect of one of the key provisions of the directive would also seem to call for a uniform interpretation of the concept of a human embryo within the Union.' and added he could not see, 'how such a categorical prohibition, applying in all Member States, could exist on the basis of concepts which were not common.' [19]

Defining a human embryo

28.18 The AG stated that Directive 98/44 gives no definition of the concept of a human embryo, and nor does its drafting history, so he therefore looked to three different sources: 'the legislation of the Member States, the provisions of the directive and current scientific information.'[20]

Member state legislation

28.19 Regarding the legislation of Member States, the AG said, 'it must be stated that one would search in vain for evidence of a unanimous conception.' Quite simply there is no consensus or agreement on what is meant by a 'human embryo'. He cites two distinct approaches or groups in defining the term: 'the first considering that the human embryo exists from fertilisation and the second ... that it is from the time when the fertilised ovum has been transplanted into the endometrium.'[21]

Directive 98/44

28.20 The AG said that the provisions of Directive 98/44 provided an important indication of the meaning of a human embryo. He noted:

> 'It is the human body, at the various stages of its formation and development for which it demands protection when it declares it expressly unpatentable ... The body exists, is formed and develops independently of the person who occupies it.'[22]

Again, in interpreting Directive 98/44, the AG noted the importance of the reference to ethics, stating that can be easily explained 'since biotechnology

---

18 Ibid, para 59.
19 Ibid, para 60.
20 Ibid, para 64.
21 Ibid, para 67.
22 Ibid, para 73.

affects living matter, and here in particular the human being.'[23] Furthermore, he noted that the Directive 'stipulates that patent law must be applied so as to respect the fundamental principles safeguarding the dignity and integrity of the person.'[24] He equally noted that:

> 'the Union legislature stresses the principle whereby inventions must be excluded from patentability where their commercial exploitation offends against *ordre public* or morality and points out that those two concepts correspond in particular to ethical or moral principles recognised in a Member State, respect for which is *particularly* important in the field of biotechnology.'[25]

Current scientific information

28.21 Thirdly, the AG contended:

> 'current scientific information leads us to the desired definition [of a human embryo] based on both what it offers in terms of specific knowledge and the inferences which can be drawn from its silences.'[26]

Science can tell us much and answer many questions but it cannot definitively answer when a human person, warranting legal, moral and ethical value, begins. As the AG stated, whilst contemporary science can provide in-depth knowledge of the biological process from conception to birth, at present it cannot, however, say when the human person truly begins. In answering the question of when the human person truly begins with 'indisputable scientific precision', he added:

> 'It must be acknowledged that, at the current state of knowledge, this question can only be answered in the negative because it is impossible, at present, to detect the appearance of life, perhaps because we are unable to define it.' [27]

28.22 The AG set out his opinion clearly:

> 'Science teaches us – and it is now universally accepted, at least in the Member States – that development from conception begins with a few cells, which exist in their original state for only a few days.'[28]

He continued that these were totipotent cells, whose main characteristic is that each of them has the capacity to develop into a complete human being:

> 'They hold within them the full capacity for subsequent division, then for specialisation, which will ultimately lead to the birth of a human being. The full capacity for subsequent development is therefore concentrated into one cell ... Consequently, in my view totipotent cells represent the first stage of the human body which they become. They must therefore be legally categorised as embryos.'[29]

23 Ibid, para 75.
24 Ibid, para 76.
25 Ibid, para 77.
26 Ibid, para 79.
27 Ibid, para 81.
28 Ibid, para 84.
29 Ibid, para 85.

Furthermore, the AG added that, on the basis of this definition, he considered that every totipotent cell, whatever the means by which it has been obtained, is an embryo and that any patentability must be excluded. He added:

> 'This definition therefore covers unfertilised ova into which a cell nucleus from a mature cell has been transplanted and unfertilised ova whose division has been stimulated by parthenogenesis in so far as, according to the written observations submitted to the Court, totipotent cells would be obtained in that way.'

28.23 Then the AG distinguished totipotent from pluripotent cells, stating that the embryo's growth:

> 'is stimulated by the initial totipotent cells, at a still very early stage in its development, the embryo is formed not of totipotent cells, but of pluripotent cells, which lie at the heart of the patent filed by Mr Brüstle.'[30]

These cells can develop into all kinds of cells, even organs in the human body, but the main difference is that they cannot develop separately into a complete human being. Pluripotent cells:

> '...are already the sign of diversification which, as the cells multiply, will subsequently result in specialisation and diversification, leading to the appearance of the organs and all the individual parts of the human body which will be born.'

In further explaining the cellular biological development, the AG noted that:

> 'One of the first stages attained when the totipotent cells have given way to pluripotent cells is called the blastocyst ... the thing to which the totipotent cells have given way is the product of their own special nature, the thing for which they exist ... Whilst, in themselves, totipotent cells hold the capacity to develop a complete human body, the blastocyst is the product of this capacity for development at a certain moment ... It is therefore one of the aspects of the development of the human body and constitutes one of the stages.'[31]

On that basis:

> 'Accordingly, it must itself be categorised as an embryo, like any stage before or after that development. It would otherwise be paradoxical to refuse legal categorisation as an embryo for the blastocyst, which it is the product of the normal growth of the initial cells.'[32]

Logically, if the earlier totipotent cells warrant legal protection and are classified as an embryo, then axiomatically the later, more developed blastocyst, a fortiori, must be similarly protected or safeguarded and accorded embryonic status. The AG contended that to deny the blastocyst being defined as an embryo and so be protected by Directive 98/44 'would essentially diminish the protection of the human body at a more advanced stage in its development.'

28.24 The AG was emphatic too that:

---

30 Ibid, para 93.
31 Ibid, para 94.
32 Ibid, para 95.

'in accordance with the principle of dignity and integrity of the person, Directive 98/44 prohibits the patentability of the human body, at the various stages of its formation and development, including germ cells ... This shows that human dignity is a principle which must be applied not only to an existing human person, to a child who has been born, but also to the human body from the first stage in its development, ie from fertilisation.'[33]

However, he agreed with the position expressed in the national legislation of a number of Member States, that 'a pluripotent cell in isolation cannot therefore be regarded as constituting an embryo in itself.'[34] He noted that most Member States took the view that pluripotent stem cells were not human embryos, citing Germany and the United Kingdom. In German law, for example, this follows directly from the distinction between pluripotent cells and totipotent cells. Under para 8(1) of the ESchG, therefore, the human embryo includes any 'totipotent' cell removed from an embryo. In the United Kingdom, the law provides that stem cells obtained from a human embryo at the blastocyst stage are not included within the concept of a human embryo, partly because they are incapable of further development.

28.25 The AG stated, therefore:

'Given that embryonic stem cells, taken in isolation, are no longer capable of developing into a complete individual, they can no longer ... be categorised as human embryos. These cells have been removed at a certain stage in the development of the embryo and they are not capable, in themselves, of resuming that development.'[35]

He continued, at para 101, that embryonic stem cells must be regarded as elements isolated from the human body within the meaning of art 5(2) of Directive 98/44, and referred to Brüstle's explanation to the ECJ that:

'embryonic stem cells are obtained from the internal cellular mass of the blastocyst, which is then removed. An element of the human body, in the course of its development, has therefore been isolated in order to proliferate the cells contained in that cellular mass.'

He added:

'Moreover, the Union legislature also seems to regard an embryonic stem cell as an element isolated from the human body, since recital 7 in the preamble to Directive 2004/23EC, which sets standards of quality and safety for tissues and cells intended for human applications, states that the directive also applies to adult and embryonic stem cells.'[36]

28.26 That said the AG was troubled that it was not possible to ignore the origin of this pluripotent cell. He said there was no problem per se with it coming from an embryo (ie a blastocyst), but significantly added the caveat 'provided only that its removal does not result in the destruction of that human body at the stage of its development at which the removal is carried out.'[37] The

---

33   Ibid, para 96.
34   Ibid, para 98.
35   Ibid, para 100.
36   Ibid, para 102.
37   Ibid, para 103.

major snag and ethical issue was that the embryo (ie blastocyst) will inevitably be destroyed after removal of the stem cells. As the AG highlighted:

> 'The pluripotent stem cell in the present case is removed from the blastocyst which, as I have previously defined, itself constitutes an embryo, that is to say one of the stages in the formation and development of the human body which the removal will destroy.'[38]

The AG rejected Brüstle's argument:

> 'that the problem of patentability which hinges on the removed cell, the way in which it has been removed and the consequences of such removal do not have to be taken into account seems unacceptable, in my view, for reasons connected with *ordre public* and morality.'[39]

He added that even though the claims under the patent did not specify that human embryos were used for the exploitation of the invention, when they actually were, the patentability of such an invention must be excluded:

> 'If that were not the case, the prohibition under Article 6(2)(c) of Directive 98/44 would be easy to circumvent, since the person applying for a patent for his invention would only have to "neglect" to specify in the patent claims that human embryos were used or destroyed ... That provision would then be deprived entirely of its effectiveness.'[40]

Sadly patenting this type of embryonic stem cell research also necessitates the destruction of human embryos and therefore is contrary to *ordre public* and morality as enshrined in Directive 98/44. The AG was emphatic that:

> 'It must therefore be agreed, if only for the sake of consistency, that inventions relating to pluripotent stem cells can be patentable only if they are not obtained to the detriment of an embryo, whether its destruction or its modification.'[41]

Certainly clear from an ethical viewpoint.

28.27 The AG reiterated:

> 'cells are removed from the human embryo at the blastocyst stage and they necessarily entail the destruction of the human embryo ... To make an industrial application of an invention using embryonic stem cells would amount to using human embryos as a simple base material.'

Human embryos are not merely a base material, a commodity or product to be exploited for commercial gain. As he added:

> 'Such an invention would exploit the human body in the initial stages of its development ... It would seem pointless, indeed superfluous, to mention again the references made to ethics and *ordre public*.'[42]

The AG flagged up an exception to the prohibition of patentability, which was laid down by Directive 98/44 itself, namely where the invention has therapeutic or diagnostic purposes which are applied to the embryo and are useful to it.

---

38   Ibid, para 104.
39   Ibid, para 105.
40   Ibid, para 108.
41   Ibid, para 109.
42   Ibid, para 110.

He contended that the deliberate use of the term and concept 'for industrial or commercial purposes' in Directive 98/44 demonstrates the clear contrast between such uses and inventions for therapeutic or diagnostic purposes which are applied to the human embryo and are useful to it.[43]

The AG said:

'Since exceptions must be interpreted strictly, they must be reserved for the specific case stated in Directive 98/44 … Use for industrial or commercial purposes requires large-scale production, which is in any case out of all proportion to, for example, the number of operations carried out or potentially carried out *in utero* on an embryo to correct a malformation and to improve chances of survival.'[44]

He said that patenting the industrial and commercial exploitation of cell cultures intended for pharmaceutical laboratories with a view to manufacturing medicines presupposes that the more the technique allows cases to be treated, the greater the production of cells, requiring recourse to a proportional number of embryos which would therefore be created only to be destroyed a few days later. He therefore posed the question:

'Would a definition which essentially authorises such a practice be consistent with the concept of *ordre public*, and with an ethical conception which could be shared by all the Member States of the Union? It is clear that it would not.'[45]

ECJ JUDGMENT

28.28 The ECJ delivered its judgment on 18 October 2011[46] when it answered the three questions referred to it by the German court for its preliminary ruling. This hinged largely on the interpretation which should be given in particular to Art 6(2) of Directive 98/44.

What is meant by the term 'human embryos' in Art 6(2) of the Directive?

28.29 The ECJ stated that according to settled case-law the need for a uniform application of EU law and the principle of equality require that the terms of a provision of EU law which makes no express reference to the law of the Member States for the purpose of determining its meaning and scope must normally be given an independent and uniform interpretation throughout the EU. Therefore, given that the text of the Directive did not define 'human embryo', or contain any reference to national laws regarding the meaning of that term, it must be regarded for applying the Directive as designating an autonomous concept of EU law, which must be interpreted in a uniform manner throughout the EU. That conclusion was:

---

43 Ibid, para 111.
44 Ibid, paras 112–113.
45 Ibid, para 114.
46 Case C-34/10 Oliver Brüstle v Greenpeace e.V. 18 October 2011, European Court of Justice (available at: http://eur-lex.europa.eu/LexUriServ/LexUriServ.do?uri=CELEX:62010CJ0034: EN:HTML)

'supported by the object and the aim of the Directive [which sought] a harmonisation of the rules for the legal protection of biotechnological inventions, to remove obstacles to trade and to the smooth functioning of the internal market.'[47]

Crucially the ECJ held:

'The lack of a uniform definition of the concept of human embryo would create a risk of the authors of certain biotechnological inventions being tempted to seek their patentability [in Member States which have the] narrowest concept of human embryo and are accordingly the most liberal as regards possible patentability, because those inventions would not be patentable [in the other Member States.] Such a limitation would adversely affect the smooth functioning of the internal market which is the aim of the Directive.'[48]

28.30 The ECJ furthermore held that that conclusion was also supported by the scope of the listing, in Art 6(2) of the Directive, of the processes and uses excluded from patentability. Moreover, Art 6(2) allows Member States no discretion with regard to the unpatentability of the processes and uses which it sets out, since the very purpose of this provision is to delimit the exclusion laid down in Art 6 (1).[49]

28.31 Significantly the ECJ said, concerning the meaning to be given to the concept of 'human embryo' in Art 6(2) of the Directive, that although, the definition of human embryo is a very sensitive social issue in many Member States, marked by their multiple traditions and value systems, the ECJ was not called upon in the preliminary reference to broach questions of a medical or ethical nature, but had to restrict itself to a legal interpretation of the relevant provisions of the Directive. In addition, the meaning and scope of terms for which EU law provides no definition must be determined by considering, inter alia, the context in which they occur and the purposes of the rules of which they form part. Also:

'the preamble to the Directive states that although it seeks to promote investment in the field of biotechnology, use of biological material originating from humans must be consistent with regard for fundamental rights and, in particular, the dignity of the person.'[50]

The ECJ pointed in particular to recital 16 in the preamble to the Directive, which emphasised that 'patent law must be applied so as to respect the fundamental principles safeguarding the dignity and integrity of the person.'

28.32 The ECJ then referred to previous ECJ rulings which held that Art 5(1) of the Directive provided that the human body at the various stages of its formation and development could not constitute a patentable invention.[51] The ECJ noted that additional security was offered by Art 6:

47 *Brüstle v Greenpeace*, para 27.
48 Ibid, para 28.
49 Ibid, para 29.
50 Ibid, para 32.
51 Ibid, para 33.

'which lists as contrary to *ordre public* or morality, and therefore excluded from patentability, processes for cloning human beings, processes for modifying the germ line genetic identity of human beings and uses of human embryos for industrial or commercial purposes.'

Also, importantly the Court noted that Recital 38 in the preamble to the Directive states that this list was not exhaustive and that all processes the use of which offends against human dignity were also excluded from patentability.

28.33 The ECJ held, therefore, that the context and aim of the Directive showed that the EU legislature intended to exclude any possibility of patentability where respect for human dignity could thereby be affected, and it followed that the concept of 'human embryo' within the meaning of Art 6(2)(c) of the Directive must be understood in a wide sense. The ECJ concluded accordingly that any human ovum must, as soon as it was fertilised, be regarded as a human embryo within the meaning and for the purposes of applying Art 6(2)(c) of the Directive 'since that fertilisation is such as to commence the process of development of a human being.'[52]

28.34 Very significantly too, the ECJ held:

'That classification must also apply to a non-fertilised human ovum into which the cell nucleus from a mature human cell has been transplanted and a non-fertilised human ovum whose division and further development have been stimulated by parthenogenesis. Although those organisms have not strictly speaking, been the object of fertilisation, due to the effect of the technique used to obtain them they are, as is apparent from the written observations presented to the Court, capable of commencing the process of development of a human being just as an embryo created by fertilisation of an ovum can do so.'[53]

Then the ECJ stated that regarding stem cells obtained from a human embryo at the blastocyst stage, it is for the referring court to ascertain, in the light of scientific developments, whether they are capable of commencing the process of development of a human being and, therefore, are included within the concept of 'human embryo' within the meaning and for the purposes of applying Art 6(2) of the Directive.

What is meant by the expression 'uses of human embryos for industrial or commercial purposes'? Also did it include any commercial exploitation within the meaning of Art 6(1) of the Directive, especially use for the purposes of scientific research?

28.35 The ECJ noted that the purpose of the Directive was not to regulate the use of human embryos in the context of scientific research. Rather it was limited to the patentability of biotechnological inventions:

'[With regard] solely to the determination of whether the exclusion from patentability concerning the use of human embryos for purposes of scientific

52 Ibid, para 33.
53 Ibid, para 36.

research or whether scientific research entailing the use of human embryos can access the protection of patent law, clearly the grant of a patent implies, in principle, its industrial or commercial application.'[54]

The ECJ further contended that Recital 14 in the preamble to the Directive supported that interpretation. Furthermore it noted that by stating that a patent for invention entitled its holder to prohibit third parties from exploiting it for industrial and commercial purposes, it indicated that the rights attaching to a patent were, in principle, connected with acts of an industrial or commercial nature.[55]

28.36   Crucially the ECJ held:

'Although the aim of scientific research must be distinguished from industrial or commercial purposes, the use of human embryos for the purposes of research which constitutes the subject-matter of a patent application cannot be separated from the patent itself and the rights attaching to it.'[56]

The ECJ also held:

'The clarification in recital 42 in the preamble to the Directive, that the exclusion from patentability set out in Article 6(2)(c) of the Directive "does not affect inventions for therapeutic or diagnostic purposes which are applied to the human embryo and are useful to it" also confirms that the use of human embryos for purposes of scientific research which is the subject-matter of a patent application cannot be distinguished from industrial and commercial use and, thus, avoid exclusion from patentability.'[57]

Is an invention unpatentable even though its purpose is not the use of human embryos, where it concerns a product whose production necessitates the prior destruction of human embryos or a process for which requires a base material obtained by destruction of human embryos?

28.37   The ECJ said this question was raised in a case concerning the patentability of an invention involving the production of neural precursor cells, which presupposed the use of stem cells obtained from a human embryo at the blastocyst stage. It noted that it was apparent from the observations presented to the Court that the removal of a stem cell from a human embryo at the blastocyst stage entailed the destruction of that embryo. The ECJ therefore held:

'an invention must be regarded as unpatentable, even if the claims of the patent do not concern the use of human embryos, where the implementation of the invention requires the destruction of human embryos ... In that case too, the view must be taken that there is use of human embryos within the meaning of Article 6(2)(c) of the Directive. The fact that destruction may occur at a stage long before the implementation of the invention, as in the case of the production of embryonic stem cells from a lineage of stem cells

54   Ibid, para 41.
55   Ibid, para 42.
56   Ibid, para 43.
57   Ibid, para 44.

the mere production of which implied the destruction of human embryos is, in that regard, irrelevant.'[58]

CONCLUSIONS

28.38 Whilst the Advocate General's opinion and the ECJ decision relate to the patentability of certain biotechnological inventions involving the use of human embryos, and whilst the ECJ emphasised that defining a human embryo was a very sensitive social issue in many Member States with multiple traditions and value systems, and that the ECJ was not called upon to broach questions of a medical or ethical nature, but rather to confine itself to a legal interpretation of relevant provisions of the Directive, nevertheless, the decision surely impacts on the legal and ethical status of the human embryo, and probably will result in a decline of use in human embryos for research purposes, if that use cannot be protected by patents. The ECJ's decision could, therefore, have a devastating impact on the development of embryonic stem cell research in the EU. Thousands of desperately ill patients in the EU might be alarmed that a new scientific avenue with the potential to yield considerable therapeutic benefits to alleviate their suffering was effectively being blocked off. Scientists in the field might be tempted to take their research elsewhere to less hostile regulatory jurisdictions. However, others would counter that the decision signalled that at last the courts and the law were standing up for the rights of the human embryo and robustly setting out very clear ethical and moral bright lines concerning its uses or misuse.

28.39 Those ethical bright lines appear to be, on the basis of the AG's opinion, that in the light of Directive 98/44 the definition of a human embryo applies from fertilisation to the initial totipotent cells and to 'the entire ensuing process of the development and formation of the human body,' including the blastocyst.[59] In addition, unfertilised ova into which a cell nucleus from a mature human cell has been transplanted or whose division and further development have been stimulated by parthenogenesis are also included in the concept of a human embryo, insofar as the use of such technologies would result in totipotent cells being obtained. By contrast, taken individually, pluripotent embryonic stem cells are not included in that concept because they do not in themselves have the capacity to develop into a human being.[60] Equally, a further ethical bright line and no-go area is that an invention must be excluded from patentability in accordance with Directive 98/44:

'where the application of the technical process for which the patent is filed necessitates the prior destruction of human embryos or their as base material, even if the description of that process does not contain any reference to the use of human embryos.'[61]

Finally, Directive 98/44:

'must be interpreted to the effect that the exception to the non-patentability of uses of human embryos for industrial or commercial purposes concerns

---

58   Ibid, para 49.
59   *Brüstle v Greenpeace eV*, AG's Opinion, para 115.
60   Ibid, para 116.
61   Ibid, para 117.

only inventions for therapeutic or diagnostic purposes which are applied to the human embryo and are useful to it.'[62]

28.40 The battles patently evident in Parliament throughout the passage and eventual enactment of the 2008 Act concerning the creation of human admixed embryos, permitting the creation of saviour siblings, restricting abortion availability, deleting the 'need for a father clause', and regarding the welfare of the child would appear to be reoccurring, albeit in the context of patent laws, (ie interpreting Directive 98/44 and defining a human embryo for the purposes of that EU law) in the EU legal system, with no sign yet of conclusion.

---

62   Ibid, para 118.

Chapter 29

Conclusion

INTRODUCTION

29.1   The Human Fertilisation and Embryology Act 2008 (the 2008 Act), which came into force on 1 October 2009, signalled an evolutionary, rather than a revolutionary, regulatory development in the sphere of assisted reproduction medicine. The vast majority of the regulatory structure and the legal parameters encapsulated in Human Fertilisation and Embryology Act 1990 (the 1990 Act) remains intact, as did the great bulk of the ethical bright lines marked out by the Warnock Report in 1984. As Bob Dylan famously said in his song, 'The times they are a changing' – so too with the overarching legislative regime. The world of assisted reproduction in 2009 and indeed in 2012 is a different one to that in 1990, with nearly 20 years of scientific, therapeutic and research developments occurring over that period. Social attitudes have equally not remained static or inert either, so it is only right and proper that the law should reflect those changes and remain fit for purpose in 2012, and also be able to address new medical, ethical and legal challenges that emerge in the immediately foreseeable assisted reproduction landscape.

WELCOME NEW FEATURES OF THE 2008 ACT?

29.2   There were a number of significant changes made to the original 1990 Act by the 2008 Act. Clearly much of the assisted reproduction legislative and regulatory infrastructure remained intact and unaltered.

29.3   First, the 2008 Act permitted the creation of a new type of embryo, the human admixed embryo, for research purposes, broadly subject to the same legal and ethical restraints and limitations as human embryos. Fundamentally, their use for research must be licensed by the HFEA, they cannot be developed beyond 14 days nor experimented on beyond 14 days, and clearly their use must be necessary or desirable for research purposes, as permitted by the 2008 Act. Crucially they cannot be implanted in a woman to produce some type of hybrid baby, even if that were technically or biologically feasible. For many peers and MPs, not to mention critics outside Parliament, this was a scientific and ethical step too far, if not a sharp slide down the ethical slippery slope. However for a greater number of peers and MPs, and many supporters outside of the legislature, the legislative green light for the creation and use of human admixed embryos was a necessary, timely and welcome development, equipping scientists and researchers with potentially more human-like embryos to experiment and research on, without the necessity of having to use human embryos.

29.4   Again the specific legalisation allowing the creation of saviour siblings for clearly articulated, limited circumstances was a very important and arguably beneficial step. It gives hope to the parents of a sick, existing child that their child might be saved from a debilitating and painful disease, as well as for the suffering child itself. Balanced against that are the minimal risks of harm to the saviour sibling, who is created not just in the hope that, eg, cord blood could be harvested from their umbilical cord, a tissue-compatible and disease-free source, but who was created as much because the parents wanted another, much-loved child. Children were not in 1990 and would not in 2009 become commodities created only for their usefulness to others. This was even more apparent in Parliament's decision to outlaw sex selection of, eg, embryos or gametes, except for serious medical reasons.

29.5   The jettisoning of the 'need for a father' clause in s 13(5) of the 1990 Act, a clause which might be seen as either redundant or unfair, and its replacement by the ostensibly less discriminatory, fairer, more human rights compliant 'need for supportive parenting' clause in the welfare of the child provision (ie s 13(5)), although opponents would claim this was politically correct, more bureaucratic, nebulous and vague, and an unnecessary legislative change, graphically illustrated the social changes that had come about in the United Kingdom by 2009, compared to 1990, when the 1990 Act was enacted. In 1990, the 'need for a father' clause was inserted as a strategic compromise to get s 13(5) through the House of Lords, given that half of the peers only wanted eg IVF to be made available for married couples. Attitudes to who potentially could be a parent had certainly changed completely by 2009 in the United Kingdom. Times certainly had changed, and there was much angst and wrangling in Parliament over the messages and signals, mixed or otherwise that this reform or retrograde step, depending on whose stance was considered, sent out from Parliament. However, it remains to be seen whether this change makes any difference at all to the practical workings of the welfare of the child provision in clinical practice. The jury is out on whether the change is symbolic or instrumental legislation, or possibly a bit of both.

29.6   The many provisions in the 2008 Act reconfiguring family structures following assisted reproduction techniques were aligned and in keeping with existing legislative changes conferring legal recognition of different unions such as gay and lesbian couples in, eg, the Civil Partnership Act 2004. Therefore for example a civil partner of a lesbian mother could, post-October 2009, become the parent of an IVF conceived child, using eg donated sperm, as indeed could a lesbian partner not in a civil partnership if the agreed female parenthood conditions were satisfied. Again for some this just represented recognition of the reality that families come in all shapes and sizes. There is no ideal version, and no type of family structure should be discriminated against, nor any type favoured or given preferential treatment, especially as manifested in the law of the land. For others this was the thin end of the ethical wedge, leading to lies being put on birth certificates (documents which should be accurate historical records), and undermined fundamentally the traditional, nuclear and long accepted genus of a family: father, mother and children. Just because there were broken families, caused eg by divorce, separation, death, or abandonment, did not give the legislature *carte blanche* to deliberately manufacture or at least condone or legitimise their intentional creation.

29.7   Clearly the statutory approval of the creation and use of human admixed embryos for research purposes in the 2008 Act, in conjunction with the existing research being undertaken using human embryos, is potentially another major boon for the continued growth of stem cell research, which offers the promise of yielding beneficial research that hopefully will translate into the development of a number of treatments and drugs for a variety of diseases and disabilities that afflict numerous patients in the United Kingdom. The United Kingdom has traditionally been at the vanguard of such research, but the huge number of ethical, legal, moral, social and medical issues surrounding this exciting branch of medicine and research were all too evident in the battlefields being fought so vigorously by both supporters and opponents of embryonic stem cell research in the United States and in the European Union. These legal and ethical fights are likely to continue, if not escalate, in the future.

29.8   Even though the 2008 Act ultimately did not amend the existing law of abortion as contained in the Abortion Act 1967 as amended, by inclusion of any of the Parliamentary amendments seeking respectively to cut the gestational time limit for abortion to various earlier times, to increase the amount of information a woman seeking abortion is given, to extend the 1967 Act to Northern Ireland, or to cut the two doctor requirement to one, nevertheless the impassioned and informed debates served to remind the public of the vitality of their elected representatives on highly controversial moral and ethical issues involving their individual consciences. Incontrovertibly Parliament is indeed the national bioethics commission, the country's moral compass and supreme assisted reproduction regulator and that is unquestionably a good thing and long may it continue. That is evident in its decision to scrap the independent, specialist regulatory body, the HFEA, which has been discharging its statutory duties and oversight of the assisted reproduction business for the past 20 years, but seemingly is going to be abolished in 2013. However, the rush to get rid of useless, expensive, wasteful, ineffective quangos – in itself a good thing – does not necessarily mean getting rid of effective and useful arm's length bodies (ALBs) like the HFEA is a good move, nor transferring its various functions to several other existing and continuing healthcare ALBs or quangos. It might transpire it is a very bad, retrograde decision indeed.

RECENT CONTROVERSY REGARDING ABORTION

29.9   The highly charged nature of the abortion issue and some of its more unsavoury possible consequences was evident in a couple of reports in the *Daily Mail*. On 8 May 2012 the *Daily Mail* reported on pills 'smuggled out of China ... Sold as "stamina boosters", the capsules have been found to contain the powdered remains of dead babies and aborted foetuses.' Apparently border control officers in South Korea 'say they have foiled 35 smuggling attempts since August, involving more than 17,000 pills made from the corpses of infants.' For many, not just pro-life advocates, this practice is thoroughly ethically repugnant.

29.10   The second *Daily Mail* article on 12 May 2012 referred to this trade in these 'macabre pills' as 'a sickening, cannibalistic and illegal trade' and highlighted the connection between the state one-child policy in China and the use of unwanted/discarded foetus bodies and parts in manufacturing these allegedly therapeutic/healing pills thus: 'This grotesquely unsavoury industry appears to cash in on China's strict family planning laws, which limit most families to just one child each and are said to result in 1.3 million abortions a year, the equivalent of more than 35,000 terminations a day.'

29.11 In marked contrast the *Guardian* on 28 May 2012 reported the concerns of Tony Falconer, President of the Royal College of Obstetricians and Gynaecologists, who 'called the rising use of vigils and human chains' at abortion clinics 'distressing and humiliating for those preparing to have a termination', and 'an unwelcome and worrying development that could also deter younger doctors from opting to perform abortions.' In a number of cases in the USA, a tiny minority of protestors took their opposition to abortion to deadly extremes by murdering doctors performing abortion procedures. Dr Falconer, when '[a]sked if he was worried that doctors here could become a target too', conceded that 'We don't have any evidence for that, but that could be a worry. It's obviously not as bad but it seems to be going down that line.' Thankfully fights in the UK about the abortion issue and reforming/tightening regulation are fought out verbally in our Parliament (inter alia) without recourse to violence.

29.12 On 29 May 2012, the *Daily Telegraph* reported that a Christian mental health worker who was sacked after voicing opposition to abortion is suing the NHS, accusing it of having a 'dangerously totalitarian' approach to dissent on the issue. It reported also that: 'Margaret Forrester, a Roman Catholic, was dismissed for "gross professional misconduct" after giving a colleague a booklet highlighting potential physical and psychological damage some women suffer after an abortion', that 'She was told that the booklet, in which women who had terminated pregnancies in the past spoke of their regrets, could amount to "offensive" material', and furthermore that: 'She accuses the Central and North West London NHS Trust of breaching her freedom of religion and freedom of speech in its treatment of her.' However, it was further reported that: 'A spokesman for Central and North West London NHS Foundation Trust said: "The trust thoroughly disputes these allegations and will continue to defend its position vigorously. We are confident that we will be able to successfully defend these claims."'

29.13 Again the highly ethically and emotively charged nature of the abortion issue was evident in a series of articles in several newspapers concerning the allegedly widespread phenomenon of repeat abortions in the NHS. The *Daily Mail* reported on 14 May 2012 that of the 189,574 abortions that took place in 2010 in England and Wales 'more than 64,000 terminations were on women who had already aborted a foetus in the past', and moreover 'Across all age groups, a total of 85 women had an abortion despite having had seven previous terminations.' The *Daily Mail* claimed these numbers of terminations translated into very stark monetary terms; namely, 'The Health Service is spending around £1 million a week providing repeat abortions', or '£1,000 each'. Is this further evidence of abortion on demand, de facto if not de jure, and abortion being offered as a form of contraceptive, not as an option of last resort? Furthermore the *Daily Mail* alarmingly reported on 26 May 2012 that:

'Out of 38,269 teenagers having terminations in England and Wales 5,300 had already had at least one, according to NHS figures released under the Freedom of Information Act. Three had their eighth abortion, while another two had their seventh ... Four teenagers had a termination for the sixth time, 14 had their fifth, 57 had a termination for the fourth time and 485 went through the procedure for a third time.'

29.14 Commenting on these incredibly high and worrying figures, on 29 May 2012 the *Daily Telegraph* stated: 'The Department of Health said about 63,300 women – 36 per cent – had repeat abortions last year, compared with 34 per cent in 2010. This was the biggest rise ever recorded in one year', and moreover 'one in four abortions to women under the age of 25 was a repeat termination.' Regarding the fact that repeat abortions rose again in 2010, and the alleged fact that contraception is more widely available than ever before, Michaela Aston of Life observed 'It is particularly disturbing that repeat abortions rose again. This is a clear indication that the original intent and spirit of the Abortion Act is being widely flouted and ignored.' Is this further evidence of doctors, the gatekeepers of the Abortion Act 1967, not discharging their sentinel duties properly, or of the vagueness and deliberately wide nature of the provisions of the Abortion Act, which effectively permits abortion on demand following a cosmetic, rubber-stamping exercise by (nominally) two doctors? Or is it just supply meeting demand, and the law and its agents (the medical profession) dealing with the reality (however intuitively repellent the frequency or individual circumstances) of unwanted pregnancies in 'notionally autonomous' individuals?

29.15 Finally on 24 May 2012 the *Daily Mail* reported that the 'BBC is facing fierce criticism after revealing it will make broadcasting history by airing a radio show live from an abortion clinic', including 'interviews with staff and some of the women choosing to terminate their pregnancy.' For pro-life supporters this was tantamount to free publicity/propaganda air-time being given to the pro-abortion lobby. By contrast pro-choice advocates regarded the development as being potentially educational and informative for women contemplating having an abortion. The abortion battleground continues to rage.

RECENT CONTROVERSIAL USES OF ASSISTED REPRODUCTIVE TECHNOLOGIES

29.16 In the *Daily Mail* on 3 May 2012 Lord Winston voiced his concerns about the setting up of a clinic in London which allows women 'to "insure" against infertility by "banking" bits of their ovaries while they are still well under 30, allowing them to conceive later in life'. Lord Winston conceded that 'In one way this is incredibly impressive' and 'It sounds wonderful' given that 'It could empower women, allowing them to improve their education, gain new skills and become highly successful in the workplace – without jeopardising their chances of eventually raising a family.' Nevertheless this infertility development 'is not merely deeply worrying, it is also utterly immoral.' He flagged up a number of concerns about the procedure, namely that 'nearly all the eggs are in the outer skin of the ovary. In order to bank tissue, the surgeon, using a telescope, has to strip the outer coat – or at least one third of it – and will be able to remove a piece of ovary containing around 60,000 eggs.' He added that 'It sounds good, but this procedure is likely to damage the ovary and cause adhesions, which will make natural conception even less likely.' Also, he contended, 'stripping the ovary in this way may itself bring on a premature menopause – which would be devastating for the woman.' In addition Lord Winston noted that 'Replacing the tissue is also a fraught process. Once it is put back into the body after thawing some years later, there is no guarantee the graft will take.' Furthermore there is the possibility that 'women may be left with dead tissue inside them – a focus for infection.' He cited a further worrying potential problem with the procedure, namely that 'the freezing process may cause subtle damage to the eggs' and that 'We have no real idea if the babies born as a result of this procedure will be genetically damaged.' This is in keeping with the lower live birth rate using frozen embryos as opposed to fresh embryos in infertility treatment. Significantly too Lord Winston was worried that: 'To date, after more than 12 years since this procedure was first done in humans, only 17 babies have been born worldwide' and 'What is shocking is that some doctors are offering this as a treatment to humans, when they should be doing research first.' Lord Winston concluded that scientists should rather, inter alia, be directing their attentions to 'finding out why so many eggs die in the ovary' instead. He noted that a 16 week old foetus had 'seven million microscopic eggs' in her ovaries, that 'By the time that girl is born, probably fewer than two million of those eggs will be left', and furthermore that 'This continues after birth so the average teenager will have over 400,000 eggs left. Over the next 40 years, virtually all those eggs will have gone until she, now a middle-aged woman, will be menopausal.' Lord Winston observed tellingly that 'This loss of eggs, by a process called cell death, seems to be quite natural and goes on all the time.' Sadly the reality in recent years of changed social/work circumstances with women putting off having families to pursue careers does not change this iniquitous biological reality of massive egg cell death in a woman's body. Nature sadly is yet again red in tooth and claw!

29.17 On 26 May 2012, in a similar but significantly different context, it was reported in the *Daily Mail* that 'Doctors have carried out the world's first successful womb transplant', on Derya Sert, 'in a breakthrough that could allow thousands of young women to fulfil their dream of motherhood.' Mrs Sert had been born without a womb and had received a healthy womb from a dead donor, which was 'working well' for her. Mrs Sert was 'due to start IVF treatment in Turkey in September in the hope of conceiving a longed-for child.' The potential beneficial implications and repercussions of this pioneering transplant surgery, followed by IVF, for a considerable number of infertile women in the UK cannot be underestimated. The *Daily Mail* noted that 'In Britain alone, there are at least 15,000 young women who were born without a womb or have had it removed due to cancer or another illness.' Clearly the benefits of this assisted reproductive breakthrough have to be weighed against the potential risks, burdens and harms, namely organ rejection, complications of IVF and pregnancy, delivery of the baby by caesarean section and risks of the woman developing cancers or diabetes. Yet again the 'natural' biological urge in the vast majority of people to be a parent and to have children drives and fuels assisted reproductive research and treatment developments, prompting scientists and assisted reproductive medicine specialists to channel their energies and talents into meeting these pressing infertility demands.

29.18 On 12 May 2012 the *Daily Mail* reported that 'Thousands of Cambridge students have been targeted by a firm offering up to £750 to egg donors.' Seemingly leaflets were stuck in the pigeonholes of University of Cambridge students '…making an emotive plea to help a couple unable to have children'. The leaflet stated, inter alia, that the couple were 'looking for a real-life angel to be our egg donor.' The *Daily Mail* commented that 'The development appears to be a result of an increase in the amount of "compensation" that can be given to donors [since 1st April 2012 – raised to £750] … and may confirm fears of a rise in "egg brokers" profiting from dealing in human lives. The targeting of elite students also raises concerns about attempts to create "superbabies".' Some would contend this development is hardly surprising given the acute shortage of human eggs, the not insubstantial medical/physical difficulties in harvesting them from the perspective of the egg donor and the now increased payments/compensation (some would contend inducements) offered to would-be egg donors. Altruistic donation appears to be being replaced, seemingly by commercial incentives and the demands of a market.

29.19 Worryingly too on 6 May 2012 *The Independent on Sunday* reported on research carried out at the University of Adelaide in Australia and noted that: 'The new study – believed to be the most comprehensive such research in the world – indicated that the risk of defects [birth defects including heart, spinal and urinary tract problems, limb abnormalities and cleft palates] ... was different for various infertility treatments. Following examination of more than 300,000 births, researchers found that couples who did not need fertility treatment had a 5.8 per cent of having a baby with a birth defect, while the defect risk rose to 8.3 per cent where parents underwent assisted conception.' The study's leader, Professor Michael Davies, 'insisted the research team did not "want to scare people", pointing out that the vast majority of babies [presumably 91.7 per cent!] are born healthy.' The *Independent on Sunday* observed: 'Not all treatments were equally risky, the survey suggested. The results showed that in vitro fertilisation (IVF) posed the least risk to women opting for assisted conception, with defects occurring in 7.2 per cent of pregnancies. IVF's main alternative, intracytoplasmic sperm injection (ICSI), which involves the injection of a single sperm directly into an egg, was found to pose a higher risk, with major birth defects occurring in 9.9 per cent of births, almost one in 10.' In fairness Professor Davies conceded there were several theories why ICSI appeared a riskier procedure, namely the potential use of damaged sperm or damage caused by manipulation of the sperm and egg in the laboratory (ie was it because of a flawed/damaged sperm or alternatively a flawed/damaged infertility treatment), and stated that: 'There are factors associated with ICSI that require further research'. Given that the use of ICSI is becoming more prevalent in licensed clinics in the UK (more ICSI treatments occur now compared to conventional IVF), this research gives cause for great concern. Another worrying finding of the research was 'a tripling of risk among the small number of women who used the drug clomiphene citrate to stimulate ovary production. The drug, which is cheap and widely available on the internet, is known to cause foetal abnormalities if the woman taking it is unaware that she is already pregnant.' Those opposed to assisted reproductive technologies/research would draw great succour from this research and conclude that assisted reproduction was harmful to the unborn children created by the technology, to the prospective parents of that child and damaging to wider society as well.

29.20 Following on from this article, *The Mail on Sunday* reported on 13 May 2012 that Dr Dan Poulter MP, a former obstetrician and gynaecologist and member of the House of Commons Health Select Committee, is to recommend an investigation into ICSI, in the light, inter alia, of the Australian research, and 'This could force the fertility regulator, the Human Fertilisation and Embryology Authority (HFEA), to examine its extensive database on ICSI treatments in the UK for evidence to support restricting its use.' The article claimed moreover that: 'To date, the database – one of the largest in the world, with information dating back 20 years – has not been used to assess if there is a link between ICSI, which accounts for 52 per cent of all IVF treatments, and birth defects.' Dr Poulter stated he would be recommending the Committee 'carry out an evidence session on ICSI followed by a report and an inquiry', and added: 'We've got to have a look at what action the regulatory body, the HFEA, is taking to address that and to use its data. There's no point in having a body that spends millions to maintain a database if it doesn't do anything when there are concerns.' Dr Poulter added that: 'We need to make sure the regulatory body is fit for purpose.' The HFEA responded that it would 'welcome' any application to use its data to investigate a link between fertility treatment and birth defects, adding that the Australian research 'will be considered by our Scientific and Clinical Advances Advisory Committee when it next meets in June' (ie June 2012). Hopefully further research will discover and determine whether eg ICSI is indeed significantly riskier for/potentially more harmful to future children than is conventional IVF or natural conception.

29.21 On 14 May 2012 the *Independent* reported that 'IVF clinics in the UK are practising aggressive fertility treatments that are putting women and children at unjustified risk, experts say', and that 'The commercially driven industry uses unnecessary procedures, high doses of powerful drugs and risky interventions to help desperate couples spending thousands of pounds to conceive', but by contrast, 'a milder, safer approach to IVF could provide equivalent success rates over a longer period at a lower cost and could enable the NHS to double the number of patients treated for the same budget.' Professor Geeta Nargund, head of reproductive medicine at St George's Hospital, London, stated: 'High-dose stimulation can have distressing side effects on the woman, the most serious of which is called ovarian hyper-stimulation syndrome (OHSS). This condition in its severe form is potentially fatal and women have died. A recent confidential inquiry into maternal deaths in the UK showed that OHSS was now one of the biggest causes of maternal mortality in England and Wales.' The *Independent* further noted that 'There were almost 30,000 cases of OHSS – which can cause chest pains, shortness of breath and, in rare cases, kidney failure and death – between 1991 and 2007 in the UK, according to figures obtained from the Human Fertilisation and Embryology Authority (HFEA) in response to a request under the Freedom of Information Act', and hence issued a warning 'about what can happen when commercial principles are introduced into health, which is that safety concerns can start taking a back seat.' Desperation for children should not blind regulators, doctors or would-be parents into ignoring risks detrimental to creating healthy children.

29.22 On 22 May 2012 *The Times* reported that the National Institute of Clinical Excellence (NICE) had published draft guidance on provision of fertility treatment, under which 'women up to the age of 42 who have been unable to conceive naturally would become eligible for at least one cycle of IVF treatment, at a cost of £3,000.' This if approved would replace the 2004 NICE guidance 'upper age limit' of 39. The new draft guidance 'is also recommending for the first time that gay and lesbian couples would qualify for the treatment if they have tried unsuccessfully for a baby using artificial insemination at private clinics.' It also recommends that 'women should be offered three cycles of IVF after just two years of trying for a baby, rather than three.' Given that the majority of IVF is offered privately in fee-paying clinics and that, as Professor Adam Balen of the British Fertility Society states, 'The 2004 guidance was not universally followed around the country. There are some primary care trusts that fail to fund any treatment' (a fact clear from much empirical research on the availability of NHS IVF), one could be forgiven for being cynical and sceptical about the effectiveness and intrinsic worth of the draft guidelines. As Susan Seenan, deputy chief executive of the Infertility Network, stated in the same article: 'New guidelines are pointless if they are not put into practice and people are suffering every day because some PCTs continue to flout the NICE guidelines.' The intractable, controversial issue of access to infertility treatments rumbles on seemingly unabated.

29.23 On 3 June 2012, *The Mail on Sunday* reported that Prime Minister David Cameron 'has thrown his weight behind a controversial technique to prevent incurable hereditary diseases that will result in the birth of children with three parents', and which could potentially 'eradicate devastating genetic diseases such as muscular dystrophy.' The process 'involves taking the nucleus out of the egg of a mother carrying faulty mitochondria – the "batteries" that power cells – and transferring it into a healthy egg donated by another woman, resulting in a disease-free baby.' The ethical snag however being that '[this] means the child would contain genetic material not only from his or her mother and father but also from the donor, though scientists say only tiny amounts would come from the third party.' The promise of this new IVF technique is great. Indeed *The Mail on Sunday* recognised this by stating: 'Mutations of the DNA within mitochondria can cause around 50 untreatable diseases, affecting about one in 5,000 births', and if the procedure was introduced it could save 'the lives of about 100 children a year.' But Josephine Quintavalle rather contended that the new science 'is an attempt to genetically modify the human species, creating an abnormal embryo using donor components from three or more adult sources, passing on these changes to future generations, with who knows what awful consequences.' Balancing the possible future benefits and burdens/harms of this groundbreaking science is very problematic.

THE FUTURE

29.24 As stated earlier, the imminent demise of the HFEA as the specialist, independent, statutory regulator in the sphere of certain assisted reproductive treatments, embryonic research and use of donated gametes and embryos does not signal the end of the regulatory regime governing these areas, still less the repeal of the Human Fertilisation and Embryology Acts 1990 and 2008 or the scrapping of the Code of Practice. The functions of licensing and policing the various clinics under the aegis of legislation and Code of Practice, and generally monitoring embryonic research, will still continue, albeit these functions will be distributed to other healthcare regulatory bodies or ALBs. That may or may not save some money – how much or little, no one can say for certain – but whether the enforcement and effectiveness of that future, new regulatory regime is better or worse is very much a moot point. It is highly likely that with further anticipated advances in embryonic stem cell research, not to mention research using human admixed embryos, and probably the existing (2012) research permitted purposes being extended and increased in the future, and with no apparent evidence of a decline in demand for IVF and other infertility treatments, whatever form future regulatory oversight takes and wherever it is located, it will unquestionably be kept very busy.

29.25 Hopefully the very solid foundations laid by the Warnock Report, the 20 years' experience and expertise of the HFEA, as manifested in the latest incarnation of the Code of Practice,[1] and the generally sound ethical principles and legal rules enshrined in the 1990 and 2008 Acts will not be ignored, forgotten or discarded by future Parliaments when they try to map out legislation to regulate this vitally important area of medicine and research.

1   8th edition (2009).

Index

(All references are to paragraph numbers)